THE BOYS OF THE ARCHANGEL RAPHAEL:
A YOUTH CONFRATERNITY IN FLORENCE,
1411–1785

Beni Culturali e Ambientali (photo: Konrad Eisenbichler)

KONRAD EISENBICHLER

# The Boys of the Archangel Raphael: A Youth Confraternity in Florence, 1411–1785

UNIVERSITY OF TORONTO PRESS
Toronto Buffalo London

Toronto Buffalo London
Printed in Canada

ISBN 0-8020-4329-1 (cloth)
ISBN 978-1-4426-1303-4 (paper)

Printed on acid-free paper

**Canadian Cataloguing in Publication Data**

Eisenbichler, Konrad
The boys of the Archangel Raphael : a youth confraternity in Florence, 1411–1785

Includes bibliographical references and index.
ISBN 0-8020-4329-1

1. Compagnia dell'Arcangelo Raffaello (Florence, Italy). 2. Confraternities – Italy – Florence – History. 3. Confraternities – Italy – History. 4. Florence (Italy) – Church history. I. Title.

BX814.C65E58 1998 267'.2424551 C97-932410-6

University of Toronto Press acknowledges the financial assistance to its publishing program of the Canada Council for the Arts and the Ontario Arts Council.

This book has been published with the help of a grant from the Humanities and Social Sciences Federation of Canada, using funds provided by the Social Sciences and Humanities Research Council of Canada.

in memory of
Māra Ezerkalns
(1951–1994)

# Contents

# Acknowledgments

While working on the Arcangelo Raffaello, I contracted many debts, some of which I know will be impossible to repay in full. First and foremost among them stands my debt to Ludovica Sebregondi; her knowledge of Florentine sources, her invaluable advice, and her spontaneous generosity have enriched my work and the time I have devoted to it.

In Florence I am indebted to a number of scholars who facilitated my research, and in particular to don Gilberto Aranci, Amanda Blake, Roberto Fuda, the late Fr I.P. Grossi OP, Giovanna Lazzi, Sandra Marsini, Silvia Meloni Trkulja, Paola Peruzzi, Paola Pirolo, and Raffaella Maria Zaccaria. Their assistance and advice was often instrumental in my search for confraternity documents and other records. I am also grateful for the help I received, with so much kindness and patience, from all the staff at the Archivio di Stato di Firenze and the Biblioteca Nazionale Centrale di Firenze, where the bulk of my research was carried out. The same is true for the staff at other Italian institutions that, over the course of several years, allowed me to use their manuscripts, books, and resources: the Archivio Arcivescovile di Firenze, the Kunsthistorisches Institut in Florenz, the Laurenziana, Marucelliana, and Riccardiana libraries, the Biblioteca Comunale di Firenze, the Museo di Firenze Com'Era, the Ufficio Catalogo della Soprintendenza per i beni artistici e storici delle provincie di Firenze e Pistoia, the Biblioteca Berenson at the Villa I Tatti, and the Biblioteca Comunale degli Intronati di Siena. Finally, I am sincerely thankful and obligated to Ann Lind and to her children, Tony and Grazia Acanfora, who on many occasions opened their Florence home to me and made me feel both welcomed and *a casa* with them.

The scholarly support and kind advice I received from many learned colleagues across the disciplines and the globe were very important for me. In particular, I wish to recognize the contributions made by professors Benjamin Arbel, James Banker, Christopher Black, William R. Bowen, John Brackett, Guido Burchi, Giovanna Casagrande, Stanley Chojnacki, Edward English, Kathleen Falvey, Philip Gavitt, Paul Grendler, Kristin Lister, Roberto Melzi, Jacqueline Murray, Nerida Newbigin, John Paoletti, Elizabeth Pilliod, Lorenzo Polizzotto, Michael Rocke, Alan Shepard, Nicholas Terpstra, and Paolo Viti. Some read sections of my work and offered constructive criticism, others answered queries and solved cruxes, while still others asked me unexpected questions that led me to inquire further of the documents.

Antonio Ricci and Roberto Buranello were valuable research assistants in Toronto, while Ilaria Taddei cheerfully provided some last-minute assistance in Florence.

Don and Irene Bean, who hosted me for a time in their beautiful 'Sunny Skies' retreat in Muskoka, gave me an idyllic setting in which to start writing.

The kind of primary research that is at the basis of my study, the months spent perusing documents in archives and libraries abroad, would have been an unmanageable financial burden were it not for the generosity of several Canadian institutions. Victoria University in the University of Toronto has, without fail, supported me and my work over the past two decades; in particular its Office of the President and the Northrop Frye Centre have on more than one occasion alleviated the financial costs of research, while its Centre for Reformation and Renaissance Studies, with its marvellous collection, staff, and associates, has provided a stimulating setting in which to develop and test my ideas. My research on the Arcangelo Raffaello was also at times financed by the University of Toronto and the Social Sciences and Humanities Research Council of Canada.

This book has been published with the help of a grant from the Humanities and Social Sciences Federation of Canada, using funds provided by the Social Sciences and Humanities Research Council of Canada.

Lastly, I wish to acknowledge the patience, support, and professionalism of the staff at the University of Toronto Press, and in particular Suzanne Rancourt, who encouraged me to submit my work to the Press, and Judy Williams, who helped me prepare the typescript for publication, as well as the two anonymous scholars who reviewed my work and so enthusiastically recommended its publication.

A tutti, grazie!

KONRAD EISENBICHLER
16 March 1997

# Abbreviations

| | |
|---|---|
| AAF | Archivio Arcivescovile di Firenze |
| ACSG | Archivio della Compagnia di San Girolamo, Firenze |
| ASF | Archivio di Stato di Firenze |
| BCI | Biblioteca Comunale degli Intronati di Siena |
| BNCF | Biblioteca Nazionale Centrale di Firenze |
| Bolaffi | *Dizionario Bolaffi dei pittori e degli incisori italiani.* Torino, 1976 |
| Cap. | *Capitoli*, statutes or chapter(s) |
| cod. | *codice*, volume |
| Colnaghi | Colnaghi, D.E. *A Dictionary of Florentine Painters from the 13th to the 17th Centuries*, intro. Harold Acton, Mina Gregory, Piero Marchi, Carlo Malvani. Firenze: Archivi Colnaghi, 1986 |
| Conv. Sopp. | Conventi Soppressi |
| Crs | Compagnie religiose soppresse da Pietro Leopoldo |
| *DBI* | *Dizionario biografico degli Italiani.* Roma: Istituto dell'Enciclopedia Italiana, 1960–current. |
| fasc. | fascicule |
| f.n.n. | folio not numbered |
| Laur. | Biblioteca Laurenziana, Firenze |
| Patr. Eccl. | Patrimonio Ecclesiastico |
| p.n.n. | page not numbered |
| Ricc. | Biblioteca Riccardiana, Firenze |
| SMN | Santa Maria Novella, Firenze |
| Thieme-Becker | *Allgemeines Lexikon der bildenden Künstler von der Antike bis zur Gegenwart.* Leipzig, F.A. Seemann, 1909–50; rpt. 1965–6, 37 vols. |

# THE BOYS OF THE ARCHANGEL RAPHAEL

# Boys in Hoods: An Introduction

During the festivities for our Patron the Archangel Raphael, two of our brothers had an argument, or came to blows, in our oratory. For this reason this morning the 11th [of January] they were reprimanded by our Father Corrector, and warned in front of the entire Confraternity, and he had them ask forgiveness of each other, and gave them a small penance to do.[1]

With these words, the scribe for the youth confraternity of the Arcangelo Raffaello recalled a fist-fight that had broken out two weeks earlier, on 31 December 1561, in the confraternity's oratory during one of its most important services of the year – the celebration in honour of the confraternity's titular saint, the Archangel Raphael. The event is exceptional – the only such reference to a fist-fight inside the oratory in nearly four centuries of history. As such, it really should not be used as the opening lines for a volume on an association of youths that, on the whole, were much better behaved. It does, however, point to the nature of youths, then and now, and to the fact that the confraternity did succeed, at least officially, in socializing the young men enough to teach them to avoid violence. In light of what other scholars have revealed about premodern Italian youth, this would make the confraternity's contribution to the peaceful development of Florentine society noteworthy in itself.[2] There are, however, quite a number of other contributions that, together with this one, make youth confraternities an important element in the life of young men, in particular, and of Florentine society, in general, in premodern times.

Children and youths have recently attracted much attention from scholars, and rightly so. Christiane Klapisch-Zuber has revealed, for example, that youths under the age of twenty-four constituted 50.2 per cent of the Florentine population in the tax census (the *catasto*) of 1427–30.[3]

Florentines themselves were extremely concerned with the spiritual and material needs of this large segment of their population. In his *Charity and Children in Renaissance Florence*, Philip Gavitt has described how the foundlings' hospice in Florence, the Ospedale degli Innocenti, served a community and an ideal that were very much a concern for fifteenth-century humanists and for the citizenry of Florence alike. As he indicates throughout the volume, compassion and charity went hand in hand with humanist belief in the perfectibility of the individual and society. Before Gavitt, an older group of youths, adolescents, had attracted the attention of Richard Trexler, who, in his ground-breaking article of 1974, 'Ritual in Florence: Adolescence and Salvation in the Renaissance,' described the role young men played in the social fibre of urban Florence and the manner in which the youths themselves were 'acculturated.' Gavitt's and Trexler's work is part of a recent interest in the history of youth that finds its roots in Philippe Ariès' *Centuries of Childhood* (1965), and blossoms into John Boswell's *The Kindness of Strangers* (1988) and David Kertzer's *Sacrificed for Honor. Italian Infant Abandonment and the Politics of Reproductive Control* (1993), or into collections such as *Enfance abandonnée et société en Europe: XIVe–XXe siècle* (1991) and *Infanzie. Funzioni di un gruppo liminale dal mondo classico all'Età moderna.*

It is, however, a history that runs the risk of contextualizing childhood within anachronistic parameters. Ottavia Niccoli points out that:

> to study children with reference only to their correlation with family structures is anachronistic because, in many cases, this means applying to a previous era – for example, the beginning of the modern age – affective and relationship models that originate, for the most part, in the nineteenth century and are, in any case, post-Rousseaunian. Furthermore, it has been pointed out that there are spaces (particularly vast in the period we are discussing) 'in which children manage to socialize in an independent and original manner ... just as there exist places that are alternative to the family and appear not to be documented at all ... they are the areas of the non-history of infancy.'[4]

In part, the present work fits into this growing field of interest in children and youths in premodern Europe and seeks to fill a gap in the neglected history of these groups: the youth confraternity. Within these lay religious organizations youths socialized in an extra-familial context, engaging in a complex corporate life that included devotional, administrative, educational, and festive activities. My work, however, is different from that of previous historians of childhood, in that it is not grounded in the solid bedrock of social history. It is, instead, a wide-ranging, even interdisciplinary view of one youth confraternity's life and practices seen primarily through its own documents.

Previous scholarship on youth confraternities has been limited to the confraternities' role in public display and festivity. Their theatre, music, art, and participation in urban ritual have overshadowed their primary existence as a devotional and educational institution. John Henderson admits, from the very start, that in his volume *Piety and Charity in Late Medieval Florence* (1994) 'boys' confraternities ... will only be touched on by reference to the growing literature concerning their performance practices.'[5] In fact, such had been the case with earlier scholars as well, who examined youth confraternities for what they could tell us about music, art, or theatre. Musicologists, such as Guido Burchi, John Walter Hill, or Edmond Strainchamps, found a wealth of information on early composers and musicians in the documents of the Arcangelo Raffaello. Art historians such as Ludovica Sebregondi, Anna Padoa, Giovanni Pagliarulo, and others have discovered commissions, payment records, attributions, locations, and other valuable information on artists and artworks in the archival documents of Florentine confraternities. Theatre historians such as Nerida Newbigin or myself have long argued for a contextualizing of early Florentine theatre within the confraternal organizations active in that city. Some scholars have also sought to provide readers with a historical, social, religious, or educational context for confraternities. But these were, on the whole, token gestures to apprise the reader of the complexity and variety of facets that constitute early modern youth confraternities.

While Ronald F.E. Weissman did not consider youth confraternities at all in his volume *Ritual Brotherhood in Renaissance Florence* (1982), and John Henderson (1994) considered them only with respect to their 'performance practices,' Christopher F. Black did devote a very brief subsection to them in his *Italian Confraternities in the Sixteenth Century* (1989). In it he rightly pointed out that 'these societies filled many needs, social and religious, in the preparation of members for adulthood ... The juvenile confraternities provided religious and secular education, organised entertainments such as ball games, and dramatic productions. They may have been designed to protect youths from sodomitic attacks by their elders, or restrain their own inclination ... These youth societies became involved in politics, most notably at the end of the century in the struggles between supporters and opponents of fra Savonarola and his republicanism.'[6] These few pages merely hinted at the complexity of organized lay religion among Italian youths.

What was needed was a detailed description of what, exactly, these youth organizations did, how they did it, and why. To fill this need, I have chosen to examine the youth confraternity of the Arcangelo Raffaello in Florence, founded by an anonymous gold-leaf worker in 1411 and suppressed by grand-ducal decree in 1785. My study will be, in some ways, a monograph describing this organization from its beginning to its end, an institutional biography as it were. During the course of the examination, I will look at its history, its governing structures, its devotional practices, its membership, its possessions, and its secular activities. This will inevitably lead to strong centrifugal forces that, emanating from the central core of the confraternity of the Arcangelo Raffaello, will push towards other confraternities, other disciplines, and other interests.

Along with Weissman and Henderson, I tend to view the confraternal movement as a continuum. With roots in the pagan associations of classical times, it became a Christian phenomenon in the Middle Ages, flourished in the thirteenth through the fifteenth centuries, underwent a transformation in the sixteenth, and, in Florence, drew to a close at the end of the eighteenth century.[7] While Weissman and Henderson stop with the fifteenth century, my overview actually comes to a focus in the sixteenth and progresses, past the Tridentine reforms, into the seventeenth. In a way, the confraternity members of this later period are the 'courtiers of God' whom Weissman identifies in his chapter on confraternities in the sixteenth century, but they are also the courtiers of their society, playing, as Trexler suggests in his essay on 'Adolescence and Salvation,' a social and a ceremonial role in the life of their city.

## Invisible History

While confraternities and their contribution to the fabric of society may have been very much in view to their contemporaries – enough to elicit government mistrust and suppression, ecclesiastical concern and control, popular support and membership – they are, as mentioned above, invisible history to us today. Confraternities were both everywhere and influential. Although they gathered or touched a large segment of the population, they have not yet found a place in the standard histories of the period, or even in the histories of religion or of 'the Church.' This is surprising, for they were often one of the points of contact in the tension between lay and religious. Similarly, as Kathleen Falvey points out, their contribution to the mystical traditions of the Latin West still needs to be examined.[8]

For the average person in late medieval and early modern times, the confraternity could acquire a relevance that went well beyond what we, today, might find in it. At a time when the 'official Church' spoke a language that was not understood by the vast majority of the faithful, celebrated mysteries behind rood screens, excluded the laity from active participation, and assumed for itself dignities and prerogatives that separated it from the people, membership and participation in a lay confraternity provided the average person with the possibility to pray to God or the saints in one's own vernacular, to see directly and to participate actively in the rituals of devotion, and, to use Weissman's felicitous phrase, to join in 'ritual brotherhood.' What, then, was '*the* Church' to a confraternity member? We should not discount the possibility that it may have been *the* confraternity that provided a language of devotion, a context for sacrificial action, a social network in Christ, a basic education in Christian faith and morals, and a closer bond with God above and mankind below.

It is worth noting that the documents of the Arcangelo Raffaello do not speak of theological questions. In the sixteenth century, for example, they do not pause to consider the revolutionary import for Christianity of events north of the Alps. It would be difficult to use these documents as sources for a history of religious debates. However, by their very existence as a record of activities, they do outline a religious life that was seen, by its followers, as spiritually fulfilling and worthy of sacrifice. They describe a Catholicism that may not be actively engaged in the fight against heresy, Protestantism, or the Infidel, but rather one that is quietly and conscientiously working to improve the spiritual and moral life of its adherents. John O'Malley has recently suggested that it is time to reconsider the standard questions – not what caused the Reformation, but what Catholicism was like in the sixteenth century; not *the* Church as an institution, but Religion in its multiplicity of aspects; not the history of religion bound by the usual time frames, but free to extend itself on the long continuum of history; Catholicism not as a monolith, but as variations on a theme.[9]

With these questions in mind, then, my efforts to narrate and describe the life of the confraternity of the Arcangelo Raffaello from 1411 to 1785 move away from the usual periodization in order to examine a multiplicity of activities, drawing together devotion and the arts, education and instruction, processions and plays. Such an approach will help us focus more clearly on how religion was lived by the average Florentine young man. The questions, then, revolve more on what it meant to be a member of a confraternity, why youths joined the organization, what was the sociology of membership, what were the influences that acted upon the group, what were the activities they engaged in, what was their weekly routine. These are in part answered by the confraternity's own records.

## The Confraternity's Documents

My work on the Arcangelo Raffaello is thus firmly based on the confraternity's own documents: its statutes, minutes, account books, and a variety of other documents the youths felt were important enough to preserve. Like the Cumean Sibyl, they speak to us with many meanings and with the sound of a thousand voices. The statutes, for one, are the prescriptive documents that tell how the founders or the reformers imagined the confraternity should be. The minutes, on the other hand, are descriptive documents that tell what the membership actually did, or, more precisely, what the scribe thought the members had done that day. The financial records tell where the confraternity drew and spent its money. And the assortment of other documents gives an insight into the confraternity's dealings with other people, usually by way of a legal text.

Among all these documents, my own preference has been for the *ricordi*, the minutes of meetings (both business and prayer meetings) and descriptions of special events at the confraternity. David Herlihy speaks of the value and importance of personal records in his introduction to Christiane Klapisch-Zuber's *Women, Family and Ritual in Renaissance Italy*:

> The *ricordanze*, like the surveys, are marvelously precise in the information they supply; they usually cite exact dates for the events recorded and exact prices for properties sold or acquired. They admit of some statistical manipulation, as Klapisch-Zuber's work in several places illustrates. But more interesting than the embedded numbers are the descriptions they offer of social practices, including social rituals. They show in detail how the Florentine family managed its domestic affairs, and they uniquely illuminate the ceremonial aspects of domestic life. They tell us, for example, how servants or wet nurses were selected, and who they were; they take us through the many rituals associated with marriages and christenings; and they show us the gifts exchanged between bride and groom, and their respective kin.[10]

The same could be said for the *ricordi* of confraternities. They narrate the usual routine of devotions and work, they describe special events that break that routine, and they reveal the special interests of the membership in general and of the scribe in particular – and all the time they give names, names, names. If the statutes tell us what was the 'text' on which the confraternity was based, the *ricordi* tell us what was the context in which that text was played out. Thus, while the statutes are normative documents that relay the prescriptive testimony, the *ricordi* are the descriptive testimony that provides us with a glimpse into the reality of confraternal life for the individuals whose names, ignored by conventional histories, survive in the confraternity's memoirs.

My primary aim, therefore, has been to let the *ricordi* speak for themselves. For this, I have generally adopted a descriptive-narrative voice that, in a way, tells the story of the youth confraternity of the Arcangelo Raffaello. In so doing, I have consciously chosen as clear and simple a language as I could, *pace* my academic training, avoiding jargon, whether historical or critical, so as to reach as wide an audience of specialists and non-specialists as I could. I was moved to carry out such a work by the fact that a narrative description of a confraternity's life, either over the long term or in its more immediate, day by day routine, was not available either in English or in Italian; and by a belief that the history of lay religious associations in early modern times, the religious education and training of youths, the nature of amateur theatre or spectacle, art, and music are aspects of our culture that would interest not only scholars but also the educated reading public. This desire to describe and narrate has not, however, supplanted the scholar's need to examine critically. Analyses have been integrated into the descriptive narrative, together with ample transcriptions from the original documents and references to similar situations in other youth confraternities.

I have also sought to use a multidisciplinary approach, with one eye firmly focused on the history and the other on the culture in which the confraternity functioned. In so doing I have sought to offer readers and scholars alike a view into the world of the average young person in premodern Florence, of lay religious practices, and of mid-level creativity that is not the exception, but the norm. It is, in a way, that world of popular consumption that, until recently, has often been ignored.

## Confraternities as Culture

The confraternal movement is, in itself, a very complex phenomenon. It contains a variety of elements emblematic of premodern lay piety – intense personal devotions, a commitment to piety and charity, prayer, liturgy, ceremony, festivity, an unfaltering cult of relics and sacred images, devotion to the saints, and so forth. It is also a forerunner of the reforming movements of the sixteenth century, be that through its emphasis on lay participation in devotional activities, or in its commitment to instruction in the faith, or in its quasi-mystical adoration of the Sacrament, or in the pageantry of its devotional rituals. As Roberto Rusconi rightly points out, 'in the case of confraternities, one encounters a phenomenon not only with religious implications, but also cultural ones, in the widest sense of the term. One need only remember, for example, that the entire poetic and musical repertoire of vernacular *laude* was compiled, over the course of centuries, specifically for the rituals that were performed within confraternities.'[11]

The cultural aspect of confraternities, and its contribution over time to society, must therefore not be ignored or underestimated. Much has already been done, for example, to examine their theatrical activities, though not often enough with an eye to the context of the event. Similarly, music and art historians have eagerly sifted through confraternity records in search of archival documentation to substantiate their dating and attribution of artworks, or to shed further light on an artist's biography. In this volume I will delve into theatre, art, and music not in order to contribute more details to an already complex picture (though this will inevitably occur), but rather to suggest the variety and versatility of a confraternity's contribution to the arts in general. Because culture is not restricted to the performing or the visual arts, I have also sought to provide the reader with an image of the confraternity's spiritual life, of its routine devotional activities, of its administrative structures, and of its history. Taken in its entirety, this picture of the confraternity of the Arcangelo Raffaello should go a long way in describing what a confraternity of young men did and how it contributed to the needs and the quality of life both of its members and of its city.

## Dates

Until 1750 Florentines computed the year *ab incarnatione*, that is, from 25 March, the feast of the Annunciation when, according to Christian thought, God became incarnate in Jesus. Because of this, Florentine documents dated between 1 January and 25 March bear a date that is one year behind our current computation. To avoid confusion, dates falling in this period will be given in double notation. Thus the date 1 February 1560/1 (given as 1560/1.2.1 in appendix 4) will indicate the first of February in the year 1560 according to the Florentine system (*stile fiorentino*) and 1561 according to our contemporary system (*stile comune*). In 1750 Florence officially switched to the modern computation with New Year's on 1 January, and thus dates from 1750 on will not require correction.

## Transcription and Translating Standards

In transcribing from original manuscript sources, I have expanded abbreviations, rationalized the u/v and i/j fluctuation, and modernized punctuation and capitalization practices. I have, however, retained the orthographic idiosyncrasies (and inconsistencies) of the various documents. Because the vast majority of documents cited were written fairly quickly as routine journal entries with no literary pretensions and no expectation that they would be read by a 'public,' scribes were not always consistent with, or even careful about, their spelling and grammar. In citing from manuscript sources I have not attempted to correct spelling or grammar errors, but to provide original citations that respect scribal variants and idiosyncrasies – sometimes even within the same document.

In the same manner, in transcribing from early printed sources, I have also retained spelling and punctuation as in the original.

In translating from original manuscript sources, I have standardized punctuation and, at times, simplified sentence structures in order to adhere more closely to contemporary English usage. Unless otherwise indicated, all translations are mine.

## Names of Confraternities and Their Saints

Names of confraternities have been kept in the original Italian, while names of saints have been rendered into English. Thus Arcangelo Raffaello is the confraternity, while Archangel Raphael is the archangel after whom the confraternity was named.

1

# A City of Confraternities

Confraternities were everywhere in premodern Europe and played an important part in the lives of devout Catholics of all social classes. Some regions and cities, Tuscany/Umbria and Florence in particular, were fertile territory for the growth and proliferation of these lay religious associations. The following pages will offer an overview of the situation in Florence by focusing especially on the Dominican church of Santa Maria Novella and its fundamental role in welcoming and fostering the development of lay devotional interests. The notion of confraternities composed exclusively of youths will then lead to a detailed discussion of who, exactly, was a 'youth' in premodern Italy: when one was a *putto*, a *fanciullo*, or a *giovane* becomes an important question especially for those of us who are dealing across linguistic, temporal, and geographic barriers.

## Florence and Confraternities

Late medieval and Renaissance Florence was rich in lay confraternities. The first were founded in the mid-thirteenth century by the Dominican preacher St Peter Martyr. By 1400 there were 52 confraternities in the city. At the end of the fifteenth century the tally had risen to 156. By the mid-eighteenth century, when Giovanni Lami published his monumental work on the Florentine church, he was able to identify 309 lay confraternities.[1] Though such growth may seem impressive, Florence was not unique in experiencing a phenomenal increase in lay religious organizations.

The situation was similar in the countryside around Florence. More than twenty years ago, Charles M. de la Roncière provided scholars with a listing of 136 confraternities extant in the Florentine *contado*, 130 of them founded before 1400. As de la Roncière himself pointed out, this was merely a first sampling with no pretensions to be exhaustive.[2] Though some attention has been focused on confraternities in Tuscany outside Florence by historians such as Amleto Spicciani (for Pescia), Oretta Muzzi (for San Donato in Poggio), and James Banker (for Borgo San Sepolcro), there is still much to be done.

Most areas in the Italian peninsula reveal a similar increase in the number of lay confraternities in the fourteenth and fifteenth centuries. As Brian Pullan points out, the momentum carried on into the sixteenth century:

> In Genoa between 1480 and 1582, the records mentioned 134 associations which could be described, if rather loosely, as confraternities ... At least 124 others arose after 1582, and in the mid-eighteenth century about 200 confraternities were in being at the same time. Eighty-four confraternities were founded in Rome during the sixteenth century ... Venetian evidence suggests that in 1521 there were at least 120 small confraternities in the city, as well as five large ones, and that by 1732 the total number of such societies ... had reached 357.[3]

Gennaro Maria Monti, the first to attempt a systematic examination of the confraternal movement in central and northern Italy, not only revealed the numerical and geographical extent of the movement, but reminded scholars of its antiquity and longevity. His two-volume study was, for over fifty years, the authoritative work in the field and still provides scholars with invaluable references to pursue and insights to develop. More recently, Christopher F. Black, in a work that limits itself to the long sixteenth century, has provided a much more detailed description of Italian confraternities across the peninsula, with special attention to groups active in urban centres other than the standard Florence, Venice, and Rome.[4]

A number of other contemporary scholars have made important contributions to the history of Italian confraternities. The movement of the *Bianchi* has recently been the focus of a magisterial volume by Daniel Bornstein. Music in confraternities has received book-length attention by Cyrilla Barr, Jonathan Glixon, and Blake Wilson, while a number of articles have been contributed by Guido Burchi, Tim Carter, Dennis J. Dutschke, John Walter Hill, and Edmond Strainchamps in particular. Confraternities in the Veneto have been studied by, among others, Lester K. Little and Giuseppina De Sandre Gasperini, while Venetian *Scuole grandi* have attracted Patricia Fortini Brown, Brian Pullan, and many more. Bolognese confraternities have been the focus of Mario Fanti's numerous works, and Nicholas Terpstra has just published an important volume in English on them. Milanese and Lombard confraternities have been eagerly studied by a prolific group of scholars including Danilo Zardin, Marina Gazzini, Riccardo Bottoni, and Marina Olivieri Baldissarri. Several important works on the Genoese *casacce*, dealing especially with their rich artistic heritage, have appeared from the pens of Fausta Franchini Guelfi, Pier Luigi Gardella, Edoardo Grendi, Gianni De Moro, and a number of local historians. Confraternities in Urbino have been examined by Luigi Moranti. Umbrian confraternities have been studied for many years under the encouragement of the Centro di Studi sul Movimento dei Disciplinati, headed by Fr Ugolino Nicolini. His death has left a vacuum that has not yet been filled. The rich vein of Umbrian lay spirituality has been tapped by Giovanna Casagrande, Kathleen Falvey, Olga Marinelli, Nerida Newbigin, Luisa Proietti Pedetta, and many others. Roman confraternities have been studied by many scholars, including Anna Esposito, V. Paglia, Barbara Wisch, and Jean S. Weisz. Recently, confraternities in Puglia have received their much-deserved attention at the hands of an energetic group of scholars that gravitates around the Centro di Storia Religiosa in Puglia: Liana Bertoldi Lenoci, Vincenza Musardo Talò, Antonietta Latorre, Pietro Di Biase, Francesco Fella, Carmine Maci, Antonio Tripodi, and others. Not even Sardinia has been left out, with a volume on flagellant confraternities by Fr Antonio Virdis.[5]

The Italian peninsula was certainly not the only setting for such a flowering of lay religious organizations. Other areas, especially France and Spain, also reveal a remarkable increase in confraternities during this period. Long ago the Abbé Martin (d. 1776) noted the extensive growth of lay religious associations in Normandy, where, over the period of just two centuries, ecclesiastical authorities officially approved more than 1,220 confraternities in about 760 parishes. Much more recently, Jacques Chiffoleau noted their proliferation in the Avignon area in the years 1360–1500 and considered a number of factors that could have fostered such a development – the Black Death and its aftermath, the development of extravagant funeral rituals, the change in mental images of death, as well as the transformation of thirteenth-century political confraternities into fourteenth-century devotional and charitable associations. In assessing these factors, and conscious of the long and ancient history of confraternities, Chiffoleau admitted, however, that he was, for the moment, unable to establish a direct link between the phenomenal growth in lay confraternities and the demographic, economic, and social crises of the thirteenth and fourteenth centuries.[6] This wealth of confraternities has led to a wealth of scholarship in French-speaking areas. Among other historians who have contributed one could mention in passing Andrew E. Barnes, Noël Coulet,

Marie-Hélène Froeschle-Chopard, Gabriel Le Bras, Alain Tallon, Marc Venard, and Catherine Vincent, just to name a few.

A similar flowering of confraternities elsewhere in Europe has also provided scholars with plenty of material for their research. The extensive success of the confraternal movement in Spain has fed the scholarly minds of historians such as William A. Christian Jr, Maureen Flynn, Linda Martz, Miguel Luis López Muñoz, Susan Verdi Webster, and A.J.R. Russell-Wood. The Netherlands have drawn the attention, among others, of Valentijn Paquay and Paul Trio. English and Irish confraternities have been studied through the 'guilds' system by a multitude of historians, of whom I need mention but Colm Lennon, Geoffrey Martin, and Alexandra F. Johnston. There have been recent studies even on confraternities on Malta and in the Ukraine and Byelorussia.[7]

The confraternal movement of early-modern Europe need not be restricted to the Christian experience. The presence of Jewish confraternities in Germany and their similarity to Christian religious guilds were briefly discussed some time ago by Jacob Rader Marcus.[8] There were a number of Jewish confraternities in Spain and Italy as well. Brian Pullan refers to a confraternity of German Jews in Venice. David B. Ruderman examines the Ferrarese situation and concludes that, although 'the Jewish association was essentially dissimilar from the Christian society ... the goals and procedures of the Jewish and Christian organizations were not totally dissimilar.' Elliott Horowitz not only sheds light on Jewish confraternities in Verona, but also reveals the existence of Jewish youth confraternities – one founded in Asti in 1619 and another in Verona extant before 1586 (when it was absorbed into an adult confraternity).[9] Further research will probably reveal the presence of Jewish confraternities in other areas of Italy and of Europe. Similarly, confraternities have also been identified within the Moslem world in early-modern times. Recently, a three-year international project was undertaken to carry out a comparative analysis of Moslem and Christian confraternities within the context of Mediterranean society; its results are eagerly awaited.[10]

Such proliferation of lay religious organizations is, among other things, an indication of the religious fervour of the late Middle Ages and early Renaissance. In the case of Florence and Italy, some scholars have sought to identify the development of lay confraternities with the religious revival of the thirteenth and fourteenth centuries, fostered primarily by the two great Mendicant orders of the late Middle Ages, the Dominicans and Franciscans.[11] It is not a coincidence, then, that in Florence the two great Mendicant churches of Santa Maria Novella and Santa Croce were the focal points from which lay confraternities developed and radiated into the city.[12]

## Santa Maria Novella and Confraternities

The Dominican church of Santa Maria Novella, in the west end of town, became from an early time the major centre for Florentine lay confraternities. It readily made its cloisters and chapels available to them. The first such group was the Compagnia delle Laudi, founded by St Peter Martyr in 1244, but others soon followed. Fr Stefano Orlandi, a Dominican historian of that church, claimed with pride that one of the fruits of his order's ministry in Florence was the large number of 'pious societies and confraternities' that found lodging at Santa Maria Novella, and then lists fourteen of them.[13] Another Dominican historian of that church, Fr Vincenzo Fineschi, lists at least twenty-four confraternities which, at different times between the thirteenth and eighteenth centuries, met in the convent, cloisters, or church.[14] More recently, a lay historian, Massimo Papi, showed that Santa Maria Novella was at the forefront of the phenomenon of lay religious associations both in an absolute sense (that is, with respect to all other Florentine churches) and in a relative sense (that is, with respect to the other orders), and that its initiatives, at least in the thirteenth century, were systematically imitated by the other churches and orders operating in Florence.[15]

In the thirteenth century, the lay confraternities established under the patronage of the Dominican order sought to win salvation not only for the souls of their members but also for those of non-members. In line with the spirit of the order that fostered them, confraternities associated with the Dominicans often exhibited polemical or anti-heretical intentions.[16] Massimo Papi suggests it is not mere coincidence that the establishment of the first lay confraternities took place at Santa Maria Novella at a time when the Dominicans, through the tribunal of the Inquisition, were in fact conducting a 'political campaign' against Ghibelline factions in Florence by conveniently accusing them of heresy.[17] His conclusion is that confraternities were 'both pawns and players on the political chessboard of the thirteenth-century. The Order of Preachers used them as part of its anti-imperial politics in an attempt to favour the papal side at a time when the crisis between the two powers was most acute.'[18]

The major characteristic of confraternities associated with the Dominicans, however, was not so much their inquisitorial nature, or their political overtones, or their active militancy against heresy, but rather their devotional and charitable activities. They were, in fact, confraternities that met primarily in order to sing the praises of God and his saints; hence the term *laudese*, often applied to them. As an external manifestation of their internal commitment to the love of God, they then carried out particular charitable works for the benefit of their members and of society at large. Some of the most famous charitable confraternities in Florence, though not necessarily associated with the Dominicans, were the Compagnia dei Neri, whose particular act of charity was to comfort and escort criminals condemned to death, and then, if necessary, to give their bodies the dignity of a Christian burial; another was the Misericordia, still operating today, which provided then and now a first-aid and ambulance service; another was the Buonomini di San Martino, also still extant and active, offering financial assistance to citizens temporarily suffering economic distress. Although the confraternities just mentioned were some of the most visible and widely respected charitable organizations in Florence, a myriad of other confraternities offered a variety of assistance ranging from dowries for young women to commemorative masses for members.

## Youth Confraternities

Alongside such confraternities, which gathered adult men and/or women to pray and carry out a charitable work, there were also a number that were composed exclusively of young men, aged approximately thirteen to twenty-four. These, too, were *laudese* associations that gathered to pray and sing lauds in honour of God, the Virgin, and specific saints. They did not carry out personal penance for the benefit of their and their neighbour's souls, nor did they carry out one of the traditional works of mercy. Instead, their major focus of interest, after the obvious devotional intent, was to instruct their young members in Christian faith and morals. One such group, the first one in fact to be established within the city of Florence, was the Compagnia dell'Arcangelo Raffaello, also known as della Scala or della Natività.

The Arcangelo Raffaello was not the junior branch of an adult organization. It existed independently, of itself and for itself. The young men that it comprised looked after their secular and devotional needs generally free from adult interference – free, that is, except for the advice and guidance they received from the only two adults who held positions within the organization, the layman who was their guardian father and the priest who was their father corrector. It is clear from the administrative structure and from the activities of youth confraternities that, within the context of their organization, the young men enjoyed a remarkable amount of independence and initiative.

The devotional and religious activities of a youth confraternity included the recitation of the Office, the singing of religious songs (either vernacular *laude* and church hymns in Latin), commemoration of its deceased members, the celebration of the Forty Hours, and, outside their oratory, participation in processions and pilgrimages. Its secular activities included the election of officers, the maintenance of their oratory and rooms, the management of their financial and economic investments, the implementation of the decisions reached at business meetings, negotiations and contracts with persons or organizations outside the confraternity, and so forth. Within the context of the confraternity's educational program, the youths learned and taught catechism, delivered sermons, staged plays, learned music and singing, and generally imbibed the basic elements of a responsible and devout Christian life. For this reason youth confraternities were sometime known as *scuole di dottrina*, schools of doctrine.[19]

## Age Terminology

When examining youth confraternities, the question of terminology for age classifications needs to be clarified. The terms used by confraternities at the time to indicate their members, be it in Latin or in Italian, do not translate easily into English.

As Ottavia Niccoli points out, the Latin *puer*, found in phrases such as *societas puerorum*, indicated a male under the age of fourteen. As such, the individual was considered a child, something that was implied in the Italian term *puerizia*. Fourteen, she continues, was the age at which, according to Justinian, a boy reached sexual maturity and, coincidentally, appeared as a *bocca* ('mouth') in the Florentine *catasto*, the census used for the purpose of determining a family's taxable wealth. Though still nothing more than a statistic – the *catasto* records do not generally give the name of each *bocca* – the young person thus entered into the city's census and tax register to be counted and to be used as a taxable deduction. It is worth noting that at about this age a young Florentine male could become a full member of a youth confraternity, the general parameters for such organizations being thirteen to twenty-four years of age.[20]

An Italian equivalent for the Latin *puer* could at times be the term *bambino*, as we see used in the title of Niccoli's article on street gangs of young males, 'Compagnie di bambini ...' *Bambini*, however, is far more appropriate to the lower rather than the higher end of the age spectrum for *puer*, that is, for someone around the ages of five to ten rather than ten to fourteen. Confraternity documents themselves do not use it, for it would indicate children well below the minimum enrolment age of thirteen. For these reasons, therefore, *bambini* is not a suitable term for the subjects of our study.

A more appropriate Italian translation for *puer* might be *fanciullo*, a term that is often found in phrases such as *compagnie di fanciulli.* Christiane Klapisch-Zuber points out that in fourteenth- and fifteenth-century Tuscany a *fanciullo* was 'a child who had arrived at the age of reason and attained the age of speech but was nevertheless not yet an *adolescente* or *ragazzo* 16–20 years old.' Anyone younger than that, she adds, 'was described by diminutives of *fanciullo* or by words such as *putto*, *bambolino*.'[21] Confraternity and other documents do, in fact, use the term *fanciullo* very often to indicate their younger members who were not yet in the *giovani* category.

The difference between *fanciullo* and *giovane*, however, was somewhat fuzzy. In 1558, for example, the records of the Arcangelo Raffaello say that the father corrector asked all '*fanciulli* aged fifteen years and less' to leave the oratory so as to allow the older members to hold a special meeting at which they voted to accept into the confraternity several *giovanetti* – apparently the very *fanciulli* that had been asked to leave.[22] The confusion between *fanciullo* and *giovane* is aggravated even by official documents. When the 1560 copy of the Arcangelo Raffaello's statutes transcribes the 1442 papal bull that recognized and approved the confraternity, the heading for that page reads 'Copia d'una bolla apostolica della autorità et libertà della Compagnia et de' *fanciulli* et de' guardiani di quella' (emphasis added). The 1468 statutes and their 1560 copy, however, contain phrases such as 'et queste constitutioni et Capitoli che hanno a istituire et ordinare la vita et i costumi de' *giovani* et nutrirgli nel timore di Dio' (emphasis added) or 'per lo Guardiano intendiamo uno di maggiore età prudentia et experientia che non sono e *giovani* della scuola' (emphasis added).[23] Even the last phrase, 'giovani della scuola,' undermines the suggestion that school-aged youths were called *fanciulli* and youths over the age of fourteen were called *giovani.*

*Giovani* is, in itself, an ambiguous term. In his *Public Life in Renaissance Florence*, Richard Trexler defines *giovani* as males between the ages of twenty-four and thirty and then argues for a differentiation between them and *adolescenti.* On the basis of this differentiation he then postulates that, while 'adolescents' up to the age of twenty-four were active in confraternities, the *giovani* aged twenty-four to thirty were excluded from participation either in confraternities or in government. This, according to Trexler, left the *giovani* in an undetermined socio-political space and was a contributing factor to the violence perpetrated, with the tacit acceptance of Florentine culture, by groups of young men in this age group. Trexler also argues that the *giovani*, stymied by their exclusion from political office, were relegated to a purely festive role within Florentine society, a role that found its outlet in the 'youth confraternities' (Trexler's term) that appeared and disappeared within the pattern of Florentine festive life. At this point, Trexler notes that unlike their Venetian 'counterparts,' the Compagnie della Calza, the Florentine groups existed on an ad hoc basis, for the purpose of embellishing a particular feast, and were then disbanded once the event was over.[24]

Although Trexler focused his attention on an age group that was clearly present as a social and festive phenomenon of Florentine life in the fifteenth and sixteenth centuries, it is important to point out that the groups of young men he identifies did not constitute 'confraternities,' but rather groupings of merry-makers more akin to festive *potenze*.[25] They did not have a religious or an educational component, they did not own and manage physical wealth or possessions, and they did not enjoy, as he himself notes, continuity over time. It is inappropriate, therefore, to call these ad hoc festive groups 'youth confraternities' or to include them in a discussion of lay religious organizations.

Similarly the term 'adolescents' for young men aged twenty to twenty-four is also tricky. Klapisch-Zuber points out that in the *Convivio* Dante, following Avicenna, viewed *adolescentia* as an 'age of growth' extending from birth to '25 full years of age' – hardly a useful category for our discussions. On the other hand, Klapisch-Zuber adds, another tradition, drawing upon Isidore of Seville and transmitted by Vincent de Beauvais, did subdivide this extensive period into three shorter spans: '*infantia*, from birth to 7 years; *pueritia*, from 7 to 14; and *adolescentia*, strictly speaking, from 15 to 28 years.'[26] This categorization provides an age bracket for adolescence that approximates the limits suggested by the *Oxford English Dictionary*, which defines 'adolescence' as the period between childhood and adulthood, placing it for males at fourteen to twenty-five years of age.[27] Though the *OED* definition approximates fairly closely the age group of the youths that constituted the confraternities, the term 'adolescent' is ultimately inappropriate, for the documents of Florentine youth confraternities themselves do not use it. Indeed, they seem consciously to avoid it – perhaps because it suggests lack of maturity and therefore harbours negative implications.

One is thus left with the observation that Latin, Italian, and English terminology are neither clear nor consistent. In his often cited article 'Ritual in Florence: Adolescence and Salvation in the Renaissance,' Richard Trexler uses the terms 'boys,' 'adolescents,' and 'youths' as if they were synonyms. He is followed in this by such major scholars as Ronald F.E. Weissman and Christopher F. Black. John Henderson, on the other hand, is consistent, but uses an inappropriate term: 'boys' societies.' The ironic twist to the entire question of terminology might be found in John Walter Hill's articles on the Arcangelo Raffaello, where he finds himself in the unenviable position of arguing for significant adult membership in youth confraternities of the seventeenth century, while at the same time still referring to them as *boys'* confraternities.[28]

For the purpose of the current study, I will cut the Gordian knot by overriding the ambiguity of the Latin and Italian terms and referring to confraternities for males aged approximately thirteen to twenty-four as 'youth confraternities.'[29] Only when the original term *puer*, *fanciullo*, or *giovane* is clearly used in the original documents in a restrictive and exclusionary fashion will I attempt to render it with something other than the generic 'youth.' The inclusiveness of the term 'youth' will thus allow me to discuss the membership of the confraternity, composed of prepubescent children, adolescents, and young men in their early twenties, without fear of excluding one or the other category. Admittedly, when in the seventeenth century the membership of the confraternity gradually changes to include males over the age of twenty-four, my use of the term 'youth' will become much more circumspect.

## Youth Confraternities in Italy

Florence is unusual for both the presence and the success of youth confraternities. John Henderson sees the phenomenon of lay religious associations for young men as a 'peculiarly Florentine' feature, adding that 'although there are references to similar organizations in the Veneto and Rome, they were neither so numerous nor involved in such elaborate festive pageantry as in Florence.'[30] Indeed, before the renewed interest in the education of the young fostered by the sixteenth-century *Scuole di Dottrina Cristiana* and by the Tridentine reforms, there were hardly any youth confraternities anywhere else in Italy.

Perhaps the lacuna is only a lack of perception, not of fact. It may well be that further and more careful archival research will identify and bring to light youth confraternities active in early-modern times in other cities of the peninsula. Edoardo Grendi, for example, has identified about twenty-nine youth confraternities active in Genoa in 1460–1528, though he admits to difficulties in determining the exact age group of members of these *societates juvenum* and the extent of their lay religious nature. His 'alternative reading' for these organizations is, in fact, to consider them within the context of 'generational alliances engaged, in a different way, in a strategic program of political and ceremonial prestige.'[31] Such an interpretation, however, would align these Genoese groups more closely with Florentine *potenze* and Venetian Compagnie della Calza than with the lay religious youth confraternities we are examining.

A century ago Pietro Vigo identified a youth confraternity active in Pistoia in the early sixteenth century, and it, by all accounts, does seem to resemble those of Florence.[32] In 1969 Vittorino Meneghin, OFM, found two youth confraternities in the Veneto established by fellow Franciscans – one founded in 1499 in Feltre by fra Timoteo da Lucca under the title *Societas puerorum militantium sub sacratissimo nomine Iesu* (which the people soon started to call the Compagnia dei soldatelli di Gesù), and another founded in c.1503 in Verona by fra Giacomo Ongarello da Padova (d. 1517) under the name of Compagnia del Nome di Gesù in San Procolo. More recently Anna Esposito has pointed to the 'compagnia et oratorio di S. Pietro et S. Paulo,' which had been established 'to sustain with discipline and the best manners' the souls of adolescents, and which later, together with several adult confraternities, joined the Roman confraternity of the Gonfalone.[33] Lester K. Little has discovered a youth confraternity in Villa d'Ogna, a small village thirty-five kilometres north-east of Bergamo, and has even published its 1474 statutes. Nicholas Terpstra has pointed to the Compagnia di S. Girolamo, 'one of the few youths' confraternities in Renaissance Bologna.'[34] Documents from the Arcangelo Raffaello indicate the formation in 1585 of a youth confraternity by the same name in Portoferraio.[35] Clearly, further archival research is necessary, both in larger and smaller centres, before a true count can be made and an extensive study of the entire phenomenon of lay religious associations for youths can be undertaken.[36]

Until such a time as a global picture can be drawn, we must devote our energies to a closer examination of specific confraternities for youths in order to provide future scholars with the individual descriptions, histories, and analyses of the phenomenon. The author of the present volume, the first to be completely dedicated to a youth confraternity, hopes other scholars will follow it with a number of similar studies, each contributing to a fuller and more revealing picture of the associative practices of youth in early modern Europe.

2

# The Founding of the Arcangelo Raffaello and the Development of Youth Confraternities in Florence

The confraternity of the Arcangelo Raffaello was founded in 1411 by a gold-leaf worker whose name has not come down to us.[1] An early description of the foundation of the confraternity, dating it precisely to 27 December 1411, can be found in a manuscript from the *buca* of San Girolamo that, for a short time, was associated with the Arcangelo Raffaello:

> Resumé of the Statutes of the Company of the Nativity of Christ, of the under-age brothers, and their intentions ... having been founded and having received their own name on the 27th of December 1411, the feast-day of our glorious apostle and evangelist the blessed messer St John, our first advocate, in which day we will celebrate our principal feast of the pure and sweet and good Child Jesus, for whose love we will visit the needy poor at least once every eight days with bread and wine, and with devotion ... and we will meet together in charity every fifteen days to praise God ... as the four dear-in-Christ elder brothers of the Company of Saint Mary of Piety [*buca* of San Girolamo] will instruct us, whom God gave us to govern us and keep us. Since they are honest men, and good examples, we wish them to be our governors for life.[2]

The manuscript then lists the four members of the *buca* who were given responsibilities over the confraternity of the Arcangelo Raffaello. These *governatori maggiori* were the shearer (*cimatore*) Biagio di Lorenzo, Francesco Bianciardi, Bindo Guasconi,[3] and Bartolomeo di Teccio. Three priests, each with an assistant, were appointed to look after the spiritual needs of the youths: fra Raffaello di Ser Benedetto became *rettore et consolatore* assisted by M.o Alviso del Carmino; fra Paolo from the convent of Ognissanti, assisted by fra Jacopo Landi from Santo Spirito, was made *padre spirituale* with responsibilities for confession and for the instruction of novices; and Ser Antonio di Stefano from San Lorenzo became father corrector, charged, with the help of Ser Antonio from Santa Lucia de' Magnoli, with 'le corretioni de' fratelli,' that is, with assigning penances as necessary.[4]

## The Blessed Carlo Guidi da Montegranelli

There is no extant list or further information on the original members of the Arcangelo Raffaello. One of the other men associated with its beginnings is the Blessed Carlo Guidi da Montegranelli (c.1360–1417),[5] founder of several pious groups, both religious and lay – the order of the Eremiti di San Girolamo di Fiesole,[6] for example, and the confraternity di Santa Maria della Pietà, called *buca* of San Girolamo.[7] An entry in the *ricordi* of the *buca* of San Girolamo recalls a 'fervoroso discorso' in praise of the Blessed Carlo Guidi delivered by the eighteenth-century Florentine savant Domenico Maria Manni, who included in it much information on Guidi's life and on the *buca*. In that same discourse, Manni pointed out that Guidi had promoted the cult of the Archangel Raphael and was to be counted as one of the founders of the youths' confraternity of the Arcangelo Raffaello.[8] Although Manni claimed to have drawn his information from a manuscript in the library of the convent of Santa Maria Novella and from other documents consulted in writing his history of the church of Santa Felicita, I have been unable to corroborate his claim from original sources. In 1761, shortly after Manni, Giuseppe Maria Brocchi published Manni's claims in his biography of the Blessed Carlo Guidi.[9] Their claims, however, are very late, and remain unsubstantiated by contemporary evidence.

## Vespasiano da Bisticci

The earliest contemporary reference to the confraternity of the Arcangelo Raffaello so far located comes from the Florentine biographer and bookseller Vespasiano da Bisticci in his life of Cardinal Cesarini. After praising the cardinal for his deep spirituality and describing his participation in the devotional and penitential practices of the *buca* of San Girolamo, Vespasiano tells how the cardinal urged him to join the youth confraternity headed by Antonio di Mariano, that is, the confraternity of the Arcangelo Raffaello:

> There was, and there still exists today, a company in the Hospice of Lemmo named after St Jerome. It meets every Saturday night to recite the office and to take the dis-

cipline, which is a devout thing to do, and especially in those days, for it included many men of means and of very sound morals. Having heard of their reputation, [Cardinal Cesarini] went there most Saturdays, accompanied by two or three men from his household. Once inside, he would dismiss those who had accompanied him, and they would return for him at the time he would tell them. He would enter in the oratory and, having done his devotion, he would sit at the governor's desk, and would ask the governor to sit beside him. He would stay for the entire office, and take the discipline like everybody else. When they came to the discipline, there used to be so many tears and sighs and such wonderful devotion that no heart could have been so hardened as not to be moved; especially when Bartolomeo di Ser Benedetto would speak, for he was such a good and devout man, and was so powerfully skilled in speaking, that there is no man, however hardened, whom he could not have moved. As I have said, the cardinal was very devoted to this company. When I was not yet very old, one day when I went to his Eminence, he asked me if I belonged to any youth confraternity. I answered I did not. See the unheard of charity of the master! He said to me: 'I want you to join the confraternity of Ser Antonio di Mariano; you will tell him I sent you.' And so I did. I tell this to point out that when it came to the well-being of his neighbour he took care not only of great matters, but also the small details. He then asked me if I wished to be a priest, for it would help me with my studies and would give me a benefice on which to live. He told me to think about this for a fortnight. At the end of the fortnight he asked me what I wanted to do. I answered that I did not wish to be a priest. He answered that if he could help me in other ways, he would. He was all love and charity.[10]

The connections Vespasiano draws between the spirituality of the cardinal and his care for the young are indicative of the strong contemporary interest in the education of the young that, in our case, is evidenced throughout the documents of the Arcangelo Raffaello right up to the seventeenth century.

## Early Meeting Sites

It is not certain where the confraternity met in the first twenty years of its existence. There are indications it changed sites several times. Perhaps, at the very beginning, under the leadership of the nameless gold-leaf worker (*battiloro*) mentioned by Del Migliore, it met in various different places. As the group gained stability, however, it settled temporarily in the Ospedale di San Paolo, which faces the piazza at the opposite end from the Dominican church of Santa Maria Novella. It then moved to rooms made available to it 'in the ancient houses of the Buonavolti of San Pancrazio.'[11]

The uncertainty in determining or in establishing precise meeting places is an indication of the precariousness of the confraternity's existence in the period 1411–30. Such a situation is understandable. The confraternity of the Arcangelo Raffaello was the first, and until 1427 the only lay religious confraternity of young men in Florence. It had no previous or comparable sister institution to support it spiritually or temporally in establishing itself in the city.

## The First Four Youth Confraternities

On 8 September 1427, however, the Arcangelo Raffaello gave birth to a second such organization. Twelve youths left the parent group and established a confraternity of their own. They moved to the convent of San Marco, at that time occupied by the Silvestrini monks.[12] There, the new group, headed by the shearer Biagio di Lorenzo,[13] called itself the Compagnia della Purificazione della Vergine Maria e di San Zanobi, but became known also as the Compagnia di San Marco, from the name of its host institution.[14] The separation was amicable, and the two groups retained close ties for the rest of their 350-year existence. They observed, for example, a ritual of reciprocal annual visits on the feast-day of their patron saints, referring to it as a 'brotherhood and union.'[15] Their choice of a name for the new company is suggestive of the new group's own awareness and acknowledgment of their debt and relationship to the parent organization – the Purification of the Virgin follows upon and finds its *raison d'être*, as it were, from the Nativity.

The reasons for the division into two different confraternities are unclear. Age or numbers may have played a role, as may have the more 'apostolic' desire to increase the number of such companies in Florence. This last possibility is suggested by a copy of the statutes of the confraternity of the Purificazione which clearly state that the second group was established 'so that this praiseworthy and charitable work would be carried out in more places.'[16] It is not unthinkable that eminent men, aware of the important role to be played by confraternities even among the youth, would have fostered, or perhaps even proposed, the creation of new sodalities.

Quite independently from the Arcangelo Raffaello and the Purificazione, a third confraternity, this time under the patronage of St John the Evangelist, was established in Florence in 1427.[17] Its statutes were officially approved in 1427 by Tommaso di Bordella, vicar to Amerigo de' Corsini, archbishop of Florence.[18] They tell how the confraternity first met on

8 May, the feast of the apparition of the Archangel Michael on the peninsula of the Gargano, and how, in 1427, it was meeting in the church of Santa Trinita of the Ingesuati, in the parish of San Lorenzo. On 27 August 1438 the Gesuati friars sold their convent for three hundred florins to Luigi d'Urbano Bruni, 'a devout man who wanted to buy it ... for a certain society or company of youths that was started there and had been received by the priests when they resided there.'[19] The sale took place the following day, but Bruni did not, at this time, designate the beneficiaries of his purchase. This he did several years later, on 29 July 1441, when he named not the youths' confraternity of the Vangelista, as the above document would lead us to believe, but the *buca* of San Paolo.[20] Perhaps as a result of this unexpected redirecting of the gift from the youth confraternity to the *buca*, in the years 1441–50 the Vangelista abandoned the church of Santa Trinita for the cloisters of Santa Maria Novella.[21] On 18 July 1450 they returned to Santa Trinita, now owned by the men of San Paolo, where they continued, well into the eighteenth century, to dispute the men's ownership and rights to the site.[22]

The confraternity of the Vangelista is one of the most important groupings of young men in fourteenth-century Florence and deserves greater attention. By the end of the century it had not only become an important venue of Florentine youth spirituality but also played a role in the political fibre of the city. Its close ties with the Medici are undeniable, especially with Lorenzo's two younger sons, Giovanni (later Pope Leo X) and Giuliano (later duke of Nemours). On his triumphal return to Florence in 1515, Giovanni de' Medici, now Pope Leo X, showered his generosity on it because, in words attributed to him, he had frequented it for some time and had nearly been brought up in it.[23]

Lorenzo himself composed a religious play, the *Rappresentazione di Santi Giovanni e Paolo*, as a Carnival entertainment commissioned and produced by his son Giuliano for a performance at the Vangelista on 17 February 1491.[24] From the mid-sixteenth century, plays began to be staged quite often in the confraternity, so much so that it eventually built a *teatro* to accommodate them.[25]

The fourth youth confraternity of the early Quattrocento was dedicated to St Nicholas of Bari and was known by the pseudonym of il Ceppo.[26] The group had met somewhere in the Oltrarno as early as the late thirteenth century. In 1417 they moved across the Arno into the parish of San Jacopo tra' Fossi, where they built their own oratory next to the Spedale dei Santi Jacopo e Filippo della Torricella, known as the Ceppo delle Sette Opere di Misericordia. The *buca* of San Girolamo Oltrarno moved with the youths, and was granted the use of their oratory. In 1530 the men of San Girolamo Oltrarno moved back to the other side of the Arno, to a site on the dreadfully steep Costa San Giorgio, sharing it with the youth confraternity of Sant'Antonio da Padova. The youths of San Niccolò, instead, moved in temporarily with the confraternity of Santa Maria della Croce al Tempio. In 1565, the youths made their last move, into their own brand-new oratory at the corner of via del Fosso and via della Badessa, built on land they had acquired in 1561. Of the four youth confraternities founded in the early fifteenth century, it is the only one to have survived to the present day. It continues to meet at the 1565 site, though today the intersecting streets are called via Verdi and via Pandolfini and the average age of the mixed-gender membership is well above that of youths.

The creation and growth of youth confraternities in the early decades of the fifteenth century suggests that Florentines felt a strong need for such lay religious organizations of young men. There are many reasons for such a need. The simple fact of popular piety was certainly a motivating force. A variety of more complex reasons, such as the desire to educate the young in the Christian faith, also played a part. The statutes of the confraternity of the Arcangelo Raffaello point out that the founder's intention was, in fact, to educate young men in the Christian faith and life.[27] The desire to involve the youths in activities more profitable to social and civic life than the unbridled rowdiness their years might otherwise elicit is yet another factor to be considered. These could include not only devotional or educational activities but also physical ones. The presence in later years of a ball court (*pallottolaio*) next to the rooms and oratories of some confraternities indicates that sports in general, and ball games in particular, were an active component of confraternity life.[28] Confraternity members also staged plays, sang, played instruments, organized feasts, participated in public celebrations, and thus became engaged in a variety of socially acceptable bonding and educating activities.[29]

## Ambrogio Traversari

Soon after youth confraternities began to show signs of success and popularity, the clergy began to show an active interest in them. The local clergy certainly had had an interest in them earlier – the simple fact that the youths were given meeting rooms in or near churches and convents points to early attention and support. By the 1430s, even the higher clergy became aware of their importance and fostered their work.

In 1435 Ambrogio Traversari, Florentine humanist and general of the

Camaldolese monks, wrote two letters to Pope Eugenius IV, then residing in Florence. In the first, Traversari described briefly the nature, organization, and activities of the youth confraternities in the city:

Hear now something equally pious, most Holy Father: Our city has several societies of noble, middle-class, and poor boys ['puerorum']. At the head of each is a faithful, grave, religious, and God-fearing man who rears these [boys] and who, in secular dress, drills the recruits for the militia of the Eternal King. Following their rule, they observe continence in everything. They flee from inane spectacles and all games, and they abstain also from the idle talk [of the games and spectacles]. They confess more frequently, and take communion often. And while during the remaining days of the week they exercise their individual trade under the supervision of their relatives, on Sundays and feast days they all meet at a designated place where they give themselves over to the praise of God ['divinis laudibus'] and use their time for worthwhile colloquies. When however they have left their childhood years behind, they transfer to another group where older people meet, and continue in similar works. Many of them, once they have tasted the goodness of innocence, enter the religious life.[30]

In the second letter, written that same year, Traversari expanded the description and underlined the educational aspects, social and spiritual, of such confraternities:

The leaders of the city are repeatedly pleased to send their sons to be nourished in this school and to be educated in this school of Christian virtue. In it nothing impious is learned, nothing other than good habits is imbibed ... [Through this training] they often remain innocent amidst the obscene raillery of criminals ... On Sundays and feast days, when greater license for lasciviousness is usurped, they gather together, and after salubrious admonitions, they either recite the psalms or sing hymns together. And if perhaps someone has occasionally or lightly violated the rules, penance is meted out and the crime is confessed. Formed and indoctrinated in this way, they return to their parents' homes and, the parents being presented with such a specimen of religion, the boys [contribute] through example and incitement to the good morality of the family ... [If the boys] decide to remain laymen, they retain the taste of supernal grace which they receive in their tender years. To whatever magistracies of the city they are elected, they cultivate justice before all else.[31]

Traversari, who was fully aware of the educational value of such organizations and of their larger potential for moulding future secular and spiritual leaders, pointed them out eagerly to the pope.

## Pope Eugenius IV

The pope, however, was not unaware of youth confraternities himself. Even before Traversari's two letters, his attention had been drawn to them, and in particular to the confraternity of the Arcangelo Raffaello. In 1430 Eugenius IV attended the performance of a Nativity play staged by the youths of the Arcangelo Raffaello at the church of San Pancrazio. The pope was so impressed by what he saw that he took the youths under his wing, granted papal approval to their constitution (*capitoli*), gave them space for a permanent oratory and meeting rooms next to the Ospedale della Scala,[32] gave official approval to their name (the Company of the Nativity of Our Lord), and assigned them a patron saint under whose protection to meet (the Archangel Raphael).[33]

A few years later, in 1442, Pope Eugenius IV, still residing in Florence, issued a bull (24 June 1442) recognizing only four youth confraternities in that city – those of the Natività or Arcangelo Raffaello, the Purificazione or San Marco, San Giovanni Evangelista known as the Vangelista, and San Niccolò del Ceppo.[34] He also established a system whereby new youth confraternities could be authorized only with the approval of a papal commission composed of the prior of the Dominican convent of San Marco (at that time the saintly friar Antoninus Pierozzi), the abbot of the Florentine *badia* (at that time don Ignazio Franchi da Genova),[35] plus the guardians of the four original confraternities. This same papal commission was also charged with approving the appointment of future guardians for the youth confraternities in the city. It has been suggested that this last regulation was set in place to prevent confraternities from unilaterally removing and replacing their guardian fathers, but I have not been able to find contemporary references to substantiate such a view.[36]

## The Other Five Youth Confraternities

As a result of such strict regulations, the number of youth confraternities in Florence did not increase as noticeably as that of adult confraternities. While in the fifteenth century the number of adult confraternities grew from 52 to 156,[37] that of youth confraternities increased from four to nine. Three were approved in 1453–4 – those of Sant'Antonio da Padova, San Bernardino, and Santa Brigida.

The confraternity of the Annunciazione e Sant'Antonio da Padova was also known as San Giorgio, from the name of the church where it met in the fifteenth century, and, in the sixteenth, from the name of the street on which its oratory stood.[38] In the local slang, the confraternity was also known as 'la Cornacchia' ('the crow') or 'la Gazza' ('the magpie'), two irreverent and quasi-sacrilegious terms poking fun at the iconology of the Annunciation.[39] According to its own records, the confraternity was founded in August 1441, and was granted meeting rooms by don Placido Catanzio, prior of the church of San Giorgio sulla Costa, next to that church's chapel of Sant'Umiliano.[40] Forced to vacate its premises in September 1520 to make room for the nuns of St Verdiana, the confraternity purchased part of a house on the Costa San Giorgio from Francesco di Jacopo Canigiani and restructured it to its needs. A room reputed to have been St Catherine of Siena's bedroom when she resided with the Canigiani during a visit to Florence was turned into the sacristy, and the rest of the building into an oratory. Once the work was completed (1533), the men of the *buca* of San Girolamo Oltrarno joined the youths and built their own oratory and rooms on top of those of Sant'Antonio.

The confraternity of San Bernardino and Santa Caterina was founded in 1461 by Paolo di Michele, but was soon placed by the archbishop of Florence under the care of the shearer (*cimatore*) Lionardo di Paolo.[41] At first the confraternity met in the church of Santa Maria Alberighi on the Piazza degli Alberighi, in the Quarter of San Giovanni. On 22 March 1489/90 it associated itself with the *buca* of Sant'Antonio Abate, which was meeting at that time in the church of San Cristofano del Corso degli Adimari, and the two together moved to the old Cistercian convent of Cestello, which was then located in Borgo Pinti, on the site of the present-day church of Santa Maria Maddalena de' Pazzi.[42]

The confraternity of Santa Brigida, which took its name from the church where it met, is mentioned in the 1454 processional list. Nothing more, however, not even the founding date, is known about it.[43]

At a later time, sometime before the end of the fifteenth century, two more confraternities for youths were formally ratified and added to the official list – Sant'Alberto, and San Bastiano.

There is very little information extant on the youth confraternity of Sant'Alberto dei Fanciulli, also known as Sant'Alberto Bianco from the white gowns the youths wore. It was founded in 1419 and met in the cemetery of the church of Santa Maria del Carmine until 1565, when it amalgamated with the adult confraternity of the Assunta detta del SS. Crocifisso.[44]

Little is also known about the confraternity of San Bastiano dei Fanciulli. It was founded in 1460 and was closely associated with the *buca* of San Jacopo Oltrarno, which met by the church of San Jacopo Sopr'Arno.

In the mid-sixteenth century, the confraternity performed at least thirteen plays, most of them of a very secular nature, composed by the notary and dramatist Giovan Maria Cecchi. Although suppressed in 1785, its documents were not transferred to the Archivio di Stato but remained with the *buca* of San Jacopo Oltrarno, which is still extant and operative.[45] It was known, in a jocular way, as the company of the 'Freccione' ('the big arrow'), a reference to its patron's iconology. In a comic poem entitled 'In lode della Compagnia di San Bastiano,' the mid-sixteenth-century Florentine poet and dramatist Anton Francesco Grazzini poked fun at the confraternity by praising its music master and its actors, and lamenting that its small oratory was its only drawback.[46]

Writing in the 1530s, the historian Benedetto Varchi mentioned that there were nine youth confraternities in the city. Varchi describes them as 'compagnie de' fanciulli' and says they met every Sunday and on holidays of obligation to sing Vespers and the other Divine Offices under the direction of their guardian father and their father corrector. And he also mentioned that they participated in the processions of the clergy for St John's and other solemn feasts.[47] The youths took part in these processions wearing their white confraternal robes, a symbol of their innocence, and carrying their confraternity's banner (*segno*). At times some of the youths donned costumes to represent their patron saint surrounded by angels. Occasionally, especially in the context of the St John's parade, they actually staged *tableaux vivants* or short plays in the course of the procession.[48]

## The Prestige of Youth Confraternities

Although few in number, the youth confraternities enjoyed great prestige. The confraternity of the Arcangelo Raffaello, the first to be independently founded and to receive papal attention, claimed pre-eminence among them. A seventeenth-century description of the confraternity, apparently drawn up during an archiepiscopal visitation, begins with the comment: 'This is the first and foremost of the four Doctrines established by the Glorious St Antoninus Archbishop of this city, and by tradition we say that the other confraternities had their beginnings in this one, which existed before them in those times.'[49]

The Arcangelo Raffaello's traditional pre-eminence was reflected in processional lists, where it received pride of place, coming last in the sequence of youth confraternities. St Antoninus's official regulation for the procession in 1454 reflected and visualized this order of precedence by decreeing a processional pattern that was clearly based on a seniority system, with the youngest confraternity marching first and the eldest last. Thus the youth confraternities had Santa Brigida first in the line-up, followed in order by the Compagnia di San Jacopo detta del Nicchio, San Bernardino, San Giorgio detta di Sant'Antonio da Padova, San Giovanni Evangelista, San Marco detta della Purificazione, and the Arcangelo Raffaello detta della Scala.[50] The processional order could, on occasion, give rise to competitions that turned violent, as when the men of the adult confraternities of San Lorenzo in Palco and of the Carità came to blows, with both fists and torches, inside the Duomo during the Corpus Christi procession.[51] Such undignified behaviour in a sacred space reflects, among other things, the importance and prestige attached to processional position. Surprisingly enough, the youth confraternities never descended to physical violence to assert their prestige, for they recognized the pre-eminence of the Arcangelo Raffaello and regulations established by St Antoninus until all but one of the youth confraternities were suppressed by grand-ducal decree in March 1785.

# 3

# At the Ospedale della Scala (1430s–1530)

The prestige garnered by the confraternity of the Arcangelo Raffaello was due not only to its primogeniture among the youth confraternities in the city, but also to the patronage and support it received from people in authority. Cardinal Cesarini recommended it to youths of promise, such as Vespasiano da Bisticci. Ambrogio Traversari spoke highly of youth confraternities in his two letters to the pope and probably expanded on his views or emphasized the work of individual groups in his conversations with the pontiff. Eugenius IV, on his part, was clearly pleased with the activities of the Arcangelo Raffaello and supported the confraternity's need for suitable accommodations. The following pages will examine the Arcangelo Raffaello's different meeting sites in the fifteenth century, and consider in depth the importance and significance of its eventual location within the complex of the Ospedale della Scala, from which it took one of its unofficial names – the Compagnia della Scala.

## First Locations

Before the confraternity was able to acquire its own rooms and oratory next to the Ospedale della Scala, it met at two other locations. Del Migliore mentions that in the fifteenth century it first met at the Ospedale di San Paolo, then in the 'ancient houses of the Buonavolti of San Pancrazio,' and finally next to the Ospedale della Scala.[1] Unfortunately, no documentary description of the confraternity's quarters in any of these sites has survived – if it ever existed. In order to envision the confraternity's three locales during the first century of its existence we must therefore reconstruct the sites from information culled from a variety of secondary sources and from the present urban configuration of the area.

The Ospedale di San Paolo stands at the southern end of piazza Santa Maria Novella. Its loggias still grace the piazza, a little the worse for their age and the weather. We have no indication, however, of where exactly (if ever) the confraternity met in the Ospedale.[2] The confraternity's second site, 'in the ancient houses of the Buonavolti of San Pancrazio,' is an even more elusive indication. The 1427 *catasto* lists the Buonavolti holdings, saying that Marco and Alessandro di Bartolomeo Buonavolti, the only Buonavolti registered in Florence, had their family house in the parish of San Paolo (not San Pancrazio, as Del Migliore claimed) on a lot bordering the street on one side, on another the Ospedale di San Paolo, for one-third of another the house of Angiolo di Piero Manetti, for one-quarter that of Matteo di Nofri d'Azzo, for one-fifth the friars of Santa Maria Novella, and for one-sixth the Ospedale di San Paolo again – and does not mention at all the presence of any confraternity on or next to that site.[3]

Today, the church of San Pancrazio, which stands on a tiny square at the intersection of via della Spada and via de' Federighi, has been deconsecrated and turned into the museum for the works of the contemporary sculptor Marino Marini. Two stone lions, much corroded by the weather, lie silently on guard at either side of the church steps. The portico and entrance have been protected by enclosing them with an enormous glass wall that suggests that the church itself is an *objet d'art* in a display case.[4] In 1430 the youths performed a Nativity play in this church in the presence of Pope Eugenius IV and the Florentine Signoria. Since it seems that the youths, and not another group, organized the event, we can infer that relations between the youths in the confraternity and the clergy of San Pancrazio were amicable and co-operative. Pope Eugenius IV, who attended the performance, was so impressed by it that he became a patron of the confraternity and granted the youths quarters next to the Ospedale della Scala.[5]

## The Move to via della Scala

It seems that by 1427 the youths of the Arcangelo Raffaello had already been meeting in rooms off the via della Scala they rented from the Benedictine monastery of San Silvestro.[6] Now, with the pope's personal intervention, they were able to renew their lease and expand their quarters. When the rental contract came up for renegotiation in 1435, the pope issued a bull asking the abbot of San Salvi fuori le Mura to continue to allow the youths to use the site next to the Ospedale della Scala where they had been meeting 'for some time,' and which they had restored at their own expense.[7] There are no documents indicating the nature of the restoration work, but we can assume it involved the necessary alterations to convert the space into a standard confraternity complex with oratory and rooms (see below, ch. 5, pp. 61–70, for a detailed description of the 1690 complex at Santa Maria Novella). The confraternity's right to these spaces was reiterated again in a legal instrument of 1 July 1438.[8] Subsequently, on 10 November 1439, in yet another bull, the pope asked the abbot to allow the youths to rent part of the garden adjacent to their oratory for a yearly sum of two florins.[9] In July 1440 the youths began a fund-raising campaign among members and friends to purchase the garden, and were able to acquire possession on 28 July 1440.[10] Finally, on 22 June 1442, two other papal bulls confirmed the youths' possession of the site, pointed to the need for further expansion, and granted them space in the adjacent monastery of San Silvestro to be used by the older members of the confraternity. As these documents indicate, the Arcangelo Raffaello was thriving not only spiritually but materially as well.

The confraternity, it seems, was growing and attracting more members than its present site could accommodate. One of the 22 June 1442 bulls points out that the San Silvestro site, which had housed the Benedictine nuns transferred to Sant'Agata, was being requested so that members over the age of nineteen could have a place to meet separately from the younger members of the Arcangelo Raffaello.[11] For an annual rent of two pounds of wax, to be paid to the abbess of the Roman monastery of Santa Maria in Julia,[12] the youths received the second site, and the older members began to use it for their meetings. Two days later, on 24 June, Pope Eugenius IV issued the bull recognizing only four youth confraternities in Florence (see above, ch. 1, p. 30). Because the bull does not speak of a separate confraternity at the San Silvestro site, it is clear that the group of older Arcangelo Raffaello members was not considered a new confraternity. This division into two subgroups within one confraternity, one consisting of older youths and one of younger boys, reappeared sporadically in later years. On such occasions, the two groups invariably remained equally part of the confraternity of the Arcangelo Raffaello.

The division by age was clearly reached for reasons of convenience, and not because of a fundamental change in the concept of a youth confraternity. Had it been otherwise, the confraternity would have split permanently into two different organizations, one for youths aged thirteen to eighteen and the other for youths aged nineteen to twenty-four, as was to be the case in 1443 with the Bolognese youth confraternity of San Girolamo.[13] The separation into two subgroups within the same organization may have been precipitated by a question of space. The Scala site was probably becoming inadequate, too small for a growing confraternity that had attracted favourable attention from the pope and his cardinals. The purchase of a garden plot adjacent to the Scala site indicates that the confraternity was also expanding its scope and interests by giving its members the opportunity to take part in games and other open air activities (see below, chs. 15–17 for a discussion of ball games and theatrical productions). Space requirements, therefore, were becoming an important concern for the confraternity. A similar division into younger and older subgroups – that is, into a morning and an evening *tornata* – would resurface at later times, again in periods of exceptional growth in memberships and activities (see below, ch. 6, pp. 74–8).

## The Site on via della Scala

The impressive complex of the Ospedale della Scala, at the south-east corner of via della Scala and via Polverosa (today's via degli Orti Oricellari), has undergone major alterations since the fifteenth century. It is possible, however, to identify the site given to the Arcangelo Raffaello as the chapel and rooms that run southward along the old via Polverosa (ill. 1).[14] The north exterior wall of the Scala complex, running eastward along the via della Scala, displays to this day some carved stone markings bearing the crests of the Ospedale (the three-rung ladder with a cross above it) and of the Pollini family (three wheels and a horizontal bar), but there are no ownership markings on any exterior walls to suggest that the confraternity of the Arcangelo Raffaello might have owned rooms in the complex. The Arcangelo Raffaello was clearly a tenant, not an owner of the site it had been granted.

Though merely a tenant, the Arcangelo Raffaello found itself very well situated. Its rooms and oratory were located within one of the major charitable institutions in Florence. The Ospedale had been founded in 1351 by Sandro di Cione Pollini on the model of the famous Sienese hospice of the same name. The youths were also neighbours, across the street, with their patron, Pope Eugenius IV, who resided in the apartments at the back of the convent of Santa Maria Novella (with an entrance directly from via della Scala). And across the via Polverosa stretched the Orti Oricellari, the gardens of the Rucellai family, where in the 1510s–20s some of the most eminent and acute minds of Florence would gather to discuss political and philosophical questions. The location was prime real estate, especially for a lay religious organization that consisted of young men under twenty-four years of age. The youths used it to their advantage and tied themselves closely to the site by adopting for themselves the name and the image that came with it.

## The Confraternity and the Ospedale

In fact, close proximity with the Ospedale della Scala gave the confraternity of the Arcangelo Raffaello one of its epithets and its monogram. The Ospedale, which had lent its name to the street that ran in front of it, now also lent its name to the youth confraternity that met with its walls. The confraternity of the Arcangelo Raffaello, already known as della Natività from the play it performed, now also became known as the confraternity of the Scala from the building complex in which it had found a home. It adopted not only the name, but also the Ospedale's monogram, the three-rung ladder with a cross above it, personalizing it with the addition of the letters N, D, A, and R at the sides of the ladder, a clearly understood acronym for 'Dominus Noster Archangelus Raphael' (see ill. 6).[15] The association between the Ospedale and the confraternity remained so ingrained in the Florentine psyche that the epithet and the monogram continued to be applied to the confraternity even after its 1530 move from the Ospedale della Scala to the convent of Santa Maria Novella.

Proximity with the Ospedale also brought the confraternity association with the hospice's founders and patrons, the Pollini family. Cione di Lapo Pollini (d. 1348) had founded the Ospedale in 1313 on the model of the well-known hospice by the same name in Siena. At first the Ospedale had only a dozen beds, but it quickly grew in size and scope. It began, for example, to welcome abandoned children, thus becoming a precursor for the better-known Ospedale degli Innocenti, into which it was eventually incorporated in September 1535.[16]

The Pollini family, whose coat of arms was displayed on the outside walls of the Ospedale, lived nearby, in a palazzo on piazza Santa Maria Novella. It continued its association with the youths even after the confraternity moved to other quarters. Membership lists of the mid-sixteenth century contain the names of several Pollini youths, among them Cammillo d'Antonio, who served as its administrator (*provveditore*) in the 1570s.[17]

However, in spite of close ties and associations with the Ospedale and the Pollini, the question of rights to the site at the Scala remained unsettled. It surfaces, for example, in a 1491 document by Zanobi di Niccolò Pollini in which he confirms, on behalf of himself and the other procurators of the

Ospedale della Scala, the confraternity's possession of land adjacent to the Ospedale.[18] The confirmation is signed in the library of the convent of San Marco and in the presence of fra Girolamo Savonarola, prior of the convent of San Marco, Bartolomeo de Cenis di Gualdo, vicar of the archbishop, Malatesta Sacramoro, canon of the cathedral,[19] and Dom Ambrogio di Marchionne and Dom Andrea, both of the Badia.

The autograph copy is in the hand of another cathedral dignitary, the *proposto* Giorgio Antonio di Ser Amerigo Vespucci, a noted humanist and teacher, and uncle to the famous explorer.[20] The persons in the group do not constitute the papal commission established in the bull of 24 June 1442, and thus cannot be considered to be a supervisory body, of sorts, for the confraternity's dealings. They are, however, a group of eminent clerics representing the foremost components of Florentine religious life: the curia, the cathedral, the convent of San Marco, the Badia. Their presence indicates ecclesiastical interest and concern at the highest level for the affairs and actions of the confraternity. The involvement of Savonarola and of two men who were later to become eminent converts to his movement is also noteworthy – their role is not clear, but their presence suggests that the confraternity may already have had ties with the Dominicans.

The 1491 confirmation of land-holdings may have been a document necessary for physical improvements to be made to the fabric of the building or to the confraternity. Internal renovations, in fact, were carried out shortly thereafter, in January 1492, when a fund-raising drive produced enough money to replace the choir stalls (*coro*) and the light fixtures (*chandellieri*) in the oratory.[21] Among the contributors we find Giorgio Antonio Vespucci, who had notarized the 1491 document, Francesco di Zanobi Pollini, son of the procurator for the Ospedale della Scala, and an anonymous friend of Dom Ambrogio di Marchionne, the representative from the Badia.[22] External work in the garden was undertaken a few years later when an addition was made to a garden wall built a few years earlier by order of the Otto di Balia to separate the confraternity's garden from an adjacent burial site that held about eight thousand victims of the 1478 plague.[23] The wall was raised an unspecified amount, a symbol perhaps of the distancing and the enclosing that was taking place, physically as well as figuratively, at the end of the Quattrocento in Florentine confraternities.

## The Silence of 1494–1530

The years between 1494 and 1530 were, in fact, a difficult period for all Florentine confraternities. This was a time punctuated by political and health concerns that led to the intermittent closure of all confraternities. As a result, there are no documents extant touching on the Arcangelo Raffaello site in these years. We may assume that the confraternity was no longer in a financial, or even a psychological, position to contemplate significant public activities, expansion, or even renovations to its site. The halcyon days of papal patronage were over, and the uncertainties of a new regime's mistrust were forcing all confraternities to avoid attracting attention. The Arcangelo Raffaello would have to wait until the 1530s for the dust of the Savonarola and Soderini years to settle and for a new, more favourable political regime to allow it to expand and prosper.

# 4

# Prelates, Princes, and Priors

The confraternity's new location on the via della Scala made the youths neighbours of the pope, whose own apartments at the back of the convent of Santa Maria Novella had an entrance from that same street. Such proximity was, in effect, further consolidation of the confraternity's prestigious position as a group fostered by, and close to, a pope whose many years of residence in Florence had made of him an important figure in the life of the city. This chapter will examine the contacts that the Arcangelo Raffaello and, in passing, other youth confraternities enjoyed with the individuals that held the religious and political reins of the city during the fifteenth century – the saintly archbishop Antonino Pierozzi, the ruling Medici family, and the reformer Girolamo Savonarola.

## St Antoninus

Eugenius IV's stay in Florence is often seen within the context of the high-water mark of the Ecumenical Council of 1439, which convoked and sought to reunite the churches of eastern and western Christendom. Although unable to resolve the schism that divided the Greek and Latin Church, the pope did succeed in his more localized contributions to the spiritual health of Christendom. In Florence, for example, he fostered the spirituality and piety of the people in a variety of ways. His support of youth confraternities has been mentioned above (see ch. 2, p. 30). He also reformed several important Florentine monasteries. Vespasiano da Bisticci recalls that he introduced the observant Dominicans in San Marco and convinced Cosimo the Elder to subsidize generously the renovations of that convent. He introduced the reformed Benedictine congregation of Santa Giustina da Padova at the Badia and instituted the practice of annual appointments of abbots.[1] In San Salvi he introduced the Benedictine monks of San Giovanni Gualberto (also known as the Vallambrosians) as well as the practice of annual appointment of abbots. Similar reforms were brought about to the monasteries of Settimo, Cestello, San Donato, the Badia in Fiesole, and others.[2] In all of these changes, Vespasiano points out, the pope sought to replace conventuals with observants, a clear indication of his intentions to reform the clergy and correct some of the abuses that had come under attack from contemporary reformist movements and the Council of Basel (1431–49).

Pope Eugenius IV's most important and effective intervention in the religious life of Florence was, however, the appointment of Antonino Pierozzi (1389–1459), prior of the convent of San Marco (1439–44), as archbishop of the city.[3] The diminutive friar, who refused to shed his Dominican robes for the rich trappings of his new office, had a profound effect on Florentine religious life that continued well past his own episcopacy (1446–59) and made of him an icon of Florentine spirituality. His canonization in 1523 merely confirmed what Florentines, then as now, believed about their beloved archbishop.

Among his many reforms, Antoninus undertook a thorough examination of Florentine confraternities. He did this from the vantage point of personal experience with such organizations. He had been, in fact, father corrector of two of the most stringent flagellant groups in Florence – the *buca* of San Girolamo and the *buca* of San Paolo.[4] He had also regularly visited youth confraternities and had taken part in the catechesis that was the hallmark of such schools.[5] In his reform of confraternities, Antoninus insisted that they write or revise their statutes and that they bring them to him for official archiepiscopal approval. The youth confraternity of the Purificazione, for example, obliged, and had their *capitoli* approved by him on 3 April 1448.[6] The Arcangelo Raffaello, on the other hand, seems not to have submitted its statutes for Antoninus's approval – the earliest copy extant, and apparently the first one to be drawn up, bears the date of 25 October 1468, and the approval of Giuliano di Antonio da Montelupo, suffragan bishop Florence.[7]

The Purificazione probably responded sooner to Antoninus's directions because its ties with him were that much closer. Richa claims Antoninus, while still a friar, had been its 'spiritual director,' that is, father corrector.[8] Then, as prior of the convent of San Marco, Antoninus had extensive and official contacts with all three lay organizations meeting in areas under his jurisdiction: the Purificazione, the Magi, and the silk weavers' confraternity or the Arte di Por Santa Maria.[9] Such contacts extended to what could be considered active support, for it was during Antoninus's priorate that the convent of San Marco granted the youths of the Purificazione a parcel of land on which to build their oratory. One of Antoninus's own patrons, Cosimo the Elder de' Medici, paid for the construction of the oratory and, on 29 June 1441, officially gave the keys of the building to the youths of the Purificazione.[10] That same day, the Purificazione also confirmed its statutes and reaffirmed Piero di Mariano Muzi as its guardian father.[11] These three elements – building, statutes, guardian – are thus closely linked not only one to the other but also to the temporal and spiritual powers that were *de facto* patrons to the youths – Cosimo de' Medici and Antoninus Pierozzi. Because of these connections, it is fair to suggest that the 1448 statutes brought for official approval to Archbishop Antoninus were, in fact, the ones drawn up and approved by the confraternity in 1441, a document, therefore, that the archbishop himself must already have known and, possibly, helped to draw up.

The Purificazione was not the only confraternity with *capitoli* already in place well before Archbishop Antoninus requested them. The youth confraternity of San Giovanni Evangelista, for example, had a set of statutes, complete with official approval by Tommaso della Bordella, vicar of the Florentine archbishop Amerigo Corsini, as early as 1 July 1427.[12] A confraternity 'Memoria' indicates that its *capitoli* were personally approved by Antoninus himself on 29 April 1451.[13] The evidence from the Purificazione and the Vangelista would suggest that the Arcangelo Raffaello also had statutes in place and officially approved well before the 1468 date of its earliest extant set, but unfortunately the hard evidence for this suggestion has not yet been discovered.

Besides insisting that confraternities have appropriate and approved regulations, Antoninus also made sure that the Christian doctrine they taught was similarly appropriate and approved. He himself was a prolific writer of compendia, confessionals, treatises, and other such tools to assist the clergy in the teaching of Christian doctrine and morals. Until recently, it was generally assumed that he had also composed a short manual in Italian to be used to teach Christian doctrine in the youth confraternities of Florence. Richa even claimed that the volume was written specifically for the youths of the Purificazione.[14]

The manual was first published in Venice in 1473 by the printer Cristoforo Arnoldo as an appendix to Antoninus's *Omnis mortalium cura* and was entitled *Libreto dela doctrina christiana: la quale è utile et molto necessaria che i puti pizoli et zovenzelli l'impara per sapere amare servire et honorare Idio benedicto: et schivare le temptationi et peccati.* It enjoyed an immediate and extensive editorial success, with about a dozen editions in the fifteenth century alone.[15] The work has been described as 'one of the oldest booklets of this type, a true catechism in the modern sense of the word.'[16] It has also been seen as a complete text, one that functioned fully in the youth confraternities of Florence as a venue for the catechises of the young.[17]

Others, however, have questioned the authorship and integrity of the volume. More than fifty years ago, Emilio Sanesi pointed out that the many elements of Venetian dialect present in this text (and here I might just point to expressions such as *puti pizoli et zovenzelli* or spellings such as *libreto* found in the title itself) indicate that this is not a Florentine work but at best a Venetian 'rewriting of a text by Antoninus, carried out after his death.'[18] More recently, serious doubts have been raised by Gilberto Aranci, who points out that even a preliminary analysis of the *Libreto*, taking into consideration the manuscript tradition and Antoninus's other works of moral education, indicates that this cannot be one of his works. It is, instead, a good example of the summary 'charts' that were often appended to moral or spiritual works and were included to help priests instructing or preparing the laity for confession. Aranci suggests that the true author of this *Libreto* probably used the moral works of Antoninus hand in hand with other similar doctrinal 'charts' in order to compile the one in question. Aranci then adds that the manual is clearly a work to be used by 'instructors,' that is, by the clergy, and not something to be placed directly in the hands of the catechumen. And he concludes by pointing out that it is an incomplete text, in that it lacks some of the most important elements of the genre – for example, it does not contain the 'Our Father.'[19]

Whether or not Antoninus composed the *Libreto* or *Dottrina cristiana* for youths in confraternities, his concern with preaching and teaching in lay religious organizations is evident. His episcopal constitutions clearly express it and warn the laity against discussing matters of faith in 'any company or gathering.' As Richard Trexler points out, Antoninus was prepared to be quite strict on this matter: 'He has heard that certain doctrines have been questioned in these meetings, and this smacks of heresy. This will either stop, he warns, or he will take action against those suspect of heresy, and he invites anyone knowing a heretic to denounce him "so we can proceed against him."'[20] The diminutive Dominican was a fiery reformer who would not tolerate heterodoxy in faith, teaching, or practices. For Antoninus lay confraternities were an important component of the city's spiritual life. As such they needed to be carefully supervised by qualified clergy and kept firmly in line with orthodox Christian teaching.

## Cosimo de' Medici

A similar attitude that supports but also seeks to control lay religious organizations is found among the Medici, and especially in Cosimo the Elder and Lorenzo the Magnificent.

Cosimo's patronage of the youth confraternity of the Purificazione has already been noted through his most generous gift – the oratory he built for them on land donated by the friars of San Marco. Although this is certainly part of the extensive rebuilding and decorating program Cosimo subsidized throughout the convent of San Marco, it is also an indication of his own commitment to providing a Christian education for the young. Del Migliore suggests that, by fostering the youth confraternity of the Purificazione, Cosimo may also have intended to foster youthful vocations in favour of the Dominicans at that convent.[21]

Cosimo's patronage, however, was not without a more pragmatic intent. The Purificazione's own *capitoli* reveal the extent of the Medici imprint in the confraternity's rooms and a possible reading of the relationship between Cosimo and the confraternity:

> [the confraternity] meets next to the friars of San Marco in a place that was rebuilt, that is, was built by Cosimo di Giovanni di Bicci de' Medici for this purpose and for the salvation of his soul, as is written in his account book for the building ['muraglia'] on pp. ___; which indicates that he paid for everything himself and he did this for the confraternity of Mariano [Muzi].
>
> And in the entrance to this place there is a chapel dedicated to Sts Cosmus and Damian, and the above-mentioned Cosimo gave us a painting ['tavola'] with the two saints painted on it, that is, Sts Cosmus and Damian, to serve for the altar of this chapel: behind this chapel there is our oratory named the Oratory of the Purification of the Virgin Mary, mother of Jesus Christ, and of St Zenobius, with sacristies and other rooms belonging to this place, a court, a well, and a garden.
>
> And the above-mentioned Cosimo gave us this in the year of the Incarnation of the Lord Jesus Christ 1444 on the 29th of June, the feast-day of Sts Peter and Paul, and we made a solemn procession of all the brothers of this school dressed in white, and he had Ser Alesso di Matteo give us the keys of the said place on his behalf and he built the said place with the permission of the friars of San Marco and the said friars freely donated and gave him the land on which to build the above-mentioned place, for they were certain that it was a good thing. And we intend to praise God at our meetings and to pray God for the said Cosimo, that he might grant him grace because of this good deed he has done, and that he may gain eternal life for it.[22]

Not only was Cosimo de' Medici looking for his just reward in the hereafter, but the presence of the Medicean patron saints, Cosmus and Damian, both in the name and over the altar of the chapel in the entrance to the confraternity, clearly points to a more immediate purpose – the iconographic and very visible demonstration of Medicean power and patronage over the Purificazione. In a less visible but equally significant manner, Cosmus and Damian reappear in the invocations that open some of the confraternity's account or minute books well into the sixteenth century.[23]

Cosimo was clearly asserting his own and his family's influence over the confraternity. Lorenzo Polizzotto rightly points out that Cosimo jealously guarded his patronage rights not only over the Purificazione but also over the other two confraternities meeting in San Marco – the Magi, and the Arte di Por Santa Maria – and passed such rights to his successors, 'for they enabled the Medici to enhance their own popularity and to use the confraternities as instruments of informal political supervision and control.'[24]

**Lorenzo de' Medici**

Such rights and powers eventually devolved to Cosimo's grandson, Lorenzo de' Medici. Rab Hatfield's ground-breaking article on the confraternity of the Magi clearly illustrates the extent of Medicean, and especially Laurentian, control over the Magi. Hatfield's work has rightly been cited and used as a starting point for further inquiry by a number of subsequent scholars – Trexler, Weissman, Newbigin, Polizzotto, myself, and others. The irony is that for a long time Lorenzo's membership in, and patronage of Florentine confraternities were hardly considered, let alone studied, either by his biographers or by Florentine historians, and this in spite of the fact that he belonged to, and was an active patron of, at least six such groups: the Magi, San Domenico, Gesù Pellegrino, Sant'Agnese, the *congrega* of the Neri, and the *buca* of San Paolo. The Magi actually directed his funeral procession, the Neri asked him to reform their constitution and membership, and so did the *buca* of San Paolo, while other confraternities eagerly welcomed him not only for the patronage he could bestow, but also for the prestige they could garner from his name on their membership rolls.[25]

Lorenzo's active participation at confraternity meetings, however, was not exemplary or even regular. The extensive records from the *buca* of San Paolo, the confraternity that most reflects his personal involvement in the lay religious associations of his time, clearly indicate that, unless he held a major office in the confraternity, his attendance was sporadic at best. In the case of the *congrega* of the Neri, which he thoroughly reformed and firmly placed within the Medicean sphere of influence, there is no record that he ever even set foot inside the oratory, let alone took part in its devotional or charitable life. Sant'Agnese, one of the oldest *laudesi* confraternities in Florence, was influenced by Lorenzo late in the Quattrocento using methods similar to those already employed with the Magi, San Paolo, and the Neri.[26]

Although clearly a devout Christian, Lorenzo had reasons other than personal devotion for associating himself or his name with a variety of Florentine confraternities. As Ronald F.E. Weissman succinctly pointed out, 'Lorenzo's many memberships offered him the chance to benefit from a broad range of penitential, festive, and charitable works performed by some of Florence's most distinguished lay brotherhoods, as well as the chance to extend his patronage by belonging to several quite different societies having quite different social bases.'[27]

Political purposes are also evident in Lorenzo's patronage of the youth confraternity of San Giovanni Evangelista, in which he enrolled at least two of his sons, Giovanni and Giuliano. For Giovanni we have no reliable records to suggest the extent of his participation in the activities of the Vangelista. Passing through Florence in 1515, on his way to meet King Francis I in Bologna, Giovanni, now Pope Leo X, visited the Vangelista, took part in a morning tornata, blessed the well, and generously dispensed 'many noteworthy privileges, and many specific indulgences to all who were inscribed in the confraternity's membership rolls.'[28] It was perhaps on this occasion that Leo X pronounced the words later attributed to him by Del Lungo: 'Let them have all they ask for, for we long frequented this School in our youth, and were almost raised in it.'[29] For his brother Giuliano, on the other hand, we have the well-known contemporary description from Bartolomeo Masi's *Ricordanze*, which tells how for Carnival 1491 Giuliano produced a play and organized suitable refreshments in the confraternity.

The play was the *Rappresentazione sacra di santi Giovanni e Paolo*, composed for the occasion by Lorenzo de' Medici at his son's request and staged the second day of Lent, 17 February 1491, in the garden of the Vangelista. I have discussed elsewhere in greater detail the socio-political aspects not of the play itself, but of its production by a scion of the ruling family and in a confraternity closely linked to it.[30] Previous scholars had already identified a political discourse evident in the text and had tried to see in it Lorenzo's own political views or praxis. My point was to suggest that the context of the performance was in itself an important political statement. And I also suggested that rather than focus on Lorenzo, which is what previous scholars had all done, one should focus on his son Giuliano, in that the complex and multi-faceted work of producing a play of these proportions was, in itself, a noteworthy feat. As *messere* for that Carnival's festivities, Giuliano was responsible for supervising the building of an extensive outdoor stage, scheduling rehearsals and performance, organizing costumes for a large number of amateur actors, obtaining ecclesiastical permission to perform the play during Lent, and arranging for suitable refreshments (*colazioni*) for the youths and their guests, as well as looking after a number of smaller details that needed immediate attention.

Though the twelve-year-old Giuliano undoubtedly had a lot of assistance, not only from fellow members of the confraternity but also from his family connections, the credit for the success of the event devolved entirely upon him, such was the nature of public display in Medicean Florence. This was not a purely formal attribution, voiced to garner favours from the Medici, but rather it was truly believed by contemporary sources.

We find, for example, not only that Giuliano is credited for the event in a completely private diary such as the one by his confraternity brother the coppersmith Bartolomeo Masi, but also that arrangements for the performance are made in his name, not his father's or anyone else's, even in documents as distant from the confraternity or Medicean partisans as the accounts of the Florentine Duomo. An entry of 29 January 1491 in the Duomo records indicates clearly that Giuliano, not his father or anyone else from the family or the confraternity, was the person in charge:

> Item to be given as asked, 20 firwood planks and 10 planed boards to Giuliano of Lorenzo de' Medici for the feast to be celebrated in the confraternity of St John the Evangelist.[31]

A week later, on 5 February, another entry in the Duomo's accounts suggests that further assistance had been or was being sought, and that it was being given, though this time in Lorenzo's name, not Giuliano's:

> Item, that all wood necessary for the feast of Saints John and Paul be lent to Lorenzo de' Medici and to whoever represents him and asks [for it] in his name, and [that] a clear and careful account be kept by the deputies of this Opera [del Duomo].[32]

Events and records of this sort indicate clearly that Lorenzo de' Medici was using confraternities for the advancement of his and his family's prestige in Florence. Rather than suppress and alienate them, as earlier republican governments had sought to do, Lorenzo joined them, enrolled his children and collaborators in them, and, like his grandfather Cosimo the Elder, assisted them in their activities. In so doing he brought them into his agenda of Medici dynasticism.[33]

## Girolamo Savonarola

The fall of the Medici in 1494 and the rise to political power of the current prior of the convent of San Marco, fra Girolamo Savonarola (1452–98), constituted a setback for Florentine confraternities. In spite of his active recruitment of young men for the purpose of renewing the moral fibre of the city, the Dominican friar and prophet was not a strong supporter of youth confraternities *per se*. Savonarola, it seems, preferred to use younger boys in his fight against the decadence of Florentine society.[34] Youth confraternities, composed of males aged thirteen to twenty-four, were not suitable because their well-established and well-structured internal organization, and their strong tradition of self-government, were obstacles in his attempts to control them. Younger boys, on the other hand, not yet members of a confraternity, could be more easily manipulated. Trexler examines contemporary sources and points out that 'the average age of Savonarola's *fanciulli* was lower than that of the earlier boys' confraternities' and that 'the age group from eighteen to thirty warily eyed, but did not participate significantly in the movement.'[35]

While he did not rely on established confraternities, Savonarola did borrow and adapt their administrative structure. This is most evident in the manner the children of Florence were organized by fra Domenico da Pescia, the fellow Dominican and, eventually, fellow martyr whom Savonarola had placed in charge of reforming the youth of the city. He gathered the children into four large bands, one for each of the four traditional *quartieri* of the city – San Giovanni, Santa Croce, Santa Maria Novella, and Santo Spirito.[36] Each group had a leader called the custodian (*custode*), with authority and power to enforce all regulations and lead the children in his charge to reform their lives ('migliori opere'). Four counsellors (*consiglieri*) assisted the *custode* and advised him. Beneath this executive of five, there was a slate of officers (*magistrati*) who were entrusted with a variety of specific tasks. The first group were the peace givers (*paciali*), whose duty it was to maintain peace among the children and resolve discord either within the group or with the rest of the children in the *quartiere*. Then there were the marshals (*ordinatori*), who organized them for processions or kept them sitting in the appropriate order in the Duomo when they assembled to hear

Savonarola's sermons. The marshals also sent away the older youths ('e' maggiori') who did not belong to the organization. The third group were the correctors (*correttori*), whose responsibility was to chastise, in a brotherly and 'evangelical' way, all those children, whether male or female, who had been delinquent or had worn 'vanities.' The fourth group were the almoners (*elemosinieri*), who collected alms for the shamed-faced poor ('poveri vergognosi') during processions. On Carnival and on all feast-days they stood at street corners with a crucifix and candles on a makeshift altar and again collected alms. The pseudo-Burlamacchi offers a charming though probably not completely truthful picture of how the children did this:

> they stood there very modestly and waited for respectable persons to pass by, and then they took the beautiful vase they had placed on the altar and, bowing graciously, they asked for alms for the poor, and each citizen offered what he wanted, and this was done in order to root out the abuses and the perverse customs of Carnival.[37]

Fifth there were the polishers (*lustratori*), who went around Florence looking for crucifixes and images of saints 'in places where of necessity it is customary to pass water,' and they either whitewashed them or removed them, for they thought it irreverent to have such images in such places. The last group were the inquisitors (*inquisitori*), whose duty it was to seek out gamblers and card players and to dissuade them from engaging in such activities. This last group is perhaps the best known, for their work has often been taken as emblematic of what all the Savonarolan children did, and of the civic discord they caused. Schnitzer, failing to perceive the irony of his phrase, calls them a youth police ('polizia dei fanciulli'), something I find chillingly evocative of the youthful bands in the Maoist Cultural Revolution.[38] Yet even a contemporary pro-Savonarolan source such as the pseudo-Burlamacchi was (un)consciously aware that there were difficulties with the *inquisitori* and pointed out that armed guards had to be assigned to the children, supposedly for their own protection. He describes their activities as follows:

> on feast-days throughout the year, after lunch and after Vespers, [the inquisitors] roamed the entire city, inside and out, [seeking out] places where there were gamblers, and they took away their cards and dice and tables and all their playing instruments, and sometimes their money, and they gave it to the poor, and they obtained all this with kind and sweet words ... The terror and fear these children

[raised] was such that when players heard them coming they dropped everything and ran away. Sometimes, nonetheless, some players said a few foul words to them, and some beat them up, but the children bore everything patiently. Hearing of this, their fathers took it badly and ordered the office of the Eight to give each *quartiere* one of its soldiers to escort and defend [the children]. Seeing this, the enemies of truth were afraid. And so the children purged the city, both inside and out, of games.[39]

Gamblers and others had reason enough to be afraid. Trexler points out that the *inquisitori* who carried out these raids were not the children, but rather the adolescents in the group, young men in their late teens, and that many belonged to some of the most powerful families in the city.[40] The combination of age and social rank must have intimidated many a person. So also must their number and group behaviour. Schnitzer points out that 'they moved around in groups of 25 or 30, and they struck dread and fear especially in gamblers [who] took to flight as soon as they heard them coming near.'[41] Today we would call such behaviour 'swarming' and rightly condemn it ourselves.

Eventually the Savonarolan attempt to organize the Florentine youth into bands by *quartieri* did not close down youth confraternities, nor did it really exclude them from participating in similar activities. Lorenzo Polizzotto has pointed out that the confraternity of the Purificazione was literally taken over by the Piagnoni and remained a locus of Savonarolan ideals long after the friar's death.[42] Passerini noted that the confraternity of San Niccolò del Ceppo was among the greatest admirers and followers of Savonarola, eagerly taking part in the burning of the vanities.[43] Even the Vangelista seems to have joined in the spirit of the times. In his biography of the merchant and navigator Giovanni da Empoli, his uncle Girolamo says that:

on feast-days [Giovanni] always went to the confraternity of the Vangelista. And note that at that time all the youths, and especially those in confraternities, at the urging of the Reverend Father fra Girolamo from Ferrara, who at that time was preaching against vices and the dishonest sins that were committed in the said city [of Florence], and especially against games and curses, the said youths gathered together, and they established officers among themselves, that is *messeri*, counsellors, and other officers, who went throughout the land to put out games and other vices.[44]

What were these vices? Contemporary records do not fail to list them –

violent games, gambling, cursing, effeminacy, and sodomy. The pseudo-Burlamacchi gives a vivid description of the sad state in which Savonarola had found Florence's youth:

they had long been nourished in many bad habits, for they had been given great licence and freedom to entangle themselves in all vices (with their ornaments and hairstyles they looked like young girls, or rather like public harlots with their impure speech and deeds), and especially in that unspeakable vice, an abominable thing to say, gamblers, gluttons, vainglorious, lascivious, and mixed up in many other sins.[45]

Needless to say, the pseudo-Burlamacchi points out that Savonarola quickly brought these wayward youths back to purity and to the simplicity of a Christian life, so much so that they became an example for the entire city.[46] There is in this an echo of Ambrogio Traversari's comment to Pope Eugenius IV, and of the premodern belief in the potential of youth to teach their elders through their purity and innocence.

Savonarola's supposed success in reforming the Florentine youths must, however, be taken with a grain of salt. Even the pseudo-Burlamacchi fails to note the inherent contradiction in his description of the youths' conversions to a Christian life and their continued violence in defence of such a life. Having described how Savonarola was able to dissuade his young followers from engaging in pitched battles with stones ('fare a' sassi'), a common event, often associated with Carnival, and one that occasionally killed some of the young participants or escalated into full-fledged battles between different parties in the city,[47] the pseudo-Burlamacchi proudly describes how Savonarola's young elite was able to rout a group of *compagnacci* who had tried to disrupt their procession. The incident occurred when Savonarola's young followers were processing through the city.[48] Just past the church of Santa Trinita and the Palazzo Spini, at a place called, quite appropriately, 'la Pancaccia,' a group of *compagnacci* started throwing stones at the youths, who, however, quickly responded in kind and eventually scattered the trouble-makers. This, the pseudo-Burlamacchi concluded, was a miracle, for, as he pointed out,

the Spirit of the Lord inspired the minds of the faithful and the lovers of the truth of Christ so that they took off the gowns they wore above [i.e., probably their confraternal or processional gowns], wrapped them around their left arm in the manner of a shield, and responded with stones themselves, forcing [the *compagnacci*] to retreat. Nor should you think these were low and ignoble persons, but [rather they were] some of the first in the city both in mind and counsel, and thus they resisted them and they scattered the enemies of God.[49]

Clearly, the evangelical message of turning the other cheek had not been fully accepted by Savonarola's youthful followers. And in the end Savonarola's reform of the youth of Florence did not take. Aside from the social problems caused by the bands of marauding *inquisitori* and the tension that rose between his teen-aged followers and the post-teenage youths in the city, there were also political concerns that militated against a restructuring of how the young were to be organized. When in March 1496 the young Savonarolans marched in procession to the Signoria and presented their proposals for a reform of youth organizations and morals in Florence, a package that had already been approved by fra Domenico da Pescia and by Savonarola, the city fathers thanked them profusely and were even moved to tears, but then set the package aside, and left it 'in pendente.'[50] There was, in fact, opposition to the package not only from other, non-Dominican preachers who thundered from their own pulpits against an administration by *fanciulli*, but also from politically sensitive Florentines who, in Trexler's words, saw this novelty of reorganizing the youth of the city along the lines of civic administrative areas (the *quartieri*) as 'an attempt to enforce the *fanciulli* morality upon the citizenry with governmental authority, using the internal political structure of the city as a base for this reform.'[51]

The Savonarolan episode did not lead to a restructuring of the administration of youth devotions and Christian education in Florence through the establishment of *quartiere* organizations, nor did it eliminate the traditional cross-city youth confraternities that had been established in the previous eighty years. It did, however, instil in some confraternities, the Purificazione in particular, a *Piagnone* undercurrent that was to be felt for some time thereafter. The Savonarolan episode also marked the end of that period of relative stability that saw the growth of Florentine confraternities and the beginning of a period of political and social instability that, for about fifty years, militated against further expansion.[52]

## The Post-Savonarolan Years

The turmoil of the Savonarolan period and the ensuing political uncertainties disrupted the smooth functioning of all confraternities. From 1494 to about 1540, confraternities in general were suppressed or closed for either political, military, or sanitary reasons.[53] The major precedent for direct government intervention had been set by the Florentine Senate on 19 October 1419 when, suspecting that confraternities had become dens of dissent and political subversion, it decreed their general closure.[54] Throughout the fifteenth century, the Florentine government periodically closed down confraternities for shorter or longer periods of time and went so far as to prohibit franchised males over the age of twenty-four who had served or were eligible to serve in elected office (the *veduti* and *seduti*, as they were called) from participating in confraternities.[55]

Such measures were most often taken at times of political tension. In 1494, the unstable political situation in Florence, brought about by the collapse of the Medicean regime, the rise of the Savonarolan party, and the threatening advance into Italy of King Charles VIII of France, led to a similar suppression (22 September).[56] In 1513, the same context in reverse – that is, the collapse of the Soderini republic and the rise of the Medici faction – led the Council of Eight to issue another edict, again closing all confraternities (4 September).[57] Then, in 1527, an edict from the officers of sanitation closed them for fear of the plague that had struck the city (3 June).[58]

While in the fifteenth century Archbishop Antoninus had come to the defence of confraternities against the closures and prohibitions imposed by the civic government, the Florentine Church of the early Cinquecento took no apparent interest in defending lay religious organizations. These were uncertain years, rendered more chaotic first by the ineffectual Soderini republic and the machinations of the Medici faction, and then by the malaise of the Medicean rule of Pope Leo X, who governed Florence through his cousin Giulio de' Medici, archbishop of Florence (1513–32), and his two young, incompetent nephews, Ippolito and Alessandro.

The confraternity of the Arcangelo Raffaello suffered from all these vicissitudes. The worst blow came in 1529–30 when, as a result of the imperial siege, it was forced to vacate the rooms and oratory on the via della Scala and turn the space over to the nuns of San Martino al Mugnone, who had had to abandon their convent outside the city walls. On 21 March 1530/1 the nuns' temporary residence at the Scala site was made permanent, and the youths of the Arcangelo Raffaello found themselves dispossessed of the quarters granted to them by Pope Eugenius IV a century earlier.[59]

With the loss of their rooms and oratory on the via della Scala, the confraternity ended the first period of its history. It had been a period of growth and consolidation, a period in which the confraternity established a place for itself and for similar associations in the social and religious fibre of the city. Its activities and aims had been accepted and integrated into

Florentine life in a manner unknown in other Italian cities. In 1529–30, as Florence faced the besieging imperial armies that were to change it permanently from a republic into a duchy, the confraternity of the Arcangelo Raffaello sacrificed its gains for the well-being of those in greater need and went begging for temporary accommodations at the doors of the convent of Santa Maria Novella. The friars' help gave the confraternity a new start and marks the beginning of a second period in the life of the youths of the Arcangelo Raffaello characterized again by growth and prominence.

# 5

# The Move to Santa Maria Novella

The 1529–30 imperial siege of Florence marks the turning point in Florence's history from republican to ducal government. The long traditions of elected leadership which, after the return of Cosimo de' Medici from his Venetian exile (1433–4), had been a mere pretext for *de facto* Medici rule, were now supplanted by the imperially sanctioned reality of aristocratic and hereditary Medicean government. In 1531 the Emperor Charles v made Alessandro de' Medici duke of Florence with right of male succession and gave him his own natural daughter, Margaret of Austria, in marriage. Florence thus became a satellite state in the orbit of Hapsburg imperial politics, and its leader a relative by marriage to the most powerful ruling family on the continent. Everything, including the confraternity of the Arcangelo Raffaello, changed to accommodate and reflect the new reality.

For the youths of the Arcangelo Raffaello, the change began with the imperial siege of Florence (October 1529–August 1530). Its immediate effect was the loss of the confraternity's oratory and meeting rooms, which were given to the nuns of San Martino al Mugnone, forced to abandon their convent outside the Porta al Prato by the imperatives of military threat and defence.[1] The youths' eviction from their location at the Scala was at first meant to be temporary, but it became permanent in March 1531 when Giovanni Stasi, the apostolic commissioner in Florence, acting on instructions from Pope Clement vii, confirmed and authorized the nuns' new location in the Scala complex, thus compensating them for the loss of their convent outside the city walls.[2] As a result, the youths of the Arcangelo Raffaello were obliged to seek new permanent quarters. This chapter will discuss that move and the confraternity's new, and better, location on the Piazza Santa Maria Novella.

## At the Convent of Santa Maria Novella

On 10 June 1533, two years after the siege and its disastrous effects on the Arcangelo Raffaello, the friars of Santa Maria Novella granted the youths temporary accommodations in their convent in rooms that had previously belonged to four adult confraternities whose membership had been decimated by the 1527 plague – those of San Jacopo later called Sant'Ignazio Martire, San Vincenzo Ferreri, Spirito Santo, and San Zanobi.[3] Until the 1527 plague struck, these had been, for the most part, prosperous confraternities with a respectable number of members. A census carried out in about 1527 counts 250 members in the confraternity of San Vincenzo *di disciplina*, 250 again in the Spirito Santo, and 200 in San Zanobi. Compared with the 70 friars and 35 *conversi, chierici, cuochi,* and *ortolani* in the convent of Santa Maria Novella, the size of the defunct confraternities using rooms in the convent was, generally speaking, significantly larger than that of their host institution. With their demise, however, the convent regained possession of the rooms and, as fra Domenico Ducci noted, 'was left like owner and heir' to their possessions.[4]

No sooner had the youths entered the vacant sites than negotiations were undertaken to clarify and legalize their presence, rights, and obligations. Archival records from the 1530s and 1540s point to continued negotiations at first with the representatives of the inactive confraternities and then with the friars of Santa Maria Novella. By early 1534 agreements were signed with the surviving members of the Spirito Santo and San Vincenzo Ferreri whereby the men simply ceded their rooms and some of their furnishings to the youths.[5] By February 1541/2 the youths and friars also reached an agreement, though in this case it seemed more of a cautious *modus vivendi* acceptable and honourable to both. The document recognized the Arcangelo Raffaello's acquisition not only of the rooms and oratories, but also of some of the furnishings and some of the rights and obligations belonging to the four inactive confraternities.[6] They received, for example, furnishings from the confraternities of San Vincenzo and the Spirito Santo, including a relic of St Vincent, several paintings including one of the saint and one of the Holy Spirit, some liturgical paraments, books, bookstands, doors, the choir stalls, and even a gallery (*sopalcho*).[7] From the confraternity of the Spirito Santo they received the friars' obligation of five low Masses each year, some land-holdings in diverse parishes, and an annuity from an inheritance managed by the Ospedale di San Paolo.[8] In return, the confraternity was to pay a yearly fee of 42 *lire* to the convent of Santa Maria Novella for the rooms it occupied.[9]

The caution evident in the 1530s and 1540s in the negotiations with the friars of Santa Maria Novella for space within the convent precinct continued in subsequent years. The friars had agreed to give the youths of the Arcangelo Raffaello 'totum situm' of the confraternity of San Vincenzo, 'non totum situm' of the confraternity of the Spirito Santo, and 'partem situm' of the confraternity of San Zanobi on the understanding that the youths open an entrance directly onto Piazza Santa Maria Novella.[10] The adult confraternities that had previously used these spaces had gained access to them from inside the convent. The men would walk through the convent's main gate, proceed into the cloister of the Sindicheria, turn left, and then enter their rooms through ground-level doors under the south colonnade. Apparently, such an arrangement had not disturbed the friars. After all, in 1505 the two adult confraternities of the Spirito Santo and of San Vincenzo Ferreri had even contributed to the building of the cloister, a favour for which they were allowed to place their escutcheons on several pillars along the south corridor of the cloister.[11]

Such an arrangement and such claims on the internal space of the cloister were not, however, transferred to the youths of the Arcangelo Raffaello. The youths, in fact, were not only instructed to open their own door directly onto the piazza, but were even given permission to remove and relocate some of the ancient marble sarcophagi that ran along the front of the convent and the church so as to clear space for the door they were to open. The sarcophagi were monumental coffins belonging to some of the oldest and most prestigious of Florentine families. The fact that they could be moved to make way for the restructuring of the confraternity's quarters reflects the nature of the relationship that had developed between the youths and the friars, but also indicates the high esteem Florentines had for the Arcangelo Raffaello.

## The View from the Piazza

The Arcangelo Raffaello's new location, facing as it did onto one of the major squares of Florence, next to the entrance to the senior Dominican convent and church in the city, was much more prestigious than the old one on the via della Scala. The via della Scala ran from the far end of the piazza, along the back of the convent, till it arrived at the city walls by the Porta a Prato – a lateral, not a main artery in the urban landscape of Florence. The new location, instead, was front-row seating, placing the youths of the Arcangelo Raffaello in full view of the city, on a large and important piazza (ills. 2–4). The site facing the piazza of Santa Maria Novella, the extensive complex of oratories, rooms, and space within the Dominican convent, and the permission to relocate the sarcophaghi are all indications of the confraternity's privileged position in the spiritual and social fabric of sixteenth-century Florence.

A few early illustrations of piazza Santa Maria Novella help us reconstruct the external appearance of the confraternity building during the three centuries the confraternity inhabited it.

An aerial view of the piazza from the 1584 Bonsignori map shows an oratory-type building on the site of the confraternity of the Arcangelo Raffaello – but it is mislabelled as the oratory of the confraternity of San Benedetto Bianco (ill. 2).[12] By size alone, it is an impressive building, several times longer than any of the houses fronting on the square. It has the two-pitched roof (*tetto a capanna*) typical of Florentine confraternities. If Bonsignori's details can be trusted, a cross stood at the front peak of the roof, and a large window dominated the back wall. The Bonsignori image was slavishly repeated in several subsequent views of the city, even though at a certain point in time it no longer reflected the contemporary urban landscape.[13] We cannot, therefore, assume that subsequent views based on Bonsignori are reliable indications of the true appearance of the oratory in later years. And, as will be evident from images discussed below, it may not be reliable for the 1580s either.

One of the earliest visual records of the façade of the Arcangelo Raffaello comes from a fresco at the Palazzo Ruspoli in Rome.[14] The image shows the piazza and the façade of the church viewed from a height well above the rooftops of the Ospedale di San Paolo at the south end of the piazza. On the left, between a row of three houses and the front gate of the convent, the oratory of the confraternity of the Arcangelo Raffaello is easily identifiable by its strikingly different two-pitched roof. Its façade has a door, two windows, and an *oculus*, or round window. In its simplicity and frugality of form the oratory depicted in this fresco displays the standard features of Florentine confraternity buildings.

An early seventeenth-century view of the same piazza by Cristofano Allori, seen again from the Ospedale di San Paolo at the south end, but this time from ground level, also shows the façade of the confraternity of the Arcangelo Raffaello (ill. 3).[15] The front door is clearly visible, with its two-pitched overhang mentioned in a note of 1570.[16] So too are the second-floor windows that open onto the piazza. The façade also seems to have decorations on it, possibly the *pittura* by Michelangelo Cinganelli depicting stories from the book of Tobit that was paid for by Baccio Comi and unveiled on 8 September 1595.[17]

The major structural difference between this view and the Palazzo Ruspoli fresco is the shape of the roof. In the 1608 Allori drawing the roof is flat and level with the top of the convent wall, with a roof-line that runs parallel to the front of the building, as is the case today. The more traditional *capanna* roof of the confraternity of San Benedetto Bianco, on the other hand, is clearly visible to the immediate right (east) of the church of Santa Maria Novella. It appears, therefore, that major structural alterations had been made to the building housing the confraternity of the Arcangelo Raffaello. The fact that the confraternity's roof was apparently a good place from which to watch events taking place on the Piazza Santa Maria Novella suggests that it may have been flat, and not peaked, as early as 1566 (thus giving the lie to the Bonsignori map mentioned above). In April of that year, in fact, the scribe recorded that a large number of people had come across the roofs from as far away as via della Scala in order to see a grandiose Carnival entertainment organized on the square, and this had, inevitably, damaged the structure:

> Because this past Carnival a wooden castle was erected in Santa Maria Novella and in front of the church, extending from our confraternity to the houses across from the old piazza, and because there had been jousts arranged by Signor Aurelio Fregoso and because a lot of people and an infinite number of persons had come to view these shows, the roofs [*sic*] of our confraternity were filled with people, who came through the back along the rooftops from as far away as via della Scala, so that the roofs suffered a lot, and many tiles and gutters were broken, knocked out of place, or damaged, and in order to protect the awning over our first door onto the piazza from being broken we had it removed and placed it in the confraternity, and we had all the roofs reset and repaired, and we had the cornices placed back and redone, and Baccio Comi paid [for the repairs] and gave me, Girolamo [di Maestro Luca] L. 11.13.4 *piccioli* [to pay] for these expenses.[18]

The flat-roof theory is supported also by a sixteenth century fresco in the Palazzo Vecchio attributed to the School of Vasari. It shows the confraternity with a simple façade, as in the Palazzo Ruspoli fresco, but with the levelled roof present in the Allori drawing.[19]

One of the most striking aspects of the building's exterior in the early seventeenth century would have been the frescoes painted on the façade by Michelangelo Cinganelli and unveiled on 8 September 1595.[20] No visual record remains, but we know that the frescoes illustrated stories from the Book of Tobit.[21]

An eighteenth-century view of the piazza by Vincenzo Tarchi and

Michele Ciocchi, this time drawn facing directly west towards the convent entrance, shows the façade of the confraternity; by this time, however, there are no frescoes on it.[22] The building has now become a four-storey structure, level with the house next door (ill. 4).[23] First published by Richa in 1755, this illustration clearly shows what the confraternity looked like following the construction of a house on top of it in the years 1736–49 (see below, ch. 21, pp. 293–4).

An early nineteenth-century view, published by Lorenzo Bardi, also faces in the same direction. It shows further but relatively minor alterations to the façade. By this time the building looks very much as it does today.[24]

The extensive changes in the exterior appearance of the confraternity building indicate a continual interest in improving it, either by way of decorations or construction around the front and on top of it. The youths clearly had the necessary funds to subsidize such projects and, at a certain point in time, the initiative and originality to change the appearance of their building's exterior away from the traditional format for Florentine confraternities.

## The Interior of the Confraternity

No contemporary floor plan or description of the confraternity oratory and rooms in the convent of Santa Maria Novella has survived. After the 1785 suppression, the site was turned to secular use, and the rooms and oratories underwent such major physical alterations that they no longer reflect, or even suggest, their previous confraternity use or format. They have now been incorporated into the building which houses the Hotel Minerva.[25] No one would recognize part of the confraternity's oratories in the hotel's lobby or its second-floor breakfast room, whose windows overlook the Chiostro della Sindicheria. From the piazza, the only distinguishing remnant of the original confraternity building still visible today is a small, three-foot-wide portion of roof that slants from the north wall of the Hotel Minerva down towards the convent. This is probably the remains of the peaked *capanna* roof that originally covered the confraternity building. The current façade of the Hotel Minerva contains a vertical pilaster dividing the front of the building into two sections, and this probably indicates the original divide between the houses of the Mazzinghi (the southern section of the building, four windows wide) and the confraternity (the northern section, five windows wide).[26]

From inside the convent's cloister, one can distinguish the rear of the confraternity's oratory and the back of a two-storey house that was built above the confraternity in the 1740s. No other structures remain to suggest that an important confraternity once had oratories and rooms on that site.

Although no floor plan for the building's internal division has survived, the arrangement of the spaces can be visualized in part from confraternity records and other sources.[27]

Before a front door was opened onto the piazza, access to the confraternity was obtained from inside the cloister of the Sindicheria in the convent of Santa Maria Novella. Members passed through the large convent doors, through the small entrance courtyard, and arrived into the Chiostro della Cantina (today della Sindicheria). A door at the far left corner of the cloister led into the oratory of the confraternity of San Vincenzo Ferreri, which had been meeting there since at least 1460. An image of the saint was painted on the wall next to it, while the acronym M DPT VK was carved on the escutcheon of the capitals of at least two columns on that side of the cloister.[28] Further down, the door in the middle of the south wall under the fourth arch lead into the oratory of the confraternity of San Zanobi, present at that site since at least 1467. The same entrance lead to the second-floor rooms of the confraternity of Sant'Ignazio Martire (extant 1475–1520), which used the second-floor oratory belonging to the adjacent confraternity of San Pietro Martire. Back on the ground floor the third door, at the far end just past the south-west corner, led into the oratory of the confraternity of the Spirito Santo, which had been meeting there since 1439. Its symbol, an inverted dove of the Holy Spirit, was carved on the escutcheon on the capital of the corner column. In summary, when the confraternity of the Arcangelo Raffaello received these sites, it obtained a total of three ground-floor oratories, and a number of rooms above them. By the time Fr Modesto Biliotti (1531–1607) wrote his description of the convent in 1586, all three doors had already been walled up and extensive internal restructuring had taken place.[29]

The internal spaces had been restructured, the cloister-side doors walled up, and a new door into the confraternity had been opened directly from the piazza. This last item was one of the conditions imposed by the friars on the youths in their settlement of June 1533.[30] Biliotti encapsulates the changes in his brief comment that, when the confraternity received the sites, it demolished many walls and built one large confraternity complex, which, as could be seen, was truly noteworthy, sufficient to its needs, and appropriately decorated.[31]

These extensive renovations had important repercussions and implications. The new door giving access to the confraternity directly from the piazza, for example, necessitated the removal and relocation of some of the marble sarcophagi (*avelli*) that run along the outside wall of the convent and church of Santa Maria Novella. The sarcophagi were an integral element not only of the fabric of the church and square, but also of the relationship between the Dominicans and the families that had chosen to be thus interred. They marked a line between ecclesiastical and public space. And they defined at least part of the urban context in the area – to this day, via degli Avelli, running alongside Santa Maria Novella, takes its name from them. For the youths to receive permission to relocate some of these monumental tombs in order to open an entrance into the confraternity is an important indication of the reputation and connections they enjoyed.[32]

The interior restructuring involved changes to the structure of parts of the convent complex itself. It is not surprising, therefore, to see that the 1533 agreement drawn up by Fr Lorenzo di Filippo Strozzi clearly stipulated that any alterations should be made only with the approval of the prior and friars of Santa Maria Novella and by the apostolic commissioner in Florence, at that time Fr Giovanni Stasi.[33]

The internal restructuring created a new series of spaces which amounted to twelve different rooms. From the front door off the piazza one entered into a large room (*stanzone* – the Italian word itself suggests this was a sizeable space) that in turn led to the change room where the brothers donned their confraternal robes (*spogliatoio*). From the *spogliatoio* one could go upstairs to a room (*stanza di sopra*) that led, on the right, to a storage room (*arsenale*). Behind it were two rooms for musicians (*prima Stanza dei musici* and *seconda Stanza dei musici*), as well as the musicians' loft (*terrazzino dei musici*), which opened onto the oratory below. There was a small room behind the organ (*stanzino dietro all'organo*) and a small room for the servant (*dove si trattiene il servo*) which opened onto the oratory (*dà in Compagnia*). Back at ground level, a door led from the *stanzone* into the large oratory (*compagnia*) where the youths met. At the opposite end from the door stood the oratory's altar and, behind it, a vestry (*sagrestia dietro l'altare*). Past this vestry there was a second, smaller oratory (*tornantino*), where the youths held their morning *tornata*. This reconstruction accounts for the three original oratories on the ground floor, which were now turned into the *compagnia*, the *tornantino*, and the *stanzone/spogliatoio* nucleus. The upstairs rooms once belonging to the confraternity of Sant'Ignazio Martire were turned into the storage room, the two rooms for the musicians, and the servant's room.

A 1690 inventory of objects in the confraternity, drawn up by Marc'Antonio Seminari, a member of the Arcangelo Raffaello, can be used to reconstruct the confraternity's rooms, their contents, and their function.[34] It is thus an important document because it provides us with a rare glimpse into a late seventeenth-century confraternity, complete with a listing of its significant holdings in ecclesiastical furnishings and works of art. It is therefore useful to follow it room by room and reconstruct, as it were, the confraternity's space and wealth.

## A Walk through the Confraternity's Rooms

When a brother stepped into the building from piazza Santa Maria Novella, he entered into the large *stanzone*, where he was immediately presented with icons of the confraternity and its devotional life. Directly in front of him, above the door to the oratory, hung a painting by Jacopo Chimenti called l'Empoli depicting an angel in the act of presenting a youth, dressed in confraternity robes, to the Virgin Mary.[35] With this image, the brother could visualize not only the special bond that united him with the Archangel Raphael, patron and protector of the confraternity, but also the reward of his devotion to the archangel – entry into the heavenly court under Raphael's sponsorship and subsequent protection under the mantle of the Madonna of Mercy.

To the left of the entrance hung Orazio Fidani's *Tobias Healing His Father's Blindness* (ill. 8), a clear reminder not only of Raphael's gift of healing, but also of Tobias's obedience, service, and dedication to his old father.[36] To the right hung Lorenzo Lippi's *Crucifixion* (ill. 7), a gift of the artist to the confraternity when he was its *governatore* (September–December 1647).[37] Two large walnut candlestick holders, carved and gilded, stood in front of the *Crucifixion*, giving it an added element of devotional focus. The two works were so highly regarded that they were noted in Gaetano Cambiagi's eighteenth-century guide to Florence.[38]

By their very position in paintings on opposite walls of the *stanzone*, the confraternity's two patron saints – the Archangel Raphael and St Mary Magdalene – acted as mirror images for each other, one participating in the joy of a son's healing of his father's blindness, the other in the pain of a mother's grief at the death of her son. The *Crucifixion* hanging on the right wall was complemented, in a way, by the anonymous *Pietà*, painted 'in maniera antica,' hanging above the entrance door.[39]

On the whole, the iconography in the large entrance hall was carefully balanced and intricately cross-referenced. There were images of the Archangel Raphael at the front and left, and images of Christ at the right and back, both sets representing a 'healer' descended from heaven. Within each pair, one image depicted an event drawn from Scripture (the healing of

Tobias's blindness and the Crucifixion) while another visualized an imagined event (the presentation of a confraternity youth to the Virgin and the Pietà). The iconology in the *stanzone* was further enhanced by still other links. The Virgin herself formed a connecting thread from the front to the back of the room, first as the Mother of Mercy who welcomed the devout into her protection, and then as the Mother of Sorrows who lamented over the loss of her Son. The confraternity's two patron saints also reinforced the iconological program by suggesting further connections from left to right through their presence at a moment of healing, be it physical or spiritual. All in all, the iconology in the *stanzone* presented a complex series of interacting references to healing, salvation, and mercy which would not have been missed by the youth or the visitor entering the hall.

Once inside the entrance hall, the *confratello* would proceed, through a lateral door, into the *spogliatoio* to don his confraternal garb. In the *spogliatoio* a locked wooden trunk contained pillows covered in a variety of fine fabrics (brocade, damask, ermine, silk, velvet, and satin); some were even trimmed in gold or silver. A large armoire, ten *braccia* long (about five metres)[40] divided into sections, held 104 confraternal gowns for members (64 *grandi*, 20 *medie*, 20 *piccole*), and an assortment of liturgical vestments used by the priests officiating at services. Like the pillows, the vestments were also made with a variety of fine fabrics and many were enriched with gold or silver threads. Several of these vestments were decorated with their donors' family crests (Galli, Portinari, Vanni, Vitolini). There were also fine cloths to cover special objects such as lecterns, altars, crosses, statues, and paintings. Fifteen altar frontals (*paliotti*), made with expensive cloths and illustrated with scenes or emblems suitable for the different feasts and commemorations of the confraternity's liturgical year, were also stored in this armoire. Some of the altar frontals bore crests belonging either to their donor's family (Quaratesi, Strozzi) or to the confraternity (the emblem of the Scala), and at least one was decorated with an image of the souls in Purgatory painted by a famous artist, Lorenzo Lippi.[41]

Among the works of art kept in the *spogliatoio* were Lorenzo Lippi's crucifix, which he painted in one day for the obsequies of Agnolo Galli; the confraternity's canvas *segno*, painted on both sides with the Archangel Raphael and Tobias;[42] the old canvas *segno*, no longer used in processions, bearing an image of Mary Magdalene and Jesus;[43] a small painting of St Francis; a life-size canvas of St Dominic believed by the youths to be the portrait of fra Santi Contini, OP, who had been their father corrector from ca. 1606 to 1626; a painting of a pelican; and two crosses (one wooden, one alabaster).[44] The ceiling itself was adorned with a fresco by Benedetto Cinganelli.[45]

On a mezzanine storage area in the *spogliatoio* there were diverse decorations and objects required to set up the *parato* for the devotion of the Forty Hours, including a number of raisers, a baldachin, a *paliotto* (with the arms of the Anichini), and a *piviale* (with the arms of the del Chiaro). A large unlocked wooden box contained a variety of cloths and objects used for funerals or memorial services. Among these, there was a *segno*, in gold-embroidered silk, depicting the Archangel Raphael that was used in funerals, where it was placed at the feet of the deceased to indicate that he had been a member of the confraternity. In a locked box there were a number of books, including the four different copies of the *capitoli* and a number of important documents (wills, etc.). Another box contained the bulls, privileges, and permissions the confraternity had received over the course of time. Elsewhere in the armoire there were religious and devotional books, volumes of receipts, *ricordi*, membership lists, and other confraternity records. A second armoire contained a large number of wooden and brass vases. There was also a writing desk, and in its drawer a number of manuscripts of various works by Jacopo Cicognini, including six plays, various works on St Mary Magdalene, and nine volumes of his writings bound in cardboard. There were benches, two racks of pegs for hanging the confraternity robes (*cappellinai*), two hourglasses, a quilted curtain (*portiera*) to be placed outside the confraternity's door, a carpet that covered the top of the entire armoire, and a large chest, containing three different locked compartments, whose keys were kept by three different members.

Having donned his confraternity robe, the *confratello* now returned to the *stanzone* and entered into the main oratory, the *compagnia*. The oratory was a special space. Here was where the youths gathered to carry out their devotions, recite the Hours, hear Mass, and take Communion. But here also was where the confraternity met to discuss business, hold elections, and even stage entertainments. This space thus enjoyed an ambivalent status, both sacred and profane. It was not a church and did not function as such; that is, it was not open to the public and did not have an exclusive role as a place of worship. Rather it was more of a private chapel for the sole use of confraternity members, who would, at times, turn the space over to non-devotional purposes. Because it was not a church, it was not subject to a number of ecclesiastical restrictions, such as the Lenten prohibition against musical performances in general and organ playing in particular, an important factor in the development and vitality of musical oratorios in confraternities during Lent and Passiontide.[46]

As he stepped inside, the confraternity brother walked between the desks of the guardian father and the father corrector at either side of the door. They were made of pine, but painted to look like much more expensive walnut. The desks had back panels that ran, together with the pews, along the length of the entrance wall, around the corner, and down the side walls until they reached the stone steps of the altar at the opposite end of the oratory. Along the side walls there were two rows of lateral pews, the back one raised up from the front one and forming, with its kneeler, the back panel for the front pew. A wooden balcony for the musicians (*terrazzino*), also painted walnut, projected from the wall above the guardian's and the corrector's desks and ran the entire width of the entrance wall. It had been built in November 1641 on the suggestion and at the expense of Alberto del Vivaio, who also donated the organ housed in it. A wooden tablet under the balcony and above the door into the *compagnia* recalled Alberto's generous gift to the confraternity, as did his family's coat of arms proudly displayed on it.[47] Above the balcony, in the middle of the entrance wall, there was an oval painting by Jacopo Vignali showing the Archangel Raphael and Tobias.[48] It had a gilded wooden frame and a brass sconce (*viticcio*) that, alone, weighed three pounds.

At the far end of the oratory there was a raised presbytery with altar. Four walnut doors with brass handles opened off the presbytery, two from the sides and two from the back. The wooden altar was painted white with gilded lining and had an altar stone (*pietra sacrata*). The *predella* was in walnut, with the confraternity's crest in the middle, and, since it had been donated by the guardian father Alessandro Dami, it displayed his family crest at the sides. At the rear of the altar there was a two-tiered platform, and at its sides two wooden pedestals painted walnut with inlaid gilded borders and arabesques, and the arms of their donors, the Comi brothers. Six brass candlesticks stood on the two-step platform, together with a cross and crucifix with brass stand. The vault behind the altar had a fresco depicting an angel choir in adoration of the Trinity. The confraternity's interest in music was clearly expressed in the fresco, for the adoring angels held or played a variety of instruments, including flutes, viols, organs, harpsichords, harps (or citharas), clavichords, sistra (a type of rattle), and pan-pipes. Domenico Torsi, writing in 1603, observed that the artist had painted them so well that the viewer would think he heard 'un non so che d'insolita armonia.'[49]

At the back of the presbytery was the sacristy. Here, between two windows, hung Piero di Cosimo's painting depicting the Virgin Mary with the Infant Jesus in her arms, St Dominic (or Vincent) on the right and St Jerome on the left, while four angels hovered above her head.[50] Above it hung an oval canvas of God the Father painted and donated by Piero Dandini, a member of the confraternity.[51] In the sacristy there was also a half-roundel *tavola* depicting a variant of Jacob's dream, which had, besides the figures of God the Father, Jacob, and the heavenly ladder full of ascending and descending angels, the Archangel Raphael leading a number of confraternity brothers to the ladder. The painting bore the inscription 'Venite haec est Domus Dei, et Scala Coeli.'[52] There was also a canvas roundel depicting the Pietà 'in a wooden frame painted walnut, very ancient,' a processional crucifix, complete with a red taffeta cover, brass sconce, and a lamp which alone weighed six pounds, and twenty-one tablets containing indulgences, obligations, lists of officers, and antiphons, all hanging on the sacristy walls. Somewhere in the room there were also the five window panes used to close the four windows on the façade and the one lateral window in the building. A walnut armoire, 4.5 *braccia* (2.65 metres) long, held at least thirty-two cloth hangings (*paramenti*) used on special occasions to cover completely the walls of the oratory, the *stanzone*, or the *terrazzino*; three quilted curtains (*portiere*) for the door that led into the oratory and the two doors off the presbytery; fifty-two wooden candlestick holders, engraved and decorated in silver; six wooden angels holding silver-coloured sconces; a gilded wooden monstrance, carved by Baccio del Bianco, with crystal lunette. A wall closet held more candlestick-holders, vases, a terracotta Madonna with the Infant Jesus in her arms, and two Infant Jesuses (one terracotta, the other papier mâché) used on Christmas Eve for the crèche. There were seven more trunks, some containing confraternal robes, others for the exclusive use of the guardian father, the sacristans, or the brothers. The sacristy also contained a wooden confessional, painted walnut. A small wooden crucifix by Bernardino Poccetti stood on top of another armoire that held a variety of administrative and devotional objects,[53] among which were the confraternity's voting urns, the peace-tablets (*paci*), a number of *tavolette* to place on the altar on various feast-days, not to mention more sconces, imitation flowers, a number of *morti* (images of the skull and cross-bones). Still another armoire held fifteen brass candlestick-holders, and more liturgical objects. Last, but not least, the sacristy had a well, complete with a rope and bucket.

From the sacristy the *confratello* would proceed into the *tornantino*, the smaller oratory used for morning services. Again he passed between a set of desks for the guardian father and the father corrector, and entered into a devotional space which was, to a great extent, similar to the main oratory described above. The walnut pews again extended around the corner, down the side walls, and reached the presbytery at the opposite end. The pews comprised twenty-nine seat boxes, of which the two nearest the altar could not be opened because of the altar rail. The altar in the *tornatino* was made of stone. It had its own altar stone, a two-tiered walnut predella, a gilded leather altar frontal with a walnut-coloured wooden platform with gilded linings and tin-plate (*latta dorata*) decorated with four chiaroscuro cherubim. On the altar there were six brass candlestick-holders, a cross with a brass pedestal and two bas-relief lead peace-tablets (*pace*), with gilded frames.[54] On the altar there was also a three-tiered cabinet containing the confraternity's collection of twenty-seven reliquaries holding a variety of relics (including the Wood of the Cross and a relic of St Mary Magdalene). Among the devotional images in the *tornantino* there was a canvas depicting the Archangel Raphael and Tobias hanging behind the altar, six canvases about two *braccia* high attributed to Santi di Tito, two unframed half-ovals about one *braccio* high depicting St Jerome and St Bernard respectively, and, above the entrance, a painting of the Madonna of the Misericordia.[55] This last item is described as a Madonna with a number of youths dressed in the confraternity's robes gathered under her mantle held open by two angels; at one side St Mary Magdalene is held aloft by angels, while on the other there is a Nativity scene; under the painting there is a frieze decorated with stories from the Book of Tobit – in short, it contained most of the confraternity's icons. The inventory points out that the painting had previously hung above the altar in the *tornatino*, but was moved to the opposite wall, above the entrance door, to make room for the painting of the Archangel Raphael.

Going back to the *spogliatoio* and then upstairs, one found the first storage room, containing a large number of paintings, including sixteen canvases painted in chiaroscuro depicting the Passion, donated by the Comi brothers and used for the decorations for Holy Week,[56] more *morti*, and other materials used for funeral or memorial services, for Holy Week, for theatrical entertainments, and other festivities.

The room to the right, called the *arsenale*, contained two wooden altars used in the *stanzone* during special feasts or for the Exposition of the Sacrament, wooden raisers, predellas, a prie-dieu, fifteen extra benches to be used in the oratory when attendance was high, five ladders, a coffin for children and another for adults (the latter decorated with the Archangel Raphael and Tobias), a variety of stage props including sixteen backdrops representing a woodland scene, seven representing a city view, and one representing a forum, four pieces of proscenium, two pieces of sky, and other stage materials. On another shelf in the *arsenale* there were ten large canvases, seven by Lorenzo Lippi and three in chiaroscuro by Baccio di Bianco, all ten depicting stories from the Book of Tobit.[57]

Proceeding into the first room for the musicians, one found two chiaroscuro works by Baccio del Bianco depicting stories related to the Archangel Raphael, an old *cassone*, a small table, a wooden stand for the *buonaccordo* (which had currently been taken home by Filippo Rustichelli), two reading stands, and a clothes-rack. The second room for the musicians contained only a large lantern (*lanternone*) and three candlestick-holders used in the musicians' balcony (*terrazzino*). Here there were three benches that ran along the three walls of the loft, a stool, and a five-keyboard organ, now in disrepair, donated to the confraternity by Alberto del Vivaio.

The servant's room contained two clothes-racks, two wooden chests, and a variety of utensils he clearly needed to carry out his work.

## Conclusion

It is clear, from this long and detailed description, that the confraternity made, on the whole, quite a stunning impression on its visitors. It not only enjoyed the use of an ample set of rooms, but also owned an extensive variety of objects, both sacred and profane. Some of these objects were made of precious materials while others were of noteworthy artistic value. Rich clothes, large wooden armoires and boxes, and gold and silver objects, sometimes by the dozen, reflected the confraternity's prosperity, connections, and status. The presence of two separate oratories, at a time when other youth confraternities were obliged to share theirs with an adult confraternity (see above, ch. 2, pp. 27–8, 31–2), further underscored the Arcangelo Raffaello's wealth and self-sufficiency. The materials stored away in the arsenal point to the confraternity's active involvement in theatrical representations (for which see below, chs. 16–17). The presence of family crests on the balcony, altar frontals, and other objects reveals the strong personal involvement of members of these families with the Arcangelo Raffaello, and reaffirms the confraternity's ties with the Florentine nobility, especially in the wake of the process of ennobling (*nobilizzazione*) that had taken hold of many Florentine confraternities from the mid-sixteenth century onward.

The comfortable rooms and their splendid decoration were not, however, an instant achievement, and neither was the ennobling that had turned the devout young men of earlier times into 'courtiers of God,' as Weissman called confraternity brothers in the grand duchy.[58] The change occurred over time in the sixteenth and seventeenth centuries as the confraternity, in the wake of the disastrous years between the death of Lorenzo to the ascension of Cosimo I, re-established itself, renewed its devotional life, and reached out to attract devout and capable young men. This renewal process will be the subject of the next chapter.

# 6

# Rebirth

By the mid-1550s, the confraternity's increasing wealth, membership, and self-assurance had reached the point where it could look with pride at its activities and accomplishments. This new prosperity is reflected in the decision taken by the two adult officers, the guardian father Antonio di Giovanni *cuoiaio* (leather worker) and the father corrector Fr David da Raggiuolo, OP, to begin once again to keep an official written record of the confraternity's activities.[1] Their inspired decision allows us to examine this renewal in many ways. In this chapter we will follow it by noting the rebuilding and renovations that were undertaken, and the growth in membership, activities, and reputation that ensued.

## The Flood of 1557

Less than a year after the decision to keep detailed records was taken, the disastrous flood of 13 September 1557 took a heavy toll on the confraternity's books and belongings. Unseasonably heavy rains had swelled all the Tuscan rivers, and in particular the Arno. In Florence the water pressure from the swollen river brought down all the bridges except for the Ponte Vecchio. The Arno then overflowed its banks and covered two-thirds of the city in mud and water. Contemporary chroniclers report that this flood was even worse than the 1333 one described by Giovanni Villani. In fact, it has been superseded only by the more recent flood of 4 November 1966.[2] The contemporary chronicler Giovan Battista Adriani recalls that convents, in particular, were worse hit because 'they are built in low-lying areas.'[3] The statutes and most of the records of the confraternity of the Arcangelo Raffaello were damaged beyond repair. As a result of the flood, very few documents from before 1557 have survived, not only for the Arcangelo Raffaello but for all nine youth confraternities in Florence.

After the flood, the *capitoli*, which had been lost and then recovered, were diligently and painstakingly recopied.[4] The *ricordi*, on the other hand, were either lost or irreparably damaged and discarded. Only in 1563 did the confraternity begin once again to keep regular records of its activities. Except for a few brief interruptions, they continue to 1785 and provide us with a full chronology and history of the confraternity to the day of its suppression by order of Grand Duke Pietro Leopoldo.

## Renewal and Rebuilding

After the flood, repairs to the building and restocking of necessary materials became an immediate priority. In 1558 a voluntary fund-raising campaign was launched among the members to finance repairs to the leaking roof and the damaged choir stalls, as well as to purchase new gowns and linens.[5] Work on the choir stalls began on 1 July 1559 and continued for just over a year until 31 August 1560 at a total cost of 92.11 *lire*.[6] The leaking roof was repaired in December 1559. A special collection in January 1560 raised 73.2.8 *lire* from fifty-three donors to restore the front door to the confraternity and its awning, damaged this time not by the flood but by recent festivities in piazza Santa Maria Novella.[7] Clearly, the brotherhood was eager to fix as necessary the damaged fabric of its building and willing to dig into its own pockets in order to do so. On Florentine New Year's Day 1560, as if to give thanks for a good past year and publicly recognize personal contributions, the *provveditore* Carlo Ghettini drew up a list of benefactors who had helped in the restoration of various confraternity objects and property.[8]

The following year, restoration and renewal continued. In early January 1561 a new front door was installed and re-covered at a cost of 7.4, *lire* using walnut from the old door, and then two cabinets (*tabernacoli*) were built at a cost of 21 *lire* to house the two confraternity banners.[9] In August a collection was raised to commission a new reliquary for the confraternity's many relics.[10] And, as if to underline the changes taking place in the confraternity, in January 1563 several paintings were relocated – the painting of St Vincent, which the confraternity believed to be by Domenico del Ghirlandaio, was moved from the large entrance hall (the *stanzone*) to the Oratory, while the anonymous Madonna of the Misericordia, with appropriately devout confraternity youths under her mantle and St Mary Magdalene and the Nativity on either side, was moved from the oratory to the *stanzone*.[11] The *ricordi* explain that the paintings were switched so that they would not be damaged by the youths' ball-throwing – a clear indication that the entrance hall was being used for somewhat rowdy activities and this was putting at risk some of the valuable objects in it. The relocation of the pseudo-Ghirlandaio into the oratory and the anonymous Madonna into the *stanzone* probably sought as well to effect a change in the tone while, at the same time, reflecting a changing attitude in the confraternity.

The confraternity's evident resurgence quickly attracted further donations and gifts. In June 1564 the Franciscans from the convent of Ognissanti gave to the Arcangelo Raffaello the goods (*masserizie*) currently in their possession but once belonging to the confraternity of the Capanna.[12] It may not be a coincidence that the following year the youths stopped using a priest from the Dominican convent of Santa Maria Novella as their father corrector and opted instead for a Franciscan from the convent of Ognissanti.

Further voluntary fund-raising campaigns were launched. In 1565 there was a drive to pay for improvements to the walls (*muraglia*).[13] Renovations to the roof were carried out again in 1566 and in 1573. The confraternity became so concerned with its exterior appearance that even adjacent buildings came under its critical gaze. In July 1573 the youths reached a formally notarized agreement with their neighbour, Giovanni di Raffaello Mazzinghi, obliging him to remove an unsightly projection (*schrignio et gonfio*) that jutted out from his house above the roof of the confraternity.[14]

## Membership Growth

As these repairs were undertaken and the confraternity was renewing the fabric of its building, membership was growing by leaps and bounds. A list of youths who enrolled between 1563 and 1586 contains the names of 1,821 brothers, indicating an average increase of 79.2 members per year. A similar list for the years 1580–1620 contains 1,822 names, revealing a drastic drop in average yearly increases (down to 45.6 new members per year), though still an active pattern of enrolment well into the seventeenth century.[15] This level of growth is impressive, especially when compared with that of other youth confraternities. The membership rolls of the confraternity of the Purificazione, for example, indicate that in the years 1580–1620 it enrolled 471 new members, for an average of 16.4 per year, significantly less than the 45.6 per year the Arcangelo Raffaello was attracting in those same years.[16]

It is not surprising, then, to see that the Arcangelo Raffaello once again chose to establish a *stretta* or subgroup (or, as they called it, a morning *tornata*) for youths aged fifteen years and older.[17] The 1468 statutes gave the guardian father the right to establish a special gathering composed of youths aged fifteen and older, and men who had passed the maximum statutory age limit for membership in the confraternity. This subgroup was to meet separately from the main body of the confraternity as the guardian would indicate. The statutes were also firm in pointing out that 'no one should dare to say that such a gathering is a separate confraternity, for it is a spiritual exercise under the direction of the guardian father.'[18] In it, the older youths were to be instructed in 'the Office and discipline discreetly' as the guardian's own conscience suggested.

A 1581 agreement among fifty-two youths formally set up a *stretta* for members over fifteen years of age.[19] Such a special gathering had existed at least twice before in the confraternity's history. We have already seen how in 1442 members aged nineteen and over were granted a separate meeting site within the convent of San Silvestro by Pope Eugenius IV.[20] In 1560 as well, a number of older members had been meeting for morning services separately from the main confraternity. This 1560 subgroup found it necessary to discuss whether youths who had not been formally enrolled in the evening *tornata* could be accepted directly into the morning *tornata* without prejudice to the statutes. An entry for April 1560 records that two youths had came up for election into the subgroup. One of them was a member of the confraternity, had been participating in its evening *tornata*, and his candidacy had been properly posted the previous Sunday. The other youth, Giovan Battista di Bartolomeo *scultore*, however, was not officially a member of the confraternity and his name had not been posted a week earlier. Someone probably questioned his candidacy, for when his name came up for voting the guardian father Antonio di Giovanni went on record saying that membership in the evening *tornata* was not a prerequisite for membership in the morning *tornata* because 'this [morning] *tornata* is a spiritual exercise, as the statutes say, and not another confraternity.' All that was necessary, the guardian pointed out, was that the candidate be at least fifteen years old and be well known to all the members of the subgroup, and that the guardian authorize his entrance. This said, Giovan Battista's name went up for voting and he was elected, notwithstanding four negative votes.[21]

In both 1442 and 1560 the presence of a subgroup was concurrent with a period of growth fostered in part by the patronage or encouragement of eminent clergymen – Pope Eugenius IV in the 1440s and fra Santi Cini in

1558–9. It was also a gathering of older youths, as the 1468 statutes do recommend. And it is quite possible that it met to carry out devotions and 'discipline' that would not be as suitable for the younger members (possibly even the practice of flagellation, for which see below, ch. 11, pp. 143–7). The 1581 case is, however, slightly different. On this occasion the growth in membership evident in the confraternity seems to have been determined more by internal than external factors. There is no evidence of an eminent patron or an active father corrector giving lustre or providing inspiration to the confraternity. Rather, it was the youths themselves who were spearheading the renewal and growth evident in those years. Probably because of such self-motivation, general membership and the morning *tornata* prospered well into the next century.

The Arcangelo Raffaello was not alone in setting up such subgroups. Perhaps the most famous subgroup is the 'Group of Fifty,' also known as the Congrega de' Neri, that was part of the adult flagellant confraternity of Santa Maria della Croce al Tempio. As their special work of mercy, the Neri comforted and escorted persons who had been condemned to death, and then buried their bodies.[22] Similar subgroups, though not with such highly visible or charitable functions, also existed within youth confraternities. The Purificazione, for example, had a *tornata segreta* dedicated to the Trinity, with its own enrolment books and ricordi.[23]

The *tornata segreta* at the Purificazione was restricted to youths aged fourteen and older.[24] It had been meeting since at least the mid-sixteenth century, and it too seemed to prosper late into the following century. Enrolment figures for the confraternity, although incomplete, indicate an enrolment of about a dozen youths per year. A document of 1664 describes clearly the dual nature of this confraternity:

Our company of San Marco is divided into two special gatherings, that is, a main and public one under the invocation of the Purification of the Most Holy Virgin Mary and Saint Zanobius, in which all brothers, adult or otherwise, participate, as well as those who are not enrolled as brothers, and then one that is secret and is under the invocation of the Most Divine Trinity, in which only those adult members who have joined and are listed in it can participate. At each group's meeting the guardian father and all or some of the four counsellors elected every four months from the membership of the secret congregation must participate.

Public meetings under the invocation of the Purification and St Zanobius take place in the main oratory ['basilica maggiore'] every Sunday and holiday of obligation throughout the year ..., on Christmas morning and then for the three masses, on the morning and evening of the Purification of the Most Holy Virgin, the mornings of the feasts of the Ascension, St Zanobius, Corpus Domini (and then to the public procession), the Octave of the Santissimo and then procession with the clergy of San Lorenzo, the vigil of St John the Baptist and then the public procession, St James on the 25th of July, the first Sunday of October it participates in the procession for the Rosary with the priests of San Marco, and it meets for meditations every Thursday evening throughout the year.

The secret congregation meets under the invocation of the Most Holy Trinity in the smaller oratory ['basilica minore']) about one hour after the ringing of the first Ave Maria on the following days: every Sunday morning throughout the year, and on the mornings of Holy Thursday and Good Friday.[25]

Though not the norm, such subgroups were periodically established well into the eighteenth century. In 1747 the youth confraternity of Sant'Antonio da Padova e San Giorgio de' Fanciulli reactivated a lapsed *stretta* of twelve members originally established in 1709.[26] Already by 1709, however, the devotional component had given way to the promotional one – the purpose of the 1709 *stretta*, named in honour of the Annunciation, had been to oversee the annual exposition of the Sacrament on the first Sunday of Lent (Quadragesima) and to contribute two pounds of wax to the confraternity.

The presence of a subgroup within the larger organization suggests that youth confraternities occasionally functioned as two units – a general confraternity that gathered all qualified youths, and, within it, a more restricted confraternity that gathered only those older youths who had demonstrated a more profound sense of devotion or commitment. Through such a two-step system of membership, the Arcangelo Raffaello and other youth confraternities were able to identify and direct their more promising members towards greater involvement in the devotional life of the confraternity and of the Christian community as a whole. Nearly all the fifty-two members who enrolled in the 1581 *stretta* at the Arcangelo Raffaello, for example, became visibly active in the confraternity in the years immediately following. Their names appear regularly and repeatedly in the roster of officers and in the activities recorded in the documents.

## Growth in Activities and Reputation

By the mid to late sixteenth century, hand in hand with the increase in membership, there was also significant growth in devotional and educational activities at the Arcangelo Raffaello. They will be described in greater detail in subsequent chapters. For the moment it suffices to point out that there was an increase in sermons delivered by the brothers, in religious plays staged for the edification and entertainment of members and friends, in attendance at public processions, and in the lavishness of festive celebrations.

The confraternity's reputation for devotion and talent soon attracted eminent visitors, who came especially to attend its sung Vespers. The papal nuncio Valerio Monaldeschi della Corbara and an entourage of monsignors and cathedral canons heard Vespers in the confraternity on All Souls' 1583.[27] His successor, Giuseppe Donzelli, archbishop of Sorrento, visited the confraternity for All Souls' 1586, just a few months after his arrival in Florence.[28] The Arcangelo Raffaello's contribution to the devotional life of the city was once again publicly recognized by the pope, who issued a bull granting a plenary indulgence to all those who visited the confraternity on the Monday and Tuesday after Easter to participate in the devotion of the Forty Hours.[29] The archbishop and even members of the grand-ducal family soon became regular visitors on the confraternity's special feast-days.

The youths' reputation spread even outside Florence. On 2 June 1585 the confraternity received a letter from Domenico Mellini of Portoferraio asking the youths for a copy of their statutes so that a confraternity of the Arcangelo Raffaello recently established in that town could model its own *capitoli* on them.[30]

## Renovations

At this point, major improvements on the site were undertaken. During the time of the *guardiano* Girolamo di Maestro Luca (1573–7), Baccio and Domenico Comi underwrote the expenses for extensive renovations to adapt the entire site previously occupied by the three defunct confraternities of Sant'Ignazio, San Vincenzo Ferreri, and the Spirito Santo to the needs of the Arcangelo Raffaello (see above, ch. 5, pp. 61–3) and then in June–September 1586 they had all the choir stalls refurbished. Michelangelo Cinganelli painted the exterior façade of the confraternity with stories from the Book of Tobit (unveiled on 8 September 1595), while his son Benedetto painted the confraternity's vaulted ceiling (unveiled on 25 December 1596).[31]

## Important and Influential Members

The confraternity's growing reputation for devotion and success soon attracted high-quality youths, both in a spiritual and in a secular sense. The young Piero di Lorenzo Niccolini, future archbishop of Florence, enrolled on 1 January 1588, sponsored by the assistant vice-*guardiano* Niccolò Antifassi.[32] Niccolini would later be described with pride as 'one of our brothers since his youth.'[33] In a spurt of active involvement he would serve as sacristan (May–August 1590), counsellor (September–December 1590), and choir master (January–April 1591), and even deliver a lay sermon on 15 April 1591 as part of the confraternity's devotion of the Forty Hours. Later, as canon of the cathedral, he would return to recite Mass in the confraternity for its patron's feast-day (31 December 1606 and 1607). And then as archbishop of Florence he would continue to be a regular visitor at this event, often accompanied by Grand Duke Ferdinando II and other members of the grand-ducal family (31 December 1636 and following). His insistence in 1636 that the confraternity's statutes be revised and rewritten had significant long-lasting effects on the confraternity's devotional and administrative life (see below, ch. 8, pp. 104–10).

In later years, other brothers from the Arcangelo Raffaello would also proceed to a distinguished ecclesiastical career. Alessandro Marzi Medici, Francesco Maria Machiavelli, Baccio Aldobrandini, Alamanno Salviati, and others were elevated to the cardinalate.[34] Giovanni Buonaccorsi became bishop of Colle (1645–81), and Lorenzo Della Robbia bishop of Fiesole (1634–45).[35]

Less exalted but nonetheless important as an indication of the spiritual vitality of the confraternity is the significant number of brothers who entered the Church. Del Migliore comments that Cosimo the Elder de' Medici had given rooms in the convent of San Marco to the Compagnia della Purificazione so that the youths, 'by frequenting this company and this convent from an early age would develop an affection for this order ['religione'] and would then be inclined to take its habit.'[36]

Lorenzo Polizzotto points out that in the years between 1501 and 1536, fifty of the sixty-seven youths from the Purificazione who joined a religious order became Dominicans, most of them at San Marco. Such a high number of religious vocations and high interest in the Dominican order he rightly attributes to the 'careful tending' of the confraternity by Savonarola and some of his most eminent followers.[37] Such statistics do not hold for subsequent lists. A similar list of religious vocations covering the years 1577–94 reveals that only ten of the nineteen youths who entered orders during those years became Dominicans, and of these San Marco received only four.[38] A much later list, for the years 1685–99, reveals an even more noticeable drop – eight in all, and only two professed with the Dominicans at San Marco.[39] Apart from the post-Savonarolan period, the religious vocations from youths in the Purificazione indicate a wide choice of orders that lasted well into the late seventeenth century, ranging from the well-established Dominicans to the new orders of the Catholic reformation.

While Cosimo de' Medici would not have been pleased with the noticeable drop in religious vocations or in interest for his beloved convent of San Marco, Grand Duke Cosimo, on the other hand, should have been very pleased with the vocations emanating from the confraternity of the Arcangelo Raffaello. Here vocations appear to have been not only more abundant in numbers but also more advantageous for the host convent. A list of religious vocations from the Arcangelo Raffaello for the years 1556–61 indicates that twenty-four of the twenty-seven brothers mentioned became Dominicans at Santa Maria Novella.[40] Twenty-seven in five years is a significantly high contribution to the ranks of the clergy, even considering that two youths eventually withdrew because they did not have the strength to continue (the scribe glossed their entries 'non potette reggere') and a third was removed by his father ('cavatone dal padre').

A fuller list of religious vocations, covering this time the years 1441–1593, is found in the records of the youth confraternity of Sant'Antonio da Padova detta di San Giorgio.[41] It gives the names of 189 brothers who entered the religious life over the course of those 152 years. Of these, the largest proportion became monks – 46 at the Badia in Florence, 47 at the Badia di San Salvi, 6 at the Badia di San Salvatore a Settimo, 20 at Monte Uliveto, 3 in Vallombrosa, 2 at the Certosa, 3 with the Camaldolese, 14 with the Augustinians at San Donato a Scopeto, and one with the Augustinians of Santo Spirito. All the others, except for one who joined the Jesuits, became friars – 17 at San Marco, 4 at Santa Maria Novella, 15 at San Francesco, 2 at the Carmine, 4 with the Capuchins, and 6 at the Gesuati. From the fifteenth century on, the confraternity of Sant'Antonio da Padova met in its own building on the Costa San Giorgio, which it shared with the men of the *buca* of San Girolamo Oltrarno. Both these factors – an independent location and association with a *buca* rather than a convent – may have had a role to play in the choice, evident in the figures from this confraternity, of the monastic over the conventual life.

Unfortunately, Sant'Antonio's consistency in keeping such records is not to be found in the papers of the Arcangelo Raffaello or of other youth confraternities. Reliable long-term comparative studies are therefore not possible, and we must satisfy ourselves with the suggestion that youth confraternities did, in the fifteenth and sixteenth centuries at least, foster vocations, and that they generally favoured the order of their host institution.[42]

Young men who would later excel in more secular fields also joined the confraternity. Several members of the Camerata dei Bardi had been in the Arcangelo Raffaello and continued to be closely associated with it. Girolamo Mei, mentor to the Camerata, is entered on a membership list of the Arcangelo Raffaello for the 1550s.[43] Filippo di Giovanni Bardi, the organizer of the Camerata, entered the confraternity in about 1575, and so did his two brothers Camillo and Cosimo di Giovanni Bardi, as well as Giulio Caccini and Piero Strozzi.[44] By 1587 the Arcangelo Raffaello also included Jacopo Corsi (1561–1602), Piero and Carlo Rucellai, and the sons of Filippo Strozzi and Nero del Nero.[45]

A number of visual artists were also connected with the Arcangelo Raffaello. This had been the case already in the late fifteenth and early sixteenth centuries when Cosimo Rosselli and then Antonio *miniatore* were appointed guardians of the group.[46] Donations in kind from the late sixteenth and early seventeenth century indicate that the confraternity continued to attract artists as members. The *miniatore* Bartolommeo Traballesi (d. 1585), for example, painted the Nativity in the confraternity's 1560 copy of the statutes, while his brother Francesco (1544–88) painted a terracotta *Raphael with Tobias* moulded by another member, Giovan Battista di Benedetto *scultore*.[47]

Along with youths who would dedicate their lives to the Church or to the arts, the confraternity also attracted the scions of some of the most eminent Florentine families. Illustrious surnames such as Acciaiuoli, Adimari, Aldobrandini, Altoviti, Antifassi, Antinori – just to remain in the A's – abound in the pages of the Arcangelo Raffaello. A number of its noble members were eventually knighted. Several youths who enrolled in these years became Knights of St Stephen, the highest secular honorific granted by the grand duchy – among them Giovanni Cosimo and his brother Panfilo del cav. Cesare Gherardini (both enrolled on 25 March 1581), Camillo di Giovanni de' Bardi (enrolled on 7 May 1581), Noferi del cav. Francesco Vagnucci (enrolled 10 July 1583), and others. Some, such as Aghinolfo di Giovanni de' Bardi (enrolled on 7 May 1581), Vincenzo di Dionigi Carducci (enrolled 6 January 1582) and Bernardo di Messer Giovan Gualberto Vecchietti (enrolled 31 March 1587), became Knights of Malta.[48]

The grand-ducal family was soon to follow. On 31 December 1589 the Grand Duchess Christine of Lorraine, recently arrived in Florence as wife of the Grand Duke Ferdinando I, attended Vespers at the Arcangelo Raffaello. She showed great interest in the youths' devotions and their talent for singing, so much so that she returned several times and, exactly two years later, agreed to enrol her first-born son, the future Grand Duke Cosimo II, into the confraternity.[49] From that day on, all the Medici sons, to the end of the dynasty, enrolled into the Arcangelo Raffaello.[50] And so did the sons of foreign rulers and nobles. Ferdinando Gonzaga, heir to the duchy of Mantua and a close personal friend of Cosimo II enrolled on 1 November 1605. Their close friendship would eventually prompt Cosimo to marry his sister Caterina to Ferdinando, now duke, and thus strengthen the already strong political and personal ties between Florence and Mantua. One of England's most (in)famous adventurers, Sir Robert Dudley, titular duke of Northumberland, now living in Tuscany and serving the Medici in a number of crucial military and administrative roles, enrolled three of his sons in the Arcangelo Raffaello – Cosimo, Carlo, and Ambrosio (24 August 1623).[51]

Admittedly, the sons of the Medici or the Gonzaga or the Dudleys never became active participants in the confraternity's devotions, administration, or festive activities, but their mere presence on the membership rolls and their periodic attendance as spectators at some of the more splendid events mounted by the youths did bring lustre to the confraternity.

And the lustre translated into an increase in general membership. While enrolment figures in the five-year period immediately preceding Cosimo II's enrolment (1586–90) had averaged 26.8 new members per year, in following five-year period (1591–5) they averaged instead a more than doubled 55.6 new members per year. The average remained consistently high until 1615–19, when it dipped to 26.6 per year (these years coincide with Cosimo II's chronic illness, and this perhaps may have had an effect on confraternity enrolment). The enrolment in 1620 of Cosimo II's four sons – Ferdinando, Giovan Carlo, Mattias, and Leopoldo – temporarily skyrocketed enrolment to a high of 88. While figures sagged again in the next five years (37, 43, 62, 37, 17), the enrolment of two Medici nephews in 1626 bounced the figure back up to 57. Similarly, when don Lorenzo de' Medici enrolled in 1630, new memberships for that year jumped to an astronomical 118 and remained consistently high to 1637, the last year included in the fascicule started in 1579 to record entrance fee payments.[52]

By the seventeenth century the confraternity had thus regained not only its physical wealth, but also its reputation as one of the most eminent Florentine schools of doctrine – to use the term loosely. Its membership rolls were filled with the names of the scions of the most eminent Florentine families, its devotions attracted a number of devout young men, its services and building were embellished by a nucleus of talented artists, and its finances were sustained by dedicated donors and a steadily growing number of dues-paying members. Secure in its devotional, financial, and cultural position in the city, the Arcangelo Raffaello was also participating in, and adapting itself to, the spiritual renewal ensuing from the Council of Trent and the Catholic Reform movement. The next chapter will consider how the confraternity and the Church dealt with each other in this period of renewal and reform.

# 7

# The Confraternity and the Post-Tridentine Church

The Church hierarchy in the fifteenth century had been, on the whole, supportive of youth confraternities. The Camaldolese General Ambrogio Traversari had praised their role in the spiritual and moral education of the laity, Pope Eugenius IV had recognized them officially and granted them both permanency and prestige, and Archbishop Antoninus had given them devotional and administrative consistency by overseeing the composition or revision of their statutes. On the whole, the interventions of the hierarchy in the devotional, spiritual, and administrative life of youth confraternities had strengthened the movement while, to a certain extent, limiting it to the few organizations it officially approved and supported.

The political and social instability that characterized Florentine life between Savonarola and Duke Cosimo I, on the other hand, took its toll on organized lay spirituality. At every political crisis, governments of the day either closed down confraternities or banned them from meeting. Thus republican governments legislated against them in the wake of the expulsion of the Medici (December 1494 and August 1495), or during the constitutional crisis of 1502. The restored Medici did the same on several occasions after returning to power (1513, 1514, 1515, 1516), or during the Buondelmonti-Alamanni conspiracy (1522), or on the eve of the last Republic (1527). The Republic itself closed them down, supposedly for health reasons, during the pestilent (and turbulent) period of 1527–30. With the final Medici restoration, the government again legislated against them (1530), and so did Cosimo I immediately after the assassination of Duke Alessandro and again before the battle of Montemurlo (1537).[1]

Though not always directly affected, since most of the bans applied to adult confraternities only, the youths of the Arcangelo Raffaello were not immune from the political realities of the times. The most evident effect of this growing series of political crises was the loss of its meeting site on Via della Scala, ceded in the wake of the siege of 1529–30 to the displaced nuns of San Martino, and the subsequent break of its affiliation with the prestigious Ospedale della Scala, itself a victim of the times.

By the mid-sixteenth century, although relocated in rooms in the convent of Santa Maria Novella, the Arcangelo Raffaello was not thriving spiritually. Aware of a certain laxity and decadence within the organization, the members themselves sought to renew their spiritual life. The following pages will trace how this spiritual renewal was effected primarily by forming closer ties with the recently reformed Dominican convent of Santa Maria Novella and hiring a father corrector from among the convent's reformed clergy. We will then follow the confraternity's move from Dominican to Franciscan, Theatine, and then, once again, Dominican confessors. We will also examine the effect on the confraternity of episcopal visitations and post-Tridentine reforms.

## The Priests from Santa Maria Novella

In 1558, the newly appointed confraternity scribe, Zanobi Buonavolti, recalled a series of decisions and agreements touching on the choice for a new father corrector. Buonavolti explained that the confraternity had suffered a decline in both morals (*buon chostumi*) and practices (*usanze*) attributable in part to the lukewarm participation of previous father correctors who, having to come from as far away as the Badia or from the convent of San Marco, had not regularly attended to their duties. Buonavolti also mentioned the recent reform of the convent of Santa Maria Novella, and indicated that the confraternity now wished to associate itself more closely with the reformed convent. In so doing, the confraternity clearly hoped to benefit from the convent's renewed spiritual life and thus undergo a renewal of its own.

In 1556, in fact, the convent of Santa Maria Novella had been forcibly transferred to the Roman province of the Dominican order. The move obliged the friars to abandon the 'Conventual' and join the 'Observantist' fold of the order, that is, to return to the rigorous observance of their original rules. Those friars who did not agree, and there were many, were allowed to leave Santa Maria Novella and enter convents in the Roman vicariate. Those who remained, together with the friars of San Marco, who, with the physical support of soldiers lent to them by the *Otto di Guardia*, literally marched in and 'occupied' Santa Maria Novella, saw the transfer as a triumph of reformist practices and ideals. The entire move was not without its painful moments. Fra Angelo Bettini, for example, had to be censured for his behaviour towards one of the friars from Santa Maria Novella. There were also political overtones to the transfer, for it had been proposed to the master-general of the order, fra Stefano Usodimare, and to Pope Paul IV Carafa by none other than Duke Cosimo I, whose own program of religious reform in Florence was as single-minded as it was self-interested.[2] About ten years earlier, Cosimo had expelled the Dominicans from San Marco and sought, in this manner, to rid himself of the continued Savonarolan, and therefore anti-Medicean, elements active in that convent. His expulsion of the Dominicans met with such strong opposition from Pope Paul III Farnese and a number of cardinals that he was eventually obliged to allow the Dominicans back. Though apparently defeated, Cosimo I in fact won the day because few of the original friars did return to San Marco and the reconstituted convent, composed for the most part of new friars, remained, as in fact it had become, obedient to Medici regime.[3]

It is clear, then, that in choosing to associate itself with the friars of Santa Maria Novella the confraternity of the Arcangelo Raffaello was making a conscious decision to align itself with the reformist ideals emanating, with strong government backing, from the Observant convent of San Marco.

The guardian father Antonio di Giovanni therefore approached the prior of nearby Santa Maria Novella to ask for a father corrector from that convent. The prior, fra Matteo Strozzi, at first ignored the request.[4] Then, after repeated entreaties from the guardian father and after having sought the advice of fra Angelo Bettini, his provincial superior, he agreed to satisfy the confraternity's request.[5]

The prior's slow and methodical response to the guardian father is indicative of the cautious relationship between convent and confraternity. Even after twenty-five years of living next to each other and signing a number of rental agreements, convent and confraternity had not developed a close relationship. When it came to hiring priests to serve as father correctors, the youths of the Arcangelo Raffaello had continued to turn to the Benedictines at the Badia or to the Dominicans at San Marco rather than seek the friars on the other side of their oratory wall. The prior of Santa Maria Novella, for his part, was uncertain about fostering a closer connection with the youths who were renting rooms in his convent. When they eventually asked for the services of a priest from his convent, the prior delayed and consulted with his superior.

When, on his superior's advice, the prior finally agreed to provide a father corrector for the confraternity, his choice fell on fra Davit da Raggiuolo. This was a wise choice, one that proved very satisfactory for both the confraternity and the convent. Fra Davit was instrumental in ironing out difficulties between the friars and the youths, and in ensuring that mutually suitable agreements were reached. Zanobi Buonavolti points out that the youths were pleased with the newly appointed father corrector because, unlike his predecessors, he attended to his duties regularly. Although fra Davit retained his position for only two years (October 1556 to June 1558), his success is measured by the confraternity's interest in continuing to retain a Dominican from Santa Maria Novella and by the calibre of his successor, fra Santi Cini.

## Fra Santi Cini (1524–70)

Fra Santi Cini was an important figure in sixteenth-century Florentine spirituality.[6] A man of profound spirituality, with strong Savonarolan leanings, he was a personal friend of two Florentine saints, St Philip Neri and St Catherine de' Ricci. He was also actively involved in the fostering of devotion and the growth of religious organizations in Florence. In this context he is remembered as the founder of the confraternity of San Tommaso d'Aquino (1566), composed of young noblemen who participated in both spiritual exercises and works of mercy in the community.[7] One of his contemporaries and a fellow Dominican recalls him, saying:

> Fra Santi Cini, a Florentine, took the habit at San Marco. He was a priest of some learning, singular goodness and devotion. He preached in Florence, Rome, Naples, and in many other cities with great results. He had been especially gifted by God in being able to touch the heart and move to tears [with his preaching]. He was very good in private conversations, by means of which (and with his preaching) he led many young noblemen to the service of God, and he converted many sinners to the right path. He was a priest of much abstinence and very little sleep. He founded in Florence the devout and noble Oratory of St Thomas of Aquinas. He was a prior at Fiesole, in Florence, and elsewhere. He was humble and benign, in sum a great servant of God, and for a time he was my teacher and prior. He passed to a better life most devoutly on the octave of St Thomas of Aquinas in the year 1570, the forty-sixth of his life, when he was preaching the Lenten services at the Duomo of Viterbo, and he was buried at the Madonna della Quercia, with many tears from those fathers. May he rest in glory.[8]

Fra Santi's influence on the confraternity of the Arcangelo Raffaello was felt most profoundly on the confraternity's devotions and activities, which he reformed and renewed as soon as he was appointed father corrector in

August 1558. The manner in which he carried out the reforms is noteworthy, for it illustrates his collaboration with the older members of the group and his concern that the correct procedures be followed (something which did not seem to have concerned his predecessors). Buonavolti's entry in the *Ricordi* again sheds light on the situation:

Having been deprived of our father corrector fra Davit, who was appointed master of novices by his prior, we were granted in exchange Fr fra Santi Cini, a friar in the said church of Santa Maria Novella, and he was very gladly accepted by us. And so he began to exercise his office with the greatest love and charity. And because the company, having been for some time without a father corrector, had become somewhat lax, that is, it did not observe some of the regulations it had been given, he decided to begin to redress it with some regulations. Therefore, in order to have a good start, we gathered on the morning of St Lawrence, the 10th of August, and when we finished our usual orations and devotions, Holy Mass was said, and when it was finished everyone sat down and [fra Santi Cini] sent out all brothers aged fifteen and under. And he proposed many things and regulations. And because there were many brothers who had not been entered and accepted in the morning *tornata* and some in the day *tornata*, it was decided, for the sake of brevity, that they all be accepted by our other brothers, and so they went to the middle [of the oratory] and our father corrector spoke briefly to them exhorting them to be fervent [in their devotion] to the house. And having carried out all these ceremonies and made these decisions he presented some youths and asked us to be pleased to accept them, and they were voted upon one by one like the previous [youths], and they all were elected unanimously, and their names will be listed below, and first the older youths

Tommaso di Zanobi Mormorai
Michele di Raffaello delle Colombe[9]
Giovan Francesco di Leonardo Giuntini
Simone di Giovan Domenico Coresi
Domenico di Cristofano Cignioni [possibly Cignani or Cignozzi]
Antonio di Giuliano Segni
Vittorio di Pellegrino dell'Ancisa[10]
Bernardo di Gabriello Naldini
Antonio di [blank] sarto
Lodovico di Giovanni Ginori
Francesco di Giovan Battista Nelli
Zanobi di Simone de' Ricci
Cosimo di Girolamo da Firenzuola

Andrea di Giovanni Nelli
Dorateo di Bernardo Fiorelli
Pagolo di Lorenzo delle Rede
Michele di Vincenzo delle Rede
Pandolfo di Bartolomeo Galli
Pierantonio di Pagnozzo Ridolfi[11]
Pagolo di Girolamo Pagoli
Antonio di Tommaso del Seta
Vincenzo di Ser Giovanni Goteschi
Bernardo di Bartolomeo Gondi
Francesco di [blank] Giullini
Jacopo di Simone cardaiuolo
Giovanni di Meglio di Giovanni
Jacopo di Meglio di Giovanni

And when all these ceremonies were finished, he had all these youths go to the middle and he admonished them, and he showed them the manner in which they were to act both when they entered the confraternity and when they took part in the offices, and how to do the roll call ['rassegna'] at every *tornata* and how to assign penances ['dare le correzioni'] as our statutes order. And in this manner he began such a good endeavour, and may it please the Lord to grant it a good middle and an excellent end.[12]

Less than a year later, in June 1559, fra Santi Cini informed the confraternity that he was being transferred to the convent of San Marco and would be unable to continue in his duties as father corrector. His efforts at reforming the confraternity by giving it order and direction had been successful and appreciated, so much so that the following August he was invited back for a visit to help celebrate the feast of St Lawrence, which the confraternity now saw as the anniversary of its renewal. That year the confraternity scribe records that it was fra Santi who 'the previous year on that day reintroduced some regulations and manners that in the past, because of little care, had fallen into disuse.' The celebrations expanded the following year, when the scribe mentions that the youths 'honoured' the feast by setting up some decorations (*parato*), reciting an *esempio* from the life of the saint, and eating watermelons.[13] The feast continued to be celebrated with watermelons for several years (see below, ch. 12, pp. 157–9).

The appointment of fra Santi's successor further speaks to the close ties now existing between the convent of Santa Maria Novella and the confraternity. When Cini was transferred to San Marco, the youths of the Arcangelo Raffaello chose not to retain him but asked the prior of Santa Maria Novella for a new father corrector. In spite of Cini's good work with the group and his renown and prestige in Florence, the confraternity preferred to lose someone of his stature than to weaken its bond with the convent. It was a bond which, in the years 1556–61, had led twenty-five youths of the Arcangelo Raffaello to enter the Dominican Order at Santa Maria Novella and thereby help to build what could be seen as a personal relationship between the youths and the friars.[14]

## Franciscans, Theatines, and Dominicans

In spite of the Arcangelo Raffaello's close ties with the friars of Santa Maria Novella, this new relationship with the convent did not last long. In 1565 the youths again changed orders. Rather than return to the Dominicans of San Marco or to the Benedictines at the Badia, they reached instead an agreement with the Observant Franciscans at Ognissanti for a father corrector from their convent. The choice of a Franciscan from a convent several streets away in lieu of a Dominican from the convent on the other side of their oratory wall suggests a deliberate message. Whatever this message may have been, the records, unfortunately, remain silent. The change seems to have been greatly successful, if only because the new arrangement with the Friars Minor of Ognissanti continued uninterrupted for forty-one years (1565–1606).

In the course of the seventeenth century the youths changed orders several times. After the Franciscans of Ognissanti they returned to the Dominicans of Santa Maria Novella for twenty-five years (1606–31), tried the Theatines for nine (1631–40),[15] went back to the Dominicans for at least thirty-eight (1640–75), and eventually settled with the Franciscans, with whom they stayed for most of the eighteenth century (from at least 1727 to 1785).[16] The see-saw relationship with the Dominicans of Santa Maria Novella reinforces the previous observation that the confraternity and the convent had a difficult friendship. Physical proximity and the obligations dependent on the space given to the youths clearly made for an uneasy bond between the two organizations.

Another aggravation for the friars of Santa Maria Novella must have been the confraternity's independent status and frame of mind. This independence, however, was not to last long. The Council of Trent and the reforms it engendered had a much more severe effect on the confraternity's vitality than all the vicissitudes – political, legal, or spiritual – it had suffered in the fifteenth and sixteenth centuries.

## Episcopal Visitations (1573, 1634)

Episcopal visitations, one of Trent's strongest recommendations, brought a change in the confraternity's life. The visitation records of the late sixteenth century, in particular those of Archbishop Antonio Altoviti in 1568 and those of Archbishop Alessandro de' Medici (1587), are incomplete.[17] Their official visits to the Arcangelo Raffaello are not to be found in them. The confraternity's own records, however, do mention Archbishop Altoviti's personal visit of 1573, though they tell us only that he was welcomed into the oratory, prayed, and toured the site.[18] Although these records do not provide us with the archbishop's own observations and conclusions, they indicate that he showed special interest in the group.

Archbishop's Altoviti's interest may have been more than polite inquiry into the confraternity's quarters and activities. One of the novices who entered the Arcangelo Raffaello shortly after his visit was one of his assistants – the twenty-eight-year-old priest Ser Girolamo da San Miniato.[19] Together with him, Raffaello di Ser Francesco Gucci 'd'età d'anni 30,' Giovanpaulo di Francesco Salvucci 'lanaiuolo d'età d'anni 26,' Raffaello di Carlo Federighi 'd'anni 20 in circha,' and Ottaviano di Stefano da Ripa 'd'anni 22' joined the confraternity that day.[20] Three of the five were clearly over the statutory age limit for membership in the group. This raises the suspicion that all or some of them may have been strongly recommended ('planted' may be a better word) by the archbishop. The recommendation of high prelates has already been encountered in this confraternity – in the fifteenth century Cardinal Cesarini had suggested the Arcangelo Raffaello to Vespasiano da Bisticci (see above, ch. 2, pp. 24–5). But while Cardinal Cesarini's intentions seem to have been above board (the youth was, after all, within the required age limits), those of Archbishop Altoviti (if he was responsible for these enrolments) could be viewed with suspicion.

The archiepiscopal records of the 1634 visitation by Archbishop Pietro Niccolini offer another insight into the relationship between the local curia and the confraternity. Archbishop Niccolini had been, in his youth, an active member of the confraternity of the Arcangelo Raffaello.[21] Once past the age limit, Niccolini had returned to the confraternity to participate in the annual feast in honour of the Archangel Raphael. He had returned as canon of the cathedral in 1606 to celebrate the patron's feast-day Mass. As archbishop he visited the confraternity in 1625 and thereafter.[22] When, therefore, Niccolini returned to the confraternity in 1634 to carry out his official archiepiscopal visitation, the youths welcomed him into their hall as a brother (*fratello*). One would expect, as the youths certainly did, a favourable disposition on the part of the archbishop towards the confraternity that had helped to shape his spirituality. Sixty years earlier, Pope Leo x had showered favour on the youth confraternity of San Giovanni Evangelista for exactly this reason.[23] Archbishop Niccolini was expected to have a similar soft spot in his heart for the confraternity of his youth.

While this may have been true as far as Niccolini's personal attendance at the confraternity's feast-days was concerned, it certainly did not hold true with respect to his official position as chief administrator and pastor of the Florentine flock. Niccolini's first-hand knowledge and personal experience with youth confraternities made him aware of their profound need for reform and updating. As his predecessor St Antoninus had done in the 1440s and 1450s, so too Niccolini sought to address the perceived laxity or irregularity in confraternal life by reforming and authorizing the statutes that governed them. On his official archiepiscopal visit to the Arcangelo Raffaello, when he was shown the confraternity's statutes, Niccolini plainly told the youths to put aside the rules by which they had governed themselves for 150 years and write a new set of statutes that reflected current devotional and administrative practice in the confraternity and that he himself would then approve.

The confraternity at first objected to the prospect of abandoning the document by which it had governed itself for so long. In an attempt to save the reputation and the validity of their statutes, on 12 February 1635 the youths brought both the 1468 original and the 1560 copy to the archiepiscopal curia and asked that the latter be authenticated as a true copy of the former. A clause attesting that it was, indeed, a true copy was added at f. 20r of the 1560 set, and then signed in a large italic hand by Archbishop Niccolini himself and, below him, in a finer script, by his chancellor Giuseppe Barni.[24] Clearly the youths felt that if the archbishop forced them to change their ancient statutes, they would first ensure that he acknowledged their authenticity. Although the youths obtained the authentication they sought, their victory was hollow, for they were still obliged to set the document aside and come up with a new version. That March, they elected four brothers to rewrite the *capitoli*. When the revisions were complete, the new statutes were brought to the archbishop, who approved them and formally presented them back to the confraternity on their patron's feast-day, 31 December 1636.[25]

If all the youths were being asked to do was to draft a set of statutes that would reflect their current practices, why were they so quick to object? Perhaps they wished to retain the old ones for the prestige they enjoyed –

according to tradition, they had been drawn up by St Antoninus himself (though this is very dubious, seeing that by 1468 the saintly archbishop had been long dead). A less idealistic and more cynical answer would be that the youths were aware of, and appreciated, the fact that current practice was based on a superficial observance of the statutes and that the drafting of new ones would, in fact, oblige them to adhere more strictly to a document – not to mention the fact that the process of drafting new statutes could, as we say in the vernacular, open up a whole new can of worms.

There was no reason to fear the proverbial can of worms. As had been the case with Pope Eugenius IV, Ambrogio Traversari, and St Antoninus, Archbishop Niccolini understood very well the intention and scope of confraternities, and especially youth confraternities. What Niccolini wished to accomplish, and what the new statutes did, was not to raise questions or problems, but rather to outline and define more precisely the confraternity's structure of government and devotions, and ensure that they conformed to current religious regulations.

The new statutes were thus laid out in two clearly differentiated sections, the first dealing with the administrative structure, the second with the rituals and spiritual life of the confraternity. The two sections were preceded by a Proem outlining the history and intentions of the confraternity. The administrative part indicated clearly the responsibilities of each official in the organization, from the guardian father to the hired servant. The second section regulated the conduct of services and the behaviour expected of members inside and outside the confraternity. Within these parameters, there was little that was new, except for the fact that what had been traditionally expected was now officially written out in detail. As such, the statutes formalized unstated, but generally held assumptions about the life of the confraternity and its members. There was, however, a very significant addition to the new statutes: the creation of the position of the twelve curators (*conservatori*). This, as I will propose in the following chapter (see pp. 104–5), was a change that contributed significantly to the process of removing control of the confraternity from the hands of the youths themselves and placing it into those of adult supervisors – a process that, in fact, had begun in the 1560s–70s in the wake of Tridentine reforms.

## Post-Tridentine Reform

Ever since the Council of Trent, in fact, confraternities had come under close scrutiny and control by the local bishop and his curia. The council itself had affirmed the right of bishops 'to visit ... confraternities of laymen, even those that are called schools or are known by some other name' and had instructed 'administrators, whether ecclesiastical or lay, of revenues of ... confraternities ... to render to the ordinary each year an account of their administration.'[26]

In Florence the decrees of the local synods from 1573 to the beginning of the eighteenth century seem to be intent on the progressive emasculation of the confraternities' independent spiritual life. Archbishop Altoviti's 1573 synod declared that confraternities were to abide by the archbishop's will regarding their participation in processions, they were to submit to archiepiscopal visitations, laymen were forbidden to preach on questions of faith and religion, and there was to be no eating or drinking in the oratories.[27] Clearly the synod was trying to regulate activities and bring them in line with Tridentine reforms. However, by curtailing lay preaching, for example, the synod was taking away one of the most important of confraternal practices. Granted, laymen could still speak to their confraternity brothers on matters of general morality, but the vitality of unrestricted lay preaching was, unavoidably, undermined.

The synods convoked by Archbishop Alessandro de' Medici in 1610 and 1619 placed further severe restrictions on the educational activities of youth confraternities. The teaching of Christian doctrine and the performance of plays drawn from sacred history were both explicitly forbidden. Christian doctrine was to be taught in the parish, the synods decreed, and no plays drawn from the Old or New Testament or from the lives of the saints could be performed in churches, societies, or public places without the express permission of the archbishop's ordinary (*ordinarius*). In trying to control or suppress abuses, the Church was thus undermining the activities that had been an integral and vital part of youth confraternities.

Christian doctrine did continue to be taught in youth confraternities for some years to come; however, it was taught from published catechisms approved by the authorities and it was learned by rote, a chapter each Sunday. Similarly, laymen did continue to recite sermons, but these eventually dwindled under the express wrath of subsequent decrees and reaffirmations of synodal directives against the practice.

After the mid-seventeenth century, the records of the confraternity of the Arcangelo Raffaello contain no references to plays, and few to sermons, or instruction on Christian doctrine. The confraternity had settled down to a quiet routine of Matins, Masses, Vespers, and the unending stream of memorial services for the ever-growing number of deceased brothers and benefactors.[28] By the eighteenth century the confraternity's only other activities were the supervision of its accumulated wealth, the distribution of dowries from the interest earned by its trust funds, and the performance of an annual oratorio for the feast of the Archangel Raphael (31 December).

Before this stagnancy set in, however, the confraternity of the Arcangelo Raffaello had enjoyed a century of unparalleled vitality. From the mid-sixteenth to the mid-seventeenth century the youths of the Arcangelo Raffaello had grown in number and importance, commissioned and staged plays, organized musical events, participated in public rituals, attracted powerful new members, and, in some cases, contributed significantly to the Christian education and vocation of its members. During these one hundred years, the confraternity had blossomed into full maturity. Its activities during this period form the nucleus of the following chapters.

# 8

# Statutes and Administrative Structures

An inventory of goods compiled in 1690 lists four different copies of the confraternity's statutes, all kept in a box on top of the cabinet in the change room.[1] They are the *capitoli* drawn up in 1468, their 1560 copy, a fine copy of the new *capitoli* of 1636, and their copy for everyday use. This chapter will examine these different sets of statutes and discuss the most important aspects of the administrative structures they outlined.

## The Statutes of 1468/1560

The 1468 *capitoli* were approved on 20 October 1468 by Giuliano di Antonio da Montelupo, bishop of Citharea and vicar of the archbishop of Florence.[2] They are described in the inventory as the confraternity's original statutes, bound in embossed black leather but not gilded, written on vellum parchment, and damaged beyond use or repair in the 1557 flood.[3] The volume was again damaged by flood waters in 1966. It has now been restored, rebound (preserving as much of the original binding and cover as possible), and is once more available for consultation.[4] It consists of twenty-three vellum folios, recently foliated in pencil. The gatherings are bound in embossed black leather with no traces of gilding present. The original ornamental embossing on the front and back leather covers is still visible.

The first folio is blank. The second contains the usual preliminary paragraph, which says, among other things, that the confraternity was founded in 1411 under the name of the Nativity of Our Lord Jesus Christ, and currently meets and resides in the quarters granted to it by Pope Eugenius IV near the Ospedale of Santa Maria della Scala in the city of Florence.[5] The page is illuminated with a beautiful floral motif along the top, bottom, and left margins. The initial letter of the text is an oversized, gold-leafed capital

A. A little up from the bottom left-hand corner there is an illumination, now barely visible, depicting the Mother and Child, an appropriate subject for a confraternity dedicated to the Nativity. At f. 24 a smaller piece of vellum, about one-third the size of a page, has been bound into the gathering. It bears the date 20 October 1468 (in a later hand) and then, below the date, in two columns, two prayers, one for afternoon Vespers ('Il giorno al Vespro'), the other for evening Matins ('La sera al Mattutino'). At the bottom of the sheet there are two musical staves of five lines each, with square notes, bar lines, and traces of lyrics beneath them.

Because of water damage incurred in the two floods, the entire volume is quite difficult to read. A comparison of chapter headings and pagination with those in the 1560 copy, however, reveals such a close match that we can conclude the 1560 volume to be a faithful copy of the earlier document. The 1560 copy, therefore, becomes a valid alternative for the original in the study of the first extant statutes.

The 1560 volume consists of parchment pages bound in red leather embossed with arabesques.[6] There are no traces of gilding on the cover. The volume consists of three octavo gatherings, with an extra sheet added at the front and rear for a total of twenty-six folios. The embossed binding also contains the letters and clover leaves as follows:

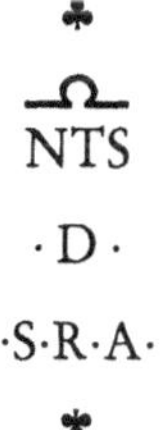


Two leather clasps, now broken and missing, once held the volume closed. There are twenty-seven lines per page. The hand is a very clear roman. The incipit page and the chapter headings are written in red ink, while the rest of the text is in black ink. Confraternity records indicate that the transcription was carried out between 28 December 1559 and 1 May 1560, expenses incurred were borne by a number of benefactors, Bartolomeo Traballesi painted a Nativity 'in the middle of the book,' and the completed volume was formally presented to the guardian father on Corpus Domini 1560.[7] This is the volume shown to Archbishop Niccolini on his visit to the confraternity on 6 September 1634 and which he wished the youths to set aside in favour of a new set of statutes to be approved by him.

The 1468 statutes, which regulated the life of the confraternity for at least 150 years, contain a prologue and nineteen short chapters that outline and define the organization's governing structure. A copy of the 1442 papal bull that recognized the confraternity and granted it certain privileges, and the 1468 archiepiscopal approval, are appended at the end.[8] Their 1560 copy contains as well a description of how the original volume had been damaged in the 1557 flood and recovered by a 'loving brother' who tried in vain to copy the contents, and then how it was successfully recopied two years later by a group of brothers who employed the technique of reimmersing the volume in clear water in order to decipher – not without some difficulty – what had been written on the ruined pages.

## The Guardian Father

According to the 1468 statutes, the functioning of the confraternity was overseen by a guardian father (*padre guardiano*) chosen by the papal commission set up by Pope Eugenius IV's bull of 1442. The confraternity recommended that, with the approval of the members of the commission, its governor (*governatore*) should also be included in the decision. If it were possible, the outgoing guardian father was to provide the commission with a list of three candidates to be considered and voted upon in sequence. The successful candidate was to be at least thirty years old, a man of upright morals, and preferably a layman. His term of office was unspecified. Some incumbents served the confraternity for just a few years, while others remained in place for decades, and still others for life.[9] The assumption was that a guardian father would serve for life or until he himself chose to step down. There is no indication in the documents that any guardian father was ever asked to resign or otherwise forcibly removed from office.

Confraternity records from the sixteenth century name Antonio di Mariano Muzi as the first guardian father of the Arcangelo Raffaello.[10] The Florentine book dealer and biographer Vespasiano da Bisticci mentions that Antonio was guardian when Cardinal Giuliano Cesarini attended the Council of Florence in the retinue of Pope Eugenius IV (1439).[11] He was still in office in 1453, when his name appeared as one of the signatories in the document approving the election of the guardian of the youth confraternity of Sant'Antonio da Padova.[12] Such dates indicate a tenure in office of at least fourteen years. His term was probably much longer, but it has not been possible at this time to determine its exact length.

The 1457 *catasto* declaration gives us an insight into Muzi and his family. He claims to be fifty-three years old, and married to the thirty-two-year-old Monna Papera di Simone da Filicaia,[13] with whom he had five daughters and three sons – nine-year-old Girolamo, three-year-old Mariano, and one-year-old Piero; the daughters are not named in the *catasto* entry.[14] Antonio points out that his eighty-four-year-old mother, Monna Nanna, lived with him, as did Monna Bartolomea, the widow of his brother Piero di Mariano, along with her two sons.[15] The entire extended family of fourteen resided in the house Antonio owned in Borgo Pinti, in the parish of San Pier Maggiore.[16] The Muzi had a coat of arms,[17] and Antonio himself enjoyed the right to bear arms.[18] He died in 1494. The family, which was registered in the San Giovanni quarter, *gonfalone* Chiavi, died out in the second half of the sixteenth century.[19]

During his lifetime Antonio held several important public offices in Florence, among them notary of the Signoria (1452), notary of the Tratte (1475–83),[20] and secretary of the Comune (1483).[21] He is better known and more important for his work in the Florentine Chancery, first under Carlo Marsuppini, then as vice-chancellor under Poggio Bracciolini (1456),[22] and soon thereafter as second chancellor (1457–94), a position in which he actually replaced Poggio as chancellor during the interregnum before Benedetto Accolti's appointment (1458).[23] Once in charge, Accolti placed Muzi back in the less important Second Chancery probably because, as Robert Black suggests, Muzi was a notary 'without any apparent humanist education' and thus not a suitable partner in Accolti's humanist program.[24]

Although Antonio was the first guardian father of the confraternity of the Arcangelo Raffaello, he was not the first to govern or direct the youths. In the early years of its existence the confraternity was led on an ad hoc basis by the anonymous gold-leaf worker (*battiloro*) who first gathered the youths together. The office of *padre guardiano* was, in fact, a later development.

The importance of this position and the respect it elicited from the youths are evident in the several benefits, both temporal and spiritual, that in time were bestowed upon present and past incumbents. By the sixteenth century the confraternity remembered its first four guardian fathers with individual yearly commemorative services. In the seventeenth and eighteenth centuries it honoured all deceased guardian fathers *en bloc* on the first Sunday after Epiphany. It also provided a burial crypt in the oratory floor for the guardian fathers who chose to be so interred. Such was the case, for example, with Antonio di Giovanni *cuoiaio* (d. 9 April 1563), and Lorenzo di Goro Benizzi (d. 10 September 1595). In a way, this common burial crypt allowed deceased guardian fathers to remain 'present' in the confraternity. In the seventeenth century the guardian father was given rent-free accommodations in the house in Borgo Ognissanti the confraternity had inherited from Baccio and Domenico Comi.[25] Starting in 1732, in lieu of accommodations, the guardian father began receiving an annuity of 20 *scudi* (or 140 *lire*) drawn from the rental income from the house.[26]

The importance the youths attached to the position of guardian father for the well-being of the confraternity is evident in the concerns expressed in a short play staged by the confraternity in June 1582.[27] Since the resignation of Ser Ceseri Galletti (December 1581), the confraternity had been unable to secure a suitable willing candidate for the post of guardian father. In an effort to come to terms with the problem, they staged a play in the hall. Its message was clear: the present difficulties in finding an upright man willing to lead the confraternity were a direct result of the degeneration that had overcome the confraternity's rituals and devotions. The confraternity's own moral state and the quality of the guardian father it could attract were thus closely linked in the minds of the brothers. By their collective piety and devotions the youths contributed to the honour and reputation of the confraternity, thus attracting men of high quality to participate in its practices, and this, in turn, sustained the confraternity's spiritual and devotional life. It was a symbiotic relationship that depended on unquestioning grass-root support and exemplary executive leadership.

The guardian father thus enjoyed near-absolute authority. He received respect and obedience from all the youths, for he was seen as the agent of God within the confraternity.[28] He could warn, chastise, punish, or eject – temporarily or permanently – any member who undermined his authority or whose life and behaviour he considered inappropriate. He was also the final authority on the interpretation of the statutes.[29] On his own authority, the guardian father appointed suitable brothers to serve the confraternity in a number of quarterly posts – the two sacristans (*sagrestani* or *camarlinghi*), the administrator or scribe (*provveditore* or *scrivano*), the two masters of novices (*maestri de' novizi*), and the two peace-givers (*paciali*).

## The Quarterly Officers

The guardian father conducted the quarterly election of the four major officers of the confraternity – the governor (*governatore*) and the three counsellors (*consiglieri*). The governor, who was to be at least seventeen years old, oversaw the functioning of the confraternity and acted as guardian father in the latter's absence. The counsellors, who were to be at least fourteen years old, served as an advisory body to the guardian and the governor, and participated in the charitable work of visiting and assisting ill or infirm brothers. To be considered for these posts, a brother had to have been a member of the confraternity for at least a year. A statute of limitations (*divieto*) prevented incumbents from being re-elected to the same office for a specified length of time – a year for the governor and eight months for the counsellors. Similarly, four months had to elapse before a counsellor could be elected governor.

The guardian father, governor, and three counsellors together selected the youths who held the other quarterly offices, those of administrator/scribe, sacristans, masters of novices, and peace-givers. The administrator or scribe kept a record of confraternity activities, decisions, and elections. He was sometimes also charged with keeping a record of members and their entry-fee payments. The two sacristans or chamberlains (*camarlinghi*) were responsible for opening the building, maintaining the rooms and altars, keeping accounts of donations to the sacristy, and looking after some of the confraternity's goods. The two masters of novices taught new members confraternal rituals and prayers, and then accompanied them into the confraternity oratory for their induction ceremony. The two peace-givers carried out the ritual of the sign of peace at the appropriate times in the confraternity's ceremonies. The ritual entailed the use of *tavolette*, hand-held tablets bearing a suitable religious image – often a depiction of the Crucifixion on one side and the patron saint on the other.[30] It is worth noting that the 1468 governing structure consisted of twelve persons in total, a figure whose biblical connotations would not have passed unnoticed by either the brothers or the authorities who approved their statutes.

## The Father Corrector

The only other adult in the service of the confraternity aside from the guardian father was the father corrector (*padre correttore*), the priest who tended to the spiritual needs of members by celebrating divine offices in the confraternity, hearing confessions, and advising the youths on matters of personal spiritual concern. He was generally chosen by the prior of the convent with whom the confraternity had reached an agreement for such a service. The 1468 statutes do not describe or mention this position, thus indicating that the youths considered the incumbent to be not a member but an 'employee' of the confraternity.[31] In fact, the account books record the payment of yearly fees for his services, and the scribe's minutes recall the agreements and arrangements for such services reached, from time to time, with different convents.[32] The relationship between father corrector and confraternity was seen, therefore, as a business agreement, and did not resemble the close personal relationship that bound the guardian father and the youths. Perhaps the lay nature and lay government that characterized the confraternity would have been compromised if the father corrector had been considered a full member of the brotherhood.

## The Selection and Induction of a New Guardian Father

The difference in attitude towards the two adults who participated in the confraternity's life is best reflected in the manner they were received into the group. While there was no ritual associated with the arrival of a new father corrector, the installation of a new guardian father was carried out with solemnity and ceremony. The tone was set not only by the pomp of the ritual itself, but also by the presence in the oratory of the abbot of the Badia, the prior of San Marco, and the guardians of the other youth confraternities. The ceremony contained several emblematic moments. First, the new guardian father was robed in a white gown and led through the rituals used for the induction of a novice into the brotherhood (see below, ch. 9, pp. 116–17). Then, while he knelt at the altar and the youths sang the Te Deum, all in turn approached him and exchanged the sign of peace with him. When this was done the guardian father moved to his desk at the opposite end of the oratory, sat, and listened to an oration delivered by either the abbot of the Badia or the prior of San Marco (or their representative), encouraging him to guide the confraternity with justice and sanctity, and inviting the youths to give him their obedience and reverence. The sacrament of Communion followed and then the ceremony ended.

The description in the statutes was the recommended format for such a ceremony. It was not, however, always followed. Some newly appointed guardian fathers chose to assume their charge quietly and simply. Such was the case with Girolamo di M.o Niccolò di M.o Luca, who, on the last Sunday of April 1563, entered without ceremony (*semplicemente*) into the confraternity and made his own vows of obedience to the statutes.[33] Other times the ceremony was altered in parts. On 2 September 1582, for example, two significant alterations were made for the installation of Antonio di Pasci da Colle.[34] First, the candidate, who had been asked to wait in Santa Maria Novella, was led into the oratory by the five *provveditori* who constituted the selection committee that had proposed his name. Second, the exhortation to the new guardian father was delivered by the confraternity's father corrector, frat'Antonio Cignori. These small but significant changes, considered alongside the fact that there is no indication in the documents that any member of the papal commission was present at the ceremony, suggest that the commission had not been directly involved in the selection. The new incumbent had been chosen by a committee struck by the confraternity itself and then approved by a vote at a general confraternity meeting (12 August 1582). Only after he had been thus selected did the confraternity forward his name to the papal commission for a perfunctory approval (17 August 1582).

On several occasions from the mid-sixteenth to the early seventeenth centuries, the confraternity chose its own guardian father and then presented his name to the papal commission for approval. Twice the confraternity's choice for a new guardian father was not presented to the commission until long after the candidate had been elected and had assumed his duties – Guglielmo Cavalcanti, elected on 6 January 1606, was not presented to the commission until six months later, on 21 June 1606, while Benedetto Bellosi, chosen on 5 December 1599, was not forwarded until a year later, on 4 December 1600. Although such cases may be extreme examples, they do indicate there was a time lapse between the practical selection and formal approval of a new guardian father. This time lapse, which in most cases was only a few days, does point to a lapse in *de facto* authority for the papal commission. Instead of being the body that selected the new guardian father, the papal commission became the body that recognized him publicly. By not selecting, the commission was also not deciding. By granting a perfunctory approval, the commission was acting as a rubber stamp that offered little more than public recognition of a previously concluded arrangement.

## Changes to the Administrative Body

The new pattern of selection and induction of the guardian father is symptomatic of a number of developments in the confraternity. By the mid-sixteenth century, the governing structure of the confraternity itself had grown to accommodate new activities and obligations. The 1468 statutes had described a slate of twelve officers. In the 1560s, when records began once more to be routinely kept, the slate of confraternity officers elected every four months had grown to at least twenty-four persons – without, however, eliciting any revision of the statutes. Two more sacristans had been added (*sagrestani*), as well as four *infermieri* (who were responsible for visiting infirm brothers), two brothers *sopra la confessione* (whose duties, apart from what their title suggests, are not very clear),[35] and a variable number of *ordinatori de' cori* (who co-ordinated the work of the choir).[36] Twenty years later the structure again expanded to include two *cerimonieri*, as well as more peace-givers (*paciali*) and *infermieri*, thus bringing the total number of officers to about thirty. On several occasions the figure even rose to the biblically charged number of thirty-three.[37]

## The 1636 Revisions

The growing disparity between the structure outlined in the statutes and the structure operative in the early seventeenth century was undoubtedly in Archbishop Niccolini's mind when he asked for a revision of the statutes. Another contributing factor may have been the perceived irregularities in the process of selecting a guardian father. In 1563, Girolamo di Niccolò di Luca had been chosen by the papal commission in meetings held in the chambers of the abbot of the Badia.[38] The commission was composed of the abbot of the Badia, the sub-prior of San Marco (fra Pier Filippo Gianfigliazzi), the three guardians of the confraternities of San Marco (Benedetto Mori), San Niccolò del Ceppo (Domenico *merciaio*), and San Giovanni Evangelista (Ser [blank] Buglioni), as well as the governor of the confraternity of the Archangel Raphael (Vittorio di Pellegrino Dell'Ancisa), and the document was notarized by Ser Francesco di Domenico Ricchi.[39] Later, as we just saw, the papal commission was instead kept at a distance from the selection process. Strictly speaking, the practice was not correct and needed to be re-examined.

One of the most significant aspects of the revised statutes of 1636 is therefore the attempt to regulate the appointment of guardian fathers.[40] Instead of relying on the 1442 papal bull, or on ad hoc confraternity practices as they had recently developed, the new statutes outlined a new structure and process for the selection of future guardians based on a new position in the confraternity's administrative rostrum – the twelve Curators (*conservatori*).

The curators were adults elected by majority vote in a general confraternity meeting. Candidates for the position had to be at least thirty years old, and had to have shown, by their church attendance and alms-giving, that they were men who would bring honour and benefit to the confraternity. In a general way they acted as an advisory body to the guardian father. More specifically, they constituted the selection committee that appointed the new guardian father from a list of three candidates established by majority vote in the confraternity's general assembly. Each curator was encouraged to visit the confraternity at least twice a year and inquire about its spiritual and temporal well-being. And, just as important, no festivity, dramatic representation, or 'other similar novelty' could be undertaken without the curators' approval.[41]

The authority and power granted to the twelve curators, not to mention their age and obvious socio-economic status, point to a change away from youth and towards adult government. Such a change is in contrast with the regulations in the original statutes, which had clearly stipulated that only confraternity members under the age of twenty-four had a right to vote – and hence decide – on confraternity matters. At that time past or older members had been allowed to attend services, but not to participate in the government of the confraternity.[42] Now instead they were given a most important role in ascertaining the proper functioning of the confraternity and in selecting its most senior officer. At this point, it can be argued, the confraternity of the Arcangelo Raffaello begins to be less of a youth confraternity and more of an adult confraternity, a change that will become most evident in the eighteenth century.[43]

The revised statutes of 1636 also regulated and defined the confraternity's dealings with its father corrector. The previous statutes had not discussed this position at all (see above, p. 101). The new set, instead, devoted a brief but complete chapter to it. Generally speaking, the chapter reiterated and specified the attributes and activities already pertaining to it. The father corrector had to be a priest of most excellent reputation, both learned and virtuous, who would celebrate Mass at every *tornata*, administer the sacraments of confession and communion to the brothers, instruct them in the path of virtue, watch over their souls, ardently promote the cult of God, and visit infirm brothers as necessary.

In the revised statutes of 1636 two significant innovations were introduced in the unstated but generally understood role of the father corrector. The first was, again, a regularization of the manner of appointment. Contrary to previous practice, when the father corrector was chosen by the prior of the convent with which the confraternity had reached an agreement for such a service, the candidate for the position was now to be selected by a committee composed of the guardian father, the governor, the administrator/scribe, and the twelve curators. This allowed the confraternity to circumvent the need for agreements with convents and orders for the services of one of their priests, to gain greater control over the choice of candidates, and to appoint priests from either the secular or religious clergy. In the long run, the confraternity did continue to draw its father correctors from the religious clergy, primarily from the Dominicans or

Franciscans, but at times it also opted for Theatines, Vallambrosians, and others.

The innovation in the process of selection is reflected in the manner in which the priest's honorarium (*limosina*) was paid. In the sixteenth century, the honorarium was given to the priest's convent. From 1581 to 1597, for example, a yearly donation of 24 *staia* of grain was made to the convent of Ognissanti in return for the services of the father corrector, who celebrated Mass every Sunday and Holy Day.[44] The agreement with the convent of Santa Maria Novella in the 1620s involved an actual exchange of priestly services: in return for a father corrector from that convent, the youths were to pay another priest to celebrate Mass at Santa Maria Novella.[45] After the 1636 reforms and throughout the eighteenth century the yearly *limosina* was a straight payment of 35 *lire* to the priest himself, not to his convent, thus indicating a direct businesslike relationship between the individual and the confraternity.

There are important implications in this new process and relationship with the father corrector. On the negative side, the priest was hired by a selection committee composed of thirteen adults and two youths, and this undermined the youths' influence on the important decision-making processes of their confraternity. On the positive side, the confraternity was, in effect, buying a specific person's services, and not a general service from an organization. If the choice of a new father corrector was well made, the arrangement could develop into a longer-lasting, more personal relationship between the youths and their confessor than had been the case previously.

A case in point would be the relationship the confraternity developed with fra Santi Contini, OP, who guided the youths from 1606 to 1626. At his death, the confraternity celebrated obsequies for him in the oratory, complete with a *parato*, special decorations, and commissioned inscriptions.

At the front of the oratory one could see the large Crucifix from the *stanzone* ... and opposite to it, above the door that leads into the oratory, there was a portrait of the same father [Contini], and below it an *impresa* that represented threshed grain and a strap ['correggiato'] next to it with the motto *Per quem mundati*, which alluded [to the fact that] the good corrections of the father had had a similar effect on our souls, and this *impresa* was devised by Dr Jacopo Cicognini. The *stanzone* was also all decorated, and not only the walls, but the entire vault, which was in the form of a pavilion ... and there were some poems attached there in praise of the deceased. The door into the oratory looked like an entrance into a cave, for all its ornaments were hidden ['chiusi'] and it was all wrapped in funeral hangings of black serge ['rasce'], and above it there was a large placard held up by a skeleton with open arms, and on it were written the words of Signor Alessandro Adimari, a famous poet of our times

To Santi Contini,
a man not lacking
in integrity of doctrine, elegance of manners, innocence of life
and a most distinguished son of the Patriarch of the Dominicans,
who now appears as a teacher to this Gathering,
as many students on earth, so many angels in heaven,
is worthy of associating with the Archangel Raphael,
his lamenting sons
beg him to raise the ladder of heaven
to the Almighty God, [and] moved by devotion
repay with this display.[46]

And at the front door there were five [pieces of] black and white serge, the colour of the Dominican Fathers, with two large Deaths to indicate that it was a funereal [design]. At the set hour for the Office, we began with much devotion, assisted by many theologians and honourable fathers of that same Dominican order, and our new corrector father fra Lorenzo Ridolfi, etc. There was music [sung by] very rare voices, and harmonies [made by] viols, as well as violins, organ and other musical instruments, all of which increased the devotion. When the office was finished Giuseppe Lapi, one of our good brothers, delivered a compendium of the deceased father's praises in a succinct and well-wrought oration, narrating all his virtuous works and his career to the end of his life, with so much effect that he moved us to tears, and fully pleased everyone. And so, when the office was done, all were given leave to go, and the following morning several Masses were celebrated for the salvation of his soul, for may it please God to lead him to his Heavenly Fatherland where he may intercede for us, his spiritual sons, so that we too may be worthy, after this short life, to proceed to the eternal one.[47]

When he died, fra Santi Contini had been the longest-serving corrector the confraternity had ever had. In earlier times, the confraternity had not sought to foster such long-term arrangements, even with very suitable priests. In 1558–9, for example, it had preferred to lose the services of a devout and distinguished man, fra Santi Cini, rather than sever its ties with the convent of Santa Maria Novella (see above, ch. 7, p. 89). Father correctors generally served the confraternity for relatively short lengths of time. Fra Santi Contini's immediate predecessor and his three successors, all

Dominicans like him, stayed in office for significantly shorter lengths of time than he had – three for one year only, and one for three years.

This all changed with the implementation of the 1636 statutes, which seem to have altered the confraternity's relationship with its priest. The one Theatine who held the post during the writing of the new statutes stayed in office for nine years (1631–40). The six Dominicans who next served the confraternity (1640–78) stayed for six, ten, three, thirteen, three, and three years respectively. The incumbencies of these later Dominicans suggest that the longer lengths of time are not a factor of the order but of a changed attitude. Extending such an examination to 1785, the results are even more striking. Except for the period 1678–1702, when the confraternity seemed unable (or unwilling) to retain a regular father corrector, for the remainder of its existence (1702–85) it enjoyed the services of eight devoted priests who stayed from a minimum of four to a maximum of twenty-three years. A listing of average years of service illustrates this change:

| Dates | Order | Number of incumbents | Average length of service |
|---|---|---|---|
| 1556–65 | Dominicans | 5 | 1.8 |
| 1565–82 | Franciscans | figures unavailable for these years | |
| 1582–1606 | Franciscans | 4 | 4 |
| 1606–31 | Dominicans | 5 | 5 |
| 1631–40 | Theatines | 1 | 9 |
| 1640–77 | Dominicans | 6 | 6 |
| 1678–1702 | undetermined | 8 | 3 |
| 1702 | Franciscan | 1 | 1 |
| 1702–26 | Vallambrosians | 3 | 8 |
| 1726–85 | Franciscans | 5 | 11.6 |

A second innovation in the job description of the father corrector, though it undoubtedly reflects a practice already in place, was the explicit indication that he should 'be aware' of the content of lay sermons to be recited by confraternity brothers. Such a statement reflects the changed attitude within the Church, in the wake of the Council of Trent and subsequent diocesan synods, towards lay preaching.[48] The Church was successful first in restricting lay preaching to matters of morals rather than dogma, and then in emasculating it completely. By the eighteenth century, lay preaching in the confraternity of the Arcangelo Raffaello had all but disappeared.

Other detailed job descriptions were also incorporated into the description of the official positions outlined in the 1636 statutes. Thus certain officers were given explicit instructions on when to arrive at the confraternity, where to sit or stand during services, which and how many account books to keep, and so forth. The results were, certainly, greater efficiency, administrative continuity, ceremonial decorum, and the like. At the same time, however, they restricted the incumbent's actions. And, ultimately, such regimentation of a layman's personal religious and spiritual devotions, to say nothing of his charitable volunteer work on behalf of the community, had a long-term effect that contributed, in its own way, to the waning of interest in the organization. In tandem with other factors, some internal and some external, the confraternity's own rigorous governing structure eventually led to its fossilization and demise.

By the early seventeenth century, the guardian father, who previously had received no material compensation for his work in the confraternity, was given free accommodation in a house belonging to the confraternity. In the eighteenth century, when incumbents came from a social class that owned and lived in luxurious palaces, the material reward of free accommodation in a middle-class house in Borgo Ognissanti was no longer attractive, and thus they began to capitalize on the rental option available to them from Comi's will (see above, p. 100). In 1732, the guardian Sigismondo Landini and two representatives of the confraternity, Tommaso Medici and Gaetano Pasquali, reached an agreement with Carlo Maria di Luca Ducci whereby Ducci received in perpetuity the use of the house in Borgo Ognissanti for a yearly rent to be paid directly to the present and future guardians of the confraternity. Ducci also received the right to use and alter the house as he wished so as to incorporate it into the adjacent house, which he had already purchased from the Buonomini di San Martino.[49]

In 1756 the money used to compensate the guardian father was changed from the rental income from the house in Borgo Ognissanti to that of the house built above the confraternity itself.[50] As a result, the hidden revenue that went from the tenant in Borgo Ognissanti directly to the guardian father became visible in the confraternity account books because it now passed from the tenant in Piazza Santa Maria Novella through the confraternity to the guardian father.

The honorarium of 20 *scudi* (i.e., 140 *lire*) that the guardian received from this revenue is more than the total of the two dowries of 60 *lire* each given yearly to two deserving young women of marriageable age. It is also several times the annual honorarium of 7 *scudi* (i.e., 35 *lire*) given to the father corrector for his services to the organization, or the paltry sum of

12 *lire* that constituted the annual income for each of the confraternity's two hired servants. It is superseded only by the *maestro di cappella*'s income of approximately 50 *scudi* (i.e., 350 *lire*) annually.[51]

The guardian father's annuity and his noble rank point to a changed attitude towards the confraternity. The enthusiastic elders and the youths who had sacrificed their free time to participate in the group's spiritual life had disappeared, and men more interested in the realities of social rank and material rewards had taken over. As the confraternity's activities and its very *raison d'être* were altered by the directives of the Council of Trent, by the changed attitudes of the ensuing Catholic Reformation, and by the religious climate fostered by the grand-ducal court of the later Medici, the members of the Arcangelo Raffaello found themselves holding positions which, in many cases, were little more than honorific titles. Peace-givers, visitors to the infirm, masters of novices became empty phrases reflecting positions rather than purposes. The membership dwindled and grew older. The legacies left by departed members were applied to trust funds that generated dowries for young women with meagre resources.

The confraternity's administrative structure thus changed into a small consortium that met weekly to hear Mass and annually to decide on the recipients of their two dowries. The confraternity records for the entire eighteenth century reveal little else but the tedium of regular services, the inevitable memorials for recently deceased brothers, the selection and bestowing of two dowries, and the annual performance of an oratorio on the feast of the Archangel Raphael. The governing structure had fossilized into a roster of tired administrators who looked after the confraternity's spiritual, financial, and cultural obligations with an exceptional lack of imagination and enthusiasm.

9

# Membership

The nature of the individuals who constituted the membership was of vital importance for the confraternity. The process that identified suitable new members, drew them to the confraternity, inducted them, and eventually released or, in the case of undesirable members, expelled them was clearly outlined in the confraternity's statutes. These expectations were then reaffirmed in the induction ceremony itself. Members were expected to conform to a high moral code in every aspect of their daily life, and so behaviour was monitored both inside and outside the confraternity's building. In this chapter we will examine the selection process, the age and moral requirements required of members, the motivation behind a young man's wish to join a confraternity, and the induction and departure ceremonies, and we will look at one member in particular, Vittorio Dell'Ancisa, as an example of the 'ideal' confraternity member.

## Selection

Confraternities that actively sought to drag youths away from the streets and to draw them into oratories or schools of Christian doctrine would encourage their members to prowl the city in twos, searching for youths that needed redeeming. This practice, sometimes known as 'fishing' (*pescare*), was quite alien to the Arcangelo Raffaello.[1] Its prospective new members were not drawn from the youths roaming the streets of Florence, but from the circle of friends, relatives, and business contacts that revolved around members. This allowed the confraternity to be very selective in the type of person it chose to welcome.

A first screening was carried out by the individual confraternity brother who, having noticed someone's interest or vocation, suggested membership to him and then officially sponsored his candidacy in front of the entire confraternity. Acceptance into the organization was not automatic on sponsorship, but was determined by a combination of factors: evidence of personal vocation, age requirements, a good reputation, a scrutiny, and a formal induction ceremony. All these elements were clearly outlined in the confraternity's statutes.

The first requirement was that the candidate be 'guided by a good spirit': in other words, that he have a true vocation for the lay religious life. To determine this, the 1468 statutes instructed the masters of novices to examine the candidate thoroughly. If they concluded that he was, in fact, a suitable candidate, the statutes then instructed the masters to send the youth to confession to one of the confraternity's approved confessors. If the latter also agreed that the candidate was suitable, the youth's name was then 'published' in the confraternity; that is, it was publicly announced and posted in the oratory so that all members could take note and discuss his candidacy. At the following *tornata* all members present voted on him. If the candidate received more than 75 per cent of the vote in favour, he was then allowed to pay his fee and undergo the formal induction ceremony.[2]

This five-step selection system – spontaneous request, examination by the masters of novices, examination by a confessor, debate within the confraternity, general vote – sought to ensure a high standard not only in the spiritual or religious aptitude of prospective members, but also in the quality of the secular life they led. In fact, when the 1468 statutes say that the candidate's name should be 'published' in the confraternity, they also add the explanation 'so that the brothers may gather information about him' ('acciò che i fratelli se ne possino informare'). Whatever members discovered about the candidate was to be reported at the following *tornata* just before those present were asked to vote on him. This step in the selection process thus determined and acted upon a subtle but important factor in Florentine life – the question of a person's *reputazione*.

The 1636 statutes retained these guidelines, but were even more explicit in outlining the reasons and the means. From the very beginning of the chapter on new members they explain that 'it is very important for the company's spiritual profit that one consider very well who are the brothers that are accepted among us.'[3] When it comes to the public inquiry into a candidate's *reputazione*, they instruct members to make sure they inquire about the candidate's name, family, age, and sponsor. The 1636 statutes also modified an important step in the process: the committee that scrutinized the candidate before he was even proposed to the membership as a whole was now to be composed not only of the masters of novices, but also of the guardian father, the governor, and the three counsellors. To allow time for the general membership to gather the necessary information, the 1636 statutes insisted on a minimum time lapse of ten days from the time the name was 'published' to the time the vote was taken. And to ensure that the decision reflected the confraternity's will, a quorum of twenty members was stipulated for the vote. The only concession the 1636 statutes made to facilitate a candidate's entry was to lower the percentage of the total votes necessary for successful election from three-quarters to two-thirds of members present.

## Standards of Behaviour

Careful scrutiny was necessary because a member's *reputazione* and his behaviour, both inside and outside the Arcangelo Raffaello, reflected back on the confraternity itself. For this reason the confraternity took an active interest in the morals and behaviour of its members. There were activities that were encouraged and activities that were not acceptable. The 1468 statutes spell them out clearly in the chapters 'On Life and Good Manners' (ch. 10) and 'On the Conversation of Brothers Outside the Confraternity' (ch. 13).

A member had to be obedient and committed to the Church, the guardian father, the statutes, his parents, and his elders. He was required to recite certain prayers at key moments of the day. He was to be chaste and, 'if he has that most precious and angelic gift,' he was strongly encouraged to maintain his virginity. He had to give alms. He had to go to confession monthly to one of the confessors affiliated with the confraternity and present the 'seal' (that is, a certificate attesting to the confession) to the guardian father. He had to take communion in the Arcangelo Raffaello at Christmas and on Pentecost ('Pasqua dello Spirito Santo') and at any other times the guardian father decreed.

A member of the Arcangelo Raffaello was not, on the other hand, to be a gambler or to watch people gamble. He was not to curse, swear, gossip, or tell lies. He was not to frequent taverns or go at night to locales where there was 'dishonest' dancing, music, or singing. Similarly, he was not to go to places where jousts, fights, or other such entertainments were held. Should one of the brothers lapse into any of these practices, fellow brothers were obliged to speak to him, reprimand him, and seek to bring him back to the right path. On the third reprimand, the unrepentant youth was to be erased ('raso') from the confraternity's roll. There was to be no third or even second chance, however, for any member who fell 'into that wicked and horrible vice of sodomy' – in his case the statutes bluntly said that 'the guardian father should evict him immediately, with grave weight on his conscience.'[4]

**Expulsion**

This last anathema, sodomy, is perhaps a red herring. In the fifteenth and sixteenth centuries, the term was used to encompass a variety of sexual activities, both homo- and heterosexual. Preachers such as St Bernardino of Siena railed against the so-called 'Florentine vice,' civil authorities legislated harsh punishments for it, and even today modern scholars try to suggest that 'youth companies were set up to control the homosexual proclivities of adolescents.'[5]

There is no evidence, however, that 'the vice' constituted a serious concern, or activity, in Florentine confraternities. As Michael Rocke points out, 'the religious confraternity may ... on occasion have had sodomitic undertones. At least this is what some accusers charged, a claim as intriguing as it is difficult to document.'[6] Rocke then gives a few examples of such accusations, all referring to alleged sodomy by members of adult, not youth confraternities – San Zanobi and the *buca* di San Paolo in particular.[7] The suggestion that sodomy may have been fostered by participation in a *buca*, where men met overnight to flagellate themselves in a semi-darkened oratory and then slept on straw mattresses laid out in a common dormitory room, is perhaps not surprising. It remains, however, more of a quasi-erotic fantasy than a documentable historical fact. And it is restricted to situations predicated by a different set of circumstances from those operative in a youth confraternity. Finally, Rocke's conclusion that sodomy in Florence 'seemed merely a natural extension of other formal, informal, and affective ties that bound males in this society together' points clearly to work environment, neighbourhoods, and personal preferences as operative factors in the sodomy equation.

The anathema against sodomy in the statutes of the Arcangelo Raffaello and other confraternities is also such a standard clause that it becomes a commonplace. And, as with all commonplaces, it is ultimately meaningless. In the entire 374-year history of the Arcangelo Raffaello, no brother was ever expelled for 'sodomy' – though mere statistics would suggest that there ought to have been at least a few youths who, if for no other reason than adolescent curiosity and experimentation, found the all-male context of the group an ideal forum for inquiry into alternative sexuality.

There is also the possibility that those responsible for upholding the statutes may have purposely chosen to deal with alleged sodomy among confraternity members in a more quiet manner. In fact, had a youth been publicly exposed and then expelled for sodomy, there would have been dire consequences not only for him but for the confraternity itself. If one member was guilty, were others not suspect? And had not the confraternity which had allowed its sacred spaces to be used for lewdness not become a venue for sin and therefore in urgent need to be cleansed or perhaps even eradicated? The repercussions of sodomy on the confraternity would therefore act as a deterrent not necessarily for the act – since adolescents are seldom restrained by threat – but for the accusation and chastisement that lay in the hands of adults who knew and understood the full effect of any public action on this matter.

A similar attitude is noted by John Brackett, who points out that several Florentine government agencies with jurisdiction over morals – the Onestà, the Conservatori dell'Onestà dei Monasteri, the Otto di Guardia, the Conservatori di Leggi, and the Ufficiali di Notte – preferred to assess light fines rather than prosecute to the full extent of the law, 'because judges could not bring themselves to subject real people to harsh afflictive penalties.'[8] And Michael Goodich observes that 'while repressive, even barbaric, legislation against sexual offenders had everywhere become the norm, it is difficult to judge the degree of compliance, except in instances where charges of sexual immorality were linked with political nonconformity.'[9] And this, in fact, may have been at the root of the charges levelled against the confraternities of San Zanobi and the *buca* of San Paolo.

What did attract action and chastisement was another type of behaviour. After all, the youths were not all model children, and they misbehaved as much as youths do today. A revealing entry for 11 January 1561/2 offers humourless modern scholars a reminder of the nature of children and youths everywhere:

> During the festivities for our Patron the Archangel Raphael, two of our brothers had an argument, or came to blows, in our oratory. For this reason this morning the 11th [of January] they were reprimanded by our father corrector, and warned in front of the entire confraternity, and he had them ask forgiveness of each other, and he gave them a small penance to do.[10]

It was, in fact, behaviour of this sort that did result in ejection from the confraternity. Shortly after the incident mentioned above, the youth Ottavio Pollini was 'erased from the confraternity rolls and excluded ... for having caused arguments on several occasions, and for having played cards several times after having been reprimanded for this, and for having broken the gilded garland on the confraternity door, and for many other things which are better left unsaid.'[11] Similarly, Tommaso di Stefano Chiari was expelled on 2 June 1609 for having punched a brother at the confraternity door.[12] This kind of behaviour clearly was not tolerated and aroused official opprobrium. However, it should be noted that it rarely appeared in the confraternity records – the three examples just cited are the only ones I was able to find for the Arcangelo Raffaello. The youths of the Arcangelo Raffaello, it seems, were not 'rowdies,' but on the whole well behaved, talented, and devout servants of God. The reason for this may lie not so much in the natural predisposition of early modern Florentine youths to be 'good,' but in the confraternity's thorough screening and selection process.

## The Induction Ceremony

Once a youth had been judged morally upright and suitable for admission into the confraternity, he was allowed to undergo the official induction ceremony. This was the solemn and highly symbolic liminal experience that constituted his 'entry' into the closed and select group of the Arcangelo Raffaello.

On the appointed day the novice entered the oratory and, as instructed by the statutes, greeted everyone in Italian with the salutation 'God grant you peace.' He then proceeded to the altar and knelt there. The guardian father intoned the psalm 'Miserere mei Deus,' and then the rest of the brothers joined in. When the singing was completed, the guardian father turned to the novice and said, in Italian, 'What do you ask for?' To which the novice was required to answer, 'The glory of God and the peace of this company.' The guardian then said, 'We beg you to observe the commandments of God and the statutes of this company, and you will receive from this eternal consolation.' To which, the entire membership said 'Amen.' At this point the guardian father solemnly placed a white confraternal robe on the novice and pronounced, this time in Latin, the exhortation (rich in Pauline echoes from Ephesians 4:24) 'May God put on you the new man, who has been created according to God.' The membership answered, again in Latin, 'In justice, sanctity, and truth.' When the robing was finished, everyone sang the hymn 'Veni creator spiritus' and at its conclusion recited the prayer to the Holy Spirit. This was followed by the hymn 'Te Deum laudamus,' during which time the inductee exchanged the sign of peace with each of the brothers in the oratory using the appropriate *tavoletta*, or painted tablet. At the end of the 'Te Deum' and the exchange of peace, everyone recited the prayer of perseverance. Finally, the new member was disrobed of the white confraternity gown and led to the next available seat on the pews that ran the length of the oratory, thus bringing the ceremony to a close.[13]

As can be seen from this brief description, the official ceremony was highly charged with meaning. The candidate underwent a ritual interrogation and robing at the altar, the confraternity's most sacred space. The white gown not only symbolized purity and innocence, but also referred back to the penitential aspect that was at the basis of the late-medieval confraternal movement. In fact, the confraternity documents refer to the gown as a 'veste da battuto,' a flagellant's gown. Its only decoration was the confraternity's emblem on the right shoulder – the manger scene, complete with ox and ass.[14] The use of Latin at the moment of robing added solemnity and dignity to the action. And the singing, also in Latin, of two of the most important and ancient Christian hymns, one a supplication to the Holy Spirit to descend upon the assembled brothers and the other the Church's most solemn hymn of praise, elevated the ceremony to quasi-liturgical status.

It should be noted, finally, that the entire ceremony was without benefit of clergy. The authority figure standing at the altar, interrogating, robing, and accepting the candidate, was the guardian father, a layman. The father corrector, the only official clergyman in the confraternity, though he had examined the candidate earlier in order to determine his suitability, played no role whatsoever in the actual induction ceremony.

## Age Requirements

According to the 1468 statutes, new members entering the Arcangelo Raffaello were to be no younger than twelve and no older than twenty years of age.

There was only one exception, and it applied to youths aged nine to eleven. In their case, the guardian father could personally allow them to enter the confraternity unofficially, without ceremony and without a vote. As a token of their commitment eventually to join the confraternity, they paid all or part of their entrance fee, as the guardian father decided. To distinguish them from full members, they were called 'pilgrims' (*pellegrini*), perhaps to indicate that they were 'on the road,' so to speak, towards their destination. As 'pilgrims' they were required to go to confession monthly, as other members did, but did not have the right to vote at confraternity meetings. When they reached the age of twelve, they were to undergo the usual procedure of scrutiny, vote, and ceremony in order to make their full entry into the organization.[15]

Youths older than twenty years of age were not, according to the 1468 statutes, to be allowed to join the confraternity. By the 1570s, however, this regulation had fallen into disregard. As has been pointed out above, for example, Archbishop Altoviti's visit to the Arcangelo Raffaello in 1572/3 was followed a short time later by the entry into the confraternity of his twenty-eight-year-old assistant Ser Girolamo da San Miniato and, at that same election, of the thirty-year-old Raffaello di Ser Francesco Gucci, the twenty-six-year-old Giovanpaulo di Francesco Salvucci, and the twenty-two-year-old Ottaviano di Stefano da Ripa, all noticeably above the upper entry limit.[16]

Their enrolment into the confraternity at an older age was not, however, unusual for that time. Though the majority of new members did fall with the statutory limits, there were exceptions, and they were not all politically motivated. I suggested earlier that Ser Girolamo da San Miniato may have been 'planted' by the archbishop in order to report back on the activities of the confraternity (see above, ch. 7, p. 91). But other older members joined because they clearly possessed the spirituality, devotion, and commitment the confraternity sought out and wished to foster.

## Vittorio di Pellegrino Dell'Ancisa (1537–98)

One such case is Vittorio di Pellegrino Dell'Ancisa. The twenty-one-year-old youth joined the Arcangelo Raffaello in the general induction sponsored by fra Santi Cini in August 1558 (see above, ch. 7, p. 88). He soon took an active role in the organization, holding many offices, sometimes even consecutively. He served as *sagrestano*, *governatore*, *cerimoniere*, *festaiuolo*, and *provveditore*.[17] Several times he represented the confraternity in dealings with external organizations – he reached agreements with the friars of Santa Maria Novella in January 1561 and 1562; he was part of the search committee for a new *guardiano* in April 1563. He is often listed among the communicants and cited as a donor to the confraternity.[18]

These were formative years for Dell'Ancisa, especially because of the guidance he received from fra Santi Cini, the confraternity's father corrector. He was one of the first to join the special *tornata* within the Arcangelo Raffaello dedicated to St Lawrence that fra Santi had organized for older and more devout members.[19] Then, in 1568, having long passed the age limit for the Arcangelo Raffaello (Dell'Ancisa was now thirty-one years old), he joined the adult confraternity of San Tommaso d'Aquino, which had been founded by fra Santi Cini. In 1569 he joined the Oratorians of St Philip Neri, a personal friend of fra Santi, and became a priest. In this new congregation Dell'Ancisa enjoyed a long, distinguished career in both Florence and Rome.

As a priest, Dell'Ancisa is especially noted for his active involvement in charitable works and for his dedication to hearing confessions at the Duomo of Florence. In 1587/8 he founded the Ospedale della Carità, in Via della Scala, to assist destitute young women and pilgrims. This last charitable work, however, attracted the attention of evil tongues and other defamatory critics who undermined his work and contributed to the poverty, disenchantment, and lack of success that characterized his last years.[20]

## Motivation

Why would an exceptional young man such as Vittorio Dell'Ancisa or the average Florentine youth join a confraternity? The question why someone would join has not often been put by scholars, not even for adult organizations. In discussing Jewish youth confraternities, Horowitz proposed the traditional argument usually applied to Christian confraternities: 'both to serve as an example to the elders of the community and, no less importantly, to keep the younger element off the streets.'[21] These are motives that might spur parents and adults in authority to encourage their young to attend – as Ambrogio Traversari's letter to Pope Eugenius IV clearly implies – but they do not necessarily tell us what motivated the young men themselves to join such an organization. Horowitz offers another suggestion that is clearly indebted to Trexler's earlier comments on the ambivalent position of young men in society and to Weissman's emphasis on confraternities as social networks:

> Between the social worlds of schooling and marriage (separated, often enough, by a gap of a decade or more) the youth confraternity was the most viable form of social belonging available to [youths] ... Since most men were marrying well after eighteen, [the Jewish youth confraternity] Zerizim became, from 1625, essentially a bachelors' society, but also, it appears, the hub of social activity among the under-thirty set of Jewish males in Asti.[22]

The confraternity as a social club is a possible way of interpreting the situation, especially in the seventeenth and eighteenth centuries, when the membership grows predominantly older and 'entertainments' – plays, music, decorative ensembles – become a recurring feature of confraternal life.

Another, more traditional view is echoed by Christopher Black, who suggests that 'in looking at early modern confraternities we can recognize such societies, at their best, as trying to fulfil the needs of the poor and deprived – physical needs for food and shelter, but also social and emotional needs, in alleviating loneliness, dishonour, spiritual deprivation or ignorance.'[23] The picture seems rather more bleak than is warranted, for not all confraternity members were, by definition, materially, emotionally, or spiritually 'poor and deprived.' Black's description applies more correctly to the poor souls who were forced by circumstances to seek the assistance of charitable confraternities such as the Misericordia, Buonomini, Bigallo, and others, not to the devout volunteers who worked within such organizations.

The question of motivation needs to be rephrased. In Andrew Barnes's words, we need to determine 'the rewards confreres saw themselves as receiving' rather than the needs that were being satisfied, and this is not easily done.[24]

One reason scholars have tended to avoid approaching the question from the direction of the rewards to be gained may be the lack of reliable documentation on what the individuals themselves privately expected from their participation. The salvation of one's soul is, clearly enough, one reward not to be discounted. But this could be achieved through other means as well, so why join a confraternity?

The silence of the records on this point is deafening. I have found no confraternity document that speaks of, or even hints at, the reasons why a young man would join the Arcangelo Raffaello, or any other youth confraternity for that matter. Similarly, personal diaries and *ricordanze*, a rather popular genre that has offered historians many an insight into fifteenth- and sixteenth-century Florentine life, have also maintained strict silence on this matter. It is as if the secrecy of the confraternal hood had been extended to cover not only identity but also motivation. Among the many personal diaries and *ricordanze* from Renaissance Florence only two, to my knowledge, contain autobiographical references that give us an insight into why a youth joined a confraternity.

The first is an autobiographical reference from Vespasiano da Bisticci, and it reveals that as a young man he had joined the Arcangelo Raffaello not because of any personal commitment to a spiritual life, but to follow through on a strong recommendation from the devout Cardinal Cesarini, then residing in Florence:

When I was not yet very old, one day when I went to his Eminence, he asked me if I belonged to any youth confraternity. I answered I did not. See the unheard of charity of the master! He said to me: 'I want you to join the confraternity of Ser Antonio di Mariano; you will tell him I sent you.' And so I did. I tell this to point out that when it came to the well-being of his neighbour he took care not only of great matters, but also the small details. He then asked me if I wished to be a priest, for it would help me with my studies and would give me a benefice on which to live. He told me to think about this for a fortnight. At the end of the fortnight he asked me what I wanted to do. I answered that I did not wish to be a priest. He answered that if he could help me in other ways, he would. He was all love and charity.[25]

It is clear from Bisticci's narrative that the young man had no vocation for the priestly life and that he joined the Arcangelo Raffaello only on the cardinal's personal recommendation. The motivation, in this case, was completely self-serving on both parts, for the cardinal was clearly trying 'to place' (as we would say today) a gifted young man into the clergy, and Vespasiano was clearly trying to curry favour with an eminent personage who could provide him with a good career.

Another autobiographical record on joining a youth confraternity in fifteenth-century Florence comes from the diary of the coppersmith Bartolomeo Masi, who joined the company of San Giovanni Evangelista in December 1490:

I recall how, on 21 December 1490, Piero my brother and I Bartolomeo entered on this day into the Company of the youths of San Giovanni Evangelista, which is located between San Barnaba and Santa Maria Madre. There were about twelve of us youths entering that day, and among us there was, for one, the shoemaker Giovanbattista d'Andrea, who was then and is still our neighbour. And the guardian father of the company was the brass worker Cristofano di Miniato, with a shop by the archbishop's palace. The following Carnival Giuliano di Lorenzo di Piero di Cosimo de' Medici was master of ceremonies; and he organized three beautiful snacks for all the youths in the company, with many baked goods and cream-filled cornets ['cialdoncini'] and round cakes ['berlingozzi'] and Trebbiano wine, and it was a marvellous thing. He then organized a play in the confraternity garden, with a stage that went the entire length of the loggia as far as the mount, and with a stage set as beautiful as could be; and this play was presented on the second day of Lent in that year ... Lorenzo de' Medici, the father of the above-mentioned master of ceremonies, attended the performance, with many other eminent men and so many people that it was a marvellous thing. And all the youths in the confraternity stood on stage, especially those who were wearing a fine cloth gown ['veste di drappo'], and Piero and I Bartolomeo were among them.[26]

As was the case with Vespasiano da Bisticci, so too Masi's description of his entry into the confraternity reveals no religious or devotional motivation. It points, instead, to the presence in the organization of other neighbourhood youths and the elaborate Carnival *festa* organized by Giuliano de' Medici, complete with sweets, wine, a play, and eminent guests.

But surely not all youths joined a confraternity to please a potential patron or to take part in festive occasions with neighbourhood friends or with the sons of eminent Florentines, as seems to have been the case with Vespasiano and Bartolomeo. In examining the motivation that led people to join penitential confraternities in southern France, Andrew Barnes, who is the only scholar to have posed the question of motivation in depth, concluded that 'entrance into a confraternity conferred on an individual the publicly recognized status of penitent. This status had religious connotations of a higher level of lay piety and devotion. In order to maintain this status an individual had to remain in good standing within the confraternity, which implied participation in its devotions.'[27]

I would venture to suggest that in the case of Florentine youths a similar question of 'status' led them to join the confraternities that were being founded for them and by them in the fifteenth century. This was not necessarily a 'social' or 'political' status, but rather the recognition that a youth in a confraternity had a more profound sense of spirituality and devotion. This is evident in Vespasiano da Bisticci's comment on why Donato Acciaiuoli joined first a youth confraternity and then, when he was older, a *buca*:

> In his childhood ['pueritia'], in order to flee young men who were without good habits, Piero and Donato and his preceptor entered a youth confraternity, where one lived with great regard for [good] habits, and he did everything [possible] in order to form himself well in good habits. Then, when he was older, he entered into a night company called San Girolamo, and when he was in Florence he went there every Saturday without fail, and stayed the night, and slept on a straw mattress ['saccone']. He was its governor several times, and during the *discipline* they carried out there he used to deliver admirable exhortations, and he was the reason for an infinite amount of good because of the example he set with his own life.[28]

In Donato Acciaiuoli's case, the motivating force was not temporal gain, but a strong sense of devotion and spirituality. His case is perhaps not unusual. The renewal of spirituality in fifteenth-century Florence, fostered by the work of such pious individuals as the Blessed Carlo Guidi da Montegranelli, Ambrogio Traversari, St Antoninus, and others all the way to

Girolamo Savonarola, is an aspect of Renaissance Florence that has been much overlooked by contemporary scholars. Recently, through the indefatigable work of historians such as Arnaldo D'Addario, for one, the role of the Church in Florentine intellectual and spiritual life in the fifteenth and sixteenth centuries has attracted much-deserved attention. It is a role that points to a close partnership between humanism and religion, especially in the context of education.

Education, in fact, is one of the other factors that must have drawn youths to join confraternities. As Del Migliore pointed out, the Arcangelo Raffaello had been founded by a gold-leaf worker in order to educate the young in the Christian faith.[29] The Arcangelo Raffaello and other youth confraternities soon became known as 'Dottrine' exactly because they taught Christian doctrine to youths. But together with doctrine, prayers, and devotional rituals they also taught the youths some of the skills necessary for success in the highly competitive world of Renaissance Florence – oratory and rhetoric, rational social intercourse, organizational and administrative skills, and so forth. Some of the youths were able to acquire a musical education, as well, while others with artistic talents were commissioned to provide decorations for a variety of special events. In other words, the confraternity was a training ground and first place of expression for many Florentines who subsequently became individuals of renown in their fields.

## An Elite Organization

By the late sixteenth and early seventeenth century the Arcangelo Raffaello had acquired such a reputation that, as Guido Burchi pointed out, one became a member of the Arcangelo Raffaello not so much to belong to a social elite as to belong to an intellectual and cultural elite that constituted a Florentine *avant-garde* of artists as diverse as the painter Cristofano Allori, the sculptor and architect Giovambattista Caccini, the painter, writer, and poet Lorenzo Lippi, the painter and set designer Baccio del Bianco, the sculptor and architect Felice Gamberai, the engineer Pier Francesco Silvani, the poets Giovan Maria Cecchi, Jacopo and Giacinto Andrea Cicognini, Giovanni Nardi, Girolamo Bartolomei, and Ottavio Rinuccini, not to mention musicians such as Piero and Ferdinando dei Bardi, Jacopo Corsi, Giulio Caccini, Vincenzo Galilei and Jacopo Peri.[30]

The motivation to join not an artistic but a social elite was, nonetheless, also a factor and should not be overlooked. Bartolomeo Masi's pride in having joined a confraternity that included 'Giuliano di Lorenzo di Piero di Cosimo de' Medici' – note the complete genealogy – is undeniable. As Florence moved from a republican to a ducal and then grand-ducal society, the social context and role of confraternities changed accordingly. Ronald F.E. Weissman has already drawn our attention to this ennobling process (*nobilizzazione*) in Florentine confraternities in the sixteenth century.[31] But, as Weissman points out elsewhere, this was not something new. Already a hundred years earlier, after Lorenzo de' Medici joined the *buca* of San Paolo, membership in that organization jumped significantly (from about 175 in 1470 to about 200 the following year) and changed quality, for, 'unlike the largely plebeian membership of the early years of the confraternity, by the 1470s San Paolo had attracted a significant number of members of families linked to the regime.'[32]

This process and its effects are evident in the Arcangelo Raffaello as well. The best indication of its presence is the increase in enrolments when a member of the Medici family joined the confraternity. From 1579 to 1590 the average yearly entrance fee payments had been 34; then, once the Grand Duchess Christine of Lorraine visited the Arcangelo Raffaello in 1591 and, in January of the following year, enrolled her first-born son, Cosimo II, into it, the yearly entrance fee payments jumped to 53 and 62 respectively, an increase of 55.9 per cent and 82.3 per cent over the previous twelve years. For the years 1591–1602 the average number of yearly fee payments remained high, at 51.6, an increase of 51.8 per cent over the previous twelve years. For the next seventeen years (1603–19), yearly fee payments averaged 40.4. In 1620, however, when all four of Grand Duke Cosimo II's sons joined the Arcangelo Raffaello, entrance fee payments more than doubled to 88. There was a significant drop to 37 the following year, 1621, probably caused by Cosimo II's death and the uncertainty about Medicean presence in the confraternity. His sons' continued patronage, however, must have inspired confidence, for entrance fee payments in the next sixteen years (1622–37) averaged 51 per year, with a high of 118 in 1630 when Don Lorenzo de' Medici joined the organization.[33]

Medici patronage remained a hallmark of the Arcangelo Raffaello, and helped to maintain high membership. Though we do not have a complete run of entrance fee payments, the documents that have survived indicate that enrolment and payment of fees remained consistently high throughout the seventeenth century.

In the eighteenth century, however, payments of entrance fees dropped significantly and the confraternity began to coast towards its eventual demise. Without the renewal brought about by continued new enrolments, the confraternity slowly but surely changed into an organization for adult and older males. Fewer and fewer adolescents appear in the records, and more and more adults (some quite advanced in age) constitute the membership. This is clearly an indication that the youths' confraternity had ceased to be a vital force. By the mid-eighteenth century the situation had became so extreme that the executive was obliged not only to lower to twelve the number of members necessary for a quorum, but also to institute a lottery whereby at each prayer meeting a large candle (*candelotto*) was awarded to one of the members in attendance. But even these measures and bribes did not produce a turnaround – there are too many meetings where the recorded attendance is a suspicious twelve, and many meetings carried out with a recorded number of fewer than the twelve required members in attendance.[34]

The change towards an older membership was tied to changes both within and without the confraternity. The Council of Trent and the decrees of subsequent Florentine synods had undermined some of the fundamental activities of youth confraternities, especially those touching upon education in the Christian faith (see above, ch. 7).

Similarly, the 1636 rewriting of the statutes had introduced changes that favoured older members. The statutes had, admittedly, lowered the minimum age requirement from nine to seven years of age, but they had also removed the upper age limit. Also, while the 1468 statutes clearly said that members twenty-two to twenty-five years of age were to prepare themselves and exit the organization, the 1636 statutes had no such clause.[35] Nor did they describe a 'departure' ceremony, as the earlier statutes had. Since there was no incentive, instruction, or ceremony to encourage older brothers to leave, members lingered on and raised the average age in the group.

## Departure

Not only had the 1468 statutes declared that youths of a certain age were obliged to leave the confraternity, but they had also provided for a departure ceremony to mark that moment. Like the entrance ceremony, it was a solemn ritual with a number of significant moments.

On an appropriate day, at the end of the usual recitation of the Office, the departing brother knelt in the middle of the oratory and recited the psalm 'Miserere mei Deus' in Latin, alternating verses with the other members. When the psalm was finished, the brother moved to the altar and knelt there. The guardian father robed him with a green gown and placed a garland of olive branches on his head. As the statutes indicate, the olive branches symbolized perseverence and the garland was the crown of virtues patiently learned and good habits faithfully maintained in the confraternity (which here is called 'nostra scuola'). While the guardian father thus robed the young man, the other brothers sang the hymns 'Laudate Dominum omnes gentes,' 'Laudate pueri Dominum,' and 'Benedictus Dominus Deus Israel.' During this time the guardian father also offered the sign of peace to the departing brother, using the appropriate *tavoletta*, and then the brother did the same with all the other members present. When the singing and the exchange of peace were finished, the guardian father recited the prayer of perseverence. Everyone then sat, and the departing brother could, if the guardian father so indicated, eat a 'light and sober snack' with the brothers, at the end of which the 'Te Deum laudamus' was sung. The prayer of perseverence was recited for a second time, 'for this virtue alone is crowned victorious.' The guardian father then delivered a sermon dealing with the young man's departure, in order not only to comfort him and give him a few words of wisdom for his future life but also to comfort all brothers in the confraternity. The departing brother then spoke, encouraging his brothers and pointing out the benefits he himself had received from membership in the organization. The statutes add that he should do so 'as God inspires him,' indicating that this may have been an extemporaneous, unrehearsed speech. At this point the departing brother bowed to the altar, the guardian father, and the brothers, and, escorted by two white-clad brothers carrying his secular clothes (probably his cloak or jacket), went to the confraternity's front door. Here the two brothers removed the green gown from him, gave him his own clothes, and told him to go forth in the peace of the Lord.[36]

As in the case of the entrance ceremony, the departure ceremony was also conducted entirely by a lay person, the guardian father. It included the singing of Church hymns, the exchange of the sign of peace, and the solemn hymn of praise 'Te Deum laudamus.' There was no ritual interrogation by the guardian father this time, but instead words of warning and encouragement. Several new elements, appropriate for the occasion, were introduced. A small communal meal recalled the numerous occasions when the confraternity ate and celebrated together. Perhaps it also echoed the 'last supper' motif, underlining and solemnifying the breaking of ties in the imminent departure. The young man himself now delivered a speech encouraging his brothers to persevere and recognizing publicly the benefits he had received from membership in the organization. He was, in other words, an example for others to follow in their own path towards Christian adulthood. His success in staying the course was symbolized by the olive crown, and his entry into the next stage of life by the green of his new gown. He was no longer a *fanciullo* who wore the white of purity and innocence, but a *giovane*, soon to assume civic and social responsibilities appropriate to verdant adulthood and maturity.[37]

Though no longer a *fanciullo* or a member of the Arcangelo Raffaello, the young man could still attend confraternity meetings. With the guardian father's permission he was welcome to take communion in the confraternity on feast-days and to take part in all its devotions. If he did so he was, however, required to continue to behave well, live honestly, and abide by the statutes. Though still attending, he could no longer voice his opinion at meetings, or vote, or hold office in the confraternity.

If, on the other hand, the young man preferred not to continue attending the *compagnia di fanciulli*, then the guardian father was to advise him on which adult confraternity best suited him and do what he could to help the youth enrol in it. This was done, the statutes point out, so that the youth 'could keep on God's path more easily, for it would not do for a *giovane* to remain loose.'[38] Unfortunately there are no records to indicate which adult confraternities the guardian father recommended to any of the youths departing from the Arcangelo Raffaello.

# 10

# The Teaching of Christian Doctrine

In his description of the Arcangelo Raffaello, the seventeenth-century erudite Filippo Leopoldo Del Migliore points out that the confraternity was founded by an anonymous gold-leaf worker who gathered young men (*giovanetti*) together in order to teach them Christian doctrine.[1] Del Migliore describes the man as 'un uomo spirituale,' thus suggesting that the initiative was grounded in that individual's own strong commitment to Christianity and lay evangelism. The founder's personal initiative was soon modified, first by the group's brief association with the *buca* of San Girolamo and then by papal approval and regularization. The teaching of Christian doctrine by a layman was thus funnelled into the officially sanctioned spirituality of fifteenth-century Florence.

A similar initiative, by a similarly 'spiritual' man, is noted by Paul Grendler in his *Schooling in Renaissance Italy*, when he mentions that a confraternity was founded in Bologna around 1425 from an initiative of Niccolò Albergati to teach Christian doctrine to youths twelve to twenty-one years old:

> Albergati began to visit churches on holidays in order to teach the elements of Catholicism to boys. A schoolteacher and a few other laymen accompanied him. By 1425 he had formed a twenty-four member lay confraternity of teen-age boys and adults to carry on the catechetical instruction. The group soon split into separate confraternities, one for adults and a second for youths aged 12 to 21. Mid-century statutes of the latter confraternity exhorted its teen-age members to go out into the streets every Sunday in order to teach the boys found there 'la sancta doctrina.'[2]

We do not know how, exactly, the anonymous gold-leaf worker in Florence first instructed the youths at the Arcangelo Raffaello. We may safely assume that he and those who followed him in the fifteenth century taught them the basics of the Christian faith by having them memorize a few simple prayers and lists of appropriate beliefs. Grendler points out that in the sixteenth century such teaching was often based on two specific types of books – a *Summario* and an *Interrogatorio*. The *Summario della vita Cristiana* was a small booklet, usually a duodecimo of only sixteen pages, that began with the name of IESUS, followed with the words for the sign of the cross, the Pater Noster, Ave Maria, Credo, Salve Regina (all in Latin), and then listing, in Italian, the Ten Commandments, the two precepts of the law of grace, the canons of natural law, the four cardinal virtues, the seven gifts of the Holy Spirit, the seven spiritual and the seven corporal works of mercy, the seven capital sins and their seven opposite virtues, the three powers of the spirit, the five senses of the body, the seven sacraments of the Church and the ten Commandments of the Church. The *Interrogatorio* was a large book containing 120 to 200 questions and answers, and thus became a more advanced and thorough venue for instruction.[3]

There are no such books extant for the Arcangelo Raffaello, though we do know that the confraternity did produce them and use them. The 1636 statutes, for example, refer to a 'Christian Doctrine composed by us and printed in 1584,' but I have been unable to track down the work.[4] In April 1610, the confraternity paid fifteen *lire* to have fourteen *libri da Compagnia* bound professionally by the printer 'all'insegna del Pellegrino.'[5] This may well have been a reissue of the 1584 volume. From journal entries in following years we learn that this was a catechism book divided into chapters, for we find the youths learning their Christian doctrine one chapter at a time on subsequent Sundays. In the spring and summer of 1643, for example, the scribe notes that the youths learned their *dottrina* a chapter at a time from Sunday, 19 April to Sunday, 27 September, from Lorenzo Vanni, a member of the Arcangelo Raffaello. We also learn that the book they were using was divided into fourteen chapters and that most chapters were covered over the course of two consecutive Sundays.[6] And, from the number of books bound, we can also infer the number of youths being instructed at the time – in the 1610s, anything up to about a dozen and a half.

We do not find a *Summario* mentioned in the records of the Arcangelo Raffaello, though on one occasion in 1582 there is a reference to what might be construed as one. At the end of a short play depicting a member's encounter with Tobias and the Archangel Raphael, the latter distributes to all present a printed sheet (*una carta stampata*) containing a list of items very similar to the one described by Paul Grendler: the twelve articles of faith, the Creed, the Ten Commandments, the seven sacraments of the Church, the three theological virtues, the four cardinal virtues, the seven gifts of the Holy Spirit, the two commandments of charity, the seven spiritual works of mercy, the seven temporal works of mercy, the seven mortal sins, the four things a Christian must always keep in mind, the five senses of the body, the commandments of the Church, the precepts a good Christian must observe, the six sins against the Holy Spirit, and the eight Beatitudes.[7] The archangel's intention, as he himself points out, was that members should memorize these items in order to return to the confraternity's original purpose and intentions – the Christian education of the young:

> Let everyone study this, let everyone learn
> through this the ways of a Christian life,
> because this is nothing but the law
> of Christ and of his Church, to which everyone
> who wishes to be saved is beholden.
> Through this your forerunners already
> left in the world good reputation of themselves
> and they commanded well, and you have
> lapsed in this, that every day there should resound
> in your ears each of these precepts
> so that each of you may keep them in his mind.
> What did you expect? That this building
> would still stand without this stone,
> [this stone] on which this place was founded,
> for the purpose of introducing young men
> into the path of God through his precepts?'[8]

The archangel's words recalled the confraternity's original purpose, but probably also brought to mind the confraternity's more recent renewal at the hands of fra Santi Cini (1558–9) and his devout followers – members such as Vittorio di Pellegrino dell'Ancisa, who had now grown up and moved away, leaving the Arcangelo Raffaello with a well-deserved reputation, but without the energetic drive of the reformers of the 1560s.

## The Blessed Ippolito Galantini (1565–1619)

Such drive and energy were not lacking in Florence, or in a number of individuals committed to the teaching of doctrine. One of these was the young Ippolito Galantini. As his hagiographer put it, Galantini was born of 'poor but honest parents,' the eldest of four children.[9] His interest in the teaching of Christian doctrine first became apparent in 1570 when the boy, aged only five at the time, began gathering together other boys, teaching and preaching to them. Such was the reputation he soon acquired that at the age of twelve he was enrolled by Jacopo Ansaldi to assist him with the teaching of Christian doctrine in Florence and was given a charge to that effect at the church of Santa Lucia del Prato. A few years later, the seventeen-year-old Galantini was asked to replace Bernardo Rutilensi as guardian father of the parish confraternity of Santa Lucia – an appointment that bespeaks the youth's reputation for devotion and sanctity. He immediately set out to reform the confraternity's statutes and to increase its membership. He drew young men to the study of Christian doctrine by going out into the streets in search of boys who were in need of reform – his hagiographer specifies children who were addicted to gambling and rough games – in order to bring them back with him to the confraternity for devotions and instruction. This was not an unusual practice, for 'fishermen' (*pescatori*) were to be found among Savonarola's young followers and are also documented at other times and in other places of Italy as well.[10] Galantini eventually established his own catechetical group, the Congregazione della Dottrina Cristiana, also known as the Vanchetoni (or Bacchetoni), taught extensively in Florence, and was even called to other cities such as Lucca, Volterra, Pistoia, and Modena. After his death, he was declared Venerable and eventually Blessed (1825).

As with most saintly people, so too with Galantini a strong personal commitment to evangelism did not exist without opposition. His reforming fervour appears not have been welcomed by the entire membership of the confraternities he directed, for often we find him mired deep in controversy. Some of the members at Santa Lucia clearly did not espouse his ideals and eventually brought him so much grief that he was obliged to give up his post. Undaunted, he accepted an appointment as guardian of the confraternity of San Salvatore, but difficulties followed him there, as well, as they did later at San Domenico, where he held the post for two years. At San Lorenzino he served for a very brief time before he was obliged to resign.[11] While his hagiographer interprets these vicissitudes as the inevitable trials and tribulations of a saint, we might see in them instead the intransigence of the committed reformer at loggerheads with the less dedicated, yet tenaciously lax (if I may be permitted the oxymoron) conservative element of the membership.

## Dott. Jacopo Ansaldi's Visit to the Confraternity

Galantini's zeal and intransigence may give us an insight into the answer given by the Arcangelo Raffaello's assistant substitute guardian father Niccolò Antifassi to dott. Jacopo Ansaldi during the latter's visit to the confraternity on 28 July 1585.

The scribe Alessandro Ghettini recalls that Vespers on that day was attended by the Rev. Jacopo Genovese, a priest of the cardinal archbishop's, and Jacopo Genovese, who had been 'chosen by His Eminence to introduce the [teaching of] Christian doctrine in confraternities and youth schools.'[12] After Vespers, Genovese delivered a 'long sermon' in which he 'commanded that [the confraternity] should set about learning such doctrine.' Members of the Arcangelo Raffaello, with their own long tradition in such teaching and learning, were probably not amused by what must have seemed to them not only Ansaldi's Johnny-come-lately effort, or Genovese's presumption in telling them what to do, but also by what could well have been a barbed reference to the confraternity's recent lapse in instructional fervour (as the play of June 1582 suggested; see above, pp. 129–30). Niccolò Antifassi answered politely but firmly on behalf of the confraternity, saying that they would not fail to do as Genovese ordered, that as a rule the confraternity every day had someone read out a tablet containing the entire *dottrina*, and that on occasion the youths themselves delivered a lesson from it, and this they would continue to do.[13]

Antifassi's firm answer contains a reaffirmation of the confraternity's long-standing commitment to teaching the doctrine and pointedly informed the two visitors that the youths of the Arcangelo Raffaello were already practising what the archbishop's appointee was preaching. The exchange may have been that much more politically charged if one considers that the Arcangelo Raffaello was at the moment without a duly appointed guardian father – Niccolò Antifassi was merely assistant substitute guardian father to Zanobi Buonavolti, who was himself only substitute guardian, not elected but appointed by the father corrector in the wake of the death, one year earlier, of the confraternity's duly appointed guardian father, Antonio di Pasci da Colle (d. 6 July 1584). With Buonavolti and Antifassi sharing responsibilities as temporary replacements, the confraternity may well have feared the archbishop's intervention and the possible imposition of an unwanted guardian – someone such as the young, energetic, and committed (but already controversial) Ippolito Galantini, for example.

In appointing Ansaldi, in fact, the archbishop had not only given him the authority to introduce the teaching of Christian doctrine in the confraternities of Florence, but also to appoint the necessary instructors and to ensure that standards and consistency were maintained throughout the city. If this had been Ansaldi's purpose during his visit to the Arcangelo Raffaello, possibly with the covert intention of giving the nod to his companion, the Rev. Jacopo Genovese, as the confraternity's instructor, the Arcangelo Raffaello clearly won the day – no one was then or ever appointed by Ansaldi to teach doctrine at the confraternity.

## Dott. Jacopo Ansaldi's *Dottrina Cristiana*

Had he been appointed, how would the Rev. Jacopo Genovese have instructed the youths of the Arcangelo Raffaello? Without a doubt he would have used Ansaldi's own textbook, published that very year – the *Dottrina cristiana. Nuovamente ristampata, & publicata per ordine dell'Illustriss. & Reverendiss. Cardinal di Firenze. Da insegnarsi, & esercitarsi dalli Curati, & Guardiani di Compagnie de' Fanciulli della suo [*sic*] Diocesi per publica utilità* (In Firenze: Appresso Francesco Tosi, e Comp., 1585). This was a good-sized volume of 108 pages, with plenty of material for a teacher or a student to use.

In the preface to the archbishop, Ansaldi pointed to the growing interest in the teaching of Christian doctrine to the youth in Florence by recalling his own appointment as instructor of doctrine to the confraternity of the Purificazione, the founding and growing reputation of the Compagnia della Dottrina Cristiana di S. Bernabà in via dei Tessitori, and the desire of the parishioners of Santa Lucia sul Prato to establish among themselves a confraternity by that name to teach Christian Doctrine (p. 3). His own published edition of the *Dottrina Cristiana* was thus meant to serve the interests and needs of this growing popular movement in the city.

In order to facilitate the learning process and make it more pleasant for the young, Ansaldi arranged his *Dottrina* so that it could be sung in the manner of psalms. He defended this choice with nine specific reasons: (1) singing allowed students to learn and remember the doctrine more easily, (2) children (*putti*) and youth (*giovani*) would linger more happily at church and at the confraternity, (3) those who could barely speak or read [*sic*] would be able to learn the doctrine through singing, (4) it would be easier to teach it, (5) it would deter the youth from singing corrupting songs, (6) those who heard it but did not come to the confraternity would nonetheless learn it, (7) children (*fanciulli*) would learn to sing with ease, (8) they would thus imitate the practice of the Roman Church, which sings day and night the Canonical Hours, and, lastly, (9) they would emulate the angels in heaven who continuously sing 'Holy, Holy Lord God' (pp. 12–14).[14]

Ironically, the actual doctrine occupies just less than a quarter of the volume (pp. 25–53). The rest is taken up by the order of Vespers (pp. 53–62), the litanies (pp. 62–7), nineteen vernacular *laude* and *lodi* (pp. 68–99),[15] and a set of rules on proper civil and Christian behaviour (pp. 99–108). The volume, in other words, moves from being a listing of doctrinal statements to being a service book and, at the end, a book of manners. The connection between good doctrine and good behaviour is clearly laid out. In this, Ansaldi is firmly rooted in the traditional view of youth confraternities as schools not only of good doctrine but also of good morals, a training ground for both the Christian and the citizen.[16] By extension, Florence was to become the *civitas Dei* its citizens had already postulated for at least the previous two centuries.

Ansaldi's interest in the connection between doctrine and behaviour was already evident in his earlier work, the *Discorsi spirituali et civili, secondo il catechismo per instruttione di giovani desiderosi far profitto nella vita spirituale et civile* (1583). The second part of this volume taught men of letters, merchants, and youth how each of them should carry out a good examination of conscience. The third section was entitled 'Lessons and discourses on good manners and behaviour' and was addressed solely to the young.[17]

In his writings and his service to the cause, Ansaldi was merely reflecting the continued strength of lay religion in Florence, a strength based on active lay participation (Ansaldi himself was not in orders) and on strong ecclesiastical and government support. As early as the fifteenth century, Pope Eugenius IV, Ambrogio Traversari, and Archbishop Antonino Pierozzi had fostered youth confraternities for the contribution they could make in teaching Christian doctrine. It had been traditionally believed that the saintly archbishop had even composed a manual of Christian doctrine for use specifically by the youths of the confraternity of the Purificazione (see above, ch. 4, pp. 43–4). More recently, Grand Duke Cosimo I had supported the translation into Italian, and publication in Florence, of Juan de Valdes's catechism. In all these cases, fostering the spirituality of lay youth had been paramount.

## The Rev. Lorenzo Vanni

Such support did not disappear in the seventeenth century. In fact, another period of renewed interest in the teaching of Christian doctrine at the Arcangelo Raffaello can be seen in the 1630s–40s. This time the renewal was spearheaded by Lorenzo Vanni, a member of the confraternity but also a priest at the basilica of San Lorenzo. The first reference to it appears in an entry of 20 May 1632 when the scribe recalls that the Rev. Lorenzo Vannni, 'one of our most devoted brothers,' delivered a discourse (*ragionamento*) on that day's festivity and on 'doctrine,' pointing out 'the fruits one can gather in teaching it and in practising it,' and he then offered to undertake such teaching himself starting the very next Sunday. The scribe brings the entry to a close by noting that everyone was pleased; they all sang the hymn to the Holy Spirit, and then some children (*fanciulli*) entered the confraternity as novices. It seems evident that Vanni's exhortation and readiness to teach doctrine were in fact tied to the entry of novices and to the desire to encourage them to learn the doctrine – which they did, throughout the summer.

That following 19 September, the scribe records a small play on the Trinity recited by twelve children (*fanciulli*) under the direction of Lorenzo Vanni, who had composed the 'most devout dialogue' himself. The actors were probably the novices in the catechism class who, having completed their course of study, were now displaying their knowledge and skills to the older members of the confraternity. In fact, at the end of the event, all twelve of the participants received prizes 'in order to encourage the children to engage themselves eagerly in such exercises of virtue ['virtù']' – much like the year-end convocation *cum* talent show one still finds in many schools today.[18] A somewhat similar term-end event is noted for 27 September 1643, when, after Vespers, Vanni had his students recite the last chapter of the *Dottrina* and then dismissed them for the term so that 'they may at their ease go and enjoy the air at their villas.'[19]

Aside from the observations that these were clearly the children of well-to-do parents with villas on the hills of Tuscany, and that the process of *nobilizzazione* was by now entrenched at the Arcangelo Raffaello, one should also note that the chapters were being taught with the help of music. When another renewal of teaching doctrine was undertaken in 1652, the confraternity 'decided to take up again the *Dottrina* already printed for use by [the] confraternity and arranged so as to be sung in the manner of psalms by the Very Reverend Messer Lorenzo Vanni, Canon of the collegiate of San Lorenzo.' The scribe adds that the collegiate church of San Lorenzo itself 'and many other churches and parishes' used this work to instruct their own youths.[20] The singing of the catechism is indicated in the 1636 statutes, which say that the 1584 volume was arranged 'so that [Christian doctrine] can be sung with great ease, like the Psalms.'[21]

The Rev. Lorenzo Vanni was not only an eager participant in the Arcangelo Raffaello's mission to educate the young, but also a noteworthy donor to the organization. To support his own involvement in the teaching of doctrine, he donated seventy-two *Dottrine* to the confraternity; the high number of copies suggests that with time the exercise may have attracted more students than had been the case in the 1610s. He also made donations in support of religious services at the confraternity – a parchment choir-book bound in leather with a tondo on one side depicting the Archangel Raphael and Tobias, and another on the other side with the arms of the confraternity, both enclosed within engraved brass frames; a large Roman breviary bound in black leather, with steel clasps and brass tacks at the corners; a priest's missal, also bound in black leather; and a large variety of liturgical vestments, all of them made of expensive fabrics and richly decorated.[22] He also enrolled his two nephews, Orazio and Filippo di Niccolò Vanni, into the confraternity.[23]

Vanni's interest in the Arcangelo Raffaello and in teaching Christian doctrine was part of a tradition in Florence that went back to the founding of youth confraternities. After an initial success in the first half of the fifteenth century, fostered by committed laymen and supportive churchmen, the movement experienced a revival in the second half of the sixteenth century, on the wake of Catholic reform ideals. For the Arcangelo Raffaello we have already noted the presence of highly devoted members, such as fra Santi Cini and Vittorio di Pellegrino dell'Ancisa. In other confraternities other young men took part in a similar movement for the religious instruction of youths.

## Not Really a Dottrina

By the late sixteenth and early seventeenth century, the impulse to teach Christian doctrine to the young had developed its own momentum and had created its own confraternities, rightly called *Scuole della Dottrina Cristiana* or, sometimes, *Compagnie di Dottrina*.[24] Although the term was occasionally applied to the Arcangelo Raffaello, it did not properly belong to it. A seventeenth-century list of Florentine confraternities correctly differentiated between the twelve *compagnie di giovani* then active in the city (the Arcangelo Raffaello and the other youth confraternities mentioned in this study), and the nine *compagnie di dottrina*, that is, those 'di San Carlo, di San Piero Maggior, della Resurrezione, di San Michele della Pace, di San Giovanni in Verzaia, della Pietà a San Piero Gattolini, di Santa Lucia in sul Prato, del Nome di Dio in via de' Tedeschi, della Concezione dietro a San Remigio.'[25]

The standard schools of Christian doctrine gathered youths from four to fourteen years of age. The Arcangelo Raffaello, on the other hand, had, from its beginning, attracted youths aged thirteen to twenty-four and was now, from the late sixteenth century on, including adult men well over the original statutory age limit of twenty-four.[26] Furthermore, the schools of Christian doctrine were closely tied to parishes and their priests, while the youth confraternities remained city-wide organizations transcending parochial boundaries. Although the teaching of Christian doctrine had been the primary charitable activity of the Arcangelo Raffaello at its founding, and had remained an important component of its life up to the mid-seventeenth century, by the eighteenth century it had ceased to be one of its activities because, as the *provveditore* Filippo Guidotti pointed out in 1783, the confraternity no longer had young men enrolled in it and the teaching of Christian doctrine was now, by decree, the purview of the parish.[27]

# 11

# Religious Rituals

The confraternity's spiritual life consisted of a communal and a personal component. The communal component took place on Sundays, all holy days of obligation, and on certain feast-days as established by confraternity custom or decided upon by the guardian father. At these times the brothers gathered in the oratory as a community to pray and to conduct confraternity business. The personal component, instead, was nurtured privately by each brother in his everyday activities outside the confraternity walls, in line, however, with the confraternity's moral and devotional standards.

The communal spiritual life of the confraternity revolved around a yearly cycle of formal religious rituals that, eventually, came to include the recitation of Matins and Vespers, the celebration of Mass, the veneration of the Blessed Sacrament in the Forty Hours, the observation of feast-days of particular significance to the confraternity, the commemoration of deceased brothers, and participation in public processions.

By the seventeenth century, the Confraternity met three times on Sundays and major feast-days – in the morning, afternoon, and evening. The morning service (Office and Mass) was celebrated very early in the day, generally shortly after dawn and after the first Mass at the nearby convent of Santa Maria Novella. The afternoon service (Vespers) took place after lunch, and the evening service (Matins) after the evening Angelus.

Both communal activities and personal conduct were expected to adhere to guidelines established in the *capitoli*. Not only rites and ceremonies, but also the behaviour of members inside and outside the confraternity was to reflect the group's purpose of helping young men grow into devout and God-fearing Christian citizens. From the moment they stepped inside the confraternity's front door, the youths thus entered into a world of prayer and ritual that was both an island away from, and a training ground for, life in the world.

In this chapter we will examine the ceremonial aspect of the youths' devotions, from the simple actions of respect required of them as they entered the confraternity to the structure of their prayer meetings. An examination of records suggesting the practice of self-flagellation will reveal that the nature of this devotional ritual at the Arcangelo Raffaello is both complex and uncertain. The chapter will close with a few words on the personal devotions members were expected to carry out on their own.

## Arrival at the Confraternity

The 1468 statutes give us an insight into the atmosphere and attitudes that were fostered from the first moment a brother crossed the threshold into the confraternity.[1] Arriving for a service, a brother was met at the front door by a confraternity member who could be either one of the masters of the novices, whose duty was, in fact, to welcome members and instruct novices on confraternity rituals, or someone so deputized by the guardian father. Only one brother stood guard at the door at any one time. When another deputy or master of the novices arrived, the new arrival replaced the incumbent at the post. This sequence of guard changes continued until all brothers had arrived. At the door the brothers exchanged the Italian salutation 'Go in peace.' Upon entering the oratory, the new arrival greeted his assembled brothers with a similar Italian salutation, 'God grant you peace,' proceeded to the altar, where, kneeling, he silently recited a prayer (the statutes stipulated at least a Hail Mary), and then went to sit at the next available space on the pews that ran, laterally, along the sides of the oratory. In order to avoid idleness or conversation while waiting for the service to start, as soon as six or more members were gathered the guardian father asked one of them to read from Holy Scripture or all of them to sing a *lauda* or a psalm. In the meantime, a bell rang to call brothers into the oratory. Those who arrived after the service had begun knelt on the ground until signalled by the guardian father to proceed to the pews.

The 1636 statutes also provided guidelines for entering into the confraternity oratory.[2] Their instructions reveal a greater emphasis on ritualistic formality and decorum. The concern for externals is evident in the very first sentence of the chapter dealing with rites and ceremonies: 'Let rites and ceremonies in praise of the Lord be carried out with decorum, gravity, fervour, and a spirit of devotion, and therefore let the rubrics in the breviaries, missals, and Roman Rituals be especially followed, as well as those ceremonies which are generally accepted as appropriate in this Confraternity.'[3] The instruction is then supported by a Latin citation from Deuteronomy urging Israel to hear and keep the ceremonies it has been given. The citation itself is highly charged – it constitutes Moses' opening words to the Hebrews as he is about to read them the Decalogue: 'Israel, listen to the statutes and the laws which I proclaim to you this day. Learn them, and be careful to observe them' (Deuteronomy 5:1).

The 'statutes and laws' which the youth of the Arcangelo Raffaello were about to receive in the 1636 *capitoli* were not, however, the high moral rules of the Ten Commandments, but rather the superficial veneer of ritual formality. The youths were instructed to enter into the confraternity with modesty, wearing appropriate apparel ('in abito ben composto'). Once inside, they were to kneel to the Crucifix in the *stanzone*, and then, with a devout heart ('raccolto il suo Spirito'), enter into the oratory, proceed to the altar of the Virgin where they were to kneel, recite a Hail Mary, and kiss the ground. They were then to stand up, turn, and bow to the painting of the Archangel Raphael, to the guardian father, and then to the governor before proceeding to the pews to take their place 'according to their rank.' The devout simplicity of the 1468 statutes had clearly been replaced by a strictly structured sequence of ritual formalities that revealed, at the very least, a baroque fascination for exteriors.

A similar interest in exteriors infuses the ensuing guidelines on when to sit or stand during services. And again the practices to be followed are supported by Latin citations, this time from Cassianus and Thomas à Kempis. In a fashion, the youths were being told to conduct themselves as if they were the monks of Egypt described by Cassianus, or followers of Thomas à Kempis's *devotio moderna*.

Such changes in the ritual for entering into the oratory had, in part, already been incorporated into confraternity practice. Reverence not only to the altar but also to the guardian's desk constituted part of the revisions to the statutes enacted by the guardian Luca Vigna in 1618/19. At that time the masters of the novices were to instruct new candidates that, on entering the oratory, they were to put on their confraternity robes,[4] bow to the altar and then to the guardian's desk, kneel with both knees, and take their cue on when to stand or sit from the other members of the confraternity.[5]

Such attention to formality did not make the youths comparable to the hermit monks of Egypt or the Augustinian monks of the Netherlands, but rather to the elegant entourage that now revolved around the grand-ducal court. The brothers' interests and practices in the seventeenth century ran more towards formally structured ritual and less towards spiritually disciplined religion. In fact, in the confraternity records of the time, the devotional component of the confraternity's celebrations is often omitted. In its place one finds instead only the matter-of-fact comment that the Office was recited, or enthusiastic recollections of the splendour and beauty of particular occasions. Phrases such as 'splendido apparato ... da tutti a meraviglia lodato et ammirato'[6] thus became the guidelines by which the confraternity measured and wished to remember its devotional activities.

## *Tornata*

The confraternity's standard activity was the prayer/business meeting (*tornata*). The 1468 statutes describe the order to be followed for the *tornata.*[7] Once the guardian father thought that a sufficient number of brothers had gathered, he instructed one of the youths to recite the opening Latin solicitation 'Jubbe domine benedicere,' to which the guardian responded, 'Cogitationes, et actus nostros in sua pace disponet Dominus omnipotens.' The choir answered with an 'Amen' and the service began. First a short lesson was read (in Latin), urging the brothers to beware and the Lord to be merciful. Then the 'Confiteor' was recited, either by one or all the assembled brothers. The antiphon and prayer to the Archangel Raphael followed.[8] At this point the brothers could recite either the penitential psalms with their appropriate litanies, or the Vesper of the Virgin with the gradual psalms (Psalms 120–34), or a different office as decided by the guardian father. If the penitential or gradual psalms were recited, they were to be followed by the hymn 'Laudate pueri dominum,' whereas if the Vesper of the Virgin was recited, it was to be followed by the more appropriate 'Magnificat.' The guardian father then asked a brother to pronounce some general intercessions (*raccomandazioni*) on behalf of past and present members. The Creed followed, with prayers to the Trinity, Our Lady, the Holy Innocents, St Mary Magdalene, and the Archangel Raphael, and the prayer of perseverance. Then the brothers recited the Salve Regina and another Hail Mary. Every first and third Sunday of the month the guardian father was to correct those brothers who had in some way erred against the confraternity statutes or committed some other chastisable act. Brothers who wished to confess publicly were invited to do so at this time, humbly and devoutly, provided their faults were 'appropriate to be confessed to the congregation.' Confraternity business was then carried out. Once business was completed, the guardian father 'rang' the Ave Maria (i.e., the Angelic Salutation), the brothers made their donation to the altar, and the congregation was dismissed.

The order of service outlined in the 1468 statutes presents a well-regulated sequence, with a variety of devotional moments and the opportunity for alternative prayers at different times in the service. It also allows for a combination of devotional, penitential, and administrative moments to suit the needs of the confraternity. It is, furthermore, a completely 'lay' order of service, which, by not incorporating any of the sacraments, can be conducted without the participation or even presence of an ordained priest.

Such is not the case with the order of service outlined in the 1636 statutes. First of all, the new statutes describe a precise sequence of prayers that adhered, much more closely, to the canonical hours observed by the clergy. The need for such a routine was substantiated with cited references to St Luke (Acts of the Apostles) and St Proculus. In the morning, as brothers were arriving, those present sang the Litanies of the Lord, while in the evening they read from a religious (*spirituale*) book. The office always began with the hymn to the Holy Spirit, 'Veni Sancte Spiritu,' and finished with the Angelic Salutation. After morning Matins the father corrector celebrated Mass and gave communion to the brothers, who were instructed to receive it devoutly ('con divozione'). In the afternoon they recited Vespers, and in the evening the Matins from the Small Office of the Virgin, 'who is the wonderful foundation of all religion.'[9]

The three evenings of Holy Week, as well as the three evenings including and following Easter, the Office of Our Lord was sung. On Shrove Tuesday and All Souls', the Office of the Dead was recited. Collections for the needs of the confraternity, lay sermons, or confraternity business took place after the conclusion of these services. Once this was done, the brothers recited the usual closing prayers, the father corrector gave the blessing, and all were dismissed.

The revised order of service reveals several important developments in the confraternity's devotional practices. First of all, it points to a realignment of devotional practices in step with those of the Church. By adopting the canonical hours and the Divine Office, and by inserting the celebration of Mass into its morning service, the confraternity lost its freedom to generate and conduct its own rituals of worship. With the demise of services created and conducted by the laity, the clergy began to play a more important and vital role in the rites and ceremonies of the brotherhood. As a consequence, the devotional thrust changed. While, for example, in the fifteenth century the confraternity regularly carried out a confessional ritual, in the seventeenth it emphasized instead the sacrament of communion. It thus moved from being a confraternity with *laudese*/penitential overtones to being one with sacramental intentions. Such a change reflects the

Tridentine efforts to curb penitential or flagellant confraternities and to favour, instead, devotional sodalities, especially those dedicated to honouring the Sacrament.[10]

Similarly, the greater emphasis on ceremonies and singing redirected the devotional thrust from prayer to spectacle.[11] The chapter outlining the order of services, for example, closes with a citation from St Isidore, instructing brothers to sing well, with a full, sweet, and mellifluous voice reflective of the sound and melody of sacred religion.[12] Eventually, this concern with spectacle and singing led the confraternity to become a showcase of talented youths for visiting and local dignitaries to admire and patronize. This was especially true when the confraternity celebrated special occasions, such as, for example, the feast of its patron saint, the Archangel Raphael.

## Flagellation

Flagellation, a practice usually associated by the general public with medieval and Renaissance confraternities, was not, strictly speaking, part of the Arcangelo Raffaello's ritual. The group was a *laudese*, that is, a praising confraternity, not a group of flagellants (*battuti* or *disciplinati*) intent on doing penance for their and society's failings. Furthermore, the confraternity had been established as a teaching institution, whose aim was to educate young men in the Christian faith and life. This differentiated the youths from the strictly *laudese* groups and distanced them even further from flagellant organizations such as the *buche* or adult confraternities that did use the scourge.

This is not to say that the concept of flagellation was not, in some ways, present in the Arcangelo Raffaello. The confraternity's official garment, for example, was clearly modelled on the gown and hood of flagellant confraternities, so much so that it was called a 'flagellant's gown' ('veste da battuti'). In 1560, the Arcangelo Raffaello decided to use the revenue of 49 *lire* from the indulgence granted by Pope Pius IV to make 'twenty-two flagellant gowns, both large and small, which the house greatly needed.'[13] The term used, and the size and number of gowns required, suggest that all the youths present at services wore such penitential garments.[14] One must be cautious about conclusions, however, for the habit does not the monk make, nor does the wearing of a flagellant's gown necessarily indicate that the actual practice was carried out.

Another term often associated with flagellation, discipline (*disciplina*), also appears in the confraternity's *ricordi*. The scribe often recalls that the brothers 'did the discipline' ('fecero la disciplina') or 'took the discipline' ('presero la disciplina'). As Bossy points out, by the sixteenth century, if not even earlier, the term *disciplina* had lost its traditional connotations of 'penitential whipping' and acquired the new meaning of 'examination of conscience,' that is, the 'systematic interior monitoring by the individual of his own life.'[15] Thus, in the case of the Arcangelo Raffaello practices, the phrase most probably indicates that the youths carried out an internal self-examination as part of the penitential component of their devotions.[16] Such an interpretation is substantiated by the 1636 statutes, which say that in its 225-year history the confraternity had 'grown in discipline,' meaning devotion.[17]

The phrase could also, admittedly, indicate the use of a ceremonial scourge, called a *disciplina*, or even the actual practice of flagellation.

One occasion when it clearly refers to the scourge, but could also refer to the act of flagellation, is recorded in 1562, when the scribe writes:

> We gathered at our usual place on the morning of Pentecost in very good number and we celebrated the Most Holy Matins of the Virgin in the large oratory. When we finished the Matins and the other usual prayers we began to sing the psalm 'Deus misereatur nostri' and proceeded, two by two, into the morning oratory ['tornata della mattina'], and each brother took the discipline from the sacristans who were giving them out at the door. When everyone was at his place and the governor had said a few words, we carried out the devotion ['si fece di poi la devotione']. When it was finished a chapter was read as is usual, and since the altar was set our father corrector celebrated the Most Holy Mass, and when it was finished he gave communion to thirty-five of our brothers.[18]

The description fits quite well into what we know was the flagellation ritual carried out in flagellant confraternities.[19] The only major elements missing are the communal meal that preceded it, the darkened oratory, and the closed doors. These are present, instead, in the Good Friday flagellation ritual described in detail by the confraternity's scribe in 1687. Because it is the only detailed description of such a ritual to survive from the Arcangelo Raffaello, it is worth reporting in full:

> In the morning, after [first] Mass in Santa Maria Novella, the brothers who had been invited the previous evening to participate in the function that will shortly be described, gathered one after the other in the *stanzone* of our confraternity, whose door had been left partially open ['socchiuso']. After a brief prayer to the Crucifix, each person retired to the *tornantino* [the smaller, morning oratory] where, in order to carry out what we had determined to do, one of them read some meditations on

the Passion of Our Lord Jesus Christ. Our father corrector arrived at that time, and since the number of brothers was complete, our guardian father ordered that everyone enter the oratory in twos, continually singing the psalm *Miserere*, [to partake of] the repast prepared by our beloved brother Ser Giovanni Lapi. Going out of the *tornantino* there were, at the door of the oratory, two of our brothers in [their confraternal] gown who offered water for the hands. The father corrector on the right and the guardian father on the left entered together into the oratory, and then the brothers, and then, after a brief prayer at the altar, they proceeded in good order to the upper pews and went to the other end, near the desks, where a large *ciambella* with anise, a round bread, and a small flask of water, with its crystal cup and napkin, had been prepared for each person. And after the father corrector had blessed the table, everyone began the repast, including the father [corrector], while one of our brothers continued to read meditations on the Passion. When the repast was finished, the father corrector pronounced a devout speech, and when he finished he left [the room]. And when the sacristans had blown out all the candles and closed everything up, one of our brothers sang the *Recordemini fratres carissimi*. When it was finished the brothers carried out the discipline ['fecero la disciplina'] and at the same time the Abbot Pitti delivered a devout sermon, after which the signal for the brothers to stop was given, and two of our brothers sang the verses of the Passion. When the door to the oratory was opened, the Crucifix was brought in, accompanied by Anton Filippo Ridolfi, who had been assigned the oration, and by four other [brothers] with lighted candles in hand. When they reached the altar they all knelt, and the orator began the oration with great feeling. When he finished, he placed the crucifix on the floor, where a carpet ['strato'] had been prepared, and he adored it, and then all the brothers [adored it], all the while singing the *Stabat mater*. When this function was finished the Crucifix was brought back to its place, thanks was given, and everyone went to his own devotions.[20]

This is clearly a case of flagellation, carried out according to standard practices. It involved a few, select individuals from the confraternity who met early on Good Friday morning to perform the ritual. It was repeated the following year, for the scribe clearly states that 'all ceremonies as in the previous year were carried out with great devotion.'[21] It then disappears from the records, which return instead to what had been the standard description of the confraternity's Good Friday rituals:

Good Friday, the 18th. In the evening the Office was sung with good music, and when it was finished the oration to the Most Holy Crucifix was delivered by Andrea Salvini, our brother, with spirit, devotion, and universal satisfaction, and when the Angelic Salutation was said the *tornata* ended.[22]

The word 'devotion' could, at times, indicate the Good Friday flagellation ritual. The Latin term *devotio* had been used as early as 1260 in an edict of the commune of Perugia to refer to the flagellation ritual of that city's *disciplinati*.[23] It was a widespread movement, which involved not only devout men, but women and children as well. An anonymous Paduan chronicle narrates:

Such was the fear of God engendered in them that nobles as well as the low-born, old men and young, children of only five years, processed through the *piazze* of the city stripped to the waist. Covered in shame ... they marched two by two each carrying a whip with which they continuously beat themselves on their shoulders until the blood began to flow, uttering groans and shrill lamentations ... Indeed not only by day but truly also by night with lit candles and in the coldest winters, hundreds, thousands and ten thousand processed through the cities and churches, prostrating themselves with humility in front of the altars, led by priests with crosses and banners.[24]

The chronicler Marchionne Stefani (1336–85) tells that for several days in 1375 processions of twenty thousand or more people, including as many as five thousand flagellants, wound their way through the streets of Florence, singing lauds and carrying reliquaries. Stefani makes it a point to note that among the flagellants there were youths as young as ten years of age.[25]

These early references to children participating in public processions and flagellating themselves are closely tied to particular public penitential movements. Such general movements do not recur in subsequent centuries, but occasional penitential processions, with flagellants, do reappear from time to time. As late as 1522 Baldassar Castiglione described one such procession in Rome and pointed out that there was 'a great number of little boys ['puttini'], all naked from the belt up, who went on procession flagellating themselves and calling for mercy saying *Parce Domine populo tuo* ... and with them there are people that make them proceed in order and give them food ... [and] this praying by those innocent [youths] moved people greatly, and so may the Almighty be moved and let him hold back the sword of justice that is certainly about to strike in many ways, and the Turk is one of the worst.'[26] Such processions, however, were not the norm. It is clear from Castiglione's words that the presence of children flagellating themselves was highly unusual.

When these references are considered in context, the suggestion that the youths of the Arcangelo Raffaello flagellated themselves regularly remains untenable. The regular Good Friday ceremony consists of the Office, a devotion, an oration, and the ritual of the Adoration of the Cross. There is only one explicit description of a flagellation ritual, and it is very late (1687). The confraternity's extant records do not describe or speak directly of a flagellation ritual at any other time in its history. The manner in which the 1687 'devotion' is entered and described in the records suggests that it was an extraordinary event. More than anything else, it probably reflects a moment of extreme pietism within Florentine society during the reign of Cosimo III, and not a general practice.[27] The suggestion that flagellation was a regular Good Friday devotional ritual and that the scribe simply did not enter it into the *ricordi* because it was not 'special' is refuted by the unending stream of prosaic entries recalling devotional practices that occurred with monotonous regularity.

Our modern mind harbours, undeniably, a morbid curiosity about ritual flagellation, especially when carried out by a group of men meeting in private, behind closed doors, and in the dark – as was generally the case in medieval and Renaissance confraternities. There is also a strong inclination on our part to say that youths did not indulge in such severe mortification. These responses, however, are conditioned by modern assumptions and attitudes. They are more of a hindrance than a help in examining the entire question of ritual flagellation.

The only conclusion we can draw from the records of the Arcangelo Raffaello is that its members did, indirectly, imply flagellation in the habit they wore, the objects they occasionally used, and the practices they sometimes carried out, and that on two occasions at least, late in the seventeenth century, a small group of them did actually take the scourge. Aside from this, it is difficult to claim that self-flagellation was a common practice in the youth confraternity of the Arcangelo Raffaello.[28]

## Personal Devotions

According to the statutes, a brother's devotional life was not to be led only in the context of confraternal meetings, but also in the world at large. Already in 1435 Ambrogio Traversari, as we saw earlier (ch. 1, above), had noted that the youths applied the moral teachings they received in the confraternity to their conduct in the world and thus, with their example, inspired those around them to improve their ways. The statutes thus advise the youths to recite certain prayers throughout the day, conduct themselves appropriately, and avoid untoward activities.

The 1468 statutes instructed brothers first of all to be obedient to the Church, to the guardian father, and to the confraternity statutes, as well as to their father and mother, and to their superiors. They then instructed the youths to recite certain prayers: five Our Fathers and five Hail Marys every day, one Our Father and one Hail Mary each time they sat down or rose from the table, and seven Our Fathers and seven Hail Marys every Monday for the souls of the deceased. Every morning each brother was to hear Mass (or be present at Elevation). And if he visited a site where the Sacrament was present, he was to recite seven Our Fathers and Hail Marys. This cycle of prayers was supplemented by regular contribution to the collection plate (one *quattrino* every Sunday and holiday of obligation), by fasting on appointed days, monthly confessions, and twice-yearly communion in the confraternity (at Christmas and Pentecost).

These actions were then complemented by appropriate behaviour both inside and outside the confraternity. Brothers were to keep themselves chaste and, if they had 'that most precious and angelic gift,' to remain virgin. Those who married were to observe the sacrament as the Church commanded. Brothers were not to play or watch games, especially those forbidden by the Church. They were not to curse, gossip, or lie. And they were not to frequent taverns or night spots where 'dishonest' dancing, music, or singing took place. They were not to take part in jousts (*giostre*), fights (*schermaglie*), or other such spectacles of the masses (*expectaculi popolari*).[29] A second chapter in the 1468 statutes (ch. xiii) repeats some of the above instructions (modest demeanour, obedience to parents, meekness with everyone) reiterates the injunctions against games and gambling, and adds an immediate ejection from the confraternity for anyone who should fall into 'the wicked and horrible vice of sodomy.' The brothers were urged to gather on Sundays and feast-days in groups of youths of similar age and visit churches or other pious sites, converse of God, virtue, and Sacred Writ, read sacred writings and lives of the saints, and attend sermons, vespers, and divine offices.[30]

The 1468 statutes thus outline not only a ritual, but also a way of life that each brother was expected to follow. Prayers were complemented by actions, and unacceptable behaviour was identified and forbidden. By listing undesirable practices, those who drafted the statutes pointed out clearly the evils the confraternity was trying to counteract: idleness, cursing, gaming, rowdiness, and sodomy.

By the seventeenth century the confraternity's demographics had changed and the older, wealthier membership appeared not to be as concerned with behaviour outside hall. Although the revised statutes of 1636 give detailed instructions on behaviour and rituals inside the confraternity, they do not discuss a brother's behaviour or devotional life once he stepped outside.

Under the rubric 'General and particular duties,' the 1636 statutes recall King David's words 'I will freely sacrifice unto thee I will praise thy name, O Lord' (Psalm 54:6) and suggest that brothers do the same; but they do not outline the times and manners of such prayers, nor do they explicitly refer to actions and behaviour to be eschewed. They limit themselves, instead, to recalling that brothers ought to lead their lives 'under the glorious banner of our saintly father the Archangel Raphael' and recite, as a sign of their subjection (*vassallaggio*) to him, the hymn, antiphon, and prayer usually sung in his praise. The statutes' other directive on personal devotions touches upon the commemoration of deceased brothers, urging the living to offer the *tornata* immediately following a brother's death for the salvation of the deceased man's soul and to say, privately, a Rosary for the same intention.[31]

There is not, in the 1636 statutes, the concern evident in the 1468 statutes with the frequency and type of devotions to be carried out outside the confraternity itself, nor with behaviour to be avoided. Unlike the 1468 statutes, the 1636 ones never once use the word *vizio*. Clearly, the newly reformed confraternity was not concerned with monitoring its members' behaviour outside the confraternity walls. Although a certain type of conduct was obviously preferable, the confraternity itself did not dictate the manner of that conduct. The individual thus became an independent believer who attended the regular meetings of his confraternity as if he were attending those of any other organization to which he belonged; in return, the organization did not impose strict guidelines on his behaviour elsewhere. The change is subtle, but the shift in direction is drastic. No longer was the confraternity brother obliged to go out into the world to spread the Good News through his personal example, as Traversari had observed and the 1468 statutes had dictated, but he came into the confraternity to find comfort and faith through highly formalized rituals, exquisite music, and amazing spectacle. This, in short, reflects the post-Tridentine spirituality of the confraternity, whereby ritual devotions within a very localized setting supplanted the educative and evangelical components of the confraternity's life. In post-Tridentine Catholicism, the parish church became the official site for Christian education and evangelism, thus turning the confraternity into a private, devotional, and contemplative retreat for its members.

# 12

# Confraternity Feasts and Devotions

Aside from the regular schedule of weekly prayer meetings and daily personal devotions, members of the Arcangelo Raffaello celebrated a number of feasts that held specific meaning for them. First and foremost was the festivity in honour of their patron, the Archangel Raphael, which they observed annually on 31 December. The feast-day of their advocate, St Mary Magdalene, was observed in late July. For a time in the mid-sixteenth century, the early August feast-day of St Lawrence was also commemorated at the confraternity. As the years passed and older members died, the feast of All Saints' became particularly important, for it linked current members with their deceased predecessors. Then, in the wake of post-Tridentine sacramental reaffirmation, the devotion of the Forty Hours also became a significant (and expensive) annual ritual at the Arcangelo Raffaello. In this chapter we will examine each of these feasts, describe how the youths celebrated them, and gauge their importance for the confraternity.

## Feast of the Archangel Raphael (31 December)

The 1468 statutes mention only one feast-day the confraternity was to celebrate, that of St Mary Magdalene (22 July). Those of 1636 drop St Mary Magdalene and mention instead the feast-day of the Archangel Raphael, Shrove Tuesday, Wednesday in Holy Week, Maundy Thursday, and Good Friday.[1]

The revised list is indicative of a changing confraternity. By the late sixteenth century, the feast-day of St Mary Magdalene, the confraternity's spiritual advocate (*avvocata*), lost its major significance for the youths, so much so that its observance was transferred to the Sunday following the feast-day. The feast-day of the confraternity's patron saint (*protettore*), the

Archangel Raphael, on the other hand, which the confraternity celebrated on 31 December, had gained in importance and was added to the confraternity's list of obligatory holy days. By the seventeenth century it had become 'la nostra festa principale,' and a contemporary description of the confraternity noted charmingly that 'there is no reliable information as to why it is celebrated on this day, except that it is an ancient practice, and some claim that in such a day St Tobias returned to his father's house.'[2] For my part, I would venture a guess that the reason might perhaps be tied to the fact that the confraternity's first permanent location, next to the Ospedale della Scala, was in the convent of San Silvestro, whose feast-day falls on 31 December.

There may be several reasons for the change from a July to a December feast. One may be the weather – late July is not a comfortable time to be in Florence. Such a simple and mundane fact may have become an important consideration as confraternity membership changed to include a significant number of upper-class youths whose families did, in fact, move to country villas to escape the summer heat.[3] Late December, on the other hand, did not see an exodus of brothers to their family's estates, and therefore was a more suitable time for a collective celebration of the confraternity's patron saint.

In line with this observation, the confraternity's changing demography may very well have been a factor. As it began to draw its membership from a wealthier and nobler social class, youths from bureaucratic or aristocratic families closely tied to the Medici court would naturally have had a lesser interest in the penitent hermit Magdalene and a greater interest in the beautiful archangel Raphael, 'one of the seven angels who stand in attendance on the Lord and enter his glorious presence' (Tobit 12:15). In their minds that 'Lord' could easily have been either the One in heaven or the one in the Palazzo Pitti. And, as it happened, the one in the Palazzo Pitti was a member of the Arcangelo Raffaello himself.

Lastly, the confraternity's fortunes rose significantly after the Grand Duchess Christine attended the confraternity's celebrations for the feast-day of the Archangel Raphael in 1591. She had been so impressed by the youths' singing and devotions that she enrolled her son, the future Grand Duke Cosimo II, into the brotherhood. The greater emphasis on the feast-day of the beautiful archangel rather than the penitent hermit may therefore also be in honour and commemoration of such princely interest and participation in the confraternity, not to mention in gratitude to the archangel himself for having somehow contributed to the confraternity's advancement on earth.

The feast of the Archangel Raphael thus developed as the confraternity's showpiece, as the once-yearly celebration of itself and its prestige. The scribe's description of the 1563 festivities is particularly informative, for it indicates not only that in the mid-sixteenth century special attention was being given to the feast and that the youths had already altered their devotional rituals to conform with the Roman Ritual (*Rituale Romanum*), but also that the feast incorporated more secular activities such as the distribution of blessed bread and the staging of a theatrical event. Planning started several weeks before, at the beginning of December, when a number of youths were appointed *provveditori* and *festaiuoli* to supervise the preparations and to run the special events at the feast.

In 1563 four youths were chosen to supervise, and twelve to organize, the feast. Another four were appointed to arrange for the *panellini*, the small buns with the confraternity's emblem impressed on them that were to be distributed to all present,[4] and they were given twelve more youths to assist them in this task. In all, thirty-two youths were charged with the preparations for the event.

The feast-day started with a solemn High Mass at the confraternity's main altar, celebrated by a Dominican priest from Santa Maria Novella as part of that convent's yearly obligations to the confraternity. The Office of the Virgin Mary was then recited, followed by a Low Mass, again at the main altar, celebrated this time by the father corrector. Communion was then given to past and present members. At this point the canonical sequence of prayers came to an end and the *tornata* proceeded to the more secular aspects of the celebration.

After communion, as all the brothers sat in their pews, the four *provveditori* in charge of providing the *panellini* came into the oratory together with their twelve *festaiuoli* dressed in white confraternal robes. The *festaiuoli* carried containers (*bacini*) full of bread, and sang a *lauda*. They all bowed first to the altar and then to the guardian's desk at the other end of the hall. They then knelt in a semicircle in front of the altar. The father corrector blessed the bread. He then took each garland of flowers from on top of the bread in each container, placed it on the head of the *festaiuolo* who had carried the basket, and then blessed the garlanded youths.[5] The *festaiuoli* then carried away the containers, still full of *panellini*, while the confraternity sang a *lauda* and the father corrector went to sit at his place. From his place at the desk he signalled to a youth who entered into the oratory dressed not in confraternal robes but rather in costume as the little boy Tobias. The youth recited some admonitory verses to the confraternity's outgoing and incoming officers (the change of officers would take place the following day, on 1 January). Tobias then declared that he wished to distribute the *panellini* himself with the assistance of two Virtues. At this point he went to the door of the smaller oratory (*tornantino*) used for morning prayers and called out two more youths, who entered dressed as the allegorical figures Humility and Obedience and addressed some more verses to all present. Then Tobias called out the twelve *festaiuoli* who had earlier brought out the baskets of *panellini*, and, with the help of Humility and Obedience, they distributed the buns to all present while the confraternity sang the Te Deum antiphonally. Tobias then gave everyone licence to go, the Ave Maria was rung, and the youths departed.

The confraternity reconvened in the afternoon for Vespers, sung with organ accompaniment. At the end one of the youths delivered a sermon. In the evening the youths reconvened for a third time to recite Matins and hear a second sermon, this time from their father corrector.[6]

The sequence of rituals (Masses, Vespers, Matins) and the distribution of *panellini* remained a constant in the celebration of the feast of the Archangel Raphael. The theatrical interlude with Tobias, on the other hand, was not always included. Other times, such as in 1591 when the Grand Duchess Christine of Lorraine was present, the youths, dressed as angels, simply sang madrigals and other lyrical pieces. They then proceeded to distribute the buns to all present, including the grand-ducal party.

By the mid-seventeenth century, the youths indulged themselves in elaborate decorations for their feast-day, as the *ricordo* for 31 December 1642 points out:

The first *stanzone* was all decorated with tapestries, above which were hung large paintings by well-known artists. The paintings had very rich ornaments. Around them were draped brightly coloured cloths of taffeta or twill and pine branches. By the oratory door there was an exquisite painting of the Madonna, with a gilded frame. Around this painting and the door red taffeta was hung to form drapes and bows in marvellous order. The altar in the *stanzone* was richly decorated with silver vases and candlestick holders, with plenty of lights and flowers.

The oratory was all decorated with red and yellow taffeta. There were paintings by known artists all around, with rich ornaments. Above them there were pine branches, and below them cotton wool festoons that went all the way around the oratory. Festoons representing apples, fruits, and flowers held by angels were hung on the wall above the balcony for the musicians, and the arms of the del Vivaio family were visible on them since Alberto del Vivaio, our brother and benefactor, had paid for them. The wall by the altar was likewise decorated with red and yellow taffeta. Cotton wool and pinchbeck festoons beautifully arranged hung from the window jambs and from the painting above the altar. The altar was enriched with a great number of lights, candlestick holders, and silver vases, very beautiful and very rich reliquaries, fresh flowers and dried flowers, all arranged in the most beautiful manner.

This display was similar to those that were set up in past years.[7]

The opulence evident in these displays was stunning, so much so that in 1649 the scribe feels the need to comment, saying that the apparatus that year 'was one of the richest and most noble in many years, and for this reason it was deemed appropriate to describe it in the *ricordo* so that youths would be moved to give themselves eagerly to the service of God.' The scribe then concludes, not without betraying his own insecurities about such displays: 'May it please the Blessed Lord that the conscience of the brothers and their devotions compare with the apparatus and the richness of the festivity so that under all aspects service to God and the well-being of the Confraternity be comparable.'[8]

By the end of the seventeenth century, the scribe's assessment of the feast had lost any spiritual considerations and was based on purely secular criteria. The entry for 31 December 1687 is emblematic in its brevity and directness: 'The feast was very beautiful not only because of the magnificent decorations but also because of the quantity of silver objects that were on the main altar.'[9] The silence about any devotional or festive elements of the celebration and the unabashed interest in the display of silver objects underscore the assumption that only the quality of the decorations and the display of confraternity wealth were worthy of mention.

The feast was clearly the highlight of the confraternity's devotional calendar. As such it was attended by the guardians of the other major Florentine youth confraternities, in particular those of the Purificazione, San Giovanni Evangelista, and San Niccolò del Ceppo, whose presence strengthened the bonds and reaffirmed the pre-eminence of the four original youth confraternities in the city.

From the late sixteenth century, the feast was also attended by members of the grand-ducal family. The Grand Duchess Christine of Lorraine and her ladies and gentlemen in waiting attended the feast in 1590, 1591, and several other times afterwards. In the seventeenth century, subsequent grand duchesses, not to mention the grand duke himself, his brothers, visiting dignitaries, the archbishop, members of the higher clergy, and eminent Florentine bureaucrats, also attended the confraternity's feast. When Archbishop Niccolini attended in 1646 he turned the occasion into a reaffirmation of his special interest and care for the confraternity of his youth:

> In the afternoon we did not recite Vespers, but kept the confraternity open all day long. There constantly was a large number of people participating in the confraternity, and in particular Monsignor Archbishop, our brother, who said that he still felt affection for the Company and had been very eager to come over in person to the Company and to the festivities to show the brothers that he remembered them and will always hold the place and all the brothers under his continued protection.[10]

The pre-eminence and importance of this feast in the confraternity's festive calendar did not lead, however, to the creation of a special liturgy in honour of the Archangel Raphael. All descriptions of the celebrations indicate that the youths were satisfied, liturgically, with the celebration of Masses, and the recitation of the standard Vespers, and Office for the 31st of December. These rites were embellished with music, sermons, the recitation or singing in costume of a few appropriate verses, and with the distribution of *panellini* to all present. There is no indication in the surviving documents that the readings for the Masses, Vespers, and the Office had anything to do with the Archangel Raphael or the Tobias story. Christ and the Virgin Mary remained at the centre of the confraternity's liturgical devotions by virtue of the standard rites of Mass, Vespers, and Office, while the archangel and his young charge were consigned, instead, to the youths' non-liturgical imagination by having them literally walk into the hall after communion, talk to those present, and distribute food. Tobias and the archangel thus entered into the young men's imagination not as devotional but as celebratory objects, as part of a festive mythology created by costume, recitation, and acting.[11]

### St Mary Magdalene

St Mary Magdalene was the confraternity's 'spiritual advocate' (*avvocata*). Her feast-day was celebrated in the Arcangelo Raffaello as early as the fifteenth century, when it was the only special festivity to be so recognized in the 1468 statutes – 'The times when we must gather for our orations and devotions shall be all the holy days of obligations commanded by the Holy Church and especially ['maximamente'] the day of St Mary Magdalene after dinner.'[12] By the late sixteenth century she had begun to share her special place with the Archangel Raphael and to be referred in the *ricordi* as the confraternity's co-titular saint (*contitolare*).

The confraternity's celebrations for her feast-day on 22 July (or on the Sunday following) conformed to the pattern already described for the feast of the Archangel Raphael – *festaiuoli* were appointed a few weeks in advance, the celebrations contained both liturgical and secular elements, and the event was attended by guardians from the other confraternities. In 1585, for example, the confraternity's scribe recalls that on Sunday, 7 July, fourteen *festaiuoli* were appointed for the forthcoming feast. Then on Sunday, 28 July, he writes that the confraternity gathered in the morning in the oratory, which had been beautifully decorated with gilt leather and with portraits of illustrious persons around the walls above the lateral pews. The Office of the Virgin was sung by confraternity youths accompanied by Raffaello di Ser Francesco Gucci on his *buonaccordo*,[13] and then Mass was celebrated. Once the services were finished, five costumed youths entered into the oratory, one dressed as St Mary Magdalene and the other four as angels. The Magdalene youth, Camillo Rondinelli, recited a few verses, and then the *festaiuoli* distributed to each person a bunch of flowers and a ring-shaped sweet cake (*berlingozzo*). At the end the Ave Maria was sung and everyone was dismissed. The scribe also recalls that the guardian fathers of the three other confraternities mentioned in the 1442 papal bull attended the festivities. Their presence was part of the annual series of reciprocal visits among the four original confraternities. In the afternoon Vespers were recited. The scribe points out that on this occasion Fr. Jacopo Genovese, a priest of the cardinal archbishop of Florence, and Jacopo Ansaldi, who had been appointed by the archbishop to supervise the introduction of the teaching of Christian doctrine in schools and youth confraternities, attended Vespers.[14]

The obvious parallels between the celebrations of the Archangel Raphael and St Mary Magdalene suggest that they were, by and large, viewed in the same vein. The distribution of baked goods, *panellini* for one and *berlingozzi* for the other, linked them together, as did the recitation of sermons and the occasional inclusion of a theatrical presentation. The latter, to be sure, was not always present, but it is clear that when the youths did stage theatrical representations they seemed to prefer to do so on the feasts of the Archangel Raphael or St Mary Magdalene.

The reasons why the youths should originally have been interested in St Mary Magdalene are not clear. Some suggestions, however, can be advanced. For one, the confraternity did find its roots in the penitential movement that swept Florence and Italy at the end of the fourteenth and beginning of the fifteenth century. It would be natural, then, for the youths or their adult supporters to choose a penitential figure, especially one whose own conversion away from a life of carnal sin to a life of prayer and penance could draw young men away from the flesh and towards the spirit. It may not be a coincidence that the repentant prostitute should be brought to the youths' attention and devotions just as they, in the flower of their adolescence and manhood, discovered their sexuality and risked falling, like the Magdalene, into the sinful world of the flesh. Examining how Florentines viewed *fanciulli* and *giovani*, and differentiating between the two age groups, Richard Trexler points out that the *giovani*, aged twenty-four to thirty-five, were given a free rein to satisfy their sexual urges.[15] In a way, then, the redeemed prostitute could be seen as a suitable protector and deterrent for youths about to enter this phase of unbridled sexual expectations. Other penitential figures would not have served the purpose as well. The penitent St Jerome, an elderly cardinal and a learned Church Father much venerated in some adult confraternities, would not, for example, have been as pertinent.

Another reason might be that both the Magdalene and the Archangel Raphael were considered to be 'healers.' This correlation is strikingly made in a painting of *St Mary Magdalene, the Archangel Raphael and Tobias with Commissioner* (Firenze, Fondazione Horne), in which both the saint and the archangel are depicted carrying vials of ointment in their hands.

The Magdalene was also especially venerated by the Dominicans as a great protector of their order. The Dominican churches and convents of Florence observed her feast-day, as did the confraternity of Santa Maria Maddalena de' Bianchi, which met near the hospital of Santa Maria Nuova.[16] It is not unfeasible that St Antoninus, or perhaps a later Dominican who took an interest in the youths of the Arcangelo Raffaello, may have fostered such a devotion in the confraternity. Such, in fact, had been the case in the youths' commemoration of St Lawrence.

## St Lawrence

According to the confraternity's records, on 10 August 1558, the feast of St Lawrence, the father corrector, fra Santi Cini, OP, had set in motion a renewal and reform of the confraternity's lax practices and devotions. The following year, on the anniversary of this event, the youths commemorated it by constructing a small set (*parato*) on which one of the youths recited an *esempio* from the saint's life and sang a *lauda*, by saying Vespers, and then by consuming a watermelon snack:

On Saturday 10 August, before Vespers, one of our brothers recited an example from the life of St Lawrence, and then said his *lauda*. Then Vespers started, and when it was finished one of our elders called upon some of the younger members to distribute, with the help of two other youths, the watermelons ['cocomeri'] that were in some basins. Everything was done with fine order. And while we ate the melons, one of our brothers played a lyre and some other brothers sang *laude* and spiritual things. We began to celebrate this feast in the year 1559.[17]

Not only is the manner of the festivity significant – containing as it did recitation, singing, prayer, and food – but so is the scribe's concluding comment. After describing the celebrations he adds 'and so St Lawrence was taken up with our other advocate saints.'[18] By 1563 the saint had entered so much into the confraternity's spirituality that he was included in the invocation at the beginning of the volume of *Partiti e deliberazioni* together with the other saints whom the confraternity had traditionally held in special reverence – the Archangel Raphael, the Holy Innocents, St Mary Magdalene, and St Jerome.[19]

The nature of the festivity for St Lawrence is slightly different, however, from the celebrations already described for the other patron saints. On the feast-days of the Archangel Raphael and St Mary Magdalene, there is never any indication that either the *panellini* or the *berlingozzi* were consumed on the premises. On the feast of St Lawrence, on the other hand, the water-melons were actually eaten on site.

Food, I would argue, played an important part in confraternity life and ritual. We are clearly not dealing, in this case, with the indecent bacchanalia that Martin Luther alleged were taking place in confraternities where 'you have nothing but gluttony, drunkenness, useless squandering of money, howling, yelling, chattering, dancing, and wasting of time.'[20] We are, on the other hand, becoming aware of the importance for confraternity brothers not only of sacramental communion but also of communal eating. Nerida Newbigin has already pointed out the importance of food in the *feste* of the confraternities of Sant'Agnese and of the Spirito Santo.[21] In a somewhat different context the same insight could be applied to the *panellini, berlingozzi*, and *cocomeri* consumed by the youths of the Arcangelo Raffaello. There is, in these three items, a definite festive element. The first two have a quasi-sacred connotation – the baked breads and sweets were blessed, distributed to the membership, and then taken home to be consumed, supposedly with some kind of reverence, within the family. It was a way of bringing the confraternity's feast out of the oratory and into the home. And, in some way, it reminds us of Ambrogio Traversari's comments to Pope Eugenius IV about the youth going home and influencing their parents with their example. The *panellini*, distributed for the feast-day of the Archangel Raphael, were stamped with the confraternity's emblem and some were even brought, in an official manner, to the grand duke himself.

Their sacrality, through their connection with the host – which also bore a stamp – is undeniable. The watermelon feast, on the other hand, is something quite different. This is not a quasi-sacred, baked product to be consumed with respect, but 'fun' food that cannot be eaten with dignity. One is led to wonder, therefore, whether fra Santi Cini may not have been more astute and jovial than his saintly reputation would at first lead us to believe – the presence of twenty watermelons and many more teenaged males eating them together must have turned this celebration of the confraternity's recent renewal into a lively *festa del cocomero*, that is, into a relaxed summertime activity. The bonding it celebrated and promoted was something the teenaged males of fra Santi's group would have understood and appreciated much more readily than the sacramental rituals of the *panellini* and *berlingozzi*. And this may, in part, explain the immediate success of the newly founded festivity.[22]

Eventually, however, St Lawrence did not remain an important figure in the confraternity's devotional calendar. The saint's presence in the invocation was the first to disappear. In 1581 the *scrivano* Girolamo Adriani did not mention him at the beginning of his *Ricordi e Partiti*.[23] The August feast-day continued to be celebrated with watermelons for a few more years. In 1583, the *scrivano* Alessandro Ghettini entered it into the record and recalled that several watermelons (*cocomeri*) were distributed to the youths, a gift from Domenico Comi.[24] Soon thereafter, however, they are no longer mentioned and the feast-day passes without any special event or recollection on the part of the confraternity. St Lawrence clearly did not last, possibly because of lack of strong interest in him, possibly because the special morning *tornata* ceased to be as active, and possibly because the very manner of the celebration was no longer attractive to the membership. Or, as in the case of the feast-day of St Mary Magdalene, the heat of summer and the changing demography of the confraternity had simply undermined participation at the event.

## All Saints'

Another feast closely associated with fra Santi Cini, who is credited in the *ricordi* with having determined the manner of its celebration, was that of All Saints' (1 November). The 1559 description runs as follows:

> The morning of All Saints' we gathered in the usual place in the manner of last year, as established and decreed by our father fra Santi Cini, our former corrector, who decreed that this *tornata* be held every year on such a day, considering how useful

such a *tornata* would be. And he decreed that there be communion and other prayers and petitions [recited] for the deceased. Last year we exhibited the Sacrament from the morning of All Saints' to the morning of All Souls', but no Mass was celebrated since we were not able to obtain one that morning from either Santa Maria Novella or anywhere else. This year, however, a morning Mass was celebrated by [a priest from] Santa Maria Novella, and so we did not exhibit the sacrament since we had had this service. Then, after the seven Penitential Psalms and the litanies with a Requiem Aeterna we recited the first Nocturn of the Dead, and when it was finished the father [corrector] delivered an exhortation and then celebrated Holy Mass, after which he distributed Communion to about [blank] brothers. Because it had rained in the morning we were not as many as last year, nevertheless we were not few.

I, Carlo [Ghettini], the current scribe, urge all those who will read this entry to ensure that this devotion be carried out, not only to have Mass celebrated, but also to expose the Sacrament on the morning of All Saints', as we did last year and as was ordered by fra Santi, for this will please the Highest God very much and you will benefit and help those poor souls who await such a day with great expectation, and this I urge you as much as I can, begging you also that the same be done for me.[25]

By the 1580s this simple celebration, consisting of a Requiem Mass, Communion, prayers, and the exposition of the Sacrament, had grown to include extensive musical presentations and the presence or participation of eminent guests. As in the case of the confraternity's other major feasts, an elaborate *apparato* was set up in the oratory. In this case, it consisted primarily of a catafalque and accompanying funereal decorations.

The nature of the occasion soon gave free rein to a mannerist or even baroque penchant for the lugubrious, as is evident in the description of the 1583 *apparato* and celebrations. That day the illustrious guests included Giuseppe Donzelli, archbishop of Sorrento, at the time papal nuncio to Florence,[26] Giovan Battista Milanese, retired bishop of Marsi,[27] Mons. d'Aragona,[28] and several other canons from the Duomo.

The musical components of the feast were ornate and various. The Office was sung by two of the brothers, the lessons were sung by the young singers from the company, after each nocturne a madrigal was sung. The Miserere and the Benedictus were arranged by Michelangelo Mollazzi, a member of the confraternity and its long-time *maestro di cappella*.[29] After the Office, fra Andrea from the convent of Santo Spirito delivered a sermon on death with such liveliness ('con tanta leggiadria') that all were satisfied ('soddisfatti'). Clearly the form, and not the content, had made an impression. The music, the guest speaker, and the honoured guests had attracted such a crowd that four rows of chairs at each side of the oratory were not enough to accommodate all the spectators, so some had to stand in the middle of the oratory and the overflow spilled out and filled the *stanzone*.[30]

The following year, 1584, music again played a spectacular role in the commemoration of All Saints'. Because Michelangelo Mollazzi was no longer *maestro di cappella*, the confraternity made do with two other members. Raffaello Gucci taught some younger members the music for the lessons, while Giulio Caccini, who was at that time *maestro di cappella* at the grand-ducal court, orchestrated the three madrigals that had been sung the previous year. Caccini also brought along a young castrato who lived with him.[31] The castrato's contribution must have been impressive, for he accompanied himself on a lyre and sang the Miserere and the Benedictus from inside the catafalque that had been erected in the middle of the oratory, in alternating verses with the choir, all of which made for 'un bel sentire.'[32] The castrato's special vocal qualities must have made an eerie impression, as of a voice from the grave, and his duet with the choir the chilling effect of a dialogue with the dead. A similar lugubrious technique was again used in 1585 when Raffaello Gucci, hidden in the catafalque, played his *buonaccordo* and sang solo as if from the grave.

As time passed, the festivity become an occasion to remember those who had died in the past year. And as the confraternity's success in the late sixteenth and early seventeenth century had swelled the membership rolls, so too it increased the number of recently deceased brothers who needed to be remembered in the mid-seventeenth century. Carlo Ghettini, the 1559 scribe, had asked that the devotion be carried out from year to year so that he, too, might enjoy the benefit of such services. By 1651, the current scribe recalled that 330 masses for the repose of the souls of departed brothers had been celebrated in the confraternity that year.[33] It seems as if the organization was fast becoming a society for the commemoration of the deceased. Inevitably, a significant portion of the members' devotional time was taken up by the obligations they were accumulating with the souls of their departed brothers in Purgatory.

The burden imposed by the deceased both by way of commemorative masses and attendance at funerals is evident in a decision of 1651 no longer to accompany the bodies of deceased women to burial. Escorting the deceased to their grave had long been a confraternal practice. In recent years, however, the confraternity had been called upon to escort not only their deceased brothers, but their relatives as well, including even some women. The situation had become critical, and the confraternity was thus obliged to re-examine its charity. To solve the problem it decided that henceforth it would accompany only its own members, and then only when specifically asked to do so.[34] Although this regulation did alleviate the burden, it did not solve the problem entirely, for the confraternity remained, even throughout the seventeenth century, firmly committed to the continued commemoration of its departed brothers. As its role in the education of the young was being undermined by the changes in religious education introduced by the Council of Trent and the synodal decrees that followed it (see ch. 7), the confraternity slowly changed its focus towards the needs of its deceased members.

## The Feast of the Purification, or *Candelora*

On 2 February, the confraternity celebrated the feast of the Purification of the Virgin Mary with a particular ceremony and a visit to its sister confraternity of the Purificazione della Vergine e di San Zanobi, detta di San Marco. The first record of such an event dates from 1582, though subsequent references indicate that at least some components of the feast had been in place for some time.

The confraternity met in the morning to recite the Office. The father corrector then blessed some candles and distributed them to all present (hence the name *Candelora*), after which he celebrated a Mass, the brothers took communion, recited a final Hail Mary, and were dismissed. At this point the guardian father, accompanied by a few brothers, went to the confraternity of San Marco to attend their principal feast, which, as their official name Compagnia della Purificazione della Beata Vergine Maria indicated, fell on this day. In this manner he continued the tradition of annual reciprocal visits among the guardians of the four original youth confraternities. In the afternoon Vespers were said. In the evening Matins were recited and one of the brothers delivered a sermon.[35]

The feast was clearly celebrated quite simply. The distinguishing feature was the blessing and distribution of candles. Only once was something more elaborate organized. On Saturday, 2 February 1585 a play by the notary and dramatist Giovan Maria Cecchi was staged in the evening after Matins had been recited and after a brother, Amerigo di Alessandro Temperami, had delivered a sermon.[36] Like the performances for the feast of the Archangel Raphael or of St Mary Magdalene, the play too was strictly tied to the day's commemoration, for it dealt with the presentation of Jesus to the Temple.[37] What was unusual, however, was that the play had been staged at least twice before, once elsewhere for an unspecified group and once just a few days before, on Sunday, 27 January, for the confraternity brothers. This performance, however, did not lead to a permanent elaboration of the *Candelora* ceremonies. It clearly remained a one-time experience which was not repeated in following years.

*Candelora* thus remained a feast associated not with the confraternity of the Arcangelo Raffaello per se, but with the Church's liturgical calendar and with the bond that united all the youth confraternities of Florence. The Purificazione was the second-oldest youth confraternity in the city, having been founded sometime before 1427 as an offshoot of the Arcangelo Raffaello itself (see above, ch. 2, p. 26). By visiting its oratory and participating in its annual feast, the guardian and brothers of the Arcangelo Raffaello were thus reaffirming and strengthening their common bond.

## The Devotion of the Forty Hours

In the wake of the Council of Trent, devotion to the Sacrament entered into the confraternity's religious ceremonies not only by way of the celebration of Mass and the taking of Communion, but also through the ritual of the Forty Hours (*Quarant'ore*).

The ritual traces its origins to the medieval practice of symbolically 'burying' the consecrated host in a special tabernacle during the Holy Week triduum to recall the period of Jesus' burial in the tomb, from late afternoon on Good Friday to sunrise on Easter Sunday. In so doing, the devout Christian was not only recalling a crucial moment in Salvation history, and adoring the consecrated host, considered to be the body and blood of Christ, but was also participating actively in this re-enactment of Salvation history by keeping 'guard' over the body of Christ with prayer and adoration. By the thirteenth century this Easter devotion was already known as the *Quadraginta horarum horatio*, from the forty hours that supposedly elapsed between the burial and the resurrection. It was not until 1527 in Milan, at the confraternity of the Santo Sepolcro and at the suggestion of the priest Antonio Bellotto (d. 1528), that this devotion extended to other special feasts, such as Pentecost, the Assumption, or Christmas. It soon spread outside the confraternity and into local churches. In Milan, St Antonio Zaccaria, founder of the Barnabites, was one of its most ardent supporters. The Capuchin Giuseppe Plantanida da Ferno di Gallarate (d. 1556) formalized the practice in writing and spread the devotion outside Milan. In 1537 Pope Paul III Farnese bestowed several indulgences to the devotion, and so did his successors, who, taking their cue from St Carlo Borromeo, further formalized and patronized it. In Rome the devotion found an early sponsor in St Filippo Neri and in the Compagnia della Morte, which carried it out every third Sunday of the month in the church of San Lorenzo in Damaso.[38]

The Arcangelo Raffaello in Florence adopted the Forty Hours as part of its yearly cycle of devotions. It seems the devotion was at first celebrated at Pentecost (*Spirito Santo*). Then, in 1572, it was transferred to the 'second day of Easter,' that is, on Easter Monday.[39] The ritual quickly grew to include an elaborate set (*apparato*) and a rigorous attendance schedule to ensure continual presence and adoration throughout the stipulated forty hours. By Easter 1583 the confraternity was appointing *cerimonieri* to organize not only the Easter festivities but the ensuing devotion of the Forty Hours as well.[40] By the seventeenth century the *apparato* had grown in splendour to rival the Christmas and the All Saints' sets. A description of the 1642 set will serve to indicate the baroque extravagance that by then was being showered on the yearly adoration of the Sacrament.[41]

The *stanzone* was decorated floor to ceiling with tapestries. On the walls hung a number of paintings by famous artists in gilded frames decorated with festoons (*goccioli*) of brightly coloured twill (*saie*). The altar of the Crucifix, at the right, carried a display of the confraternity's many relics, set in precious silver reliquiaries and surrounded by an appropriate number of lamps. Five years later Lorenzo Lippi's *Crucifixion*, a 1647 gift of the artist, would be placed on this altar, thus adding further lustre to its already rich decoration.

The walls of the oratory were decorated with sixteen canvases (4 × 3 *braccia* each) depicting the Passion, each decorated with twill festoons. The canvases had been donated by Domenico and Baccio Comi and were a chiaroscuro work by an anonymous artist. The oratory's high altar was contained in a small temporary chapel formed by an arch resting on two pilasters. The structure took up the entire front of the oratory and included two large lateral doors, richly decorated. The arch itself (*apertura*) was decorated with an image of the Flood, something that had been suggested and devised by the current guardian father, Giulio Guazzini.

The scribe explains that the image depicted the moment in which God said to Noah 'Arcum meum ponam' ('I will place my rainbow,' Genesis 9:13). It included an illustration of the dove returning with an olive branch in its beak and the crow feeding on cadavers. The ark was shown resting on Mount Ararat in Armenia, with water still around it. God the Father was depicted above the rainbow, while under it hovered an image of the Sacrament and of the dove of the Holy Spirit. Rays of light from the Sacrament and the Dove were shown drying the fields below and making plants grow. Above the arch there was a large tablet inscribed with the biblical verse 'Arcum meum ponam in nubibus, et erit signum federis inter me, et inter terram' ('I do set my bow in the cloud, and it shall be a token of the covenant between me and the earth,' KJV, Genesis 9:13). Two lateral tablets bore the inscriptions 'Et recordabor federis mei quod pepigi vobiscum' ('And I will remember my covenant which is between me and you,' KJV, Genesis 9:15) and 'Nequa quam ultra maledicam terre propter hominem' ('I will not again curse the ground any more for man's sake,' KJV, Genesis 8:21). Another tablet read 'Fiat pax in virtute tuam' ('Peace be within thy walls,' KJV, Psalm 122:7, Vulg. Psalm 121:7). And at the front of the *stanzone* there was yet another with the inscription 'Haec reparat iris iras' ('This rainbow repairs wraths'; the verse is not biblical).

The scribe glosses these images and inscriptions by pointing out that just as God, angered by mankind's sins and operating within the law of Justice, sent the Flood to renew the world, so too, under the law of Grace, he sent the flood of Christ's precious blood to make amends for Adam's sin and thus regenerate mankind through the death of the Redeemer. As the ark saved the human race and the different species of animals, so too the Cross saved mankind. The dove with an olive branch in its beak is a representation (*figura*) of the peace struck between God and mankind through the workings of the dove of the Holy Spirit. The crow feeding on cadavers is a representation of those who will not reap the fruits of the Passion of Christ but continue to linger on the dead bodies of earthly and sensual concerns. The rainbow is a sign that God will no longer take his revenge on mankind, but will keep his 'bow' unarmed towards those who have repented for their sins and have sought refuge in him.

The temporal chapel and its illustrations were the work of two members of the confraternity, the architect Pierfrancesco Silvani and the painter Lorenzo Lippi.[42] The scribe points out that the two artists went personally out of their way to ensure that everything was done and arranged perfectly, out of love for the confraternity and not for personal gain. In so doing, the scribe concludes, they showed themselves to be 'true followers and brothers of our Protector the Archangel Raphael.'

The confraternity remained open for the three days of devotions comprised by Easter Sunday and the Forty Hours. A large number of people, both members and non-members, visited the site to view the *parato* and participate in the adoration. They also came to hear a number of sermons recited by some of the younger members of the confraternity ('fanciulletti di puerile età').

On the third day, after evening Matins, the devotion ended and the substitute father corrector carried the Sacrament in solemn procession back to the appropriate tabernacle in the smaller oratory, accompanied by confraternity youths wearing their gowns and carrying torches.

Financing such an elaborate set and decorations was, obviously, a burden. Already in 1619 the carpenter's work and materials alone cost 20 *scudi*, the equivalent of one year's rent from the house the confraternity owned in Borgo Ognissanti or the yearly honorarium that was later given to the guardian father.[43] The confraternity had been fortunate enough to obtain, early in the seventeenth century, a testamentary endowment to assist in bearing the expenses for the Forty Hours. In a January 1604/5 codicil to his will, Domenico Comi left his farm of La Casellina in Ponte a Greve to his adopted son Filippo del Riccio and his heirs on condition that part of the revenues be used, among other things, to pay for the Forty Hours at the Arcangelo Raffaello.[44] Soon thereafter, however, the expenses incurred in the Forty Hours rose to such levels that Filippo del Riccio (who had by then changed his surname to Comi, in honour of his adoptive father) found them to be a severe burden. In 1622 he informed the confraternity that his wife would pay only 30 of the 40 *scudi* required because the 'poor harvest and other accidents' did not permit them to subsidize the expense in full. By 1661 Filippo's son, Domenico Comi the Younger, could not afford to pay at all and petitioned the grand duke to free him from this obligation.[45] It appears that eventually the Comi were obliged to forfeit the farm at La Casellina and hand it over to the confraternity, which thus acquired directly the rental income used to subsidize its three expenses of *panellini*, Forty Hours, and regular masses from the clergy of Santa Maria Novella.

The confraternity continued for some time to indulge itself in setting up an elaborate display and decorating its oratory lavishly. Two of the reasons for such opulence must have been the need to maintain the reputation it had acquired for such a spectacle and the honour it gathered from the annual visit by the grand duke and his family, who came to view and adore the Host in such a 'splendido apparato.'[46] Generous funding was somehow made available even as late as 1687. In time, however, the scribe ceased to wax eloquent about the splendid *apparato* or the princely visits, thus suggesting that the devotion became a more subdued event, a clear indication that funding was no longer sufficient to subsidize an elaborate display.

# 13

# Processions

The confraternity of the Arcangelo Raffaello participated in both public and private processions. In June, for example, it took part in the procession to honour the city's patron, St John the Baptist. In May/June it joined in the Corpus Domini procession. It also took part in occasional processions organized by the Florentine clergy, such as those to welcome the Madonna of Impruneta to Florence or to solicit God's favour or temper his wrath, as the case might be. Privately, the confraternity accompanied the bodies of deceased members to burial, or joined with the friars of Santa Maria Novella to honour the relic of St Thomas Aquinas. These and other processions constituted part of the confraternity's religious life at different times of the year and at different periods in its 374-year history.

Dress and behaviour in procession was strictly regulated by the confraternity statutes and the guardian father's authority. The 1468 statutes insisted that each brother own a white linen gown with an image of the Nativity on the right shoulder to be kept at the confraternity (not at home) and worn in public processions as the guardian father decided. In procession the brothers were to walk in good order, carry themselves with gravity and modesty, and have their minds at peace, so as to be a good example to people. They were also to sing hymns or lauds, as they were told. The confraternity's banner (*segno*), which bore an image of the Archangel Raphael guiding Tobias, was to be carried in the procession, adorned as the guardian father indicated.[1] The 1636 statutes are more specific, adding that the brothers should also wear a white belt, carry the rosary (*corona*) in their hands, and walk in twos with the shorter brothers at the front and the taller ones at the back, and that the guardian father should come last with 'the usual *segno* in his hands.'[2] The brothers should walk silently, 'step by step,' with decorum. Psalms or hymns could be sung, as directed by those with the authority to do so – probably the guardian father, the *maestro di cappella*, or the choir masters. In a funeral procession for a deceased brother a bier was to be carried in lieu of the *segno*.[3]

The 1636 statutes further mention that the confraternity generally participated in the 'solemn processions' for Corpus Domini and St John the Baptist 'by invitation,' presumably from the appropriate ecclesiastical authorities. Invitations to other processions, it says, were not to be accepted without permission from the guardian father, the *governatore*, the *provveditore*, the *consiglieri*, and the *conservatori*. In the case of funeral processions for non-members, the permission of the guardian father or, in his absence, the governor, sufficed, though they were to grant it not simply out of charity, but also if the good reputation of the confraternity was enhanced by it.[4]

Processions were thus a costumed, formalized ceremonial event, strictly regulated by both the old and new statutes, entered upon by invitation, and accepted on the basis of the good reputation that would accrue to the confraternity because of such participation. They were an act, therefore, not simply of devotion, but also of public display and honour through which the confraternity both bestowed and acquired reputation.

## The St John's Procession

The most important civic and religious festivity in Florence was organized to honour the city's patron saint, St John the Baptist, on his feast-day (24 June) and the days immediately preceding it.[5] There were civic and religious processions, horse races, offerings to the cathedral, and religious ceremonies. The chronicler Matteo Palmieri recalls that by the mid-fifteenth century the festivities included a secular parade (*mostra*) on the 22nd of June, a procession of the clergy and confraternities on the morning of the 23rd, and, that same evening, a horse race (*palio de' barberi*). The morning procession on the 23rd included not only the clergy and confraternities of Florence, but also a number of floats (*edifizi*) that constituted a veritable cycle play.[6]

In 1454, Archbishop Antoninus, concerned about the secular elements present in the procession of the clergy, revised the structure and the order of events: the *mostra* was moved up to the 21st, the parade of floats was separated from the procession and moved to the morning of the 22nd, and the procession of the clergy and the confraternities was kept on the morning of the 23rd.[7] Describing the new festive program, Matteo Palmieri identifies twenty-two different sections in the new parade of floats on the morning of the 22nd:

1 / the cathedral clergy and youths
2 / the youth confraternities of the Vangelista, led by Iacopo di Biagio *cimatore*, and of Sant'Antonio da Padova, led by Onofrio di Filippo di Bartolommeo, *calzaiuolo*
3 / the float of the Archangel Michael with a representation of the fall of Lucifer
4 / the youth confraternities of the Archangel Raphael, lead by ser Antonio di Mariano Muzi, and of the Purification, led by his brother Piero di Mariano Muzi
5 / the float of Adam, with the play of the Creation
6 / Moses, on horseback, with the people of Israel
7 / the float of Moses, with the play of the Ten Commandments
8 / prophets and sibyls, prophesying the Incarnation
9 / the float of the Annunciation, with its play
10 / the Emperor Octavian, with the Sibyl and his escort
11 / the Temple of Peace, with its play
12 / the float of the Magi
13 / the Magi, with their escorts
14 / the horseback escort of Pontius Pilate
15 / the float of the Burial of Christ
16 / the float of Limbo
17 / the float of Paradise
18 / Mary and the Apostles who were present at the Ascension
19 / the float of the Ascension
20 / the riders, escorts, ladies, and cast of the play of the Living Man and the Dead Man
21 / the float of the Living Man and the Dead Man
22 / the float of the Final Judgment.[8]

The Arcangelo Raffaello's participation in these festivities is thus documented first in its presence at entry no. 4, and secondly in its staging of entry no. 11. In describing float no. 11, in fact, Palmieri says it is the '*Temple of peace* with the float of the Nativity in order to stage its play.' He then describes an incident where a drunken German spectator climbed on the float, threw the actor impersonating the Emperor Augustus into the crowd in the piazza, and then attempted to climb one of the columns of the temple, only to find that 'some youths who were atop the temple as if they were angels and therefore had batons in their hands beat him fiercely and, not without some difficulty, made him fall to the ground.'[9]

With the expulsion of the Medici and the advent of Savonarola, a more stringent reformer than the saintly (and pro-Medicean) Antoninus, the parade of floats was suppressed. Such government action may have been influenced by political as well as religious considerations. The parade, in fact, could have had strong Medicean associations by virtue of Lorenzo de' Medici's uncanny ability to appropriate civic rituals and festivities to his family's interests. By funding, organizing, or participating in *armeggerie*, *trionfi*, parades, and other such events, the Medici in general and Lorenzo in particular had been able to present themselves as princely patrons of Florentine civic rituals. Whether as the formal entry of Pope Pius II (1459), the joust organized in his honour, or the proposed changes in the St John's parade, the Medici political and cultural agendas were always present in the event.[10] It is not surprising, then, that Savonarola and the post-Medicean governments of 1494–1512 would have wanted to do away with possible reminders of the previous rulers.

Soon after the collapse of the Savonarolan and Soderini regimes, however, the Florentines, strong in their appreciation of festive events, reinstituted the St John's parade.[11] And in 1514, in the wake of the Medici restoration, the parade was reorganized. The new sequence, though simpler, clearly followed the 1454 prototype:

1st The fall of Lucifer and his followers
2nd The creation of Adam and his story
3rd The Annunciation of Our Lady and its mysteries
4th The Nativity of Saint John the Baptist
5th The Nativity of Christ and his story
6th The Resurrection of Christ
7th When Saint John baptized Christ
8th The Ascension of Christ
9th The Assumption of Our Lady
10th The living man and the dead man[12]

And so the parade survived, with variations, throughout the sixteenth century. The confraternity of the Arcangelo Raffaello continued to participate, though not always with a Nativity float. The theatre historian Alessandro D'Ancona cites from the unpublished diary of Antonio da San Gallo to point out that in 1549 'a confraternity, called the Holy Angel Raphael, put on the battle of David and Goliath, and David stood on top of a triumph [a triumphal cart] and recited seven verses in front of the palace of His Excellency [the Palazzo della Signoria], who was at a window and could hear it all very well.' The confraternity then sang a madrigal and one of the youths delivered a prosopopoeia, that is, a speech in verse in the persona of King David. By then, however, such theatrical and dramatic contributions to the St John's festivities were not the norm. Antonio da San Gallo concludes his description by saying that 'when the playing ['recitare'] was finished, the entire procession of priests and friars followed in order, which I will not mention because one sees it every year.' What is recorded, in other words, are the exceptional, not the usual moments in the celebrations.[13]

What was more usual, for the youths of the Arcangelo Raffaello, was to join in the celebrations for St John's by participating in the religious procession of the 23rd. According to Archbishop Antoninus's regulations, the city's nine youth confraternities were to walk second in this procession, following the different orders of friars. Within their group, the youths marched in order of seniority, with the youngest confraternity first and the eldest at the place of honour, at the end. The Arcangelo Raffaello, as the first confraternity to be established, thus came last, immediately after the confraternity of the Purificazione detta di San Marco.[14] The youth confraternities probably made a striking appearance. In listing all the festive events held on 23 June 1577, the chronicler Bastiano Arditi points out that 'on the eve of St John's there were beautiful processions, above all that of the youth confraternities, triumphal carts with music, voices, instruments together.'[15] While Arditi's entry is unclear on its own, we can easily connect it with what we know from other sources to understand that the youth confraternities marched with a wagon and contributed with both vocal and instrumental music.

Processional wagons consisted of an everyday wagon decorated with platforms and scenery appropriate for the occasion. In April 1565 the Arcangelo Raffaello acquired such a processional wagon partly as a gift, and partly as a purchase. The records explain that the guardian father, Girolamo di M.o Luca, asked Mons. Benedetto Nerli, archbishop of Volterra, and Alessandro d'Ottaviano de' Medici, on several occasions to donate to the confraternity a pageant wagon that had been used for the *mascherata* the previous carnival. At that time, the wagon had been the 'float of Nature,' complete with a 'triumphant Nature' sitting on an elevated throne at the back. The bishop and Alessandro de' Medici, who apparently had paid for the construction of the float, eventually agreed to donate the float to the youths. However, the cart's wheels and flatbed belonged to the Arte de' Mercatanti, and the confraternity eventually had to enter into negotiations with the Arte to purchase the wagon itself.[16]

In spite of such costumes, music, and pageant wagons, the overt secularism and dramatic components of the fifteenth-century processions described by Palmieri and Sangallo are not as evident in the sixteenth century. A 1582 *ricordo* indicates how confraternal participation had been significantly scaled down:

Saturday, 23 June, the vigil of St John the Baptist.
Having gathered early in the morning, our father corrector celebrated Mass. We then placed ourselves in order to go in the procession. [Some brothers] dressed up as the Archangel Raphael and Tobias, with a choir of about twelve angels who sang continually a madrigal composed by one of our beloved brothers and ran as follows:

The Heavens rejoice today
Happy and gay for the birth
Of him who was worthy of washing in holy water
The divine word who showed the world
That he came from the chaste and fecund
Womb of Mary and lives forever.
Now we, angels of highest heaven,
Announce to you the joy and song
Of those heavenly souls in this holy day.[17]

The 1582 participation with the Archangel Raphael, Tobias, and a choir of twelve angels was, itself, an exceptional event. In 1583 and 1584 the majority of 'the older brothers' chose not to dress in costume, but simply to process in their confraternal robes and carry the confraternal banner.[18] Tobias, the Archangel Raphael, and accompanying angels reappeared in the 1587, 1588, and 1589 processions, but, again, they did not become the norm.[19]

Even if the brothers did not contribute a *tableau vivant*, they did provide a number of participants to the procession. In 1454 Palmieri had noted about thirty youths from the Natività and the Purificazione at section no. 4 of the procession – he did not mention, however, how many participated in the play at section no. 11.[20] The confraternity's scribe in the mid-seventeenth-century, instead, kept a meticulous record of the number of brothers attending processions, and this allows us to draw a small but significant attendance chart for the three major processions the youths attended in the decade from 1640 to 1650:

| Year | *Number of brothers participating in the processions for* *St John's* (23 June) (city wide) | *Corpus Domini* (morning) (city wide) | *Corpus Domini* (afternoon) (*quartiere* S.M. Novella) |
|---|---|---|---|
| 1640 | 68 | 88 | 94 |
| 1641 | n/a | n/a | n/a |
| 1642 | 84 | 100 | 90 |
| 1643 | 92 | 122 | 106 |
| 1644 | 64 | 108 | 90 |
| 1645 | 40 | 90 | n/a |
| 1646 | 50 | 95 | 82 |
| 1647 | 81 | n/a | 82 |
| 1648 | 92 | 110 | 90 |
| 1649 | 91 | 112 | 88 |
| 1650 | 85 | 100 | 90[21] |

These attendance figures indicate that by the mid-seventeenth century participation in the St John's procession was several times higher than what Palmieri had indicated for the mid-fifteenth century. It was not as high, however, as that for the two Corpus Domini processions, one the city-wide procession from the Duomo, the other the procession of the Dominican clergy from Santa Maria Novella through the *quartiere*. The figures indicate that the St John's parade, though of enormous importance to the city and to Florentines in general, did not attract as many participants from the Arcangelo Raffaello as the Corpus Domini city-wide procession or, most of the time, as many as the local procession in the *quartiere*.

There may be several reasons for such a difference in attendance. One may lie in the post-Tridentine emphasis on sacramental devotion and its consequent ritual exhibition of the consecrated Host. By the mid-seventeenth century, the consecrated Host, rather than the city's patron saint, may have held a more important place in the confraternity's processional priorities.

Another reason may be tied to the changes in the demographics of the Arcangelo Raffaello itself. The older members, who were growing in number, may have considered it inappropriate for them, individually, to march publicly near the front of the procession as a *fanciullo* and as a symbol of the innocence and promise of Florentine youth. By 1700, in fact, the changed demography of all youth confraternities had eventually forced a change in their place in the ecclesiastical procession for St John. In his guide to the churches and religious festivities of Florence, Lodovico Antonio Giamboni points out that the four 'Compagnie di Dottrine di fanciulli' walked in front of the 'Compagnie d'huomini e giovani.' These four 'Dottrine,' that is, the confraternities of the Resurrezione, San Michele della Pace, San Giovanni in Verzaia, and Nome di Dio, had not been included in the 1454 and 1514 lists. The Arcangelo Raffaello is entered not among them, but with the 'huomini e giovani,' as are also several of the youth confraternities mentioned in the two earlier lists. All these are then followed by the regular clergy, the monks, and others.[22] By the eighteenth century, then, the youth confraternity of the Arcangelo Raffaello had joined the ranks of the adult confraternities, at least in the official ecclesiastical procession for the city's patron saint, and its place as a youth confraternity had been taken over by the *Dottrine* that had developed in the wake of the Council of Trent.

## Corpus Domini

Another important ecclesiastical and civic procession was the one held in the morning of the variable feast of Corpus Domini. The earliest direct references to the Arcangelo Raffaello's participation in this procession are from the 1560s. On 29 May 1562 the confraternity scribe recorded that the youths 'accompanied the Holy Sacrament.'[23] In these years the feast was also associated with the confraternity's own devotion of the Forty Hours, and thus *festaiuoli* were appointed to oversee both events.[24] The brothers would gather at the confraternity in the morning, recite Matins and hear Mass, and then proceed to the cathedral to join in the archbishop's Mass and procession. Attendance was high. The chart above for the period 1640–50 has already shed light on relative figures. Such numbers were present even earlier, as some occasional references from the *ricordi* clearly indicate.[25]

The Arcangelo Raffaello's participation in the procession was limited to attendance and singing. There is no indication it ever included plays, pageants, *tableaux vivants*, or even costuming, as did the procession for St John's. The 1583 entry, for example, reports that the confraternity attended the procession, during which it sang the 'Pange lingua' in 'canto fermo,' as well as 'many other psalms,' then, on their return, when they reached Santa Maria Novella, they began singing the Te Deum and thus singing entered into the confraternity.[26] And, in this simple manner, participation continued into the eighteenth century.[27]

## Procession in Honour of the Relic of St Thomas Aquinas

In 1640 the confraternity added another procession to their Corpus Domini program – they began to participate in the yearly procession organized by the Dominicans of Santa Maria Novella to honour their relic of St Thomas Aquinas. The procession took place after Vespers on the afternoon of Corpus Domini and extended throughout the *quartiere* of Santa Maria Novella.

The confraternity's participation was part of a recent rapprochement in the delicate relationship between the Dominicans of that convent and the Arcangelo Raffaello. After some years of having used Theatines as father correctors (1631–40) and having even asked and received aggregation with that order (1633), the confraternity had now returned to seek the services of the Dominicans. Their new father corrector, fra Agostino Rondinelli, OP, was, in fact, the priest who had served them in 1630–1 and who had been released from duty because, on the orders of his prior, he had ceased to come to the confraternity to celebrate Mass.[28] Whatever the difficulty may have been that had led the prior of Santa Maria Novella to instruct Rondinelli not to serve the confraternity, it was now resolved, and Rondinelli began not only to celebrate the required Masses (1640–6) but also to draw the confraternity closer to his convent. Participation in the procession to honour the Dominicans' great theologian and teacher was something he himself had suggested in order to increase co-operation between the two organizations.

Such participation was, however, strictly based on the formality of the Dominicans extending an invitation and the confraternity accepting it. The *ricordi* carefully register the confraternity's deliberations and 'gracious acceptance.' In 1640, for example, the scribe recalls that 'having been asked ['pregati'] by the prior of Santa Maria Novella and by our father corrector [fra Agostino Rondinelli, OP] to participate in the procession for the relic of St Thomas Aquinas, the brothers, with the permission of our guardian father and *provveditore*, were pleased to attend, and ninety-four of our brothers attended.'[29]

In 1702, however, relations with the convent once again deteriorated and the confraternity turned to the Franciscans of Ognissanti for a father corrector. Understandably, the following year they voted not to accept the Dominicans' invitation on the grounds that they had no obligation to do so. In 1704 they again turned down the invitation, and then, the following year, stood firm in their decision even in the face of a notarized order from the archbishop to attend, again claiming they had no such obligation. The confraternity was apparently successful in its adamant refusal, for in the following years the entry for Corpus Domini recalls its participation in the morning procession at the Duomo, but not in the late afternoon procession in the ward of Santa Maria Novella.[30]

Participation in the procession that carried the relic of one of the major Dominican saints through the streets of the ward that took its name from the Dominican church of Santa Maria Novella was highly significant. It demonstrated visibly the confraternity's participation not only in the rituals and the spiritual life of the Dominican order, but also its submission to that order's authority in the *quartiere*. To be absent from the sanctification of the ward by the Dominicans, and from their spiritual *prise de pouvoir* over it, constituted a refusal, on the part of the confraternity, to be considered, among other things, a local organization. While the friars would have liked the confraternity to join them in order to increase the size of the procession and, inevitably, the local prestige of the order, and while the archbishop would have like them to participate in order to obtain their submission to local ecclesiastical powers (parish priest or parish church), the members of the Arcangelo Raffaello instead reaffirmed their existence as a city-wide lay religious organization independent of parish authorities. And they did so even against the notarized order of the archbishop. In order to do so the confraternity must clearly have had the self-assurance and conviction that came from a long history of independence, and from a solid socio-economic standing in the city.

## Occasional Processions

Such prestige, whether spiritual or secular, was, in fact, one of the reasons why the confraternity of the Arcangelo Raffaello was asked, or chose, to participate in public processions, especially those that were decreed, on an *ad hoc* basis, by the appropriate authorities. Thus, in times of grief or jubilation, need or thankfulness, the youths were asked to join with the clergy and people of Florence to implore or praise God through the streets of the city.

When Florence suffered drought for six months in 1562, for example, the youths took part in a penitential procession intended to appease God's obvious anger against the city and the world.

13 [September 1562], the second Sunday of the month. A procession was held to ask for God's mercy, since through many signs he has shown himself to be very irate with us, first since it has not rained for more than six months, [then] because most

of the world is full of heresies, and [then] because those few Christians that are left are, for the most part, dissolute and improper ['scorretti'] in vices and sins, so much so that they are displeasing to Our Lord God. Instead of our *segno* we carried our crucifix, accompanied by two torches, and we went barefoot on this procession, starting at 9 o'clock. We went to Santa Maria del Fiore, to San Marco, to San Barnaba to visit the Vergine della Quercia, who had been brought into Florence for this reason, and from San Barnaba [we went] to San Lorenzo and to Santa Maria Novella, and from there we returned to the confraternity where we brought to an end the day that had thus begun.[31]

The penitential aspect and the implied connections with the processions of the *Bianchi* are evident in the confraternity's white gowns, the bare feet, and the carrying of a crucifix rather than a *segno*.[32] There is no indication or even suggestion of flagellation in this or on any other occasion when the brothers joined a procession. There is, however, a clear suggestion that the natural calamity, the drought, was seen as one of a variety of scourges the Lord was inflicting on a dissolute world.

The youths thus processed to calm an angry God whose wrath had expressed itself, among other ways, through inclement weather. In 1589 they processed to Santa Maria del Fiore to join in the Forty Hours decreed by the grand duke in an attempt to stop the rains and restore the 'serenity of the air.'[33] They asked the same boon in 1652 when they processed to San Marco to visit the exposed body of St Antoninus.[34] In 1654 they asked for rain, instead, processing to the cathedral to honour the relic of the True Cross that had been placed in public view, to the SS. Annunziata to pray at the miraculous image of the Virgin, and then to San Marco to see the exposed body of St Antoninus.[35] An insight into the manner and a glimpse of the atmosphere that surrounded such processions even in the mid-sixteenth century may be gleaned from an entry in the travel diary of the Venetian Bartolomeo Fontana:

I passed Sunday night in Terni, and here there was a procession throughout the land at three hours in the night and all the children ['mamoli et putti'] walked with the confraternity of the flagellants ['la schola de battudi'] and with burning lights, crying out the litanies and other orations in a loud voice on account of the great rains that had been falling every day for perhaps five months already. And they processed in the falling rain and at that time, and this was an awesome ['pauroso'] thing to be seen.[36]

The youths also participated in propitiatory processions to sue God for victory in war. This was particularly important when the fighting was directed against the heathen enemy. On Sunday, 28 April 1560, the confraternity joined in a procession to seven different Florentine churches in order to benefit from the Great Jubilee declared by Pope Pius IV and to 'offer assistance to the great undertaking of King Philip against the Turks at Tripoli.'[37] In 1645, they processed to San Marco to visit the exposed body of St Antoninus in order to ask not only for the success of the wars against the Turks but also for rain.[38]

There were, also, processions without such urgent needs. In 1561 the youths joined with all the other confraternities in a procession to San Marco and to the SS. Annunziata to pray for the success ('buon esito') of the Council of Trent.[39] On 9 May 1589 the confraternity took part in the solemn procession through the city on the occasion of the translation of the uncorrupted body of St Antoninus from its original burial site to the Salviati chapel, as Archbishop Alessandro de' Medici had asked all confraternities to do.[40] Such processions, however, were few. Devotion and honour were generally bestowed through regular, annual processions such as those for St John's or Corpus Domini.

## The Procession to the Vergine della Pace

For a brief period in the late sixteenth century, the youths made an annual pilgrimage procession to the church of the Virgin of Peace ('Vergine della Pace') outside the city gate at San Piero Gattolini.[41] The church had been built in 1566 to house a miraculous image of the *Madonna della Neve* painted on a tabernacle that had survived the disastrous siege of 1529–30. In 1573, Archbishop Altoviti rededicated the church to the Virgin of Peace, a name change that was associated with the Florentine victory over the Sienese at Marciano (1555). Popular devotion blossomed around the image and interested even the Grand Duchess Christine of Lorraine, who enlarged the church and build a convent next to it. Grand dukes Cosimo II, Ferdinando II, and Cosimo III continued to embellish the building throughout the seventeenth century.[42]

The youths' procession to the image took place on the 24th of August and included the singing of Matins, prayers, and hymns. The fullest description of this event is found in the 1584 *ricordo* that runs as follows:

> We gathered on the morning of the feast of the Apostle St Bartholomew and, since it was our custom on that day to go on procession to the Virgin of Peace outside the gate at San Piero Gattolini, all the brothers were given their white confraternal

gowns and placed in order. We left the confraternity at the tenth hour carrying the most holy Cross, with two lighted torches, and its bearers walked bare-footed. As soon as we stepped outside the confraternity we began singing the seven penitential psalms in a soft voice, together with the litanies and the prayers. When we arrived outside the gate, near the Virgin, having finished the prayers, we intoned the hymn to the Virgin, that is, the 'Gloriosa Domina,' and we all entered into the church. When it was finished and we were all kneeling, we recited the oration and its verses, and then we began the holy Matins, with the Invitatory ['Invitatorio'], and the 'Quem terra pontus aethera,' always on our knees. When it was finished and we were given the signal we left and returned to the confraternity, and all along the road we recited the holy Matins. We arrived at the end of the Benedictus, so, without taking off our gowns, we finished. Our father corrector was waiting to say Mass, along with many brothers who had not been in time to come with us, though there were some who followed us without wearing the confraternity gown. When Mass was finished some of our brothers took Communion, and then, after the offering to the altar, everyone was dismissed. That afternoon the youths ['fanciulli'] recited the Holy Vespers, as usual, and at the end they read from the tablet of the commandments and from the [booklet] of Christian doctrine, and everyone was dismissed.[43]

Confraternity records do not suggest any reason why the youths of the Arcangelo Raffaello should, for a few years in the late sixteenth century, carry out a ritual procession to a devotional shrine of the Virgin. Their history had not been that of a Marian cult, nor were they involved, previously or thereafter, in an independent pilgrimage procession of their own to any shrine. Other confraternities had. The men of San Filippo Benizi, for example, did carry out a formal yearly pilgrimage to the Servite hermitage of Monte Senario.[44] Aside from the few years in question, however, the youths of the Archangel Raphael never took part in such a devotional exercise. For lack of further information the entire event remains, unfortunately, shrouded in mystery.

# 14

# Sermons at the Arcangelo Raffaello

Alongside the weekly recitation of matins and celebration of Masses, one of the major regular activities at the Arcangelo Raffaello was the recitation of sermons. Since the last century, scholars of Renaissance theatre, philosophy, and culture have mentioned *en passant* the importance of sermons delivered in confraternities. Alessandro D'Ancona drew connections between confraternity recitation of sermons and religious *laude*.[1] Drawing on Isidoro Del Lungo, Benedetto Neri claimed (incorrectly) that Agnolo Poliziano had been a member of a youth confraternity where, in his younger years, he had 'practised piety and eloquence' by delivering four sermons – two on the Eucharist, one on the Passion, and one on the Washing of the Feet.[2] As I have demonstrated elsewhere, Poliziano did compose these four sermons for recitation in a youth confraternity, but he did this as an adult and for recitation by youths in a confraternity, not by himself.[3]

In the last decades, Paul Oskar Kristeller, Cesare Vasoli, and Olga Zorzi Pugliese have touched on the sermons delivered by Giovanni Nesi in 1472–97 in several Florentine youth confraternities, among them those of San Niccolò del Ceppo (13 December 1472), Sant'Antonio da Padova (7 April 1474), and the Arcangelo Raffaello (11 April 1476, 25 February 1477/8).[4] More recently, quite an array of men from the Neoplatonist circles of Laurentian Florence have been tied to confraternities – Angelo Poliziano, Donato Acciaiuoli, Alamanno Rinuccini, Francesco Berlinghieri – as well as disciples of Ficino such as Marco Parenti, Filippo Carducci, Bernardo Canigiani, Giovanni Cocchi, and Pierfilippo Pandolfini.[5] No one, however, has studied the phenomenon of lay religious sermons in youth confraternities in detail or conducted a thorough study of it. Such a study would take into account not only the texts and personalities involved, but also confraternity records, for they offer an insight into the routine, practice, and manner of such oratory.

This lack of attention on the part of scholars may, in part, be attributable to the scarcity of texts available. The few that have survived (four by Poliziano, four by Giovanni Nesi, one by Machiavelli, possibly one by Alamanno Rinuccini, ten by Giovan Maria Cecchi, for example) are but a minimal part of what was, undoubtedly, a vast and varied production. If one considers that youths recited sermons on nearly all major feast-days of the year, and often organized Lenten or Advent series of sermons, it becomes painfully clear that an extensive corpus of lay religious works has been lost to us. Paul Oskar Kristeller has already pointed out that 'the practice of preaching in the Compagnie is mentioned so frequently in the statutes, and this kind of literature is so likely not to be recorded or else to escape scholarly attention that its known specimens must be considered as a rather small selection from a much larger volume of sermons actually composed and delivered.'[6]

One must not confuse, therefore, what has come down to us with what was composed. In his study on sermons in confraternities, Ronald F.E. Weissman declared that 'although frequently associated with boys' confraternities, few of the sermons were, in fact, the work of adolescents' and added that '[Giovanni] Nesi, the adolescent, was *atypical* in delivering sermons at the ages of sixteen, eighteen, nineteen, twenty, and twenty-two' (my emphasis).[7] This is not quite correct. First, Nesi's age when he delivered his sermons fits perfectly well within the statutory age limits for membership in youth confraternities – thirteen to twenty-four years of age. Second, although the few extant sermons recited in youth confraternities were composed by adults, the vast majority of sermons were, in fact, composed by the youths themselves. The point of the entire exercise, as is evident from the statutes of these organizations, was to give youths practice not only in oratory but also in composition and rhetoric by having them write their own sermons and then deliver them to their peers. The assumption that the hundreds and hundreds of sermons composed in Florence for recitation by youths in their confraternities could all have been ghost-written by adults is tenuous at best. Kristeller does suggest that in the Quattrocento the practice of ghost-writing spread from letter writing and public orations to the composition of sermons, but he does not say that it became the norm. Furthermore, his observation is primarily drawn from Poliziano's letter of 1490 to the Venetian humanist Girolamo Donato, and is thus based on a single case that points to the exception, rather than the rule.[8] The rule, on the other hand, is clearly indicated by the sixteenth-century records of these same confraternities, where scribes recall, year after year, that it was the youths themselves who composed and delivered their own sermons. Giovanni Nesi, therefore, was not 'atypical,' but very much typical both because of his age and because he delivered his own sermons.

That is not to say, however, that only youths delivered sermons in their confraternities. The Arcangelo Raffaello documents indicate clearly that sermons were delivered by three different types of persons: the father corrector, an outside adult guest, or one of the youths in the confraternity. While the father corrector addressed the youths in the morning *tornata*, guests and youths spoke in the evening, and sometimes in the day *tornata*. On all occasions the sermon was incorporated into the religious rituals of that meeting and day. And the purpose of the exercise was always in tune with the educational aims of the confraternity, for sacred oratory was seen as a means to foster and advance the Christian education of the young.

### Sermons by the Father Corrector

The father corrector delivered sermons not every Sunday, as we would expect from contemporary practice, but only on feast-days. They were given at the morning *tornata*, during the course of Mass. Unlike modern-day practice, they came not after the Gospel reading but after the canon and before the distribution of Communion. We read, for example, that on the feast of the Purification of the Virgin (2 February) 1581/2,

> We gathered in the morning at our usual place in time, sung the Hours solemnly, made our usual devout devotion, and when it was finished the candles were blessed and distributed, then Holy Mass was celebrated and when it was finished, after having delivered a most beautiful sermon, our father corrector gave communion to twenty-eight of our fathers and brothers, then we made the offer to the altar, and then we made a little offer for the servant [Pasquino]. God be praised.[9]

Given the nature and the regularity of such sermons, we can suppose they took their cue from the day's readings or festivity. And, given the lack of any text or even description of the contents, we can further suppose that there was nothing spectacular about them. Like many a Sunday homily – especially when it is delivered to a younger congregation – the father corrector's sermons may have been delivered extemporaneously, without any formal pretensions in the areas of content, form, or delivery. The confraternity scribe himself invariably describes them as long and either devout or beautiful, but adds nothing more.

### Sermons by Guests

Sermons by guests were relatively few and tended to be delivered at particular times of the year by city priests with a special interest in religious oratory. Most often, they were the preachers charged with the Advent sermons at a city church, and tended to visit and address the confraternity on All Saints' (1 November). Thus on 1 November 1581 the scribe recalled that 'the preacher from Santo Spirito who was to preach the following Advent delivered a most beautiful sermon that lasted about an hour and when it was finished our guardian father exhorted us to draw some fruit from what His Reverence had said to us.'[10] Immediately following that Christmas, on 1 January 1581/2, another guest, this time the priest that had delivered the Advent sermons at the Duomo, visited and spoke to the confraternity.[11] Neither of these individuals is mentioned by name in the records, indicating that the scribe (or the youths) had been impressed more by the position than the man who held it.

In fact, only on rare occasions is the guest preacher's name mentioned in the records. In February 1582/3 the youths invited Fr Marcellino Vangelista, a Franciscan who was preaching the Lenten sermons at the Duomo and was 'beloved' of the confraternity ('nostro amorevole'), to deliver a sermon in conjunction with their celebration of the Forty Hours.[12] The purpose of the guest sermon was to edify the youths, but it was also timed to inspire them to attend that preacher's Lenten sermons. Two months after Fr Marcellino had spoken to the youths, on Sunday, 17 April, the guardian father had the confraternity cut short its Sunday morning devotions (only Matins was recited) in order to allow the youths to go to the Duomo to hear the priest's last Lenten sermon. In his memoirs, Francesco Settimani describes Fr Marcellino as an observant Franciscan, and then immediately adds 'who was truly an evangelic preacher' ('ch'era veramente un Predicatore Evangelico'). His preaching, Settimani continues, attracted so much attention that notices were posted against him and the people remarked that the Grand Duke Francesco I had been conspicuously absent at the friar's sermons. The friar, who began to suspect a plot against him, raised his oratory accordingly, challenging 'Florence' to make a martyr of him and chastising it as a den of thieves and a public harlot:

Florence, I hear you want to kill me: I leave it to you, for you have already killed other preachers. Know, Florence, that this will be my crown. Would God that we were at the beginning of Lent. Open your eyes [and see] your thieves. Florence, they have made a public harlot of you. Woe to you. Woe to you.[13]

It is not surprising that such strong invectives against the moral corruption of contemporary Florence, and the obvious reference to the execution of Girolamo Savonarola, would not please the grand duke, whose personal relationship with the Venetian courtesan Bianca Cappello was then a source of scandal to many. In inviting such a controversial preacher to their oratory, the youths of the Arcangelo Raffaello were revealing a penchant for fire and brimstone that, perhaps, had not been evident from their more ceremonial or festive activities.

The following 1 November, the youths invited Fr Andrea, a friar at Santo Spirito, to their evening service. He must have been a charming preacher, with a much more attractive and less tempestuous oratorical style. The records tell that he delivered his sermon 'with so much gracefulness ['leggiadria'] that everyone was satisfied.'[14] Unfortunately, they do not explain what constituted this 'gracefulness' or how it was appropriate to that day's festivity – All Saints' – and the friar's theme for that day – death.

In those same years there were sermons from Fr Gregorio, a Jesuit from the church of San Giovannino dei Gesuiti (or degli Scolopi), dealing with the Eucharist and prayer (17 April 1582); from frat'Agostino da Eboli, an Observant Franciscan from the convent of Ognissanti (1 November 1582); from Fr Arcangelo, a Servite then preaching at the Duomo, who spoke on angels (31 December 1582) – an appropriate topic for that day, since the youths were celebrating the Archangel Raphael.[15] The different orders and churches represented in this brief sample suggest that the youths were not limiting themselves to a particular order, church, or preacher but were drawing upon the variety of resources available to them. And their interests in guest preachers ran from the men who were charged with a series of high-profile sermons (the Advent or Lenten sermons) to popular speakers with oratorical panache.

Occasionally the guest speaker was a major ecclesiastical figure literally 'visiting' the confraternity. Archbishop Antonio Altoviti toured the site and attended evening Matins on 11 January 1572/3, but he did not address the group – he limited himself, instead, to blessing the congregation at the end of the service and granting each of the youths present a forty-day indulgence.[16] Had he spoken, his sermon would probably have been more of an address than a homily. Such was the case in 1587, for example, when his successor, Archbishop Alessandro de' Medici, paid a visit to the confraternity. The scribe recalls that after Matins had been sung the archbishop 'went to sit on the altar platform ['predella'] and delivered a beautiful sermon exhorting us to frequent such a spiritual exercise [i.e., the confraternity], and [saying] that he had been very edified in seeing that everything was proceeding in excellent order.'[17]

Not all visitors, however, came to praise. Some, like the Rev. Jacopo Genovese, a priest of the cardinal archbishop, visited the confraternity on 28 July 1585 together with Jacopo Ansaldi, who had been appointed by the archbishop to oversee the teaching of Christian doctrine in the schools and confraternities of the diocese. In the course of a long sermon, Genovese 'ordered that [the confraternity] should set in place the teaching of such doctrine.' Proud of their long tradition of Christian education, and possibly a little annoyed at being told what to do by an outsider, the confraternity responded through the acting guardian father, Niccolò Antifassi, who pointed out 'that they would not fail to do what he was asking, and that ordinarily every day a tablet containing all the doctrine was read out, and that sometimes the youths delivered a lesson [sermon] based on it, and they would continue to do so.'[18]

## Sermons by Youths

In fact, sermons delivered by the youths were quite common in the confraternity. Such direct, personal involvement in the devotional and educational life of the group was one of the hallmarks of its lay spirituality. The youths not only governed themselves but also instructed and encouraged each other in leading a Christian life and learning the basic elements of the faith and the tradition. Sermons by and to their peers thus constituted a significant part of the activities of youth confraternities. And, unlike those of the father corrector, they were delivered much more often and regularly, usually after Matins at the Sunday evening *tornata*.

These sermons were generally composed by the youths themselves, though outside sources suggest that, at least on some occasions, the young men drew upon more experienced persons to ghost-write for them. In a letter of 22 April 1490, for example, Angelo Poliziano complained to his correspondent, the Venetian diplomat and humanist Girolamo Donato, that he was being harassed with requests for all sorts of epigrams and compositions, including 'little religious sermons for confraternities.'[19] In 1558 Giovan Maria Cecchi, the popular contemporary dramatist, composed several such sermons to be recited by the youths of San Giovanni Evangelista.[20] In the introduction to 'The pious readers,' Cecchi points out that he had undertaken to compose this series of short explications of the Epistles and Gospels for the ecclesiastical year in response to the entreaties of some of his friends, and that he intended this work to be for no other purpose than 'to be read or learnt by heart in parts and be recited in exhortation of confraternities, and not for sermons to be preached from pulpits' (p. 23). Although Cecchi intended to write one sermon for each Sunday and feast-day of the year, thus forming a complete homiletic cycle of *sermones de tempore et de sanctis*, the collection consists of ten specimens only. They start, appropriately enough, with the beginning of the ecclesiastical year – one sermon for each of the four Sundays of Advent. Cecchi then provides three sermons for Christmas day – night, morning, and High Mass – and one each for the feasts of St Stephen (26 December) and St John the Evangelist (27 December). The sequence then breaks, jumping to a meditation on death to be delivered at All Souls' (2 November).

Both Poliziano's and Cecchi's sermons were written for recitation in the youth confraternity of San Giovanni Evangelista. Similar sermons may also have been ghost-written for the Arcangelo Raffaello, but there is no indication of this in the surviving records.

It seems, instead, that the youths of the Arcangelo Raffaello generally composed their own orations. In the 1470s the young Giovanni Nesi, for one, composed and presumably delivered to the confraternity two sermons in Italian. The first, on humility, was delivered by the twenty-year-old Nesi on 11 April 1476 and the second, on charity, two years later on 25 February 1477/8.[21]

Another learned youth, Giovanni di Donato Cocchi, recited an 'Oratione del corpo di Christo' at the Archangelo Raffaello on 23 March 1474/5 and one on penitence at the youth confraternity of Sant'Antonio di Padova.[22] Cocchi was clearly a young man with intellectual potential. He became part of Ficino's group at the Platonic Academy and eventually prior of the Academia Ficiniana (November–December 1493).[23]

As with the sermons by the father corrector and by guest preachers, sermons delivered by youths were also generally keyed to that day's readings or festivity, though at times they did touch upon more general topics drawn from Christian doctrine. On occasion, they were even linked together into a logical sequence. We thus find that in early 1582 a number of youths took turns delivering sermons on the Ten Commandments. Pier Lupivecchi began the series in the evening of Monday, 1 January, with the first two Commandments: 'To love only one God, and not to mention his name in vain.' He was followed the following Sunday, 6 January, by Vincenzo Allegri speaking on 'Sanctify the feasts'; Antonio Minerbetti continued on 14 January with 'Honour thy father and thy mother'; Lorenzo Galli on 21 January with 'Thou shalt not kill'; Girolamo Adriani on 28 January with 'Thou shalt not commit adultery.' After a pause throughout the month of February, the series continued with Matteo Corboli on 4 March with 'Thou shalt not steal'; Stefano Nemi on 11 March with 'Thou shalt not give false witness'; Lodovico Tempi on 18 March with 'Thou shalt not covet the possessions and the wife of another.'[24] Later that spring a similar sermon sequence was delivered on the three spiritual virtues (20 May–3 June 1582); that fall the four cardinal virtues were featured (28 November–26 December 1582); and the following winter/spring the seven mortal sins (2 January–17 April 1583).

The 1580s appear to be particularly rich in oratorical activity at the Arcangelo Raffaello. This may be due in part to the personal interests of the official scribe, and his personal views on what was 'memorable' enough to merit mention in the *ricordi.* Girolamo Adriani, who kept the *ricordi* from 1 November 1581 to 2 January 1582/3, had a first-hand interest in sermons – he delivered three in the years he served as scribe (28 January and 28 November 1582, 2 January 1582/3). This, however, does not seem to be a strong reason – his successor, Alessandro Ghettini (who served from 2 January 1582/3 to 3 September 1587), did not deliver sermons, but did continue recording them. Another reason may be the father corrector's or the guardian father's own interest in having the youths give sermons. Fra Antonio Cignori, who was corrector throughout the 1580s, may be partly responsible for the interest in oratory – he was probably the priest who commissioned Giovan Maria Cecchi to write a play for the youths. More probably, however, the acting father corrector, Zanobi Buonavolti, may have been the moving force behind the wealth of sermons delivered by the youths in those years. His two terms in office, January to August 1582 and then again July 1584 to May 1591, do coincide with the flurry of oratorical activities, be they religious or dramatic.[25]

Then, again, youths themselves also seemed eager to participate. Some contributed a sermon a year. Among them are Mariotto di Bandino Stefani (with a sermon in 1581, 1582, 1584, and 1585), and Matteo di Piero Corboli (with a sermon in 1582, 1583, and 1584). Others spoke twice in a year: Antonio di Lionardo Tempi (6 June, 5 December 1582), Francesco di Mariotto Steccuti (24 and 25 December 1581), Pier Luigi del Borgo (15 April, 31 December 1582), Antonio Rigogli (2 February, 17 March 1585), Silvestro di Baccio Aldobrandini (29 and 31 December 1585), and Alessandro di Giuliano Franceschi (2 February, 26 March 1586, who delivered both his sermons twice). Apparently some were especially keen to mount the podium and speak at length on the topic that chance or the guardian father had given them. In January 1583, for example, during a weekly sequence of sermons on the seven vices, Piero Lupivecchi sermonized his peers for three consecutive Sundays on the vice of lust.

In the day, after Vespers were finished, Piero Lupivecchi, whose turn it was to speak on lust, went to the usual desk where all other speakers ['lettori'] go, and beginning his lesson he divided his topic into three parts, since the subject matter was long, and that day he spoke on one part, saving the other two for next Sunday, all in good order.[26]

Such enthusiasm for preaching and detailed analysis of a topic may have been admirable, but it could also lead to abuses. Piero Lupivecchi's extensive discussion on lust, which was obviously a topic of interest to him, could, on the other hand, have annoyed some of his peers. Although on 16 January the scribe seemed impressed by Piero's tripartite approach and drew attention to it, on the following two Sundays he was clearly less inclined to speak of it, mentioning only that on 23 January Piero 'returned to the speech he had left [unfinished] the previous Sunday and, not finishing it, kept it for the next Sunday,' when he finally 'finished his lesson on lust.'[27]

By the early seventeenth century, a need was clearly felt to establish some rules about sermons. In his 1619 partial revision of the statutes, the guardian father Luca Vigna included a rubric that said:

Because it is not reasonable for anyone to assume the authority to have sermons delivered by youths ['fanciulli'] in public in our evening or day *tornate*, we order that in the future no sermons can be delivered as in the past if they have not been seen and approved in writing at the bottom by the guardian father, and if he has not heard them rehearsed at least twice, and this [is commanded] also because they are too long and tedious, or not well delivered, [so that they] bring not honour but rather shame on the Confraternity and on those same people that deliver them.[28]

Aside from dealing with the problems of undue length, audience boredom, or speaker's inability, Luca Vigna's revisions may have been intended to bring the practice of lay preaching more in line with Tridentine and other ecclesiastical regulations. The Council of Trent, and subsequent diocesan synods, had expressed concerns on the matter of laymen delivering sermons, publicly interpreting Scripture, discussing dogma, or assuming the responsibility for educating the young in the Christian faith.

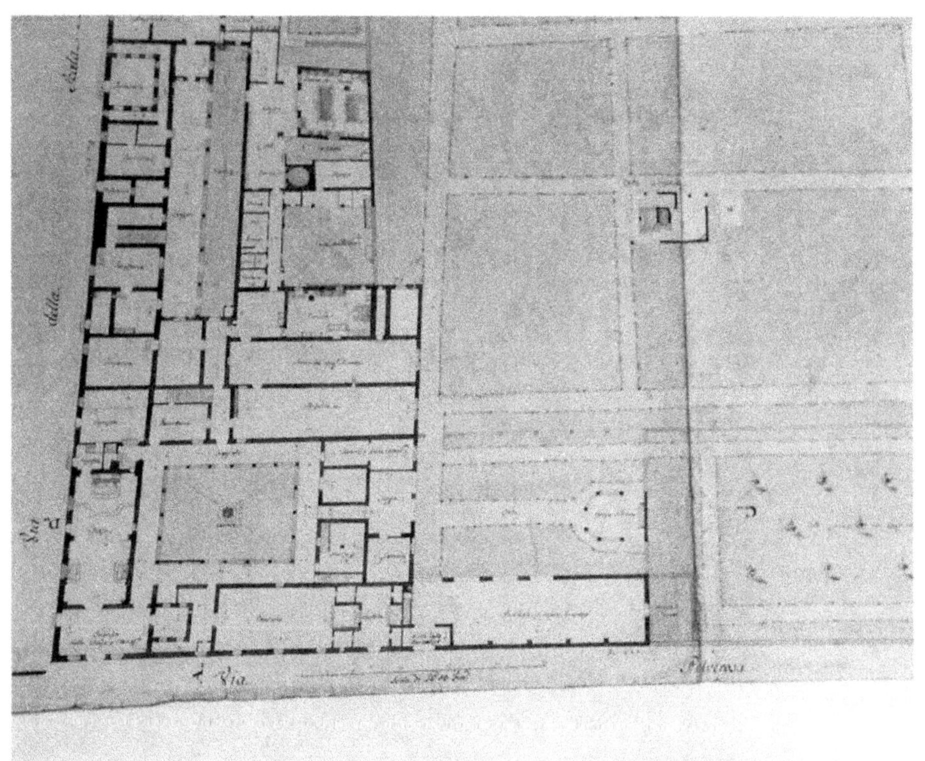

1 Floor plan and cross-section of the Ospedale della Scala, 1787. Florence, Museo di Firenze Com'Era (photo: Konrad Eisenbichler)

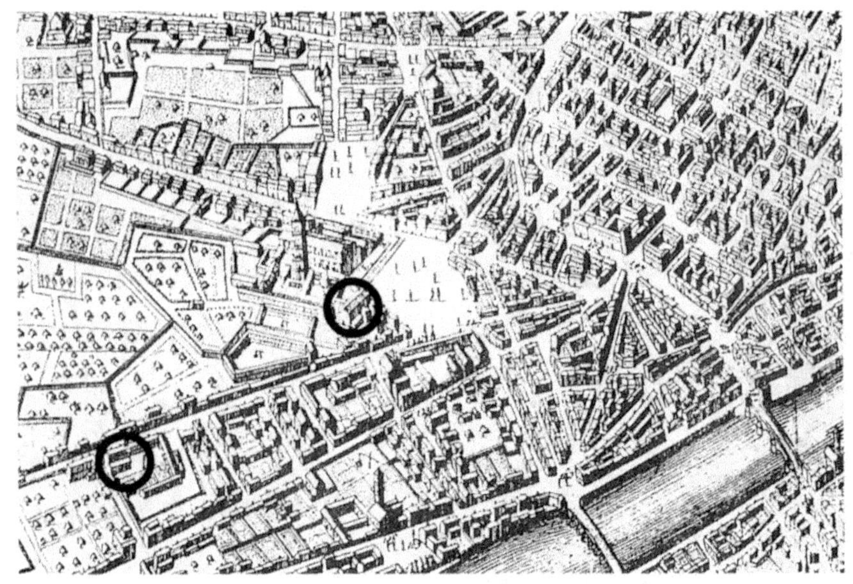

2 Bonsignori map showing via della Scala and Piazza Santa Maria Novella, 1584. Florence, Museo di Firenze Com'Era (photo: Konrad Eisenbichler)

3 Cristofano Allori (?), *View of Piazza Santa Maria Novella*, c. 1608. Paris, Louvre, Dép. des Arts Graphiques, Inv. 33

4 Vincenzo Tarchi and Michele Ciocchi, *View of Piazza Santa Maria Novella*, from G. Richa, *Notizie istoriche delle chiese fiorentine*, vol. 3, 1785

5 Anon., *The Archangel Raphael and Tobias*, 1563. ASF, Crs 164.36/38, f. 1r. Reproduced by permission of the Ministero per i Beni Culturali e Ambientali (photo: Konrad Eisenbichler)

6 Anon., *The Archangel Raphael and Tobias, with the Monogram of the Compagnia dell'Arcangelo Raffaello*, black and white cut-out glued on the cover of a working copy of the 1690 inventory. ASF, Crs 155.1/3, fasc. B, f.n.n. 90r. Reproduced by permission of the Ministero per i Beni Culturali e Ambientali (photo: Konrad Eisenbichler)

7 Lorenzo Lippi, *Crucifixion with Our Lady, St John, and St Mary Magdalene*, 1647. Florence, Museo di San Marco, Inv. 1890, no. 2115

8 Orazio Fidani, *Tobias Healing His Father's Blindness*, 1654. Florence, Uffizi (on deposit at the NATO headquarters, Brussels, since 1988), Inv. 1890, no. 7612

## Post-Tridentine Interventions by Ecclesiastical Authorities

Attempts to regulate the activities of Florentine lay confraternities were not new. Pope Eugenius IV, in his bull of 1442, had recognized but also restricted youth confraternities (see above, ch. 2, p. 30). St Antoninus and subsequent archbishops had sought to bring them into line by insisting that their statutes receive archiepiscopal approval. In Florence, the decrees of provincial and diocesan synods from 1573 to the beginning of the eighteenth century clearly point to the Church's progressive interference on their spiritual and educational life.

Archbishop Altoviti's 1573 Provincial Synod declared that confraternities were to abide by the archbishop's will regarding their participation in processions, they were to submit to archiepiscopal visitations, unauthorized laymen were forbidden to preach on questions of faith and religion, and there was to be no eating or drinking in the oratories.[29]

The synods convoked by Alessandro de' Medici in 1610 and 1619 placed severe restrictions on other educational aspects of youth confraternities, such as the teaching of Christian doctrine or the staging of religious plays. Christian doctrine was to be taught in the parish, the synod decreed, and no plays drawn from the Old or New Testament or the lives of the saints could be performed in churches, societies, or public places without the express permission of the archbishop's Ordinarius.

The 1645 Diocesan Synod, convoked by Archbishop Pietro Niccolini, reaffirmed previous rulings and then voiced its own interdiction, using derogatory turns of phrase to refer to lay preaching:

> the laity should not speak in public, that is, give sermons in private within confraternities and societies, on pain of punishment as decreed above, against which abuse we object most strongly, completely and strongly, condemning the temerity of certain lay persons in this city who, discounting even the synodal constitutions of the most high popes, freely *make words* everywhere in confraternities. [italics mine][30]

Niccolini had had first-hand experience with youth confraternities. At the age of twelve he had joined the Arcangelo Raffaello, introduced into the group by the acting guardian father, Niccolò Antifassi (1 January 1587). At ages fourteen and fifteen he had been active in the group as its *sagrestano* (May–August 1590), counsellor (September–December 1590), and *ordinatore de' cori* (January–March 1591), and had even delivered a sermon on the Sacrament during the Eastertime devotion of the Forty Hours

(15 April 1591).[31] His attempts at revising confraternal practices, therefore, were founded on direct knowledge of the situation.

The 1681 and subsequent synodal decrees regarding confraternities seem fairly mild in comparison to the earlier ones. This is an indication that previous regulations had had their effect. In reading the records of the Arcangelo Raffaello one finds that references to sermons recited by laymen within the confraternity dwindle by about the middle of the seventeenth century. Sermon series on the Ten Commandments, the Virtues, or the Vices disappear completely and instead sermons are recited only at Christmastime or on the occasion of a special feast.

By the eighteenth century, sermons at the confraternity are quite rare. Together with the staging of sacred plays and the teaching of Christian doctrine, they had ceased to be a component of the confraternities' mission in education. With the loss of one of its major *raisons d'être* – the education of the young in Christian doctrine – the confraternity was turning into a school for more secular interests. In particular, it had become a showcase for young talent. Already by the mid-seventeenth century the 'long and devout' sermons had turned into exhibition pieces for young orators. The scribe recalls that on All Souls' (2 November) 1642, 'a small young boy ['fanciullino'] of the Milanesi, a brother of ours, delivered a most beautiful discourse on the pains of Purgatory with more than ordinary quickness and vivacity, leaving the brother all in high admiration [of him].'[32] The sermons that followed were delivered by youths who are described as 'a tender youth from among our brothers' ('giovanetto de nostri fratelli') such as Giovanni Francesco Pandolfini (9 November 1642) and Luigi di Carlo Strozzi (7 December 1642). Shortly after Christmas a six-year-old son of Cosimo Perotti delivered a sermon in which 'he spoke and gestured so exquisitely ['raramente'] that everyone was amazed' (27 December 1642). The following Easter, there were several speakers, described either as 'tender youths and children of few years' ('giovanetti et fanciulli d'infantil'età') or as 'a child of few years' ('fanciullo di poc'età') (5 April 1643).[33] And they all drew a crowd.[34]

It appears that by the mid-seventeenth century, instead of educating their peers, the youths were entertaining their elders. The confraternity had changed from being an organization that taught Christian faith to the young into a school that taught them oratorical arts more appropriate to public display than personal devotion. More specifically, it sought to develop their talents in the fields of public speaking, as we have seen in this chapter, and in the areas of theatre and music, as we will see in the following chapters.

# 15

# Fun and Games

As the journal entry that opens the introduction to this volume clearly indicates, children are often inclined to physical violence. Educators have long realized this and have therefore sought to temper the tendency by providing the young with acceptable physical outlets – play and exercise. This chapter will first examine the presence and nature of youthful violence in premodern Italian society, and then describe and discuss the manner in which youth confraternities tried to redirect their members' pent-up physical energies into socially acceptable activities.

## The Violence of Children

In her article on the social role of children in early modern Italy, Ottavia Niccoli describes the amount and extent of physical violence present in the group behaviour of *fanciulli*, especially in the fourteenth and fifteenth centuries. The 'punishment' they meted out on the bodies of executed criminals, for example, reveals not only the brutal violence that was a commonplace in the society of the time, but also the freedom to be violent that was tacitly granted to such 'gangs' of children roaming the streets. Niccoli explains that group violence was accepted because it was part of the 'institutional role of children to punish and mock, according to a superior level of justice, those who have provoked the hostility of the community against them.'[1] Even staged (but very real) battles between children, Niccoli suggests, fulfilled a ritual role in early modern society. Many times, however, and especially in the street fights that broke the peace of urban life, their behaviour had no useful social function – it was simply a form of gang or internecine violence that needed to be controlled and eliminated. Civic and religious leaders sought to ban such behaviour and to redirect this tendency for violence towards more useful social goals. Savonarola's use of groups of young men to enforce some of his social reforms is well known.[2] What was needed, however, was not legislation but social change.

Eventually, a change in attitude took place in the sixteenth century that no longer saw youthful aggression as a prophetic sign of a supernatural will expressing itself through 'innocent' children, but simply as a form of unacceptable social behaviour. Niccoli suggests that one of the new elements that fostered this change was the post-Tridentine emphasis on education of the young through the Schools of Christian Doctrine. By drawing children aged six to fourteen into quasi-sacred spaces where they were taught the basic elements of the faith and of a renewed morality, such schools fostered a 'refusal of the street,' as Niccoli calls it, that changed the street 'from a place of ritual games to a venue that offered quick passage from home to school to church.'[3]

Given the physical exuberance of the young, it would have been useless, however, to expect a group of confraternity brothers always to behave like the 'angels' they were often asked to impersonate in the plays they staged or in the public processions they marched in. If the confraternity, or the school of doctrine, was to be a valid place for their devotional and spiritual education, it also had to take into account their need for some sort of physical outlet and for appropriate non-devotional activities that would help release some of the energy natural to their age. What the youths needed was to temper their devotions with some form of physical relaxation.

The youths were probably familiar with the well-known story of St Benedict and the archer. In the prologues to two of his plays, Giovan Maria Cecchi, who wrote several plays for the Arcangelo Raffaello, recalls the legend. He tells how one day a hunter passing by St Benedict's monastery saw the monks running about, happily playing ball. The hunter was somewhat surprised to see such a frivolous pastime in a Benedictine monastery. St Benedict, sensing the man's disapproval, approached him and engaged him in a conversation on the functioning of the crossbow the hunter was carrying. The hunter explained to the abbot how the crossbow worked, and showed him how one loaded it. He then unloaded it, released the tension, and continued with the conversation. The saint then asked if he could try loading the crossbow himself and, with the hunter's permission, did so. When the saint did not release the tension after unloading the crossbow, but carried on chatting instead, the hunter nonchalantly took the crossbow back and released the tension himself. The abbot asked the hunter why he had done that, and the hunter explained that if a crossbow is kept constantly taut it will eventually weaken and become useless. At that point the saintly abbot smiled and said: 'So it is with my monks as well.'[4]

Such a legend was not merely a pleasant story from the medieval hagiographical corpus used to give spiritual meaning to an otherwise worldly activity, but also a Christianized example for Quintillian's observation that he approves of play in the young because 'all our pupils will require some relaxation, not merely because there is nothing in this world that can stand continuous strain and even unthinking and inanimate objects are unable to maintain their strength, unless given intervals at rest, but because study depends on the good will of the student, a quality that cannot be secured by compulsion.'[5]

The father corrector and the guardian father of the Arcangelo Raffaello clearly adhered to the same philosophy and allowed the youths space and time within the confraternity's walls for some physical merry-making as well as for devotions.

There remained, however, the question of what was an appropriate pastime for youths in a confraternity. Card games, dice, and gambling obviously were not, for they were closely associated with taverns and similar unsavoury places. The 1468 statutes had clearly stated a member 'was not to indulge in any game or watch any game, and especially not those forbidden by Holy Mother Church. He should not gamble, or curse, or spread rumours, or tell lies. Brothers should not frequent places where there are taverns, or go at night to places where there are dances or music or vulgar songs. Nor should they take part in jousts, fights, or other spectacles for the masses.' A brother who had been led by bad company to play with dice, the 1468 statutes went on to say, should be twice warned and corrected, but on the third occasion he should be expelled from the confraternity.[6] Such was the case with Ottavio Pollini, who was expelled from the Arcangelo Raffaello on 25 May 1562 'for having caused arguments on several occasions, and for having played cards several times after having been reprimanded for this, and for having broken the gilded garland on the confraternity door, and for many other things which are better left unsaid.'[7] Although Ottavio Pollini was probably not an easy youth to deal with, anyway, his behaviour does suggest how important it was, for the confraternity, to find a suitable outlet for its young members' excess energies.

Several such outlets were, in fact, available within the confraternal setting. Already in the fifteenth century, soon after it first started to meet, the confraternity began to put on theatrical representations, and continued to do so well into the seventeenth century (see the following chapter). It also involved the youths in singing, even to the extent of providing a paid teacher to train them (see ch. 18). Both, however, were rather tame activities that did not quite offer the kind of physical outlet the youths really needed to keep them away from rowdier behaviour in the taverns or streets of the city. As in the case of the Benedictine monks from Cecchi's prologues, the youths needed a sport to exhaust their energies. And what better sport, then or now in Italy, than a ball game.

## The *Pallottolaio*

By the mid-sixteenth century, several youth confraternities in Florence owned a ball court (*pallottolaio*) where their members played ball games. By 1624 there were *pallottolai* at San Giovanni Evangelista, San Giorgio, San Bernardino, San Domenico, and Sant'Alberto Bianco dei Fanciulli, as well as at the Arcangelo Raffaello.[8]

As the records of Sant'Antonio da Padova indicate, the existence of a *pallottolaio* in the confraternity complex helped the youths 'flee scandal or worse trouble.' For this very reason the confraternity of Sant'Antonio da Padova decided in December 1610 to build one in its garden 'so that our youths can entertain themselves on feast-days after divine office.' The current governor, Guasparri di Pierfrancesco Landini, was put in charge of the project, and he met the challenge by having the structure built in stone, thus giving it not only a sense of permanence but also greater durability. Construction costs were to be recuperated over time by charging individual players for use of the court.[9]

The Sant'Antonio document unfortunately leaves a blank space where the dimensions of the court and the regulations for its use were to be entered. We do know, however, that the walls and pillars were painted white and that there was a roof over it – in February 1630/1, while the confraternity was closed during the quarantine elicited by the current plague, the *pallottolaio* was whitewashed, and then in July-September 1633 a wooden roof was placed over it and the old walls and pillars painted afresh.[10] In a 1624 affidavit, the youth confraternity of San Bernardino described its *pallottolaio* as 'path for playing ball' ('un viottolo per giocare alle pallottole'), thus indicating that the court was more of a narrow corridor than a wide field.

As the youths of Sant'Antonio realized, *pallottolai* had to have rules to regulate their use 'so that things should proceed with order, and [so that] we might avoid scandals.'[11] Trouble, however, was not easily avoided, especially when neighbours complained about the noise.

Such was the case with the youth confraternity of Sant'Alberto Bianco, which met in the Carmine district. In 1624, its neighbour, the cav. Pesciolini, brought a suit against them at the ecclesiastical tribunal. The confraternity responded by gathering affidavits attesting to the presence of *pallottolai* in other confraternities. In its affidavit, the Arcangelo Raffaello pointed out that it had not one but two *pallottolai* and that they were located under some windows of the Mazzinghi house next door. In their defence plea, the youths of Sant'Alberto Bianco referred specifically to the situation at the Arcangelo Raffaello and noted that the Pesciolini, who were renters, did not need be concerned about noise, since the Mazzinghi, who actually owned their house, had no complaints at all about the presence of *pallottolai* under their windows. To shore up their defence further, the youths of Sant'Alberto Bianco pointed out that as early as the past May they had rented a garden (*orto*) next to their building and *pallottolaio* and wished to use it for 'virtuous deeds, such as comedies or religious plays as has often been done in Florence, pious works such as religious discussions, lessons on the lives of saints, sacred songs, and other chaste and permissible pastimes as are carried out in similar places and in nearly all other confraternities in this city.' Their plea, however, fell on deaf ears, for the archbishop ruled against them, ordering them not to play *pallottole* or *piastrelle* or any other game, or to make any inappropriate noise under pain of an interdict for the confraternity and a fine of 25 *scudi* (175 lire) for each of the individuals involved.[12] The judgment was severe, but perhaps merited. The game of *pallottole* does not seem to have been a quiet sport.

Eventually, even the Arcangelo Raffaello was obliged to remove its *pallottolaio* to another location. By 1656 we find it located in the garden of the guardian father's house in via della Scala. The entry in the records notes that it had been built there because the Arcangelo Raffaello 'knew how necessary it was for the youths in the confraternity always to have a place where they could go for recreation and where they could gather on festive days after the usual *tornate* and also on half-feast days in order to gather honestly and thus spend the free time that is so dangerous for youth.' Eight members signed the document pledging to pay the necessary rent of sixteen ducats and any other expenses necessary to maintain the *pallottolaio*.[13] By 1658 the situation had changed slightly. The house was now inhabited by Raffaello and Lorenzo Del Soldato, two brothers very active in the Arcangelo Raffaello, and a new group, this time composed of fifteen members, undertook to oversee the management of the *pallottolaio*, its track (*viottolo*), and its finances. The confraternity, the document reiterates, had paid for the construction of the *pallottolaio* on the understanding that it would be refunded the expenses from the ball court's daily earnings.[14] It is evident that although the confraternity was quick to defend the usefulness of a ball court for the moral well-being of its members, it still expected the venture eventually to be self-funding – which it had not yet become after at least two years of operation.

By the eighteenth century, ball courts disappear completely from the records of the Arcangelo Raffaello. Perhaps ecclesiastical regulations against such games within the contexts of confraternities were having their effect, or perhaps the membership was growing older and less inclined to participate in such strenuous sports.

## Arcadia

Although in the eighteenth century the members of the Arcangelo Raffaello appeared not to engage themselves in sports, those of Sant'Antonio da Padova, on the other hand, developed a refined interest in salon games – cards and billiards. By 1728 they had actually set up a room for such table games and had even given it a name, 'Arcadia,' that betrayed not only the confraternity's pretensions at elegant erudition, but also the new spirit of the times and the confraternity's abysmal fall from Christian devotion or spirituality. In January 1728 the 'Arcadia,' which had been managed till then by twelve brothers, was turned over to a consortium of sixteen members, who went by the rather pompous title of 'Accademici.' An inventory of the objects from the room temporarily transferred by the confraternity to the 'Accademici' reveals that the room contained a variety of games, in particular card games and billiards (*trucco*).[15] Though perhaps more elegant, it was, in purpose, possibly not unlike our contemporary pinball arcades.

The game of *trucco*, which was one of the main attractions in the 'Arcadia,' was a type of billiards. According to a sixteenth-century poem by Nicola Martelli, the game was invented at the beginning of that century in either Naples or Mantua and was brought to Florence from Naples by Pandolfo Pucci, where it was at first called *gugole*.[16] The game became quite the rage in fashionable circles in the seventeenth and eighteenth centuries as the French kings, Louis XIII and then Louis XIV, made it one of their favourite pastimes. But, as in the fictitious River City, Iowa, of *The Music Man*, so too in Florence this early form of pool eventually ran afoul of the local authorities. In Florence, Grand Duke Peter Leopold forbade the game in 1781, and the confraternity of Sant'Antonio was left with little choice but to sell their equipment.[17]

## Conclusion

Though they originally sought to keep youths away from taverns and off the streets, especially during the dangerous period of Carnival time, confraternity sports and games eventually became in themselves a source of temptation for members and an object of disapproval for 'right-minded' people. Ball games disturbed neighbours and landed confraternities in court. Ball courts were expensive to build and maintain and eventually had to be given over to consortia to manage them. Card games ran afoul of the original fifteenth-century statutes that had viewed them as cause enough for reprimands and ejection from the confraternity. And billiards, then as now, was ... not nice?

One recreational activity that did flourish in youth confraternities for close to two and a half centuries, however, was theatre. Whether as a form of 'honest entertainment' at Carnival time, or as a pedagogical tool in the confraternity's continuing efforts to instruct the young, or as a devotional component in the annual ritual of celebrations, confraternity theatre successfully blended probity with the risqué, learning with fun, reverence with amusement. The next chapter will examine its development within the confraternity of the Arcangelo Raffaello.

# 16

# Theatre in the Confraternity

At different times in its annual calendar of feasts and devotions, as well as at different moments in its 374-year existence, the confraternity of the Arcangelo Raffaello organized theatrical performances that were either inserted into its devotional life or performed separately as a special event for members and friends. In line with current theories on play-acting and education, the performance of plays by youths in confraternities was seen both as a moment of relaxation and as an opportunity for education. The Horatian maxim of *delectare et docere*, so often repeated in the prologues of fifteenth- and sixteenth-century plays, served as a mark of antique authority and as an indication of contemporary views on the role of theatre. The content of the plays, the oratorical exercise of learning and performing parts, and the administrative experience of staging and producing a play all served to educate the youths who worked on the event. This chapter will examine the recreation/education rationale behind the performance of theatre within youth confraternities and then discuss the four most important yearly occasions for theatrical performances at the Arcangelo Raffaello in the fifteenth and sixteenth centuries: Christmas, the St John's procession, and the feast-days of the Archangel Raphael and of St Mary Magdalene.

## Plays as Recreation

The staging of religious plays was seen as an activity that kept youths away from less reputable pastimes such as gaming, dicing, and drinking. By being involved in an event that aimed to be spiritually uplifting, and one whose organization and production taught participants basic lessons on successful management and positive interpersonal skills, the youths were thus engaged in an entertainment that was morally acceptable. It is not unusual, therefore, for the *ricordi* to refer to plays as 'honest entertainment' ('onesto trattenimento') for both participants and spectators.

The 1636 statutes of the confraternity of the Arcangelo Raffaello speak clearly about plays in confraternities. Under the rubric 'Regarding Honest Recreation,' they say

> 'that honest and gentle ['soavi'] entertainments lift and fortify the soul greatly, as the Holy Fathers bear witness with their example ... Thus, with the guardian father's permission, ... the brothers may once a year restore themselves in a pleasant villa, or stage a virtuous comedy or a sacred representation, to be recited with the appropriate decorum and retaining modesty in speech, gravity in actions, fleeing noises ['strepiti'], obscenities, gossip, and undue licence, all the while remembering the words of the Orator: When we give our spirit to pleasant pastimes, we will remember truth and decorum.'[1]

All youth confraternities performed plays at Carnival and at other appropriate times of the year. In some confraternities, plays eventually became such a common occurrence that permanent structures were built to accommodate them. In 1563, for example, the confraternity of San Giovanni Evangelista asked for permission to build a permanent stage (*palco*) in its stanzone for the performance of its annual plays.[2] Other confraternities rented or purchased land adjacent to their oratory complex in order to have an area in which to stage plays or play ball. In their 1624 plea in defence of their *pallottolaio*, the youths of Sant'Alberto Bianco claimed the garden had been rented expressly for them 'to exercise themselves in honest activities, such as comedies and pious representations staged many times in Florence, pious works such as devout gatherings, lessons from the lives of the saints, divine lauds, and also other permissible and modest pastimes as are usually carried out in other similar places and in nearly all other confraternities in this city.'[3]

Plays, in fact, had long been a regular activity of Florentine youth confraternities and were often composed by persons with close connections to them. Piero di Mariano Muzi, the guardian father of the Purificazione and brother to Antonio di Mariano Muzi, guardian to the Arcangelo Raffaello, composed a play on the prodigal son theme for his youths to perform.[4]

The most famous fifteenth-century Florentine religious play, the *Rappresentazione di SS. Giovanni e Paolo*, was composed by Lorenzo de' Medici at the request of his son Giuliano for performance in the confraternity of San Giovanni Evangelista (17 February 1490/1).[5] In the sixteenth century, Giovan Maria Cecchi wrote at least twenty-eight plays for at least four different Florentine confraternities.[6] Further research into confraternity drama will eventually point to the large corpus of plays commissioned by, composed for, or performed in confraternities, and will shed light on staging practices that eventually evolved into the elaborate settings and technical virtuosity of Renaissance and baroque theatre.[7]

## The 1430 Nativity Play

The 1430 performance of a Nativity play in the presence of Pope Eugenius IV and the entire Florentine Signoria is a defining moment in the history of the Arcangelo Raffaello. The performance is viewed by the seventeenth-century antiquarian Ferdinando Leopoldo Del Migliore as the event that led to the confraternity's subsequent good fortune in receiving from the pontiff a permanent meeting site, official statutes, a name, and a patron saint.[8] The general public and the confraternity itself must have viewed the event in a similar vein, for the youths soon became known as the confraternity 'of the Nativity' and were called upon to perform the play on special occasions. As if to mark this development, an image of the Nativity was placed on the right shoulder of the confraternity's official gown worn on public processions. The play that endeared the children to the pope thus became the visual representation of the confraternity's public and private image.

Unfortunately, no first-hand record of the event has come to light. A description of the performance, if it was ever entered in the confraternity's *ricordi*, and the text, if it was ever preserved in the confraternity's files, may have been severely damaged or destroyed at several points in the confraternity's life – they may have been lost in the 1557 flood, for example, or during one of the several suppressions the confraternity suffered at the hands of the government. The text itself may have been an ephemeral work, composed explicitly for the 1430 performance in the church of San Pancrazio and discarded soon thereafter. Although much evidence is lacking, it is clear that the confraternity had established a reputation for itself, thanks, in part, to the Nativity plays it performed in the 1430s and for many years thereafter.

## Nativity Plays in the St John's Parade

By the mid-1400s, the Arcangelo Raffaello's Nativity play had, in fact, become one of the component parts of the annual St John's procession and parade. A few years earlier, the entire event had drawn the attention of one of the Eastern delegates to the Ecumenical Council of Union (1439). His description of what appear to be plays performed during the St John's parade is brief but revealing:

On the 23rd of June they hold a great procession and a great feast, attended by the entire population. In it, they present prodigious things, nearly miracles, or representations of miracles. For they resurrect the dead; St Michael stomps on demons; they crucify a man who plays the part of Christ; and they represent the Resurrection of Christ; they make men play the part of Magi, and with men they represent the birth of Christ; with shepherds, and the star, and the animals, and the crèche. Then, they go in procession with statues, relics of the saints, and images, and crosses worthy of reverence; always with trumpets and other musical instruments in front. What can one say about the fact that they had a monk represent St Augustine and they placed him twenty-five *braccia* high, and he walked about and preached. And they also represent hermits with beards, and they walked high up on wooden legs; a striking spectacle! And we also saw some statues, some very big, some tall, process heavily along. What can one say about St George, who put on the miracle of the dragon? Having done all these things on the 23rd (on the 22nd, in fact, they had placed their riches on show and displayed a great quantity of gold and silver and much clothing), the day of the feast they consecrated about a hundred banners in the church of S. Giovanni, then about thirty wooden castles, but very well done; then a great quantity of candles and torches; then some men who had been kept in prison, with crowns and olive branches.[9]

The secular aspect of this procession not only surprised the visiting Orthodox dignitary, but was unacceptable to a later archbishop of Florence, Antoninus Pierozzi. In 1454, Antoninus sought to separate the procession's clerical and secular elements by decreeing that henceforth the clergy would process on the morning of 23 June, the eve of St John's, while the parade of floats would wind its way on the morning of the previous day, 22 June.[10]

The St John's parade of floats is of interest to historians of theatre. In her collection of fifteenth-century Florentine religious plays, Nerida Newbigin argues convincingly for a reinterpretation of this parade as a cycle play.[11] She bases her argument in part on the 1454 description of the event by the chronicler Matteo Palmieri, who records that year's order of festivities. Palmieri's narrative clearly indicates that the St John's parade was composed of at least three different elements – parade, cavalcade, and floats – all intermingled and all connected sequentially to form a unified narrative. The floats served as pageant wagons for the performance of a number of plays that were interspersed with the parade and cavalcade, and which contributed to the narrative of the event. In describing the parade, Palmieri tells of an unusual incident that occurred when float no. 11 arrived in the piazza and its occupants were about to begin their play:

'11. *Templum pacis* with the float of the Nativity in order to stage its play.
*Intervention of a crazy man.*
It happened that, as the float arrived in front of the Palazzo of the Signoria and Octavian dismounted from his horse and went up inside the float, that is into the temple, in order to begin the play, a crazy German wearing only a wet shirt came along and asked: 'Where's the King of Rome?' Somebody answered him saying: 'There he is,' and pointed to Octavian. The German went up onto the float, and since many thought he was part of the play no one prevented him from doing so. First he seized the statue that was in the temple and threw it into the piazza, then he turned to Octavian, who was dressed in very rich purple with gold brocade, grabbed a hold of him and sent him upside-down into the people in the square. Then he attached himself to one of the temple's columns and tried to climb up to where there were some youths on top of the float dressed up as angels, who, from up there, beat him fiercely with some batons they had in their hands and, not without some difficulty, made him fall to the ground. When he got up and tried to climb back up, he was beaten with many clubs, both from above and from below.'[12]

Palmieri's description indicates that the youths of the Arcangelo Raffaello participated in the event not just by marching in the parade, or by simply staging a *tableau vivant*, but by actually performing a play on their own pageant wagon. It also gives us several insights into dramatic performance and audience participation at a Florentine festival. It indicates, for example, that the performance not only took place on the pageant wagon, but could move to and from street level. Actors could mingle with, and come out from, the audience – some of whom obviously moved with and became part of the parade. For the drunken German to be mistaken for an actor, costume must have included contemporary garb. Palmieri's description also reveals the resourcefulness and resilience of the youthful actors, who, as avenging angels from on high, could intervene into the 'action' and physically force an unwelcome intruder from their stage.

## The 1573 Nativity Play by Giovan Maria Cecchi

Although the Nativity plays performed by the Arcangelo Raffaello in the fifteenth century have been lost, a Nativity play composed for and performed by the confraternity in 1573 has survived – Giovan Maria Cecchi's *Atto recitabile per alla Capannuccia. Per il natale di Nostro Signore* (*Scenic act to be performed at the manger. For the birth of Our Lord*). Cecchi composed the work at one go and in a hurry on 29 November 1573, 'the eve of St Andrew's,' and sent it that same day to a certain Messer Piero, who had commissioned it, with a covering note inviting the recipient to alter it as he thought necessary, for 'time is short, and I have not had the leisure to revise it.'[13]

The play is more of a devotional interlude than a dramatic work. It contains allegorical figures (Vigilance as the prologue, Human Nature, Peace, Charity), Old Testament prophets (David, Solomon, Isaiah), and sibyls (the Eritrean and Cumean sibyls). They either recite their lines or sing them solo or in chorus. The verses are written in a variety of forms (sextets, septets, octaves, or free hendecasyllabic verse).

Structurally, the work is a triptych. After the prologue recited by Vigilance, three allegorical figures appear on stage (Human Nature, Peace, Charity) and recall how postlapsarian history has been a history of waiting for the arrival of the Redeemer foreshadowed by several Old Testament figures – Abel, Noah, Abraham, Isaac, Jacob, and Moses. When Human Nature, Peace, and Charity finish reciting their individual parts, the three prophets and two sibyls appear and sing in turn their respective prophecies. When they are done the curtain drops to reveal the manger (*presepio*) while a choir of angels sings a 'Gloria,' arranged as a madrigal. The prophets and sibyls sing another madrigal, and thus bring their contribution to an end. At this point the play returns to the three allegorical figures, who now adore the manger scene and, reciting their praises of the new-born babe, identify in him the Old Testament patriarchs who had prefigured the redemption; 'Here is the second Adam ... here is the just Abel ... here is the more just Abraham and the more perfect Isaac ... here is the most worthy usurper of Jacob ... here is the true Moses.' The play then ends with everyone, actors and audience, processing to the manger to kiss the Christ-child.[14]

The three sections of this 'dramatized' triptych are: (1) an allegorical segment in which sacred history up to the birth of the Redeemer is seen as a period of waiting punctuated by a series of precursors to the promised Redeemer; (2) a devotional interlude in which Hebrew prophets and pagan sibyls sing their prophecies and attest to the arrival of the Redeemer (literally, the unveiling of the manger); and then (3) another allegorical segment in which the Christ-child is identified as the Redeemer who supplants his Old Testament precursors. There is no dramatic action or tension in this play. Historical events are interpreted allegorically, the action on stage limits itself to the unveiling of the manger, and what follows is merely an explication of how the manger scene reflects and surpasses sacred history. The emphasis is placed on the devotional and spiritual aspects of the event, all with an underlying tone of instruction – after all, the play was being staged and performed by youths for their edification and devotion. Music (singing) and ritual (the procession to kiss the Christ-child) elevate the play towards a religious celebration appropriate for the season.

The entry for 24 December 1586 in the confraternity's *ricordi* sheds light on the context for the unveiling of the *presepio* on Christmas Eve:

Since it was the eve of the Nativity of our Lord, we gathered at the fourth hour in order to unveil the most sacred *presepio* and we sang Matins. And because the church of Santa Maria Novella was not yet open, many women came and stayed until it opened, continually singing psalms and hymns. Then we went to kiss the Child, since our assistant *provveditore* had had a beautiful *presepio* set up, with a great number of angels, so that it looked like Paradise, with many lights. And at the eighth hour, as the church opened, everyone took his leave.[15]

There is, in the *ricordi* entry, an interesting mixture of devotion and performance, of private and public events, and of prayer and waiting, rendered all the more theatrical by the presence of adults of both sexes – women, as well as men, are mentioned in the entries for other years (1583, 1584, for example) – whose role is akin to that of spectators. There are also elements, such as the singing of hymns or the processing to kiss the child in the *presepio*, that clearly connect the ritual in the *ricordi* entry with Cecchi's *Atto recitabile per alla Capannuccia*.

## The Raphael and Tobias Plays

Plays touching on the Archangel Raphael and Tobias were also an important component of the confraternity's dramatic repertoire. The archangel was, after all, the confraternity's patron saint and namesake, while the young Tobias was emblematic of all youths in the confraternity. Short plays that enacted a visit from the Archangel Raphael or his companion Tobias thus entered into the confraternity's rituals, usually to illustrate how the archangel who guided and instructed the Hebrew youth could also guide and instruct his Florentine devotees.

Most Raphael/Tobias plays were performed, as one would expect, on the day the youths celebrated their annual feast and patron saint (31 December). During the 1563 festivities, for example, the youth Tobias walked into the oratory to take part in the confraternity's annual celebrations. After the usual several morning Masses in the confraternity, Matins, the blessing of the special bread with the confraternity's emblem stamped on it (*panellini*), and the singing of the *lauda* 'Hyerusalem dominum,' the youths sat at their places as a brother dressed as Tobias entered the oratory. The scribe tells that Tobias then 'recited many verses' reprimanding the outgoing officers whose term was drawing to a close that day, the guardian father, and the incoming officers, and admonishing them, saying, the Archangel Raphael who had sent him did not wish the confraternity to forego the traditional distribution of the *panellini*. To this purpose the archangel had sent Tobias and two Virtues, Humility and Obedience, to assist in the distribution. After the youths had sung another *lauda*, Tobias went to the door of the *tornatino* and called forth the two Virtues, who entered and recited, each in turn, a few verses. Then, with the help of the twelve *festaioli*, Tobias and the two Virtues distributed the blessed bread. When all was done, Tobias dismissed the youths.[16]

Although not a 'play' in the traditional sense of the word, the costuming, impersonation, recitation of verses, the 'action' present in calling out other 'characters,' and the sense of 'spectacle' on the part of the audience indicate that a simple theatrical event had been performed. It had been smoothly integrated into the devotional ritual – Masses, Matins, Lauds, distribution of blessed bread – and into the festive context of that occasion – the celebrations for the patron saint. Although the 'play' purported to issue a reprimand to the outgoing officers and say some words of warning to the incoming slate, there is no indication that either group had done anything to deserve such words. The performance, therefore, was morally gratuitous and festively appreciated.

There were times, however, when Tobias and the archangel appeared explicitly to chastise. Such was the case, for example, on 3 June 1582. That afternoon, the youths had gathered for their usual devotional routine – Vespers and then a sermon on charity recited by one of the brothers. After the offering to the altar was collected, however, Zanobi Buonavolti, the acting guardian father, invited everyone to move to the entrance hall (*stanzone*) where the youths saw a play, at first described briefly and then transcribed in full in the *ricordi*.[17] The day of the performance was Pentecost Sunday, a day in which there was no tradition in the confraternity for festive or devotional entertainments. This, and the full transcription, invite a closer examination of the event and the circumstances.

The argument of the play centres on the degeneration of the confraternity's ritual and devotion. A young man, who has been a member of the

Arcangelo Raffaello for seven years, accompanies a pilgrim to the confraternity and tells him, with regret, that the group's devotion and practices have reached a very low point. Members, he says, attend only 'out of habit,' they no longer carry out the devotions and rituals of old, they no longer compete with each other in charity and devotion, they do not obey their officers, nor are they eager to volunteer to assist the confraternity. In fact, they no longer linger in the confraternity after services to learn Christian doctrine, but 'flee' away as soon as Vespers are ended. The older members, adds the youth, are the worst, for they mock the rituals, disobey the guardian father, do not bother to confess regularly, and object to being reprimanded in public. To aggravate the entire situation, the confraternity now finds itself without a guardian father and seems unable to attract anyone to the position. Knowing the youths cannot improve their situation on their own, the youth expresses his wish for a guardian father strong enough to restore the confraternity's rituals, devotions, and reputation. At this point the pilgrim reveals himself to be Tobias, encourages the youth to turn to their patron saint, and then prays to the Archangel Raphael to intervene. The archangel appears, accompanied by two other angels, all three singing a madrigal. He then urges the youths to reform by remaining true to their statutes, which are still wholesome (*sani*), and by adhering to God's law. To help the youths know this law, the archangel asks Tobias and the two angels to give to each youth in the hall a sheet of paper containing a listing of the following: the twelve articles of faith, the Creed, the Ten Commandments, the seven Sacraments of the Church, the three theological virtues, the four cardinal virtues, the seven gifts of the Holy Spirit, the two commandments of charity, the seven spiritual works of mercy, the seven temporal works of mercy, the seven mortal sins, the four things a Christian must always keep in mind, the five senses of the body, the commandments of the Church, the precepts a good Christian must observe, the six sins against the Holy Spirit, and the eight Beatitudes.[18]

The play is thus clearly intended to reprimand and admonish the youths for a perceived decline in devotional practices, and to suggest that their inability to secure a new guardian father was a direct result of such decline. The previous guardian father, Ser Ceseri Galletti, had resigned because of advanced age on 10 December 1581. By June 1582, the confraternity's selection committee had still been unsuccessful in finding a suitable and willing replacement. The play, the reprimand it contained, and its exhortation to prayer and diligence were thus intended to lead to a personal reform that would improve the confraternity and, in turn, attract a suitable candidate for the vacant post. In the eyes of its contemporaries, the play was probably a success, for, two months later, on 12 August, Antonio di Pasci da Colle, a schoolteacher in Florence living in the quarter of Santa Croce, agreed to serve. He was approved by the papal commission on 17 August and formally installed on 2 September.[19]

It is not possible for us to determine whether the play led to a reform which, in turn, convinced Messer Antonio to accept the position. It is possible, however, to identify the play's intentions and appreciate the role such presentations played in the confraternity. Those who had organized the play, and especially the acting guardian father, Zanobi Buonavolti, certainly considered such activities to be educational and effective. In their eyes, the play had achieved its goal.

Not all appearances of Raphael and Tobias involved reprimands – gratuitous or deserved, as they may have been. Occasionally the pair cheerfully joined the youths to march with them in public processions. In 1582, for example, they and an angelic choir joined the confraternity in the St John's procession and sang a madrigal composed by one of the youths.[20]

At least once the pair returned to the confraternity in a play that did not reprimand the youths or invite them to join in a confraternity ritual, but rather re-enacted on stage an episode from the apocryphal book of Tobit. This occurred on 5 February 1624 when the youths performed Jacopo Cicognini's *La celeste guida* (*The Heavenly Guide*), a 'regular' play that was then published the following year.[21] Cicognini's dedicatory letter and his brief description in the preface to the reader, as well as the long description of the event in the confraternity's records, attest to an elaborate and elegant Carnival-time production. Even the court diary recalls the event, saying the grand-ducal couple and their children attended the performance, which lasted three hours, and they 'remained at their chairs without Residence. It was well acted, with beautiful costumes.'[22]

Because the scribe's description is one of the most detailed in the records, it is well worth citing in full to illustrate the wealth of skills and resources available at the confraternity:

Our Company, wishing to represent for one time the happy and glorious return of our great father and protector, the Archangel Raphael, and seeing that the general membership was so inclined, arranged in that enthusiasm for the composition of this sacred representation. When the parts had been assigned, it was staged with full display and exquisite music and costumes, all by the youths from our Company. For this reason it has seemed appropriate to make a special memoir both of the work and the music that went with it, as well as of the stage set ['apparato'] and other details, as follows.

The author envisioned not the entire history of young Tobias, which usually begins with his departure, but rather his return, accompanied by that heavenly guide the Archangel Raphael [who was going] under the name of Azarias. In his work [the author] did not overstep the span of twenty-four hours, in which the action [of the play] was envisioned. Besides what the story tells, he introduced many events suitable to the [different] parts, grave, humorous, and new, since the story, which in itself is bare of incidents and events [and] restricted to one day, could not contain anything else but the return of the young man and the healing of his father. For this reason it was necessary to adorn it. And with all of this, the parts and events that were added were connected to the marriage of Sarah and the young Tobias and not detached from it, nor were they separated from the characters in the sacred story, as can be well understood from the play.

It was staged this past Carnival, and what elicited no less pleasure than marvel was that our Most Serene Lords expressed their wish to favour us with their most desired presence even before our invitation [had been sent], which would have been done after the first performance, which, as usual, is a dress rehearsal in front of the women. For this reason the oratory was quickly set up and the work was presented as had been planned for their presence.

When the silk curtains were raised, which thus raised formed on their own an ornament and festoon for the arch that had been placed high in the ceiling, one saw a most beautiful stage set representing the city of Nineveh. Straight ahead was the city gate, with towering walls, and outside the gate one could see a country scene with long fields and tall mountains in the distance. And on stage one saw the following characters.

Prayer knelt in the middle, with a small antique altar in front of her, and on the altar a thurible that let out perfumed smoke. She was accompanied by Charity and the Seven Works of Corporal Mercy, dressed in appropriate costumes and holding in their hand objects that indicated each character's qualities. After a musical piece ['sinfonia'] by various instruments they sang in praise of the works of charity.

Then Prayer, with a most sweet ['soave'] voice showed how the works of mercy, when joined with Prayer, were welcomed by God. This was done with good foresight, since one was about to stage the play of young and old Tobias which, because of their charity and prayers, were so welcome to God.

Since the site was not [large enough] for machines, or for [easy] set changes for suitable interludes, the dramatist ['poeta'] sought to ennoble the representation in the best way the confraternity oratory allowed, and thought that if music and dance were occasionally woven on purpose into the play, they would relieve the spectator's tedium at the familiar events of the narrative. Thus, at the end of the third act, after old Tobias had gone with some of his relatives to pray God for the safe return of his son and had distributed alms to some poor girls, to serve as dowries, [the dramatist] had twelve youths dressed as girls appear on stage, six of whom sang and six danced with a movement that was very majestic, something between a walk ['passeggio'] and a dance ['ballo'], quite different from the last [dance]. This brought much delight because of the skill of both the choreographer and the composer, which in their genres was admirable. And the spectators could not tire of watching it, and thought it finished too soon.

Nor was the appearance and arrival of young Tobias less beautiful, or the healing of his father, which brought tears most devout and sweet [to the eyes]. The same [was true] with [the appearance of] Sarah, dressed most superbly, accompanied by twelve maidens from Media as well as by a choir of noble young men from Nineveh and other relatives and characters who had gone to greet her. As they were entering into the city through the gate straight ahead, the maidens sang and repeated some verses they had begun [singing] in the distance, so beautiful and harmonious that they filled the hearts of the spectators with infinite pleasure.

Then, after the appropriate greetings to old Tobias and his wife, [young Tobias] ordered that the slaves who had led the camels to the gate be unchained and be freed. These, happy at the bridegroom's order, began a most beautiful dance for eight youths, all from our Company, some of whom were dressed in a flesh-pink colour ['colore incarnato'] and other in deep blue ['turchino'] laced in silver in the same pattern, with caps laced in gold or silver and lined in silk ['tocca'], as were also the sleeves, and they showed most nobly. The dance was accompanied by a clever ['artificioso'] song sung by the same young maidens from Media.

After the slaves, the maidens, and all the other persons in the choir left, only old Tobias, his wife, and the newlywed couple remained on stage. They called for Azarias and offered him half their wealth, but he thanked them and revealed himself for who he was. In the act of revealing himself, the Archangel Raphael shook and filled the hearts of all the spectators with most sweet awe and an uncommon fright. At the same time, with unexpected marvel, he changed costume and form, for first he had appeared to be a pilgrim. Nor could one tell how, for those clothes and hat were removed as if by a miracle of God ['divinamente'], so that in a flash he transformed himself from a pilgrim into an angel dressed in a light cotton gown that was flesh-coloured with white interfacing and adorned in satin, and it was all laced in gold, and with the appropriate wig ['capelliera'], so much so that the spectators could not hold back their tears and, all filled with spiritual consolation, they concluded that the scope and intentions of the youths of the Confraternity had been attained and every pleasure had resolved itself in most devout concern ['compuntione'].

When the fifth act of the play had ended, the Archangel Raphael appeared again, accompanied by the Seven Works of Corporal Mercy, as if he were about to return to his heavenly homeland. Then, of a sudden, the forum and the gate of the city of Nineveh widened and the sky opened, and the Eternal Father appeared in a most bright and sublime throne, adored by angels. And from the heavenly seat a ladder made of clouds descended to the earth, on which the Archangel Raphael climbed in slow steps, leading with him the above-mentioned Virtues, singing all the while. When he arrived at the feet of the highest God, he explained in a most sweet voice what he had done for the good Tobias, in fulfilment of His command. Then, having recommended his devout servants and children [to God], and having prayed His Divine Majesty that He make the brothers of that Confraternity heir to His heavenly kingdom, and having heard the answer of the King of the world, all happy he changed those clouds into a golden ladder. And there remained, at the conclusion of the work, the Confraternity's own emblem. After the angelic choirs had sweetly sung while the heavens closed up again, the ladder disappeared, and the forum and the gate returned to their proper places, such a noble and virtuous undertaking was brought to an end with devotion and universal applause.

So that no one should remain cheated of the merits and praises that are his due, either because of the expenses [he underwrote] or because he had engaged himself in such praiseworthy work, one will list, though in a disorderly manner not respectful of any order of precedence, all those who have taken part in it.

Headmasters ['capi'] of the play: our father corrector fra Santi Contrigni, our guardian father Messer Francesco Fiorvigna, Lorenzo Galli, Mario Stefani, Cosimo Portinari. Author of the work: Dr Jacopo Cicognini, one of our brothers. Composer of the music: Giovanbatista da Gagliano, our *maestro di cappella.* Choreographer of the dances: Santi Commessari. Responsible for the stage set, scenery, and related expenses: Cosimo Portinari, Ferdinando de' Bardi, Lionardo Tempi. Responsible for the music and related expenses: Lorenzo Galli, the brothers Nicolò, Giulio, and Giovanni di Antonio Buonaccorsi. Responsible for all the lights and lighting of the stage set, which was all done with wax torches: Francesco Cavalcanti, Giovan Battista del Rosso. Responsible for the dances, and related expenses: Cav.re Agnolo Dassi, Vincenzio Giraldi, Agnolo Galli. The following danced: Vincentio Giraldi, Luigi and Alfonso d'Antonio Antinori, Camillo and Francesco d'Alessandro del Nero, Tommaso di Salvetto Salvetti, Giovanni di Vincenzo Tatti, Zanobi Salvini. In the same dance these [youths] were instructed by Francesco Fontani and Cosimo, students of the above-mentioned Santi Commessari, choreographer of the dance. The above-mentioned Cav.re Agnolo Dassi, Vincenzo Giraldi, Agnolo Galli, Cammillo and Francesco del Nero, Luigi and Alfonso Antinori paid for their own costumes.

It should not be left unsaid that in this representation all the costumes were not only very appropriate, and all in the ancient way without hats, capes ['ferraiolo'] or swords, which are modern civil clothes, but long for older characters and for the youths jackets ['giubbe'] down to the knees of such materials that they were beyond belief for the viewers, not only because the costumes were made of velvet and all full of gold, and the tinsel ['canutiglie'] was real and good, but many were also made with gold interfacing ['telette d'oro'], and were brand new, and of various colours, that on stage they made such a fine show and represented so many heroes. Among [such costumes] that of the above-mentioned Francesco Cavalcanti stood out [and drew much] admiration, in red velvet all embroidered with tinsel and gold bars, as well as that of Ferdinando de' Bardi, so rich both in its material and in the quality of its gold lace, and also the costume embroidered with towers, a symbol of his family, which he arranged for one of the youths in the choir. Nor was the costume of the same [Ferdinando de' Bardi] less admirable when he appeared dressed like a maiden from Media, for it seemed to be all glimmering and full of trembling stars on account of the lights that reflected on the artful costume. To which one should add the costumes of the youths in the choir, among which there was a green one, full of flowers in bloom, embroidered in gold with roses, worn by Giovan Battista Bartoli. Among others, an admirable, rich, splendid and noble costume was the one worn by Giovanni Battista del Rosso, who was, like all the others, in a general costume ['in universale'], since the older youths were dressed in long gowns of purple velvet and other colours.

But among all, like the sun among the stars, the costumes of Tobias and his bride Sarah seemed admirable to the spectators' eyes. Appearing at the end [of the play] surrounded by so many maidens, [Sarah] reinforced her beauty with such a sumptuous fine wool dress, flesh-toned ['incarnatina'] and white, adorned with satin and with gold lace in the manner of Media, that truly there was no one who did not praise it greatly.

The other costumes for the choir, the Works of Mercy, the angels, and in particular the clever costume the Archangel Raphael put on and took off, and a quantity of well-devised, designed, formed, and rich hats and caps, were the work, expense, and effect of the imagination of the most devoted Cosimo del Bianco, who on this, and many other occasions, has always deserved universal praise.

The costume of Astradoro was admirable, and that of Rullo, the foolish servant, for its whimsical design, and which was made at the expense of him who played the part, and also that of the young page, and finally everyone's in particular, and in general they were most appropriately dressed, but each had made the effort to have his cap ['berrettone'] specially made, and from the materials, jewels, and feathers it was evident that they had competed in expense and in imagination.

The patron of this spiritual representation and devout undertaking was the most illustrious Signor Piero de' Bardi, Count of Vernio, a man famous for combining nobility with virtue.[23] He worked so that everything went well and in order. And this was the kind result of his praiseworthy and welcomed manners, due to which everything went happily. The father of the del Nero brothers, besides the great care he took in finding costumes, showed himself to be so zealous for the glory of the

Confraternity that even behind the stage and on every occasion he did not avoid any undertaking, and there was no place where he did not show a sign of his affection.

The general producers ['provveditori generali'], and worthy of much praise, [were] Antonio del Soldato and Antonio Vitolini.

| *Cast of characters* | *Names of the performers* |
|---|---|
| the elder Tobias | Antonio del Soldato |
| Anna, his wife | Francesco del Bianco |
| Tobias, his young son | Lionardo Tempi |
| Sarah, his bride | Donato Alamanni |
| Rosetta, servant in the house | Giovanni Buonaccorsi |
| Delio, that is, Oristilla | Ferdinando de' Bardi |
| Domitio, a doctor | Giuseppe Lapi |
| Rullo, his foolish servant | Paolantonio Folchi |
| M.na Gioia, weaver | Lorenzo Stefani |
| Habat, old man, cousin of Tobias | Giulio Buonaccorsi |
| Corinto and | Francesco Cavalcanti |
| Lidio | Giovambatista del Rosso |
| Sbarra, servant to Corinto | Niccolò Buonaccorsi |
| Falchetto, page to Lidio | Francesco Salvini |
| Astradoro, a false hypocrite of Cabala | Alessandro Dami |
| Vitale, a foreigner | Francesco Stefani |
| Azarias, that is, the Arc. Raphael | Alfonso Peri |
| Choir of noble youths of Nineveh | Giovan Battista Bartoli |
| | Piero Lenzi |
| | Alessandro Galli |
| Zaffiro, young slave to Sarah | Carlo Galli |
| Prologue | Alessandro Galli |
| | Giovan Francesco Medici |

The prompter, for the actors as well as for the exits of the musical choirs, the dances, scene changes, and machines, was Vincenzo Ruotoli.

The musicians were for the most part students of the above-mentioned Giovan Battista da Gagliano and other famous musicians he had called upon.

Alfonso di Jacopo Peri interpreted not only the part of Azarias, but also that of Charity, singing with his usual grace, and at the end he sang the part of the Archangel Raphael. And the music was by the same Jacopo, his father. And let this suffice as a praise of one and the other, since their abilities are known to everyone.

The work was staged several times, and once especially on the specific invitation of gentle ladies, and thereafter in front of a large audience of noble and virtuous men.

It was all dedicated to the honour of God and to the glory of our great patron and father, the Archangel Raphael, and not for any other purpose or for human consideration, [but] begging him to receive the affection of our hearts and be our guide and most secure escort so that after the pilgrimage of this life [we may] arrive at the eternal homeland.[24]

As this long description indicates, the Arcangelo Raffaello not only had a lively interest in theatrical productions, but also the energy, ability, skills, and resources necessary to mount spectacular multimedia entertainments for the enjoyment of the Medici court and the Florentine nobility. It could call upon a variety of artists, from painters to musicians, from amateur actors to choreographers, not to mention wealthy patrons and eager volunteers, all of whom co-operated to ensure success and achieve honour for the confraternity. Pride in their abilities and achievement is evident in the scribe's detailed description.

Also evident is an interest in the theory of drama and, consequently, a certain critical acumen, for the scribe touches upon the three unities – time, place, and action. In particular, he points to and defends the author's inclusion of action that was not, strictly speaking, drawn from the Book of Tobit but was felt to be necessary for the theatrical and dramatic success of the play. Such observations echo Cicognini's own, later discussion published in the introduction to the 1625 edition of the play. 'Since one must not present [on stage] events that go beyond the space of twenty-four hours, and knowing that the healing of the old father did not contain action that would allow for the large number of characters, the variety of dances, and of pleasant and unexpected events sufficient for a five-act play ['rappresentatione'], for this reason it was necessary to make use of invention.'[25]

This coincidence indicates that there were lively discussions in the confraternity or, at least, among some of its members and sympathizers, on current dramatic theory in particular and on the art of theatre in general. The significant difference between the scribe's comments expressed in a private document – the *ricordi* – and Cicognini's views expressed in a public introduction to the reader is to be found not in the literary and theoretical aspects of the question, but rather in the very important and immediate concern to steer clear of the local Inquisitor. While the confraternity and its sympathizers may have understood the special role of theatre in education and may have been better able to separate fact from fiction, the general public or a zealous Inquisitor may not have been as subtle. Cicognini therefore bluntly points out:

So that the sacred story may always remain intact, you must recognize, oh judicious readers, to be pure truth only that which applies to the healing of [old] Tobias and the words of the Archangel Raphael before his disappearance, and so as to be better understood and for caution's sake, we have marked [the text] taken from the history of Tobias with a bolder script. The rest you must consider to be [material] inserted so that scenes may develop smoothly, yet within the rules [of drama], which is evident in the care that has been taken to raise only Sarah and her husband, who are the heroes [of the story], to be the subject of the main action, without [including] any other marriage at the end [of the play], for reasons that to you, as intelligent persons, are very well known.[26]

The critical acumen expressed by the scribe in his *ricordo*, the youths' association with a major contemporary Florentine dramatist and an important musician, as well as the elaborate stagecraft evident from the descriptions of the play, all indicate that the confraternity was a forum for dramatic and theatrical experimentation. In a more general way, the Nativity and the Raphael/Tobias plays indicate clearly that such experimentation was present over a long period of time, from the early fifteenth to the mid-seventeenth centuries. However, although the Nativity and Raphael/Tobias plays seem to be the most common subject matter for such theatrical interests, they do not constitute, in themselves, a continuum. The confraternity's interest in theatre, in fact, encompassed other subjects and other figures, and reflected and adapted itself to changing times and official attitudes. The remainder of this chapter will thus turn to the plays in honour of St Mary Magdalene, to the ecclesiastical pressures that were brought to bear on the confraternity's theatrical activities, and to its response to such pressures.

## St Mary Magdalene Plays

St Mary Magdalene was the confraternity's 'advocate' saint (*avvocata*), and as such she was honoured by the youths with a special celebration on the Sunday following her 22 July feast-day.[27] On a few occasions the records indicate that a short theatrical work was staged in her honour. After morning Mass on 28 July 1585, for example, 'Camillo Rondinelli recited some verses dressed up as St Mary Magdalene and accompanied by four angels,' and then the traditional sweetcakes (*berlingozzi*) and flowers were distributed to all present.[28] Rondinelli's verses were probably sung and accompanied by Raffaello Gucci on 'his instrument,' the *buonaccordo* he often played in those years in the confraternity.

Two short one-act plays touching on St Mary Magdalene written for and staged by the confraternity of the Arcangelo Raffaello are Giovan Maria Cecchi's *Disprezzo dell'amore e beltà terrena* and *Duello della vita attiva e contemplativa*, both composed in 1580–7.[29] The confraternity *ricordi* for these years, however, do not mention their performance. On 28 July 1624, on the other hand, they do register an elaborate performance of a play by Giovan Maria Cecchi entitled *Dialogo per la festa di S.M. Maddalena* (*Dialogue for the Feast-day of St Mary Magdalene*). The attribution and the detailed description of the action reveal that it was none other than his *Duello della vita attiva e contemplativa*, which had clearly remained in the confraternity's files.[30]

The *ricordi* point out that the decision to decorate the confraternity, set up a stage in the oratory, and present a play, 'in order to keep up the devotion towards the Most Holy Penitent Mary Magdalene,' was taken by the guardian father Francesco Fior Vigna, the governor Giovan Francesco Grazzini, and the sacristans.[31]

The *stanzone* was immediately decorated with green and yellow taffeta, and with paintings by well-known artists. Several large oval portraits of the saint, with carved wooden frames gilded *all'antica*, were hung in the oratory and decorated with sheets of white twill interspersed with fir branches. A stage was erected at the foot of the altar and, in place of a stage set, rows of vases were placed across it to conceal the musicians and to function as exits for the actors. Then, on Sunday, 28 July, the play was performed.

The allegorical figure of Conversion recited the prologue. At first she appeared covered in a frightening ('orrido') mantle, but then, after a few verses, she removed it and revealed a beautiful white costume meant to represented the state of purity of a converted soul. She spoke of St Mary Magdalene, and thus introduced the subject matter of the play. When she finished her lines, Active Life entered from one side of the stage, a silver shovel in her hand, while Contemplative Life appeared on the other side, hands crossed on her chest and in an ecstatic pose. Contemplative Life narrated with pride how Mary Magdalene had been one of her followers. Then Active Life followed, praising herself by taking pride in Martha, the Magdalene's sister. The two allegorical figures debated the relative merits of their particular ways of life until Peace suddenly appeared and put an end to the discussion by pointing out that both paths lead to paradise. In the meantime, Pride entered on stage accompanied by Vainglory and Stubbornness, all three falsely dressed as young maidens. They were accompanied by Virginity, Married Life, and Widowhood, whom they were trying to entice into their way of life. However, realizing that the latter three were in fact heavenly virtues, the first three departed in shame. At this, Conversion called them back, and they reappeared, dressed this time quite differently, in monstrous and horrid outfits that visualized for all present the ugliness inherent in Pride and in those who sin from it. When these 'monsters' left the stage, Active and Contemplative Life returned. When the sound of a very sweet melody led them to wonder what it could be, Contemplative Life explained that it was the sound of the blessed spirits in heaven rejoicing at the memory of Mary Magdalene's arrival. A curtain now dropped, and the saint herself appeared hovering in mid-air, supported by angels. Singing most sweetly, she described the peace of the blessed and urged the audience to do penance and to seek heavenly glory. And with this the *Dialogo* came to an end.

At this point the scribe concludes saying that the spectators cried with pleasure ('piansero per dolcezza') and lists the actors:

| | |
|---|---|
| Conversion | Cammillo Sommai |
| Active Life | Ferdinando de' Bardi |
| Contemplative Life | Giovanni Buonaccorsi |
| Peace | Vincentio Giraldi |
| Pride | Francesco Salvini |
| Virginity | Alessandro Galli |
| Married Life | Donato Alamanni |
| Widowhood | Benedetto Nerli |
| St Mary Magdalene | [Piermaria di Michelangelo] Cinganelli |

That Sunday after solemn Vespers, the scribe adds, a large number of brothers and members of the nobility, including foreigners, visited the confraternity, and, he reports, they all commented on the originality of the *apparato*, the beauty of the paintings, and the richness of the altars and of the usual reliquaries that had been placed on them, all of which was done, so the scribe claims, not for worldly ambition or honour, but for the glory of God.

Similar *dialoghi*, though not as dramatically developed, continued to be performed occasionally. In July 1644, for example, the scribe records that a *Noli me tangere* play was staged for the feast-day and that it was sung throughout:

That day solemn Vespers were sung, and when they were finished our brother Luca Fantoni delivered a very beautiful oration in praise of the saint, and then a musical dialogue was sung by three young brothers of ours ['fanciulli nostri fratelli'], that is, by Girolamo Bernardi dressed like the gardener who was the Risen Lord, Giovanni Filippo Rucellai dressed as St Mary Magdalene grieving because she had not found her Lord in the sepulchre, and Giovanni Battista Vantucci representing the Angel, with a choir of angels behind, and they all performed very well, and it all ended with applause and general praise.[32]

In spite of these examples, and even though the confraternity considered St Mary Magdalene its 'advocate' and duly celebrated her feast-day, an independent tradition of theatrical performances in honour of the saint did not really develop. As in the case of the feast-day of the Archangel Raphael, the descriptions of the theatrical activities included in the celebration suggest that these were exceptional events, indicative more of occasional theatrical activity than of a regular festive practice. Furthermore, while the archangel and Tobias did occasionally appear at times other than 31 December, St Mary Magdalene remained strictly tied to her late July feast-day.

In summary, neither the two patron saints nor the Nativity itself generated recurrent theatrical activity for their respective feast-days. The only regular yearly 'performance' in the fifteenth and sixteenth centuries may have been the confraternity's contribution to the annual St John's parade, though even it may have been limited to intermittent periods within these years. To find records of a more regular pattern of theatrical activity we must look to the first half of the seventeenth century, to a time when the confraternity was to number among its members and sympathizers some of the major dramatic, musical, and artistic figures of contemporary Florence and enjoy the attention and patronage of the grand-ducal court. Ironically, this theatrical activity was to be centred not on the confraternity's religious festivities but on the more secular period of Carnival time. And it was to flourish in spite of stringent ecclesiastical regulations against theatre in sacred spaces. Before examining the confraternity's theatrical activity in the seventeenth century, it is therefore advisable to review the Church's attitudes and regulations on theatre in the post-Tridentine period.

# 17

# Theatre in the Seventeenth Century

Theatre in youth confraternities changed significantly in the sixteenth and seventeenth centuries. First of all, the revival of classical theatre at the end of the fifteenth century, and especially the revival of the comedies of Plautus and Terence, led to the creation of a new dramatic genre that combined ancient form and contemporary subject matter – the erudite comedy. Secular, and often critical of some aspects of contemporary society, the new genre could be found everywhere. Secondly, princely patronage often supported and encouraged the theatrical entertainments mounted by youth confraternities. Splendid sets, elaborate costumes, music, and dancing became ever more common in oratories and halls that were, at other times, intended for devotion and prayer. In the wake of the reforming spirit of the Council of Trent, ecclesiastical regulations against plays in sacred spaces, and in particular against secular plays, were therefore not slow to follow. At the same time, as the century waned, erudite comedy ceded its primacy to other forms of theatre. Youth confraternities thus adapted themselves both to ecclesiastical directives and new fashions in courtly entertainment. This chapter will follow these changes at the Arcangelo Raffaello. It will also briefly examine the presence of props and scenery in the confraternity, and point to the youths' developing role as performers and entertainers.

## Secular Plays in Sacred Spaces

The performance of plays within religious settings – churches, convents, or confraternities – has always been viewed by ecclesiastical authorities with suspicion. One of the concerns is that plays may not reflect with due accuracy and devotion the sacred episodes they re-enact. Another is that performers or spectators may not behave with the decorum appropriate to such subjects. A third is that sinful activities may be exhibited or, perhaps, even exalted in a religious space.

In fact, Italian religious drama in the fifteenth and sixteenth centuries – to say nothing of its secular counterpart – did give ecclesiastical authorities reason to be concerned on all three counts. An anonymous fifteenth-century sacred representation of the Nativity not only brings to the stage several snacks, songs, and dances by the shepherds, but also ends with a gruesome Slaughter of the Innocents that leaves King Herod wildly jubilant and triumphant.[1] Lorenzo de' Medici's *Rappresentazione di SS. Giovanni e Paolo* (1491) included extensive secular discussions on political praxis and theory, battle scenes, banquets, and other such action. Castellan de' Castellani's *Rappresentazione del figliuol prodigo*, dating from the beginning of the sixteenth century, had vivid tavern scenes complete with drunkards, gamblers, and prostitutes. It is not surprising, therefore, that such secular aspects included in religious plays performed in 'sacred' surroundings would not be acceptable to Church authorities.

In the sixteenth century, with the meteoric rise in popularity of the theatre of antiquity, and especially of the comedies of the Roman dramatists Plautus and Terence, plays that were completely secular in subject matter, tradition, and form became so popular that they too entered into the halls of religious organizations and often replaced the *sacre rappresentazioni* that had held the stage there in the previous century. Giovan Maria Cecchi's plays from the 1540s and 1550s, for example, though composed for such lay religious groups as the confraternity of San Giovanni Evangelista or that of San Bastiano de' Fanciulli, were thoroughly secular, firmly modelled on, and indebted to, pagan Plauto-Terentian comedy. And they were also peppered with situations and matters not necessarily appropriate for an adolescent audience or cast.

Cecchi's most famous play, *L'assiuolo* (*The Horned Owl*),[2] was first performed in 1549 by the Company of the Monsignori in the Sala del Papa in the convent of Santa Maria Novella, the very same hall in which Pope Eugenius IV had held his audiences a little over a century earlier. It depicted two cases of successful seduction by first-year students at the University of Pisa and the permanent adulterous relationships they established with two young married women of that city. Aside from putting on stage and deriding the usual lustful old lawyer, the play also presented an old bawd who, though dressed in the habit of a tertiary, had not stopped practising her previous profession. As if to increase the immoral overtones of the play, the ploy used by the seductors to obtain access to their ladies' beds depended, in part, on events at a comedy performed by cloistered nuns in a convent. In one particularly important scene (III.iv), Cecchi had the lustful old lawyer exclaim:

> Comedies, comedies, comedies. I've grown tired of them, you and your nuns. If they really must, and they say they do, they should tend to other things and not comedies. Is this the time to put on comedies, eh? They should let the Duke's company or the Cardinal's put on comedies, and they should stick to weaving.

At this, the young woman who had received the brunt of his indignation responded:

> Good God, Messer Ambrogio. The poor girls are made of flesh and bones just like us and they must have some relaxation after all. What do you want them to do?

thus anticipating St Benedict's comment to the archer in the prefaces to two of Cecchi's later plays.[3] At this point the old man noticed the bundle of clothes the young woman had collected for the nuns and, on inspecting it, was shocked to note that 'men's coloured stockings, and ... breeches' were being brought to nuns in a convent.

The entire episode was cast in a humorous tone, for Cecchi clearly intended to poke fun at the old man who objected to the nuns' diversions. At the same time there may be some unintentional self-criticism. One could easily argue that this play illustrated how St Benedict's wise rule about the need for relaxation had been interpreted so loosely that it had played a part in leading four young people to commit fornication and adultery, thereby placing their immortal souls in grave peril.

In the mid-sixteenth century, secular plays of this sort were commissioned and performed in most youth confraternities, usually with the full knowledge and support of those responsible for the confraternity's well-being, morals, and honour. On 25 December 1565, for example, the youths of San Bernardino presented Francesco d'Ambra's *La cofanaria*, complete with magnificent intermezzi, as part of the wedding celebrations of Francesco I de' Medici and Joanna of Austria. The play and the intermezzi met with such success that they were described in the published accounts of the festivities.[4]

In 1570 the confraternity of San Bernardino staged another play newly composed by their brother the dramatist Francesco D'Ambra. The records do not mention the title, but they do say that the guardian father, Ser Piero dal Ponte a Sieve, 'a notary and a citizen of Florence, actuary of the archbishop of Florence,' had at that time taken a leave of absence from the position because of another appointment in the city – he had been named *procuratore* – and that his substitute was the Rev. Jacopo Bartoli, 'a Florentine priest.' They then go on to say that the play's performers were the priest's own students, 'all sons of Florentine gentlemen.'[5] At the San Bernardino, the clergy in charge and the confraternity's sympathizers clearly did not object to the performance of secular comedies of sexual intrigue and seduction.

Other ecclesiastical authorities and persons with a more profound sense of morality or religion did, however, find such events objectionable. The old lawyer in Cecchi's play may have been introduced as a figure of ridicule, but his views on the performance of plays in sacred spaces were clearly shared by some of his contemporaries. In the wake of Counter-Reformation spirituality, the cultural climate was changing, and some writers and performers, and the public, were adapting to it. Cecchi himself underwent a change of heart in about 1557 to the extent that he stopped writing scurrilous comedies and began writing religious plays, instead.[6]

## Ecclesiastical Regulations against Plays in Sacred Spaces

The changes are evident in the Church's regulations on confraternities and on drama in religious settings. The Council of Trent, for one, had sought to exercise greater control over confraternity activities by insisting that bishops include them in their regular visitations of the churches in their diocese. These regulations were reiterated by the second Florentine diocesan synod (1573). Although Archbishop Antonio Altoviti had not included confraternities in his original 1568–9 visitations, he did subsequently visit them. On 11 January 1572/3 he toured the Arcangelo Raffaello and then took part in its devotions.[7] The subsequent confraternity decision to fix the leaky roof, the enrolment into the confraternity of at least one priest from the archbishop's retinue, and the unusually large attendance (120 brothers) at the following St John's procession are just a few indications that the archiepiscopal visit had led to physical improvements to the building, closer ties between the confraternity and ecclesiastical authority, and an increase in participation.[8]

In 1577, Altoviti's successor, Archbishop Alessandro de' Medici, who would eventually be elected Pope Leo XI, forbade the performance of any plays in confraternity oratories. As D'Addario points out, the archbishop felt that the house of God was to be a house of prayer, and the performance of any plays, even on religious subjects and completely chaste, would have profaned the sacredness of the place.[9]

The archbishop's decrees, however, did not eradicate plays from confraternities. The youths of the Arcangelo Raffaello, for example, adapted to the new circumstances and found other venues for their theatrical activities. Thus plays were performed in the entrance hall (*stanzone*), that is, outside the consecrated space of the oratory proper but still within the confraternity complex (on 1 June 1582). Or they were performed away from the confraternity, for example at the Franciscan convent of Ognissanti, 'to give [the friars] a bit of recreation' (on 3 March 1584/5). A third alternative was to 'revive' in the confraternity those plays the youths had already staged at a reputable site outside the confraternity. Thus in 1585, after their father corrector, Antonio Cignori, had commissioned them to perform a play elsewhere on the occasion of a special mass by one of his 'disciples,' the youths restaged it again in the confraternity with some simple scenery and in the presence of a large audience ('molto populo') who kept silent and was very pleased.[10] Yet another way to sidestep ecclesiastical regulations was to integrate the plays into the confraternity's meeting and devotions. On 1 June 1582, as we saw above, youths dressed as the Archangel Raphael, Tobias, and a Pilgrim performed a short play at the end of that day's services on the need to renew the confraternity's devotional life.

The desire of some confraternities to continue to mount plays in their halls had at least one victim: the guardian father of the youths of San Bernardino. In 1578, the newly elected guardian, Benedetto Biliotti, who was a member of the adult confraternity of San Benedetto and also of the flagellant *buca* of San Girolamo, refused to allow the youths to perform a comedy on the grounds that 'he had objections of conscience' on these matters. When the youths ignored his scruples and performed the play anyway – Raffaello Carraresi's *Il veduto* – Biliotti considered himself deeply offended and resigned.[11] The following year the youths, unperturbed by the previous year's experience, staged Alfonso Lenzi's *Carino*, and in 1580 his *La Cintia*, 'all with wonderful intermedi and new stage sets.' The Grand Duke Francesco I himself attended the Carnival day performance of the last play.[12]

Clearly, some confraternities continued to indulge their taste for secular comedies unconcerned with archiepiscopal prohibitions or their guardian father's scruples. They may have been encouraged in this by such high-placed personages as the grand duke himself, whose attendance granted the performers his tacit but public support. Such support should not, however, be seen as an example of Church/State antagonism – with his presence at plays Francesco I was not necessarily playing political power games with the archbishop, but merely reflecting the taste of his court and the practices of his father.

## Grand Ducal Patronage of Confraternity Performances

A *memoria* from the confraternity of San Giovanni Evangelista, in fact, points out that on several occasions Cosimo I, together with his wife and children, had attended their plays. As a result of one particularly noteworthy performance, Cosimo had even granted the youths and their theatre (*teatro*) his high patronage and had enrolled himself in the group – something that was then done by all subsequent Medici grand dukes.[13]

The Arcangelo Raffaello also attracted grand-ducal attention and membership. In 1589 the newly arrived Grand Duchess Christine of Lorraine attended Vespers for the 31 December festivities in honour of the Archangel Raphael.[14] She returned a few months later for Easter 1590, and then again for Vespers on 31 December 1591. On these occasions the confraternity had sung Vespers with musical accompaniment by Raffaello Gucci. In 1591 the devotions were enhanced by a costumed choir consisting of three angels, one of which was the Archangel Raphael, interpreted by Bernardo di Raffaello Carraresi. An angel holding a silver vase in his hand – perhaps the Archangel Raphael, since he is often depicted carrying a vial containing the fish-ointment used to cure old Tobit's blindness – sang 'his life' in a delicate and angelic voice.[15]

On this last occasion, the grand duchess was so visibly moved by the youths' singing and devotions that the acting guardian father, Niccolò Antifassi, took advantage of the situation and asked a favour of her: noticing that the grand duchess had been pleased, he asked her to honour the confraternity by enrolling her newborn son, Cosimo II, in it. The grand duchess was at first surprised by such a request ('ne restò confrandata'), but then agreed with pleasure.[16] The future Cosimo II thus became a member of the Arcangelo Raffaello at the age of seven months. Although there is no record of him ever attending any meetings or devotions, his name on the membership roll was sufficient to give the confraternity the lustre of princely participation. Unfortunately for the Arcangelo Raffaello, Cosimo II died young (1621) and therefore was not able to bestow extensive patronage on the confraternity. But the connection had been made, and his son, the Grand Duke Ferdinando II, together with other members of the grand-ducal family, did make it a practice to honour the confraternity with their membership and regular attendance at plays and festivities.[17]

## Sacred Plays in Sacred Spaces

In spite of ecclesiastical regulations about plays in confraternities, the Arcangelo Raffaello managed to stage plays without raising objections from the authorities or from local moralists. Unlike the youths of San Bernardino, those of the Arcangelo Raffaello were working in concert with their senior officers. In fact, in the 1580s the initiative for their theatrical productions had come not only from the youths but also from their elders, and in particular from their acting guardian father Zanobi Buonavolti (1584–91) and their Franciscan father corrector fra Antonio Cignori (who served them from at least 1582 to 1592). The plays had been simple representations of angelic visits, or devout plays touching on the gospel narratives composed, on several occasions, by the most eminent contemporary dramatist in Florence, Giovan Maria Cecchi. When Archbishop Alessandro de' Medici visited the confraternity on 6 January 1586/7 – two days after the youths had staged a play drawn from that day's gospel narrative, the flight into Egypt – he had no reprimands for them. Instead, he praised them for their devotions and urged them to continue, 'having seen that things were going extremely well.'[18]

Other youth confraternities also adapted their theatrical events to changing times and sensibilities. On 31 December 1606, the youth confraternity of San Jacopo detta del Nicchio, for example, celebrated the feast of the Archangel Raphael with 'a beautiful representation, similar to the one that in past years was staged at the Scala' (that is, at the Arcangelo Raffaello).[19] Other confraternities presented Christmas plays akin to those of the Arcangelo Raffaello. On 25 December 1619 the youths of Sant'Antonio da Padova e San Giorgio de' Fanciulli staged a *Rappresentazione dei pastori* 'with a very rich *presepio*, a choir of angels with a Paradise, and a cloud with an angel that guided the star, and other beautiful things.'[20]

## Plays in the 1620s–1630s

After the flurry of theatrical activities at the Arcangelo Raffaello in the mid-1580s, an extensive interest in mounting plays did not resurface in this confraternity again until the 1620s. The play that marks the beginning of this new period of theatrical activity is a revival of Giovan Maria Cecchi's *L'Acquisto di Giacobbe* – which the *ricordi* call *Commedia della benedizion di Giacob*.[21]

Compared with the presentations of the previous century, this event was, without a doubt, a major undertaking. The play was performed a total of five times – twice 'for the women' (Sunday, 11 and Wednesday 21 September 1622), twice 'for the men' (Sunday, 18 and Monday, 26 September), and once for the court (Friday, 23 September). This last performance was attended by the Grand Duke Ferdinando II, his mother the Grand Duchess Maria Maddalena, his uncle Don Lorenzo de' Medici, his brothers as well as his brother-in-law Duke Federigo of Urbino, and Cardinal Alessandro Marzi Medici.[22]

The mere size and logistics of the event dislodged confraternity orations – on 11 September the recitation of the Office took place in the entrance hall 'because the oratory and the *tornatino* were obstructed by the comedy.' Some of the major figures of the contemporary music scene were involved: Jacopo Peri composed the music for the scene of the Archangel Raphael and God the Father, while Giovan Battista da Gagliano, brother to the better-known Marco, composed the music for the scenes with the angels and the shepherds, as well as for the orchestral interludes (*sinfonie*). The stage set and costumes were devised by the painter Cosimo del Bianco. Vincenzo Ruotoli suggested that Cecchi's play be improved by the addition of a third act and a scene with Jacob's ladder. The poet and dramatist Jacopo Cicognini obliged by composing the desired additions and by making alterations to the other acts as well.[23] Lorenzo Galli and Mario Stefani were appointed 'capi della commedia,' while Meglio Coppo was named *camarlingo* and *provveditore* for the show. The entire event was financed with donations from the guardian father, Francesco Fior Vigna, and twenty-three other members. From the description of the event in the confraternity *ricordi*, it is evident that the Old Testament story of Jacob's blessing was little more than a convenient excuse for an extravaganza of music, stage sets, costume, and technical skills.

This 1622 performance marks the Arcangelo Raffaello's return to public theatrical activity and points to a very different approach to theatre in the confraternity. On Christmas Day 1622, just three months after the multiple performances of Cecchi's revised and expanded play, the confraternity staged a *Mistero della redenzion umana* by Jacopo Cicognini, which was attended on the 27th by the grand-ducal family and published two years later as *Il Gran Natale di Christo Salvator nostro*.[24] In early 1624 the youths presented Cicognini's *La celeste guida*, a play drawn from the Raphael and Tobias story (see above, ch. 16, pp. 207–14). The following July, on the occasion of the festivities for St Mary Magdalene, a *Dialogo per la festa di Santa Maria Maddalena* was presented. Although the scribe does not give the dramatist's name, the description of the play clearly indicates that this was Giovan Maria Cecchi's *Duello della vita attiva e contemplativa*, composed for the confraternity nearly fifty years earlier and now revived.[25]

A little more than a year later, a *Rappresentazione dei pastori cantata dentro con ritornello* was presented on Christmas 1625. The event appears to be a revival of Cicognini's 1622 play *Mistero della redenzion umana*. In his prefatory remarks to the published version, dedicated to Prince Ladislaus of Sweden and Poland, Cicognini points out that 'the subject of this labour of mine is, in itself, most eminent, and as such it was already worthy of being presented by the noble actors of the famous company of the Arcangelo Raffaello, also known as the Scala, and to have as spectators all the Serene Highnesses of Tuscany.'[26] The publishing licences granted and recorded in the volume indicate that Cicognini's decision to publish the work was reached shortly after its second performance – he obtained the archbishop's permission on 6 January, the Inquisitor's on 15 January, and Niccolò dell'Antella's on 20 January.[27]

The play contains a prologue recited by Lucifer as he rises out of the ground. It then follows with a debate among three allegorical figures – Human Nature, Sin, and Death. The manger scene (*presepio*) is then uncovered and Human Nature is seen kneeling inside it. The shepherds enter and exit singing, and then the archangels Raphael and Gabriel with assorted angel choirs do the same. Finally the heavens open to reveal another choir of angels, this time singing a Gloria. The varied musical components, the allegorical figures, the uncovering of a *presepio*, the opening of a 'heaven' with angel choirs in it, not to mention Cicognini's own words, tie the published play to the Arcangelo Raffaello and its Christmas-time devotional shows, much as had been the case with Cecchi's 1573 *Atto scenico per alla Cappannuccia* – which, incidentally, also contained singing, three allegorical figures (Human Nature, Peace, and Charity), angel choirs, and an unveiling of the *presepio*.

A similar devotional play was performed for Christmas 1639. This was an elaborate affair, with scenery and music which the scribe felt worthy of being described in detail in the *ricordi*.[28] The basic set was the one the youths had used the previous spring to stage a tragedy. It had now been adapted to the new requirements by the painter Lorenzo Lippi, a member of the confraternity, who added a hut (*capanna*) to the original backdrop and included the Virgin, St Joseph, and two richly clad angels in the act of adoring the Christ-child lying in the manger between the ox and ass. All figures were life-size and drawn in perspective. The scene and setting were unveiled in the morning, after services, and were so impressive that the confraternity remained open all day to allow the general public to visit and view the *presepio*. That evening at Matins the confraternity was filled to capacity. In place of the final motet, a group of brothers costumed as shepherds entered into the oratory singing and marvelling at the brightness lighting up the midnight sky. At that moment a cloud appeared in the heavens carrying an angel who announced to them the birth of the Messiah. When the cloud arrived in the middle of the stage set, it suddenly disappeared among other clouds and the manger scene was revealed. The shepherds knelt in front of the Christ-child and adored him, singing in solo or in choral recitative their love and devotion for him with such effect that they moved the audience to tears. They then sang *ritornelli* and accompanied themselves with shepherds' instruments ('con instrumenti pastorali'). The heavens then opened to reveal many angels, who, with their own instruments, joined the shepherds in singing and making music. After the heavens closed, the shepherds departed, leaving the audience, in the words of the scribe, wanting the entire *Rappresentazione* to be staged once again for the benefit of those who had not been present at this performance.

## Scenery and Props

The youths in the confraternity and their supporters were clearly acquiring a taste for elaborate theatre. And they were also acquiring the physical materials necessary for such productions. The 1583 inventory already listed four pieces of scenery (*prospettiva*).[29] One hundred years later the confraternity's holdings had increased appreciatively. The 1690 inventory contains a variety of scenery and other bits of stage set:

> Four pieces of scenery representing a city view, and they are the best that are in the confraternity ... A sign that is placed in the first room of the entertainment and says 'Entertainment only for those who frequent the confraternity' ... Three more of the above in a walnut frame, used in the same manner ... Two planks with decorations around the edges, painted, that seem to be two baskets, to be placed in front of the scenery to hide the lights ... Sixteen pieces of scenery representing woods. Four pieces of proscenium consisting of four canvases on frames with stones painted on them. Seven pieces of scenery representing a city view. A forum for a city view. Two pieces of Heaven hinged together. Two frames with a canvas on them that is plastered, so it can be painted, made to be placed on the large windows in the oratory when there is a festivity so that there is less light and also for greater decoration.[30]

Some of these stage materials were even lent out for the asking. An entry of 18 January 1635/6 recalls that some brothers asked to borrow the confraternity's backdrops (*prospettive*) in order to use them at Giovanni Francesco Ferroni's house, where they were performing some improvised comedies.[31] Although confraternity members were involved, the entertainment was carried out independently of the confraternity and therefore no record was kept of it. There is also no record of whether the backdrops were ever returned. One would hope they were, though a confraternity decision six months later seems to cast doubts on the trustworthiness of the youths who borrowed them. On 3 August 1636 the confraternity decided that whoever lent out or used confraternity objects for personal purposes would be excommunicated.[32] Firm as it may have been at the moment, the decision did not last long – ten years later, in 1646, the youths revoked their threat and again allowed members to borrow confraternity objects.[33] The reversal was probably necessitated, as will become evident below, by the plays the youths had then begun to perform in private houses.

## Performances in Private Houses

Private performances, especially at Carnival time, were very much the vogue in early seventeenth-century Florence. A noteworthy collection of thirty-one of Giovan Maria Cecchi's plays in the archive of the Rosselli del Turco family suggests the number of plays performed privately at Carnival time and exemplifies the venues for such presentations. Many are transcriptions done by Stefano Rosselli, an avid collector of Florentine plays and keen amateur actor. They include *Le pellegrine*, *Il debito*, *L'ammalata*, *L'andazzo*, *Gli sciamiti*, *La conversione della Scozia* – all transcribed in the early 1620s from the author's autograph originals. This collection also indicates that *L'ammalata* was 'performed in Florence in via San Gallo at the house of Signor Benedetto Gucci for Carnival in the year 1624'; *Il figliuol prodigo* was 'performed in Florence at the house of the Signori Agnolo and Lorenzo del Turco, in via de' Ginori' sometime after 12 January 1617/18 (the date of the transcription);[34] *I contrassegni* was 'composed in 1585 and performed for Carnival in 1623 at the house of Signor Benedetto Gucci in via S. Gallo,' and so forth.

On 20 January 1633/4 the confraternity decided to flee the moral dangers of the approaching Carnival by keeping itself busy staging a play 'outside the Confraternity.' Aware that they did not have the time to commission a new play, they consulted with their guardian father and father corrector and chose to stage instead one of the more famous Florentine plays of the previous century, Sforza Oddi's *Commedia de' morti vivi*. The play, based on the Achilles Tatius's tale of Leucippe and Clitophon, had been composed in 1576 and had already been revived on several occasions by other groups.[35] They then asked their current governor, Francesco Orlandini, to find a suitable locale. Orlandini asked and received permission to use the 'Palazzo Medici in via Larga' – probably not the current Palazzo Medici-Riccardi, but the Casino of Cardinal Leopoldo de' Medici further north on the via Larga.[36]

The confraternity then appointed their current *provveditore*, Antonio del Soldato, as producer, and put Baccio del Bianco in charge of the stage set. Baccio had the confraternity's large stage stage set (*scena grande*) brought to the Palazzo and then adapted it to suit the play. He painted a backdrop that depicted Naples, with a large seaport in the distance, and supervised the building of the entire set. To enrich the performance, a concluding eight-part dance was choreographed and directed by Francesco Fontani, 'most expert in this profession.' The rich costumes for the dancers were paid for by Francesco Orlandini and the confraternity's current first counsellor, Vincento Giraldi. The play was performed twice for a group of invited gentlewomen and their husbands and for a large number of Florentine nobles. Men and women were seated in separate areas, and could be accommodated very well because, as the scribe noted, 'the place could hold a lot of people.' The scribe then lists the cast of characters and the performers:

| | |
|---|---|
| Antonino, from Ragusa, friend of Ottavio | Niccolò Luna |
| Moretto, a Neapolitan juggler | ... Corsini |
| Luigi, a Neapolitan gentleman and second *innamorato* | Francesco Guardini |
| Oranta, a Neapolitan gentlewoman, in love with Ottavio | Lorenzo Guardini[37] |
| Fabbritio, servant to Luigi | Vincenzo di Niccola Capponi |
| Marcone, majordomo for Oranta | Giovanni Casini[38] |
| Giovanna, his wife | Carlo Baldesi |
| Beccafico, foolish servant to Oranta | Messer Giuseppe Panci |
| Ottavio, a gentleman from Ancona, first *innamorato* | Raffaello Carnesecchi |
| Alessandra, under the name of Rossana, slave to Oranta, in love with Ottavio | Adriano Roncioni |
| Tessandro, husband to Oranta, and Jancola, from Capua | Alessandro Dami |
| Rabacchio, servant to Ottavio | Carlo Simoni |
| Prologo, ad lib. | Giuseppe Lapi[39] |

The permission to use the Casino, the attendance of the cream of Florentine nobility, the personal contribution of an eminent artist such as Baccio del Bianco or of the dance instructor Francesco Orlandini, not to mention the personal financial contribution made by a number of persons so as to stage this event with the decorum and style appropriate to the audience and the location, all point to the high reputation the confraternity enjoyed in the city and the support it could muster in order to put on a fine show.

It was a reputation that continued for a long time and saw the youths perform again at the Casino. For Carnival 1645/6 they staged three performances of an 'opera morale' by the 'Dottore et Poeta' Camillo Lenzoni, with music probably by their current *maestro di cappella* Niccolò Sapiti, and dances choreographed by Filippo Franceschi. The audience included both Medici cardinals (Leopoldo and Gian Carlo), Don Lorenzo Medici, and most of the Florentine nobility.[40]

The personal interest in theatre evident in the Florentine upper classes and in individual members of the Arcangelo Raffaello was deeply shared by the confraternity's current guardian father, Giulio Guazzini, 'Cancelliere delle Decime di S.A.S.'[41] In June 1638, the recently appointed Guazzini informed the youths that he had composed a play and wished to have it performed somewhere in the city, preferably in the confraternity's garden.[42] The youths immediately obliged, and on the following feast-day of St Mary Magdalene they themselves staged it.

This was a three-act play entitled *Lo schiavo ritornato*, and the confraternity scribe, perhaps out of respect for the guardian father, perhaps out of pride for the richness of the performance, entered a long, detailed description of the event, the setting, the participants, and the patrons who underwrote the expenses.

## Currying Favour with the Medici

One more play, Rinaldo Strozzi's *Tragedia di SS. Cipriano e Giustina*, performed in February 1639/40, brings to a close a period of extensive theatrical activity.[43] Perhaps four plays in eight months was an excessive burden for the confraternity. There is no record of another performance until two-and-a-half years later, August 1642, when the youths staged a second play by their guardian father. The occasion – the birth of Grand Duke Cosimo III – and the confraternity's intentions – a blatant attempt to curry favour with the ruling family – were the motivating factors in this return to the stage.

On that occasion, the youths staged Guazzini's *Il morto risuscitato* (*The Resurrected Dead Man*).[44] The work was performed three times in the confraternity's 'small court' (*corticina*): twice for the women (on 24 and 29 August), and once for the men (on 31 August). The confraternity clearly saw the birth of another Cosimo as an auspicious event not only for Tuscany, but for itself as well. Undisguised by the scribe's baroque description lies the confraternity's hope that Cosimo III may become its special grand-ducal patron, thus taking the place of his deceased namesake.

## A Return to Plays at Carnival

Perhaps revived by, or pleased with, the August attempt to curry favour, the confraternity returned the following February to the performance of Carnival plays. This time, however, the play was mounted not at the confraternity, but at the house of Giulio Guazzini, its guardian father. The work was Jacopo Cicognini's *La vergine prudente*, performed on 15 February 1642/3.[45]

From the *ricordi* we learn that the house, on via della Scala, was chosen because it had a very large and suitable place for such an event. The Carnival-time performance took place on the advice and with the permission of the father corrector and the guardian father so as to keep the youths actively involved and in practice, and to keep them away from the opportunities usually available at that time of the year to waste time and endanger virtue. The confraternity chose Cicognini's play because it was seen as an exemplary piece, 'very honest, and yet pleasing [and] grave [*grave*] because of the choral music and the characters that appear in it.' Actors were selected from the brothers most apt for the parts and the subject, and instructed 'to perfection.' The play was performed four times – the first and second time for an audience of ladies (*gentildonne*) related to the actors or to other confraternity members, and the other two times for the men. The expenses were incurred by the cast and the production crew. Antonio del Soldato, the current governor of the confraternity, was singled out for having paid for the lumber for the stage set. The costumes were rich and beautiful. Each act had appropriate choral music composed by Baccio Baglioni, the confraternity's *maestro di cappella*. The scribe then concluded, saying that 'it has seemed befitting to write this memoir so as to encourage those who follow us to involve themselves in similar virtuous actions.'[46]

Although there is no record of a Carnival performance in 1643/4 – possibly because it may have been organized independently, outside the confraternity complex – such encouragement did not fall on deaf ears. Three devotional dialogues were performed in 1644, one on Palm Sunday, one for the festivities in honour of St Mary Magdalene, and one in early August.

The Palm Sunday dialogue, *Sopra la preparazione da farsi alla prima comunione*, was recited by four youths and ended with a prize-giving ceremony for the younger members who had been taking part in the Christian doctrine instructions.[47] The untitled St Mary Magdalene dialogue performed in July of that year was, instead, a trio on the *Noli me tangere* motif sung by Girolamo Bernardi in the role of the resurrected Jesus, Giovanni Filippo Rucellai in the role of the grieving Mary Magdalene, and Giovanni Battista Vantucci in the role of the angel. The latter was accompanied by a choir of angels.[48] The August dialogue, *Sopra l'amor divino*, was recited after Vespers by Lorenzo Frescobaldi and Benedetto Comparini.[49]

The confraternity was clearly returning to a more active theatrical schedule. For the 1644/5 Carnival another major play was staged, again at the house of the guardian Giulio Guazzini. It was *Don Gastone*, a play by Giacinto Andrea Cicognini, a member of the Arcangelo Raffaello.[50] The scribe's description of the event is nearly identical to that of the 1641/2 Carnival play. The same reasons for the location and the performance are given, and the same financial arrangements are mentioned. The music, however, was now composed by unnamed members of the confraternity 'under the direction of the *maestro di cappella* [Niccolò Sapiti].' And the performance was repeated five times, again to a segregated audience of ladies (on 12, 15, and 19 February), married couples (22 February), and men (24 February). On one occasion, César de Bourbon, duke of Vendôme, attended the performance.[51] And again the scribe concluded that the record had been written in order to inspire future members to continue in such virtuous actions.

The following Carnival, on 9, 12, and 18 February 1645/6, an *opera morale* by Camillo Lenzoni was performed three times at the Casino of Cardinal Leopoldo de' Medici on the Via Larga, across from the convent of San Marco.[52] The 'greater part of the nobility of Florence' again attended the last performance, including both Medici cardinals (Gian Carlo and Leopoldo), and Don Lorenzo de' Medici. The expenses were incurred, as usual, by the cast and crew of the production. Costumes were 'most noble and rich, and the music most beautiful.' This time the play ended with a dance for gentlemen composed and choreographed by Filippo Franceschi, a member of the confraternity.

There is no mention of theatre at the Arcangelo Raffaello, whether devotional or Carnival-time performances, for eleven years, from February 1645/6 to 17 June 1657, when the youths staged their last play – Jacopo Cicognini's *Amor fraterno*.[53] The work, whose title may be seen to be emblematic for the confraternity itself, was a revival of an earlier composition that had already been staged by the confraternity at the villa of the Buonaccorso family at Castello di Poggio and then at the *pieve* of Monte Reggi, 'when it was held by the Very Rev. Messer Luca del Vigna, son of Messer Francesco Fiorvigna our guardian at that time' (i.e., between 1619 and 1637). In a letter of 22 January 1631/2 Jacopo Cicognini writes, 'The Company of the Scala is presenting a moral work of mine that does not last two hours ... and it is performed by the flower of nobility, and very exquisitely, and it is entitled *Amor fraterno*, and it depicts city people and country people in a villa near Fiesole.'[54]

In 1657 the play was again staged outside Florence, this time at Ambrogio Baldesi's villa 'La Quercia.'[55] Since the guardian father, the father corrector, the governor, and a number of brothers were to attend the event, the confraternity decided to forego Vespers in the oratory and to recite them, instead, in the chapel next to the villa. First there was a sit-down meal, with the youths who were performing sitting at a table by themselves, and the elders and the other youths at another table. When the meal was over, everybody moved to the chapel and recited Vespers, joined this time by more brothers who had arrived in the meantime from Florence. At 20 o'clock (2 p.m.) the play was performed. It had a prologue recited by 'Constancy and Imeneus' that had been composed by Francesco Baldovini and set to music by Piero Sanmartini. There were also two ballets by 'very modest [chaste?] young men' ('giovanetti modestissimi'). The audience was composed not only of confraternity youths who had been guests for lunch, but also of a large number of 'other brothers' and of Florentine nobles who had come from the city to their villas in the area. The show ended at 23 o'clock (5 p.m.), to allow everyone to return with ease to Florence.[56]

## The End of Theatre at the Arcangelo Raffaello

The 1657 revival of Jacopo Cicognini's play marks the end of dramatic representations by the confraternity. From August 1642, when the youths had staged Giulio Guazzini's play *Il morto resuscitato* in honour of the birth of Cosimo III, no play had been performed in the confraternity complex. Some 'dialogues' were recited or sung as late as August 1644, but they did not aspire to serious dramatic representations. The staging and performance of elaborate plays may have continued, possibly until 1657, but they must have been Carnival or summertime entertainments held not in the confraternity halls but at private houses and villas. For this reason they become private events organized by groups of friends and do not appear in confraternity records.

The records that do speak of confraternity plays in the seventeenth century reveal that the Arcangelo Raffaello had not only adhered to post-Tridentine ecclesiastical regulations concerning plays in sacred spaces, but had also followed the guidelines of its 1636 revised statutes. The chapter on 'Dell'onesta recreazione' had said 'that honest and gentle ['soavi'] entertainments lift and fortify the soul greatly.' It had encouraged the youths to linger in the confraternity garden in 'holy and joyous conversation' or to hold, once a year and with their guardian father's approval, 'a recreation in some delightful villa, or organize some virtuous comedy or sacred representation' to be performed with the appropriate decorum.[57]

Such practices did not entail a major change for the Arcangelo Raffaello. As far back as the mid-sixteenth century, the records indicate that the Arcangelo Raffaello had not abused its taste for theatre. The works it staged were usually simple representations that could easily be incorporated into its devotional life and did not raise concerns about the propriety of such activities in consecrated halls. Unlike the youths of the confraternity of San Bernardino, those of the Arcangelo Raffaello did not stage secular plays against the wishes and scruples of their guardian father. On the contrary, they and their superiors worked in unison to offer their brethren 'honest and pleasant entertainments.' On those occasions when the confraternity seemed engaged in a flurry of theatrical activities, the plays were clearly aids to their devotional and moral life, and attuned to the readings or the celebrations of the day. Even in the seventeenth century, when Carnival-time performances entered regularly into the confraternity's calendar of events, the plays drew their subjects from biblical or hagiographical sources.

Ironically, only in 1636, when the confraternity was engaged in the process of revising its statutes,[58] was there a suggestion that some brothers were interested in, or performing, non-religious drama. The 'improvised comedies' staged that Carnival at the house of Giovanni Francesco Ferroni do not, however, reappear in following years. Secular plays, appropriate for Carnival or summer performances, soon moved to private houses or villas. The performances that remained inside the confraternity complex eventually amounted to nothing more than simple devotional presentations where music, more than any other activity, began to take centre stage.

From 1658 to 1686 there is a gap in the confraternity *Ricordi – Libro F*, which covered these years, has been lost. When the next *libro* picks up the narrative, the staging of plays has disappeared completely and given way to the performance of musical oratorios.

# 18

# Music in the Confraternity

More than any of the other arts, music was probably the Arcangelo Raffaello's most important contribution to cultural life in Florence. The membership as a whole, and the most musically gifted youths in particular, received musical training and were then given an opportunity to perform in public. Coupled with the presence within the membership of youths with talent in the visual arts and in theatre, this proved to be a powerful mixture that produced, especially in the late sixteenth and early seventeenth century, a critical mass of gifted young men who, without exaggeration, helped to change the course of European musical history. In this chapter we will glance at some of these individuals and the confraternity's musical activities. Together with training and performance, the chapter will also devote some time to the organs used in the confraternity, and in particular to the vicissitudes surrounding an organ once belonging to the astronomer Galileo Galilei. The increased use of large instruments and choirs led to the need for larger performance space, and this in turn led to the construction of a musicians' loft within the oratory. Music thus changed the physical appearance of the confraternity. Lastly, the chapter will close with an examination of the new vogue at the Arcangelo Raffaello in the late seventeenth century for the performance of oratorios.

## Musical Names

Several music historians have already examined the activities and membership of the Arcangelo Raffaello – Guido Burchi, Tim Carter, John Walter Hill, and Edmond Strainchamps in particular – and pointed to the presence of important musicians and the performance of innovative works by this confraternity. Girolamo Mei, Giulio Caccini, Marco da Gagliano and his brother Giovanni Battista, Jacopo Peri, and Vincenzo Galilei are just some of the illustrious musicians whose names appear in the documents of the Arcangelo Raffaello. So do those of many of the members of the Camerata dei Bardi, which has traditionally been seen as the birthplace of opera. It may be possible to argue that opera traces some of its roots *through* the Camerata into the Arcangelo Raffaello itself, whose mixture of song and action predates Jacopo Peri's 1598 *Dafne* by several years. According to John Walter Hill, the youths of the Arcangelo Raffaello had already performed a 'dramatization' that was completely sung from beginning to end five years earlier, on 31 December 1593 – it consisted of a madrigal attributed to Ottavio Rinuccini and set to music by either Giulio Caccini or Jacopo Peri.[1] I will point out below that this date should be moved up several years, for the records show that the youths had staged a sung play as early as February 1584/5.

The flourishing of musical theatre at the Arcangelo Raffaello was not a sudden or fortuitous event. It grew out of a long tradition of musical, theatrical, and visual interests that found its own roots in the confraternity's original mandate to educate the young and foster their devotional life.

## Laudate pueri Domino

Already in the fifteenth century the confraternity of the Arcangelo Raffaello was teaching music to young males and giving them an opportunity to perform in public. In so doing, it was following the mandate given to youth confraternities by Pope Eugenius IV's bull of 1442. Music, however, had been a component of its devotional and pedagogical aims even earlier. Evidence of such early interest comes from two marble panels sculpted by Luca della Robbia in 1421–38 for the choir loft in the Florence cathedral.

In his article on the panels, Robert Mode argues convincingly for a reconsideration of the models used by della Robbia. He points to the 'problems of identification' raised by 'the type of youthful choristers and celebrants' found in these marble reliefs and says that they are not 'the lively *putti* that dominate Donatello's pendant structure' but 'mainly older children and adolescents.' Focusing on the two so-called Alleluja side panels that 'depict male youths with a sharpened naturalism that distinguishes them from the more ideal groupings in the two registers across the front,' Mode argues that 'in seeking their models ... Luca selected members of adolescent confraternities in Florence who engaged in holy song as a regular spiritual exercise.' Mode argues against an identification that would see in them the youths in the cathedral choir school founded by Pope Eugenius IV with a bull of 23 March 1435/6. In his view, the youths depicted in the panels are 'no organized vocal ensemble,' such as the newly formed, quasi-professional choir under the direction of such illustrious musicians as Guillaume Dufay or Antonio Squarcialupi would have been, but rather 'an eager complement of adolescent choristers' more akin to the non-professional singers from the youth confraternities that had already been in existence in Florence for ten or twenty years. Mode further points out that 'the ages, types, and informal presentation of these youths confirm this derivation.'[2]

The panels do, in fact, present a charming and lively mix of children aged about ten to twelve and adolescents aged about fifteen to seventeen – very much the age group that frequented youth confraternities. Their relaxed posture and, in the case of some, their distraction suggest a less structured context than would have been present in a cathedral choir established and subsidized by a pope then resident in Florence. Such choristers could easily be found at the Arcangelo Raffaello.

Fifteenth-century confraternity statutes also reveal the presence of music in youth confraternities. Although they do not use the word 'musica' itself, the 1468 *capitoli* of the Arcangelo Raffaello do say that the youths were to sing 'hymni et salmi et laude.' They mention in particular the 'Te Deum laudamus,' 'Laudate pueri Dominum,' 'Magnificat,' 'Laudate Dominum omnes gentes,' 'Benedictus Dominus deus Israel,' and 'il Credo maggiore.'[3] What is worth noting, aside from the fact that these are all fairly standard hymns, is that they all, including the Credo, are in Latin. The youths were thus clearly taught to perform in Latin, as well as in the Italian vernacular of the *laude* – none of which, incidentally, are mentioned by title in the statutes.

Confraternity records support the statute's suggestion that Latin hymns were more common than vernacular *laude*. In the case of the Arcangelo Raffaello, the records, which begin to be kept regularly in the 1560s, recall the singing of standard Latin hymns, but very rarely that of vernacular *laude*. The few cases when such *laude* are recorded are invariably linked either with Christmas or the feast of the Archangel Raphael (31 December) and are strictly focused on the Nativity scene – clearly an indication of the more 'popular' aspect of the *laude* and the celebration.[4] Though the absence of regular records for the fifteenth century does not allow us to draw as firm a conclusion for that period, it is probably safe to assume on the grounds of the 1468 statutes that the singing of Latin hymns would have been a more common practice in youth confraternities than the singing of vernacular *laude*. Though this seems to contradict the received wisdom that has *laudesi* confraternities singing mostly, if not solely, vernacular *laude*, it should be kept in mind that youth confraternities, with a strong mission to educate the young, would have sought to teach and foster a more 'elevated' or 'educated' singing than the 'popular' vernacular songs of Christmas pageants or devotional adult confraternities.[5]

The 1636 *capitoli* of the Arcangelo Raffaello also mention the performance of music in the confraternity. The word itself appears, once, to indicate that some of the responses or 'cantiche' could either be recited or 'in musica' – a phrase that could even suggest instrumental accompaniment. The verb 'to sing' (*cantare*), on the other hand, appears fairly often in phrases referring to the 'singing' of Matins, Vespers, Lessons, Antiphonies, psalms, hymns, and the prayer to the Archangel Raphael.

Most important, however, the 1636 statutes formally introduce a new set of officials whose duty was to oversee the choir. This was clearly an *ex post facto* creation, since the confraternity had long before included a set of *ordinatori de' cori* in its regular slate of officers, though there had been no statutory support for the position at that time. Already in the 1560s the Arcangelo Raffaello was naming three to eight of its members to the post at each of its periodic elections (January, May, September), and, at least then, it appears that a wide cross-section of the membership filled it, from someone like Pagolo di Giovanbattista Genozzi *orafo* to someone like Lorenzo di Lorenzo de' Medici (both elected for January–April 1564). As the sixteenth century progressed, however, the 'ennobling' of the membership can be seen in the names drawn for this position, as well – in May 1588, for example, the *ordinatori* were Guglielmo Antinori, Antonio Maria Aldobrandini, Francesco Sernigi, Baldino Panciatichi, Antonio Baldesi, and Francesco Ganucci.

The duties of the *ordinatori de' cori* were not formally enunciated until the 1636 statutes declared that the *cerimonieri*, as they were now called, 'are expected to prepare the choir for the celebration of the Divine Office according to the Roman rite, appoint the more practised brothers as leaders ['imponitori'], singers of the antiphonary ['antifonari'], and to other posts. For this reason they must arrive for prayer meetings at the Confraternity early and teach them the ceremonies and rehearse the singing with them.'[6] The reference to the *imponitori* recalls the lack of a conductor in the della Robbia panels and the presence of older youths who seem much more focused on their singing than their younger confrères.

The presence of *imponitori* and the lack of a conductor do not negate, however, the participation of professional musicians either as performers or instructors at the Arcangelo Raffaello.

The first regular instructor to appear in the records is a semi-professional, the furrier (*vaiaio*) Michelangelo di Jacopo Mollazzi, hired on 1 July 1563 to teach music to ten of the confraternity children (*giovanetti*) for a fee of 2.5 *scudi* per month (30 *scudi* per year).[7] He is still active twenty years later, when he appears in the records for June 1583 as 'maestro di nostra Cappella della Musicha,' a title that was subsequently applied to all music teachers at the Arcangelo Raffaello and clearly suggests an elevation in rank.[8]

For reasons unknown to us, Mollazzi disappears from the records immediately after this date and the confraternity spends the next eight years without an officially appointed and paid music instructor. During this period responsibility for music devolves to the membership itself, and in particular on one especially talented brother, Raffaello di ser Francesco Gucci.

## Raffaello di Ser Francesco Gucci (c.1542/3–1610)

Guido Burchi notes that we have no information on this very talented and versatile musician except for what is to be found in the records of the Arcangelo Raffaello. This is unfortunate because, as he adds, Gucci was an influential figure in the development of vocal and instrumental music in the confraternity, for 'it is exactly with Gucci that monody becomes a very frequent mode of singing at the Scala.'[9] Furthermore, shortly after Gucci's debut as a solo performer, other solo performers at the Arcangelo Raffaello include Giulio Caccini, Jacopo Corsi, Ottavio Rinuccini, the sons of Giovanni Bardi – singers, Burchi points out, that were to become the major exponents of the Camerata Fiorentina and to be directly involved with the development of opera.[10]

Raffaello Gucci had joined the confraternity at the age of thirty in the inductions of 1 March 1572/3. Given the timing and his age, his entry may have been connected with the visit of Archbishop Altoviti a few months earlier (11 January 1572/3).[11] Whatever the reason for his enrolment, he served the confraternity long and well not only by teaching his fellow brothers, but also by performing as a vocalist and instrumentalist. When he died in January 1609/10 the confraternity seems truly to have mourned his passing.[12]

When Gucci unofficially took over from Mollazzi, he had already had some experience in organizing musical performance at the confraternity – the records recall that he and Migliorotto Migliorotti had set the music for the Forty Hours celebrated on 20 February 1582/3.[13] Then, on 1 November 1584, the records note that the Lessons were sung by younger musicians ('giovanetti musici') instructed by Raffaello Gucci, 'since the confraternity no longer had a *maestro di cappella.*' That same evening the court musician and fellow member Giulio Caccini sang three madrigals in duet with a young castrato he had brought along with him for the occasion.[14] The co-operation between Gucci and Caccini, evident in their work for the Arcangelo Raffaello, is an indication of the talent and professionalism to be found in Gucci. Gucci co-operated again with Caccini and his castrato in 1589, when he performed at the festivities for the wedding of Grand Duke Ferdinando I with Christine of Lorraine.[15] That same year, on 31 December 1589, he performed again for the new grand duchess when she visited the confraternity for the feast of the Archangel Raphael. At that time Gucci played his keyboard instrument and sang verses in alternation with a choir that was accompanied by the well-known virtuoso violinist Giovan Battista Jacomelli 'del Violino,' a native of Brescia.[16] He performed for her on her subsequent visits, without, however, Jacomelli's participation, singing solo, but accompanied by several musical instruments, and alternating his part with a choir of youths.[17]

In the 1580s–90s, Gucci's own performances were stunning, to say the least. He first appears as a performer on 4 November 1584 in a polychoral rendition of the 'Miserere' and 'Benedictus' in which he accompanied himself on a *buonaccordo* (harpsichord) and alternated verses with the choir. He returns a month later, on 8 December, with his own keyboard instrument (probably the same *buonaccordo* from November) to sing the 'Te Deum,' 'Gloriosa,' and 'Benedictus.' The following year, for All Saints' 1585 (1 November), he sang and played his instrument from inside the catafalque that had been erected in the oratory – an eerie performance to say the least, but not an unprecedented one, for the previous year the same effect had been achieved either by Giulio Caccini or a young castrato he had brought along with him (the pronoun is unclear in the original).[18] Such was Gucci's skill at singing and at playing his keyboard instrument that the following year, on 2 April, Holy Wednesday 1586, in another polychoral setting of the 'Benedictus' and 'Miserere,' he sang and accompanied himself on his instrument in alternation with a mixed choir of voices and five viols, something the scribe says 'satisfied very much.' In fact, it was a *tour de force* that was repeated each of the following evenings of Holy Week. For All Saints' 1587 he joined with Giulio Romano, Lelio Lenzoni, and Niccoli castrato to sing madrigals. And so Gucci continued to sing and play on many occasions until 1600, when he withdrew from such performances (perhaps because of age, seeing that by now he was close to sixty years old).[19]

**Baccio Malespini and Marco da Gagliano**

Yet another professional musician who becomes involved with the Arcangelo Raffaello is Baccio di Ulivieri Malespini, who, as Mollazzi's official successor as *maestro di cappella*, taught and directed music at the confraternity from at least 3 March 1590/1 to the summer of 1609. As in the case of Mollazzi and Gucci, the little that is known about this musician is drawn from the Arcangelo Raffaello documents. He was recommended for the post and supported by the confraternity's *governatore*, Lionardo di Noferi Nemi and Carlo del Caccia, who argued that 'it would be well in order to keep the confraternity going ['tener aviata la Compagnia'] to hire Messer Baccio di Ulivieri Malespini as master of music and that they themselves would assume the responsibility to collect the commission that would be agreed with him.' The commission agreed was to be 30 *scudi* annually, for which Malespini was to teach music to ten confraternity youths (*fanciulli*) at no extra fee, and organize the music for all festivities during the course of the year and for all evening *tornate* during winter. Malespini was hired and served until the summer of 1609, when he was replaced by Marco di Zanobi da Gagliano.[20]

Marco da Gagliano was not new to the Arcangelo Raffaello. He had joined the organization at the age of six on 24 February 1588/9.[21] From an early time he served the confraternity in elected offices, the first of which might well have been his appointment as scribe in May 1599, a post he held until the following December.[22] From at least 1602 he had assisted Malespini in his musical duties at the confraternity. On 2 December 1607, at a time when Marco's older brother Lionardo was assistant superintendent (*sottoprovveditore*), the membership voted to replace Malespini with the eighteen-year-old Marco, offering him a yearly salary, 40 *scudi*, that was 33 per cent higher than Mollazzi's or Malespini's (both of whom had been hired at 30 *scudi* per year). Da Gagliano's higher salary was to be provided and guaranteed by a number of confraternity members who had clearly been impressed by the abilities and talent of their fellow brother. Malespini, however, was not pleased with being replaced by an 'assistant' in what seemed to be a somewhat heavy-handed internal move, and complained to Prince Cosimo II de' Medici, heir to the throne. The situation soon acquired the air of an international incident, for Cardinal Ferdinando Gonzaga of Mantua, a fellow member of the Arcangelo Raffaello, also became involved, initiating an exchange of letters with Prince Cosimo on behalf of Marco.[23] Eventually the confraternity, out of respect for their fellow member and future Grand Duke Cosimo de' Medici, grudgingly rescinded its earlier decision and reinstated Malespini, who, his honour redeemed, continued in office for another year and a half. He resigned gracefully on 28 June 1609 and was replaced, without turmoil, by the young Marco.[24]

## *Maestri di Cappella*

Marco da Gagliano served the confraternity until 1621, during which time his musical star rose high on the Florentine firmament. Shortly before, in 1608, he had been appointed *maestro di cappella* at the cathedral. Then, in 1609, he became chapel master at the grand-ducal court in Palazzo Pitti. His connections with the musical and religious establishment of Florence were further solidified when he was appointed canon (1610) and then apostolic prothonotary (1615) at the basilica of San Lorenzo, the second most important church in the city and the Medicis' traditional parish church.[25] He supervised music at the Arcangelo Raffaello for twelve years, his last documented contribution being the music for the obsequies of Grand Duke Cosimo II on 14 March 1621.[26]

When he retired from his post at the Arcangelo Raffaello, Marco da Gagliano was replaced without controversy by his younger brother, Giovan Battista, who had joined the confraternity on 24 July 1599. Though he served as *maestro di cappella* only until 1624, Giovan Battista remained active in the organization until his death in 1651.[27]

Subsequent appointments to the post followed without incident for the next century and a half and brought to the confraternity a number of highly qualified musicians – among them Piero Sanmartini (1666–74 and 1690–4), Giovan Battista Benvenuti (1674–90), Giovan Niccola Ranieri Redi (1718–36), and Bartolomeo Felici (1744–62) – most of whom held the position contemporaneously with that of chapel master at the court or at the cathedral.[28] Together with the membership of the grand-ducal sons in the Arcangelo Raffaello, the numerous visits of members of the ruling family to special events at the confraternity, and the patronage of the Medici cardinals, the double-duty of court musicians at the Arcangelo Raffaello points to the intimate connection that existed between the confraternity and the court – a connection, it should be noted, that was based not so much on shared devotional interests as on music and spectacle.

## Galileo's Organ

By the end of the sixteenth century, music at the confraternity was often enriched by instrumental accompaniment. One of the first references to instruments in the confraternity comes from Corpus Domini 1561, when the scribe recalled that Vespers were celebrated very solemnly that day, 'with many organs ... and many lauds were also sung on the organs.'[29] A similar concert of organs was recorded for the feast of the Archangel Raphael in 1563, when the scribe noted that Vespers were sung and 'many organs were played, just as in the morning.'[30] The scribe's interest in recording the accompaniment and his use of the plural suggest that the use of multiple organs was unusual. Since the confraternity did not seem to own an organ at this time, it is probable that some members had brought their own instruments from home and had improvised a keyboard orchestra, of sorts. As late as 1583 there did not seem to be a permanent organ in the confraternity, so much so that the occasional use of a small organ brought in from outside was still a pleasant novelty for the members. That April, the scribe noted that 'in the evening we recited a devout Matins of the Virgin with the usual music, and moreover we had one of our brothers who played a well-equipped small organ which pleased the brothers greatly.'[31]

The organs mentioned in these entries may very well have been similar to the small portable instruments one often sees in period paintings of angelic choirs. One such illustration, in fact, was front row centre during the youths' devotions, for it adorned the vault behind the confraternity's main altar. It was a fresco depicting a choir of angels adoring the Trinity and playing on a variety of instruments – flutes, viols, organs, harpsichords, harps (or citharas), clavichords, sistra (a type of rattle), and pan-pipes.[32]

Sometime around 1596, the confraternity acquired its own keyboard instrument – a *graviorgano* received as a gift from Baccio Comi, one of the confraternity's most generous members.[33] Comi had purchased the instrument from Galileo Galilei, whose father, Vincenzo, had been a renowned musician in his own right. Galileo himself attested to the purchase in an affidavit of 19 June 1619, from his Villa di Bellosguardo, in which he explained that the organ had been built by Domenico da Pesaro, and that he had brought it himself from Padua about twenty-seven years previously, given it on consignment to Giulio Caccini with the instruction that if Jacopo Corsi wished to buy it, the price for him would be 150 or 180 *scudi*, but for anyone else 180 or 200 *scudi*. It was eventually sold to Baccio Comi, either directly or through Jacopo Corsi, either for 150 or 180 *scudi*, and definitely not for anything under 150.[34] Giulio Caccini had already attested to the consignment and the sale (direct to Comi) in an affidavit of 30 December 1615 in which he added that he himself played that instrument on several occasions, both in the confraternity and at Comi's house when the latter had it temporarily moved there for special concerts in which Caccini performed together with Giovan Battista del Violino.[35]

An affidavit of 1620 signed by Cosimo del Bianco attests that the instrument was purchased by Comi twenty-four years previously not for himself but 'to serve the confraternity.' Because Jacopo Corsi, Giulio Guidi, and others who played it thought it had 'very little breath,' they convinced the donor to pay to replace the bellows. The work was done by 'Vincentio the organist who resided at the top of via del Campaccio.' Del Bianco is uncertain whether the price of the re-bellowing was 20 or 24 ducats (or *scudi*), but is certain of the work done because he himself carried the instrument to Vincentio's shop and went there on several occasions in the company of Raffaello Gucci to see how the work was progressing. Del Bianco notes that on many of these occasions Gucci actually played the instrument at the shop to ensure that the work was being done 'to the desired perfection.' When the job was completed, del Bianco brought the instrument back to the confraternity where it was played continually as long as Raffaello Gucci was alive (d. 1610) and then by others after him.[36]

In an earlier affidavit (1615) Marco da Gagliano declared that he, too, had often played on that *graviorgano*. However, da Gagliano had ceased to use it, because with time the instrument had deteriorated. It would have required so much work and expense to restore it and tune it in unison with other keyboard instruments then in use at the confraternity that da Gagliano had asked the *sottoprovveditore* Cosimo del Bianco some years earlier to remove it from the oratory because 'it gave great bother and would easily have been damaged.' Da Gagliano adds that unless he occasionally wished to use it during Holy Week and asked Cosimo del Bianco to bring it back, the *graviorgano* lay unused.[37]

## Legal Wrangles for the Organ

Although not used regularly, the instrument was still an important possession for the confraternity, one that it would willingly go to court for. In fact, a drawn-out legal dispute for ownership of the *graviorgano* arose in 1615 when the confraternity asked Filippo del Riccio Comi, Baccio's adopted son and now his heir, to return the instrument he had borrowed some time earlier on the occasion of his wedding to Laura del Vivaio.[38] Filippo, a member of the confraternity and its superintendent (*proveditore*) at the time of the borrowing, refused, claiming that the instrument had belonged to his father and therefore it now belonged to him. The legal battle that ensued engendered many documents and affidavits and extended over a span of five full years.[39] It also put an end to Filippo Comi's participation at the Arcangelo Raffaello – in the listing of officers for September 1614, just as the dispute was about to go to court, the entry for the *provveditore* is suddenly left blank and his name disappears from the records.[40]

The situation was complicated not only by the fact that Filippo Comi had been the superintendent, but also because other confraternity materials were also involved. In a 1615 affidavit, Cosimo del Bianco attested that when Baccio Comi was alive several confraternity possessions were stored in a room at Comi's house called 'L'Arsenale delle cose di Conpagnia.' These included 'the paintings of the Passion of Our Lord, the tapestry back-boards, sconces and other brass objects, the large candlestick holders for the altar, ... many pieces of scenery for the *apparato* of the Forty Hours and for the Crèche that is set up at Christmas.' The confraternity's servant, Pasquino di Francesco, supported this statement with his own affidavit that there used to be an 'Arsenale della Compagnia' in Baccio Comi's house and that he, Pasquino, would often go there to retrieve the confraternity's objects as needed. After Baccio's death, these objects were transferred to the confraternity because Domenico Comi, Baccio's brother, had storage rooms built within the confraternity itself especially for such use.[41] Ownership, however, was obviously questioned, for in a series of affidavits a number of persons attested that these objects were the property of the Arcangelo Raffaello.[42] Even the tax collector and the creditors of the deceased Baccio Comi were asked to testify. Alessandro Benci, an employee of the Gabella, the Florentine tax office, declared that in the statement of 1605 under item 174, containing the inventory of Domenico Comi's estate, there is no reference to an organ. Cesare Pollini's affidavit on behalf of the creditors of Baccio Comi claims that the inventory of 13 March 1613/14 listed a keyboard instrument, with two registers and bellows, but adds that Filippo Comi had declared at that time that the instrument did not belong to him but to the confraternity of the Arcangelo Raffaello.[43]

Given all this evidence, the judgment eventually came down in favour of the confraternity. At this point, however, the confraternity claimed that it would not accept an instrument that Filippo Comi had allowed to deteriorate, and insisted that it be suitably restored back to functioning order at Comi's expense. When Comi refused, the confraternity suggested that he simply purchase the instrument outright from them.

Two appraisers, Girolamo di Vincenzio Bolcioni and Stefano Soldini *strumentaio*, were engaged to determine the value of the *graviorgano*.[44]

Their report reveals not only the instrument's high value but also the beauty of its voice and appearance. They declared that it was 'a most perfect instrument not only because of its form, for it is easily portable to any location, but also because it has such a sweet sound that it easily blends in all concerts.' The instrument, they were keen to point out, had been built by 'il Pesero,' that is, by Domenico da Pesaro, one of the most renowned organ and harpsichord makers of the time, or, as they themselves put it, 'who in such instruments is celebrated as the first Maestro who has existed till now.' For these reasons, they added, one could say that the *graviorgano* was 'a joy fit for a prince, that it has no price, that its beauty, for it has been painted and gilded, allows it to be used in any most-honoured place and in the presence of any great prince.' Though they claimed that it was impossible to set a value on such an object, they did propose a minimum of 200 *scudi*, 'which anyone who desired very much to own the instrument would gladly pay for it.'[45] The decorations on the *graviorgano* consisted of the Comi coat of arms 'below' and the Archangel Raphael and Tobias 'above'; together with the gilding, they had been done by Michelagnolo Cinganelli, who, as he himself declares in an affidavit of 1620, had been commissioned to do them twenty-eight years earlier by Baccio Comi at a fee of 20 *scudi*.[46] Filippo Comi, already burdened by other financial difficulties, chose not to purchase the instrument, but returned it to the confraternity (we do not know, however, whether he had had it repaired or not).[47]

In January 1645/6 the *graviorgano* again resurfaces in the documents, this time as it is being sold to Filippo di Francesco Franceschi.[48] Though the sale to Filippo Franceschi was easy, the decision to sell was couched in so much rationalization that one becomes immediately suspicious. The entry in the record book notes that the organ was too large to fit in the balcony recently constructed for the musicians. As a result, the Arcangelo Raffaello had been obliged to keep the instrument away from the confraternity at the house of someone who would use it and not let it deteriorate. Realizing that with time and insufficient use the instrument would nonetheless decay, and that while it was in someone else's custody it was of no benefit to the confraternity, the membership seized the opportunity to sell it to Filippo for 130 *scudi*, a price which, the record adds, was quite good when one considered that such an opportunity did not come every day and that Filippo was a devoted member of the confraternity. What these comments reveal is that the *graviorgano* was a white elephant – beautiful, but useless. The confraternity could neither maintain it nor house it. It also could not readily find a buyer for it. In fact, it had already tried to sell the instrument in 1630, without success.[49]

A further problem, implied but not expressed, was that the legal battle with Filippo Comi had focused attention on the *graviorgano*'s value and its purpose – it was a valuable instrument and it had been received as a bequest from Baccio Comi to enhance the musical life of the confraternity. The confraternity could not simply sell it and pocket the money. The financially distressed Filippo Comi would gladly have done so himself, or at least sought legal recourse against the confraternity for breach of trust against his adopted father's will and then repossessed the bequest for his own use. To protect themselves from such action, and to abide by the intention of Baccio Comi's will, the Arcangelo Raffaello decided to place the income from the sale of the *graviorgano* into a trust fund whose interest would be spent to repair and maintain the instruments used in the confraternity.[50] The revenue was deposited with two wealthy members and donors to the confraternity, the brothers Lorenzo and Agnolo Galli, who managed the investment so well that it provided the confraternity with sufficient funds for the maintenance of music in the oratory well into the eighteenth century.

## The Musicians' Loft

By the mid-seventeenth century, music at the Arcangelo Raffaello had become such an important activity that it led to physical restructuring of the confraternity complex. A loft for the organ, the choir, and the instrumentalists was added in the oratory above the entrance door, and practice rooms for the musicians were built behind it in space taken from the storage area.

The balcony for the musicians was a gift of Alberto del Vivaio, a wealthy dilettante composer in his own right, who had been elected superintendent for music at the confraternity in May 1641.[51] His intention was to provide the musicians with more performance space and to house an organ that he wished to donate to the confraternity. The loft was to be built just inside the oratory, immediately above the desks of the guardian father and the father corrector. The organ intended for it was a well-furnished wooden instrument that del Vivaio thought would complement the voices of the singers better than the company's current *organetto*. The brothers agreed with him and eagerly allowed him to go ahead and build, at his own expense, the proposed loft.[52]

The work was carried out in record time. Approval was granted on 6 October and work was completed to everyone's satisfaction four weeks later, on 1 November 1641. The results were twofold. First, the quality of sound in the oratory improved because the musicians were no longer constrained by performing from the sacristy behind the altar, and also because performing from the raised balcony over the entrance door allowed for better acoustics. Second, without the musicians in the sacristy, there was more space for the celebrants to go about their business.[53] Praise was also lavished on the manner in which the loft had been constructed, easily blending in with the wooden stalls that ran along the three walls of the oratory. Behind it, on the other side of the wall, a staircase, corridor, and rehearsal room for the musicians had been constructed as a gift from Agnolo and Alessandro Galli.[54]

Del Vivaio's wooden organ, however, was probably not adequate. On several occasions in the following years the *maestro di cappella* Niccolò Sapiti had his own organ brought to the confraternity for special occasions (All Saints', Christmas, and so on). In fact, in January 1647/8 the confraternity decided to order a custom-built organ for its loft, one that 'should be seven-foot, with two principals, one of tin and one of wood, then an octave also of lead, a fifteenth, and a flute all made of lead except for the show-pipes in front, which should be of polished tin, with a wind chest, and three bellows with levers, and it should sound strong and well.'[55]

From this brief description we learn that this particular instrument had a C pipe that was seven feet long, thus producing a pitch standard a little over a whole tone higher than our modern A=440 (produced by an eight-foot pipe). Though there is evidence that seventeenth-century Italian organs were pitched higher than modern organs, this seems to be a level somewhat higher than expected. Also, since large Italian organs are usually based on sixteen-foot principals, the seven-foot principals suggest in this case a smaller organ. One of the two principals, possibly the wood rank, may have had stopped pipes in the bass, which would then have brought the range down an octave. The two principal ranks were augmented by an octave and a flute rank, both playing an octave higher than the principal, and by the fifteenth, playing two octaves higher, thus producing a combination of five ranks that, in modern terms, could be described as eight feet [sixteen?], eight, four, and two feet for the principal chorus and four feet for the flute (keeping in mind, of course, that the standard length for that organ was seven, not eight, feet). The flute rank, consisting of lead and polished tin pipes, suggests that part of it (the polished tin pipes) was placed in front of the case housing the pipes. Similarly, the tin principal may also have been exposed to view. The pipes stood on a wind chest. The three bellows with levers indicate that they were operated by hand rather than foot, much like the bellows used today to quicken a fire.[56]

Three years later the organ was in place and the confraternity, pleased with it, paid its maker, Giovanni Palmieri, 170 *scudi* for the work.[57]

The extensive and radical alteration to the fabric of the oratory and the storage room, not to mention the donation of at least two organs and the commissioning of a third, is an indication of the value placed on music in the confraternity. Professional musicians, renowned instructors, fine instruments, spaces especially set aside for rehearsal and for performance, the continued maintainance of instruments – all of these indicate long-term commitment both financial and cultural. It is no surprise, then, that music flourished at the Arcangelo Raffaello.

## Theatre and Music

There was interest in music not only for its obvious devotional uses, but also because it enriched the confraternity's theatrical presentations. Music first entered into dramatic performances by youth confraternities simply as a song or a dance to be inserted into the action, as many *sacre rappresentazioni* of the fifteenth century indicate. By the late sixteenth century, secular theatre in the confraternities and elsewhere contained much music, especially by way of the *intermedi* that graced the plays as entr'actes. At the same time, 'moral interludes' and once-act 'moralities' presented by youth confraternities as inspiration, edification, and entertainment for their fellow members contained so much music that they were eventually sung from beginning to end.[58]

One of the first such theatrical presentations in music is Giovan Maria Cecchi's lost play *La presentazione di Gesù al Tempio*, performed by some of the children in the Arcangelo Raffaello on 2 February 1584/5. The record entry is self-explanatory: 'Saturday 2 February. Some of our younger youths ['giovanetti'] represented in music when Our Lady, together with St Joseph, go to the temple to offer Jesus to Simon, a work of the above-mentioned Cecchi.'[59]

As a sung play, this performance predates Jacopo Peri's 1598 *Dafne* by more than a decade and surpasses in quality as well as in time the dramatized madrigal of 1593 mentioned by John Walter Hill as the first sung dramatization at the Arcangelo Raffaello.[60] With time and with the development of a musical theatre, sung plays become more frequent at the Arcangelo Raffaello, especially in the seventeenth century. For All Saints' 1622 a 'dialoghetto in musica' by Jacopo Cicognini was inserted before and after the office. As the scribe tells us,

> it represented the souls in Purgatory who asked to be freed from their suffering, and the Angel consoled them promising them [they would be freed] by virtue of the

Office about to be celebrated, and then when the Office was finished the Angel repeated that they had been freed, and so they flew up to heaven thanking the brothers for their prayers and the suffrages they had received.[61]

Such simple but effective sung dialogues were performed primarily for special events such as Christmas, All Saints', or the feast-day of the patron saint. For the feast of St Mary Magdalene in 1644, for example, an unattributed dialogue very reminiscent of Cecchi's own *atto scenico* on the saint is 'recited in music' at the Arcangelo Raffaello.[62] There is no doubt, therefore, that, as early as the 1580s and as late as the 1640s, such dialogues or 'moralities' were often sung from beginning to end, rather than recited.

The practice of sung plays at the Arcangelo Raffaello had begun. It did not, however, become the norm. Confraternity records continue to mention the more usual practice of incorporating song into theatrical performances or of singing madrigals while wearing costume. Members with a thespian streak, Camillo Rondinelli for one, seemed eager to don costume and recite, orate, or sing to their fellow brothers. In April 1585 Rondinelli dressed up as a Victory riding a triumphal cart, with Death and a Devil at her feet and accompanied by many angels, then on Sunday 28 July, for the feast-day of St Mary Magdalene, he impersonated the saint in the company of four angels.[63]

Musical entertainments incorporated into the performance of spoken theatre flourished and attracted the participation of many talented artists. The 1622 revival of Giovan Maria Cecchi's *L'acquisto di Giacobbe*, retitled for the occasion *Commedia della Benedizion di Giacob*, included such a variety of musical numbers that one is left wondering where the spoken dialogue was inserted. The scribe, for one, does not mention the spoken parts at all. What he does mention, instead, and in detail, is the music. The revised prologue ended with the appearance of the Archangel Raphael and Tobias singing with a choir. The stock figure of the Parasite, which Cecchi had drawn from the Graeco-Roman comedy of Plautus and Terence and the Italian *commedia erudita*, was given a hymn to sing in which he longed for Mankind to be redeemed. The third act was nearly all redone in order to delight spectators with music and machineries – as Jacob slept, the scene changed, the heavens opened, God the Father appeared on high surrounded by a choir of angels, four of whom, holding golden lilies in their hands (a clear reference to the grand-ducal and Florentine lily), sang as they descended a golden staircase (a clear reference to the confraternity itself, della Scala). God the Father also sang, 'with much majesty and greatness, representing all of himself in his verses.' When Rachael appeared at the well, a group of shepherds divided into two choirs and sang a *canzonetta* in *versi sdruccioli* (verses with the emphasis on the third-to-last syllable) 'that truly raised in all listeners a feeling of great sweetness and wonder, for which they were moved.' The music for the event was composed by Jacopo Peri and the *maestro di cappella* Giovan Battista da Gagliano – Peri writing the parts for God the Father and the Archangel Raphael, da Gagliano those for the choir of angels and shepherds, and the instrumental parts.[64]

With the growing ecclesiastical restrictions on the performance of plays in sacred spaces (see above, ch. 17), however, the Arcangelo Raffaello found itself ever more unable to stage the musical productions that had brought it so much fame. After a hiatus of about thirty years, a new genre allowed the confraternity to pursue its interests in the performance of non-devotional music – the oratorio.

**Oratorios in the Confraternity**

The period 1650–90 is marked at the Arcangelo Raffaello by the absence of plays and musical dialogues, though not of music itself, which, though probably still excellently performed, seems to have been limited to devotional purposes. Matins, for example, were often sung 'a due cori,' as had been the custom since the mid-sixteenth century. In 1655 the *maestro di cappella* Giovanni Battista Contarini composed new music for the Invitatory, 'which, because it was a new thing, was very welcomed.'[65] The chapel masters continued to be paid their usual yearly salary of 50 *scudi* annually (350 lire), and they received occasional small bonuses on certain regular feast-days – All Saints', Christmas, 31 December – suggesting that special musical events may have been held at those times.[66] A gap in the records for 1658–86 prevents us from determining whether anything new developed at the Arcangelo Raffaello in those thirty years.

Something new did, however, enter the Florentine musical scene at this time – the oratorio. John Walter Hill points out that in the period roughly from 1650 to 1750 the oratorio 'was the most accessible and pervasive genre of dramatic music in Florence during all but the summer months.'[67] From the 1650s on, the Congregation of the Oratorians of St Philip Neri at the church of San Firenze spearheaded and then sustained this development by their initiative and by the sheer number of oratorios they presented.[68] Confraternities followed suit some years later. Hill reports that at the youth confraternity of San Bernardino e Santa Caterina, the 'first unequivocal reference to an oratorio is on 27 November 1679'; at San Niccolò del Ceppo, annual oratorios for the feast of their patron saint on 6 December were produced from 1694 to 1734; at the Compagnia di S. Jacopo, there were oratorios from 1696 to 1729; similar time spans apply to the confraternities of San Sebastiano, San Francesco detto il Martello in S. Croce, San Gregorio, Gesù Salvatore, and San Pier Maggiore.[69] At the Arcangelo Raffaello, the term and the form appear in 1691. In confraternities, in other words, the development of the genre is late and, I would add, sudden.[70]

The case of the Arcangelo Raffaello can be seen as representative of this development. When in 1686, after a gap of twenty-eight years, the scribe resumes keeping a record of activities, nothing seems at first to have changed – the same sequence of devotions and musical performance of hymns and offices as in the previous century continues, the only difference being that there is no record of any 'dramatic dialogues' or theatrical performances. Then, suddenly, five years later, in 1691 the scribe records the performance of a series of *oratori* during Lent.[71] For the next few years, the Arcangelo Raffaello gives itself over to the new form, performing several oratorios every year. If we follow the schedule of performances reconstructed by Guido Burchi and John Walter Hill, the Lenten oratorios at the Arcangelo Raffaello in 1691 were as follows:

4 March 1691, *S. Agnesa*, with music by Bernardo Pasquini
11 March 1691, *SS. Giovanni e Paolo fatti martirizzare da Giuliano apostata*, with music and lyrics by Cosimo Bani
18 March 1691, *Il Martirio di S. Cecilia*, with music by Piero Sanmartini
19 March 1691, *Il Martirio di S. Vittoria*, with music by Giovanni del Violone
25 March 1691 [title and composer unknown]
1 April 1691, *Il Martirio di S. Cristina*, composer unknown
8 April 1691, *Gerusalemme destrutta da Tito*, with music by Lorenzo Cattani and lyrics by Antonio Fineschi da Radda.[72]

The manner in which oratorios were presented is worth noting. They were always performed on a temporary platform at the altar, and the audience, sometimes numbering a few hundred, was accommodated in the oratory, in the musicians' loft, in rooms with windows looking into the oratory, and even on temporary scaffolding, as necessary.[73] At the Arcangelo Raffaello, oratorios were scheduled after the evening service and were divided into two parts of thirty to forty-five minutes each, separated by an intermission during which one of the youngest members of the confraternity recited an oration praising the feast-day's saint. The pattern had been established by the Oratorians at San Firenze and had become the norm.

As Smither points out, oratorios 'had a quasi-liturgical function,' at least originally or among the Oratorians of St Philip Neri.[74] In confraternities, however, that function could often be forgotten or even ignored. By placing oratorios *after* the devotional component of their feast, by associating them with a *tour de force* public oration by a young member (clearly a reference to the confraternity's original mandate of gathering 'youth'), and by hiring professional and semi-professional musicians to perform them, confraternities clearly intended oratorios to provide delight rather than supplement devotion or offer instruction. The presence of a general audience, rather than their own closed membership, further supports such a view.

The mayhem of a crowded hall, filled with expectant visitors, and its effect on the evening's devotions (Vespers and Compline) is described in a 1712 journal entry from the confraternity of San Jacopo detta del Nicchio. Visitors lined up outside for hours waiting for the doors to open; when they entered they filled the oratory and overflowed into the cloak room and the outer corridor, and eventually they were accommodated 'right up to the musicians' stage'; although the confraternity had decided earlier to forego Vespers that day and proceed directly to Compline, when the time came to start the service it was obliged to forego Compline as well because of the crowd; and, lastly, during the performance cries of 'viva!' erupted from the audience 'in loud voices' at particularly well performed passages. As a devotional exercise or a quasi-liturgical event, this had been an abysmal failure, but as public entertainment it had succeeded, and so the scribe recorded with unconcealed pleasure that 'everything was greeted by general applause.' As Smither concludes, 'they had clearly come for a musical experience, not for prayer or edification.'[75]

Events of this sort were fairly expensive to mount. The San Jacopo scribe notes that costs and salaries were covered by a variety of persons. The composer was paid by the Marchesa Teresa Tornaquinci Borboni del Monte, to whom the work had been dedicated (a standard practice), and the members raised a collection among themselves for the altar, but when the funding came up short the treasurer was obliged to solicit a contribution from an outside source and from 'some loving brothers who had not [previously] agreed to such a burden.'[76] Even the less imposing productions cost a fair amount of money to mount. An invoice from the Arcangelo Raffaello dated 10 April attests that 97.22.8 *lire* (just under 14 *scudi*) had been collected and given to Giovanni Nardi to pay for expenses incurred in copying out the oratorios and having them printed so as to distribute them to the membership. The sum also included expenses incurred in paying several trumpet (*trombe*) and timpani players hired to embellish the music.[77] The sum is similar to the amount paid by the confraternity of San Marco to print six hundred copies of the libretto for the oratorio they performed on 26 April 1748, 14 *scudi*.[78]

Six oratorios in as many weeks, such as the Arcangelo Raffaello presented in 1691, meant not only high expenses but also a gruelling performance schedule. The fact that the series was completed without noticeable difficulty suggests that the confraternity's choir possessed a fair amount of professionalism and tenacity. A similar series of oratorios was presented during Lent and Passiontide 1692, 1693, and 1694, and the titles reveal some old and some new oratorios (see appendix 4). The confraternity was clearly developing a repertoire.

The incentive for the performance of oratorios must have come from several sources. Certainly, current taste must have accounted for some, and so did the changed membership of youth confraternities. Hill suggests that the adults who now generally belonged to and ran these organizations were not keen to stage the 'sacred plays' or 'musical discourses' of earlier times, for these genres were too closely linked with juvenile and old-fashioned activities. Instead, they 'turned their interest toward the oratorio, a more fashionable and sophisticated form of religious musical drama performed by professionals.' To prove his point, Hill points to the confraternity of San Giovanni Evangelista, which did remain a youth group and did 'continue to present religious plays instead of oratorios well into the eighteenth century.'[79]

Another factor may have been competition. The confraternity of the Purificazione, the second-oldest such institution, founded in 1427 by a group from the Arcangelo Raffaello, had begun in 1688 to perform three oratorios annually. When the Arcangelo Raffaello turned to oratorios in 1691, it did so by producing a series of six annual performances during Lent – twice as many as its sister institution. In 1697 the Purificazione increased its series to five, in 1701 to nine, and in 1706 to eleven oratorios annually. Competition had clearly set in and taken over.[80]

Perhaps the most important factor in the increased interest in oratorios may, however, have been the confraternity's new *maestro di cappella*, Pietro Sanmartini, who assumed office on Christmas Day 1690.[81] Sanmartini had served as *maestro di cappella* at the Arcangelo Raffaello earlier, in 1659–66, when he had first returned to Florence after a period of working abroad in Rome, Bologna, and Arezzo. He may well have picked up his interest in oratorios while in Rome, where the Congregazione dell'Oratorio di San Filippo Neri was extensively promoting the new musical form – though he could well have been introduced to it while still in Florence, where the Oratorian church of San Firenze led the way in number and quality of performances.[82] A noted keyboard player and composer, Sanmartini held the post of chapel master at the cathedral and served as a musician at the grand-ducal court. From 1692 he was a composing member of the Accademia Filarmonica of Bologna. What little has survived of his vast output, both instrumental and vocal, indicates that he was a competent composer who may have contributed significantly to the development of the symphony. For the Arcangelo Raffaello he composed the oratorio *Il martirio di S. Cecilia* (music now lost), performed on 18 March 1690/1,[83] and he may well have been responsible for several of the other oratorios performed at the confraternity in 1690–4.

With Sanmartini's departure from the post and the appointment of Pietro Socci, the momentum visibly slows. In 1695 the Lenten/Easter series dwindles to just one oratorio on Easter Monday and one for the feast of the Archangel Raphael. In 1696 and 1697 the confraternity performs only one oratorio, on Easter Monday. Then, in 1698 it settles down to just the one oratorio for the feast-day of its patron saint, 31 December. The practice of performing an oratorio on this feast-day dated back at least to 1692 when the choir performed *Le Nozze di Tobbia* by Antonio Fineschi da Radda, and continued until 1723 (see appendix 4).

When interest in oratorios begins to wane drastically in the 1720s, it does so at other confraternities as well. Hill's suggested explanation is that the Purificazione's initiative stimulated interest all around in the 1690s, but the financial strain of presenting oratorios – cost of constructing the platforms, paying musicians and singers, printing libretti, and other expenses – drastically curtailed and eventually stopped performances in lay confraternities The problem was twofold: wealthier confraternity brothers eventually begged off being tapped for donations to subsidize the expense, and the membership in general seems to have preferred to spend the confraternity's endowment by subsidizing dowries (for their daughters) or paying for other 'miscellaneous expenses.'[84]

A brief revival of interest in oratorios took place in 1751–2, under the direction of the *maestro di cappella* Bartolomeo Felici, himself a documented composer of oratorios.[85] The revival got off to a bit of a false start when the first performance was postponed from 31 December to 1 January 'because the musicians could not be had on account of the Opera.' The following day, however, two virtuoso singers from the theatre in via della Pergola participated in a 'solemn Oratorio for four voices' and attracted such a crowd of spectators that the confraternity was obliged to hire soldiers from the Grenadier's Guard to keep the peace and control admission to its building.[86] The following December, however, on account of the weather, very few persons attended the performance of the four-part oratorio for that year, and then the records become silent.

In 1763 the Arcangelo Raffaello's long-standing interest in music fell victim to the confraternity's financial difficulties when the guardian father and the confraternity officers decided to suspend music for the next two or three years. Lamentations that evening were sung simply, in three voices, with harpsichord (*cembalo*) and a small bass viol (*bassetto*) accompaniment.[87] Music at the Arcangelo Raffaello never flourished again as before.

# 19

# Art in the Confraternity

Although the Arcangelo Raffaello came into the public eye in the fifteenth century because of its interest in theatre, from the mid-sixteenth century it also began to attract attention because of its rapidly growing interest in the visual arts. By the time Marc'Antonio Seminari drew up the 1690 inventory, the confraternity could boast of a collection of paintings, frescoes, terracotta figures, reliquaries, and other such objects of artistic merit that was not at all negligible. Among the artists represented were Jacopo Vignali, Jacopo Chimenti detto l'Empoli, Piero Dandini, Orazio Fidani, Lorenzo Lippi, Carlino Dolci, Baccio del Bianco, Matteo Rosselli, and Jacopo Ferretti. The confraternity also had paintings attributed to Santi Di Tito, and Domenico del Ghirlandaio (but now reassigned to Piero di Cosimo). It had frescoes by Bartolomeo Neri, Michelangelo Cinganelli, and Bartolomeo and Francesco Traballesi. It had illustrations by Valerio Spada and Bartolomeo Traballesi. It had terracotta works by Santi Buglioni, Giovan Battista di Benedetto, and Michele di Raffaello delle Colombe. It comes as no surprise, then, that the confraternity earned an entry in the early guidebooks of Florence as a place not only of devotion but also with works of art that were worth a visit.[1] In this chapter we will examine who were the artists associated with the Arcangelo Raffaello, what were the artworks present in the confraternity, and what was, if any, the confraternity's iconological program. The chapter will close with a few thoughts on what it could have meant for the youths to receive, commission, create, or manage artworks.

## Artists in the Confraternity

On special occasions, such as major feast-days, or Easter, or for the annual devotion of the Forty Hours, not to mention plays or important obsequies, the confraternity could decorate its oratory with a variety of artworks and images, some of which, though kept in storage rooms, were the work of reputable artists. Stored away in the *arsenale*, for example, there were ten large canvases, several painted by Lorenzo Lippi and three painted in chiaroscuro by Baccio del Bianco (son of the better-known Cosimo del Bianco), all depicting stories from the Book of Tobit.[2] Other paintings kept in storage were anonymous, such as the sixteen chiaroscuro canvases depicting the Passion and used to decorate the oratory during Holy Week and for the Forty Hours of Easter Monday-Tuesday. Though anonymous, the fact that they had been donated by Baccio Comi, a long-time benefactor who had not been stingy in his gifts, suggests that they were reputable works, probably by contemporary artists.[3]

On other special occasions the confraternity could call upon well-known contemporary artists who were not, necessarily, members of the Arcangelo Raffaello. In 1621, for the obsequies of Cosimo II, for example, the confraternity commissioned works from Giovanni da San Giovanni, Giovanni and Sigismondo Coccapani, Cosimo del Bianco, Pandolfo Sacchi, Anastagio Fontebuoni, Felice Palma, Orazio Mochi, Agostino Ubaldini, Francesco Susini, Ottavio Vannini, and Matteo Rosselli. After the obsequies, the works were distributed among the benefactors who had contributed financially for the event.[4]

The long list of artists whose association with the Arcangelo Raffaello is attested in the confraternity's own archival documents reveals that the youths were able to draw on the services of a number of members and sympathizers with talent in the visual arts. Their presence in the extant records leads us to wonder whether such may not also have been the case for the period before the mid-sixteenth century, a time for which confraternity records are, unfortunately, unavailable.

One surviving document reveals that the painter Cosimo di Lorenzo Rosselli was guardian father in 1489/90 and another that Antonio di Tommaso *miniatore* followed in his footsteps in 1525.[5] The incumbency of two artists in the confraternity's most senior and only lifetime position leads us to think that they might have attracted fellow artists to the group or that they might have fostered artistic endeavours within the confraternity. We know nothing about what Antonio di Tommaso *miniatore* accomplished during his term in office. We do know that Rosselli's term was 'temporary,' and this may have prevented him from having an impact as guardian father.[6] He may, however, have contributed in other capacities. We know, for example, that Rosselli was involved with or contributed to other Florentine confraternities such as those of Santa Barbara dei Tedeschi e Fiamminghi, the flagellant company of San Domenico detta del Bechella, San Zanobi delle Laude, and the youth confraternity of Sant'Antonio da Padova.[7] We wonder, therefore, whether he might not have contributed some of his work to the Arcangelo Raffaello, as later member/artists did. In that case, although his name does not appear in the January 1491/2 funding drive to pay for the refurbishing of the confraternity's oratory in via della Scala, we might suspect that he nonetheless contributed in kind to the project.[8] Although this is little more than speculation, it does point to the need for further research in the involvement of Florentine artists such as Rosselli in the devotions and activities of lay confraternities.

## Donations by Artists

In the sixteenth and seventeenth centuries, a number of artists were personally involved with, and donated generously of their time and skills to, the Arcangelo Raffaello.

Lorenzo Lippi (Florence, 1606–65), for example, was an active member and strong supporter of the Arcangelo Raffaello well into his full adulthood. Not only did he attend devotions, but he also shared in the confraternity's administrative life, serving in several posts within the governing structure of the organization. A quick glance at the records reveals that he served as *cerimoniere maggiore* (January–April 1643; September–December 1645), *ordinatore di coro* (May–August 1624), *infermiere* (January–April 1645), and *maestro de' novizi* (January–April 1647), just to mention a few of the posts he held. When he donated his *Crucifixion with Our Lady, St John, and St Mary Magdalene* in July 1647 (ill. 7), he held the most senior quarterly post available, that of *governatore* (May–August 1647). The *Crucifixion* was praised in the confraternity records for its beauty and for the artistic skill it demonstrated. It was soon placed in permanent exhibition in a very public space within the confraternity complex – the large entrance hall (*stanzone*), where it was later joined by another important work, Orazio Fidani's *Tobias Healing His Father's Blindness* (ill. 8).[9] Lippi also contributed less important works to the confraternity. One such piece was a painted 'Crucifix' which he did 'in half a day' in October 1657 for the obsequies for Agnolo Galli, a benefactor to the confraternity. After the commemorative service, Lippi's crucifix was placed in storage in a closet in the entrance hall, thus indicating that the work was not of such high quality as to merit permanent public exhibition. Lippi's other works for the Arcangelo Raffaello were also kept in storage and used as decorations for specific events. Among them there was an altar front (*paliotto*) with an image of the 'Souls in Purgatory' and an undetermined number of canvases depicting stories about the Archangel Raphael.[10]

Lippi was not unusual in donating his work to his confraternity, nor was it only painters who contributed to the visual embellishment of the Arcangelo Raffaello. The seventeenth-century calligrapher and illustrator Valerio Spada, 'one of our brothers,' contributed a fine copy of the new statutes, elegantly written in a formal italic hand and decorated with putti, flowers, insects, and arabesques (see back jacket).[11] This copy was, clearly, not the one used for everyday purposes. It was used, instead, on formal occasions, such as installations, or for display purposes when important guests visited the confraternity. Like the paintings by well-known contemporary artists that met the visitor entering the confraternity, the beautifully written and decorated statutes were a sign of the group's wealth and importance.

This pattern of contributions to the confraternity's artistic wealth by artists enrolled in the organization continued in the sixteenth century as well. In July–August 1561, three artists co-operated to donate a terracotta image of the Archangel Raphael and Tobias. The figures were sculpted by Giovan Battista di Bartolomeo, fired by Santi Buglioni, and painted by Francesco di Mariano Traballesi.[12] In May of that year, Giovan Battista di Bartolomeo *scultore*, who had joined the confraternity a year earlier, donated two terracotta busts, one of St Mary Magdalene and the other of St Lawrence. The two saints were of special importance to the confraternity – St Mary Magdalene because she was its 'advocate,' and St Lawrence because on his feast-day in 1558 the father corrector, fra Santi Cini, had initiated an important renewal of devotional life within the Arcangelo Raffaello. The two busts, which were painted by Michele di Raffaello delle Colombe, were thus important icons. As such they were at first placed on display on the 'altare del perdono' and then they were to be placed at either side of the main altar in the oratory, level with the altarpiece (this, however, never seems to have been done).[13]

Another artist, Jacopo Ferretti, 'our dear and loving father,' contributed his own works, carried out restorations, paid for improvements to other paintings, and donated religious vestments as well. In March 1560, for example, he restored a *Noli me tangere* he had donated earlier, which was being used as the confraternity's *segno*, or processional banner. In 1559 he paid to have the confraternity's other *segno*, this one depicting the Archangel Raphael, regilded. He also paid for a new frame for the canvas of the Virgin that was used as an altarpiece in the *stanzone*. He had lateral panels added to the *Descent of the Holy Spirit* the confraternity had received from the confraternity of San Vincenzo and painted an Archangel Raphael and a St Mary Magdalene on them. And he also donated a red velvet chasuble with red fringes.[14]

The number and variety of works of art received as gifts from artists in the sixteenth and seventeenth centuries point to a pattern that was probably in place in the fifteenth century as well. Unfortunately the records for this period have not survived, and therefore we cannot rely on archival sources to answer the questions raised by some of the earlier artworks present in the Arcangelo Raffaello. For example, one would like to know whether the Jarvis Collection *Madonna and Child*, formerly attributed to Domenico del Ghirlandaio but now assigned to Piero di Cosimo, was, in fact, a gift of the artist to the flagellant confraternity of San Vincenzo Ferreri.[15] Similarly, one is curious about the misattribution of this painting. Why did the Arcangelo Raffaello think it was by Domenico del Ghirlandaio? Had Domenico been a member of the Arcangelo Raffaello or of the confraternity of San Vincenzo Ferrer? Had he held administrative positions in the group? Had he simply been a sympathizer? Or was the painting perhaps by someone else, possibly by someone in Ghirlandaio's *bottega*, who had been a member? The questions remain, but the pattern of a member's donation of his own 'formal' or 'occasion' pieces is clearly present in the confraternity's records.

## Patrons of the Arts

Similarly, there is also a pattern of patronage and sponsorship of the visual arts not by artists but by wealthier members with an interest in the embellishment of the confraternity's walls, ceilings, devotional objects, books, or special events.

In the 1560s–1590s, two brothers, Baccio and Domenico di Paolo Comi (both d. 1605), whom we have already met in the previous chapter as patrons of music at the Arcangelo Raffaello, actively subsidized a variety of activities in the Arcangelo Raffaello and bankrolled an extensive program of physical restructuring and decorating of the confraternity building. Domenico makes his first appearance in the records in May 1563 as *festaiuolo* for the approaching Pentecost celebrations. Baccio appears the following year as *festaiuolo* for the devotions of the Forty Hours.[16] In the forty years that followed, they paid for the internal restructuring of the confraternity complex to create a suitable entrance hall and oratory; the refurbishing of the wooden stalls in the oratory; six oil paintings depicting 'sacred stories' to be hung in the entrance hall; the painting for the building's exterior façade; the painting of the oratory's vault; and a number of smaller projects, such as Michelangelo Cinganelli's decoration of the organ purchased from Galileo Galilei and donated to the confraternity by Baccio Comi, not to mention the financial patronage of non-artistic projects.[17]

Later in the seventeeth century another set of brothers, Agnolo and Alessandro Galli, again members of the Arcangelo Raffaello, also stood out for their generosity and their patronage of art in the confraternity. In 1654 they donated Orazio Fidani's recent work *Tobias Healing His Father's Blindness*, a product of Fidani's full artistic maturity (ill. 8). They also paid for the fresco by Bartolomeo Neri on the wall behind the high altar and his frescoes around the altars and doors of the *stanzone*. On his own, Agnolo Galli paid for the paintings by Michelangelo Cinganelli on the ceiling of the oratory and on the external façade of the confraternity. Like the Comi brothers before them, the two Galli brothers were also clearly eager to contribute to the beautification of the confraternity's physical space.[18]

Other individuals also contributed to the improvement of the physical fibre of the building. In 1641, Alberto del Vivaio, recently appointed to oversee the music in the confraternity, paid for the building of a new organ loft (*terrazzino della musica*) and the installation a new instrument in it to replace the previous one, purchased by Baccio Comi from Galileo Galilei. For his initiative and financing, Del Vivaio was allowed to place his family crest on the new loft. His interest, however, was not necessarily in bricks and mortar, but in music, so much so that he later made a sizeable bequest to support the performance of music in the confraternity.[19]

There are also recorded cases of individuals who gathered together to subsidize, jointly, the commissioning of an artwork. When Giulio Del Caccia donated a gilded brass book with silver decorations containing a relic of St Mary Magdalene on 26 July 1592, two other confraternity members donated a matching reliquary containing a piece of the wood of the cross.[20] Other times, a group of members joined together to raise a voluntary collection. Such was the case in 1561, when some members commissioned a reliquiary to hold the relics of 'St Agatha, St Blaise, St Ursula, St Mary Magdalene, and many other relics received from diverse sources.'[21] To my knowledge, no research has yet been carried out to locate and identify these objects and to examine them in the context of sixteenth-century Florentine *oreficeria*.[22]

As the documents indicate, the Arcangelo Raffaello itself commissioned very little art. Its members, however, whether as artists or as patrons, donated generously to it and subsidized extensive architectural improvements to its site. By the time the confraternity was suppressed, these contributions had provided it with a rich and varied number of devotional objects with artistic merit.

In all its history, there is only one documented case in which works of art commissioned for the Arcangelo Raffaello did not remain in the confraternity. In 1621 a group of nine members joined to subsidize the expenses incurred in building the set for the confraternity's memorial service for Grand Duke Cosimo II. For their generosity they were allowed to take home the six large allegorical paintings and four life-size statues created for the event by some of the most prominent artists then working in Florence. There may be two reasons for this dispersal of confraternity art – first, the expenses incurred by the nine patrons were, admittedly, quite high, and therefore they ought to have been reimbursed in some way, and, second, the iconology of the artwork produced for this event did not at all fit the iconological program in place in the confraternity's complex.

## Iconology

The confraternity's iconology, in fact, was fairly uniform and well considered. The fundamental images were those of the Archangel Raphael, St Mary Magdalene, the Virgin, and Jesus.

The Archangel Raphael was the confraternity's primary icon.[23] He had been given to the youths by Pope Eugenius IV as their celestial patron and object of devotion. The confraternity thus took its name from him and placed images of him throughout their complex, in their books, and even on the coffin used for confraternity funerals.

The Archangel Raphael was a very appropriate icon for a youth confraternity, for in the apocryphal book of Tobit he is the angel who guides and protects the young Tobias on his journey from Nineveh to Media. He thus becomes an image of the 'guide' who directs and protects the young traveller. Allegorically, he guides the young Christian on his journey towards God and protects him from the snares of the Devil. From the fifteenth century onward, the archangel became associated in the popular imagination with the guardian angel, though this is, strictly speaking, an incorrect association. In Renaissance depictions of Raphael as Tobias's guide he is usually depicted as an effete and elegantly dressed young man in his late teens, walking alongside a much younger youth, often a mere child of eight or nine years of age. In some ways this iconology recalls the presence, within the context of a youth confraternity, of older teens and pre-pubescent boys, the first acting as role models and guides for the second. The iconology of 'Raphael as guide' and the age difference between him and his charge are evident in two naïf illustrations at the beginning of two record books from the Arcangelo Raffaello: the first depicts the archangel and Tobias walking along as a group of confraternity brothers, in their white gowns, kneel in veneration around them, while the second shows the archangel and Tobias walking along as the boy's little dog scurries beside them (see frontispiece and ill. 5).[24] Although it has now been lost, it is safe to suggest that the Raphael/Tobias pair in the anonymous *Jacob's Ladder* roundel hanging in the confraternity's sacristy also adhered to this figurative concept. Similarly, the confraternity's processional banner, because of obvious thematic connections, probably depicted the two youths on their way to or from Nineveh.

The Raphael and Tobias narrative was not, however, only a story about a journey. It was also a story about healing – Sarah's from her demons and Tobit's from his blindness. In the context of the youth confraternity of the Arcangelo Raffaello, the first healing, which allowed the young couple to consummate their marriage, was perhaps not an appropriate episode to emphasize – especially when the confraternity statutes encouraged members who had 'that most precious and angelic gift of virginity' to maintain it. The second healing, on the other hand, was more suitable. We thus find a depiction of it hanging in the confraternity's entrance hall, to the right of the main door, in Orazio Fidani's *Tobias Healing His Father's Blindness* (ill. 8). It was perhaps unusual for the confraternity to emphasize the 'healing of Tobit' episode in its iconology of the archangel. The group was not at all involved with anything 'medical,' nor does there seem to have been a significant number of budding young physicians in the organization. The only explanation can be an allegorical interpretation through which the restoration of old Tobit's sight by his young son's application of the fish ointment suggests the restoration of good Christian mores in the parents of the youths frequenting the confraternity – something that Ambrogio Traversari has suggested in his 1434 letters to Pope Eugenius IV (see above, ch. 2, p. 29).

Besides the healing of Sarah, there are other elements of the Raphael/Tobias narrative that do not appear in the confraternity's iconology. The charitable work of burying the dead, carried out by old Tobit and his son Tobias while the archangel, invisible, looked on, is not suggested anywhere in the confraternity's images or in its written records (plays, poems, etc.). Perhaps this episode was suppressed because the confraternity was, in the strictest sense, an educational rather than a charitable institution. Other confraternities, such as the Congrega dei Neri, had already assumed as their specific work of mercy the burying of the dead. The Arcangelo Raffaello did escort its own deceased brothers to their final resting place, but it did not extend this service to the public at large as part of a social consciousness or as Christian charity. I have already mentioned that the healing of Sarah from her demons did not appear in the confraternity's iconology. Her marriage with the young Tobias is also not represented, perhaps for similar reasons.

The repentant prostitute St Mary Magdalene, on the other hand, did appear regularly in the confraternity's iconological program. Her rejection of carnality and her penitential life made her a suitable role model on which the young men of the Arcangelo Raffaello could mould their lives. She appeared as the disconsolate figure at the foot of the cross in Lorenzo Lippi's *Crucifixion* hanging on the right wall in the *stanzone* (ill. 7). She was also present in the anonymous *Madonna of the Misericordia with St Mary Magdalene and Nativity* that hung above the altar in the smaller oratory. There was a terracotta bust of her by Giovan Battista di Benedetto. And she appeared on Jacopo Ferretti's processional banner and in his lateral panel for the anonymous *Descent of the Holy Spirit*, where she counterbalanced his Archangel Raphael.

The other woman in the confraternity's iconology was the Virgin Mary, who appeared as the grieving mother at the foot of the cross in Lippi's *Crucifixion* (mentioned above), and in the *Pietà* over the entrance door into the confraternity. She was also the welcoming figure in Jacopo Chimenti's *Angel Presenting a Confraternity Youth to the Madonna*, hanging over the door into the oratory and in the anonymous *Madonna della Misericordia* altarpiece in the *tornatino*. She was enthroned and surrounded by saints in Piero di Cosimo *Madonna and Child with Sts. Dominic and Jerome*, and one of the figures in the anonymous *Descent of the Holy Spirit*, both in the *sagrestia*. And she appeared also in an anonymous terracotta *Madonna and Child*. Though she was present in many images and in the prayers of the Office of the Blessed Virgin Mary, recited weekly by the youths, she does not seem to have changed the confraternity's devotional focus towards a Marian direction.

Strangely enough, the Nativity, which had endeared the youths to Pope Eugenius IV and had given them a pseudonym, did not figure prominently in the confraternity's iconological program. There were no images of it on the confraternity walls, or on its processional banners. Its only appearance was on the logo sewn onto the right shoulder of the white confraternal gown. The closest indication of a 'nativity' motif in the decorations of the building may be an anonymous *Virgin and Child* terracotta, but even that was not usually on display.

A number of 'lesser' images were also present on the confraternity's walls, not part of an iconological program focused on the Archangel Raphael, St Mary Magdalene, Jesus and Mary. As such, they do seem somewhat out of place. The figures of St Dominic, St Jerome, St Bernard, and St Francis, for example, seem odd, for none of these saints enjoyed special veneration in the confraternity. Some of these images may be explained away as unsolicited gifts received from diverse sources. The 'little canvas painting, without a frame, with St Francis on it' located in the *spogliatoio* in the 1690 inventory may be the 'little canvas painting without a frame depicting a friar' listed in the 1784 inventory. Its description and state of conservation indicate that it was clearly not an important image for the youths. It may well have come into the confraternity as a simple gift from one of the Franciscan priests who served as father correctors in the period 1565–1606. If that was the case, it may have been a 'loaded' gift from the time when the confraternity was trying to distance itself from the Dominican convent next door and was turning to the Friar Minors from the convent of Ognissanti for a father corrector.[25]

## Customizing Images

The confraternity was certainly conscious of the importance of images. I have described above how the arrangement of paintings in the entrance hall not only exhibited some of the confraternity's most valuable works of art but also created a complex set of iconographical cross-referencing between images of healing, salvation, and mercy (see above, ch. 5, pp. 64–5). For this reason, images that did not quite reflect the confraternity's iconology were, at times, customized to make them fit the 'program.'

Such was the case with the anonymous *Descent of the Holy Spirit* which the Arcangelo Raffaello received in the early 1540s from the extinct confraternity of San Vincenzo.[26] The work had originally belonged to the flagellant confraternity of the Spirito Santo, where its subject matter had reflected precisely the group's name and devotional focus. In March 1560, two lateral panels were added to it and Jacopo Ferretti painted on them the Archangel Raphael and St Mary Magdalene, the new owners' namesake and their 'advocate.'[27] By this simple technique, without necessarily invading the original image, Ferretti had managed to personalize the painting to the Arcangelo Raffaello.

Similarly, Piero di Cosimo's *Madonna and Child with Sts Dominic and Jerome* was probably altered to change an original St Vincent in adoration of the Mother and Child into a St Dominic. All that was necessary in this alteration was to paint over the iconological star on the Dominican saint's chest and add a new one over his head, thus turning him from one saint into the other. An inquiry with the museum that now owns the panel revealed that the chest area does, in fact, show traces of having been retouched.[28]

Similar retouching may also have been carried out on the anonymous *St Vincent* canvas the Arcangelo Raffaello received in the early 1540s from the extinct confraternity of San Vincenzo Ferreri.[29] The work does not appear in subsequent inventories, where instead a suspicious *St Dominic* does appear. As for the previous item, I have argued elsewhere that this painting, too, was customized to fit better into the Arcangelo Raffaello's iconology.

Not only were paintings customized, but so were objects. The confraternity's processional banners carried the Scala monogram on them, and so did many of the confraternity's religious furnishings, from altar fronts to *tavolette*. Many objects in the confraternity similarly carried the family coats of arms of the persons who had donated them. Thus in 1557 Alexo di Raffaello Lapacini placed his family's arms on two doors he had donated to the confraternity. Baccio Comi later did the same on the *graviorgano* he had purchased from Galileo Galilei and donated to the Arcangelo Raffaello. After he died the confraternity placed his arms on the marble plaque installed in his and his brother's memory in the *stanzone*. Alberto Del Vivaio placed his family's crest on the organ loft he had built in the oratory. Lorenzo Vanni's appeared on a crimson chasuble he had donated, and Giulio Del Chiaro's on a gold-trimmed, white brocade cope, complete with stole and maniple.[30] Slowly but surely the confraternity complex, furnishings, and even its religious objects were becoming 'personalized' with the mark of their donor. And these donors were, on the whole, men of rank. The *nobilizzazione* process, which Weissman had identified in the membership of confraternities in the later sixteenth century, was thus being applied as well to the confraternity's physical space and objects.[31]

## The Experience of Art

The Arcangelo Raffaello thus owned a rich variety of objects created by local artists in both the major and minor arts, as well as by talented artisans working in wood, clay, and other media. Not only the Arcangelo Raffaello but Florentine confraternities in general were rich repositories of a large variety of objects of artistic merit.[32]

The local artists who prayed, met together, and collaborated in confraternities ran the gamut from individuals who are still well known in the art-historical community to talented men whose contributions, though appreciated in their day, have not survived the passage of time and aesthetic tastes. The connection between these artists and confraternities in which they met has not yet been fully examined in a monograph study. In the case of youth confraternities it may well be that a young artist found an early venue for public expression in the ephemera created for special events such as plays and *feste*, or in the *apparati* erected for memorial services, Christmas, Easter, or the Forty Hours devotions. Events, I might add, that were attended not only by confraternity members, but by a public of nonmembers that often included nobles, the court, and the ruling family.

Just to take one example, the twenty-five-year-old Baccio del Bianco worked together with the slightly younger Lorenzo Lippi in February 1629 on the stage set for the confraternity's production of Jacopo Cicognini's play *Trionfo di Davit*. This was a special event, sumptuously done, with original music by the *maestro di cappella* Agnolo Conti, and an audience that included the grand duke and the ladies and gentlemen of his court.[33] A few years later Baccio designed on his own the set for the performance of Sforza Oddi's *Commedia de' morti vivi*, mounted by the confraternity, again with a splash, this time in the Palazzo Medici in Via Larga.[34] About ten years earlier, his father Cosimo del Bianco had devised the complicated double stage set and costumes for the September 1622 grandiose performances of Giovan Maria Cecchi's *Commedia della Benedizion di Giacob*, revised by Jacopo Cicognini and even embellished by music by Giovan Battista da Gagliano. The play, it should be noted, was staged five times and the performances were attended not only by the grand duke, his family, and his court, but also by the papal nuncio, the archbishop of Florence and his vicar, as well as the archbishops of Pisa, Fiesole, and Borgo San Sepolcro.[35] Earlier, in 1621, Cosimo Del Bianco had worked on the set for the obsequies of Grand Duke Cosimo II. Although neither his teenaged son Baccio nor the younger Lorenzo Lippi is mentioned in the records or accounts for either of these two events, it is not improbable that the two talented youngsters would have been called upon to help in the decorative aspects of the set or the *parato*.[36] The experience that both Lorenzo Lippi and Baccio Del Bianco acquired at the Arcangelo Raffaello, either by doing or by watching, stood them in good stead. Guido Burchi rightly points out that in the years 1600–40 and then again in 1669–1720 the Arcangelo Raffaello was the focus for a number of innovative artists, be they musicians or designers. He mentions in particular Lorenzo Lippi and, 'above all, Baccio del Bianco who, slightly more than twenty years old, gained his first experience at the Scala, developing in this manner that mastery which later, in

1650, earned him an invitation from Philip IV of Spain to produce spectacles for him, among which the staging of Calderon della Barca's *Perseus* has remained famous.'[37]

# 20

# The Obsequies for Grand Duke Cosimo II

One of the most visually stunning events at the Arcangelo Raffaello must have been the confraternity's 1621 obsequies for Grand Duke Cosimo II. The premature death of their beloved *confratello* and ruler was lamented and observed with an extensive (and expensive) stage set and with a formal eulogy. A detailed description and an analysis of the decorations set up in the confraternity, and of the eulogy delivered in Cosimo's praise, form the core of this chapter. They are introduced by a few words on Cosimo II himself and some closing comments about the birth of his namesake, Cosimo III.

## The Death of Grand Duke Cosimo II

On 28 February 1621, grand duke Cosimo II de' Medici died.[1] He was only thirty-two years old, but had been chronically ill for the last seven years and had not been expected to live much longer. His reign started optimistically enough when, in 1609, at the age of nineteen, he ascended to the throne on the death of his sixty-year-old father, Ferdinando I. Together with his young wife, Maria Maddalena of Austria, and his several brothers and sisters, the oldest of whom were still in their teens, he brought a breath of fresh air to the court and the city.[2]

As the Pitti Palace became a locus for the entertainments and festivities of the young Medici siblings and their friends, Cosimo undertook to expand it significantly, increasing it threefold. He thus turned the old Florentine merchant palazzo into a truly royal palace, with two imposing wings extending to the back, a large central courtyard suitable for theatrical and other festive entertainments, and a terrace with a fountain behind it. The palazzo was to be a *reggia* appropriate to his young wife's imperial dignity. Maria Maddalena was, in fact, a Hapsburg, daughter of an emperor and, later, sister to another. And Cosimo II, like his grandfather Cosimo I, loved his wife dearly. He built for her a magnificent villa at Poggio Imperiale, which changed its name to honour her ancestral dignity, and joined it to the city with the broad cypress-lined avenue that to this day, in spite of the horrific traffic that speeds along it, exudes an air of dignified grandeur.

Besides this extensive building program, Cosimo II also paid close attention to his fleet and actively sought to increase it. In this endeavour he enjoyed the assistance of the expatriate Englishman Sir Robert Dudley, an adventurer with many talents. Dudley fostered the expansion of Leghorn by improving its harbour facilities and having it declared a free port; he actively promoted shipbuilding and oversaw the drainage of the Pisan marshes, thus bringing prosperity and work to that entire coastal area.

Cosimo's small navy, his improved facilities at Leghorn, and the economic well-being of his treasury allowed him to contribute to current military enterprises. He granted docking rights to the Grand Emir Fakhr ad-Din II in his war against the Sultan Amurath IV (1613),[3] he came to the aid of Ferdinando Gonzaga, duke of Mantua, when Carlo Emmanuele I of Savoy invaded Monferrato (1613–17), and he sent troops to help the Emperor Ferdinand II break the siege of Vienna (1619) – all of this without adding to the tax burden of his subjects.

War was not, however, Cosimo's interest. He was by nature a peaceful man, more inclined to diplomacy than to conflict. He interceded, for example, on behalf of his cousin Marie de' Medici when, at the end of her regency, her son Louis XIII not only set her aside but relegated her to the castle of Blois and then, after her escape from this virtual house arrest, refused to allow her to return to court. On several occasions Cosimo was called upon by the pope and other European rulers to help mediate potential conflicts.[4]

A man of peace and civility, Cosimo lived true to the Medici tradition of supporting the arts and letters. Like his great-uncle Francesco I, he was interested in scientific inquiry as well, though as a patron and not as a practitioner. Shortly after his accession to power, he invited his old teacher Galileo Galilei back from his eighteen years at the University of Padua and appointed him 'Chief Mathematician to the Grand Duke,' with a villa on the hill of Poggio Imperiale, a very generous salary, and grand-ducal protection from the ever-present threats of the Inquisition.

Finally, the young ruler's reign was blessed with the absence of open military conflicts and with the abundance of good harvests, both of which gave the people of Tuscany a sense of economic and social well-being. To his contemporaries this was a clear indication that Cosimo's work and goals bore the stamp of divine approval. Napier would later describe him as 'a prince of gentle character, clement, tolerant and cheerful, with a friendly and social disposition, some literature, and a strong inclination to national peace and tranquillity, not only for Tuscany but throughout Europe.'[5] His contemporaries would have agreed.

The promise of a long, prosperous reign was, however, cut short by the onset, in 1614, of a chronic illness that seriously debilitated the young grand duke for the rest of his short life. An invalid in body but not in spirit, Cosimo sought to rule as efficiently as his illness would allow him. The prospect of an early death was, however, evident to all, including Cosimo himself. As the end drew near, he set up a Council of Regency for the minority of his eleven-year-old son, Ferdinando II. The council was composed of four trusted ministers, whom he named – Count Orso D'Elci, the Marquis Giovan Francesco Del Monte, Niccolò Dell'Antella,[6] and Mons. Giuliano de' Medici Archbishop of Pisa.[7] The council was overseen by his wife, Maria Maddalena of Austria, and his mother, Christine of Lorraine, as joint regents.

Napier, perhaps a little too colourfully and certainly not with an open mind, describes the two co-regents as 'two weak, untalented and bigoted women suddenly invested with power and riches.' In this assessment he is somewhat unfair to the two women – as scions of two of the most powerful ruling houses of Europe, Maria Maddalena of Austria and Christine of Lorraine were not unaccustomed to either power or riches. Diaz has recently described them, perhaps more correctly, simply as bigots. Their four chief ministers were not much better – Diaz describes them as 'a gathering of ecclesiastics and aristocrats' that allowed Tuscany to be gripped by 'a spirit of stately courtliness, immobile and feudalistic.'[8] Cosimo II's death, therefore, signalled a period of uncertainty and then decline that had begun with his illness and was to continue throughout the regency and the ensuing rule of the last Medici.

Cosimo's death touched the confraternity of the Arcangelo Raffaello very closely, not only because he had been the country's ruler but also because he had been a lifetime member of the group. He had officially joined the Arcangelo Raffaello on 5 January 1592, when his mother, Christine of Lorraine, had enrolled him at the age of seven months into the group whose singing and devotion had so impressed her on her visits in 1590 and 1591. Although he never took an active part in the spiritual or festive life of the confraternity, his name on the membership rolls gave the Arcangelo Raffaello the prestige of grand-ducal affiliation and resulted in a significant increase in membership (see above, ch. 6, p. 82). With his death the confraternity lost its most illustrious member and its most important earthly patron. It was only fitting, therefore, that the Arcangelo Raffaello commemorate his passing with an elaborate funeral *parato* and a public memorial ceremony.

The practice of confraternal commemoration on the death of the ruling grand duke was not new either at the Arcangelo Raffaello or in other confraternities. In his *Cronaca*, Giuliano de' Ricci recalls that in 1574, at the death of Cosimo I, a number of orations were delivered in his memory and mentions in particular that 'Andrea di Vincentio Alamanni [recited one] in the confraternity of the Angelo Raffaello called della Scala.'[9]

Similar orations were delivered on the death of other members of the grand-ducal family. When the Grand Duchess Joanna of Austria, wife of Francesco I de' Medici and much beloved of the Florentines, died in April 1578, an elaborate official funeral was held for her, and then 'for many days thereafter in all the confraternities of the city, there was general lament and prayers to God, with most honourable obsequies and orations recited by youths and composed by learned persons: among which the foremost were those recited by Palla Rucellai in the Company of the Agnolo Raffaello in via Maffia, and another one by Giovanni da Falgano in the Agnolo Raffaello, called the Scala, in the piazza of Santa Maria Novella.'[10]

At the death of the fourth grand duke, Cosimo II, the Arcangelo Raffaello once again set up a funereal display and on 14 March 1621 had one of its members, Giovan Francesco Ghiberti, deliver a commemorative oration.[11] Other confraternities also observed the passing of Cosimo II with a special commemorative service and oration. The youths of Sant'Antonio da Padova, for example, had one of their past members, the forty-four-year-old Jacopo Cicognini, recite 'the praises' of Cosimo II in their oratory on the same evening as the Arcangelo Raffaello (14 March 1621). In the *ricordi* of Sant'Antonio da Padova, the scribe noted that 'the oratory was filled with a great number of people, and there would have been more were it not for the weather, for it was raining heavily, and the competition from the confraternity of the Scala.'[12]

The competition must have been overwhelming. At the Scala, that is, at the Arcangelo Raffaello, an extensive and elaborate *parato* had been erected in the large entrance hall (the *stanzone*) and in the oratory. The youths of the Arcangelo Raffaello had spared no expense to honour their deceased brother. A number of account books list both the costs incurred for the event and the benefactors who underwrote them. One tally puts the total at 6,138.5.6 lire, contributed by nine different members through an average donation of 682.7 *lire* each. The total expenses may, however, have been much higher – it is not clear from the records either that all the tallies were in fact entered in the summary document or that the confraternity itself was ever able to determine the exact sum of the total expenses relating to the obsequies.[13]

The entire event was so impressive that the scribe not only recorded the expenses incurred but also wrote down a detailed description of the *parato* and transcribed the oration delivered by Giovan Francesco Ghiberti.

## The Parato for the Obsequies in the Compagnia[14]

The *parato* was one of the most splendid and elaborate funeral decorations yet set up in the Arcangelo Raffaello. It was designed by Simon Carlo Rondinelli and built by Ser Giovanni Pieroni, whom Rondinelli had hired as master builder (*architetto*).[15] The appointment may have been controversial, for Rondinelli was obliged to hire Ser Giovanni Coccapani as well,[16] and this 'in order to please Signor Giovanbattista Strozzi,'[17] one of the nine confraternity members who underwrote the cost of the display. The other eight patrons were Agnolo Dassi, Agnolo Galli, Filippo Del Nero,[18] Filippo Magalotti,[19] Giovan Battista Quaratesi,[20] Luigi Bartoli, Lorenzo Bonsi, and Piero Martellini.

At first Rondinelli wanted to build an elaborate temple in the oratory, but the room's restricted space and its low ceiling militated against the use of high-placed lamps, 'the soul and ornament of such action.' Obliged to revise his plans, Rondinelli designed instead a set that depicted an Egyptian tomb, 'dark and frightful' ('orrida e tenebrosa').

The funereal decorations did not, however, limit themselves to the 'Egyptian tomb' in the oratory. They extended out, even onto the piazza, to tell everyone passing by that the confraternity was in mourning. The façade of the building, in fact, was covered from top to bottom in funereal black serge (*rasce*). A large rectangular placard hung above the front door and bore a Latin inscription urging Cosimo, newly risen to immortality, to accept the confraternity's obsequies:

Cos. II. M.D. Etruriae Arc. Raph. Societas ademptam immortalitatem gratulatam clementissimum principem orat suprema haec funeris dona aequus accipiat si quid delatos honores nunc curat felicissimamque animam id etiam praemii manet, ut ista sentiat.

A lion's skin, held in place by a war spear, had been painted above the placard, thus making the ensemble look 'like an ancient trophy.' The skin's front paws were tied to the spear with a bow whose strings were inscribed with the Latin phrases 'Conscidisti saccum meum' on the right and 'Dimidio dierum meorum' on the left. All three inscriptions had been composed by Jacopo Soldani and painted by Paulantonio Guerrini.[21] The total height of the ensemble was 10.5 *braccia*, or 6.18 metres – the skin itself was nearly 3 metres high, the protruding spear just over a metre long, and the placard just over 2 metres high and nearly 3 metres long – thus constituting a somewhat large but well-balanced element on the otherwise plain black façade of the building.

Just inside the confraternity, the walls of the large *stanzone*, which measured 11.78 metres square, had also been covered from floor to ceiling in black serge. The ceiling had been covered in sheets of Scottish twill (*saie scotte*) to make the room look like a pavilion. From the centre of the ceiling hung a large globe of the world (*mappamondo*), a metre in diameter. The globe was lighted by an internal lamp which revealed a scroll painted on the great expanse of the sea bearing the inscription 'Orbis Universus Sepulcrum.' The scribe points out that the phrase had been drawn from Thucydides, but that the device was a fantasy (*capriccio*) of the designer Rondinelli. The pavilion ceiling was painted by Cosimo del Bianco.[22] Directly across from the entrance door was the door into the oratory, made to look like a hole (*buca*) or the opening of a tomb. Above it Rondinelli had placed a full-size skeleton by Pandolfo Sacchi, shown in the act of tearing its chest and belly open to expose a cartouche bearing the words 'Patens Sepulcrum.'[23] The only other decorations in the *stanzone* were eight large candlestick holders, each 2.35 metres high and bearing a large white candle.

Inside the oratory, Cosimo del Bianco had covered the ceiling in black cotton. A Doric chapel (*sacello*) had been erected in the farthest third of the oratory and decorated with arches, statues, and trophies. It stood separate from the rest of the tomb and occupied a space just a little shorter than the third set of pews (*manganelle*). It was, nonetheless, fairly large, measuring 6.5 metres in width, 4.70 in length, and 7 in height.

To the right of the entrance there was a niche (2.35 metres high) containing a life-sized statue of Tuscany by Anastagio Fontebuoni.[24] Tuscany was portrayed as a majestic and beautiful woman, dressed in a thin, pleated chlamys (*crespa clamide*) that reached to her feet. She wore the grand-ducal mantle on her shoulders and held the grand-ducal sceptre in her right hand. All of these are standard iconological details. Cesare Ripa adds that in her left hand she should also hold a book with the red Florentine lily on top of it, symbols of its capital city and its tradition of arts and learning respectively.[25] On either side of the niche, there were two large display cases, about 3.5 metres high, containing a variety of military trophies and ancient priestly instruments, and above them the inscriptions 'Et lituo' and 'Et armis,' drawn from Virgil. Above the niche stood a cartouche with the deceased grand duke's *impresa* – a laurel crown with the motto 'Non iuvat ex facili' – and above it the great red lily of Florence. Under the trophies there were small painting of towns, wars, conquests, sacrifices, and other such scenes devised by Rondinelli.

Directly across from the statue of Tuscany, on the left of the entrance, was a similar niche with a statue by Giovanni da San Giovanni depicting the Order of St Stephen.[26] The order was represented by a woman with the face of the goddess Pallas, armed with a corselet and wearing a brief gown. She wore the mantle of the Order of St Stephen on her shoulders and on her head a morion helmet ringed with a triple crown, civic, naval, and mural. In her right hand she held the baton of command and in her left the shield with the order's Maltese cross, which reappeared again above the niche. The figure, for which Ripa does not provide a suggested iconology, was clearly fashioned on the basis of the iconology of Tuscany embellished with the emblems already in use by the order. The trophies displayed in the two cases all referred to the order's naval exploits against the Turks, and included turbans, arrows, quivers, scimitars, and other spoils of war. The cartouche above them read 'Quae mare' and 'Terrasque metu,' an inscription again drawn from Virgil. Under the trophies there were pictures of naval battles, conquests, and similar military scenes. Inside the niche there was the grand duke's other *impresa* consisting of an 'Indian tree' (*Albero Indiano*) and the motto 'Sola solo, sola salo.'

The chapel (*sacello*) was constructed by Giovanni Pieroni. Its front was two-thirds closed. On the right crouched the heraldic lion of Florence, grieving. It was crowned with the ducal crown and rested on a globe bearing the cross and lily of the Florentine Republic. On the left lay the heraldic wolf of Siena, also grieving, and resting on a broken slab of marble bearing the black and white arms of that city. The two animals occupied a third of the platform each and represented the two principal territorial components of the Grand Duchy of Tuscany – the old republics of Florence and Siena. The middle third of the platform consisted of the two steps that led into the chapel. The construction was painted to look like olive marble, with touches of yellow and gold in all its raised edges (*risalti*), concave surfaces (*scorniciati*), and the like. The statues and trophies on it were painted to look like gold.

A flight of marble steps was visible behind the chapel. It led to an altar that seemed to be at the far end of the tomb, outside the chapel, in a niche made of black cotton. On the altar stood a large cross, 4.85 metres high, painted silver, and six ancient urns with bright lights emanating from inside of them.

In the middle of the chapel there was a platform (*sodo*) with an inscription devised by Rondinelli that read 'Principi Optimo, Patri Benignissimo, Munus Extremum.' Above it, another platform supported a coffin painted lapis lazuli with gold highlights. On the coffin itself stood a triangular spire (*guglia*), also painted lapis lazuli, with a base bearing the Medici crest with grand-ducal crown. The base was also decorated with a number of gold hieroglyphs that referred to the life and deeds of the deceased grand duke. Flames rose from a crack in the top half of the spire, and enveloped a dying phoenix from whose mouth a bright ray of golden light shot upwards towards the word GOD painted in the bright opening of a cloud-filled heaven above the coffin. In the best tradition of medieval religious painting, the ray of light bore an inscription – 'Renovatur in Celis.' On the pedestal, box, and coffin there were many ancient-looking clay oil lamps, again painted lapis lazuli. They and a number of other lamps hidden throughout the chapel filled it with light. Although the idea for the burning lights had been Rondinelli's, it was the *architetto* Pieroni who had devised the system to keep them lit over a long period of time and to keep them out of sight from the viewer.

At the four corners of the pedestal stood four life-size clay statues painted to look like marble. The first on the right was by Felice Palma and represented Prudence.[27] The scribe writes that she was depicted as a woman with two faces, looking into a mirror she held in her right hand. Her left hand rested on an anchor while a snake wound around her left arm. She wore a morion helmet garlanded with mulberry leaves. Her pedestal bore the inscription 'Prudentissimo Principi.' The figure on the front left corner, Fortitude, was by Orazio Mochi.[28] She was depicted as a robust woman armed with a low-cut cuirass and wearing a short gown, like an Amazon. On her head she wore a helmet with an oak crown. She leaned with her right hand on an oak pole which sprouted leaves at its tip. With her left hand she held a tablet (*targa*) with a picture of a lion in the act of killing a boar. The inscription on her pedestal read 'Fortissimo Heroi.' Behind her, the statue of Temperance, by Agostino Ubaldini, was visible in perspective.[29] She wore a dress that reached down to her ankles. In her right hand she held a palm branch, and in her left a bridle (*freno*). Her hair was long and loose, and she was crowned with laurel leaves. The words 'Moderatissimo Domino' were inscribed on her pedestal. 'Justice,' by Francesco di Piero Susini, stood on the back right corner.[30] She was a beautiful virgin with a severe countenance and very sharp eyes. She wore a majestic crown and a necklace with an eye carved in it. In her right hand she held a sword, lowered but ready to strike. In her left hand she held a compass. The words 'Justissimo Cosmo' were inscribed on her pedestal.

The representation of the four virtues is in line with those offered by Cesare Ripa in his *Iconologia*. The image of Prudence created by Palma, for example, is quite similar to the one in Ripa's woodcut. Ripa's emblem shows a woman with two faces looking at herself in a hand-mirror. On her head she wears a helmet adorned with a garland of mulberry leaves. With the other hand she holds not an anchor but an arrow. And a remora, not a snake, curls up the arrow (much like the snake on the staff carried by Aesculapius, the Greek god of medicine, that has become the symbol of the medical profession). Ripa explains the symbolism of his image by saying that the mirror shows that the prudent individual should know and correct his failings, and it also recalls that Socrates used to advise his students to look at themselves in the mirror every morning; the helmet represents human intellect (*ingegno*), ready and armed with wise counsel; the mulberry-leaf garland indicates that the wise individual does not act before the appropriate time, but waits for time to ripen; the remora is a symbol for delay, since Pliny said that when this fish attaches itself to a ship it has the power to bring the vessel to a standstill; and, lastly, the arrow indicates that one should not delay in attaching oneself to what is known to be good. In the description given by the Arcangelo Raffaello scribe there are some slight variants from Ripa's iconology, but they are easily attributable to the scribe's own misreading of the image he was viewing. In the case of Prudence, for example, the remora is misread as a snake, an understandable mistake. In the case of Fortitude, the scribe claims that she held a tablet (*targa*) in her left hand, while in fact Ripa claims she should be holding a shield, something much more appropriate to her overall military image.[31] It is clear, therefore, that the artists who created the four statues were very conversant with contemporary emblem iconology and used it, whereas the confraternity scribe, who misidentifies some of the details and does not offer his reader an allegorical interpretation, was less so.

Around the tomb there were five large decorative areas, two on each side of the oratory (above each of the two lateral rows of pews) and one above the front of the tomb. Each of these spaces contained a large painting in *chiaroscuro*, 2.95 metres long and 2.35 high, with a frame that added 60 centimetres more to the measurements.

The painting in the centre, above the entrance to the tomb, was by Ottavio Vannini and represented *Religion accompanied by Zeal and Humility*.[32] Religion was depicted as a majestic woman covered with a very thin veil and surrounded by light. She had a flame on her head and wings of fire. In her right hand she held an equilateral triangle. She leaned on Zeal, standing at her right side. He was depicted as a man in priestly clothes, with a mitre on his head, and a torch in his right hand. Humility stood at Religion's left side. She was depicted as a bare-footed woman dressed in a shirt. Her knees were bent, and with her feet she trampled crowns, sceptres, and other royal emblems, among which vipers and other dead snakes lay scattered about. In the background there were depictions of temples, altars, sacrifices, and other such things. The painting's frame was decorated with flames and crosses, and contained a cartouche with an elephant painted on it. In the middle, above the painting, there was a military emblem with the Medici arms and a crowned helmet.

To the right hung the painting of *Perfect Virtue*, by Giovanni da San Giovanni. She was depicted as a majestic woman dressed and armed like an Amazon. In her left hand she held a shield bearing the image of a palm tree in a wreath of holly. In her right hand she held a many-pointed Herculean club. A lion's skin billowed from her shoulders. With her left foot she crushed with a threatening and victorious air a seven-headed hydra (the heads were those of a serpent, goat, wolf, ostrich, bear, peacock, and donkey). The frame was decorated with palm and oak trees, and the cartouche bore the image of a porcupine about to strike.

Matteo Rosselli's *Piety* followed on the right. She was a beautiful young woman, with beautiful eyes, an aquiline nose, large wings, and fire emanating from her heart. With her right hand she poured out a cornucopia of flowers, fruits, and other such assorted products of the earth necessary for human life. With her right hand she held a sword and leaned on an altar. She wore a short dress that reached to her knees. The background depicted a variety of acts of human and Christian piety. The frame was decorated with hyacinths and the cartouche displayed the image of a stork.

Sigismondo Coccapani's *Magnanimity and Munificence* hung across from them, on the left.[33] Magnanimity was a majestic woman dressed like an empress and sitting on a tamed lion. Her helmet was a crowned lion's skull. She held a royal sceptre in her right hand and with her left Munificence's right hand. Munificence was similar to her, but a little smaller. Her crown contained two cornucopias full of flowers. With her left hand she scattered gold, jewels, and coins profusely. Both wore buskins. In the background magnificent constructions – mausoleums, cities, ports, armies, and the like – were visible. The frame was decorated with more cornucopias full of flowers and the cartouche bore the crowned head of a lion.

Anastagio Fontebuoni's *Good Advice and Judgment Sitting on the Rain-*

*bow* was the last painting on the left. Good Advice was depicted as a majestic old man dressed in a long robe and wearing a large gold necklace. In his right hand he held a book while with his left he pointed to Judgment. The latter was depicted as a naked young man with a compass in his left hand and a square with a mason's level in his right. There was also a four-sided stone (*pietra quadrilatera*) crushing down on the heads of a bear and a wolf. A three-headed bust – with the heads of a dog on the right, a lynx in the middle, and a lion on the left – was depicted above the stone. The painting's frame was decorated with mulberry branches and the cartouche bore the crowned head of an owl.

All the painters of these images and the sculptors of the statues described earlier were selected by Giovanni Coccapani, who had been placed in charge of all the work. Either he or his younger brother Sigismondo made sketches of the entire set.[34]

The spaces between the paintings were filled with skeletons, 2 metres high, lined up along a 2.35-metres baseboard (*basamento*). They were embellished with falling folds of white satin, devised by Sigismondo Coccapani. Under each of the paintings there was a large figure of Death with a cartouche on its chest and a large torch-holder in each hand to light the painting. Each cartouche was inscribed with a distich explaining the meaning of the painting, composed by the fifteen-year-old Antonio Peri, a youth described as gifted with poetic ability.[35] Each of the six skeletons standing between the paintings held open a scroll, and each also had a cartouche underneath it. Their six scrolls and cartouches bore the following mottos from Scripture:

| | | |
|---|---|---|
| Scroll 1 | 'Annos eternos in mente habui' | Ps. 76/77:6 |
| cartouche | 'Mori lucrum' | Phil. 1:21 |
| Scroll 2 | 'Judicia Domini iustificata in semetipsa' | Ps. 18/19:10 |
| cartouche | 'Diriges Justum' | Ps. 7:10 |
| Scroll 3 | 'Elevata est magnificentia tua' | Ps. 8:2 |
| cartouche | 'Verus Dei cultor' | John 9:31 |
| Scroll 4 | 'In sole posuit tabernaculum suum' | Ps. 18/19:6 |
| cartouche | 'Alta a longe cognoscit' | Ps. 137/138:6 |
| Scroll 5 | 'Transibo in locum tabernaculi admirabilis' | Ps. 41/42:5 |
| cartouche | 'Ecce venio' | Ps. 39/40:8 |

| | | |
|---|---|---|
| Scroll 6 | 'Quasi flos egreditur, et conteritur' | Job 14:2 |
| cartouche | 'Regnabit in secula.' | Ps. 145/146:10 |

In the space between the wall and these figures of Death, Giovanni Coccapani had hidden other lights and oil lamps. The scribe concludes the description by saying that 'these few decorations' completely filled the space available. He then adds that the pews were decorated with silver torch-holders.

The nine men who bore the expenses for the *parato* were eventually given the work of art that had been commissioned for it. The scribe thus points out that the six allegorical paintings were distributed as follows: San Giovanni's *Perfect Virtue* was given to Agnolo Dassi, Rosselli's *Piety* to Agnolo Galli, Vannini's *Religion* to Filippo Magalotti, Coccapani's *Magnanimity and Munificence* to Giovanbattista Quaratesi, and Fontebuoni's *Good Advice* to Lorenzo Bonsi. Ubaldini's statue of Temperance went to Piero Martellini, Mochi's Fortitude to Filippo Del Nero, Palma's Prudence to Giovanbattista Strozzi, and Susini's Justice to Luigi Bartoli.[36] Besides the *buona reputazione* that followed from their generous financial support, the nine donors were thus able also to take home a piece of the work they had subsidized, much of it by very reputable contemporary artists.

The artists themselves were paid generously for the value of their work. For each of the chiaroscuro paintings each artist received 126 *lire*, for the two statues of Tuscany and the Order of St Stephen Fontebuoni and San Giovanni respectively were paid 28 *lire* each, for the four statues of the moral virtues their sculptors earned 140 *lire* each, and Ubaldini received 21 *lire* for his statue of the phoenix rising from a broken pyramid. Even the minor artists, who painted filler images or prosaic placards, were amply rewarded. Francesco Corniccieri, *pittore*, received 35 *lire* for his two large skeletons.[37] Giovan Battista Lupicini, *pittore*, received 56 *lire* for his lettering, large and small, inscribed in several places in the confraternity.[38] Paulantonio Guerrini, *pittore*, received 42 *lire* for the large placard, lion skin, and Medici crest that hung on the confraternity façade.[39] Pandolfo Sacchi, *pittore*, received 38.10 *lire* for the lion and wolf at the two ends of the catafalque, and for the large skeleton above the oratory's door that welcomed visitors by tearing open its chest and belly. But the prize clearly went to Giuseppe Buonaiuti, *pittore di grosserie*,[40] who received the enormous sum of 630 *lire* for all his 'cartouches, skeletons, pedestals, emblems, decorations for paintings, gildings, and other grotesques.'[41]

Although the scribe does not give us an equally detailed description of the music for the memorial service, it was probably more than equal to the artistic and architectural elements described above. Filippo Del Nero and Agnolo Dassi, who had been put in charge of it, had in turn hired Marco da Gagliano to look after it. The scribe points out that they had done this confident that the composer/musician would be able to provide 'with his own abilities and with his impeccable taste the proper music and orchestration for the obsequies.' He no doubt did. Marco da Gagliano had been closely associated with the confraternity since he had joined it at the age of six, on 24 February 1589. He had been performing in it since 1602, and had been its chapel master since 1609.[42] His teacher had been Luca Bati, who in his time had been chapel master at the Duomo, and an active participant in the discussions and musical experiments of the Camerata de' Bardi. At the time of the obsequies, Marco himself had returned from a brief period at the Gonzaga court in Mantua and had risen to the post of chapel master at the Duomo (1608) and at the grand-ducal court (1609), as well as canon and then apostolic prothonotary at San Lorenzo (1610 and 1615 respectively).[43] His credentials were, in a word, impeccable. His contribution to the obsequies, therefore, would have been such as to honour not only the memory of the deceased grand duke, but also himself and the confraternity to which they both belonged.

Marco da Gagliano appears in the account books for the obsequies only once, when on 21 March he is paid 70 *lire* for the music for the service.[44] This occasion marks his last recorded service to the confraternity. By the time the Christmas season approached, he had been replaced as *maestro di cappella* for the Arcangelo Raffaello by his younger brother Giovanni Battista da Gagliano.[45] Himself a member of the confraternity since 1599, Giovanni Battista remained in charge of its music for only three years (1622–5), though he continued to be a member of the brotherhood until his death in 1651.[46]

Part of the expenses for music includes a payment of 7 *lire* to Maestro Girolamo Bolcioni, *organista*, for tuning the confraternity's organ. A somewhat curious 'musical' expense is the reimbursement of 35 *lire* to Cosimo del Bianco for a pair of purple stockings made of Piacenza silk and a pair of gold-laced garters, all given as a gift to Signor Loreto, *musico*.[47] Although I have been unable to determine the identity of this brightly clad musician, his attire brought an unexpected splash of colour to my reading of the account books.

Other account entries provide further glimpses into the realities of staging such a complex event. Because of the large number of candles, open flames, and painted wood in the oratory and the *stanzone*, the risk of fire was very high. The confraternity therefore spent a fair sum, 5.6.8 *lire*, to procure a number of water buckets 'rispetto al fuoco.' Security must have been a concern as well, not only for the sake of personal safety, but also to avoid unnecessary losses. We thus read that on 14 March a number of hired soldiers from the Bargello were paid 4 *lire* for keeping an eye, especially at night, on the extensive black serge hanging on the façade of the building. On the day of the obsequies, four German soldiers were paid 8 *lire* to guard the front door, and it cost another 1.6.8 *lire* to keep them in drink. And 4 *lire* were paid to four more undercover soldiers ('birri ... incogniti') keeping an eye on the serge inside the confraternity.[48] Security, therefore, had been set in place to guard against accidents, intruders, and thieves.

Not only was the physical security of people and materials a concern, but so was the reputation of the confraternity itself. And although this may seem obvious from the extensive and expensive obsequies that were planned, it is also evident in the manner the confraternity dealt with potential trouble. Just a few days before the event, a carpenter's helper had bullied another helper working with him. The confraternity, seeking 'to avoid scandal,' promptly gave him severance pay and dismissed him.[49]

The detailed expenses for food and drink given to the men working on the decorations and the set provide an insight into a working man's diet at that time. On the days before the obsequies and for a few days following, the confraternity paid for dried figs, nuts, caviar, salad, small marinated fish, bread, and wine 'for the men to eat.'[50]

Although such items may constitute an unusual diet for us today, or lead us to wonder what was the 'caviar' these carpenters and painters dined on, the records do not suggest the fare was at all unusual. Although caviar is mentioned as early as the fifteenth century as a luxury product from the East, the seventeenth-century fare given to the workers on the *apparato* was probably something produced locally and devised for fairly general consumption.[51] The more refined food seems instead to have been given as a gift to two specific individuals. One was Messer Domenico Montini, *legnaiolo*, who was given a marzipan, a tench (fresh-water fish), two flasks of wine, and four lemons 'per la sua sufficienza' for a total cost of 7.13.6 *lire*. The other was the master builder Giovanni Pieroni himself, who received four flasks of Greek wine, a small marzipan ('un marzapaneto'), four refined sugar loaves ('quattro pani di zucchero raffinato'), five boxes of quince jam cakes ('cotognato alla Portughese'), a pound of Genova paste, and six pounds of crushed pistachio nuts, for a total cost of 62 *lire*.[52]

To co-ordinate the variety of work and all the people involved in it, not to mention to oversee the expenses and keep a record of everything, the confraternity appointed its regular *provveditore*, Cosimo Portinari, as special *provveditore* for the event. The scribe (who was probably Portinari himself, since the *provveditore* generally acted as *scrivano*) recalls that Portinari 'looked after his duties day and night with the utmost devotion.'

The *parato* was so impressive that the confraternity was kept open the entire following day, Tuesday, to allow visitors to view the magnificent – and costly – decorations that had been set up in memory of Cosimo II. One special visitor that day was the new grand duke. The eleven-year-old Ferdinando II had not attended the confraternity's memorial service the previous evening. He did, however, make a brief detour from his other visits the following day to satisfy either his curiosity or the unstated obligation of viewing the display. Cesare Tinghi, who kept the ceremonial diary at the grand-ducal court, recalls that in the late afternoon of 15 March, grand duke Ferdinando II went with his mother, his brothers, two of his sisters, and the Marchese del Bufalo to visit his younger sister at the new monastery of the Crocetta. Once there, while the women remained at the monastery, the grand duke and his brothers proceeded to the confraternity of the Archangel Raphael 'to see the funeral *parato* erected for the obsequies of the deceased grand duke and returned to the new monastery where, mounting in the carriage of Her Ladyship his mother, he returned to the Palazzo Pitti.'[53]

In this official court record of the grand duke's daily activities, Tinghi makes short shrift of the entire event, indicating perhaps a lack of genuine interest on the part of the new ruler for the spiritual or religious activities of the confraternity so closely linked with his father. Ferdinando's four brothers, Giovan Carlo, Mattias, Francesco, and Leopoldo, who accompanied him to the confraternity, had just recently enrolled in the Arcangelo Raffaello.[54] They might have been the ones to suggest such a visit to him. However, like their father Cosimo II, their interest in the confraternity was also purely formal, for none of them appears to have taken an active part in the organization's religious devotions or ceremonies.

## Giovan Francesco Ghiberti's Oration on the Death of Cosimo II

Although Cosimo Portinari, the confraternity's *provveditore* and scribe, took great care to describe in detail the extensive and complex *apparato* set up for the obsequies, richly adorned with the works of reputable Florentine artists, he did not give similar detailed information for the eulogy recited in conjunction with that *apparato* at the end of the memorial service. In fact, he limited himself to a very brief comment, saying that the oration was delivered by Giovan Francesco Ghiberti, who had composed it in three days.[55] Although the oration was transcribed and has been preserved, it does not appear where one would expect to find it, that is, with the description of the *apparato* in the confraternity's *ricordi*. It is, instead, bound up in a fascicule teasingly entitled 'Memorie di curiosità' in a *filza* that is a pot-pourri of diverse and unrelated matters.[56]

What were the historical circumstances and the choices obviously made that resulted in such cryptic brevity on the one hand and a 'separated' transcription on the other? Perhaps the scribe's remark that the oration had been composed in three days could be taken as a lead in this case. It seems strange that, having had all the time necessary to construct and paint the complex *apparato*, to commission well-known artists to produce paintings and statues, and to decorate the confraternity both inside and out, the confraternity should be satisfied with a eulogy described only as having been composed in three days and then excluded from the official *ricordi*. Was Ghiberti's eulogy a last-minute effort deemed not good enough for preservation? Was there animosity between Portinari and Ghiberti that led to the scribe's omission of the oration from the description and the 'official' record? Could the eulogy have been assigned first to someone who was unable to fulfil his obligations and thus obliged the confraternity to find a new orator at the last moment? Such questions, unfortunately, remain unanswered, for I have been unable to determine the context that created such an unexpected situation.

In spite of Portinari's dismissive comments, Giovan Francesco Ghiberti's contribution to the obsequies was very respectable. His oration is a well-crafted example of the genre and compares favourably with similar works on the death of Cosimo II delivered by more renowned persons and subsequently published.[57]

Ghiberti began with a general consideration on the importance of writers in memorializing the deeds of great men. Caesar, Cyrus, or Alexander would not amount to much, Ghiberti points out, were it not for writers who, 'with their learned pens, their well-wrought words, and rhetorical flourishes, not only made little deeds appear great, but with the admirable power of their language knew how to present what in effect were vices as if they were virtues.'[58] In other words, through the commonplace debate on the power of sword and pen, Ghiberti sets the stage for a eulogy that will attempt to turn Cosimo's deeds into actions worthy of being memorialized.

Fast upon this comment, Ghiberti adds the standard *apologia* for his own feeble talents in such a task. He claims to have spent the little time he was given to compose a suitable eulogy (and here there may be a veiled reference to the context) not in considering the praises of this prince, but in deciding to abstain from such an exercise. What follows is a baroque flight into several insincere excuses for his own inability to see clearly into the question, pointing out that his intellect has 'not the eyes of an eagle, but those of a blind mole.' He will therefore leave the task of praising Cosimo's deeds to 'a more cultured, a more learned, a more fecund orator,' for 'in such a deep and vast Ocean even a more expert helmsman would be afraid of not reaching port.'[59] Lastly, Ghiberti wonders how he could possibly sing Cosimo's praises when everybody in the confraternity, the city, and the whole world knows the deeds, valour, and virtues of the deceased ruler better than he. The entire introduction, with its *apologia* and *captatio benevolentiae*, thus sets the stage for the triumph of the pen over the sword.

Moving away from Cosimo II, but also cleverly returning *ad fontes*, Ghiberti goes back to Cosimo the Elder to begin a catalogue of Medici family worthies – Lorenzo the Magnificent, Leo X and Leo XI, Giovanni delle Bande Nere and don Giovanni, Cosimo I, Francesco I and Ferdinando I. The point of the exercise is to conclude that all these illustrious ancestors pale in comparison to Cosimo II, who not only epitomizes the genius of his family but also gathers in himself all virtues, intellectual, moral, and theological. This catalogue of worthies is a fairly standard device. Michelangelo Buonarroti the Younger, Giulio Strozzi, and Francesco Maria Gualterotti, for example, all made use of it in their respective eulogies. While Gualterotti adds a few words about the maternal ancestors, and Buonarroti gives a passing nod to the 'sangue di Lorena,' Ghiberti completely ignores the maternal contribution to Cosimo's genetic inheritance.[60] Given that it was as a result of a visit from his mother, Christine of Lorraine, that the confraternity was able to count Cosimo II as one of its members, the orator's slip is even more surprising. It may simply be a slip. It may, on the other hand, be a conscious effort to ignore the deceased ruler's French side and highlight instead his imperial Hapsburg connections through his wife, Maria Maddalena of Austria.

After the catalogue of Medici worthies, Ghiberti recalls how Cosimo II splendidly embodied all four of the moral virtues. His sense of justice, both spiritual and temporal, is praised, and special mention is made of his habit of consulting widely whenever a new law was proposed so that it would be 'just, honest, and useful to his people.' This was, in fact, a characteristic noted and lauded by other eulogists as well, such as Michelangelo Buonarroti the Younger. Cosimo's temperance is evidenced by the fact that he was never seen to lose his temper or to be distressed, a point again made by Buonarroti as well. His fortitude, Ghiberti goes on to say, surpassed that of

Caesar, Alexander, Hannibal, Scipio, and all the ancients, for he was able to control his passions, something they never quite managed to do successfully. This, Ghiberti adds, is a greater victory, for what is the point of conquering great castles or, like Hector or Achilles, conquering great enemies, if then one remains prey to one's lusts and vices? Cosimo's fortitude is also evident in the strength he demonstrated during his illness. At this point Ghiberti subtly implies a Christlike quality, for he presents the illness as divine punishment for the sins not of Cosimo but of his people. The illness, Ghiberti claims, was given to Cosimo by God himself for the greater glory of Cosimo and as punishment to the people of Tuscany for their sins; 'for we were not worthy to have such a Prince, Custodian, and Father in good health.' Cosimo thus becomes the scapegoat and sacrificial lamb who suffers pain and eventual death for the redemption of his subjects. Lastly, generosity (magnanimity) is evident in Cosimo through the care he had for his people, and especially because he spared them the ravages of war – 'thefts, fires, rapes, violence, the death of friends and worthy men, the pillaging of land, the destruction of cities' – all of which obscure true fame (*gloria*). There is greater glory, Ghiberti points out, in sparing the life of a single subject than in taking the lives of thousands of enemies.[61]

Charity, 'the greatest of the theological virtues,' was so much a part of Cosimo that, Ghiberti claims, no Christian saint ever had more. The hyperbole leads the eulogist to call on the people of Florence and all of Tuscany as witnesses, reminding them of Cosimo's love for them in buying grain abroad during times of scarcity and selling it to them at great financial loss to himself. The Christological image returns as Ghiberti calls Cosimo a 'loving pelican' who feeds his brood with his own blood.[62]

Having used the *argumentum ad populum*, Ghiberti now involves the audience directly, begging pardon from them for having wandered off topic and having presumed to recount to them, Cosimo's own confraternity brothers, what they themselves already knew about their 'brother.' The eulogy thus moves from Cosimo the ruler to Cosimo the brother. Ghiberti, who as we have already seen can readily lapse into baroque hyperbole and fanciful embellishment, now actually reconstructs history by suggesting that Cosimo had such affection for the confraternity that he joined it 'di proprio moto.' In fact, Cosimo was enrolled in it by his mother when he was only seven months old, and this at the impromptu suggestion of Niccolò Antifassi, the confraternity's acting guardian father (see ch. 6, p. 81 and ch. 17, p. 223).[63] Cosimo's own lack of interest in the confraternity's spiritual life is evident in the fact that the records do not indicate that he ever attended meetings or participated in the confraternity's devotions. But

Ghiberti is prepared to ignore reality and regale his audience with what they wish to hear, rather than with what they know as a fact.

Facts, as we see, are but a small hurdle for Ghiberti, and so he gallops forward to interpret the actual *apparato* and its decorations as reflections of Cosimo's virtues. The four allegorical statues at the corners of the chapel are, appropriately enough, seen to represent Cosimo's four moral virtues. The triangular form of the mausoleum (probably the pyramid placed on top of the coffin) recalls the three theological virtues embodied in Cosimo. The chiaroscuro paintings depict how he overcame vice, while the other paintings illustrate his zeal for religion, piety, magnificence, liberality, and prudence. The interpretations are fanciful but pertinent, very much in line with the baroque mentality behind the entire setting.

The memory of such virtues leads Ghiberti to mourn the loss he and the confraternity have suffered, a loss for which, he ventures to say, the rhetorical skills of either a Demosthenes or a Cicero could not find words of consolation. Language or thought cannot express or conceive its extent, he adds, and then concludes that all they can do is thank God for his bounty in allowing the people of Tuscany, though unworthy, to enjoy for a while Cosimo's presence. Rather than mourn, the youths should rejoice that Cosimo has been transumed from this life of woe to true and eternal life from whence he can continue to be the confraternity's patron, this time from the vantage point of greater 'proximity' to God. Though Cosimo is now gone, Ghiberti points out with assurance, his fame lingers in this world, his virtues continue in his children, and his goodness survives in his subjects.

Ghiberti concludes his eulogy with a flight of praises for the new grand duke Ferdinando II. The people can rest assured and live happily for their new prince has been grafted onto that glorious tree which is the House of Austria, 'the most holy, most valorous, and most beloved to God that ever was on Earth,' and rules under the guidance of his grandmother, in whose veins flows 'the sacred and noble Lotharingian blood.'[64] And so the eulogy, which had begun with the praises of accomplishments of the Medici line, draws to a close with a paean to the nobility of the bloodlines of the royal and imperial houses of Lorraine and Austria. They were, one might add, the two houses that did in fact hold the reins of power at the moment, for Cosimo's mother (Lorraine) and wife (Austria) served as joint regents during the minority of the new grand duke Ferdinand II. Such obsequious praises are, unfortunately, a splendid example of what Diaz described as the 'spirit of stately courtliness, immobile and feudalistic [which characterized that] true and proper camarilla of pious courtiers.'[65]

As an addendum to the eulogy, the scribe has included four poems by Giovan Francesco Ghiberti – three in Latin and one in Italian – composed on the occasion of the illness and then death of the grand duke. The first, a fourteen-line poem in Latin, is entitled 'To the god-like Cosimo, for the same most serene grand duke, while ill and pledges of the same author.' Addressing the deceased grand duke Cosimo I as a 'new star' and a 'god powerful over illness,' it asks him to alleviate the suffering and illness of the people, and in particular to look upon his namesake, the current grand duke Cosimo II, on whom the well-being of the entire people of Tuscany depends. The second poem, a sonnet in Italian, elevates the deceased Cosimo I to the level of a healing saint, referring to him as 'San Cosimo' in the title and then addressing him outright as 'Saint' (*Divo*) in the poem itself. This second poem asks on behalf of all of Tuscany that Cosimo II be restored to health, not for the benefit of his people, as the first had done, but for the benefit of all Christendom, for the newly restored grand duke would be able to stand strong against the rising threats of the 'perfidious Ottoman' who was unfurling his crescent flags and disturbing the sea with hundreds and hundreds of vessels. The third poem, an eight-line composition in Latin, prepares the way for Cosimo II's eventual death by postulating that both the citizens of Florence and those of Heaven appeal to God to allow Cosimo to be with them, and God, 'the just judge of the universe,' decides in favour of the latter. The fourth and last poem, a Latin quatrain, laments the death of Cosimo II but finds comfort in the thought that Cosimo continues to live in the poetic pledges that have been offered to him and in his children. In other words, the grand duke is memorialized by the paeans of his poets and by the continuation of his dynasty.

## The Birth of a New Cosimo: Cosimo III (1642)

The survival of the dynasty and of Cosimo's name were assured, at least for one more generation, by the birth of his grandson and namesake, Cosimo III. In 1642, twenty-one years after the obsequies described above, the confraternity of the Arcangelo Raffaello was rejoicing at the birth of a future ruler. On the evening of 14 August 1642, and for the two evenings following, the façade of Arcangelo Raffaello was ablaze with hundreds of lamps (*fuochi*). Ten days later, on Sunday 24 August, the youths celebrated formally with a Te Deum and a solemn High Mass in the morning, and then with an elaborate display of lights and the performance of a play in the evening. In describing the celebrations, the scribe waxes eloquent and indulges himself in a display of baroque language and conceits:

Already those fires and lights of happiness that had been lit in every corner of our city for three evenings in a row and those public shows and regal liberality demonstrated at the happy birth that occurred on the 14th past of the first-born of the Most Serene grand duke had passed, and perhaps those warm affections that for the same reason burn in the hearts of the followers of the Archangel Raphael would have died out, if a benevolent man ['benigno'], overcome by love, moved from the depth of his entrails by gratitude, with the cape of a generous resolution, had not kept them alive and made them shine forth. Our confraternity, always grateful and intent on sublime matters, just as at the setting of the Second Cosimo it celebrated rightful funerals in his memory, it now wished, at the rising of the Third, to cry out to the Divine Goodness with a solemn Mass of the Holy Spirit and render thanks for the special favour granted to the hopes of Tuscany, and [to celebrate] with lights above the door and the roof of the confraternity.'[66]

The youths of the Arcangelo Raffaello were clearly identifying the new Cosimo with his namesake and seeing in his birth a signal of rebirth and of future glories not only for the grand duchy but also for the confraternity.

The celebrations were organized by Girolamo Bartolommei, Guglielmo Altoviti, and Agnolo Galli. In agreement with Alberto Del Vivaio, their superintendent for music, they commissioned the confraternity's current *maestro di cappella*, Baccio Baglioni, to compose the music for a solemn High Mass of the Holy Spirit. They arranged to have the confraternity decorated with all the necessary pomp and invited 150 ladies (*gentildonne*) to attend the service on the morning of the 24th.

Mass was sung by the Rev. Alessandro Venturi, archdeacon at the cathedral, with the assistance of Piero Portinari and Lorenzo Vanni as his deacon and subdeacon. All three were members of the Arcangelo Raffaello. At the end of the service the event was enlivened by a 'beautiful motet' composed by Girolamo Bartolommei and set to music by Baccio Baglioni. The motet sang the praises of Cosimo III's parents and intimated the high hopes placed on the young heir to the throne. Francesco Rondinelli,[67] for his part, had composed an inscription that was displayed in a cartouche above the door into the oratory.

In the evening, the confraternity presented a comedy composed by Giulio Guazzini, its guardian father. The play was entitled *Il morto risuscitato*, a clear example of the rebirth motif mentioned above. The performers were, for the most part, confraternity youths aged six to fourteen, with the assistance of four older members who, the scribe points out, were less than twenty years old themselves. The play was performed a total of three times (the first two on 24 and 29 August for *gentildonne*, and the last, on

31 August, for the *huomini*) and at no cost to the confraternity because Giulio Guazzini had underwritten all expenses.

Two images governed the confraternity's rhetoric on this occasion. One was the natural metaphor of the setting and rising of the sun – as one Cosimo had disappeared below the horizon, another was now rising on the horizon of the confraternity's fortunes. The second was the Christian image of the resurrection – as Jesus had died and had risen, or as St Paul says we all must die in Christ in order to rise with him, so Cosimo III was the risen 'dead man' Cosimo II.

By way of such images, the confraternity was reaffirming its past relationship with the ruling family and appropriating the future. Little did it know, however, that Cosimo III's extreme pietism and unenlightened conservatism, extended over an exceptionally long reign, would slide Tuscany further into socio-economic collapse and spell the end of his dynasty. And while Tuscany was eventually able to recover from Cosimean stagnancy thanks to the enlightened government of the house of Hapsburg-Lorraine, the same cannot be said for the confraternity of the Arcangelo Raffaello, as we will see in the next chapter.

# 21

# The Final Years

A period of apparent vitality at the Arcangelo Raffaello in the 1730s, witnessed by an ambitious building program, could not reverse a severe attendance problem. A new secular attitude towards religious organizations and Catholic piety, especially widespread among the intellectual elite, further militated against a 'rebirth' of the confraternity's spirituality. Government scrutiny in the early 1780s was only a prelude to the inevitable grand-ducal suppression of the Arcangelo Raffaello and all other Florentine confraternities. This last chapter will be devoted to the confraternity's final half-century, focusing in particular on the momentary burst of energy in the 1730s, its irreversible attendance problem, and the new secular attitudes of the intellectual and ruling elites of Tuscany. The last few pages will then trace the final moments of the Arcangelo Raffaello from the first goverment inquiries into its activities to the last actions of the State and the Church as they worked, hand in glove, to suppress it.

## A Changed Confraternity

As the confraternity entered into its third century of life, it had changed so extensively that few of its long-gone members from the fifteenth or sixteenth century would have recognized it, had they been able to return for a visit. The membership had grown much older, adults were now completely in charge, Christian doctrine was no longer taught to the young, religious plays and moralities were no longer performed by its members, attendance at the weekly services was an acute problem, and devotional life had stagnated. Music alone was still the confraternity's hallmark, but a new musical form, the oratorio, with all its ponderous complexity and intricate formality, had replaced the simple *laude* of the Quattrocento or the elegant madrigals of the Cinque-Seicento.

New practices had also sprung up. The guardian father was now paid for his efforts. The executive and officers were for the most part noblemen. Generous bequests to the confraternity were generating funds for the awarding of annual dowries to young women. An internal lottery had been set up in order to improve attendance at devotions. But none of these new developments could revitalize the confraternity's sagging spiritual or devotional life.

And the times had changed, as well. The *siècle des lumières* was not supportive of either Quattrocento lay spirituality or post-Tridentine devotional practices. The spiritual and religious morass that had gripped Tuscany under the reign of its bigoted and, unfortunately, long-lived grand duke Cosimo III could not be removed by his unhappy son Gian Gastone, the last of the Medici rulers. Florence and Tuscany had to wait for the Medici dynasty to die out before it could acquire rulers whose education, energy, and enthusiasm for a new order would bring a breath of fresh air to the country. The House of Lorraine-Hapsburg, which inherited the grand duchy in 1737, provided the initiative and leadership that finally moved Tuscany out of the lethargy into which it had fallen and into the new spirit, deeply imbued with the ideas and hopes of the French-German Enlightment that was sweeping the continent.

## The New House above the Confraternity

Perhaps by sheer coincidence, just as the old order was passing and the new one was taking over, the confraternity showed unusual entrepreneurial initiative and undertook an extensive building program. Work to extend part of the confraternity's building up to the roofline of what had been the Mazzinghi house next door (now inhabited by the Del Borgo and Targioni families) was begun in the summer of 1736. The purpose of the project was twofold: to make major repairs to the fabric of the *vestibolo*, which had fallen into severe disrepair, and to build a rental apartment above the confraternity. The process turned out to be both long and cumbersome. Work continued for at least thirteen years. During this time, access to the vestibule and oratory was so restricted that the confraternity was obliged to forego, from 1736 to 1749, its annual public celebrations for the feast of the Archangel Raphael (31 December). In 1737 the confraternity was even forced to hold its Eastertime devotion of the Forty Hours outside its building, in two chapels in the church of Santa Maria Novella – those of the Ricasoli and of the confraternity of the Pura.[1]

The building project turned out to be not only long, but expensive as well. Financial records are incomplete, but they do show sizeable yearly payments to the *muratore* Giovan Battista Cerroti for a total of at least 1,925 *lire* for the years 1736–9, plus other payments of 200 *lire* to the engineer Bernardino Ciurini (or Sciorini), of 107.10 *lire* to the Chapter of the Duomo for their support, and so forth. In April 1739 the confraternity had to redeem its investments in a number of different *monti* to pay for the expenses incurred in the project.[2]

The project also embroiled the confraternity in a civil lawsuit that went on for several years. The suit was brought by the widow of the *muratore* Cerroti, who had died shortly after completing his job. She sued the confraternity for 800 *scudi* (5,600 *lire*) that she claimed were still owed to her deceased husband. Though the lawsuit was not settled until 1754, and for the lesser sum of 400 *scudi*, the confraternity clearly did not have the necessary funds at hand, for it had to take out a loan from the Ospedale di Sant'Onofrio in order to pay the debt. Financial problems were not new to the confraternity. Already in December 1743 it had refused to refund 90 *scudi* (630 *lire*) to the heirs of its guardian father Sigismondo Landini for expenses he had incurred on behalf of the confraternity. Fortunately, the new house above the confraternity was soon rented out and began to bring in some much-needed revenue.[3]

## Attendance Problems

Construction, lawsuits, and debts were hardly over when the confraternity had to face another severe problem that could not be solved simply by borrowing money. Attendance had dropped alarmingly. Already in the 1730s the afternoon or the evening *tornata* were often cancelled for lack of participation.[4] When the guardian father sent a personal, hand-delivered letter to 360 members asking them to attend a meeting on the morning of 2 October 1746 to discuss the sale of the house the confraternity owned in Borgo Ognissanti – a major asset the youths had received as a bequest from Domenico Comi in 1604 – only 29 brothers showed up, that is, just 8 per cent of the membership.[5] Not surprisingly, at another general meeting called on 6 August 1752 to deal with low attendance and lapsed payment of dues, several drastic decisions were taken in an attempt to remedy the situation.

First of all, the Christmas extraction of the names of brothers who would choose the recipients of the two annual dowries awarded by the confraternity to needy young women would now be done from two separate bags, one containing the names of brothers who had attended more than twenty meetings that year, and another containing the names of brothers who were paid up with their dues. Since many members had not paid their dues for several years, it was decided to encourage them to rectify their status by letting them pay outstanding fees for a total of two years only, that is, for the current and immediately past year. Third, it was decided to lower the number of brothers necessary for a quorum at a *tornata* from twenty, as chapter 7 of the statutes required, to twelve. Fourth, to encourage attendance a lottery was set up. The names of all members arriving at a service before the recitation of the first psalm would be placed in a bag, and then a large candle (*candelotto*) would be awarded to the first and last names drawn from the bag at the end of the service. Fifth, the exact time of meetings was determined to be 9 a.m. during the period from Lent to All Saints', and half an hour later from All Saints' to Lent. A letter was then sent to all members informing them of these decisions and adding that the evening *tornata* would now begin fifteen minutes after the Angelus. The measures were considered so important that they were eventually forwarded to the archbishop for his approval, which he granted on 17 February 1753.[6]

The new guidelines came into effect just nine days after they had been drawn up, on Assumption Day, 15 August 1752. A description of the first extraction of the two *candelotti* was entered into the confraternity records. After the Office of the Blessed Virgin, Mass, and prayers had been recited, the guardian father ordered that the names of all members present who had arrived before the recitation of the first psalm be placed in a bag. Then he himself extracted all the names one after the other. The first to be drawn was the father corrector, fra Giovanni Francesco Colzi, and the last was Abbot Niccolino Rocco Niccolini. The *provveditore* Ferdinando Dami gave the *candelotti* to the winners, grace was said, and all were dismissed.[7]

The new incentive did not, however, improve attendance. That first time, a Tuesday, there had been twenty-nine brothers present. The Sunday following, only sixteen showed up. For the rest of the year attendance generally ranged between eleven and fourteen, and never went above eighteen (recorded twice, once on Sunday, 10 September and once on Christmas Eve).[8] Though the *candelotto* lottery clearly did nothing to improve attendance figures, the confraternity retained it to the end, probably because participants were not keen to give up their chance for a small gift from Lady Luck.

The Arcangelo Raffaello was not the only confraternity to experience attendance problems, or the only one to try to remedy the situation by establishing what were, in effect, door prizes. Its sister confraternity of the Purificazione detta di San Marco experienced the same problem and, nine years earlier, opted for the same solution.[9] The adult confraternity of Gesù Pellegrino detta dei Caponi, which also met in Santa Maria Novella, had resorted to a similar stratagem as early as 1626. Their records recall that 'since in the year 1626 the number of the brothers attending services at the Venerable Company of Mercy of Gesù Pellegrino began to dwindle, it was decided to improve attendance, at least among the current officers, by distributing to them an amount of wax every first Sunday of the month, and this was established as chapter 28 [of their statutes] and confirmed by the [archbishop's] Ordinary.'[10] The situation at the Gesù Pellegrino was clearly more severe, seeing that even elected officials were not attending services.

The youth confraternity of Sant'Antonio da Padova had experienced attendance problems since the early 1700s. In this case the problems were aggravated by the unwillingness of elected officials even to serve in their posts. In 1709–11 some confraternity members actually turned down posts and preferred to pay a fine rather than serve. Attendance became such a severe problem that on 25 May 1711 the confraternity voted to forgo its evening meetings because 'the evening was inconvenient and few came' and, except for general meetings, to gather only in the morning. Its *ricordi* for most of the eighteenth century are short and scattered, at first skipping several months and then several years at a time. And they show a variety of different hands, indicating that no one was prepared to serve regularly as the confraternity scribe. Morale and interest in the confraternity's activities were clearly at a very low and critical point.

As the original motivating spirit for confraternal devotions and practices waned, financial or economic advantages began to be the glue that held the confraternity together. In trying to solve its problems, the Arcangelo Raffaello did not consider renewing its spiritual mission, but sought instead to entice members into its hall and account books by offering them economic rewards for regular attendance and prompt payment of dues. It did not work. By 1770 participation at Sunday devotions had fallen so low that the confraternity was obliged to reduce its *tornate* to just one, in the morning, and so drop the afternoon and evening services that had been part of its devotional and administrative cycle for centuries. Clearly, there was no interest among the membership to maintain the confraternity's traditional devotional cycle.

Ironically, however, the confraternity still had a good number of paying members. The records from 1750 to 1784 show that on average 87.5 members paid their dues every year. But a pattern of diminishing enrolment was firmly in place, with membership dropping steadily from a high of 123 in 1750 to a low of 54 in 1784.[11] Clearly the pattern could not be broken by the incentives set in place in 1752 or by a reduction of duties.

## Attitudes to Confraternities

Part of the problem lay in the general attitude among the educated elite towards traditional forms of Catholic piety, and confraternities in particular. The lay spirit of French-German Enlightment had entered Tuscany with the Lorraine-Hapsburgs and had influenced the middle and upper classes of Florence, from which the Arcangelo Raffaello had been drawing its members for nearly two centuries. In time, educated Florentines not only lost their interest in what the confraternities stood for or had to offer, but even turned against them.

The eighteenth-century Florentine *erudito* Lorenzo Mehus summarized the current lay intellectual view of confraternities in his *Dell'origine, progresso, abusi, e riforma delle confraternite laicali* (1785).[12] It is a historical examination of the rise of confraternities, their periodic deterioration, and the recurring calls for their reform, both in Italy and abroad. Mehus makes his views and agenda clear from the very first sentence of his 'Prefazione':

> My intention is to consider those lay gatherings commonly called confraternities ... and to show that they are contrary to sacred laws, harmful to parish jurisdiction, and offensive to that status which, by right of divine decree, is held among their flock by rectors of churches, who in our day reside in them enjoying no respect and nearly insulted.[13]

Although Mehus admits that, ever since the fourth century, 'pious' confraternities have existed and have contributed to the well-being of Christians, he is also keen to point out that secular or immoral imitations of such groups have given rise to inappropriate practices, which, in turn, have badly misled innocent Christians. The problem first arose, in his view, in the twelfth century, when 'profane' confraternities were founded among 'private' individuals for the purpose of establishing offensive and defensive allegiances. Though bound by a formal religious oath, they had no other scope than to provide mutual assistance in a variety of matters. Mehus then connects these 'profane' confraternities with conspiracies, citing the eleventh-century Italian grammarian Papias, who, in his *Erudimento elementario*, defines the word *fratria* as *coniuratio*. The remainder of the chapter calls upon the writings of Gualterus de Coutances, archbishop of Rouen (d. 1207), John of Salisbury, Charles Du Fresne Sieur Du Cange, and others to prove that these twelfth-century 'profane' confraternities were seen as contrary and anathema to the Church even in their own time.[14]

Mehus's strongest disapproval, however, is reserved for 'the scandalous and reckless Confraternity of the Flagellants of the thirteenth century' (ch. 16). Such a movement and its practices were born, Mehus suggests, out of 'that superstitious licence in which barbarous education has lead the World.'[15] It is not difficult to see in these words the aversion of the 'enlightened' seventeenth-century lay intellectual for Scholastic or 'spiritual' education in the thirteenth century. For Mehus, the pietistic fervour of the 1260 flagellant movement is an anathema not only because of the physical act of flagellation or the use of hoods which it promoted, but also because it led the laity to heretical practices, such as hearing confessions and granting absolution themselves. Mehus concludes by accusing the flagellants of great disregard for the rights of the parishes and their priests.[16]

In fact, there was a long history in Florence for the view that confraternities could undermine the parish and its priest. Brian Pullan reminds us that 'in the early fifteenth century, the Archbishop of Florence seemed uneasy lest the confraternity become a rival to the parish priest, and anxious to protect the priest's ultimate jurisdiction over the souls of his flock.'[17] The sixteenth- and seventeenth-century decrees of the Florentine synods certainly support such a view and such a concern.

Although Mehus does mention ecclesiastical suggestions and even attempts at reforming confraternities, his greatest praise and time are spent on the general suppression of confraternities decreed in 1419 by the Florentine government. He dedicates an entire chapter to this event (ch. 20), and then another, quite lengthy one to transcribe the actual decree of suppression (ch. 21). In spite of such government action, however, Mehus points out that 'pious' confraternities were able to rise again, and again degenerated to the point of needing reform. Chapter 23 thus outlines 'the need for reform of pious Confraternities in our time.' Mehus cites, first, Guillaume Durant the Younger, bishop of Mende (d. 1328), who, in a promemoria for the Council of Vienne (France), suggested that 'it was a useful thing for the Church of Jesus Christ to suppress those confraternities that amuse themselves in banquets and in empty discourses, believing that it was more convenient to use that money to help the poor and to honour the saints to which they were dedicated.'[18] Mehus ignores the fact that Durant is clearly referring to the French *Puy*, a type of confraternity not at all pertinent to the Florentine, or even Italian, experience. He then continues along similar lines drawing upon the likes of Maffeo Vegio (d. 1458), Pope Clement VIII (d. 1605), Théophile Raynaud (d. 1663), Bernard Van Epsen, and Lodovico Antonio Muratori (d. 1750), who, 'though he favoured [confraternities] and praised them, nonetheless wanted them to be cleaned of those marks and stains that infected them.'[19]

At this point, with the support of ecclesiastical and intellectual authorities behind him, Mehus produces his own list of abuses to be found in confraternities (ch. 24). The one most in need of attention is the 'contempt in which [confraternities] hold parish churches,' forcing them to languish empty, even during the most solemn festivities of the year. This is aggravated, he adds, by competition, for confraternities schedule the celebration of Divine Offices at the same time as the cathedral or the parish does. Thirdly, in spite of council decrees dating as far back as the seventh century, confraternities continue to consume food within their locales, and subsidize it with fees that had already been declared illegal at the Council of Nantes. This last abuse, Mehus notes in a rare moment of levity, had led Guillaume Budé to observe that confraternity members in France should be called *coepuloni* because of the great banquets they held, a pun that Mehus then tries unsuccessfully to render in Italian. Fourth, some confraternities give a small sum of money to poor members when they take communion in the oratory. To Mehus this mixture of money and the Sacrament is inappropriate because it either is outright simony or gives the impression of simony, and 'in such a delicate matter one must not only keep a distance from evil, but even from the shadow of evil.' Mehus then mentions a number of papal and conciliar warnings against such a practice, from St Gregory to Gratian, St Anselm, and Gregory of Campostella. Fifth, Mehus objects to the belief, which he calls a 'superstition,' that enrolment in a confraternity somehow favours an individual's entry into heaven, 'as if through a single piece of cloth, whether white or black or of whatever other colour, and without any good work, especially without any work of charity and mercy, one could fly to the glory of the heavens, a vain opinion, presumptuous, scandalous, and abominable, that has its roots in that pernicious sect of the flagellants and which makes the individual more daring and less reticent to commit a crime.'[20]

In the final chapter Mehus praises Grand Duke Peter Leopold for his wisdom in suppressing all confraternities, gives a ten-point outline of the grand duke's program and aims in establishing a new, parish-based confraternity, and expresses his hope that 'the zeal of bishops and the duty of parish priests' will match the ruler's 'wise and pious intentions.'[21]

We thus realize that Mehus is not only expressing the views of a strictly lay, and possibly anticlerical, Tuscan intellectual élite, but is also producing an *ex post facto* defence of the grand-ducal *motu proprio* that closed down all confraternities, appropriated their wealth, and established a new system of lay charity and devotion.

## Government Scrutiny

Before the grand duke could close down all confraternities, however, he first needed to have a clear indication of their number, situation, and wealth. On 22 July 1783 a grand-ducal decree thus ordered a survey of all confraternities in Tuscany.

Early in August, fra Ugone Romani, curate of Santa Maria Novella, responsible for the description of all confraternities in his parish, inquired about the Arcangelo Raffaello's membership and activities. The *provveditore* Filippo Guidotti answered that the confraternity was founded in 1411, that its statutes were approved on 20 October 1468 by Giuliano, suffragan bishop of Florence, that its purpose was in part the instruction of youths in Christian doctrine, but that this had fallen into disuse a long time before because there was a lack of youths in the confraternity and because such education was now, by decree, to be carried out in the parishes. He added that the confraternity met at 9 a.m. on Sundays and holy days of obligation to recite the Divine Office, the Office of the Dead, other prayers, and to hear Mass. Their father corrector, an Observant Franciscan from Ognissanti, administered the sacraments of Communion and Confession. The confraternity took its turn in the Devotion of the Forty Hours every year at Easter, it celebrated the feast-day of the Archangel Raphael, and for the three days of Holy Week and for All Saints' it recited the appropriate office. It also conferred two annual dowries of 60 *lire* each to two poor young women. The membership was composed of clerics, nobles, and citizens, and each member paid an annual fee of 10 *soldi*.[22]

Guidotti's answer reveals that the confraternity had long ceased to carry out its original mission of gathering the youth and instructing them in the Christian faith. It had turned, instead, into an association of adults who used the organization as an expression of their own personal devotion, fulfilled the confraternity's obligations towards deceased members and benefactors, and managed the annual distribution of two dowries.

A second inquiry soon followed from fra Romani, this time asking for more precise information. The guardian father, the marquis Antonio Arnaldi, responded that same day, saying that there were currently 166 members in the confraternity, each of whom paid an annual fee of 10 *soldi*, that the oratory (which he called a church) and its adjacent rooms were owned by the confraternity, and that the father corrector was the Rev. Fr. Gaspero Giusti, from the convent of Ognissanti.[23]

This, along with similar information from all confraternities in Tuscany, was gathered into a compendium for the use of the grand duke and his ministers.[24] At the end of the compendium a few 'General Observations' by the compiler, Carlo Giunti, point clearly to what the government perceived to be problems. The majority of the works of mercy carried out by these confraternities, Giunti says, are '*for their own institution*' (emphasis in the original); in many of these confraternities,

centuria and *buche* officers enjoy the extra benefit of the pepper while in office,[25] and all members in general receive certain extra benefits such as the candle that is given to them on the feast of the Purification [2 February], the palm on Palm Sunday, the small breads on the feast of the patron saint, and candle butts at different times of the year. Finally, nearly all the brothers of confraternities of the Sacrament go or send someone to collect alms at church doors on Sundays for the upkeep of torches and other sacred objects used in taking the Sacrament to the infirm.[26]

Giunti's description and comments point out clearly that he was not in agreement with all the hidden profits confraternity members gained from their membership in the organization.

The grand duke, for his part, was not interested in going after small tax revenues from undeclared benefits, but set his sights on greater sources of revenue – the confraternities themselves. He ordered detailed inventories of all confraternity holdings to be drawn up. On 22 July 1784 Raffaello Rosi, assistant to the chancellor Pollini, visited the Arcangelo Raffaello and drew up its inventory, which was then signed on 6 August by the guardian father, Antonio Arnaldi.[27] Aware that he was now personally responsible to the grand duke if anything from the official inventory went missing, Arnaldi drew up his own list of the confraternity's most precious objects and then took them home for safekeeping.[28]

After all the inventories had been compiled, an exchange of notes ensued between Archbishop Antonio Martini and Grand Duke Peter Leopold, in which certain confraternities were to be exempt from the proposed general suppression. On 4 September the archbishop sent a first list to the grand duke suggesting nineteen confraternities, and then on 9 November a second list with twenty names on it.[29] Neither list contained the name of the Arcangelo Raffaello. Even the archbishop had determined that the oldest and most prestigious youth confraternity in Florence had ceased to serve its purpose.

## The Decree of Suppression

The inevitable edict of general suppression was issued as a grand ducal *motu proprio* on 21 March 1785, contemporaneously with a second edict exempting nine confraternities from the general closure and a third one establishing the statutes and regulations the nine and any new confraternities were required to follow.[30] The only one of the original youth confraternities allowed to survive was that of San Niccolò del Ceppo, and it is still active today (though it is no longer a confraternity of youths).[31]

The edict itself is a clear reflection of the grand duke's view that confraternities had ceased to serve their purpose, a conclusion he claims to have reached from the survey he had commissioned two years earlier.[32] The grand duke acknowledges that many confraternities had originally been established to provide the faithful with the Sacrament and the Word of God in times of war or civic strife when churches could not guarantee such services. He mentions St Antoninus in particular as someone who founded confraternities specifically for this purpose. He then points out that other confraternities were created instead in the years following the rise of the Mendicant orders and suggests that they may have been one of the many ways in which the survival of such orders had been facilitated, much to the detriment of 'true ecclesiastical discipline.' Still others were established for the most excellent purpose of assisting in the care of churches, escorting the Viaticum, accompanying the dead to burial, and carrying out other works of mercy. If only they had continued in this, he interjects parenthetically.

Nonetheless, the excessive number of confraternities currently active in the city of Florence, the abuses that have been introduced in them, and the fact that current circumstances have made most of them useless have obliged him to remedy the situation with a general edict. He notes that civic peace and the service provided by parish and other churches now allow anyone to attend freely to religion at any time of the day. Attendance at confraternity churches, he argues, gives one a false impression of having fulfilled one's obligations to sanctify the feast-day. And here the grand duke suggests that brothers in confraternities do nothing more than listen to Mass and blindly recite prayers they often do not even understand. This, he adds, draws them away from participating fully at parish functions, in the Catechism, and in hearing the explication of the Gospel or the moral instructions that are an essential part of religion and a duty of all Christians. The original intention of confraternities, he continues, has weakened and deteriorated, as all man-made things do, to the point that their meetings are no longer a source of edification, brotherly charity, or service to churches, but are often occasion for scandal. He then gives a list of such scandals: dissension, arguments, lust for profit, scheming in the determination of offices, alms, and dowries, independence from the local parish priest and often even animosity and spite against him, vanity, competition, unnecessary expenses and luxuries, inappropriate meals, especially when such meals are held in the countryside, and the indecent manner in which their churches are officiated.

For all these reasons the grand duke ordered the abolition of all companies, congregations, groups, *centuria*, and confraternities in the Grand Duchy, be they composed of laity or clergy, men or women. Along with them, he also included the so-called Third Orders.

He then instructed those responsible for the administration of the ecclesiastical patrimony in the different dioceses of the realm to seize, immediately, all churches, houses, books, sacred objects, possessions, and funds belonging to these groups. These same administrators were then instructed to establish a new confraternity in each parish to look after, in partnership with the local parish priest and the local bishop, the burial of the dead, the fulfilment of obligations that could not be rescinded, and any other duty belonging to the old confraternities having to do with assistance to the parish or with works of public charity. The administrators were to proceed swiftly with the clearing up of all funds and patrimonies, claiming all credit owned, and paying, with revenue from the immediate sale of furniture and goods, all outstanding debts. All real estate, funds, and goods were to be immediately appraised and sold. All confraternity churches not deemed by the local bishop to be of use for religious service or not worth keeping as public oratories were to be desecrated and sold. Administrators were not to disperse sacred objects from the confraternity churches, but to draw up an inventory of them and, together with the local bishop, to determine how the Segretario del Regio Diritto was to distribute them among the most needy churches in the diocese.[33] Again in consultation with the bishop, all officiations and benefices pertaining to confraternity churches to be desecrated were to be transferred to other churches, except for those belonging to private patrons who could defend their rights in a court of law. Charitable subsidies from old confraternities were to remain within the parish in which the old confraternity had been located. Other wealth, however, was to be incorporated into the ecclesiastical patrimony, including revenue from rental income. Subsidies were to be distributed by the ecclesiastical administrators in consultation with the local parish priest, simply and profitably, without partiality or scheming.

With the same edict of suppression, the grand duke also decreed that each parish should create a new confraternity for the express purpose of fulfilling those obligations that the old confraternities should have fulfilled. Thus, as of 1 May 1785, each parish in the grand duchy was to establish a confraternity responsible directly to the local parish priest, who was also to be its father corrector. Members were to be at least eighteen years of age and had to ask spontaneously to be included. The confraternity was to bear the name of that church's titular saint, not to have a church or an oratory of its own, or a patrimony to administer. Its function was to assist in parish functions and celebrations, lead the youth to Christian doctrine, assist the infirm, take them to the hospital, bury the dead, escort the Viaticum, and gather and distribute alms for the poor of the parish. All of this was to be carried out according to a set of general statutes for new confraternities that the grand duke had decreed that same day in a third *motu proprio*.[34]

The grand duke concluded his assessment of the old confraternities and his detailed directions for the extensive restructuring of confraternal life in Tuscany by saying he had no doubt that there would be plenty of good persons ('persone oneste') who would accept the new statutes and join the new parish confraternities. In so doing such persons would show everyone, Peter Leopold added pointedly, that if they had been members of the old confraternities, they had taken no part in the abuses that had plagued these organizations.

Peter Leopold reiterated his harsh view of confraternities a few years later in a *pro memoria* to his successor, Ferdinando III. In it he twice pointed out that there had been an 'infinite number' of confraternities in Florence and everywhere else in Tuscany. In Florence alone he had counted 264. And they had been ripe with abuses, he added. This more private document offers us an insight into Peter Leopold's personal view of confraternities:

They gathered on feast-days and recited the Office, and for the most part they served to waylay the people from the parishes and from [Christian] instruction, and they constantly fomented dissension with the parish priests on account of the authority the brothers thought they had over churches, functions, processions, etc. In the countryside they served as a pretext for festive meals. In Florence, then, there were also many night companies, where they gathered to eat all night long, and even slept there, and they heard Mass on feast-days very early, before daylight, and they spent the rest of the day hunting, or at the inn, or loafing around, and they did a thousand knavish things in the distribution of the many dowries that were given out by these confraternities, and were of a respectable amount.[35]

To remedy the situation, he had abolished all confraternities, except for 'the Misericordia, which has little revenue and takes the infirm and those who have been injured in the streets or those who have died in accidents to the hospital; those of the Vanchetoni, of the Stimate, of San Girolamo, and another four, which, however, are not allowed to open on feast-days, or to advertise, or take part in processions and functions.' Peter Leopold then added that 'these, too, should be abolished in order to dispel the thought of establishing new ones.'

In reviewing the results of his actions against confraternities, Peter Leopold was quick to point out that 'fanaticism' had been reduced, that a sizeable ecclesiastical patrimony had been established to provide for poorer churches, and that new parish-based confraternities of charity had been established to look after the local churches. He comments that the new confraternities, 'because they have no churches or revenues of their own cannot create problems.' His advice to his son, briefly put, was that 'whoever will head the government of Tuscany will do well ... not to permit the introduction of new companies or confraternities, to which the country is much inclined, and abolish even those that have been left in Florence.'[36]

The suppression of 1785 was immediate and, in the case of the vast majority of confraternities, final. Peter Leopold had assessed the general situation correctly, carried out the deed swiftly, and satisfied the need for charitable works through a more efficient system of lay confraternities and through a more equitable distribution of religious objects among the parishes.

## The Final Moments

The confraternity of the Arcangelo Raffaello met for the last time on Easter Monday, 28 March 1785. Its last *ricordo* is both brief and poignant:

Monday, 28 March. I recall how this morning 20 Masses were celebrated, and at 11:30 a.m. our father corrector went up to the altar and celebrated Holy Mass and when it was finished the singers intoned the litanies of the saints and then our father corrector recited the prayers, at the end of which the singers intoned the hymn 'Pange lingua' and the 'Tantum ergo' with the Benediction, all of which was done with good order and with decorum for our company.[37]

The final entry seems to summarize the confraternity's life, one dedicated to devotion, music, and decorum. That same day the confraternity's servant, Giovanni Tedeschi, handed over the revenue from the annual fees to the *sottoprovveditore* Filippo Guidotti, who then made the last entry in the registers of dues.[38] There is no indication here or anywhere else in the records of the confraternity's imminent demise, the expropriation of its goods, and the desecration of its oratory.

On 15 September Carlo Huart, royal administrator for ecclesiastical affairs for the diocese of Florence, sent a brief note to Archbishop Martini:

> Since the suppressed confraternity called of the Scala, situated in the Piazza of Santa Maria Novella, is to be alienated, I dare to supplicate Your Most Illustrious and Most Reverend Lordship that, whenever it should please you, you would deign to commit the profanation.[39]

The very next day, 16 September, the chancellor and secretary of the Curia, Angelo Vincenzo Del Chiaro, instructed fra Ugone Romani, the curate of Santa Maria Novella, 'to secularize and desecrate' the oratory of the Arcangelo Raffaello. The curate carried out the act and then, in his own hand, attested to it at the bottom of Del Chiaro's note of instruction. Two witnesses, Marco Paoli and Sebastiano Bianchi, added their signatures to the document.[40] A year later, on 17 March 1786, the building of the Arcangelo Raffaello was put up for sale, and on 21 March it was purchased at auction by Vincenzo di Agostino Massai and Stefano di Baldassar Stefanelli for the sum of 2,100.3.10 *scudi*.[41] The confraternity of the Archangel Raphael had ceased to exist. Its building was soon to be extensively restructured for secular use.

# Epilogue

My first intention had been to examine the Arcangelo Raffaello from its inception in 1411 to the death of its member and patron Grand Duke Cosimo II in 1621, but then friends and colleagues urged me to expand my sights to take in the entire spectrum of the confraternity's life. I am glad they did so, for it has given me the opportunity to discover, among other things, the richness and variety of the confraternity's theatrical and musical activities in the seventeenth and eighteenth centuries, its metamorphosis into a confraternity of adults, and its new-found interest in the charitable work of dowering young women. Some of this, in turn, has given me insights on what to pursue next. As Umberto Eco and others have already pointed out, books beget books. Casting aside the cynical self-consciousness of the writer, one can rephrase the witticism as 'knowledge begets knowledge.' It is my hope that my work will lead other researchers to look at youth associations in pre- and early modern times, and eventually shed more light on the place and contribution of youths to their society and its culture.

The young men of the Arcangelo Raffaello in the fifteenth and sixteenth centuries found in their organization not only a devotional focus, but also an educational opportunity and a social network that served them well in this life and the next. By praying to God and the saints, learning the basic elements of the Christian faith, and supporting one another on the journey to salvation, they were developing as citizens of both the earthly and heavenly city. Their success can be seen in the longevity of the organization they founded and managed – close to four centuries of continued existence is more than can be claimed by many an organization today. Another proof of their success can be seen in the growing age of the membership – youths remained in the confraternity till they were well past the age limit, and adults themselves were attracted to join the organization. Eventually, the older members changed its demographic profile completely. No longer was this an organization of middle- and lower-class youths interested in instruction and spiritual guidance, but an academy of adult artists and patrons exhibiting their talents and munificence, and, finally, perhaps even a club for older upper-class gentlemen interested in managing (and sharing in) the accumulated endowment.

The confraternity's continued vitality, even in the wake of such major demographic change and the ecclesiastical regulations undermining its original mandate, is a testament to the variety and strength of what it had to offer to those who joined. Its devotional life thrived through such venues as the recitation of the Office, attendance at Mass, the partaking of Communion, the devotion of the Forty Hours, the observance of feast-days, participation in public and private processions. Its commitment to education focused on morals, music, oratory, and spectacle. Its social role shifted to draw together a more homogenous group of men from the middle and upper classes, many with similar interests in the visual and performing arts.

Eventually, however, lethargy did set in, and membership dwindled. Perhaps there could eventually have been another renewal, but the spirit of the times was moving against such lay religious organizations. The 'enlightened' grand duke from north of the Alps wiped all confraternities out with a stroke of his pen. And not without the tacit support of the clergy and the general population, for, as Peter Leopold struck down the confraternities, no voice of opposition rose to stop him. Even the archbishop failed to protect them. Clearly, the times had changed. The civic and ecclesiastical authorities were keen to bring all lay devotional practices under their supervision, appropriate the accumulated wealth of lay religious organizations, redistribute it as they saw fit, and establish new groups, as poor as the proverbial church mouse, to teach doctrine and help the parish priest keep the altars adorned.

The closing moments of this history have not yet been studied in depth. Nor has anyone searched out connections between suppressions in different states – in Milan, for example, confraternities were abolished the following year, 1786, by the government of Peter Leopold's brother, the Archduke and Emperor Joseph II. The way had been prepared already under the reign of Maria Teresa by the suppression of confraternities in the smaller and less important dioceses of Lombardy, and then by the suppression of selected confraternities in Milan. The archbishop did mount some opposition, but eventually the imperial government won the day.[1]

Aside from the suppression of confraternities in the late eighteenth century, there are still many aspects of youth confraternities that need to be examined, even for earlier periods.

The membership rolls deserve the attention of a social historian able to carry out a thorough demographic study. We still need to determine exactly who joined youth confraternities and at what age, how long they remained active in the organization, and what they did once they left. Such a study would need to be divided into sample periods to analyse demographic changes over time. The role of sponsors also needs to be analysed. Was it to Niccolò Antifassi's credit that he 'brought' the twelve-year-old Pietro Niccolini, future archbishop of Florence, into the confraternity? Were there family or social connections that governed such sponsorship (much as in the baptismal 'godparent' system), or did Antifassi know Pietro to be a devout young man who would benefit from joining the Arcangelo Raffaello (or vice versa)? I suspect that an examination across confraternal boundaries may shed further light on patronage systems in Florence.

A thorough demographic study of youth confraternities would also help to shed light on why the demographic profile changed. Was it simply the loss of the pedagogical function that reduced the number of youths in the organization? I suspect not. But then, what were the other factors at play? Did the growing professionalism of confraternity events attract the involvement of adults, or did the adults who now ran the confraternity naturally demand more professionalism in their spectacles?

Similarly, financial records deserve the attention of a bona fide economic historian to assess the contribution made by youths to the micro-economy around them. The undertaking of construction projects, the commissioning of works of art, the production of spectacles, not to mention the bestowing of dowries, would suggest that youth confraternities enjoyed a sizeable income and made noteworthy transfers of funds. Were these all managed (at least until the mid-seventeenth century) by youths under the age of twenty-four? If so, what then are we to infer about age and financial responsibility in premodern times?

The spiritual side of confraternities also needs to be examined more closely. Kathleen Falvey's invitation to examine 'confraternities and the history of mystical traditions' should certainly be extended to youth confraternities as well, for several saintly individuals, especially in the sixteenth century, were closely associated with them. In this study we have encountered such deeply religious men as fra Santi Cini and Vittorio Dell'Ancisa, not to mention St Antoninus or the Blessed Ippolito Galantini. Further work on the spiritual life of youth confraternities will reveal the presence of many other individuals who found in confraternities not the political, social, educational or economic advantages we like to point out today, but a devotional focus and a spiritual strength that is far too often ignored by contemporary scholars.

The place of youth confraternities in the spiritual life of the city thus needs to be examined further. Richard Trexler's ground-breaking work of 1974 has often been cited, but not yet taken up and developed further. Lorenzo Polizzotto pointed to the survival of Savonarolan reform ideals in conventicles within adult confraternities in the 1530s – did something similar infiltrate youth confraternities? If so, is our reforming Dominican fra Santi Cini to be a suspect? Is it just coincidence that he was transferred to San Marco? Perhaps what is needed is a disciple of Arnaldo D'Addario to take up the challenge and examine the Florentine church in the sixteenth century through the spiritual life of its youth. This ought to be done, as John O'Malley suggests, by viewing Catholicism as variations on a theme and seeing 'the Church' in its multiplicity of aspects. Along the same lines, further work on fra Santi Cini, for example, or Vittorio dell'Ancisa, Jacopo Ansaldi, and other devout reformers of Florentine youths would also provide much needed information and help us to understand better the contribution of youths to early-modern Florence.

My own interests and expertise draw me to theatre and spectacle, a fertile field that will yield an abundant crop – as confraternity memoirs and financial records have already done for art historians and musicologists. But even in these areas there has been no attempt to identify and examine the full extent of the contribution made by youth confraternities.

The years I have spent reading the records of the Arcangelo Raffaello and other youth confraternities in Florence have been both enjoyable and rewarding. I especially treasured the realization that I was the first scholar to read the records for the entirety of their story, and not just to find a reference or to focus on my own area of expertise. When I finally reached the last fascicule of *ricordi* and read the scribe's entries for the confraternity's final years, I was struck by how moved I was. Sitting in the vast reading room of the Archivio di Stato, in the air-conditioned tranquillity and fluorescent light that belie the insanity of traffic on Viale Giovane Italia or the sun's unforgiving rays on via dell'Agnolo, I felt I was there, watching the confraternity close down forever. And I felt the need to mourn the loss of a friend.

Over the years, the confraternity, in all its complexity and in the variety of its incarnations, had become an old friend. Its members had come alive for me and, though not quite as in a Pirandellian play, had entered into my life. I had come to know and enjoy the company of Raffaello Gucci, always ready to sing and play on the *buonaccordo* he had brought from home – the eternal showman; and Camillo Rondinelli, ready to don costume at the drop of a hat and act in a play, often put many a smile on my face; I ran out of patience with the neurotic Jacopo Cicognini, who was always trying to steal the limelight in his own grandiose but insecure ways and passing off Giovan Maria Cecchi's plays as his own; I admired Niccolò Antifassi, willing to risk grand ducal displeasure to advance his confraternity, and I pitied the Marquis Antonio Arnaldi, overseeing the closure of the organization that had been placed in his care; for some reason I did not feel comfortable around fra Santi Cini, but instinctively trusted the elderly fra Santi Contini, a benevolent grandfather figure; I knew that Zanobi Buonavolti could always be counted upon to serve the confraternity quietly and efficiently; the shifty Filippo del Riccio, later Comi, on the other hand, abusing his position to gain possession of the confraternity's organ, did not inspire confidence; his adoptive father and uncle, Baccio and Domenico Comi, instead, seemed to be well-meaning bachelors with plenty of money and no heirs of their own. And then, through it all, the Archangel Raphael, looking on.

APPENDIX 1

# Guardian Fathers at the Arcangelo Raffaello

?–1439–53–? **Antonio di Mariano Muzi** (1404–1494). Mentioned as the guardian father of the Arcangelo Raffaello by Bisticci in the life of Cardinal Cesarini.

?–? **Lorenzo Vitegli.** Indicated as 'nostro secondo guardiano.'

?–? **Domenico delle Tarsie** [or della Tarsia]. Also indicated as 'nostro secondo guardiano' (I have not been able to resolve the crux).

?–? **Girolamo del Correggiaio.** Indicated as 'nostro terzo guardiano.'

?–1478–90 **Lorenzo Vitelli** (d. by February 1489/90). Indicated as 'nostro quarto guardiano.' In 1478 he co-signs the statutes of the Purificazione as 'Laurentius titulo sancti Raphaellis aut Scale' (BNCF, MS Magliab. VIII, cod. 1500, fasc. 11, f. 26v).

1490–? **Cosimo di Lorenzo Rosselli.** Temporary guardian in the spring of 1488/9.

?–? **Domenico di Giovanni Tasselli.** Indicated as 'nostro quinto guardiano' (the name is occasionally spelled Tarselli).

1525–? **Antonio di Tommaso *miniatore*.** Indicated as 'nostro sesto guardiano.' Already a member of the Compagnia della Vergine Maria, he required permission from Zanobi Pieri, prior of the convent of San Marco and father corrector of the confraternity of the Vergine Maria, in order to become guardian at the Arcangelo Raffaello.

?–? **Giovan Battista di Piero Nuttini.** Indicated as 'nostro settimo guardiano.'

?–? **Giovan Battista Petrucci.** Indicated as 'nostro ottavo guardiano.'

1556–63 **Antonio di Giovanni *cuoiaio*** (d. 9 April 1563). Indicated as 'nostro nono guardiano.' Buried in the confraternity's tomb for guardian fathers (at which time he is described as a 'sensale').

1563 **Meglio di Giovanni *tessitore*.** Elected on 11 April 1563 as substitute guardian, he is described as 'uno de' nostri padri.' His son, Giovanni di Meglio di Giovanni, is an active member in the 1560s.

1563–77 **Girolamo di M.o Niccolò di M.o Luca** (d. 2 September 1577). Elected and approved by the commission set up in the bull of 1442 on 16 April 1563; accepts on 23 April, takes possession 30 April, and begins his duties on 1 May.

1577–81 **Ceseri Galletti**. Resigns 10 December 1581.

1582 **Zanobi Buonavolti** (d. 1 May 1591). Substitute guardian.

1582–4 **Antonio di Pasci da Colle** (d. 6 July 1584). Elected on 12 August 1582; approved 17 August; takes possession 2 September. When he is not well in January 1583/4, Niccolò Antifassi is elected his assistant. Buried in Santa Maria Novella.

1584–91 **Zanobi Buonavolti** (d. 1 May 1591). Elected substitute vice-guardian on 6 July 1584. Niccolò Antifassi is elected his assistant on 5 August 1584.

1591–2 **Niccolò Antifassi**. Elected substitute guardian on 2 May 1591; resigns on 6 September 1592.

1592–5 **Lorenzo di Goro Benizzi** (d. 10 September 1595). Elected on 15 November 1592; approved 17 November; takes possession 22 November; buried 10 September 1595 in the confraternity's tomb for guardian fathers.

1595–9 **Niccolò Antifassi** (d. 23 May 1602). Elected substitute guardian on 10 September 1595; resigns on 2 May 1599; buried in San Marco.

1599–1603 **Benedetto Bellosi**. Elected on 5 December 1599; approved on 4 December 1600; resigns on 6 July 1603.

1603–6 **Pietro Mannucci**. Elected on 12 October 1603; takes possession on 1 November 1603; resigns on 25 April 1604, but continues to serve throughout 1604–6.

1606–10 **Guglielmo Cavalcanti** (d. 19 February 1610). Elected on 6 January 1605/6; approved on 21 June 1606.

1610–16 **Guglielmo Neri**. Elected substitute guardian on 24 February 1609/10; elected guardian in November 1610/11; resigns on 25 September 1616. He is present at the installation of Guardian Conti on 13 August 1645 (see below).

1616–18 Rev. **Tommaso Rustici**. Elected and approved on 25 December 1616; takes possession on 6 January 1616/17.

1618–19 **Luca di Francesco di Vigna** (later Rev.). Elected on 2 December 1618; takes possession on 9 December 1618; resigns on 15 September 1619. He becomes a priest and the *pievano* at Monte Reggi.

1619–37 **Francesco Fior Vigna**. Elected on 20 October 1619; resigns on

30 November 1637. He is present at the installation of Guardian Conti (below) on 13 August 1645. He is the father of the previous guardian, Luca di Francesco di Vigna.

1637–45 **Giulio Guazzini.** Elected on 14 December 1637, the first to be chosen according to the new statutes of 1636; takes possession on 25 December; resigns on 1 August 1645.

1645–9 **Francesco Conti** (d. 14 August 1649). Elected on 4 August 1645; accepts on 6 August; takes possession on 13 August 1645; obsequies celebrated 20 August 1649. Conti had been a member of the confraternity of the Vanchetoni, taking part in their spiritual exercises and in the teaching of doctrine.

1649–75 **Alessandro di Giovan Battista Dami** (d. before 27 June 1675, probably in January 1674/5). Elected and accepts on 28 October 1649. From 1646 to 1674 Dami kept the accounts of the Camarlingo (i.e., all of ASF, Crs 161.13/14 and 14/15). At his election he is described as 'fratello affettionatissimo alla Compagnia, et frequente alle Tornate.'

1675–94 **Giovanni Comparini.** He co-signs an agreement with the guardians of other confraternities on 18 November 1677 (ASF, Crs 1647.10, f. 92v). On 26 December 1690 he asks to be allowed to resign because of his advanced age and indispositions, but the confraternity refuses to accept his resignation. After Cardinal Francesco Maria de' Medici, the confraternity's patron, intervenes on his behalf, the confraternity finally grants him permission to resign on 24 January 1693/4 and he does so on 2 April following.

1694–1707 **Orazio di Ottavio Dami** (d. 1707). Elected on 31 March 1694; takes possession on 2 April 1694; obsequies celebrated on 11 December 1707. Earlier, on 9 December 1691, he had been appointed procurator 'all'interesse in causa Comi e Lapi, e terminare ogni pendenza a benefizio di nostra Compagnia.'

1707–40 **Sigismondo di Raffaello Landini** (d. December 1740). Assumes his duties on 30 November 1707. In February 1740 he expresses to the father corrector, fra Giovanni Francesco Colzi, his wish to resign and asks the confraternity to find another guardian; buried at the church of the Carmine on 17 December 1740.

1741–9 **Tommaso Gaetano de' Medici,** Balì and Senator (d. 19 December 1749). Elected on 27 April 1741; takes possession without ceremony on 22 May 1741; obsequies celebrated on 18 January 1750 and a Requiem Mass on 19 January 1750 [on this year Florentines changed their computation of the new year from 25 March to 1 January].

1750–69 **Francesco Antonio Ferroni,** Marquis (d. in 1769 at age fifty-two). Takes possession on 19 July 1750; obsequies celebrated on 4 June 1769; expenses for the obsequies, 106.10 lire. Ferroni had already been an active member of the Arcangelo Raffaello, since at least February 1741 (when he was appointed *consigliere*). He had also been a member of the *buca* of San Girolamo, contributing generously to the renovations to its fabric; of the Misericordia, and of the confraternity of San Filippo Benizi; see Sebregondi, *Tre confraternite* (1991), pp. 9–11, 30 n. 65; *La Misericordia di Firenze. Cimiteri monumentali* (1983), p. 42; *Gazzetta Toscana* 18 (1769), p. 70.

1769–85 **Antonio Arnaldi,** Marquis. Elected on 21 September 1769; takes possession on 1 October 1769.

APPENDIX 2

# Father Correctors of the Arcangelo Raffaello

Until 1556 the father corrector was either a Benedictine from the Badia or a Dominican from the convent of San Marco (ASF, Crs 160.6/7, f. 1). In 1490 the confraternity aggregated with the Benedictines of the congregation of Santa Giustina di Padova, thus indicating that at least at that time it was being served by the Benedictines (ASF, Crs 164.36/38; ASF, Crs 164.37; bull dated 20 May 1490). From 1556 to 1565 the confraternity used Dominican priests from the convent of Santa Maria Novella, and specifically:

1556–8 Fr **Davit da Raggiuolo**, OP. Appointed by Matteo Strozzi, prior of the convent, on 27 October 1556. Resigned in June 1558.

1558–9 Fr **Santi Cini**, OP. Appointed by the prior of Santa Maria Novella on 28 June 1558. On 10 August 1558 he reformed the confraternity (ASF, Crs 160.6/6, ff.6r–7r). On 11 June 1559 he resigned because the prior transferred him to the convent of San Marco.

1559–62 Fr **Angelo d'Antonio Grifi**, OP. Appointed on 18 June 1559 (ASF, Crs 160.6/7, f.9v). He was also 'maestro delli studenti di S.ta Maria Novella.' An an agreement of 1 January 1560/1 with the friars of S. Maria Novella he was to be paid 56 *lire* per year to celebrate Mass at every *tornata*; the agreement was renewed in 1561/2. On 2 July 1562 he resigned because the prior had sent him to oversee a convent of nuns in Ripoli.

1562–? Fr fra **Tommaso Cambi**, OP Appointed by the prior of Santa Maria Novella on 2 July 1562 (ASF, Crs 160.6/7). No date given for his resignation. From May 1592 to May 1595 he was prior of Santa Maria Novella (Ricozzi, 'Necrologio,' p. 318)

?–1563–? Fr fra **Matteo dalla Pieve,** OP No date of appointment or resignation; he is recorded in the confraternity in 1563 (ASF, Crs 160.6/7, f.108v).

From 1565 to 1606 the father correctors were Observant Franciscans from the convent of Ognissanti; in light of an agreement reached on 1 April 1565, the Franciscans would celebrate Mass and hear confessions in the confraternity in return for an annual offering of grain (ASF Crs 160.7/8 for the agreement, and ASF, Crs 160.9/10 *passim* and ASF, Crs 157.3/5 *passim* for the annual offerings). There is no indication of who served the confraternity between 1565 and 1582, but then the father correctors are as follows:

?–1582–92 Fr fra **Antonio Cignori** (also Cicogni or Cicognoni). Already active as father corrector before 12 August 1582. He dies in early 1592 and the confraternity celebrates his obsequies on 7 March 1592. He requisitioned Giovan Maria Cecchi to compose the play *La Dolcina* ('fatto a requisitione del rever.do padre fra Antonio Cicognoni del ordine di San Francesco Osservanti l'anno 1584,' see SI-BCI, MS I.VII.25, f. 1) and may have commissioned other plays by Cecchi performed at that time at the confraternity.

1592–4 Undetermined priest.

1594–? Fr fra **Lorenzo** [no last name given] 'comes' to the confraternity in August 1594. He may be the fra Lorenzo who is a *discepolo* of fra Antonio Cignori.

1602–6 Fr fra **Bonifazio Pacini**. He resigns in December 1606 because he is called 'ad altro governo' (ASF, Crs 162.21/22, f.263r).

On 25 December 1606 the Franciscans from Ognissanti are dismissed and the Dominicans from Santa Maria Novella are rehired (ASF, Crs 160.8/9.date; ASF, Crs 162.21/22, f. 263r). They will serve until 1631 as follows:

1606 Fr fra **Luigi Maraffi,** OP. Appointed by the prior of Santa Maria Novella on 25 December 1606 (ASF, Crs 160.8/9; ASF, Crs 162.21/22, f. 263r).

1606–26 Fr fra **Santi Contrini,** OP. Appointed sometime in 1606, he serves the confraternity until his death on 2 August 1626 (ASF, Crs 160.8/9). The confraternity celebrates his obsequies on 30 September 1626 with great splendour (ASF, Crs 162.22/23, ff. 137v-8v). Contrini was also custodian of the relic of St Thomas Aquinas at the church of Santa Maria Novella. See Ricozzi, 'Necrologio' (1980), entry 1077, pp. 291–2.

1626–9 Fr fra **Lorenzo Ridolfi,** OP. Elected on 15 August 1626 to replace the deceased Fr. Contrini, he assumes his duties the very next day. His prior formally appoints him to the position on 29 September. He resigns on 28 March 1629 (ASF, Crs 162.22/23, ff. 136v, 137–8, and 166r respectively). He serves as prior of Santa Maria Novella between November 1629 and November 1632, and then again starting from November 1636. He dies on '16 calendas februarii' 1649. See Ricozzi, 'Necrologio' (1980), entry 1135, pp. 305–6 and 319.

1629–30 Fr fra **Giovan Domenico Bonsi**, OP. Appointed by the prior of Santa Maria Novella on 1 April 1629, he resigns on 30 May 1630 (ASF, Crs 162.22/23, f. 166 and ASF, Crs 162.23/24, f.8). He serves as prior of Santa Maria Novella between May 1639 and May 1642. See Ricozzi, 'Necrologio' (1980), p. 319.

1630–1 Fr fra **Agostino Rondinelli**, OP. Appointed by the prior of Santa Maria Novella on 30 May 1630, he serves until 28 July 1631 (ASF, Crs 162.23/24, ff. 8, 27). He will return in 1640 (see below).

On 25 July 1631, Rondinelli does not go to say Mass at the confraternity because the prior of Santa Maria Novella has told him not to go out of the convent. Because of this the confraternity decides to seek another father corrector and on 28 July chooses the Theatines (ASF, Crs 162.23/24, f. 31r–v), who provide them with the following priest from 1631 to 1640:

1631–40 Fr **Vincenzo Ugoccioni**. Appointed on 30 July 1631, he serves until 22 April 1640 (ASF, Crs 162.23/24, ff. 31v, 167r).

On 15 August 1633 the confraternity decides to ask the general of the Theatines for aggregation with that order; on 24 September they send a letter asking for aggregation; aggregation is granted on 8 December (ASF, Crs 162.23/24, ff. 61r, 64r).

On 9 May 1640 the confraternity decides to return to the Dominicans of Santa Maria Novella (ASF, Crs 162.23/24, f. 168r), who then serve them until 1677 as follows:

1640–6 Fr fra **Agostino Rondinelli**, OP. Appointed by the prior of Santa Maria Novella, he reassumes office on 9 May 1640 (ASF, Crs 160.8/9; 162.23/24, f. 168). The first father corrector to be appointed after the 1636 revision of the statutes, he is approved by the twelve *consiglieri*, celebrates Mass in the confraternity on 13 May, and is installed on 17 May (ASF, Crs 163.24/25, f.n.n.). Rondinelli is often absent from the confraternity for long stretches of time. Giovan Domenico Bonsi, then prior of the convent, substitutes for him in August, and fra Alessandro Carnesecchi in September 1640; fra Giovan Gualberto Spigliati (1578–1657) substitutes for him in April 1642 (on Spigliati see Ricozzi, 'Necrologio' [1980], entry 1151, p. 308); fra Lorenzo Rucellai substitutes for him in 1643 (Crs 163.25/26, f. 173v). He dies on '8 idus augusti' 1646 (Ricozzi, p. 304); the confraternity records for 10 August say he died the previous week (ASF, Crs 160.8/9; ASF, Crs 163.25/26, f. 66v). See Ricozzi, 'Necrologio' (1980), entry 1125, p. 304.

1646–56 Fr fra **Giovan Francesco Tempi,** OP (1609–61), 'uno dei nostri fratelli,' is appointed on 24 August 1646 (ASF, Crs 160.8/9; Crs 163.25/26, f. 66v). He is prior of Santa Maria Novella in 1653–6. During his absence from the confraternity in 1656, fra Ducci substitutes for him. In August 1656 he is appointed *reggente* at the Studio in Perugia (ASF, Crs 163.25/26, f. 173v). He dies on 28 November 1661. See Ricozzi, 'Necrologio' (1980), entry 1158, pp. 311–12 , 319.

1656–9 Fr fra **Francesco Bentivoglio,** OP. Appointed by the prior of Santa Maria Novella on 19 November 1656 (ASF, Crs 160.8/9; ASF, Crs 163.25/26, f. 173v). He dies in early August 1659 'die 4a in qua solemnia sancti patris nostri Dominici caelebrantur.' See Ricozzi, 'Necrologio' (1980), entry 1152, pp. 308–9.

1659–72 Fr fra **Jacinto della Rena,** OP. Appointed by the prior of Santa Maria Novella on 31 August 1659 and resigns on 14 February 1671/2 (ASF, Crs 160.8/9).

1672–7 Fr fra **Alessandro Carnesecchi,** OP. Appointed by the prior of Santa Maria Novella on 21 February 1671/2; apparently serves until 1677 (ASF, Crs 160.8/9; see the records on payments in ASF, Crs 161.14/15, ff. 81r, 85r and ASF, Crs 165.41/49, f. 60v). In 1651–4 he served as prior of Santa Maria Novella. See Ricozzi, 'Necrologio' (1980), p. 319.

From 1678 to 1702 the confraternity is served by priests from an unspecified order. They are:

1678 Fr fra **Basilio Affatichi,** 'Correttore sostituto.' See the records of payment of 35 *lire* in ASF, Crs 161.14/15, f. 88v; ASF, Crs 165.41/49, f. 67v.

1679–82 Fr fra **Giovanni Domenico Turriti.** There are records of payments of 35 *lire* in early January in 1680 and 1682 in ASF, Crs 161.14/15, ff. 96v, 103r.

1683 Fr fra ... **Talenti,** 'Vice Correttore' (ASF, Crs 161.14/15, f. 106r).

1684 Fr fra ... **Mescoli,** 'Correttore' (ASF, Crs 161.14/15, f.n.n. at date 8 January 1685).

1685–93 Fr fra **Giovanni Domenico Turriti,** 'Padre Correttore.' Yearly payments of 35 *lire* in early January are in ASF, Crs 161.14/15 and ASF,

Crs 161.15/16 at dates). A description of his sudden death on 13 February 1692/3 is in ASF, Crs 163.26/27, f. 84v.

1693 Fr **Angelo Cocchi**, Vice Padre Correttore' (ASF, Crs 161.15/16, f.126v at date 31 December 1693). A member of the Arcangelo Raffaello, he had been reciting Lenten sermons at the confraternity for some years.

1694 there are no records of payment to father correctors for this year.

1695–1701 Fr fra **Raffaello Badi**. For records of payments of 35 lire in early January 1695, 1696, 1700 see ASF, Crs 161.15/16, ff. 61r, 79r). He dies on 25 August 1701 (ASF, Crs 163.26/27, f.171v).

1701–2 A vice-corrector fills in from September 1701 to February 1702, but his name is not given (ASF, Crs 161.15/16, f. 90v).

On 5 February 1702 the confraternity returns briefly to the Observant Franciscans from the convent of Ognissanti with:

1702–3 Fr **Antonio Buonaventura Faggiotti**. Assumes his duties on 12 February 1701/2. He dies on 10 June 1703 (ASF Crs 163.26/27, f.176v, 186r). Records of payment in ASF, Crs 161.15/16, f. 96v.

From 1703 to 1726 the confraternity is served by the Vallambrosian monks from San Pancrazio, and in particular by:

1703–7 Fr **Alfonso Foggini**. Confessor *pro tempore* of the papal nuncio (ASF, Crs 163.26/27, f.186v), on 12 July 1703 Foggini offers his services to the confraternity (ASF, Crs 163.26/27, f. 186v). Record of payments of 35 *lire* yearly in early January from 1704 to 1707 is in ASF, Crs 161.15/16, ff. 101r, 125r. He is also a paid-up member of the confraternity and on 31 December 1715 wins the extraction of one of the two yearly dowries (ASF, Crs 163.27/28, f. 81r).

1708–18 Fr don **Filippo Neri Fantungheri**. Serves first as vice father corrector (1708–10) and then as corrector (1711–18). On 8 August 1718 he resigns because he has been appointed abbot at the Badia di Figline. The confraternity celebrates the Office of the Death for him on 21 December 1720 and remembers him as 'nostro Correttore et uno de nostri Fratelli molto affezionato alla nostra Compagnia' (ASF, Crs 163.28/29 at date 21 December 1720). Records of yearly payments of 35 *lire* from 1708 to 1712 are in ASF, Crs 161.15/16, and from 1713 to 1717 in ASF, Crs 161.16/17.

1718–26 Fr don **Calisto Forzoni**, 'monaco in S. Pancrazio et de nostri Fratelli' (ASF, Crs 163.28/28 at date 14 August 1718). Records of yearly payments from 1718 to 1726 are in ASF, Crs 161.16/17.

From 1727 to 1785 the confraternity returns to the Observant Franciscans from the convent of Ognissanti. It is served by:

1727–39 Fr fra **Guido di Firenze**. Appointed in 1727 (ASF, Crs 161.16/17, f. 181v), he dies in late November 1739 (ASF, Crs 155.1/3 fasc. B, f.n.n.). Records of yearly payments of 35 *lire* from 1727 to 1738 are in Crs 161.16/17.

1739–62 Fr fra **Giovanni Francesco Colzi**. Appointed in 1739 (ASF, Crs 161.16/17, f. 136r). Records of payments of 35 *lire* yearly from 1739 to 1762 are in ASF, Crs 161.16/17 and Crs 161.18/19. He is once described as 'Guardiano del Convento d'Ognisanti' (ASF, Crs 155.1/3 fasc. B, f.n.n. circa f. 195r).

1763–73 Fr fra **Lucido Matucci**. Records of yearly payments of 35 *lire* from 1764 to 1773 are in ASF, Crs 161.18/19.

1774–80 Fr fra **Eraclio Franceschi**. Records of yearly payments of 35 *lire* from 1774 to 1780 are in ASF, Crs 162.19/20). He is deceased by 21 September 1780 (ASF, Crs 164.34/35 p. 195).

1780–5 Fr **Gasparo Giusti**. Appointed on 1 October 1780 (ASF, Crs 164.34/35 p. 196). Records of yearly payments of 35 *lire* from 1780 to 1784 are in ASF, Crs 162.19/20.

APPENDIX 3

# Chapel Masters at the Arcangelo Raffaello

| | |
|---|---|
| Crs | Archivio di Stato di Firenze, Compagnie religiose soppresse da Pietro Leopoldo. (NB: references to this collection are made only for information specifically mentioned in the entries and therefore are not comprehensive.) |
| Burchi 1971/2 | Guido Burchi, 'Musica e musicisti nella Compagnia della "Scala" di Firenze (1556–1785).' Thesis, Università degli Studi di Firenze, 1971/2 |
| Burchi 1983 | Guido Burchi, 'Vita musicale e spettacolo alla Compagnia della Scala di Firenze fra il 1560 e il 1675,' *Note d'archivio per la storia musicale* n.s. 1 (1983), 9–50. |
| *Grove* | *The New Grove Dictionary of Music*, ed. Stanley Sadie. 20 vols. London: Macmillan, 1980. |
| *Grove Opera* | *The New Grove Dictionary of Opera*, ed. Stanley Sadie. 4 vols. London: Macmillan, 1992. |
| Kirkendale | Warren Kirkendale, *The Court Musicians in Florence during the Principate of the Medici*. Firenze: Leo S. Olschki, 1993. |
| Smither | Howard E. Smither, *A History of the Oratorio*. Vol. 1 *The Oratorio in the Baroque Era. Italy. Vienna. Paris*. Chapel Hill: University of North Carolina Press, 1977. |
| Solerti | Angelo Solerti, *Musica, ballo e drammatica alla Corte Medicea dal 1600 al 1637. Notizie tratte da un Diario con appendice di testi inediti e rari*. New York/London: Benjamin Blom, 1968. |

1563–84 **Mollazzi, Michelangelo di Jacopo**, *vaiaio* (furrier). Already a member of the confraternity, he was hired on 1 July 1563 to teach music to thirty of the confraternity's younger members at a salary of 30 *scudi* per year. He continued in office until the summer of 1584.

References: Crs 160.7/8 f. 4v at date 1563.7.1; Crs 160.8/9 at date 26 June 1583; Crs 160.8/9 f. 22r; Crs 162.21/22, f. 32. Burchi, (1971/2), *passim*; Burchi 1983, 11n2, says this musician was probably an amateur and finds no other information about him except for these records; also p. 40. Not listed in *Grove*, Kirkendale, Smither, Solerti.

1584–91 No *maestri di cappella* are employed. The confraternity relied on its own members, and especially on Raffaello Gucci, 'nostro fratello,' who is on record as early as 1584 as instructing the singers.

References: Crs 160.8/9 at date 1 November 1584; Crs 162.21/22 f. 54r.

1591–1609 **Malespini, Baccio d'Ulivieri** (also known by the surnames of Malespina, Palibotri, Palibotria, Palibotra) (b. 13 September 1545, buried 29 October 1610). Appointed *maestro di cappella* at the Arcangelo Raffaello on 21 April 1591, Malespini was paid 30 *scudi* per year to teach ten brothers and to perform the music for the year. In December 1607 an attempt to replace him with Marco da Gagliano failed after the crown prince, Cosimo de' Medici, intervened saying Baccio should be retained because he had served the grand-ducal family loyally for over forty years. Malespini resigned his post on 28 June 1609.

Malespini had contacts with Jacopo Corsi, from whom he received loans (1577). In 1577–8 he taught music to the brothers Jacopo, Giulio, and Bardo Corsi. Though a castrato, he married in 1582. In 1589 he performed in the intermedi for the wedding of Grand Duke Ferdinando I.

Not to be confused with the Ferrarese ambassador in Florence, Bartolomeo Malaspina.

References: Crs 160.8/9 at dates 21 April 1591 and 11 December 1607. Burchi 1971/2, *passim*; Burchi 1983, 15n11, says that nothing more is known about this musician than what appears in the records of the Arcangelo Raffaello; Kirkendale, 118–19. Not listed in *Grove*, Smither, Solerti.

1609–21 **Da Gagliano, Marco di Zanobi** (Florence, b. 1 May 1582, d. 25 February 1642/3). Priest. Joined the Arcangelo Raffaello at the age of six and a half on 24 February 1588/9. A student of Luca Bati, in 1602 he became his assistant at the basilica of San Lorenzo. That same year he was already assisting Baccio Malespini at the Arcangelo Raffaello. In 1607 he founded a music academy in Florence, the Accademia degli Elevati, which gathered both musicians and literati; its patron was Cardinal Ferdinando Gonzaga of Mantua and its secretary Giovanni del Turco. In

1607, after an aborted appointment as *maestro di cappella* for the confraternity, Da Gagliano went to Mantua for a year, where he set the music for Rinuccini's *Dafne* (which had already had music set to it by Jacopo Peri) and presented it there for for Carnival 1607/8. Having returned to Florence, he was appointed *maestro di cappella* at the cathedral in November 1608 (shortly after Luca Bati's death), and then at the court (1609). In 1610 he was made a canon at San Lorenzo and in 1615 apostolic prothonotary as well. He was appointed *maestro di cappella* at the Arcangelo Raffaello on 28 June 1609 and served in the position until 1621. His last recorded contribution to the Arcangelo Raffaello was the music for the confraternity's obsequies for Cosimo II, on 14 March 1621.

References: Crs 162.22/23, f. 83r at date 14 March 1620; Crs 165.40/48, f. 22v at date 24 February 1588; Burchi 1971/2, *passim*; Burchi 1983, 48; Hill, 'Oratory Music in Florence, I, 119–21; *Grove*, 7:81–7 (by Edmond Strainchamps, who erroneously reports Marco's age when he enrolled in the Arcangelo Raffaello as five and a half rather than six and a half; see Hill for the correction); Kirkendale; and Solerti, *passim*.

1622–5 **Da Gagliano, Giovanni Battista** (Florence, b. 20 December 1594, d. 8 January 1651). Younger brother of Marco da Gagliano (see above). He joined the Arcangelo Raffaello on 24 July 1599 and remained a member until his death in 1651. The earliest notice of his involvement with the music in the confraternity is dated December 1619 (Burchi 1983, 48). In 1613 he was appointed instructor in plainsong to the clerics of the basilica of San Lorenzo. Later he became a salaried singer (*musico*) at the cathedral (1621) and at the court (1624). In 1643 he officially replaced his recently deceased brother Marco as *maestro di cappella* at both the cathedral and the court, a post whose duties he had already fulfilled for the previous nineteen years because of his brother's 'indisposition.' However, since Giovan Battista was not a priest, he was not granted the official title, which was reserved for a canon of the cathedral.

Kirkendale (p. 370) says that Giovan Battista was already *maestro di cappella* at the Arcangelo Raffaello in December 1620, and indicates that this is contrary to Hill's information on p. 121, but I have not been able to check his reference and therefore retain the 1621 date for the time being.

References: Crs 165.40/48 f. 65v at date 1599.7.24; Burchi 1971/2, *passim*; Burchi 1983, *passim*; Hill, 'Oratory Music in Florence, I,' 121n54; *Grove*, 7:80–1 (by Edmond Strainchamps); Kirkendale, 370–6 and *passim*.

1625–41 **Conti, Agnolo di Salvestro** (buried 11 December 1641). Began to carry out his duties at the Arcangelo Raffaello on 5 October 1625, without waiting for his official appoitment to start on 1 November. Conti was a *tiorba* player at the court.

References: Crs 162.22/23 f. 128v at date 1 November 1625; Burchi 1971/2, *passim*; Hill 'Oratory Music in Florence, I,' 125; Burchi 1983, 48 (who says he held the post to the end of 1640); Kirkendale, 381–3. Not listed in *Grove*, *Grove Opera*, Smither, Solerti.

1642–4 **Baglioni, Baccio** (d. 30 August 1649). Officially appointed on 1 November 1642. Baglioni later became chapel master at the cathedral of Livorno. He composed an opera, *Celio*, in co-operation with Niccolò Sapiti.

References: Crs 163.25/26 f. 9r at date 1 November 1642; Burchi 1971/2, I:51n17 and *passim*; Hill, 'Oratory Music in Florence, I,' 126n69. Not listed in *Grove*, *Grove Opera*, Kirkendale, Smither, Solerti.

1644–53 **Sapiti, Niccolò** (buried 11 December 1678). Priest. Appointed on 1 November 1644 and released on 1 November 1653. A pupil of Marco and Giovan Battista da Gagliano, he became *maestro di cappella* at the cathedral on 19 August 1660. Before that, he had been organist and director of music at the Oratorian church of San Firenze (1641–6), where he directed music by Giovan Battista da Gagliano. Sapiti was a prolific composer and co-operated with Baglioni in the composition of the opera *Celio*.

References: Crs 163.25/26, ff. 39r and 142v at dates 1 November 1644 and 1 November 1653; Burchi 1971/2, *passim*; Hill, 'Oratory Music in Florence, II,' 259; Kirkendale, 646. Not listed in *Grove*, *Grove Opera*, Smither.

1653–9 **Comparini, Giovan Battista** (1611–1659). Priest. Joined the Arcangelo Raffaello at age nine on 25 December 1620. On 1 November 1653 he was appointed both one of the *conservatori* and one of the *soprintendenti alle musiche*. He is described at that time as 'Sotto Maestro di Cappella del Duomo suggetto valoroso nella sua professione.' Eventually he became *maestro di cappella* at the cathedral (1654–9) and, in the words of his contemporary Giovanni Cinelli (reported by Hill, 'Oratory Music in Florence, I,' 126n73), 'he composed many good works for the Chapel, such as the Magnificat, many motets, masses, and various Vespers, which compositions move about in manuscript form through the hands of professors.' Hill adds that one of these manuscript motets is extant in Florence at the Conservatorio di Musica Luigi Cherubini, call number E.177.

References: Crs 163.25/26 f.142v at date 1 November 1653; Crs

165.40/48 f. 126r at date 25 December 1620; Burchi 1971/2, 1:52n23 and *passim*; Burchi 1983, 44n27; Hill, 'Oratory Music in Florence, I,' 126–7; Kirkendale, 646. Not listed in *Grove*, *Grove Opera*, Smither.

1659–66 **Cerri, Bonaventura** (d. 23 November 1685). Priest. Appointed at the Arcangelo Raffaello on 1 November 1659, he served until April 1666. Composer for the 'Strage de' mostri, festa a cavallo nel giorno natalizio del Sereniss. Gr. Duca Cosimo III.' He served as *maestro di cappella* at the cathedral from 1681 to 1685.

References: Crs 161.13/14 *passim*; Burchi, 1971/2, 1:52n14 and *passim*; Burchi 1983, 44; Kirkendale, 646. Not listed in *Grove*, *Grove Opera*.

1666–73 **Sanmartini, Pietro** (Florence, b. 18 September 1636, d. 1 January 1701). Priest. First appointed on 1 November 1666, Sanmartini served until March 1674; he would later be reappointed (see below, under 1690–4).

A student of G.B. Comparini, Sanmartini began his career abroad, in Rome, Bologna, and Arezzo. On his return to Florence, he served first as assistant and then, from 1686 to 1700, as chapel master at the cathedral. Burchi describes him as a 'musico particolare' at the Medici court, performing on the lute, cembalo, and organ (Burchi 1983, 45n29). He composed many operas, oratorios, and sacred and instrumental music; from 1692, was a composing member of the Accademia Filarmonica of Bologna.

References: Crs 161.14/15 *passim*; Burchi 1971/2, 1:52n22 and *passim*; Burchi 1983, 45; *Grove*, 16:472 (by Argia Bertini); *Grove Opera*, 4:168; Kirkendale, 646. Not listed in Smither.

1673–90 **Benvenuti, Giovan Battista** (d. 1691). Priest. Began serving on 1 November 1673. He was dismissed on 1 November 1690 because of 'la sua indisposizione grave assai.'

References: Crs 163.26/27 f. 54r at date 1 November 1690; records of payments from 1573 to 1690 are in Crs 157.3/5, Crs 164.37bis/40, Crs 164.38/41, all *passim*; Burchi 1971/2, 1:53n25 and *passim*. Not listed in *Grove*, *Grove Opera*, Kirkendale.

1690–94 **Sanmartini, Pietro**. Priest. For a biography see above under 1666–73. He began serving again at the Arcangelo Raffaello on 25 December 1690.

References for 1690–4: Crs 163.26/27 f. 57r at date 25 December 1690; for records of payment during this second period see Crs 157.3/5, Crs 164.37bis/40, Crs 164.38/41, all *passim*.

1694–1700 **Socci, Pietro**. Priest. Begins to serve on 1 November 1694. Socci held several positions contemporaneously. First, as a priest, he was prior of Santa Lucia dalle Rovinate. Then, aside from being chapel master at the Arcangelo Raffaello, he served for a long time as chapel master at the Oratorians' church of San Firenze (1694–1737), and at SS. Annunziata (1 February 1702 to 19 June 1707). He also directed oratorios at the confraternity of the Purificazione (1696–1700). Perhaps because of his many posts, or perhaps for lack of talent and inclination, Socci does not appear to have been a composer of oratorios (Hill, 261, found only one reference to a musical composition by Socci, a Latin motet).

References: records of payments to him are in Crs 157.3/5, Crs 164.38/41, *passim*; Burchi 1971/2, *passim*; Hill, 'Oratory Music in Florence, II,' 259–64. Not listed in *Grove*, *Grove Opera*, Kirkendale, Smither.

1700–9 **Rustichelli, Filippo**. Began to serve on 1 November 1700. Rustichelli was also an occasional paid singer (bass) at San Felice (1668–75). For the sake of sheer curiosity, I point out that Rustichelli dated his receipts of payment using the modern tabulation of the year, that is, with the year starting on 1 January, rather than with the Florentine *ab incarnatione* system starting on 25 March.

References: records of payments in Crs 164.38/41; Burchi 1971/2, *passim*; Hill, 'Oratory Music in Florence, II,' 256. Not listed in *Grove*, *Grove Opera*, Kirkendale, Smither.

1709–14 **Balassi, Francesco**. Priest. No information is available on him.

References: Crs 157.3/5 at dates 1 November 1709 and following; Burchi 1971/2, *passim*. Not listed in *Grove*, *Grove Opera*, Kirkendale, Smither.

1715–18 **Ricci, Francesco Maria**. Served at the Arcangelo Raffaello from April 1715 to April 1718. Earlier, he had served as 'second organist' at the cathedral from 1686 to an undetermined date.

References: Crs 157.3/5 at dates 19 April 1715 and following; Burchi 1971/2, *passim*; Kirkendale, 647. Not listed in *Grove*, *Grove Opera*, Smither.

1718–36 **Redi, Giovanni Nicola Rinieri** (Florence, 1685–1769). Priest. A singer (bass) as well as a composer, Redi served as *maestro di cappella* at a number of Florentine churches: the Oratorian church of San Felice (1737–69), where he also served occasionally as a paid singer (1729–42), Santa Maria Novella (1761–7), San Pancrazio (c.1729–66), San Gaetano (1760), and at the cathedral (1760–9), where he had been *sottomaestro* from at least 1753.

References: records of payments in Crs 157.3/5 *passim*; Burchi 1971/2, 1:54n37 and *passim*; Hill, 'Oratory Music in Florence, II,' 256, 264; Hill, 'Oratory Music in Florence, III,' *passim*. Not listed in *Grove*, *Grove Opera*, Kirkendale, Smither.

1736–44 No *maestro di cappella* was appointed, possibly because construction above the confraternity hindered extensive performance of music in the oratory.

1744–62 **Felici, Bartolomeo** (Florence, b. 1695, d. 12 June 1776). Often confused with his son Alessandro Felici (Florence, 1742–72). Bartolomeo Felici studied with G.M. Casini, and then directed his own music school in Florence, attended, among others, by Cherubini. Felici also served for most of his life as organist and chapel master at San Marco. He composed numerous oratorios.

References: Crs 157.3/5 and 158.4 *passim*; Burchi 1971/2, 1:54n37 and *passim*; Hill, 'Oratory Music in Florence, II,' 264–6; *Grove*, 6:457. Not listed in Smither.

1762–85 Neither Burchi nor I have been able to find documents confirming the presence of *maestri di cappella* in these years.

APPENDIX 4

# Musical and Theatrical Performances at the Arcangelo Raffaello

The following list includes plays, as well as dialogues, singing, and exortations performed in costume. It does not include processions, singing, or musical performances carried out without benefit of costume or without 'action.' And, lastly, it is a working list, and as such it does not claim to be complete. (Dates are given in the form year-month-day.)

1563.12.31 [Raphael/Tobias play].
1573.12.25 Giovan Maria Cecchi, *Atto recitabile per alla Capannuccia.*
1575.12.21 Sun. Tobias play [?].
1577.9.2 to 1581.11.1 No records were kept by the confraternity.
1580–7 Giovan Maria Cecchi, *Disprezzo dell'amore e beltà terrena. Dialogo e atto scenico di Ms Gio: Maria Cecchj fiorentino. Fatto per la Compagnia dell'Arcangiol Raff.lo detta la Compagnia della Scala* [from the manuscript's title page].
1580–7 Giovan Maria Cecchi, *Duello e atto scenico della vita attiva e contemplativa, fatto per la Compagnia dell'Archangelo Raffaello il giorno della festività di Santa Maria Maddalena* [from the manuscrupt's title page].
1582.6.3 Sun. [Tobias play].
1582.6.23 Costumed singing.
1584.12.24 Nativity play ['misterio'].
1584/5.1.27 Sun. and 1584/5.2.2 Sat. Giovan Maria Cecchi, [*La presentazione di Gesù al Tempio*; now lost].
1584/5.3.? and 3 Anonymous 'trattenimento spirituale.'
1585.4.25 Thurs. Two plays, the first the anonymous 'trattenimento spirituale' mentioned above and the second a [*Visit to the Sepulchre*].
1585.4.28 Sun. Anon. [*Triumph of Victory*].

1585.7.28 Sun. Anon. [*St Mary Magdalene with Angels*].
1586/7.1.1 Costumed singing.
1586/7.1.4 Anon. [*Flight into Egypt* and costumed singing].
1591/2.2.2 Anon. [*Presentation to the Temple*].
1592.3.30 Easter Monday, and 1592.4.3 Anon. [*Visit to the Sepulchre*].
1593.12.31 Costumed singing.
1593/4.1.2 Anon. [*Flight into Egypt*].
1594.4.12 Anon. [*Visit to the Sepulchre*].
1595.4.2 Anon. [*Visit to the Sepulchre*].
1609.12.25 Costumed singing.
1610.12.31 Costumed singing.
1611/12.3.18 Costumed singing.
1612.12.25 and 1612/13.1.6 and 10. Costumed singing.
1613.12.25 Costumed singing.
1614.12.25 Costumed singing.
1614/15.1.6 Costumed singing.
1616.12.25 Costumed singing.
1618.12.25 Costumed singing.
1619.4.1 Anon. [*Visit to the Sepulchre*].
1619.8.20, 25, 28 and 1619.9.4 Giovanni Nardi (c.1580–c.1655), *Il disperato miracolo della Vergine narrato da Cesario Cisterciense.*
1619.12.25 Costumed singing.
1619/20.2.20, 23, and 25 Giovanni Nardi (c.1580–c.1655), *Il martirio di S. Lucia Vergine e Martire.*
1622.9.11, 18, 21, 23, and 26 Giovan Maria Cecchi, with revisions and additions by Jacopo Cicognini, *Commedia della Benedizion di Giacob.*
1622.11.1 Anon. Musical dialogue among the souls in Purgatory.
1622.12.25, 26, and 27 Jacopo Cicognini, *Mistero della Ridenzion Umana.*
1623.7.23 Jacopo Cicognini, *Disprezzo d'Amore et Bellezza.*
1623/4.2.5 Jacopo Cicognini, *La celeste guida.*
1624.7.28 Giovan Maria Cecchi, *Dialogo per la festa di S.M. Maddalena.*
1625.11.9 Jacopo Cicognini, 2-part motet about souls in Purgatory.
1625.12.31 Costumed singing.
1626.11.1 Anon. [musical dialogue].
1626.12.25 Anon. *Rappresentazione dei pastori cantata dentro con ritornello.*
1628/9.2.27 Jacopo Cicognini, *Il trionfo di David.*
1631/2.1.? Jacopo Cicognini, *L'amor fraterno.*
1633/4.1.20 and 24 Sforza Oddi (1540–1611), *De' morti vivi.*
1635/6.1.18 Improvised plays at the house of the guardian father.

1638.7.20, 23, 24, ?, ? Giulio Guazzini, *Lo schiavo ritornato.*
1639.5.9, 14, and 17 Girolamo Bartolommei Smeducci (1584–1662), *Aglae.*
1639.11.1 Anon. *Purgatorio.*
1639.12.25 and 31 Anon. *Rappresentazione dei pastori.*
1639/40.2.9, 12, and 23 Rinaldo Strozzi, *Tragedia di SS. Cipriano e Giustina.*
1642.8.24 Giulio Guazzini, *Il morto risuscitato.*
1642/3.2.15, ?, ?, ? Jacopo Cicognini, *La vergine prudente.*
1643/4.3.20 Anon. *Dialogo sopra la preparazione da farsi alla prima comunione.*
1644.7.24 Anon. Dialogue [*Noli me tangere*].
1644.8.7 Anon. *Dialogo sopra l'Amor Divino.*
1644/5.2.12, 15, 19, 22, and 24 Giacinto Andrea Cicognigni, *Don Gastone.*
1645/6.2.9, 12, and 18 Camillo Lenzoni, play [no title given].
1654.11.1 motet, in dialogue form.
1655.11.1 motet, in dialogue form, on the Final Judgment.
1657.6.17 Jacopo Cicognini, *L'Amor fraterno*, with a prologue by Francesco Baldovini.
1657.7.22 [music for St Mary Magdalene's].
1658.7.28 [music for St Mary Magdalene's].
1658–86 gap in the *ricordi.*
1673.9.19 Jacopo Cicognini, *La conversione di Santa Maria Maddalena.*
1690/1.3.4 Oratorio, *S. Agnese.*
1690/1.3.11 Oratorio, *SS. Giovanni e Paolo.*
1690/1.3.18 Oratorio, *Martirio di S. Cecilia.*
1690/1.3.19 Oratorio, *Martirio di S. Vittoria.*
1691.3.25 Oratorio, *Annunciazione.*
1691.4.1 Oratorio, *Martirio di S. Cristina.*
1691.4.8 Palm Sunday. Oratorio, *Gerusalemme destrutta da Tito.*
1691.11.1 Oratorio, *La destruzione di Gerusalemme.*
1691/2.2.24 Oratorio, *Martirio di S. Caterina.*
1691/2.2.25 Oratorio [no title given].
1691/2.3.2 Oratorio, *Santa Vittoria martire.*
1691/2.3.9 Oratorio, *SS. Giovanni e Paolo.*
1691/2.3/16 Oratorio, *La strage degli Assiri.*
1691/2.3.19 Oratorio, *S. Cecilia.*
1691/2.3.23 Oratorio, *B. Lodovica.*
1692.3.25 Oratorio, *S. Cristina.*
1692.3.30 Oratorio, *Il Martirio d'Antonina e d'Alessandro.*
1692.12.31 Oratorio, *Le nozze di Tobbia.*

1692/3.3.8 Oratorio [no title given].
1692/3.3.1 Oratorio, *S. Teodora.*
1692/2.3.23 Easter Sunday. Oratorio, *S. Lodovica.*
1692/3.3.24 Oratorio, *Il legislatore ebreo.*
1693.3.25 Oratorio, *Gerusalemme destrutta.*
1693/4.3.19 Oratorio, *Martirio di S. Teodosia.*
1694.3.26 Oratorio, *Judith.*
1694.4.2 Oratorio, *Il legislatore ebreo.*
1694.4.12 Oratorio, [no title given].
1694.4.18 Oratorio, *S. Antonio da Padova.*
1695.4.4 Oratorio, [no title given].
1695.12.31 Oratorio, [no title given].
1696.4.23 Oratorio, [no title given].
1697.4.8 Oratorio, [no title given].
1698.12.31 Oratorio, *Le Nozze di Tobbia.*
1699.12.31 Oratorio, *Mosè al Mar Rosso.*
1700.12.31 Oratorio, [no title given].
1701.12.31 Oratorio, [no title given].
1702.4.18 Oratorio, [no title given].
1702.12.31 Oratorio, *S. Ambrogio.*
1703.12.31 Oratorio, *La partenza e ritorno di Tobbia.*
1704.11.1 Oratorio, *Gerusalemme destrutta da Tito.*
1704.12.31 Oratorio, *Il re Nabucodonosor.*
1705–6 Gap in the *ricordi.*
1707.12.31 Oratorio, [no title given].
1708.12.31 Oratorio, [no title given].
1709.12.31 Oratorio, [no title given].
1710.12.31 Oratorio, [no title given].
1711.12.25 Oratorio on the Nativity.
1711.12.31 Oratorio, [no title given].
1712.12.25 Oratorio, [no title given].
1713.12.31 'conforme all'anno passato,' Crs 163.27/28 f. 67r.
1714.12.31 'conforme agl'anni passati,' Crs 163.27/28 f. 74v.
1715.12.31 Oratorio, [no title given].
1716.12.31 Oratorio, *Mosè.*
1717.12.31 Oratorio, [no title given].
1718.12.31 Oratorio, [no title given].
1719.12.31 Oratorio, [no title given].
1720.12.31 Oratorio, [no title given].
1720.12.31 Oratorio, [no title given].

1721.12.31 Oratorio, [no title given].
1722.12.31 Oratorio, [no title given].
1723.12.31 Oratorio, [no title given].
1724.12.31 Oratorio, [no title given].
1726–1731 Gap in the *ricordi.*
1731–41 No plays or oratorios mentioned.
1741–5 Gap in the *ricordi.*
1751.12.31 Performance of an oratorio cancelled and rescheduled to the following evening (1752.1.1), [no title given].
1752.1.1 Oratorio, [no title given].
1752.12.31 Oratorio, [no title given].
1763.3.30 Because of heavy expenses, the performance of music is greatly reduced for the next two or three years.
1763–85 No plays or oratorios mentioned.

## Undated Performances

The title pages of three oratorios at the AAF (Compagnie VII.II.1 fasc. 2 'Arcangelo Raffaello') indicate that they were performed at the Arcangelo Raffaello:

1. *Gioasso*, with music by Giovan Niccola Ranieri Redi; datable to 1718 × 1731 (see below).
2. *I due sposi felici, Sara e Tobia*, with music by Francesco Gasparini; datable to 1712 × 1733 (see below).
3. *La liberazione del cieco nato evangelico*, with lyrics by Domenico Canavese and music by several unnamed composers; datable to 1709 × 1716 (see below).

## The title pages read:

Gioasso / Oratorio a quattro Voci / Da Cantarsi nella Venerabile Compagnia dell'Arcangiolo / Raffaello detta La Scala / Posto in Musica, e Dedicato all'Altezza Reale / della Ser.ma Violante Beatrice di Baviera / Gran Principessa di Toscana, e Governatrice della Città / e Stato di Siena / Dal Rev.do Gio: Niccola Ranieri Redi / Cappellano d'Onore, e *maestro di cappella* / di Camera della med.a A. R.e/ Altezza Reale / La Clemenza con la q.le si è depicta altre volte V. A. R.e d'accogliere le mie fatiche, mi rende ardito di dedicarle il presente componimento destinato per la musica, e se questo incontrerà la sorte med.a del Suo Reale Aggradimento non averò altro da desiderare, che la continuazione dell'alto Suo Patrocinio, del che umilm.e supplicandola pieno di riverenza e d'ossequio me le protesto. / Dell'A.V.R.e / Umil.mo Ossequios.mo et Abb.mo Ser.vo / Gio: Niccola Ranieri Redi /

Because Redi was chapel master at the Arcangelo Raffaello from 1718 to 1736, and Violante Beatrice di Baviera governed Siena between 1716 and 1731, the oratorio can be dated to the period 1718–31.

I due sposi felici / Sara e Tobia / Oratorio / a quattro Voci / da cantarsi / nella Venerabile Compagnia / Dell'Arcangelo Raffaello / detta della Scala / Musica / del Sig.r Francesco Gasparini

From Kirkendale (465, 549) we find that Gasparini was active in Florence between 1712 and 1723.

La Liberazione / del Cieco nato evangelico / Oratorio / da cantarsi / nella Venerabile Compagnia / dell'Arcangelo Raffaello / detta della Scala / Poesia / di Domenico Canavese / Dedicata / All'Ill.mi SS.ri/ Abate Carlo Ginori / e Marchese Andrea Borbon del Monte / Festaioli della detta Compagnia / Musica di Diversi

From Kirkendale (529, 436) we find that Canavese was active in Florence at least between 1709 and 1716.

APPENDIX 5

# Works of Art at the Arcangelo Raffaello

In the following list, information is arranged in the following order:

Artist (life dates). *Title of the work* (year of composition), material, size. Location. Published photographs. Description. Notes. References.

The following abbreviations have been used:

| | |
|---|---|
| AABA | Archivio dell'Accademia di Belle Arti, Filza B 'Filza 1a di documenti, lettere e carte diverse dell'Acc. di Belle Arti di Firenze dall'anno 1681 al 1790.' |
| Cantelli | G. Cantelli, *Repertorio della pittura del Seicento* (Firenze: OpusLibri, 1983). |
| Cirri | 'Sepoltuario,' BNCF MS Cirri. 13+2 vols. |
| Crs | Archivio di Stato di Firenze, Compagnie religiose soppresse da Pietro Leopoldo. |
| Follini | *Firenze antica e moderna illustrata.* Attributed to Vincenzo Follini and Modesto Rastrelli. Firenze, 1797. Rpt. Sala Bolognese: Forni, 1975. |
| Inventario 1540s | 'Inventario di maseritie della compagnia di S.to Vincentio,' ASF, Crs 155.1/3, fasc. B, f.n.n. loose leaf. |
| Inventario 1583 | 'Inventario di robbe spettanti alla Compagnia dell' Agnolo Raffaello fattosi al tempo del Guardiano Messer Antonio Pasci questo dì 25 d'Aprile 1583,' ASF, Crs 155.1/3, fasc. B, ff.n.n. [60r–63r] dated 25 April 1583; another copy is in Crs 164.38 ff. 4v–7r dated 25 April 1583. |
| Inventario 1591 | 'Inventario ... 1591,' ASF, Crs 164.36. |

| | |
|---|---|
| Inventario 1690 | ASF, Crs 164.37; there are two other copies of this inventory in ASF, Crs 155.1/3 fasc. B, docs. 27–8. |
| Lapucci | Roberta Lapucci, 'Storia di Alcuni dipinti estratti dalle compagnie soppresse da Pietro Leopoldo nel 1785,' *Rivista d'Arte* 41 (1989), 209–47. (NB: Lapucci does not distinguish between the youth and the adult confraternities of the Arcangelo Raffaello – that is, between the 'Scala' and the 'Raffa' companies – so her information must be used with caution.) |
| Patr. Eccl. | ASF, Patrimonio Ecclesiastico, 43, fasc. 32. |

**List of Works**

**Anon.** *Archangel Raphael* (pre-1690), oil (?) on wood. References: Inventario 1690, p. 23, 'Un Angelo Raffaello dipinto su l'asse contornata.'

**Anon.** *Archangel Raphael* (pre-1583), canvas with gilded white frame. Location: in 1591 it hung above the *Visione di Jacob* over the door inside the oratory; in 1690 on the altar in the *tornatino* (though previously it had hung above the door in the *tornatino*). References: Inventario 1690, p. 41; Crs 163.26/27, f. 54r at date 1 November 1690.

**Anon.** *Archangel Raphael* (pre-1591), oil (?) on wood with gilded frame, 1 1/3 *braccia*. References: not listed in Inventario 1583; Inventario 1591 item 22.

**Anon.** *Archangel Raphael and Tobias* (16th cent.), oil (?) on canvas. Location: in 1561 in an armoire (*tabernacolo*) in the *stanzone*; in 1690 in the *spogliatoio*; in 1784 in a small *sgabuzzino* just inside the *compagnia* (oratory); current location unknown. Description: processional banner painted on both sides, representing the Archangel Raphael and Tobias; with a gilded frame with the emblem of the Scala on top; with straps used to carry it in procession. Regilded in 1559 at the expense of Jacopo Ferretti and then carried in the St John procession of 23 June 1559; stored in one of the two tabernacles built in 1560 at a cost of 21 *lire* to house the confraternity's two processional banners. References: Crs 160.6/7 at date 23 June 1559; Crs 160.6/7 at date 8 January 1560; Inventario 1583; Inventario 1591, item 15; Inventario 1690, p. 9; Patr. Eccl., p. 11.

**Anon.** *Crucifix* (pre-1583), wood, 1.5 *braccia*. Location: in 1583 above the door in the oratory, in 1591 above the door in the *stanzone*, in 1784 in the *vestibolo* (*stanzone*), and current location unknown. Description: processional crucifix with veil and cover in red taffeta. References: Inventario 1583; Inventario 1591; Inventario 1690, p. 32; Patr. Eccl., p. 8.

**Anon.** *Crucifix* (pre-1690), alabaster with gilded wood frame. Reference: Inventario 1690, p. 9.

**Anon.** 16 *Deaths* [skull and crossbones?] (pre-1690), oil (?) on canvas. Current location unknown. Description: four large ones, and four smaller ones, used to decorate the oratory on All Saints'. Reference: Inventario 1690, p. 21.

**Anon.** *Death* [skull and crossbones?], (pre-1690), oil (?) on canvas. Reference: Inventario 1690, p. 21.

**Anon.** *Death* [*Good and Bad Death*] (pre-1690). Current location unknown. Description: inscribed with 'Bona. Mala.' Note: hung above the oratory's door during obsequies. Reference: Inventario 1690, p. 21.

**Anon.** *Death* or *Memento mori* (pre-1690), oil (?) on canvas, small. Inscribed 'Heri Mihi: Tibi hodie.' Reference: Inventario 1690, p. 9.

**Anon.** *The Descent of the Holy Spirit at Pentecost* (pre-1530), oil (?) on wood. Location: pre-1540 in the confraternity of the Spirito Santo and, subsequently, in that of San Vincenzo; in 1591 in the *sagrestia*; current location unknown. Description: the Holy Spirit descends on the Virgin [or on St Mary Magdalene] and the Twelve Apostles. Note: the painting was probably given to the Arcangelo Raffaello by virtue of the agreement of February 1541/2 with the friars of Santa Maria Novella (Inventario 1540s); it probably had originated in the confraternity of the Spirito Santo but was included in the list of objects from the confraternity of San Vincenzo given to the Arcangelo Raffaello (Inventario 1540s); the side panels painted by Jacopo Ferretti, one representing the Archangel Raphael, the other St Mary Magdalene, were added in March 1560. References: Crs 160.6/7 f. 19v at date 25 March 1560; Inventario 1583; Inventario 1591, item 21, 'Maddalena et 12 Apostoli quando ricevono lo Spirito Santo.'

**Anon.** *Eagle* or *Pelican* (pre-1690), oil (?) on metal sheet. Location: in 1784 in the *vestibulo* (*stanzone*); current location unknown. References: Inventario 1690, p. 9; Patr. Eccl., p. 9.

**Anon.** *Gesù Bambino* (pre-1690), painted plaster doll, flesh-coloured. Note: placed on the altar of the *tornatino* on Christmas morning. Reference: Inventario 1690, p. 34.

**Anon.** *Gesù Bambino* (pre-1690), painted papier-maché doll, flesh-coloured. Note: placed on the oratory's altar on Christmas morning. Reference: Inventario 1690, p. 34.

**Anon.** *Jacob's Ladder* (pre-1583), half roundel; oil (?) on wood. Location: in 1591 above the door inside the oratory, with the canvas of the Archangel Raphael above it; in 1690 in the sacristy; in 1784 in the *coro* in the oratory; current location unknown. Description: God the Father, Jacob, angels ascending and descending the ladder, and the Archangel Raphael leading youths from the company towards the ladder; inscribed with 'Venite haec est Domus Dei, et Scala Coelj.' References: Inventario 1583; Inventario 1591, item 19; Inventario 1690, p. 32; Patr. Eccl., p. 15.

**Anon.** *Madonna* (pre-1591), painted canvas. Location: in 1591 in a chapel in the *stanzone*, next to the street door; current location unknown. References: not listed in Inventario 1583; Inventario 1591, item 18.

**Anon.** *Madonna of the Misericordia with St Mary Magdalene and the Nativity* (pre-1563), oil (?) on wood. Location: in 1562/3 moved from the oratory to the *stanzone*, in 1583 to the *tornatino*, in 1591 placed above the altar in the *tornatino*; in 1690 and 1784 hung above the door in the *tornatino*; current location unknown. Description: altar triptych with predella; in the central panel, Madonna with several youths kneeling at her feet, two angels holding her cape; in one lateral panel St Mary Madgalene supported by angels, in the other a Nativity; on the predella stories from the Book of Tobit. References: Crs 160.6/7 f.49v at date 27 January 1562/3; Inventario 1583; Inventario 1591, item 24; Inventario 1690, p. 43; Patr. Eccl., p. 18.

**Anon.** *Madonna and Child* (pre-1690), terracotta bas-relief. Description: Virgin with Child in her arms. Reference: Inventario 1690, p. 33.

**Anon.** *Musician Angels adoring the Trinity* (pre-1604), fresco. Location: on the wall behind the main altar in the oratory, it was destroyed after 1785 when the oratory was restructured for secular use. Description: a choir of angels adoring the Trinity and playing on a variety of instruments – flutes, viols, organs, harpsichords, harps (or citharas), clavichords, sistra (a type of rattle), and pan-pipes; Domenico Torsi, 'Descrizione del l'esequie fatte nella morte del Signor Jacopo Corsi nella Compagnia dell'Arcangelo Raffaello, 1603,' MS from the library at the Villa Corsi-Salviati, ff. [41v–42r], cited in Tim Carter, 'Music and Patronage,' 93n34. Reference: Crs 160.8/9 at date 8 September 1647.

**Anon.** *The Passion of Our Lord* (pre-1690), sixteen canvases, all the same size; each 4 × 3 *braccia* circa. Location: in 1690 in the 'Stanza di sopra,' in 1784 in the *cantoria*, current location unknown. Description: sixteen canvas paintings in chiaroscuro, with wood frames painted walnut and gilded, donated by Domenico and Baccio Comi. Note: hung in the oratory during Holy Week. References: Inventario 1690, p. 21; Patr. Eccl., p. 12.

**Anon.** *Pietà* (pre-1583), oil (?) on wood, 4 *braccia*. Location: in 1583, 1591, 1690, and 1784, in the *stanzone* above the door from the piazza, current location unknown. Description: a dead Christ in his mother's lap, with other figures, painted 'in maniera antica.' References: Inventario 1583; Inventario 1591, item 17; Inventario 1690, p. 1; Patr. Eccl., p. 1.

**Anon.** *Pietà* (pre-169), oil (?) on canvas, with walnut-coloured frame 'assai antico.' Location: in 1690 in the *sagrestia*. Reference: Inventario 1690, p. 32.

**Anon.** *St Bernard* (pre-1690), oil (?) on wood, 1 *braccio* circa, with a rounded top and a yellow frame. Location: in 1690 in the *tornatino*, in 1784 in the *cantoria*, current location unknown. References: Inventario 1690, p. 42; Patr. Eccl., p. 12.

**Anon.** *St Domenic* (pre-1690), canvas (?) with gilded black frame. Location: in 1784 in the *vestibulo* (*stanzone*), current location unknown. Note: 'natural size,' believed in 1690 to be the portrait of father corrector Santi Contrini (d. 1626); in 1784 the figure is described simply as 'a Dominican.' References: Inventario 1690, p. 9; Patr. Eccl., p. 8.

**Anon.** *St Francis* (pre-1690), small canvas without frame. Location: in 1690 inside the closet in the *spogliatoio*. Note: in 1784 the figure is described simply as 'a Religious.' References: Inventario 1690, p. 9; Patr. Eccl., p. 8.

**Anon.** *St Jerome* (pre-1690), oil (?) on wood, 1 *braccio* circa, with a rounded top and a yellow frame. Current location unknown. References: Inventario 1690, p. 42; Patr. Eccl., p. 12.

**Anon.** *Tavoletta* (pre-1690), wood tablet. Note: used 'for the Lunario.' Reference: Inventario 1690, p. 9.

**Anon.** *Trionfo*. References: Inventario 1583, 'il trionfo grande con sua treggia et altre appartenenze.' (I am unable to determine what, exactly, this would represent.)

**Chimenti, Jacopo, detto l'Empoli** (1554–1640). *Madonna with an Angel and a Confraternity Youth* (17th cent.), oil on canvas (?). Location: in 1690 in the *stanzone* above the door into the oratory; current location unknown. Description: 'Our Lady with an Angel who presents to her a youth in confraternal robes, and other figures' (1690 inventory). References: not listed in Inventario 1583 or 1591; Inventario 1690, p. 1; Patr. Eccl., pp. 1–2.

**Dandini, Piero** 'nostro fratello' (1646–1712). *God the Father* (17th cent.), roundel. Location uncertain in 1690; in 1784 in the *cantoria* above the 'Virgin and Child'; current location unknown. Gift of the artist to the company. References: Inventario 1690, p. 32; Patr. Eccl., p. 12.

**Del Bianco, Baccio** (1604–56). Two *Stories about the Archangel Raphael* (pre-1690), chiaroscuro painting. Location: in 1690 in the 'Prima stanza de' Musici'; current location unknown. Reference: Inventario 1690, p. 26.

**Del Bianco, Baccio** (1604–56). Three *Stories from the Book of Tobit* (late 16th–early 17th cent.), large chiaroscuro canvases. Location: in 1784 in the *tornatino*; current location unknown. References: Inventario 1690, p. 25; Patr. Eccl., p. 18.

**Del Bianco, Baccio** (1604–56). Ostensory (late 16th–early 17th cent.), gilded wood. Current location unknown. Reference: Inventario 1690, p. 33.

**Di Bartolomeo, Giovan Battista** (sculptor, active in the 1560s). *St Lawrence* (1561), painted terracotta bust. Location: in 1561 in the cabinet in the guardian's desk; current location unknown. Notes: donated to the confraternity by the artist in May 1561 and then painted by Michele delle Colombe, 'nostro fratello.' References: Crs 160.6/7, ff. 23v, 33r at date May 1561.

**Di Bartolomeo, Giovan Battista** (sculptor, active in the 1560s). *St Mary Magdalene* (1561), painted terracotta bust. Location: in 1561 in the cabinet in the guardian's desk; current location unknown. Donated to the confraternity by the artist in May 1561 and then painted in 1561 by Michele delle Colombe. References: Crs 160.6/7 ff. 23v, 33r at date May 1561.

**Di Bartolomeo, Giovan Battista** (sculptor, active in the 1560s). *The Archangel Raphael and Tobias* (1561), painted terracotta figures. Current location unknown. Note: modelled by Di Bartolomeo, fired by Santi Buglioni, and painted by Francesco di Mariano Traballesi, all in July/August 1561, then donated to the confraternity by Di Bartolomeo in August 1561. Reference: Crs 160.6/7 f.34r at date 10 August 1561.

**Di Tito, Santi, school of.** Six paintings on religious subjects (pre-1690), oil on canvas, 2 *braccia*, with gilded black frames. Location: in 1690 in the *tornatino*; in 1784 in the *vestibulo* (*stanzone*); current location unknown. References: Inventario 1690, p. 42; Patr. Eccl., p. 2.

**Ferretti, Jacopo** 'nostro caro et amorevole padre' (active 1550s–60s). *Noli me tangere* (16th cent.), oil (?) on canvas. Location: in 1560, 1591, 1690, 1784 in a cabinet in the *stanzone*, just inside the street door; current location unknown. Description: processional banner (*segno*) depicting Christ as a gardener appearing to St Mary Magdalene, and possibly bearing the inscription 'Noli me tangere.' Notes: restored in 1560 by Jacopo Ferretti, it continued to deteriorate, getting progressively worse; housed in one of the two tabernacles constructed for the two *segni* at a cost of 21 *lire* in January 1560/1. References: Crs 160.6/7 f. 19r–v at date 25 March 1560 and 8 January 1560/1); Inventario 1583; Inventario 1591, item 16; Inventario 1690, p. 9; Patr. Eccl., p. 8.

**Ferretti, Jacopo** 'nostro caro et amorevole padre' (active 1550s–60s), *The Archangel Raphael* and *St. Mary Magdalene* (1560), oil (?) on wood. Location: in 1591 in the *sagrestia*; current location unknown. Description: side panels to the anonymous *Descent of the Holy Spirit at Pentecost* (see above). References: Crs 160.6/7, f. 19v at date 25 March 1560; Inventario 1583; Inventario 1591, item 21.

**Fidani, Orazio** (Firenze, 1606–56). *Tobias Healing His Father's Blindness* (1654), oil on canvas, 36 cm. × 197.5 cm. See ill. 10 Location: in 1690 and 1784 in the *stanzone* above the altar to the left of the main entrance; currently in Florence, Uffizi (Deposits). Inv. 1890, no. 7612. Photographs: in Cantelli, ill. 365; pre-restoration photograph in *La città degli Uffizi. I musei del futuro* (Firenze: Sansoni, 1982), 229, with note by S.M. Description: Tobias healing his father, with the Archangel Raphael and other figures. Notes: painted in 1654, it was a gift of Agnolo e Alessandro Galli to the confraternity. References: Inventario 1690, p. 1; Patr. Eccl., p. 1; AABA n. 47; C. Innocenti, in *Il Seicento fiorentino. Biografie* (Firenze: 1987), 90; Lapucci, 231.

**Lippi, Lorenzo** (Firenze, 1606–65). Several *Stories from the Book of Tobit* (17th cent.), canvas. Current location unknown. Reference: Inventario 1690, p. 25.

**Lippi, Lorenzo** (Firenze, 1606–65). *Crucifixion* (1647), oil on canvas, 370 cm × 190 cm. See ill. 7. Location: in 1647 in the *stanzone* above the altar; in 1690 in the *stanzone* to the right of the entrance; current location in Florence, Museo di San Marco, Inv. 1890, no. 2115, with provenance indicated as 'Dalla Compagnia della Scala in Firenze'; restored in 1982. Photographs: *Il Seicento fiorentino* (1987), vol. 1, fig. 76. Description: altarpiece Crucifixion, with Virgin, St John the Evangelist, and St Mary Magdalene kneeling at the cross. Notes: gift of the artist to the company on 28 July 1647. References: Crs 163.25, ff. 76r–v at date 28 July 1647; Inventario 1690, p. 1; Patr. Eccl., p. 1; Chiara d'Afflitto in *Il Seicento fiorentino. Catalogo*, 3:108; Chiara d'Afflitto in *Paradigma* 2 (1982), 111–34; Cantelli, 95; Rosanna Caterina Proto Pisani, 'Momenti del Seicento Fiorentino,' *Paradigma* 5 (1985), 148–49n55.

**Lippi, Lorenzo** (Firenze, 1606–65). *Crucifix* (17th cent.), oil on wood. Location: in 1690 and 1784 in the cabinet in the *stanzone*; current location unknown. Description: 'crocefisso in su l'asse contornato,' which Lippi did in half a day (1690 inventory). Notes: gift of the artist to the company for the obsequies for Agnolo Galli. References: Inventario 1690, p. 9; Patr. Eccl., p. 8.

**Lippi, Lorenzo** (Firenze, 1606–65). *Souls in Purgatory* (17th cent.), oil on canvas, on an altar front (*paliotto*). Current location unknown. Reference: Inventario 1690, p. 7.

**Neri, Bartolomeo**, also known as 'il Poeta a piedi' (active in the 1640s). Undetermined subject, fresco. Location: on the wall around the main altar; subsequently destroyed. Note: the brothers Agnolo and Alessandro Galli paid for the fesco. References: Crs 163.24, ff. 77, 79 at date 8 September 1647); Laur. MS Antinori 155, 'Alcune notizie delle chiese fiorentine,' f. 8v.

**Piero di Cosimo** (c.1462–1521?). *Madonna and Child with Sts Dominic and Jerome* (late 15th cent.), oil on wood, 209 cm × 205.7 cm. for the central panel with the Madonna and Child, 67 cm × 87 cm. for each of the lateral panels depicting angels; altar panel, with gilded frame and predella. Location: in 1591 in the oratory; in 1690 in the *sagrestia*, between the two windows, with a pietra serena border and a gilded wooden frame; the Madonna and Child panel is currently in the Jarves Collection, Yale University Art Gallery, New Haven; the two panels with two angels each are currently one in the Church of the Advent, Boston, the other at the Museum of Fine Arts, Boston. Notes: previously attributed to Domenico del Ghirlandaio (1449–94). Photographs: in Mina Bacci, *L'opera completa di Piero di Cosimo* (Milano: Rizzoli, 1976), 97–8, ills. 57–9; the angels alone are in Mina Bacci, *Piero di Cosimo* (Milano: Bramante, 1966), ills. 52, 52a; photographs are on file in Florence, Kunsthistorisches Institut, no. KIF 50423. Description: the Virgin with the Child standing on her right knee, St Vincent (according to the 1583 and 1591 inventories) or St Dominic (according to the 1690 and 1784 inventories) on the right, St Jerome on the left, and four angels above her head; Cirri says there were also some Confraternity brothers (8:4293). References: Inventario 1583 'tavola del altar di compagnia dentrovi S. Vincenzo, S. Girolamo et in mezo la Vergine messa in oro'; Inventario 1591, item 20, 'Madonna Gesù, con S. Vincenzo e S. Girolamo tavola d'altare con cornice di legno dorato ha una predella e altare ... sta in compagnia'; Inventario 1690, p. 31, 'tavola, si crede essere di mano di Domenico Ghirlandaio ... la Beata Vergine con Bambino Gesù in braccio, con S. Domenico [*sic*] a mano destra, e S. Girolamo a sinistra, e 4 angeli sopra la testa della Beata Vergine Maria ... sta in sagrestia, tra 2 finestre, con ornamento intorno di pietra serena e con altro ornamento di legno intagliato e dorato'; Patr. Eccl., p. 12, 'Una tavola grande dell'altar maggiore fra le due finestre rappresenta la Beatissima Vergine con Gesù bambino in braccio, S. Domenico e S. Girolamo e varii angeli di maniera antica con sua tenda gialla di tela lacera che serve per coprirla e suo ferro, è fissa nel muro'; Follini (25) claims it is by Domenico del Ghirlandaio 'la Vergine sedente col Bambino in piedi sul ginocchio destro'; the same incorrect attribution is given by Cirri, 8:4293: 'e sopra l'altare dell'Oratorio una tavola del Ghirlandaio con la Vergine e il Divino Infante e i santi Domenico, Girolamo, e alcuni fratelli della Compagnia'; Mina Bacci, *Piero di Cosimo* (Milano: Bramante, 1966), 102–3, ills. 52, 52a; Mina Bacci, *L'opera completa di Piero di Cosimo* (Milano: Rizzoli, 1976), 97–8, ills. 57–9; Padoa.

**Rosselli, Matteo** (Firenze, 1578–1650). *Madonna* (17th cent.), oil (?) on canvas. Location: in 1608 above the door into the *compagnia*; current location unknown. Note: Cosimo del Bianco paid for the canvas and the frame; the confraternity paid Matteo Rosselli 17 *scudi* for his work. References: Crs 160.8/9 at date 11 October 1608.

**Spada, Valerio** (Siena, 1613–Firenze, 1688). Script and illustrations for the 1640 statutes (1640), ink on vellum. Location: ASF Cap. Crs 627. Description: italic hand, arabesques, illustrations; the volume is bound in red velvet; ink drawings on pp. i (naked cherub in the clouds holding a banner bearing the inscription 'Proemio' and with the dove of the Holy Spirit below him), viii (naked putto sitting on stone slab leaning back to his right to pick a daisy), xviii (lily stalk with three blooms, buds, and four insects around it – a dragon fly, a house fly, a bee, and a wasp), xxvi (flower stalk with three blooms), xxxi (flower stalk with one bloom and one bud, and with an insect on the bud), xxxviii (three flower stalks, one with three blooms, the other two with single blooms), xxxxiii (three flower stalks, all single bloom), xiiii xvi, xxviii, xxxvi, xxxxvi (filigrains). Reference: Inventario 1690, p. 12.

**Vignali, Jacopo** (Casentino, 1592–Firenze, 1664). *Archangel Raphael and Tobias* (pre-1690), oil on canvas with gilded frame. Location: in 1690 in the oratory above the entrance door and the musicians' loft; current location Florence, Museo del Convento di San Marco, Inv. 1890 no. 8681, with provenance indicated as 'Dal convento di San Marco in Firenze' and dated 1622. References: Inventario 1690, p. 28; Patr. Eccl., p. 12; Lapucci, 241.

# Notes

## Introduction

1 ASF, Crs 160.8/9 at date 11 January 1561/2.
2 For the element of violence symptomatic of youth in premodern Florence and Italy, see Trexler, *Public Life,* Niccoli, and *Infanzie*.
3 Klapisch-Zuber, 98.
4 Niccoli, 348, with a footnote reference to E. Becchi's 'Premessa' in the volume *Bambini*, ed. E. Becchi, in *Quaderni storici* 58 (1984), 716 (my translation).
5 Henderson, 'Piety and Charity,' 9n19.
6 Christopher F. Black, 47–8.
7 A few confraternities still exist in Florence, but their post-suppression resurgence and their current activities digress from this monograph's focus.
8 Falvey, 'Confraternities.'
9 I draw these observations from Professor John O'Malley, SJ, who voiced them in his plenary address at the annual meeting of the Renaissance Society of America on 31 March 1995, New York, NY, and then repeated them on 17 October 1995 at the Centre for Reformation and Renaissance Studies, Toronto, Canada.
10 Klapisch-Zur, viii.
11 Rusconi, 'Tra movimenti,' 342 (my translation).

## Chapter 1

1 Lami, 3:1561–5; Meersseman, *Ordo*, 924, 1047; Monti, 1:150; Papi, 'Per un censimento,' 113–17; Weissman, *Ritual Brotherhood*, 43–4, basing himself on Varchi, 9:36; Papi, 'Confraternite,' 724; Henderson, 'Piety and Charity,' 26 and 393–432. For the similarly remarkable growth of confraternities in France in the

period 1350–1500, see Chiffoleau, *La comptabilité*, esp. 267–70. On St Peter Martyr, see Orlandi, *Il VII Centenario.*

2 De la Roncière, 'La place des confréries ... Appendices.' See also his 'Les confréries à Florence.

3 Pullan, 'Support and Redeem,' 186. Pullan draws his figures from Grendi, 'Morfologia,' 246–9; Paglia, 86, 307–15; and his own *Rich and Poor in Renaissance Venice*, 34.

4 Monti; Christopher Black.

5 This and the following list on scholarship are drawn from the 'Publications Received' rubric of *Confraternitas* 1–6 (1990–6) and do not intend, by any means, to be either complete or representative. For further information on recent scholarship on Italian confraternities, see Rusconi, 'Confraternite;' Zardin; Eisenbichler, 'Ricerche nord-americane' and 'Italian Scholarship.'

6 Chiffoleau, *La comptabilité*, 267–74. See also his 'Entre le religieux et le politique.'

7 Again, for a running bibliography of recent studies on confraternities, see the 'Publications Received' rubric of *Confraternitas* (Toronto, 1990+)

8 Marcus, esp. 74–80 and 259–60. It should be remembered, however, that in the German context the guild often functioned as both a religious and a business organization – confraternity plus guild – and because of this the German situation was somewhat different from the Italian one.

9 Pullan, *The Jews of Europe*, 113, 130, 223, 291; Ruderman, 'The Founding of a *Gemilut Hasadim* Society,' 248–57; Horowitz, 'Jewish Confraternities in Seventeenth-Century Verona: A Study in the Social History of Piety,' PhD dissertation, Yale University, 1982 (which, unfortunately, I was not able to consult); see Horowitz, 'A Jewish Youth Confraternity in Seventeenth-Century Italy' for the youth confraternities in Asti and Verona.

10 Godin, 'Les confréries.'

11 See, among others, the works of Anna Benvenuti Papi listed in the bibliography, and especially 'L'impianto mendicante in Firenze,' 'Fonti e problemi,' 'I frati della penitenza,' 'Penitenza e penitenti in Toscana.' See also Massimo Papi's 'Santa Maria Novella di Firenze'; Morghen, 29–42; Meersseman, 'Disciplinati e Penitenti' (1962), 43–72. For other parts of Italy, see Casagrande; De Sandre Gasparini, 'Benedettini' and 'Movimento dei disciplinati'; Bertoldi Lenoci; Fanti, 'Gli inizi' and 'Santa Maria della Carità.'

12 Papi, 'Confraternite e ordini mendicanti,' 727–9, and esp. 728 for a map illustrating the geographical spread of confraternities from the two foci of Santa Maria Novella and Santa Croce.

13 Orlandi, *Necrologio*, 1:xxx.

14 Fineschi, xxi–xxvii.

15 Papi, 'Confraternite e ordini mendicanti,' 731.

16 Meersseman, 'Etudes sur les anciennes confréries doménicaines,' reprinted in Italian as 'Le confraternite di San Pietro Martire' in *Ordo* (1977), 754–920; Dondaine; Papi, 'Le associazioni laiche,' 224n13; Christopher Black, 26; Housley; Lesnick, 82–5.

17 Papi, 'Confraternite e ordini mendicanti,' 729; also Papi, 'Associazioni laiche,' 227n24 and 238–9.

18 Papi, 'Associazioni laiche' 239 (my translation).

19 The term is not strictly correct, for it indicates a type of organization that developed in the early sixteenth century and became, very much, a parochial school for catechism (see below, ch. 10). One should also be careful not to confuse these *Scuole di Dottrina Cristiana* with the Lombard or Venetian *scuole*, the term used for confraternities in those areas. Similarly, Jewish synagogues could be called *scuole*; see, for example, Liscia Bemporad's article on the two synagogues in Florence, the 'Scuola Italiana' and the 'Scuola Levantina.'

20 Niccoli, 349–50.

21 Klapisch-Zuber, 96.

22 ASF, Crs 160.6/7, ff. 6r–7r at date 10 August 1558.

23 For the 1560 copy see ASF, Cap. Crs 752 ff. 17v, 1r, 2v respectively; for the 1468 original see ASF, Cap. Crs 882.

24 Trexler, *Public Life*, esp. ch. 11, 367–99. On the Compagnie della Calza see Venturi; more recently, see Muraro; Muir, 167–73 *passim*, and Chojnacki, 'Measuring Adulthood,' 380. Elsewhere, Chojnacki makes insightful comments on the political role of Venetian noblemen in their twenties as a liminal group that helped to articulate the state's ideology, something quite unlike the role described by Trexler for Florentine youths; see Chojnacki, 'Political Adulthood in Fifteenth-Century Venice.' I am indebted and grateful to Professor Chojnacki for the bibliography on the Compagnie della Calza.

25 For the role of *potenze* in Florentine social and festive life of Florence see Trexler, *Public Life*, 399–418, 510–15, *passim*.

26 Klapisch-Zuber, 95–6.

27 *OED*, 2nd ed. (1989). For women the age of adolescence is slightly different, covering the ages of twelve to twenty-one.

28 See Trexler, 'Ritual in Florence,' *passim*; Weissman, *Ritual Brotherhood*, 64n72, 213; Christopher Black, 47, 49; Henderson, *Piety and Charity* (1994), *passim*; Hill, 'Oratory Music in Florence, I,' 'Oratory Music in Florence, II' and 'Oratory Music in Florence, III,' *passim*

29 Horowitz, 'A Jewish Youth Confraternity,' 37n3, adopts the same practice, saying that 'although Trexler and others have pointed out that the term youth or "juventus" was used generally in the period under discussion with reference to

the years after adolescence (through age forty or forty-five), in this paper it is used in its modern sense as the period in life between childhood and maturity.'

30 Henderson, *Piety and Charity* (1994), 72.

31 Grendi, 'Le società dei giovani a Genova,' 523.

32 Vigo, *Una confraternita di giovanetti pistoiesi.*

33 Esposito, 100–1, citing from the papal bull of Eugenius IV, dated 1 February 1446, approving the establishment of the confraternity. Esposito adds in a footnote that the bull is found in the Archivio Segreto Vaticano, Gonfalone, mazzo B, n. 4, with a copy in ASV, Arm. 53, t. 13, f. 124r; and that it has been published, 'with several errors,' in L. Ruggeri, *L'archiconfraternita del Gonfalone* (Rome, 1866), 57–60.

34 Terpstra, 21–3 and *passim.*

35 Vigo, *Una confraternita di giovanetti pistoiesi*; Meneghin; Esposito; Little. For the Portoferraio confraternity see ASF, Crs 160.8/9 and ASF, Crs 162.21/22, ff. 63r–v, 69r both at dates in June–September 1585.

36 As this volume was going to press I came across the statutes of the youth confraternity of San Bernardino di Siena, founded in Siena in 1468, but was not able to incorporate their information into this work; see SI-BCI, MS A.X.18, 'Compagnia dei fanciulli ... Capitoli.'

## Chapter 2

1 This date is drawn from the 1468 statutes, which are the earliest extant copy (ASF, Cap. Crs 882, f. 2r), and is reiterated in their 1559 copy (ASF, Cap. Crs 752, f. 2r). It is also substantiated by the 1636 statutes (ASF, Cap. Crs 627), which claim the confraternity had been 'open' for 225 years. Del Migliore, writing his 'Zibaldone' at a much later date, gave 1410 as the founding year (BNCF, MS Magliab. XXV, cod. 418, p. 111), but I have been unable to determine his source. His dating has, unfortunately, been followed by Monti (183) and Trexler ('Ritual in Florence,' 206). The 1406 date mentioned by Hill ('Oratory Music in Florence, I,' 108n2) is also unclear; the manuscript he cites (ASF, Cap. Crs 752, mentioned above) clearly reads that the 'schola et compagnia titulata Compagnia della Nativita del nostro Signore Yesu Christo ... hebbe principio nel anno MCCCCXI' (f. 2r); I suspect he misread the final letters as VI rather than XI.

2 ACSG, Capitoli 1413/14, f. 56r. Compagnia di Santa Maria della Pietà was the official name for the *buca* of San Girolamo. On the term *buca* to indicate an adult confraternity that met overnight and practised flagellation, and on the *buca* of San Girolamo in particular, see Ludovica Sebregondi, *Tre confraternite*, 3–23. Although the Italian word *buca* may be related to the word *buco* (hole), it

does not denote 'underground chapels' (*pace* Henderson, *Piety and Charity* [1994], 3); in fact, Florentine *buche* met not only in above-ground chapels, but even in chapels on second stories of buildings; see the still-extant chapel of the *buca* of San Jacopo Oltrarno, for one.

3 In 1410 Bindo di Balduino Guasconi had been one of the thirty-three founding members of the *buca* of San Girolamo. See Sebregondi, *Tre confraternite*, 16.

4 ACSG, Capitoli 1413/14, ff. 56v–57v. All but one of these names reappear with similar responsibilities in the *buca* of San Girolamo; see Sebregondi, *Tre Confraternite*, 20n87, citing f. 48r of the same Capitoli. I wish to thank dott.ssa Ludovica Sebregondi for this information.

5 For biographical information on the Blessed Carlo Guidi, see the entry by Giuseppe Raspini in *Bibliotheca sanctorum*, 3:798–9 (where the confraternity of the Archangel Raphael is erroneously called S. Michele Arcangelo) and Brocchi, 3:195–214. For passing references see Del Migliore, *Firenze città nobilissima*, Henderson, 'Penitence and the Laity,' and Sebregondi, *Tre confraternite*, *passim*.

6 The order of the Eremiti di San Girolamo di Fiesole was founded in 1404 and suppressed in 1668. See the entry in *Dizionario degli istituti di perfezione*, 3:1204. As the author of the entry points out, the history of the order has not yet been written.

7 There were two *buche* named after San Girolamo, one meeting at the Ospedale di San Matteo (also known as the Ospedale di Lemmo), the other in the Oltrarno on the Costa San Giorgio. To differentiate between the two, the Oltrarno confraternity will be identified henceforth as the *buca* of San Girolamo Oltrarno, while the Lemmo confraternity will be identified simply as the *buca* of San Girolamo. See Sebregondi, *Tre confraternite*, *passim*. There was a third confraternity named after St Jerome, and it met at S. Maria Soprarno, but it was strictly a flagellant confraternity, not a *buca*; see Henderson, *Piety and Charity* (1994), 457n73.

8 'Fra l'altro disse ... esser egli stato il Promotore quivi della devozione verso l'Arcangelo Raffaele, et uno dei fondatori della Compagnia sotto la di lui invocazione detta la Scala ... Dette notizie disse averle ricavate da un manoscritto esistente nella libreria dei RR. PP. di Santa Maria Novella e da altri manoscritti da esso trovati nel far l'istoria della chiesa di S. Felicita.' ACSG, Deliberazioni e Partiti 1723–51, f. 868.

9 Brocchi, 3:203.

10 Bisticci, 83.

11 Del Migliore, 'Registro,' BNCF, MS Magliab. XXV, cod. 418, p. 111. Monti, 1:183, bases himself on Del Migliore.

12 Del Migliore, 'Registro,' BNCF, MS Magliab. XXV, cod. 418, p. 35. See another similar description by Del Migliore in BNCF, MS Magliab VIII, cod. 1500, fasc. 11, f. 4v–5r, included in an untitled copy of the 1478 statutes of the confraternity of San Marco. Del Migliore's statement that the parent confraternity had been meeting in the church of S. Maria de' Servi, the SS. Annunziata, is incorrect and directly contradicts his statement a few lines later on the same page that it met in the convent of San Martino, also incorrect. Until 1496 the confraternity met in rooms belonging to the convent of San Marco, but then built themselves an oratory on land in via S. Gallo belonging to the convent.

The Silvestrini were a Benedictine congregation founded by St Silvestro Guzzolini (c.1177–1267) in 1231. They were evicted from the convent of San Marco by Pope Eugenius IV in 1436 in response to strong lobbying on behalf of the Dominicans by Cosimo de' Medici and St Antoninus, at that time vicar-general of the Observant Dominicans. The Dominicans were then granted possession of the building; see *Dizionario degli istituti di perfezione*, 8:1507–19.

13 In the *catasto* of 1427, Biagio di Lorenzo *cimatore* declares himself to be fifty years old, single, and resident, with his widowed sister-in-law and her three sons aged ten to sixteen, in a house in the parish of San Lorenzo, in via Larga (today's via Cavour), near San Marco; ASF, Catasto 79, Campioni del Quartiere di San Giovanni, Gonfalone Drago, 1427, f. 409v. I am indebted to dott.ssa Sebregondi for this reference.

14 ASF, Filze di Cancelleria, 1782, doc. 172; Del Migliore, 'Registro,' BNCF, MS Magliab. XXV, cod. 418, p. 35. For confraternity documents covering the years 1379–1785 see, at the ASF, Crs 1640–86 (*filze* 1677–80 are *alluvionate*, that is, destroyed or damaged by the flood of 1966). The original statutes of 1444 are now lost; those of 1478 are in BNCF, MS Magliab. VIII, cod. 1500, fasc. 11; those of 1781 are in AAF, Filze di Cancelleria, 1782, no. 171. See also AAF, Compagnie Religiose 03.10, 03.11. For the confraternity's loose association with the *buca* of San Girolamo see Sebregondi, *Tre confraternite*, 14–15. See also Richa, 5:329–37. Professor Lorenzo Polizzotto is currently preparing a monograph study on the Purificazione.

15 ASF, Crs 163.25/26, f. 72v.

16 'E questo si fe perché in più luoghi si esercitasse questa laudabile et charitativa opera.' BNCF, MS Magliab. VIII, cod. 1500.11, f. 4v. The same document indicates that the Arcangelo Raffaello donated to the new group an altarpiece and several other objects ('consegnandoci una tavola d'altare liberamente chon altre chose,' f. 4v). The document also reveals that the statutes were revised by Piero di Mariano Muzi starting on 29 June 1444 (f. 3v) and approved by Archbishop Antoninus on 3 April 1448 (f. 22r).

17 For confraternity records covering the years 1558–1785 see, at the ASF, Crs

1237–43 (*filze* 1238, 1240, 1242 are *alluvionate*). The *capitoli*, dated 1 July 1427, are at the BNCF, MS Magliab. XXXI, cod. 11 ff. 1–9. They were displayed in the exhibition *La Chiesa e la Città* and are described by Gilberto Aranci in the published catalogue, pp. 84–5, item 4.10. See also at the AAF, Compagnie Religiose 05.17, 05.18, and 05.19. Del Migliore gives brief descriptions of the confraternity in his 'Registro' at the BNCF, MS Magliab. XXV, cod. 418 f. 41 and MS Magliab. XXVI, cod. 137ff. There are brief published descriptions of the confraternity's early years in Uccelli, *Il convento*, 64–6; Del Lungo, 194–6; and Monti, 1:188–90. Monti's description should be read with caution, for it is based on secondary sources and confuses some of the evidence (such as Bruni's beneficiaries, see below). Also, his identification of this confraternity with the one meeting in 1409 outside Florence is tenuous at best. Trexler, in his 'Ritual in Florence,' 207n3, points out that Morçay, in his *Saint Antonin*, 91, is incorrect in identifying this company with the one founded in 1388.

18 Orlandi, *S. Antonino*, 2:211, with reference to ASF, Notarile di Jacopo di Ser Antonio di Jacopo da Romena, J. n. 7 (a. 1417–27) at date 1427 (the month and day are lacking in the document).

19 Capitoli, ff. 7v, 3r. 'Memorie dell'Origine e vicende della Compagnia, compra del luogo, interessi ecc. Testamenti e Legato Rucellai 1438–1765,' ASF, Crs 1579.3, fasc. A, f. 56r. The Latin original for the legal instrument of sale is in ASF, Notarile Antecosimiano 2532, Michele Benincasa, 1433–62, ff. 85r–86v.

20 ASF, Crs 1579.3, f. 57r. Note that Uccelli, *Il convento*, 65, and others follow the incorrect lead given in the above-mentioned document and claim that Bruni donated the site to the Vangelista.

21 ASF, Crs 1579.3b, f. 486v.

22 ASF, Crs 1579.3, fasc. A, f. 58v. For the disputes see ASF, Crs 1579.3 fasc. B, 'Compagnia e Compagnia di S. Gio. Evangelista. Controversie per la proprietà del luogo 1763–1782'; see also AAF, Compagnie VII.II.1; ASF, Fondo Mannelli-Galilei-Riccardi 439, 'Fogli attenenti alla Compagnia del Vangelista e alla *buca* di S. Paolo.' For the location of the oratorio on via dell'Acqua (now via Guelfa) see Uccelli, *Il convento*, 66–7 and Paatz, 5:397–8. The site was later folded into the Istituto di Sant'Agnese dell'Opera Pia del Bigallo. Documents on the early history of the Vangelista are contradictory and confusing. I gratefully acknowledge the help of dott.ssa Ludovica Sebregondi in keeping my bearings through this material.

23 Cionacci (1680), cited in Del Lungo, 194 and also in Sebregondi, 'Lorenzo de' Medici,' 337.

24 See, among others, Eisenbichler, 'Confraternities and Carnival,' 128–39.

25 A 1752 note lists some of the major performances in the confraternity's *teatro*; AAF, Compagnie VII.II.1. For a detailed description of the stage set for a 1589

performance in the Vangelista's lawn in honour of Grand Duke Ferdinando's wedding, see Eisenbichler, 'Spazi e luoghi,' 51–62.

26 The confraternity is still extant, and its documents are kept in its own archive on site. See the authoritative work by Sebregondi Fiorentini, *La compagnia e l'oratorio di San Niccolò del Ceppo*, from which I draw my information.

27 ASF, Cap. Crs 752, 'Capitoli 1560,' f. 1r. See also Del Migliore, 'Registro,' BNCF, MS Magliab. XXV, cod. 418, p. 111.

28 See below, ch. 15.

29 For a discussion of all these activities, see below, chs. 15–20.

30 Ambrogio Traversari, 'Epistola xix,' in *Latinae epistolae*, 2:40; English translation from Trexler, 'Ritual in Florence,' 209.

31 Traversari, 'Epistola xxxi,' in *Latinae epistolae*, 2:136–7; English translation from Trexler, 'Ritual in Florence,' 209 (NB, Trexler's page reference to Traversari is incorrect). An Italian translation is found in Garin, 304.

32 See below, ch. 3, for a description of the site.

33 'l'anno 1430 per una rapresentazione della Natività del Signore che alcuni di quei giovanetti recitarono in S. Pancrazio alla presentia di Papa Eugenio 4 e di tutta la Signoria con aplauso grandissimo, se ne passarono col favore di quel Pontefice, a cui piacque grandemente la vivezza di quella gioventù veduta in quell'atto, ad abitare in una semplice chiesa dell'ospedale della Scala aprovando i Capitoli, ne' quali volse che la Compagnia militasse sotto nome della Natività del Signore et havesse per avocato l'Angiol Raffaello.' Del Migliore, 'Registro,' BNCF, MS Magliab. XXV, cod. 418, p. 111.

34 The bull is found in ASF, Diplomatico, Patrimonio Ecclesiastico di Firenze, 1442 giugno 24. It was displayed and commented in the exhibition 'La Chiesa e la città a Firenze nel XV secolo'; see the exhibition catalogue, 82–4. The bull is transcribed in Puccinelli, 310–11; and mentioned in Calzolai, *Frate Antonio Pierozzi*, 83ff., and others.

Fifteenth- to seventeenth-century transcriptions or résumés of the bull can be found in the papers of the pertinent confraternities: see ASF, Crs 164.36, ff. 9 seqq., and ASF, Crs 164.37, p. 13 in the papers of the Arcangelo Raffaello; see BNCF, Conventi Soppressi D.3.270, ff. 35r–36v, for a version appended to the statutes of San Niccolò del Ceppo.

35 Franchi, a monk from San Niccolò del Lido di Venezia, was abbot of the Badia from August 1440 to April 1444; see Puccinelli, 40.

Emilio Sanesi gives the name of the Blessed Gomes of Lisbon and says that the papal bull 'fixed' Gomes and Antoninus in their role as overseers for the appointments of guardian fathers of youth confraternities (*La vita di S. Antonino*, 97–8), but the information is incorrect because Gomes was abbot only until 1439 and then, after a few months at Santa Maria degl'Angeli, left Florence permanently for Portugal; see *La Chiesa e la Città*, 6.1 and 6.10. On the Blessed Gomes of Lisbon see *Dictionnaire d'histoire et de géographie ecclésiastiques*, 21:528–31.

36 Mode, 68, with reference back to Calzolai, *Frate Antonino Pierozzi*, 83ff.

37 Henderson, 'Piety and Charity' (1983), 26 and 393–432.

38 For the documents of the confraternity of the Annunciazione e Sant'Antonio da Padova see, at the ASF, Crs 134–7 (covering the years 1593–1785). Its 1715 statutes are in AAF, Compagnie Religiose Capitoli, 04.29. See also AAF, Compagnie Religiose 05.21 for a 1633 sentence on its continual questions with the *buca* of San Girolamo.

39 Artusi and Patruno, in their popularizing volume *Deo gratias*, 168, advance an amusing interpretation for the two epithets, saying that the black confraternal gowns worn by the youths made them look like 'birds of evil omen' with a particular tendency to loud gossip. I am not at all convinced by this, mainly because youth confraternities wore white, not black gowns. For similar jocular (and slightly irreverent) popular names given to confraternities because of some aspect of their iconology, consider the *Orciuolo* ('the jug'), given to the Compagnia di Santa Maria Annunziata in San Felice on account of the vase with a lily often included in depictions of the Annunciation, or *la Colomba* ('the dove'), given to the Compagnia dello Spirito Santo in the church of Santo Spirito because of the dove of the Holy Spirit in its emblem.

40 ASF, Crs 134.1, f. 7r–v. See also the description of the confraternity's history in Baccini.

41 For the documents of San Bernardino e Santa Caterina see, at the ASF, Crs 254–5 (covering the years 1588–1785) and Cap. Crs 839. There are also two *dichiarazioni* in AAF, Compagnie Religiose 04.06 and 04.07, dated 1678 and 1690 respectively.

42 ASF, Crs 254.2, f. 1v; see also ASF, Carte Strozziane III serie, vol. 233, f. 8v. When, in 1638, the Cistercians moved to the Oltrarno, their new church became known as 'Cestello Nuovo'; see Richa, 1:307–13, and Paatz, 4:90–1.

The *buca* of Sant'Antonio Abate was founded in 1438. Its 1502 statutes are at the Biblioteca Riccardiana, Manoscritti 1748, and were displayed in the 1980 exhibition 'La comunità cristiana fiorentina e toscana nella dialettica religiosa del Cinquecento,' Chiesa di S. Stefano al Ponte; see the published catalogue by the same title, entry 171.

43 The confraternity is first mentioned in the 1454 processional list (see below, ch. 11, p. 168). It is mentioned in Manni, 1:56–7; Paatz, 1:406; Trexler, 'Ritual in Florence,' 208–9; and Henderson, *Piety and Charity* (1994), 450, item 30. I have not been able to locate archival materials from this confraternity.

44 For confraternity documents covering the years 1558–1784 see, at the ASF, Compagnie Soppresse incamerate nel Bigallo, Compagnia della Dottrina dell'Assunta e S. Alberto dei Fanciulli detta del SS. Crocifisso e S. Alberto

Bianco. There are also a few documents in AAF, Compagnie Religiose 02.10, 03.15, and 03.16 from 1630(?), 1485–1635, and 1499 respectively. An entry for Santa Maria del Carmine in ASF, Crs 113.18, f. 127v notes that it was founded on 13 October 1419 and met 'nel cimitero del detto convento, nel canto di duo muri dietro al luogo ove si raguna la compagnia di Santa Agnesa.' I thank Nerida Newbigin for offering me this last item, previously unknown to me. One must be careful not to confuse this confraternity with the flagellant adult confraternity of Sant'Alberto Nero, also known as della Morte or dell'Ossa. In his *Piety and Charity* (1994), 444, Henderson distinguishes between a youth confraternity of Sant'Alberto and a flagellant confraternity of Sant'Alberto Bianco, but they are in fact one and the same thing.

45 Tordi, 2–3; Eisenbichler, 'The Religious Drama of Giovan Maria Cecchi,' appendix IV, 250–3; Henderson, *Piety and Charity* (1994), 447, item 17.

46 Grazzini, 2:134–5.

47 Varchi, 1:591 (bk. 9, ch. 36). Eventually the number of youth confraternities rose to twelve in all, with the addition of the confraternities of San Francesco in S. Pietro Scheraggio, San Salvatore in Ognissanti, and the Gesù in San Frediano. These later youth confraternities are mentioned in an undated manuscript at the Biblioteca Riccardiana, MS Morelli, 287; in Poccianti; and in Giamboni.

48 See below, ch. 13 for a discussion of the religious aspects of these processions, and ch. 16 for a discussion of their theatrical aspect.

49 AAF, Compagnie VII.II.1, fasc. 2, doc. 2, f.n.n.

50 There are several copies of the 1454 procession list. See the 'Regole di frati come vanno a processione secondo la nota del vescovo Antonino come mi dette Baccio Falsamonstra,' ASF, Signoria e Balia, Carte di Corredo 45, f. 18v; Forti, 'Il foro fiorentino,' ASF, Manoscritti 197, pp. 509–13 and again in Manoscritti 199, pp. 123–4; British Library, Additional MSS. 28, 178, ff. 170v–171r. John Henderson gives an English resumé of this document in his thesis, 'Piety and Charity,' (1983), 433–4. A list of 1510 echoes the same sequence: 'Innocenti 1a, S. Bastiano 2a, S. Jacopo 3a, S. Alberto 4a, S. Bernardino 5a, S. Giorgio 6a, S. Giovanni Evangelista 7a, Purificazione 8a.' AAF, Compagnie VI[1], insert 'Compagnie'; see also Sebregondi, 'Religious Furnishings,' 158n55.

51 Sebregondi, 'Religious Furnishings,' 150 and 157–8n55.

## Chapter 3

1 Del Migliore, 'Zibaldone,' BNCF, MS Magliab. XXV, cod. 418, p. 111. See above, ch. 2, p. 25, n. 11.

2 For a history, floor plans, and views of the Ospedale di San Paolo see Gold-

thwaite and Rearick, 221–306. See also Henderson, 'The Hospitals of Late-Medieval Florence.'

3 ASF, Catasto 76, Campioni 1427, Santa Maria Novella, Lion rosso, f. 353r–v. The Buonavolti registered at that house in the 1427 Catasto are M.a Mattea, widow of Bartolomeo Buonavolti, aged sixty-three, her sons Marco aged forty-two, Alessandro aged forty, Bastiano aged thirty-six, Giovanni aged twenty, and her grandson Bartolomeo di Bastiano aged three.

4 On the church of San Pancrazio, see Dezzi Bardeschi.

5 In his description of the founding of the confraternity of San Marco, Del Migliore gives two contradictory indications within the same page, suggesting that in 1427, between the San Pancrazio and Scala accommodations, the Arcangelo Raffaello met either in the church of Santa Maria dei Servi or in the convent of San Martino. Neither of these indications seems to be a reliable reference. The first site, Santa Maria dei Servi – that is, the church of SS. Annunziata – is where the confraternity of San Marco moved once it was founded – and this leads me to believe that Del Migliore momentarily confused his references and his syntax. The second location, the convent of San Martino, is clearly an anachronistic misnomer for the quarters Pope Eugenius IV gave the confraternity next to the Ospedale della Scala, a site which, after 1530, became known as the convent of San Martino from the name of the nuns who came to occupy it at that time. Both sites, therefore, are suspect. Since Del Migliore does not mention these locations again and no other document makes reference to them, they are clearly a slip of the pen on his part and, therefore, should not be given credence.

6 Carlo di Tommaso Strozzi says that the youths purchased the convent in 1427, and that it was then taken away from them in 1447 and given to the Servites; ASF, Carte Strozziane, ser. 3, vol. 233, f. 3v. I have not been able to confirm such a purchase, or subsequent loss. Richa, 5:273, says that the convent of San Silvestro, belonging to the Benedictine Order, was closed by Pope Eugenius IV in 1435 and its occupants transferred to the convent of Sant'Agata. This convent is not to be confused with the convent of San Silvestro in Borgo Pinti, founded in 1539 and occupied until 1808 by Benedictine Silvestrine nuns; see Fantozzi Micali and Roselli, 248–9.

7 'Inventario 1591,' ASF, Crs 164.36/38, f. 11r, which gives the date of the bull as 24 April 1435. The 'Inventario 1690,' ASF, Crs 164.37, p. 16, gives the date as 23 April 1435.

8 'Instrumento ... che testifica del possesso del luogo appresso lo Spedale della Scala datoli dall'abbate del monasterio di S. Salvi' in 'Inventario 1591,' ASF, Crs 164.36/38, f. 11r. See also 'Inventario 1690,' ASF, Crs 164.37, p. 16.

9 'una certa particella d'orto contiguo al loro luogo, purché li fratelli assegnino tanto in beni stabili allo Spedale della Scala che li renda ogn'anno due fiorini di

oro o più,' in 'Inventario 1591,' ASF, Crs 164.36/38, f. 11r and 'Inventario 1690,' ASF, Crs 164.37, p. 16.

10 AAF, Compagnie VII.II.1, fasc. 2, doc. 1. The document is a transcription made by dom Ambrogio di Marchionne, a monk at the Badia, on 9 January 1492/3 from a *quadernuccio* of Antonio di Mariano Muzi, begun on 4 July 1440 and continuing to 5 February 1445/6.

11 'domandavasi detto luogo per quelli che erano già pervenuti alla mezana età di 19 o venti anni per separarsi da quelli che stavano appresso lo Spedale di S.ta Maria della Scala.' See 'Inventario 1591,' ASF, Crs 164.36/38, f. 10r; 'Inventario 1690,' ASF, Crs 164.37, p. 15. The site was acquired shortly thereafter. An affidavit of 8 August 1442 claims that the abbot of San Salvi had, in fact, given it to the confraternity of the Archangel Raphael. See 'Inventario 1591,' ASF, Crs 164.36/38, f. 10v and 'Inventario 1690,' ASF, Crs 164.37, p. 16. Another bull of 11 December 1442 gives instructions on how to pay the annual rent of two pounds of wax; 'Inventario 1591,' ASF, Crs 164.36/38, f. 10v and 'Inventario 1690,' ASF, Crs 164.37, p. 15.

12 The convent eventually changed its name to S. Anna dei Funari (that, is *falegnami*, carpenters). It survived to the end of the nineteenth century, when it was demolished (1887). See Hvelsen, 340–1.

13 Terpstra, 30–1.

14 See Fantozzi Micali and Roselli, 210, for a floor plan and a cross-section of the site when it belonged to the nuns of San Martino. The original drawings are at the Archivio e Museo di Firenze Com'Era.

15 A colour drawing of the monogram is found at the BNCF, Priorista di Luca Chiari, 1630.

16 Cirri, 'Sepoltuario,' BNCF, MS Cirri, vol. 9, pp. 4597 and in particular 4599, where he says that the Ospedale functioned until the fall of the republic, when it was eventually annexed to the Innocenti. Before being transferred, however, it had temporarily moved across the street into a palazzo belonging, in 1919, to the Biondani. The final amalgamation with the Innocenti occurred in the wake of Pope Paul III's approval, dated 17 September 1535. See also Richa, 3:327–51; Passerini, *Storia degli stabilimenti di beneficenza*, 675–85; Paatz, 4:133–47. For the Innocenti and the question of foundlings in late-medieval and Renaissance Florence, see Gavitt. See also Carocci, *San Martino*.

17 The palazzo, which apparently had belonged to Cione, comprised the block formed by via dei Banchi, the Trebbio, via del Moro (which at that time was called Tana dell'Orso), and the via del Sole. Its western side constituted the south-east border of the piazza. BNCF, MS Cirri, 'Sepoltuario,' 9:4597.

Ademollo points out that Cione Pollini was not a *ciabattino* (shoemaker), but a member of the Arte della Lana and even one of its consuls in 1308. He also mentions several Pollini who held important posts in the republic and grand duchy. See Ademollo, 3:840–2.

18 AAF, Compagnie religiose, VII.II.2. The document was displayed in the exhibition *La Chiesa e la Città* and then reproduced and described in the published catalogue, item 4.11, p. 85.

19 With an annual income of more than two hundred ducats, Malatesta Sacramoro (d. 1511) was one of the wealthiest canons at the Duomo. His conversion to Savonarolan ideals and transfer to the Dominicans of San Marco was one of the several stunning conversions of those years. Sacramoro's faith in Savonarola was such that on 2 April 1498 he even signed a deposition declaring he was ready 'to enter into the fire,' that is, to undergo the trial by fire scheduled for 7 April in Piazza della Signoria to prove the righteousness of Savonarola's cause. Shortly thereafter, however, Sacramoro's devotion to the cause underwent a drastic change. When the Florentine mob attacked the convent of San Marco, Sacramoro was one of the key persons who convinced Savonarola to hand himself over to Florentine justice. Then, during the friar's trial, Sacramoro sided with the prosecution. For this reversal he was subsequently described as the Judas of San Marco (Luschino, 87). In 1508 Sacramoro asked to be, and was, transferred to the Dominican convent in Rimini, his native town, where he eventually became prior. He later became prior of the convent in Parma. See Schnitzer, *passim*; pseudo-Burlamacchi, 147, 149; Ridolfi, *Vita di Girolamo Savonarola*, *passim*; Vaglienti, 49, 53.

20 On 5 June 1497 Vespucci abandoned his rich prebend as *proposto* of the cathedral to enter the Dominican convent of San Marco in yet another astonishing conversion to the Savonarolan movement in those years. Vespucci was a man of such high moral standards that he was known as 'the mirror of Florentine piety and probity' (Bandini, *Vita*, 10). He died in 1514 in the convent of San Domenico di Fiesole. His rare collection of Greek and Latin codices, many with his own marginalia, was subsequently dispersed into the libraries of the Opera di Santa Maria del Fiore, the Laurenziana, and the convent of San Marco.

On Vespucci's conversion and possible involvement in the posthumous cult of Savonarola see Trexler, 'Lorenzo de' Medici and Savonarola,' 304–5. See also Bandini, *Vita*, 10; pseudo-Burlamacchi, 93; Ridolfi, *Vita*, 1:192 and *Life*, 127; Weinstein, 243n46. See the 'Chronica conventi Sancti Marci de Florentia,' Laur., MS Biblioteca S. Marco, 370, f. 98v for a description of Vespucci's profession in San Marco and a brief character sketch.

21 ASF, Crs 155.1/3, fasc. B, f.n.n. 3r–v.

22 The other contributors were Guglielmo di Stefano, Sandro di Bartolomeo di Berto, Geri di Zanobi del Testa Girolami, Guglielmo di Francesco *merciaio*, Guglielmo di Stefano di Ser Guglielmo, Francesco *biadaiuolo*, Piero di Filippo,

Girolamo di Giuliano, and Guido di Ser Giovanni da Pistoia. ASF, Crs 155.1/3, fasc. B., f.n.n. 3r–v.

23 The cost for the addition was one large golden florin, paid on 26 October 1495; see ASF, Crs 155.1/3, fasc. B, f.n.n.; see also the document in AAF, Compagnie religiose, VII.II.2, described by Gilberto Aranci in *La Chiesa e la Città*, 85, item 4.11. Ademollo, 3:841, says that twenty thousand victims of the plague of 1479 were buried in a *piazzetta* adjacent to what later became the chapel of the nuns of San Martino. For a summary of information on the plague of 1477–9 that infested not only Florence but much of Italy, see Corradi, 313–26.

## Chapter 4

1 For the congregation of Santa Giustina da Padova and the Florentine Badia see *La Chiesa e la Città*, 106–8.
2 Bisticci, 10–12.
3 On Antoninus see Maccarani; Morçay; Tinalli; Calzolai's many articles in the journal *Sant'Antonino nel V Centenario della morte* (1958–60); and more recently Peterson.
4 See Calzolai, 'S. Antonino e le "buche"'; Sebregondi, *Tre confraternite*, 13.
5 Tinalli, 44.
6 Del Migliore, 'Istorie,' BNCF, MS Magliab. VIII, cod. 1500, fasc. 11, f. 4v; published in Morçay, 473–4, doc. 71; partly cited in *Nuovo corpus*, 32–3n5. Sanesi, *La vita di S. Antonino*, 100, adds that Antoninus approved the statutes of San Giovanni Evangelista in 1449 and those of San Niccolò del Ceppo in 1450.
7 ASF, Cap. Crs 882. See below, ch. 8 pp. 90–104 for a discussion of these statutes.
8 Richa, 5:332.
9 Hatfield, 138.
10 Centi, 1:74, citing Calzolai, *Frate Antonino Pierozzi*, 79.
11 Del Migliore, 'Istorie,' BNCF, MS Magliab. VIII, cod. 1500, fasc. 11, f. 3v.
12 The original copy is in BNCF, MS Magliab. XXXI, cod. 11. It was displayed in the exhibition 'La chiesa e la città' (Florence, Sotterranei di San Lorenzo, 6 June–6 September 1992) and described by Gilberto Aranci in the exhibition catalogue *La chiesa e la città*, 84, item 4:10. As don Aranci points out, this is the earliest original of a youth confraternity's statutes in Florence.
13 AAF, Compagnie, VII.II. 1, f.n.n. 1r: 'le costituzioni, che furono distese successivamente per regolare le pratiche, ed esercizi di detto pio istituto, si vedono firmate di propria mano dal detto Glorioso Servo di Dio [St Antoninus] nel dì 29 Aprile dell'anno 1451 = e si conservano tutt'ora nell'Archivio di detta Compagnia colla dovuta venerazione.' See also Richa, 5:332.

14 Spinillo, 6, referring back to Richa.

15 Centi, 74. Spinillo, 6, gives the following printing history for the volume in the fifteenth century: 1473 Venezia, 1479 Venezia, 1483 Venezia and Roma, 1479 Venezia, 1483 Venezia, 1485 Milano, 1486 Roma, 1446 [*sic*] 2 eds. Roma, 1491 Roma, 1493 Roma, 1500 Roma.

16 Tacchi and Venturi, *Storia della Compagnia di Gesù in Italia* (1910), 279, cited in *La chiesa e la città*, 78.

17 Aranci summarizing P. Braido, *Lineamenti di storia della catechesi e dei catechismi. Dal 'tempo delle riforme' all'età degli imperialismi (1450–1870)* (Torino, 1991), 28–9, in *La chiesa e la città*, 78.

18 Sanesi, 'L'insegnamento della dottrina cristiana,' 18, cited and explicated by Aranci in *La chiesa e la città*, 78.

19 For all these observations, see the acute analysis by Aranci in *La chiesa e la città*, 77–8, to which I am much indebted.

20 Trexler, 'Episcopal Constitutions,' 248.

21 Del Migliore, 'Zibaldone, BNCF, MS Magliab. XXVI, cod. 137, p. 37; Monti, 1:184. See also below, ch. 6 pp. 000 for a discussion of vocations.

22 Del Migliore, 'Istorie,' BNCF, MS Magliab. VIII, cod. 1500, fasc. 11, f. 4v; published in Morçay, 473–4, doc. 71, where its location is given as 'Fiesole, Arch. di San Domenico'; partly cited in *Nuovo corpus*, 32–3n5. The *tavola* of Sts Cosmus and Damian appears in an inventory dated 1 March 1589/90 as 'Un quadro antico drentovi S.o Cosimo e S.o Damiano senza cornice,' ASF, Crs 1647.9, f. 330r. While this document gives the donation date as 29 June 1444, the confraternity statutes, on the other hand, give it as 1 July 1441; I have been unable to determine which is the correct date.

23 See, for example, ASF, Crs 1647.9, f. 1r (t.p. dated 1576).

24 Polizzotto, *The Elect Nation*, 337.

25 For the funeral procession see Trexler, *Public Life*, 458–9. For the Neri see Eisenbichler, 'Lorenzo de' Medici e la Congregazione dei Neri,' republished in English without appendices as 'Lorenzo de' Medici and the Confraternity of the Blacks in Florence.' For San Paolo see Weissman, 'Lorenzo de' Medici' (1993), 321–2.

26 For Medicean influence in Sant'Agnese see Newbigin 'Piety and Politics' (1994), 26–7; but see also the entire article for Lorenzo's interference in Florentine festive celebrations.

27 Weissman, 'Lorenzo de' Medici,' 315–16.

28 AAF, Compagnie VII.II.1, f.n.n. 1r–v.

29 'si faccia come addimando perocché nella detta Scuola usammo già assai tempo, sendo noi giovinetti e ci fummo quasi che allevati' (Del Lungo, 194) and again in Sebregondi, 'Lorenzo de' Medici,' 337. The source for Del Lungo's citation is

unclear; his text implies Cionacci's 1680 edition of Lorenzo de' Medici's *Poesie sacre*, but the closest reference I could locate in that volume is Cionacci's comment that Leo x 'quando Pontefice ritrovossi una volta in Firenze, fece alla detta Compagnia [del Vangelista] non so qual dimostrazione dell'affetto che fin da giovanetto le aveva, come de' fratelli, portato sempre' (col. 16). Perhaps Del Lungo drew his information from documents he did not cite in his notes.

30 Eisenbichler, 'Confraternities and Carnival,' 128–139.

31 'Item quod comodentur usque in petia xx assium abietum et pianatas x Juliano Laurentii de Medicis pro festo celebrando in societate s. Joannis evangeliste,' Archivio del Duomo, Delib., 1486–91, f. 78v; published in Poggi, 2:204, entry 2406. I am grateful to Professor John Paoletti for generously giving me this reference, which is unknown in scholarship on Lorenzo's play, and also to Nerida Newbigin for her suggestions on this item.

32 'Item quod Laurentio Medici et cuiucumque eum reprehensentanti et eius nomine petenti comodentur omnia ligna expedientia pro festo sanctorum Joannis et Pauli et per deputatos per dictam operam retineatur computum clarum et diligens.' Archivio del Duomo, Delib., 1486–91, f. 79r; published in Poggi, 2:204, entry 2407.

33 See, along these lines, the similar conclusions reached by Weissman, 'Lorenzo de' Medici,' 324: 'under Lorenzo it seemed better to patronize, influence and coopt [confraternities] for one's own purposes than to suppress them. Indeed, rather than maintaining authority by suppressing Florence's lay brotherhood, there is even the possibility that Lorenzo's authority was reinforced in 1471 during a crucial moment in his political ascendency, through his own participation and those of his allies in the Confraternity of San Paolo.'

34 See Trexler's perceptive remarks on Savonarola and his reform of the youth of the city in his 'Ritual in Florence,' 250–2. See also Schnitzer, esp. ch. 14, 'Savonarola e i fanciulli,' 305–21, 372–7; and, more recently, Polizzotto, *The Elect Nation*, 39–40, 123–7.

35 Trexler, 'Ritual in Florence,' 250–1, basing himself on Villani, Landucci, Nardi, Benivieni, and the pseudo-Burlamacchi, among others.

36 The following description is drawn mostly from the pseudo-Burlamacchi, *Vita del beato Ieronimo Savonarola*, 121–4. See also Polizzotto, *The Elect Nation*, 123–7.

37 Pseudo-Burlamacchi, 123.

38 Schnitzer, 311.

39 Pseudo-Burlamacchi, 123–4. For a similar description see Girolamo da Empoli, 'Vita di Giovanni da Empoli,' in da Empoli, 22–3.

40 Trexler, 'Ritual in Florence,' 253–4.

41 Schnitzer, 316.

42 Polizzotto, 'Confraternities, Conventicles,' 249–50.
43 Passerini, *Storia degli stabilimenti*, 192.
44 Girolamo da Empoli, 'La vita di Giovanni da Empoli,' 22; republished in Spallanzani, 99; the passage is cited in Trexler, 'Ritual in Florence,' 253, and Aranci in *La chiesa e la città*, 84.
45 Pseudo-Burlamacchi, 119. See also Schnitzer, 306–9; Ridolfi, *Vita di Girolamo Savonarola*, 229, with references to Nardi.
46 Pseudo-Burlamacchi, 119.
47 Pseudo-Burlamacchi, 120 and then 135–6. Even Schnitzer failed to see the contradiction inherent in this; see his *Savonarola*, 315–18, 376. On battles with stones see Niccoli.
48 Pseudo-Burlamacchi, 135, sets the event in the context of the Carnival 1498 procession for the burning of the vanities. Schnitzer, 376, dates the event instead to Palm Sunday, 27 March 1496.
49 Pseudo-Burlamacchi, 135–6 and then again in the appendix 'Trattato de' miracoli di fra Girolamo Savonarola,' 235–6.
50 Pseudo-Burlamacchi, 125–7.
51 Trexler, 'Ritual in Florence,' 254–5. The anti-Savonarolan preacher cited by Trexler was the Augustinian Gregorio da Perugia, raging against the Savonarola reform from the pulpit of Santo Spirito. See also Polizzotto, 'Confraternities, Conventicles,' 249–50.
52 See Polizzotto, 'Confraternities, Conventicles,' 250–4. See also his 'When Saints Fall Out,' and Trexler, *Public Life*, 11.
53 For a discussion of this turbulent half-century in the life of Florentine confraternities, see Weissman, *Ritual Brotherhood*, 137–79, and Polizzotto, 'Confraternities, Conventicles,' 237–58.
54 ASF, Provvisioni, Registri 109, ff. 160v–162v. See Mehus, 136–63 (see also ch. 21, below, where this work is discussed at length); Polizzotto, 'Confraternities, Conventicles,' 238–40. There were subsequent bans in 1426, 1443, 1455, and 1458.
55 See Weissman, 'Lorenzo de' Medici,' 316–17. Note, also, that Weissman points out that 'Despite a history of prohibition against confraternal activity by the Florentine political class, the *veduti* and their kinsmen continued to participate and did so in great numbers' (320).
56 ASF, Provvisioni, Registri 185, f. 6v and ASF, Provvisioni, Registri 186, f. 91v. See Polizzotto, 'Confraternities, Conventicles,' 247–8. These closures lasted only a few months; the *buca* of San Girolamo, for example, reopened on 4 April 1495; see ACSG 'Memorie,' f. 13; cited by Sebregondi, *Tre confraternite*, 5, 69.
57 ASF, Otto di Guardia e Balia, Epoca Repubblicana, Registro 223, Minute di Bandi, ff. 26r. See Weissman, *Ritual Brotherhood*, 177–80, and Polizzotto, 'Confraternities, Conventicles,' 251. This closure lasted just over a year; the

*buca* of San Girolamo, for example, reopened on 25 November 1514; see ACSG, Deliberationi e Partiti 1500–62, ff. 60v, 63r; cited by Sebregondi, *Tre confraternite*, 5, 69.

58 ASF, Otto di Guardia e Balia, Epoca Repubblicana, Registro 205, f. 2r. See Polizzotto, 'Confraternities, Conventicles,' 251–2. The length of this closure varied from confraternity to confraternity. While in the case of Santa Maria della Croce al Tempio it lasted about sixteen months (the confraternity reopened on 18 October 1528; ASF, Crs 1646.8, f. 279v), in the case of the *buca* of San Girolamo it continued, for a variety of other reasons, for fifteen years; ACSG, Deliberationi e Partiti 1500–1562, f. 112v, cited and discussed by Sebregondi, *Tre confraternite*, 5.

59 Del Migliore, 'Zibaldone,' BNCF, MS Magliab. XXV, fasc. 409, pp. 59–65. See also BNCF, MS Cirri, 'Sepoltuario,' 9:4599.

## Chapter 5

1 In a 1527(?) document, the convent of San Martino 'fuori la porta al Prato' was described as containing fifty *monache velate* and six *servigiale e fattoressa*; BNCF, MS N.A. 987 'Descrizione dei Quattro Quartieri [di Firenze],' f.n.n. 20r.

2 Del Migliore, 'Concessione dello Spedale di Santa Maria della Scala fatta alle monache di San Martino al Prato per il reverendo Giovanni degli Stazi Commissario Apostolico con il consenso della famiglia de Pollini fondatori di esso,' BNCF, MS Magliab. XXV, cod. 409, pp. 59–65. Del Migliore notes that he copied the document on 23 April 1672 from a Latin original in the possession of the nuns of San Martino dated 21 March 1530/1 and notarized by Ser Giovanni di Zenobi di Bartolo di Vannucci. Together with the transcription Del Migliore also includes Pope Clement VII's letter of instruction to Giovanni Stasi dated 4 November 1530.

3 See the convent floor plan in Paatz, 3:693. Del Migliore, 'Registro,' BNCF, MS Magliab. XXV, cod. 418, pp. 411–12; F.M. Biliotti, 'Chronica pulcherrimae aedis magnique coenobii S. Mariae cognomento Novellae Florentinae civitatis, a.d. 1586,' SMN, MS Bilioctus, pp. 126–8 – I wish to thank at this point Fr I.P. Grossi, OP, for his kindness in allowing me to read and cite from his transcription of this manuscript. Domenico Ducci, OP, 'Istorie del convento di Santa Maria Novella e delle Compagnie poste nei chiostri del Santo Convento,' BNCF, MS Conv. Sopp. B.9.432, ff. 13–14r, lists and briefly describes the confraternities that met in Santa Maria Novella; the manuscript is dated 1691. Similar descriptions are found in 'Notizie storiche sopra le Compagnie di secolari, che si adunano nel Convento di S. Maria Novella' in 'Memorie del convento, chiesa e confraternite di Santa

Maria Novella,' BNCF, MS Baldovinetti 124, f.n.n. 1r. Among several published sources, see especially Fineschi, xxii.

4 BNCF, MS N.A. 987 'Descrizione dei Quattro Quartieri [di Firenze],' f.n.n. 1r. The document, unfortunately, does not give any membership figures for the confraternity of the Arcangelo Raffaello, still residing at the Scala, probably because it was composed of youths, not adults. The catalogue entry for the manuscript dates it to the first half of the sixteenth century; on the basis of internal evidence, John Henderson dates it to 1527. Given that the three confraternities in question were decimated by the 1527 plague, Henderson's suggestion must certainly be taken as a *terminus ad quem*. For Ducci's comment, see his 'Istorie del convento di Santa Maria Novella,' BNCF, MS Conv. Sopp. B.9.432, ff. 13v–14r.

5 'Concessione delli huominj della Compagnia dello Spirito Santo et particolari fatta alla nostra Compagnia,' ASF, Crs 155.1/3, fasc. A, ff.n.n. 14r–15v; a copy precedes it on ff.n.n. 7v–8v. For the agreement with the Compagnia di San Vincenzo, see ASF, Crs 155.1/3, fasc. A, ff.n.n. 10r–12v, which includes the signatures of thirty-eight surviving members of San Vincenzo.

6 See the contract dated 6 February 1541/2, drawn up by Ser Giovanbattista di Lorenzo di Giordano; copies in ASF, Crs 155.1/3, ff.n.n. 18r–24v, dated 17 February 1541/2; ASF, Crs 160.6/7, ff. 109r–114v; ASF, Crs 160.8/9, ff. 21r–22v at date 23 April 1563 (2-page resumé in Italian). See also SMN, MS Bilioctus, pp. 127–8, and BNCF, MS II.IV.374, 'Raccolta cavata dal Sen.re Carlo Strozzi ...'

7 ASF, Crs 155.1/3, fasc. B, f.n.n.; loose leaf inserted into the volume at this point bearing the title 'Inventario di maseritie della compagnia di S.to Vincentio' on one side, and listing, on the reverse side, 'La reliquia di S.to vincentio / La croce di S.to vincentio / La tavola di S.to vincentio / La tavola dello Sp.to S.to / E cori di S.to vincentio e dello Sp.to S.to / El sopalcho della conpagnia di S.to Vincentio / E paramenti bianchi a fior d'oro e altre robe auta dalla donna di Guasparre Rucellai / Vesta della compagnia presso a' frati / Libri, leggii, usci, seramenti, pietre sacrate, calici, deschi, cataletti, tele dipinti / E altre cose atenenti a detta compagnia.' I am grateful to dott.ssa Ludovica Sebregondi and dott.ssa Raffaella Zaccaria for their assistance in transcribing this short but difficult document.

8 In 1572, the *scrivano* records that the Ospedale owed the youths the sum of 3 *lire* yearly from as far back as 25 March 1526 for a total of 138 *lire* outstanding; ASF, Crs 160.8/9, f.n.n. 24v at date 22 March 1572/3.

9 ASF, Crs 160.7/8, f.n.n. 24r at date 22 March 1572/3; receipts for such payments are in ASF, Crs 157.3/5 and ASF, Crs 158.48 *passim*.

10 ASF, Crs 155.1/3, fasc. A, doc. 1 dated 12 June 1533; ASF, Crs 164.36/38, f. 11v; ASF, Crs 164.37, p. 16.

11 'Notizie storiche sopra le Compagnie di Secolari, che si adunano nel Convento

di S.M. Novella,' in 'Memorie del Convento, Chiesa e Confraternite di Santa Maria Novella,' BNCF, MS Baldovinetti 124, f. 2r. The escutcheons are in an advanced state of neglect but still visible on the capitals of the pillars, some bearing the inverted dove of the Holy Spirit, others the acronym M DPT VK.

12 The map is found in many publications and posters. A copy is published in Mori and Boffito, facing p. xxiv. The actual oratory and rooms of the confraternity of San Benedetto Bianco stood next to the east wall of the church, in the corner formed by the nave and the east transept. They were demolished in 1866.

13 For slavish imitations, see the illustrations in Mori and Boffito, including an eighteenth-century view published in Amsterdam; Ferdinando Ruggeri's map of 1731; and Francesco Magnelli and Cosimo Zocchi's map of 1783.

14 The fresco is published in *Palazzo Ruspoli*, 191. I gratefully thank dott. Ludovica Sebregondi for discovering the reference that the fresco is in Rome; its photograph at the Kunsthistorisches Institut in Florence places it incorrectly in the Sala di Gualdrada, Palazzo Vecchio, obviously confusing it with the *Game of Soccer* fresco mentioned in n. 19 below.

15 Cristofano Allori (?), *View of Piazza Santa Maria Novella*, ca. 1608 (Paris, Louvre, Dép. des Arts Graphiques, inv. 33). Published in Thiem, ill. 94, with *scheda* on pp. 332–5 and in *Firenze e la sua immagine*, 90, with *scheda* on pp. 89–90. Thiem dates the drawing to 1608, since only one of the two obelisks erected that year is shown and seems to be attracting the attention of a small group of persons around it as if it were a novelty.

16 In January 1570 the door to the confraternity and the overhanging roof above it, which had collapsed because of celebrations held on the square, were restored. ASF, Crs 160.6/7, ff. 15v–16v.

17 ASF, Crs 160.8/9 and Crs 162.21/22 f. 186v at date 8 September 1595; Laur., MS Antinori 155, 'Alcune notizie delle chiese fiorentine,' f. 8v. See also Leoncini, 313. On Michelangelo Cinganelli (ca. 1558–1635), see *DBI*, 25:589–90; Thieme-Becker, 6:607; and Colnaghi, 74.

18 ASF, Crs 160.7/8, f. 22v at date 8 April 1566. Giuseppe Zocchi's 1744 engraving of the piazza during the 'Corsa dei cocchi' clearly shows spectators sitting on the rooftops (including on the roof of the confraternity's building), and shows that some had even brought along, and raised, what today we could call 'beach' umbrellas; see *Firenze e la sua immagine* 142.

19 School of Vasari, *The Game of Soccer in the Piazza S. Maria Novella* (Firenze, Palazzo Vecchio, Sala di Gualdrada). The image is attributed to Giovanni Stradano in Bucci and Bencini, ill. 1 facing p. 6.

20 ASF, Crs 160.8/9 at date 8 September 1595.

21 Laur., MS Antinori 155, 'Alcune notizie delle chiese fiorentine,' f. 8v.

22 For Ciocchi, see the entry in the *DBI*, 25:656. For Tarchi, see the entry in

Bolaffi, 11:20–1. Thieme-Becker has extremely brief notes on them at 6:611–12 for Ciocchi and 32:442 for Tarchi. See also the similar image by Giuseppe Zocchi from his *Scelta di* XXIV *vedute ... della città di Firenze* (1744), reproduced in *Firenze e la sua immagine*, 142.

23 *Veduta della Piazza di S.a Maria Novella.* First published in Richa, vol. 3, facing p. vi; and then in Fineschi, *S. Maria Novella*, ill. 3; and more recently in *Firenze e la sua immagine*, ill. 22.

24 The Bardi printers were active in Florence ca. 1804–51. Lorenzo himself was active ca. 1804.

25 Some readers may find it of interest that a plaque on the façade of the Hotel Minerva recalls that Henry Wadsworth Longfellow (1807–82) resided there and identifies him as an American poet, translator of the *Divine Comedy.*

26 The five-window width of the Arcangelo Raffaello building is corroborated by Giuseppe Ciocchi's 1755 engraving; see ill. 4.

27 For a visual idea of how the internal spaces of the Arcangelo Raffaello might have been arranged, one could look at the floor plan and cross-section of the confraternity of the Purificazione published in Hill, 'Oratory Music in Florence, III,' 134–5, based on drawings dated 5 July 1774 and kept in ASF, Crs 1641, fasc. E. Similarly, one could glance at the floor plan of the 'Oratorio and adjoining rooms of the Company of San Girolamo and San Francesco Poverino' from the Sepoltuario Cirri in BNCF, MS Cirri, 'Sepoltuario,' 4:2103, published in Sebregondi, *Tre confraternite*, fig. 6; or, from the same publication, fig. 36, the floor plan of the original site of the confraternity of San Francesco Poverino in via San Zanobi, from Archivio Storico del Comune di Firenze, MS 5013, 61.

28 SMN, MS Bilioctus, pp. 126–8. The portrait of the saint is no longer visible. The acronym on the escutcheons, on the other hand, is barely visible on the second and third columns of that corridor. I have been unable to expand the acronym. In the few years I have dedicated to this study, the condition of the capitals and escutcheons in this cloister has deteriorated *a vista d'occhio.*

29 SMN, MS Bilioctus, pp. 126–8; BNCF, MS Conv. Sopp. B.9.432, Ducci 'Istorie del convento di S. Maria Novella,' ff. 13r–15r; BNCF, MS Baldovinetti 124, ff.n.n. 1r–2r, 8r; Fineschi, xxi–xxii.

30 ASF, Crs 155.1/3, fasc. A, ff.n.n. 4r–v; ASF, Crs 164.36/38, f. 11v; ASF, Crs 164.37.

31 SMN, MS Bilioctus, p. 35: 'cum quatuor illa oratoria de patrum gratia, et confirmatione Clementis septimi et Pauli tertii summorum pontificum archangeli Raffaelis accepisset societas, multis deiectis parietibus, ex quatuor illis oratoriis hanc unam, quam certe insignem cernimus, sibi erexit habitationem, et suae congregationis locum, quem satis commodum, satiaque decorum reddidit.'

32 At least one of the tombs was moved as late as 1580; see the agreement allowing the confraternity to move at its own expense a tomb (*sepolcro*) from besides the

confraternity's door and place it on the sides, with the others; the agreement is dated 18 December 1580, but the copy in ASF, Crs 162.21/22 f. 28v is at date 24 April 1583.

33 ASF, Crs 155.1/3, fasc. A, ff.n.n. 5r–v. Fr Lorenzo di Filippo Strozzi was a friar at Santa Maria Novella.

34 'Inventario ... 1690,' ASF, Crs 164.37

35 Current location unknown. Listed in the 1690 inventory (ASF, Crs 164.37, p. 1) and in the 1784 official inventory compiled by the grand-ducal authorities ('Sopra la porta della Compagnia un quadro rappresentante un Angelo che presenta a Nostra Signora un fanciullo in veste da Compagnia con varie figure di mano dell'Empoli,' ASF, Patr. Eccl. 43, fasc. 32, pp. 1–2). Richa, 3:108, attributes it incorrectly to Francesco Curradi, and is followed in this by Paatz, 3:757 (who, however, locates it in the oratory), but the documents cited above do not support such an attribution.

36 Painted in 1654 and donated by Agnolo and Alessandro Galli to the confraternity. Currently on loan to NATO headquarters (Brussels) from the Uffizi (Deposits), Florence, Inv. 1890 no. 7612. Published in Cantelli, ill. 365; for a photograph of the painting before its recent restoration, see *La città degli Uffizi*, 229. See also *Il Seicento fiorentino. Biografie* (1987), 89–90, and Clarice Innocenti.

37 Currently in the Museo di San Marco, Florence, Inv. 1890, no. 2115, with provenance indicated as 'Dalla Compagnia della Scala in Firenze.' For the records of the gift, see ASF, Crs 160.8/9 at date 28 July 1647 and ASF, Crs 163.25/26, f. 76r. Also mentioned in Laur., MS Antinori 155, f. 8v. Published in Sricchia, fig. 65.

For Lorenzo Lippi see the entries in Thieme-Becker, 23:274 and Bolaffi, 6:446–7. For recent work on him see in particular Sricchia, 242–70 and ills. 39–68; D'Afflitto, 'Precisazioni,' 61–76. Lorenzo di Giovanni Lippi paid his entrance fee to the Arcangelo Raffaello on 25 September 1616 (ASF, Crs 165.40/48, f. 116).

38 Cambiagi, *L'antiquario fiorentino*, 146.

39 The *Pietà* is already listed in a 1583 inventory, where it is described as 'una sconficcatione in una tavola sopra la porta dello stanzone'; ASF, Crs 155.1/3, fasc. B, ff.n.n. 60r–63r, 'Inventario di robbe spettanti alla Compagnia dell'Agnolo Raffaello fattosi al tempo del Guardiano Messer Antonio Pasci questo dì 25 d'Aprile 1583.' In a 1591 inventory it is properly identified as a *Pietà* and described as a 'tavola di legniame' measuring 4 *braccia*; 'Inventario ... 1591,' ASF, Crs 164.36/38. The 1784 grand-ducal inventory lists it as 'Sopra la porta della Piazza una tavola dipintovi la Pietà con varie figure di maniera antica.' ASF, Patr. Eccl. 43, fasc. 32, p. 1.

40 One *braccio*, the standard Florentine unit of measure, was 0.589 metres in length.

41 The *paliotto* seems not to have survived, probably because it was already in a bad physical state in 1785. In fact, the inventory drawn up at the time of the sup-

pression describes it as 'ben lacero'; 'Filza I degli Stati delle Soppresse Compagnie Riunite al Patrimonio Ecclesiastico di Firenze, Loro Giustificazioni annesse,' ASF, Patr. Eccl. 43, fasc. 323, f. 7r.

42 The *ricordi* mention that Jacopo Ferretti 'fece ridorare il segno nostro che quando andiamo a processione portiamo, cioè del Archangelo Raffaello il quale era tutto stinto.' ASF, Crs 160.6/8 before 23 June 1559.

43 The *segno* was painted and then restored by Jacopo Ferretti. The *ricordi* describe it as 'un quadro di tela con cornice entrovi un Cristo in forma d'ortolano quando apparse alla Magdalena il quale quadro fu similmente fatto da lui [Jacopo Ferretti] più tempo fa, et al prexente fu restauto e rinovato.' ASF, Crs 160.6/8, f. 19r–v at date 25 March 1560.

44 The current location of all these works is unknown.

45 Laur., MS Antinori 155, 'Alcune notizie delle chiese fiorentine,' f. 8v.

46 For a similar brief discussion of these factors as they applied to the oratories of Roman confraternities see O'Regan, 892.

47 ASF, Crs 162.23/24, ff. 188v–189r. Alberto Del Vivaio had been elected *sopraintendente della musica* the previous 26 May 1641; ASF, Crs 162.23/24, f. 183v. Del Vivaio died on 23 November 1659.

48 Currently in the Museo del Convento di San Marco, Florence. Inv. 1890 no. 8681, with provenance indicated as 'Dal convento di San Marco in Firenze' and dated 1622. See also 'Inventario ... 1690,' ASF, Crs 164.37, p. 28 and ASF, Patr. Eccl. 43, fasc. 32, p. 12. Richa, 3:108, attributes the painting incorrectly to Carlo Dolci and is followed in this by Paatz, 3:758; the documents cited above, however, contradict this attribution.

49 Domenico Torsi, 'Descrizione dell'esequie fatte nella morte del Signor Jacopo Corsi nella Compagnia dell'Arcangelo Raffaello, 1603,' MS in the library of the villa Corsi-Salviati, ff. n.n. [41v–42r], cited in parts in Carter, 'Music and Patronage,' 93n34. I have been unable to identify the artist who painted the fresco of the Trinity, but perhaps it may be Michelangelo Cinganelli, who had earlier painted the confraternity's ceiling and the outside façade (Del Migliore, 'Registro,' BNCF, MS Magliab. XXV, cod. 418, p. 412). Much later, in 1647, Bartolomeo Neri, also known as 'il Poeta a piedi,' did some 'pitture d'ornato' around the high altar (ASF, Crs 160.8/9 at date 8 September 1647; ASF, Crs 163.25/26, f. 77r; Laur., MS Antinori 155, 'Alcune notizie delle chiese fiorentine,' f. 8v.

50 The youths attributed the work to Domenico Ghirlandaio, and as such it is entered in the confraternity inventories. The 1583 and 1591 inventories identify the Dominican saint as St Vincent, while the 1690 and 1784 inventories identify him as St Dominic. The Madonna and Child panel is currently in the Jarves Collection, Yale University Art Gallery, New Haven, while the two lateral panels each depicting two singing angels each are one in the Church of the Advent, Boston, the other at the Museum of Fine Arts, Boston. The angels have been

published in Everett Fahy, Jr, 'Some Later Works of Piero di Cosimo,' *Gazzette des Beaux Arts* 65 (1965), 206–7, 210–12 (where the author gives the dimensions of each painting as 34.5 in. x 25.25 in.); Mina Bacci, *Piero di Cosimo* (Milano: Bramante, 1966), 102–3, ill. 52, 52a. All three panels are published in Mina Bacci, *L'opera completa di Piero di Cosimo* (Milano: Rizzoli, 1976), 97–8, ills. 57–9. Venturini, 60–7, identifies the three Boston panels as coming from the confraternity of the Arcangelo Raffaello. See also Padoa, 15–16.

51 Current location unknown. For the painter Pietro Dandini (1646–1712), see Thieme-Becker, 8:346.

52 Present location unknown. The work is documented from as early as the 1583 inventory, where it is described as 'un quadro dentrovi la visione di Jacob,' ASF, Crs 155.1/3, fasc. B, ff.n.n.

53 For Bernardino Poccetti (1548–1612), see Thieme-Becker, 27:166–77; Bolaffi, 9:142–5.

54 For three fine illustrations of bas-relief, silver-framed *paci*, see *La Chiesa e la Città*, 190–3.

55 The current location of these works is unknown.

56 The sixteen canvases were all of similar size (4 × 3 *braccia* each). Their current location is unknown.

57 Current location for all these works is unknown.

58 Weissman, *Ritual Brotherhood*, ch. 5.

## Chapter 6

1 'L'anno 1556 si cominciano i Ricordi di nostra Compagnia da Zanobi di Piero Buonavolti per commissione speciale del nostro P. Correttore e del nostro P. Guardiano. In dì 29 novembre, prima domenica del santo Avvento. Correttore Fra David. Guardiano Antonio di Giovanni cuoiaio.' ASF, Crs 160.6/7, f.n.n. 21r.

2 Villani, *Cronica*, bk. 11, ch. 1, pp. 178–86. For contemporary descriptions of the 1333 and 1557 floods, as well as photographs and descriptions of the 1966 flood, see Nencini.

3 My translation from Aiazzi, 16. Giovan Battista Adriani was also professor of rhetoric at the Studio in Florence, a member of the Accademia fiorentina, and eventually official historiographer to Grand Duke Cosimo I. He composed an *Istoria de' suoi tempi* (Firenze: Giunti, 1583) that covers specifically the years 1537–74; for a brief analysis of this work, see Diaz, 219–25.

4 Agnolo d'Agnolo Brunelleschi paid for the copying, and Bartolommeo Traballesi for the illustration of the Nativity scene in the middle. ASF, Crs 160.8/9, f. 18v at date 23 June 1560. Bartolomeo Traballesi (d. 1585) worked on the *Studiolo* of the Grand Duke Francesco I and for the confraternity of the Nun-

ziata; see the entry in Bolaffi, 11:142. The Capitoli of the confraternity of San Niccolò del Ceppo were also destroyed in this flood; see Sebregondi Fiorentini, *La compagnia e l'oratorio di San Niccolò del Ceppo*, 5.

5 ASF, Crs 160.6/7 f. 8r at date 13 May 1558.

6 ASF, Crs 160.6/7, f. 27r.

7 ASF, Crs 160.6/7, ff. 15v–16v.

8 ASF, Crs 160.6/7, f. 19r–v at date 25 March 1560.

9 ASF, Crs 160.6/7, f. 30r.

10 ASF, Crs 160.8/9 at date 18 August 1561 and ASF, Crs 160.6/7, f. 34.

11 ASF, Crs 160.6/7, f. 49v; ASF, Crs 160.8/9 at date 27 January 1563. The painting of St Vincent was in fact by Piero di Cosimo. It was later moved to the sacristy and is now in the Jarvis Collection of the Yale University Art Gallery. Its two lateral panels depicting angels are respectively at the Church of the Advent in Boston and at the Boston Art Gallery.

The current location of the anonymous painting of the Virgin with St Mary Magdalene and the Nativity remains unknown. The 1690 inventory describes it as a Madonna with confraternity youths kneeling under her mantle (held open by two angels), with St Mary Magdalene at one side (supported by angels), the Nativity on the other side, and a frieze underneath with stories from the book of Tobit; see ASF, Crs 164.37, p. 43.

12 A short inventory of these *masserizie* is found in ASF, Crs 160.7/8, ff. 14r–v. For the Compagnia di San Bartolommeo detta della Capanna, which met in the Cerchi chapel in the Franciscan church of Santa Croce as early as 1439, see Henderson, *Piety and Charity* (1994), 450; Hall, *Renovation*, 164; Moisè, 426–7.

13 ASF, Crs 155.1/3, fasc. B, doc. 12, for the fundraising proposal and the promissory notes from prospective donors.

14 ASF, Crs 155.1/3, fasc. A, ff.n.n. 29r–32r at date 29 July 1573; the agreement is notarized by Antonio di Giovanni Antonio del Grasso. See also the 'Contratto della Compagnia della Scala per conto del trattare con i Mazzinghi confinanti a detta Compagnia di 26 luglio 1573 rogato da Angiolo di Ser Lorenzo Favilla' in Marucell. Cod. A.147. In the 1561 census the Mazzinghi are listed as owning two houses adjacent to the confraternity, and their household is described as consisting of thirteen persons (six males, seven females); ASF, Decima Granducale 3782, 'Descrizione del Quartiere di Santa Maria Novella, 1561.' Coincidentally, for the same census, the convent of Santa Maria Novella, next door to the confraternity, claims to house seventy-six *bocche*, all male.

15 Both lists are in ASF, Crs 164.36/38.

16 Enrolment calculations for the Compagnia di San Marco are based on figures reported in ASF, Crs 1647.9 ff.n.n. for the years 1580–93 and ASF, Crs 1647.10 for the years 1594–1620.

17 For the creation and purpose of *stretta* subgroups within confraternities, see Christopher Black, 88–9; Terpstra, esp. 28–30, 63–5, 124–5, 139–45.
18 ASF, Cap. Crs 752, f. 13r–v, ch. xiv, 'Della uscita et dipartenza de' fratelli.'
19 ASF, Crs 155.1/3, fasc. F, ff.n.n. at date 2 April 1581.
20 See above, ch. 3, p. 36. See also ASF, Crs 164.36/38, f. 10r and Crs 164.37.
21 ASF, Crs 160.6/7, f. 21r–v at date April 1560.
22 For the Neri, see 'Notizia della Compagnia dei Neri di Firenze, e catalogo dei condannati ai quali la Compagnia prestava la suprema assistenza,' in BNCF, MS ii.iv.377, ff. 180–7; Passerini, *Storia degli stabilimenti di beneficenza*, 482–96; Uccelli, *Della compagnia di S. Maria della Croce al Tempio*; Cappelli, *La Compagnia dei Neri*; and, more recently, Eisenbichler, 'Lorenzo de' Medici e la Congregazione dei Neri nella Compagnia della Croce al Tempio' and 'Lorenzo de' Medici and the Confraternity of the Blacks in Florence.'
23 For the 'Compagnia della santissima Trinita comunemente detta la tornata segreta della Compagnia della Purificazione della gloriosa vergine Maria e San Zanobi detta di S. Marco,' see ASF, Crs 1647.9, ff. 365r–368v, which lists the names of members enrolled in it from 6 May 1576 to 8 May 1594. The volume, begun by Giovangualberto di Girolamo Pagoli in 1579, has a vellum cover decorated with a coloured drawing by an unknown artist depicting the Trinity (Christ on the cross, God the Father with a papal tiara behind him, the dove of the Holy Spirit hovering near Christ's left ear, and below them the globe of the earth).
24 Youths enrolling in the *tornata segreta* in 1577–1584, for example, range in age from 14 to 30, with an average age of 17.6 years. Later, in the 1590s, a few new members are significantly older than the rest (for example, Vincenzo di Giovanni Giraldi is 50 years old, Giovanbattista Giuliani is 52, Alamanno Fontani is 34), but they are clearly exceptions and are probably enrolled merely as honorary members (ASF, Crs 1647.10, ff. 31r–34r).
25 ASF, Crs 1647.10, f. 27r.
26 ASF, Crs 134.6/7, f. 38r at date 15 October 1747. For the 1709 group, see ASF, Crs 135.7/8, f. 24r at date 14 April 1709.
27 ASF, Crs 160.8/9 at date 1 November 1583; ASF, Crs 160.6/7, f. 37; detailed description in ASF, Crs 162.21/22, f. 37r. Valerio Monaldeschi della Corbara was nuncio in Florence from February 1582 to April 1586.
28 Archbishop Giuseppe Donzelli was nuncio in Florence from May 1586 to April 1587.
29 Bull of Pope Gregory XIII dated 5 April 1585 and valid for ten years; ASF, Crs 162.21/22, f. 61r.
30 ASF, Crs 160.8/9 at dates 2 June 1585 and following; ASF, Crs 162.21/22, ff. 63r–v, 65v, 68v–69r.

31 For the choir stalls, see ASF, Crs 162.21/22, ff. 78v and 81r. For the façade and ceiling, see ASF, Crs 160.8/9 and ASF, Crs 162.21/22, ff. 185v and 196r at dates 8 September 1595 and 25 December1596 respectively, and Leoncini, 313. In the confraternity records Baccio Comi is credited with paying the expenses for both works (ASF, Crs 162.21/22, ff. 185v, 196r); Del Migliore, on the other hand, claims that Agnolo Galli paid for Cinganelli's work ('Registro,' BNCF, MS Magliab. XXV, cod. 418, p. 412). I have been unable to substantiate his claim.

For Michelagnolo di Giovanni Cinganelli (ca.1558–1635), see *DBI*, 25:589–90; Colnaghi, 74; and Thieme-Becker, 6:607. For Benedetto Cinganelli, see *DBI*, 25:589, where Michelagnolo's entry reports that Benedetto, his son, joined the Accademia del disegno on 11 July 1618. Benedetto is not mentioned in either Colnaghi or Thieme-Becker.

32 ASF, Crs 160.8/9 at date 1 January 1588.

33 ASF, Crs 162.22/23, f. 229v at date 31 December 1625.

34 Alessandro Marzi Medici (d. 1630) had served as canon at the Duomo and then bishop of Fiesole (1596–1605), before finally being made archbishop of Florence (1605–30). He is listed in the documents of the Arcangelo Raffaello as one of the novices accepted on 23 May 1566, and a later marginal note identifies him as 'Arcivescovo di Firenze'; ASF, Crs 160.7/8 f. xxiii$^{v}$.

Francesco Maria Machiavelli (d. 1653) was titular Latin patriarch of Constantinople, bishop of Ferrara, and then elevated to the cardinalate in 1641 by Pope Urban VIII. He appears in the confraternity records at ASF, Crs 160.8/9 at date 21 December 1641 and Crs 162.23/24 f. 190r.

Baccio Aldobrandini (1613–65) was made a cardinal-priest by Pope Innocent X in 1652. He appears in the confraternity records at ASF, Crs 160.8/9 at date 21 February 1652 and ASF, Crs 163.25/26, f. 125r.

Alamanno Salviati (1668–1733) was apostolic prothonotary, nuncio to France (1707), vice-legate to Avignon (1711), legate to Urbino (1717), and then was made a cardinal by Pope Benedict XIII in 1730. The confraternity recited an Office for the Dead for him on 8 March 1732/3; ASF, Crs 163.30/31, p. 251.

35 Bishop Buonaccorsi celebrated Mass in the confraternity on 30 November 1645; ASF, Crs 163.25/26, f. 56r.

Lorenzo Della Robbia had been a canon at the Duomo, bishop of Cortona (1628), and finally bishop of Fiesole (1634), where he is remembered for having built a seminary (Ammirato, *Vescovi*, 60). The confraternity celebrated his obsequies on 28 January 1645; ASF, Crs 163.24/25, f. 43r.

36 Del Migliore, 'Zibaldone,' BNCF, MS Magliab. XXVI, fasc. 137, p. 37 (my translation); also cited by Monti, 184.

37 Polizzotto, 'Confraternities, Conventicles, and Political Dissent,' 250, drawing his statistics from ASF, Crs 1646.1, ff. 160r–165r.

38 Five of the others entered Santa Maria Novella, and one San Domenico in Fiesole. Of the other nine, three became Capuchin friars, two became monks at Santa Maria degli Angeli, and one each a canon regular of St Augustine, a monk at the Certosa, a friar at the Carmine, and a Jesuit at the Gesù in Rome. ASF, Crs 1647.9, f. 290r–v.

39 Of the other six, two became Capuchins, two joined the Scuole Pie del Pellegrino, one became a Jesuit, and one entered an unspecified order. ASF, Crs 1648.11, f. 92r–v. For the Scuole Pie, see Grendler, *Schooling*, 381–90.

40 Of the other three, one each entered the Badia, the convent of San Francesco, and an unspecified convent in Florence, which could, possibly, have been Santa Maria Novella itself. ASF, Crs 160.6/7, f.n.n.

41 ASF, Crs 134.2/3, ff. 2v–6v.

42 The case in Bologna was clearly different – Terpstra calculates that 'from the 1440s into the sixteenth century, only 18 (or 4.3%)' of the members of the local youth confraternity of San Girolamo became friars; see his *Lay Confraternities*, 42.

43 ASF, Crs 162.21/22, f. 33r; also mentioned in Hill, 'Oratory Music in Florence, I,' 111n13.

44 ASF, Crs 164.36/38, f. 64r for Filippo Bardi, f. 58v for Camillo Bardi, f. 70r for Giulio Caccini, 83v for Piero Strozzi; ASF Crs 165.40/48, f. 32r for Cosimo Bardi. All these are also noted in Hill 'Oratory Music in Florence, I,' 110n11.

45 For all these, see Hill, 'Oratory Music in Florence, I,' 111–12. See also Strainchamps, 'Marco da Gagliano' and 'Music in a Florentine Confraternity,' Burchi, 'Vita musicale,' and Carter, 'Music and Patronage.'

46 Cosimo di Lorenzo Rosselli replaced the recently deceased Lorenzo Vitelli, as an inventory of articles transferred from Vitelli's estate to Rosselli indicates; ASF, Crs 155.1/3, fasc. B, f.n.n., at date 9 March 1490. Antonio *miniatore* had been a member of the Compagnia della Vergine Maria, and needed a special permission from the father corrector of that group (who was also prior of San Marco) in order to accept the post; ASF, Crs 155.1/3, fasc. F, f.n.n., at date 19 February 1524.

47 ASF, Crs 160.8/9 at date 23 June 1560 and ASF, Crs 160.6/7, f. 25r for the Nativity; ASF, Crs 160.6/7, ff. 33v–34r at date 10 August 1561 for the terracotta. For the two brothers Bartolomeo di Mariano (d. 1585) and Francesco di Mariano Traballesi (1542–88), see their entries in Colnaghi, 263. I have not been able to identify Giovanbattista di Benedetto *scultore* in the standard reference works.

48 ASF, Crs 165.40/48, *passim*.

49 ASF, Crs 162.21/22, ff. 114v–115r at date 31 December 1589 and ff. 143v–144v at date 31 December 1591.

50 Cosimo II's sons enrolled and paid their fee as follows: Ferdinando and Gian-

carlo on 24 April 1612; Giovan Carlo, Mattias, Francesco, and Leopoldo on 19 August 1620. ASF, Crs 165.40/48, *passim*.

51 ASF, Crs 165.40/48, at dates. Sir Robert Dudley (1573–1639) was the son of Robert Dudley, earl of Leicester, and Lady Douglas Sheffield. He abandoned his second wife, Alice Leigh, and their five daughters in England and moved to Europe, eventually settling in Tuscany, where he entered the employ of Ferdinando I, Cosimo II, and Ferdinando II. The three Dudley boys listed as members of the Arcangelo Raffaello are by his third wife, Elizabeth Southwell (d. 1631), with whom he had eloped from England. On Robert Dudley, see Lee.

52 ASF, Crs 165.40/48.

## Chapter 7

1 For a discussion of bans against, and closures of, confraternities, see Polizzotto, 'Confraternities, Conventicles and Political Dissent,' 237–58.

2 There is no in-depth study of the transfer and the reforms, but see the brief comments by Grossi, 514–16, and Polizzotto, *The Elect Nation*, 443–4.

3 For a description of Cosimo's expulsion of the Dominicans from San Marco, and his subsequent feud with the pope, see Amati, and, more recently, Polizzotto, *The Elect Nation*, 432–7.

4 Fra Matteo Strozzi was twice prior of Santa Maria Novella (August 1556 to April 1562 and then again July 1571 to June 1573). See SMN, MS Bilioctus, p. 49r; Ricozzi, 317–18.

5 ASF, Crs 160.6/7, f. 1r. On fra Angiolo Bettini, a 'committed Savonarolan,' see Polizzotto, *The Elect Nation*, 410–12, 443–4. Some of Bettini's sermons are extant in manuscript and are so indicated by Polizzotto.

6 On fra Santi Cini, see Razzi, 284–5; Cistellini, 'San Filippo Neri,' 93–6; D'Addario, *passim*; Grossi, *passim*; *La comunità cristiana fiorentina*, 184–5. Apparently there is some biographical information in *Il Rosario* [subsequently renamed *Memorie domenicane*] (1902), 19, and in an anonymous untitled article in *Rassegna di ascetica e mistica* 26 (1975), 312–16, but I have been unable to locate either journal.

7 On the confraternity of San Tommaso d'Aquino, see Richa, 7:68–80; Passerini, *Storia degli stabilimenti di beneficenza*, 516–18; Paatz, 5:248–56; Cistellini, 'Una pagina di storia religiosa,' 191–4; *La comunità cristiana fiorentina*, 184–7, entry 175.

8 'Fra Santi Cini, Fiorentino, professo di S. Marco, padre di sufficienti lettere, e di singolar bontà, e divozione, predicò in Firenze, in Roma, in Napoli, e in altre molte Città con grandissimo frutto. Haveva dono particolare di Dio nel muovere i cuori, e indurre al pianto. E valeva molto nei colloquij privati, onde, e

colle prediche, e con quelli, indusse molti nobili giovanetti al servizio divino: e convertì molti peccatori alla buona vita. Era padre di molta astinenza, e di pochissimo sonno. Fondò in Firenze il divoto, e nobile Oratorio di San Tommaso d'Aquino. Fu priore a Fiesole, in Firenze, e altrove. Era humile, benigno, e insomma un gran servo di Dio, e fu mio maestro e Priore certo tempo. Passò a miglior vita divotissimamente, l'ottava di San Tommaso d'Aquino, l'anno 1570, e di sua età quarantesimosesto predicando nella quaresimo [*sic*] nel Duomo di Viterbo, e fu sepolto alla Madonna della quercia, con molte lacrime di quei suoi padri. Sia in gloria.' Razzi, 284–5.

9 On the painter Michele di Raffaello Delle Colombe (d. 1580), see his entry in *DBI*, 38:31–2, and Colnaghi, 76.

10 On Vittorio dell'Ancisa, see below, ch. 9, pp. 118–19.

11 De' Ricci recalls that, in 1574, Pierantonio di Pagnozzo Ridolfi was created a mounted knight ('huomo d'arme') by Cosimo I; see his *Cronica*, 13–14 and 13n2 for the editor's references to the two laws that set up this corps of one hundred mounted noblemen who thus enjoyed the right to bear arms, a number of tax exemptions, and a peacetime monthly salary of 7 *scudi*.

12 ASF, Crs 160.6/7, ff. 6r–7r.

13 ASF, Crs 160.6/7, ff. 10v–11r and ASF, Crs 160.8/9 at date 10 August 1560.

14 ASF, Crs 160.6/7, f.n.n.

15 In 1633 the confraternity even asked and received aggregation with the Theatine order; ASF, Crs 162.23/24, ff. 61r and 64r at dates 15 August 1633 and 8 December 1633.

16 See appendix 2 for a listing of father correctors and their years in office. Bolognese confraternities also alternated between Franciscan and Dominican priests 'in order to achieve their goal'; Terpstra, 47.

17 The records for the visitations in the city are lacking, and only those for parishes outside the city survive; for a brief listing of visitations see Calzolai, 'L'archivio arcivescovile fiorentino,' 180–1.

18 ASF, Crs 160.7/8, f. xxvii$^{r}$, at date 11 January 1572/3. For a brief biography and bibliography on Archbishop Antonio Altoviti (1521–73), see his entry in the *DBI*, 2:572–3.

19 ASF, Crs 160.7/8, f. xxviii$^{r}$ at date 1 March 1572/3, where he is described as a 'prete di Mons. Arcivechovo Antonio Altoviti d'età d'anni 28.'

20 While the other four entrants do not reappear in the records, Raffaello Gucci appears many times in the 1580s–90s, occasionally contributing financially and often participating in the musical life of the confraternity as an organist, clavicenbalist, singer, and music teacher. See the entries in ASF, Crs 162.21/22 *passim*; see also below, ch. 18.

21 The *ricordo* for 31 December 1625 states that during his visit to the confrater-

nity, Archbishop Pietro Niccolini fondly remembered that he had been enrolled in it in his youth and offered to assist it ('rammentò ancora che egli era ne' suoi primi anni stato in essa descritto, et che sendo stato figliolo di questa Santa Casa, et essendo hoggi Padre, e Pastore, ne conservava grata memoria, et particulare benevolenza, offerendosi in ogni bisogno con ogni cortesia et prontezza maggiore,' ASF, Crs 162.22/23, f. 229$^{v}$). Niccolini had entered the confraternity at the age of twelve on 1 January 1588, sponsored by Niccolò Antifassi; ASF Crs 160.8/9 f.n.n. and Crs 165.40/48 at date. He served as *sagrestano* (see at date 6 May 1590), *consigliere*, *ordinatore dei cori*, and had even recited an oration on Easter Sunday 1591; see ASF, Crs 160.8/9 at dates 12 September 1590, 6 January 1591, and 15 April 1591 respectively.

22 In subsequent years, Archbishop Niccolini continued to visit the confraternity to attend its ceremonies. His presence is recorded for 1636, 1640, 1643, 1644, 1645, and 1646. In the 1640s he was often accompanied by the Grand Duke Ferdinando II, the grand duke's uncle Don Lorenzo, and César de Bourbon, Duke of Vendôme.

23 See above, ch. 4, p. 47.

24 ASF, Cap. Crs 752, f.n.n. 21r. The statement is dated 12 February 1634/5. Archbishop Niccolini's signature appears on line 6, that of Giuseppe Barni on line 7. There are remnants of the red wax with the archiepiscopal seal below the signatures.

25 ASF, Crs 160.8/9 at dates; ASF, Crs 162.23/24, ff. 83r and 107r.

26 *Canons and Decrees of the Council of Trent*, 156–7 (session 22, 'Decree Concerning Reform,' rubrics 8–9).

27 *Etruria sacra*, 'Decreta Synod. II Prov. 1573,' Cap. 1, rubric 46, p. 162, and rubric 51, p. 164; Cap. 2, p. 165; Cap. 3, p. 165.

28 In 1645, for example, the confraternity noted that in the past year it had celebrated 698 Requiem Masses for deceased brothers; ASF, Crs 163.25/26, f. 55v at date 5 November 1645. Although there was some variance in the numbers, the average for the period 1642–58 was 462.6 Requiem Masses per year; ASF, Crs 163.25/26.

## Chapter 8

1 'sopra il palco nello Spogliatoio,' ASF, Crs 164.37, 'Inventari di arredi e mobili, 1690.'

2 They are now at the ASF, Cap. Crs 882. This item has been damaged in the 1557 and 1966 floods; its 1559–60 copy is also at the ASF (Cap. Crs 752), and transcribes the 1468 authorization, 'Giuliano vescovo di Citarea, vicario e suffragano del Rev.mo Arciveschovo di Firenze.' See also ASF, Crs 164.34, p. 259.

Giuliano di Antonio da Montelupo had been a Dominican at Santa Maria Novella since at least 1422. He served the convent as *procuratore* (1430, 1435), *sottopriore* (July 1431, April 1434), *infermiere* (1434), and *maestro de' novizi* (1437) before Pope Eugenius IV made him titular bishop of Cerigo (*Lat.* Citharea; 21 June 1439), just in time for Giuliano to be one of the signatories of the Act of Union between the Latin and Greek churches (6 July 1439). He served as vicar to several bishops. As vicar of Giovanni di Dietisalvi, bishop of Florence, Giuliano consecrated the oratory of the Compagnia di San Domenico nell'Orto, detta del Bechella (1467). See Orlandi, *Necrologio*, 2:315–17 and Meersseman, *Ordo*, 2:701–3.

3 'Un altro Libro di Capitoli coperti di corame nero stampato senza dorare, scritti in carta pecora e sono questi i primi originali che per la piena et inondazione dell'anno 1557 e 13 settembre si immollarono e guastaronsi talmente che più adoprar non si potevano; onde ne fu fatta la predetta copia con non ordinaria fatica d'alcuni fratelli di quei tempi,' ASF, Crs 164.37, pp. 12–13.

4 ASF, Cap. Crs 882. A typewritten note on the verso of the front cover says that on 12 August 1967 the volume was sent to a laboratory in Budapest to be restored and was returned in 1971.

5 ASF, Cap. Crs 882, f. 2r.

6 ASF, Cap. Crs 752.

7 ASF, Crs 160.7/8, f. 25r, at date 13 June 1560. The Nativity by Traballesi, which the records say 'sta in mezo il libro,' is no longer in the volume.

8 Brocchi, 203, and Maccarani, 45, both claim that St Antoninus himself had approved the confraternity's statutes, but this claim is not substantiated by the statutes themselves or by any other confraternity document. Chronologically, it would have been impossible for St Antoninus to approve the 1468 statutes, since he died in 1459, and we have no indication of the existence of any earlier version of the statutes which he could have approved *in vitam*.

9 See appendix 1 for a list of guardian fathers of the confraternity.

10 ASF, Crs 163.38/41, f. 7v; ASF, Crs 160.6/8, f.n.n. 38; *passim*. In the confraternity records the surname is sometimes given as Mutii, Muzzi, or Murzi.

11 Bisticci, 83; see above, ch. 2.

12 'Antonius marianus custos societatis sanctae Nativitatis domini nostri que congregatur apud hospitale sanctae mariae della scala de flor.' See Orlandi, *S. Antonino*, 2:314.

13 Antonio married Papera in 1442. ASF, Manoscritti 253, Lorenzo Maria Mariani, 'Priorista fiorentino,' vol. 6, f. 1473; ASF, Raccolta Ceramelli Papiani, fasc. 3326.

14 Two of Antonio's sons attained high public office when they were elected priors of Florence, Girolamo in 1478 and Mariano in 1488 and then again in 1513. ASF, Manoscritti 253, Mariani, 'Priorista' vol. 6, f. 1473.

15 Piero also had participated actively in the lay religious movement. In 1453 he had been guardian father of the youth confraternity of the Purificazione della Vergine e di San Zanobi detta di San Marco, founded in 1427 by a group of older youths from the confraternity of the Archangel Raphael (see above, p. 26). The notebook 'Debitori e Creditori' of the Compagnia di San Marco begins with the note: 'Questo libro è della chonpagnia di Piero di Mariano ... cittadino fiorentino, popolo di San Piero Maggiore' (ASF, Crs 1649.14, f.n.n.). In his daily life Piero had worked as a *borsaio* (ibid., f. 20). He composed a play on the prodigal son theme for the confraternity of the Purification entitled *Festa del vitel sagginato* and published in *Nuovo corpus*, 29–55. See also Sebregondi, *Tre confraternite*, 14 and 66.

16 ASF, Catasto 828, ff. 459r, 462r–463v.

17 'D'azzurro, e due scaglioni abbassati in capo da un compasso aperto dello stesso,' ASF, Raccolta Ceramelli Papiani, fasc. 3326; see also ASF, Manoscritti 253, Mariani, 'Priorista,' vol. 6, f. 1473.

18 ASF, Manoscritti 253, Mariani, 'Priorista,' vol. 6, f. 1473.

19 ASF, Raccolta Sebregondi, fasc. 3721. For further information on Antonio and his family, see also the 'Cittadinario Fiorentino. San Giovanni,' vol. 1, f. 92. The Notarile Antecosimiano does not seem to contain notarial documents pertaining to Antonio's career.

20 For archival items relating to Muzi's years in this position, see ASF, Archivio delle Tratte, 11 'Deliberazioni. 1482–1491,' 44 'Notizie Antiche,' 401 'Registro dello squittinio del 1484,' and 823 'Tratte. 1482 al 1485.'

21 ASF, Manoscritti 253, Mariani, 'Priorista,' vol. 6, f. 1473; ASF, Raccolta Sebregondi, fasc. 3721.

22 Muzi's experience in the Chancery dated back to at least February 1453 (Robert Black, 100). Poggio made him his 'principal coadjutor and vice-chancellor, ... charged by Poggio with minuting the meetings of the important advisory assembly, the *Pratica*, as well as with administering ambassadorial missions'; Robert Black, 89. With the collapse of Poggio's organization, Muzi became involved in the work of other sections within the Chancery (ibid., 90). For a comment and examination of Muzi's scribal hand, a chancery *bastarda*, see ibid., 155. See also Brown, *passim.*

23 Fubini, 89n216.

24 Robert Black, 171. In spite of Muzi's obviously important role in the Chancery during a particularly difficult period, there still is no scholarly study of his career and work. For passing references to Muzi's work in the Chancery, see Robert Black; Brown; Marzi; *Il notaio nella civiltà fiorentina*, items 86, 88, 91, 145.

25 The house was located in Borgo Ognissanti, in the parish of San Salvatore.

ASF, Crs 156.2/4, fasc. A 'Compagnia e eredità di Domenico Comi, 1604–1735'; ASF, Crs 160.9/10, 'Debitori e creditori della Compagnia dell'Arcangelo Raffaello,' where, from f. 18sin 'Lascio del S.r Domenico Comi'; ASF, Crs 160.11/12, 'Entrata e uscite e ricordi del Esequie di Baccio Comi'; and ASF, Crs 164.35/36, 'Carteggi per il legato Comi e memorie sopra il medesimo, 1646–1690.' Domenico Comi's will is in ASF, Notarile Moderno 5499, Andreini Andrea, 1601–5, Testamenti, ff. 84r–92r; the house and the conditions attached to it are mentioned on f. 87v: 'perché volse che detta Casa serva et debba servire perpetuamente di tempo in tempo per il guardiano di detta compagnia et case che alcuno de' Guardiani di detta compagnia non la volessi habitare, volse detto testore che egli la possa appigionare ad altri per quel tempo che durerà il suo Governo, et le pigioni di detta Casa liberamente appartenghino al detto Guardiano.'

26 ASF, Crs 161.18/19 f. 283v at date 19 March 1731/2. For the annuity paid to the Marquis Arnaldi, see ASF, Crs 161.18/19 at dates 4 October *passim*.

27 See below, ch. 16, pp. 205–7 for a fuller discussion of this event.

28 'imperò che non da lui ma da Dio per lui siamo governati et retti,' ASF, Cap. Crs 752, f. 15v.

29 See ASF, Cap. Crs 752, Ch. 17, 'Della autorità del Guardiano.'

30 See ASF, Cap. Crs 752, ch. 6, 'Degli uficiali che debba eleggere il Guardiano.' No *tavolette* once belonging to the confraternity of the Archangel Raphael have been located. The use of *tavolette* in the peace-giving ritual of standard confraternities is to be noted, for these objects have been examined to date primarily for their use in the comforting rituals of confraternities who assisted criminals condemned to death; see Edgerton, 'A Little Known "Purpose of Art"' and *Pictures and Punishment*, esp. ch. 5; Falvey, 'Early Italian Dramatic Traditions and Comforting Rituals'; Weisz. See also ills. 16, 17, 18, and 29 in *Crossing the Boundaries*.

31 The revised statutes of 1636 do devote a chapter to the father corrector; see below, pp. 105–8.

32 See appendix 2 for a listing of the confraternity's father correctors.

33 'da per se sottometendosi a l'ubidientia,' ASF, Crs 160.7/8, f. 1v, at date 1563.

34 ASF, Crs 162.21/22, f. 16v, at date 2 September 1582.

35 There is no description of this position in either the 1468 or the 1636 statutes.

36 The number of *ordinatori de' cori* varied from three (on 12 May 1563), to four (5 September 1563), to six (2 January 1564–1 May 1565), to eight (2 September 1565–1 January 1573).

37 See, for example, the lists of 28 December 1580, 7 January 1582 (adding the guardian, governor, and three counsellors to the list), 2 September 1584 (as before), 5 January 1586 (adding the guardian).

38 'nella badia di Firenze e in camera del padre Abate,' ASF, Crs 160.6/7 f. 50v at date 16 April 1563; also ASF, Crs 160.8/9 at date 16 April 1563.
39 ASF, Crs 160.8/9 at date 16 April 1563.
40 The 1636 statutes are extant in a copy at the ASF, Cap. Crs 627, and in another at the AAF, Compagnie Religiose. Capitoli, 02.27. In the following discussion I refer to the copy at the ASF.
41 See ASF, Cap. Crs 627, ch. 3.
42 ASF, Cap. Crs 752, ch. 14.
43 A similar change occurred in the confraternity of San Niccolò del Ceppo, which, though originally a youth confraternity, eventually became – and is today – a confraternity of adults. On San Niccolò, see Sebregondi Fiorentini, *La compagnia e l'oratorio di San Niccolò del Ceppo*.
44 Receipts in ASF, Crs 157.3/5 *passim*; accounts in ASF, Crs 160.9/10 *passim*.
45 In August 1629 the agreement was clearly not working well. The new father corrector, fra Giovan Domenico Bonsi, was instructed by his superiors not to celebrate Mass at the confraternity until the youths provided the convent with a priest who would celebrate in Santa Maria Novella. The youths refused to do so and temporarily hired another priest for their needs, paying him 1.6.8 *lire*; ASF, Crs 160.12/13, f. 61v.
46 The original in Latin is easy to understand, but not to translate. It runs as follows: 'Sancti Contrinio / Integritate Doctrinae, Morum elegantia, Innocentia Vitae / Homini non impari / Divique Praedicatorum Patriarche lectissimo filio / Qui dum huic Coetui moderator extitit / Quot Alumnos in Terris, Tot Angelos in Coelis / Archangelo Raphaeli consociare dignatus est / Filij Moerentes / Et Paradisi Scalam erigi precantes / Patri Optimo, pietatis iussu / vista persolvunt.' On fra Santi Contini see also the entry in Ricozzi, 291–2, entry 1077.
47 ASF, Crs 162.22/23, f. 138v at date 29 September 1626.
48 See below, ch. 14 for further discussion of the changes in lay preaching within confraternities.
49 See ASF, Crs 155.1/3, fasc. A, ff.n.n. 226r–239v; see also ASF, Crs 161.18/19, f. 283v. The agreement was notarized by Ser Silvestro Antonio dal Poggio; the representatives of the confraternity were the Balì Tommaso di Ottaviano de' Medici, 'uno dei Fratelli e Conservadori di detta Ven.le loro Compagnia,' the *provveditore* Gaetano di Cosimo Pasquali, and the *guardiano* Sigismondo Landini; ASF, Notarile moderno 22456, ff. 78r–80r, n. 51.
50 ASF, Crs 161.18/19, f. 243v.
51 See ASF, Crs 160 and 161 *passim*. The payments to the *maestri di musica* have been transcribed by Burchi in the appendix to his 'Musica e musicisti,' vol. 2, *passim*.

## Chapter 9

1 For a description of such 'fishing,' see, among others, Grendler, *Schooling*, 338.

2 ASF, Cap. Crs 752, pp. 10r–12r. The entrance fee set out in the 1468 statutes was either 12 *soldi* or a pound of wax candles, and in the 1650 statutes 2 *lire* and a candle; ASF, Cap. Crs 752, f. 10r and ASF, Cap. Crs 627, p. 34. I should add that neither set of statutes denies admission because of a *mestiere infamante*, though the careful scrutiny of background and behaviour outlined in the statutes may, in fact, have been sufficient to exclude any candidate who plied one of the 'disgraceful trades.'

3 ASF, Cap. Crs 624, p. 32.

4 ASF, Cap. Crs 752, chs. 10 and 13.

5 Henderson, *Piety and Charity* (1994), 49, referring back to Weissman, *Ritual Brotherhood* and to Trexler 'Ritual in Florence,' but neither Weissman or Trexler, as far as I can tell, actually makes such a blunt claim. Trexler, for example, summarizes some of the contemporary concerns about badly raised boys who were 'dandified by their mothers' and 'had lost their virginity by the time they reached age fifteen'; 'Ritual in Florence,' 237–8. More correctly, Goodich links heresy and sodomy and suggests that in Perugia the confraternity of the Virgin 'was founded as early as 1233 by Peter Martyr and was presumably early entrusted with the pursuit of sexual offenders and heretics' (82).

6 Rocke, 'Male Homosexuality,' 445.

7 Rocke, 'Male Homosexuality,' 445–6; see also his 'Il controllo dell'omosessualità' (1982), 88, 128–9.

8 Brackett, 283–4. See also Davidson, 85–91, 94–6.

9 Goodich, 84–5.

10 ASF, Crs 160.8/9 at date 11 January 1561/2.

11 ASF, Crs 160.6/7 at date 25 May 1562.

12 ASF, Crs 160.8/9 at date 2 June 1609. For a chart and study of expulsions from the confraternity of Gesù Pellegrino in 1334–69, see Henderson, *Piety and Charity* (1994), 135–40.

13 ASF, Cap. Crs 752, ff. 10r–11r, ch. 10, 'What one must do when someone wishes to join our company.'

14 ASF, Crs 160.6/7, ff. 24v–25r at date 13 June 1560 describes the gowns worn by the youths in the Arcangelo Raffaello during the Corpus Domini procession as 'the usual flagellant gowns ... and each of the brothers had on his right shoulder the sign of our school, that is, the sign of the Nativity of Jesus Christ in the manger between the ox and the ass under the shed, as our Statutes decree.' Other confraternities also wore their emblem on their right shoulder; see the 'figure of Our Lady' on the right shoulder of the gown of the Purificazione, as

decreed by their 1478 Statutes in 'Istorie,' BNCF, MS Magliab. VIII, cod. 1500, fasc. 11, f. 18v.

15 ASF, Cap. Crs 752, f. 11r, ch. 12.

16 ASF, Crs 160.7/8, f. xxviii$^{r}$ at date 1 March 1572/3. The only one that day to join the confraternity and perhaps to fit within the age limits was Raffaello di Carlo Federighi, 'd'anni 20 *in circha*' (emphasis added).

17 The appointments were as follows: *sagrestano* (May and September 1559, May 1563, May 1564), *governatore* (January 1560 and 1562, January 1563), *cerimoniere* (May 1569), *festaiuolo* for various events (June 1560, August 1561, May, and August 1562, December 1563, May 1564, March 1565), and *provveditore* (September 1560, January, May, and September 1561, January and May 1562, January 1563, May 1565, January and May 1566).

18 For his donations, see ASF, Crs 160.6/7, f. 22v at date 5 May 1560. For his yearly fee payments from 1563 to 1566, see ASF, Crs 160.7/8, *passim*. For his other contributions, see the confraternity's documents for the years 1558–68, *passim*.

19 ASF, Crs 160.6/7, f. 33v at date 5 August 1561 and f. 45r at date 10 August 1562. See also Marangoni, 52–3.

20 For further information on dell'Ancisa and his Ospedale, see Cistellini, 'Una pagina di storia religiosa,' 97–101; D'Addario, 48, 52–4; Marangoni; Sebregondi, *Ordo equestris*, 9–38.

21 Horowitz, 'A Jewish Youth Confraternity' 42; see also Trexler, 'Ritual in Florence,' 210 and 263.

22 Horowitz, 53.

23 Christopher Black, 133.

24 Barnes, 'Poor Relief,' 611.

25 Bisticci, 83.

26 Masi, 15–16. The word *drappo* indicates a fine cloth either of silk or wool.

27 Barnes, 'Religious Anxiety,' 398.

28 Bisticci, 330.

29 Del Migliore, 'Registro delle compagnie di Firenze,' BNCF, MS Magliab. XXV, cod. 418, p. 111.

30 Burchi, 'Vita musicale,' 12.

31 Weissman, *Ritual Brotherhood*; see especially ch. 5, aptly entitled 'The Courtiers of God.' For a similar process active in Bolognese confraternities, see Fanti, *La Chiesa e la Compagnia dei Poveri in Bologna*, *passim*, and Terpstra, 96–8, 125–6.

32 Weissman, 'Lorenzo de' Medici,' 318–19. Weissman's observation may shed light on Rocke's comment about suspicions of sodomy in the *buca*, as noted above.

33 For a similar discussion of this phenomenon and statistics, see above, ch. 6, pp. 81–2.
34 See the discussion below, ch. 20, pp. 294–7.
35 ASF, Cap. Crs 752, f. 12r–v, ch. 14, 'Della uscita et dipartenza de' fratelli.'
36 ASF, Cap. Crs 572, ff. 12r–13r.
37 Unlike English, Italian does not have a negative connotation of immaturity for the word 'green.' On the contrary, 'la verde età,' 'gli anni verdi,' and related expressions such as 'trovarsi negli anni verdi' all have positive connotations of strength and vigour.
38 ASF, Cap. Crs 752, f. 13r.

## Chapter 10

1 'Registro delle compagnie di Firenze,' BNCF, MS Magliab. XXV, cod. 418, p. 111.
2 Grendler, *Schooling*, 333; see also his 'The Schools of Christian Doctrine.' Albergati subsequently became bishop of Bologna (1375–1444).
3 Grendler, *Schooling*, 343–5, for the *Summario* in general, and 344 for the listing; 345–52 for the *Interrogatorio*. See also Turrini, 419, for a similar list of contents drawn from northern Italian catechisms of the sixteenth century.
4 ASF, Cap. Crs 627, p. xxxvi.
5 ASF, Crs 162.21/22, f. 288r at date 4 April 1610.
6 ASF, Crs 163.25/26 at dates for the teaching; at date 27 September 1643 for Lorenzo Vanni.
7 ASF, Crs 162.21/22, ff. 12v–13r at date 3 June 1582; see also below, ch. 16, pp. 205–7. The single sheet was probably a folio meant to be folded, sewn, and cut into a sedicesimo, much like the *Summario* booklets mentioned by Grendler, or hung in a readily visible place in the youth's home. See Turrini, 420–1, for the 'cartelloni murali,' which, as he explains, were 'large sheets on which the basic notions of Christian doctrine were printed' and which were then hung in schools 'where it was not possible to see to it that each student had his/her own catechism.'
8 ASF, Crs 162.21/22, f. 15r at date 3 June 1582.
9 Sorgenti, 263. On Ippolito Galantini, see the fundamental work by Aranci, *Formazione religiosa*; see also the entry in *Bibliotheca Sanctorum* 5:1355–6; for early biographies, see Dionisio Baldocci Nigetti. Sorgenti's *Vita del B. Ippolito Galantini* (Rome, 1825) has been translated anonymously into English as *The Lives of St Joseph Calasanctius, founder of the Pious schools, and of the Blessed Ippolito Galantini, founder of the Congregation of Christian Doctrine*; for his beatification, see *Florentina beatificationis et canonizationis Ven. servi Dei Hippolyti Galantini Congregationis doctrinae christinae fundatoris* (Romae: Ex

typographia Reverendae Camerae Apostolicae, 1821). See also Richa, 4:75–86; Sanesi, 'L'insegnamento religioso'; Del Campana; D'Addario, 45–7, 290–301; *La comunità cristiana*, 120–9.

On the Vanchetoni (or Bacchetoni), see Paatz, 2:131–7. It seems that the name 'Vanchetoni' derived from their modest manner of walking (*van chetoni*, 'they proceed silently'), and 'Bacchettoni' refers to the sticks (*bacchette*) they carried when 'fishing' for idle youths in the streets of Florence; see *Bibliotheca Sanctorum*, 5:1356 and Turrini, 450n227.

10 For Savonarola's children, see above, ch. 4, pp. 49–53; for other examples, see Grendler, *Schooling* 338, and Turrini, 450–1.

11 Sorgenti, 271–308ff.

12 Ansaldi (b. 1537) was entrusted with the task by Archbishop Alessandro de' Medici in 1577. On Ansaldi, see Richa, 4:75–99; G. Sebregondi, *Repertorio delle famiglie patrizie e nobili fiorentine*, fasc. II, *sub voce*; and D'Addario, 45–6, 229. It is noteworthy that Archbishop de' Medici appointed a layman, not a priest, to organize and oversee the teaching of Christian doctrine in Florence.

13 ASF, Crs 162.21/22, f. 66v at date 28 July 1585; just published in Aranci, 375–6. Antifassi's answer also reveals the presence of *tavolette* at the Arcangelo Raffaello containing verses or prayers used during devotional or, in this case, instructional moments. The Arcangelo Raffaello's *tavolette* appear to have been closer to the ones used until recently in the Tridentine rite for the reading of the final gospel (John 1) or for the prayers of consecration, rather than to the ones used by comforting confraternities (for which, see Edgerton, *Pictures and Punishment*, or Falvey, 'Early Italian Dramatic Traditions and Comforting Rituals,' with ills. 16–17 and 29 in the same volume). The 'Inventario ... 1690' lists quite a number of *tavolette*, some with writing on them, others with illustrations, but does not mention specifically a *tavoletta* with the Dottrina on it.

14 For the teaching of catechism through song (psalmody) and the singing of *lodi* in schools of Christian doctrine in northern Italy, see Turrini, 426–8.

15 Compare this list of six *laude* and thirteen *lodi* in this volume with the silence on vernacular *laude* in the statutes of youth confraternities; see below, ch. 18, pp. 237–8.

16 On the tripartite division of such textbooks see Turrini, 420, with specific reference to the *Sommario della Dottrina Christiana*, *Dottrina Christiana* and *Lodi devote per uso della Dottrina Christiana* (Como: Girolamo Frova, 1596), each with its own title page and pagination, each clearly intended to be sold separately, but all also clearly meant to be bound together into one volume. See also Grendler, 'The Schools of Christian Doctrine.' For the connection between the teaching of Christian doctrine and the reformation of behaviour (*costumi*), see Turrini, 435–47.

17 The volume is discussed briefly in *La comunità cristiana fiorentina e toscana*,

116–17, item 100. The Italian title for the third section is 'Lettioni e discorsi sopra il buon costume e creanze.' It is not listed in Turrini's appendix.

18 ASF, Crs 162.23/24, f. 46v at date 19 September 1632. For the practice of awarding of prizes to students in catechism classes, see Turrini, 443–5.

19 ASF, Crs 163.24/25, f. 23v at date 27 September 1643.

20 ASF, Crs 163.24/25, f. 127v at date 7 April 1652. I have been unable to locate a copy of this *Dottrina* set to music by Lorenzo Vanni.

21 ASF, Cap. Crs 627, f. xxxvi.

22 The list of donations is drawn from the 'Inventario 1690' in ASF, Crs 164.37.

23 ASF, Crs 162.23/24 at date 2 June 1641. At the time Orazio was four years old and Filippo still a baby under the age of one. Orazio died the following year and was buried on 25 August 1642.

24 There are many studies on the *scuole* and catechism, but see in particular Franza, esp. 95–6 and 219–32; Pelliccia, 237–68; and, above all, Grendler, *Schooling*, esp. ch. 12, 'The Schools of Christian Doctrine,' 333–62.

25 Ricc., MS Moreni 287, 'Registro di compagnie, pievi e priorie della diocesi fiorentina,' f. 1r–v. The register also lists forty-three 'Compagnie d'Huomini' on ff. 2r–3r and eleven 'Compagnie che non vanno a Processione' on f. 3r.

26 For the age parameters of schools of Christian doctrine, see Turrini, 459. In her article Turrini refers to their students correctly as *bambini* and *bambine*, and the documents she cites generally use the terms *putti*, *puttini*, *putte*; see her appendix of sixteenth-century texts on 468–89.

27 ASF, Crs 164.34/35, pp. 258–9.

## Chapter 11

1 ASF, Cap. Crs 752, ch. 8, 'Delle tornate, et come ci habbiamo a ritrovare insieme.'

2 ASF, Cap. Crs 627, pt. 2, ch. 3, 'Dei riti e cerimonie.'

3 ASF, Cap. Crs 627.

4 'si tirino il ferraiuolo su le spalle'; the *ferraiuolo* is, strictly speaking, a cloak, but here it probably refers to the confraternal gown.

5 ASF, Crs 162.22/23, f. 63r–v.

6 ASF, Crs 163.25/26, p. 113.

7 ASF, Cap. Crs 752, ch. 9, 'Del ordine del Ufitio.' For a published description of the evening service at the confraternity of San Giovanni Scalzo in 1456, see Henderson, *Piety and Charity* (1994), 123–5; see also Barr, 24–6, for the service at the flagellant confraternity of San Niccolò.

8 At this point the 1560 copy of the statutes breaks off in mid-word, and we are left without a copy of the confraternity's prayer to the Archangel Raphael. ASF, Cap. Crs 752, f. 17v. The original 1468 statutes are, unfortunately, illegible at this point.

9 'Ipsa est totius religionis mirabile fundamentum.' ASF, Cap. Crs 627, pt. 2, ch. 2.
10 See Weissman, *Ritual Brotherhood*, 220–35, and Christopher Black, *passim*. For an earlier period, see Meersseman, 'La riforma delle confraternite.'
11 For spectacle in the confraternity, see below, chs. 16–18.
12 ASF, Cap. Crs 627, pt. 2, ch. 2, 'Dell'ore canoniche.'
13 ASF, Crs 160.6/7, f. 23v at date 1 May 1560.
14 See cover and illustrations 5–6 for examples of such garments.
15 Bossy, 126–7, but also see the entire section on 'Discipline,' 126–40. See also Barnes, 'Religious Anxiety,' 395.
16 See, for example, the following occasion: 'Ragunamoci la mattina, e in gran numero, dissonsi le hore cantando, fecesi una devota e fervente disciplina di poi si disse la S. Messa, e detta si communicarno 5 de' nostri padri e fratelli. Lodato Dio.' ASF, Crs 160.6/8 at date 24 December 1581.
17 ASF, Cap. Crs 627, pp. 1–2, 'Proemio.'
18 'Raghunamoci nel nostro solito luogho la mattina dello Spirito Santo assai buon numero de frategli e si celebrò il S.mo mattutino della vergine nella compagnia grande et finito il mattutino e altre orationi solite inposto il salmo deus misereatur nostri a coppia a coppia andamo nella tornata della mattina e ciascuno prese la disciplina da i sagrestani che sull'uscio stavano dandole, posto ciascuno al luogho suo fatto dal governatore alquante parole si fece di poi la devotione, e finita, si lexe un capitolo secondo il solito e in parte sendo parato il nostro padre correttore celebrò la S.ma messa e quella finita comunicò xxxv de' nostri frategli.' ASF, Crs 160.6/7, f. 40r at date Pentecost 1562.
19 See Calzolai, 'S. Antonino e "le buche,"' 10, and Weissman, *Ritual Brotherhood*, 92–5, for descriptions drawn from the statutes of the *buca* of San Paolo. See Henderson, 'Penitence and the Laity,' 240–3, for descriptions drawn from the Compagnia dell'Assunzione and for a description of Holy Week rituals. See also his 'The Flagellant Movement,' and *Piety and Charity* (1994), 124–5. For Bologna, see Terpstra, 62–3.
20 ASF, Crs 163.26/27, f. 7r–v at date 28 March 1687. A similar flagellation ritual is described in the records of the adult confraternity of the Arcangelo Raffaello detta del Raffa about ten years earlier, on Saturday evening, 2 January 1676/7; see ASF, Crs 142, fasc. 7, f. 1v. In their case, this was a standard Saturday evening exercise that was entered regularly in the records.
21 ASF, Crs 163.26/27, f. 25v at date 16 April 1688: 'si fecero con molta devozione tutte quelle funzioni come l'anno a dietro.'
22 ASF, Crs 163.25/26 at date 18 April 1642, Good Friday.
23 Ansidei, 1:180. See also Frugoni, 212; Henderson, 'The Flagellant Movement,' 150; Peretto, 148.
24 English translation from Henderson, 'The Flagellant Movement,' 150; the Latin original, which Henderson cites in the footnote, is in *Annales Sanctae Iustinae*

*Patavini*, ed. Philipp Jaffé, Monumenta Germaniae Historica Scriptores, 19 (Hanover, 1866), p. 179.

25 Stefani, 295–6 (rubr. 757a, I, ix,149).

26 Baldassar Castiglione, *Lettere inedite e rare*, ed. G. Gorni (Milano-Napoli, 1969), 44; cited in Niccoli, 363.

27 On the detrimental effects on Tuscany of Cosimo III's bigoted religiosity, see, among others Young, 710–28; Diaz, 493–6; and Acton, *passim*. For a less negative view, see, in the collection *La Toscana nell'età di Cosimo III*, the articles by Marcello Fantozzi, 'Il bigottismo di Cosimo III: da leggenda storiografica ad oggetto storico' (389–402), and by Gaetano Greco, 'Provvedimenti e pratiche nel governo politico della Chiesa locale nell'età di Cosimo III' (437–54).

28 Among the many studies that touch on the flagellant movement and confraternities, see Meersseman, *Ordo*; Magli; Henderson, 'The Flagellant Movement'; Bornstein. For a revealing sociological approach to the penitential movement in France, see Barnes, *The Social Dimension of Piety*, and esp. ch. 6, 'Devotional Life.'

29 ASF, Cap. Crs 752, ch. x, 'Della vita et buon costumi.'

30 ASF, Cap. Crs 752, ch. xiii, 'Della conversatione de' fratelli fuora del luogho.'

31 ASF, Cap. Crs 627, part II, ch. x, 'Degl'obblighi generali e particolari.'

## Chapter 12

1 ASF, Cap. Crs 752, ch. 8, 'Delle tornate, et come ci abbiamo a ritrovare insieme'; ASF, Cap. Crs 627, pt. II, ch. 1, 'Delle tornate.'

2 AAF, Compagnie VII.II.1, fasc. 2, doc. 2. The feast of the Archangel Raphael was universally declared and set for 24 October by Pope Benedict XV in 1921. Previously the feast, when celebrated, had varied according to country and diocese. In Spain, for example, it was celebrated on 7 May; in France on 9 or 15 July; in Venice on 22 April. Martyrologists also give differing dates: Pietro de Natalibus gives 8 May; Molano, Canisius, and Ferraris give 20 October. See *Enciclopedia cattolica*, 10:471 *ad vocem* Raffaele.

3 See above, ch. 9, for a discussion of the confraternity's changing demography. See also Weissman, *Ritual Brotherhood*, esp. chs. 2–4, for a more wide-ranging discussion of confraternal demography in Florence, and Christopher Black, 32–57, for all of Italy.

4 The 1690 inventory lists a confraternity seal, kept by the bakers (*maestri de' forni*), bearing the image of the Archangel Raphael and Tobias that was used to mark the *panellini*. A similar brass seal, kept by the servant, was used to mark the candles used in the Candelora service of 2 February. See ASF, Crs 164.37, p. 47.

5 For illustrations of confraternity youths wearing garlands, see the anonymous drawing in *La chiesa e la cità*, ill. 5.8 p. 101 and Sebregondi Fiorentini, *La compagnia e l'oratorio di San Niccolò del Ceppo*, fig. 9.

6 ASF, Crs 160.7/8, ff.n.n. 8r–9r at date 31 December 1563.

7 ASF, Crs 163.25/26, f. 13v at date 31 December 1642.

8 ASF, Crs 163.25/26, f. 99v at date 31 December 1649.

9 ASF, Crs 163.26/27, f. 21r at dated 31 December 1687.

10 ASF, Crs 163.25/26, f. 71r at date 31 December 1646.

11 I have drawn the same conclusion in my article 'Devotion to the Archangel Raphael in Renaissance Florence.'

12 ASF, Cap. Crs 752, f. 6v, ch. viii, 'Delle tornate.'

13 The *buonaccordo* is a keyboard instrument, precursor to the *cembalo* and the clavichord. See below, ch. 18 for a discussion of music in the confraternity.

14 ASF, Crs 162.21, ff. 65v–66v. See above, ch. 10, pp. 132–3, for a discussion of the significance of this particular visit.

15 Trexler, *Public Life*, 388–9.

16 Giamboni, *Diario sacro*, 145.

17 ASF, Crs 160.8/9, f.n.n. at date 10 August 1560; for a description of the 1559 *parato* see ASF, Crs 160.6/7, ff. 10v–11r.

18 'e così [S. Lorenzo] si è preso insieme con li altri nostri avocati,' ASF, Crs 160.6/7, f. 11r.

19 ASF, Crs 160.7/8, f.n.n. 1r.

20 Luther, 35:68 (see pp. 67–73 for his fuller thoughts on German confraternities).

21 Newbigin, '*Cene* and *Cenacoli*.'

22 As an aside I might point out that fish, which one would have expected in a confraternity dedicated to the archangel who helped a youth catch a fish, was not part of communal or festive meals at the Arcangelo Raffaello, perhaps because it was not as convenient to prepare and serve, or perhaps because it was more of a 'fasting' than a 'celebratory' dish.

23 ASF, Crs 162.21/22, f.n.n. 1r. The named saints invoked at this time are, in order, the Archangel Raphael, St John the Baptist, St Peter, St Paul, and St Mary Magdalene. Although the inclusion of the Baptist is understandable, it is not clear why Adriani included Sts Peter and Paul on his list.

24 ASF, Crs 162.21/22, f. 33v; see also ff. 50v (1584), 67r (1585).

25 ASF, Crs 160.6/7, f. 13r at date 1 November 1559.

26 Giuseppe Donzelli OP (d. 22 April 1588) served as 'procuratore fiscale della camera apostolica,' nuncio to Florence, and governor of Rome. He was appointed archbishop of Sorrento in 1574. He is described as 'prudente, dotto, santo pastore, benemerito di vari edifici' in Moroni, *Dizionario* (1840–79), 67:238. See also Gams, 926.

27 Giovan Battista di Raffaello Milanesi had been appointed a canon at the Duomo in Florence in 1542, bishop of Marsi in 1562, and had attended the Council of Trent. He retired from the bishopric in 1579. See Moroni, 43:139; Gams, 893.

28 This is probably the same Mons. Aragona whose passion for gambling led Pope Gregory XIII to order him out of Rome for having ignored the several papal prohibitions against the sport (25 August 1575). Mons. Aragona found company for his vice in the Florentine cardinals Maffei and Medici, who were rumoured to have gambled away twenty-seven thousand *scudi*. See Pastor, 9:865, appendix 13, 'Polizia dei costumi in Roma, 1573–1582'; the original document is, according to Pastor, at the Biblioteca Vaticana, MS. Urb. 1044, p. 517b.

29 Michelangelo Mollazzi *vaiaio* had been musical instructor to the confraternity since at least 1 July 1563, when he began to collect a salary to teach music to ten *confratelli*; ASF, Crs 160.7/8, f. 4v.

30 ASF, Crs 162.21/22, ff.n.n. at date 1 November 1583.

31 For a discussion of castrati, see Rosselli, 143–79.

32 ASF, Crs 162.21/22, ff. 53v–54r at date 1 November 1584.

33 ASF, Crs 163.25/25, f. 119v at datea 1 November 1651.

34 ASF, Crs 163.25/26, f. 117r at date 23 July 1651.

35 For *passim* references to the feast, see, in ASF, Crs 160.8/9 and ASF, Crs 162.21/22 at pertinent dates.

36 ASF, Crs 162.21/22, f.n.n. 57v.

37 'la rapresentatione et misterio quando la Vergine Maria insieme con Giuseppe vanno al tempio a hoferire Christo a Simeone, l'opera di Ser Giovan Maria Cechi.' ASF, Crs 162.21/22, f.n.n. 57v at date 2 February 1584/5. The work is no longer extant.

38 For the history and the devotion see Finnegan; Unger; Weil; as well as the entries in the *Enciclopedia cattolica* and in the *Catholic Encyclopedia*.

39 ASF, Crs 160.8/9, f.n.n. at date 16 May 1563: 'In tal tempo si faceva le Quaranta hore dello Spirito Santo – fino al anno 1572 che si fu partito di farla la festa di Pasqua di Resurrezione e si ponevano il 20 giorno.'

40 ASF, Crs 162.21/22, f.n.n. 26r.

41 The following description is drawn from ASF, Crs 163.25/26, ff. 4r–5r at date 20 April 1642. See also, in the same document, ff. 17v–18r at date 4 April 1643.

42 For the painter Lorenzo Lippi, see below, ch. 19, p. 259. For the architect Pierfrancesco di Gherardo Silvani (1620–85), see Thieme-Becker, 31:33.

43 ASF, Crs 157.3/5, f.n.n. at date 7 April 1619. For the house in Borgo Ognissanti and the guardian father's honorarium, see above, ch. 8, p. 109.

44 ASF, Crs 156.2/4, fasc. A, f.n.n. The revenue was also to pay for the *panellini* dis-

tributed at the confraternity's annual feast in honour of the Archangel Raphael (31 December) and for a number of masses from the Dominicans of Santa Maria Novella.

45 ASF, Crs 156.2/4, fasc. A, f.n.n. 75r at date 7 March 1661/2; letter from Domenico Comi the Younger to the grand duke explaining that he could no longer afford to adhere to his adoptive grandfather's will with respect to the payments to be made to the confraternity for its devotion of the Forty Hours.

46 ASF, Crs 163.25/26 and 26/27 *passim*.

## Chapter 13

1 ASF, Cap. Crs 752, ch. xvi. It seems no *segno* from the Arcangelo Raffaello has survived to the present day.

2 This was not the confraternity's *segno*, which would have been too heavy for the *guardiano* to carry – in fact, the confraternity used to pay a porter to carry it – but some other sign that identified his position.

3 ASF, Cap. Crs 627, pt. II, ch. vi, 'Delle processioni.'

4 ASF, Cap. Crs 627, pt. II, ch. vi, 'Delle processioni.'

5 The most thorough, though by now dated, discussion of this festivity is Gori.

6 For a discussion of how this parade constituted a cycle play, see Nerida Newbigin's introduction to *Nuovo Corpus*, xxx–xliii.

7 Gori, 20–1.

8 Palmieri, *Liber de temporibus* (1906), 172–3; *Nuovo Corpus*, XXIX–XXX.

9 Palmieri, 172–3; *Nuovo Corpus*, xxix–xxx.

10 See Newbigin, 'Piety and Politics,' Trexler, *Public Life*, and my 'Political Posturing.'

11 *Nuovo Corpus*, xlviii, drawing upon Landucci, *Diario fiorentino*, 133 and 180.

12 Cambiagi, *Memorie istoriche*, 65–8; Landucci, *Diario fiorentino*, 345; Guasti, *Le feste di San Giovanni*, 26–7; Gori, 22; *Nuovo Corpus*, xlviii.

13 D'Ancona, *Origini*, 1:245n1. For published contemporary descriptions of confraternal participation in the St John's processions, see *Descrizione de' trionfi mandati per i giovani della Compagnia di san Bastiano nella processione di San Giovanni Battista nell'inclita città di Fiorenza il dì XXII di giugno 1576* (In Fiorenza: ad istanza di Giovanni Wolfio inglese, n.d.); *Descrizzione de l'ordine della processione fatta la vigilia de San Giovanni Batista l'anno 1577* (Firenze: A stanza di Francesco Dini, 1577); and *Descrizzione dei trionfi mandati nella processione di s. Giovanni Battista l'anno 1577 nell'inclita città di Firenze dalle Compagnie di san Bastiano, di san Giorgio e di san Giovanni Evangelista* (In Firenze).

14 ASF, Signoria e Balia, Carte di Corredo 45, f. 18v, 'Regole di frati come vanno a

processione secondo le note del vescovo Antonino come mi dette Baccio Falsomonstre.'
15 Arditi, 161.
16 ASF, Crs 160.7/8, ff. xviiii$^{r-v}$, 102$^{sin}$, cxv$^{dex}$, 118$^{sin}$, cxviii$^{dex}$ at date April 1565.
17 ASF, Crs 162.21/22, f.n.n. 15r–v, at date 23 June 1582 and ASF, Crs 160.8/9 at date.
18 ASF, Crs 162.21/22, f. 31v at date 23 June 1583; f. 48r, at date 23 June 1584.
19 ASF, Crs 162.21/22 at dates. Youths dressed as angels were not an unusual component of Italian processions; in the case of Bologna, for example, see Terpstra, 23.
20 Palmieri, 172; *Nuovo Corpus*, xxix.
21 ASF, Crs 163.24/25 and 163.25/26 at dates.
22 Giamboni, 119–20. The 'Compagnie d'Huomini e Giovani' listed are those of Nome di Giesù in San Fridiano, San Salvatore in Ognissanti, San Bastiano da San Iacopo, San Iacopo del Nicchio, Sant'Alberto Bianco, Santa Caterina detta il Bernardino, San Niccolò del Ceppo, San Giovanni Evangelista, San Marco, Angiol Raffaello detta la Scala, San Giovanni Batista detto lo Scalzo.
23 ASF, Crs 160.8/9 at date 29 May 1562.
24 ASF, Crs 160.7/8 at dates 11 May 1564 and 23 May 1566.
25 In 1582, for example, there were 120 participants, in 1583 more than 100, in 1587 so many that there were not enough confraternity gowns to go around, etc. See the occasional references in ASF, Crs 164.32/33.
26 ASF, Crs 162.21/22 at date 9 June 1583.
27 Giamboni, *Diario sacro*, 366–7.
28 ASF, Crs 162.23/24, f. 31r at date 25 July 1631.
29 ASF, Crs 162.21/22 at date 7 June 1640.
30 See the entries in ASF, Crs 163.26/27 at dates 7 June 1703, 22 May 1704, 6 June 1705, 11 June 1705, and *passim*.
31 ASF, Crs 160.8/9, at date 13 September 1562.
32 On the movement of the *Bianchi* and their penitential processions, see Bornstein.
33 ASF, Crs 160.8/9 and ASF, Crs 162.21/22 at date 9 December 1589.
34 ASF, Crs 163.24/25 at date 28 January 1651/2
35 ASF, Crs 163.24/25 at date 23 August 1654.
36 Fontana, 59; University of Pennsylvania, MS 226 Ital., f. 42v, at date 30 March 1544. I am grateful to Professor Melzi, editor of this manuscript, for sharing this reference with me before its publication.
37 ASF, Crs 160.8/9 at date 28 April 1560.
38 'per impetrare la pioggia et per la liberatione delle guerre fatte dal Turco'; that day eighty-nine brothers participated in the procession. ASF, Crs 163.24/25 at

date 25 August 1645. See also Richa, 7:158–9 for a list of solemn expositions of St Antoninus's body from 1621 to 1728 on similar occasions – mostly desperate needs for either rain or shine.

39 ASF, Crs 160.8/9 at date 5 December 1561. The confraternities had gathered the previous year in Santa Maria del Fiore to pray for the same intention; ASF, Crs 160.8/9 at date December 1560.

40 ASF, Crs 160.8/9 and ASF, Crs 162.21/22 at date 9 May 1589. For a description of the opening of the original tomb, the discovery that the body had remained uncorrupted, the ceremonial bier set up in San Marco, and the solemn procession through the city, and for the list of major dignitaries present, see Richa, 7:147–9. See also the contemporary description by Buoninsegni.

41 There are references to it in ASF, Crs 162.21/22 at date 24 August from 1583 to 1587.

42 See Härth-Ragaller, 289–95, with several views of the façade of the church. For brief references to the image, the building, and the artwork commissioned for it, see Richa, 9:290–1; Carocci, *I dintorni di Firenze*, 2:262–3; and Sebregondi Fiorentini, 'Francesco Buonarroti,' 64. For the church of San Piero Gattolini, see Richa, 10:99–118.

43 ASF, Crs 162.21/22 at date 24 August 1584.

44 Sebregondi, *Tre confraternite*, 32–3.

## Chapter 14

1 D'Ancona, *Origini del teatro italiano*, 1:113–14.

2 Neri, 7–9. Neri draws his observations from Del Lungo, 193–5. Del Lungo published Poliziano's three vernacular sermons in his collection *Prose Volgari inedite e Poesie latine e greche, ... di Agnolo Poliziano* (Firenze, 1867), while Neri published the fourth, which is in Latin, in the 1902 pamphlet cited above. The pamphlet is rather difficult to find; fortunately, it has been reprinted photostatically in Poliziano's *Opera omnia*, 3:85–113. The four sermons have also been published, with an introduction, by Giovannangiola Tarugi, in her 'Scritti religiosi di Angelo Poliziano,' 43–108.

3 Eisenbichler, 'Angelo Poliziano e le confraternite di giovani a Firenze,' where I suggest that Poliziano composed the four sermons in 1491 for recitation by the Medici children (Giovanni or Giuliano di Lorenzo de' Medici) in the confraternity of San Giovanni Vangelista.

4 Kristeller, *Studies in Renaissance Thought and Letters*, 99–122; Vasoli, 'Giovanni Nesi tra Donato Acciaiuoli e Girolamo Savonarola,' 103–79; and Pugliese, 641–656.

5 *La chiesa e la città*, 84. For our interest, I might point out that there are tran-

scriptions of two fifteenth-century sermons recited at the Archangel Raphael in the collection BNCF, MS Magliab. Strozz. xxxv, cod. 211: Giovanni Nesi's oration on Humility (11 April 1476) and Giovanni Cocchi's on the Sacrament (23 March 1474).

6 Kristeller, *Studies in Renaissance Thought and Letters*, 103.

7 Weissman, 'Sacred Eloquence,' 254.

8 Kristeller, *Studies in Renaissance Thought and Letters*, 106

9 ASF, Crs 162.21/22, f. 8v at date 2 February 1581/2, Friday.

10 ASF, Crs 162.21/22, f. 3r at date 1 November 1581.

11 ASF, Crs 162.21/22, f. 7r at date 1 January 1581/2

12 ASF, Crs 162.21/22, f. 23r–v at date 20 February 1582/3.

13 Francesco Settimani, 'Memorie fiorentine' in ASF, Manoscritti 129, vol. IV, f. 295r–v.

14 ASF, Crs 162.21/22, f. 37v at date 1 November 1583

15 For all three examples, see ASF, Crs 162.21/22 at dates.

16 ASF, Crs 160.6/8 at date 11 January 1572/3.

17 ASF, Crs 162.21/22, ff. 84v–85r at date 6 January 1586/7.

18 ASF, Crs 162.21/22, f. 66v at date 28 July 1585, Sunday.

19 Poliziano, *Epist.* II, 13; reprinted in Poliziano, *Opera omnia*, 1:26–7. There is a rather free Italian translation of this passage in Del Lungo, 204. The letter is discussed briefly by Maïer, 245.

20 Cecchi, *Ragionamenti spirituali.* The only extant manuscript, in the hand of Cecchi's grandson, Mariano di Niccolò Cecchi, is at the Biblioteca Comunale degli Intronati di Siena, MS H.XI.55, pp. 1–106.

21 'Johannis Nesij adolescentis oratio de humilitate habita in fraternitate Natiuitatis die XI aprelis MCCCCLXXVI' and 'Johannis Nesij oratio decaritate a N.P. habita in societate Natiuitatis die xxv februarij MCCCCLXXVIJ.' The first sermon is found in two manuscript collections, one at the Riccardiana (MS 2204), the other at the BNCF (MS Magliab. Strozz. xxxv, cod. 211), while the second is only in the Riccardiana collection; for a complete description of the two codices, see Kristeller, *Iter Italicum*, 1:216–17 and 141–142; for a listing of the contents of these codices, see Kristeller, *Studies in Renaissance Thought and Letters*, 105n17. Nesi's two sermons in the Arcangelo Raffaello have been published by Cesare Vasoli as an appendix to his 'Giovanni Nesi,' 139–52. Although the titles are in Latin, both sermons are in fact in the vernacular.

22 There are manuscript copies in BNCF, MS Magliab. Strozz. xxxv, cod. 211, ff. 97v–101r and in Ricc., MS 2204, ff. 166v–171v. See Kristeller, *Iter Italicum*, 1:142, and Cosenza, 2:1029. Professor Polizzotto has kindly indicated to me a sermon entitled 'Oratione per la prima domenica di Quaresima alla compagnia

del'Agnol Raffaello' delivered by Giovanbattista Bracceschi at the Arcangelo Raffaello at an unspecified date; BNCF, Conv. Soppr. j.vii.5, ff. 358r–361v (but I have not had the opportunity to examine this work).

23 Della Torre, 725, *passim*.

24 ASF, Crs 162.21/22 at dates.

25 See below, chs. 16–17 for a discussion of theatre in the confraternity.

26 ASF, Crs 162.21/22, f. 22r at date 16 January 1582/3.

27 ASF, Crs 162.21/22, f. 22r–v at dates 23 and 30 January 1582/3 and 30.

28 ASF, Crs 162.22/23, f. 64r at date 13 January 1618/19.

29 *Etruria sacra*, 'Decreta Synod. II Prov. 1573,' 162–5.

30 'Concionandi munus, ut supra in cap. de Praedic. Verbi Dei, laici familiares sermones in Confraternitatibus, & Societatibus sub poenis ibi statutis ne exerceant, contra quem abusum vehementi spiritus fervore invehimus, nonnullorum laicorum temeritatem in hac civitate potissimum omnino damnantes, qui nihil summorum Pontificum, & Synodales constitutiones facientes, ubique per Confraternitates libere verba faciunt' *Etruria sacra*, 341.

31 ASF, Crs 160.8/9 at dates.

32 ASF, Crs 163.25/26 at date 2 November 1642.

33 ASF, Crs 163.25/26 at dates.

34 The phenomenon continues to the end of the century; see for example the sermon recited by a son of Francesco Cerretani that so delighted his audience because of his tender years (at date 26 December 1686).

## Chapter 15

1 See Niccoli, 356.

2 Among contemporary chroniclers, see da Empoli, 22–3; Landucci *Diario fiorentino*, 124–5. More recently, see Schnitzer, Trexler, and Polizzotto (for whom, see above, ch. 4, pp. 49–53), and Niccoli, 367–9.

3 Niccoli, 372–3; see also Turrini, 441–2.

4 See the prologues to Cecchi, *L'acquisto di Giacobbe* and *Il putto risuscitato*, both published in his *Drammi spirituali inediti*, 1:95–8 and 357–8 respectively.

5 'Nec me offenderit lusus in pueris' (*Inst. orat.* I.iii.10) and 'Danda est tamen omnibus aliqua remissio; non solum quia nulla res est, quae perferre possit continuum laborem, atque ea quoque, quae sensu et anima carent, ut servare vim suam possint, velut quiete alterna retenduntur; sed quod studium discendi voluntate, quae cogi non potest, constat' (*Inst. orat.* I.iii.8); Quintillian, *Institutio oratoria*, 59 and 57 respectively.

6 ASF, Cap. Crs 752, ff. 9r, 12r–v. Other youth confraternities had similar regulations outlining and forbidding unacceptable activities; see, for example, the 1464 statutes of San Bernardino, BNCF, Conventi soppressi da ordinare Badia Fiorentina 33, f. 12r–v. The statutes of adult confraternities had similiar chapters on 'della honesta vita et buoni chostumi'; see, for example, the 1495 *capitoli* of the Compagnia dell'Annunziata, ASF, Cap. Crs 314, ff. 16v–17v; or those of the SS. Nome di Gesù, ASF, Cap. Crs 613, pp. 11–16 . For a discussion of what was viewed as unacceptable behaviour, see Turrini, 441–2.

7 ASF, Crs 160.6/7, f.n.n. at date 25 May 1652.

8 ASF, Compagnie Soppresse incamerate nel Bigallo, Compagnia della dottrina dell'Assunta e S. Alberto dei Fanciulli detta del SS Crocifisso e S. Alberto Bianco, fasc. 13, 'Filza di documenti,' which contains the 'Attestationi che fanno le Compagnie nelle quali è Pallottolaio' dated 18 July 1624. I wish to thank dott.ssa Ludovica Sebregondi for having brought this document to my attention.

9 ASF, Crs 134.2/3, f. 35v.

10 See ASF, Crs 134.2/3, f. 53r at date 20 February 1630/1 for the whitewashing; ASF, Crs 134.1/2, docs. 8 and 9, dated 3 July 1633 and 16 September 1633 respectively, for the expenses incurred in that year's improvements to the structure.

11 ASF, Crs 134.2/3, f. 35v.

12 ASF, Compagnie Soppresse incamerate nel Bigallo, Compagnia della dottrina dell'Assunta e S. Alberto dei Fanciulli detta del SS. Crocifisso e S. Alberto Bianco, fasc. 13, 'Filza di documenti,' ff.n.n.

13 ASF, Crs 155.1/3, fasc. F, f.n.n. at date 1 May 1656.

14 ASF, Crs 155.1/3, fasc. B, doc. 23, dated 1 May 1658. See ASF, Crs 161.13/14, f. 44v at date 7 November 1649 for expenses incurred for improvements made to the *pallottolaio*. See also ASF, Crs 155.1/3, fasc. A, ff.n.n. 84r–85r at date 1 May 1658.

Both Raffaello and Lorenzo Del Soldato were active in the confraternity in the 1640s–50s, often holding office, especially as *paciale* or *cerimoniere*. Lorenzo Del Soldato remained active in the confraternity for at least sixty years, serving as *provveditore* from January 1686/7 to March 1694/5 and as *governatore* in September–December 1703 (ASF, Crs 163.26/27, ff. 4r, 110v, and 187v).

15 See ASF, Crs 135.8/9, pp. 134–5 at date 18 January 1727/8 for the decision to transfer management; pp. 141–7 at date 6 February 1727/8 for the agreement with the Accademici; and p. 145 for the inventory of goods transferred.

16 See Nicola Martelli, 'Del giuoco del biliardo,' a *capitolo* addressed to the same Pandolfo Pucci published by Gaetano Milanesi; the original is in BNCF, MS Magliab. ii.iv.I, f. 238. For a seventeenth-century English description of the game of billiards, see Charles Cotton's *Compleat Gamester*.

17 ASF, Crs 135.9, f. 34r at date 15 August 1781.

## Chapter 16

1 ASF, Cap. Crs 627, ff. xxxxi–xxxxii. 'The Orator' is Cicero, and the citation a paraphrase from his *De Officiis*, where, speaking of the duties of the young, he says that 'even when they wish to relax their minds and give themselves to enjoyment they should beware of excesses and bear in mind the rules of modesty' (I.xxxiv.122); Cicero, 125.

2 ASF, Crs 1579, f. 172 at date 1563 (no more precise date given); the information in drawn from the records of the *buca* of San Paolo. Both confraternities used the same oratory complex; therefore the youths asked the adults for their permission to alter the physical structure of the *stanzone*.

3 ASF, Comp. Soppr. incamerate nel Bigallo, Comp. della dottrina dell'Assunta e S. Alberto dei Fanciulli detta del SS. Crocifisso e S. Alberto Bianco, fasc. 13 'Filza di documenti' (see p. 394, note 8, above).

4 *Rappresentazione del vitello sagginato*, published in *Nuovo Corpus*, 31–55; see also Newbigin, 'The Word Made Flesh,' 363–6.

5 Published in D'Ancona, *Sacre rappresentazioni*, 3:235–68. Modern editions of the play are included in Lorenzo de' Medici's *Opere*, 2:71–114; and in his *Scritti scelti*, 549–601. A recent translation into English verse is in *Selected Writings*, 158–243. Although the literature on this play is extensive, the confraternal aspect of the play and its performance was not examined by anyone until my 'Confraternities and Carnival,' 128–39.

6 That is, the confraternities of San Bastiano de' Fanciulli, San Giovanni Evangelista, Arcangelo Raffaello detta la Scala, and Purificazione detta San Marco. See Eisenbichler, 'The Religious Drama of Giovan Maria Cecchi,' appendix 4, pp. 250–1.

7 For a discussion of late Cinquecento stage sets for confraternity drama, see my 'Spazi e luoghi.'

8 Del Migliore, 'Registro,' BNCF, MS Magliab. xxv, cod. 418, p. 411.

9 My translation from Pontani, 798–805. Pontani revises and corrects an earlier Italian translation by D'Ancona, *Sacre rappresentazioni*, 1:230–1, used and reprinted by several subsequent scholars. The Greek original is in Joseph Gill, *Quae supersunt actorum Graecorum Concilii Florentini (Concilium Florentinum: Documenta et scriptores)*, ser. B, vol. V, fasc. I (Roma: Pontificium Institutum Orientalium Studiorum, 1953), i–xiii.

10 See Gori, 21; and *Nuovo corpus*, xxxi.

11 *Nuovo corpus*, xxx–xliii.

12 Palmieri, 172–3; transcribed in *Nuovo corpus*, xxix–xxx.

13 The autograph manuscript of the play is at the Riccardiana, MS 2824, ff. 28–42. It was published in Cecchi, *Drammi spirituali inediti*, 2:127–50. The covering letter to Messer Piero appears on p. 127. Confraternity records from September

1573 to May 1581 are, unfortunately, not extant, and so I have been unable to identify more fully the Messer Piero who commissioned the play.

14 Cecchi, *Drammi spirituali inediti*, 2:146–7. Confraternity inventories indicate that the youths owned several statues of the Baby Jesus that were used for such purposes. The 1583 inventory, for example, lists 'un bambino della natività di gesso con basa dorata' (ASF, Crs 155.1/3, fasc. B, doc. 13), while the 1690 inventory lists two, one of plaster and one of papier maché, each one 'colorito color di carne, quale si mette all'altare del Tornatino la mattina del S. Natale' (ASF, Crs 164.37, p. 34).

15 ASF, Crs 162.22/23, f. 83 at date 24 December 1586.

16 ASF, Crs 160.7/8 at date 31 December 1563.

17 ASF, Crs 162.21/22, ff. 12v–15r at date 3 June 1582. Recently published in Aranci, 349–60. There is no indication of authorship for the play.

18 ASF, Crs 162.21/22 at date 3 June 1582; see also above, ch. 10, pp. 129–30.

19 ASF, Crs 162.21/22 at dates.

20 ASF, Crs 162.21/22, f.n.n. 15r–v at date 23 June 1582.

21 The letter dedicatory is dated 1 August 1625.

22 ASF, Miscellanea Medicea 755, 'Diario di etichetta,' vol. 3, f. 18r, according to Solerti, who published it in his *Musica, ballo e drammatica*, 171 – where, however, he gives the date as January rather than February. Crinò published a paraphrase of the entry (p. 265) and cited it as being on f. 6. The expression 'stettero su le seggiole senza Residenza' indicates that the grand-ducal family did not sit on special chairs on a raised platform or under a baldachin, but on normal chairs, like everyone else.

23 Piero was the son of Giovanni de' Bardi, count of Vernio (1534–1612). Giovanni was an eminent patron of letters and music in the second half of the Cinquecento, and in particular of the musicians Vincenzo Galilei and Giulio Caccini, whose careers he actively fostered. He is remembered above all as the host of that group of musicians, poets, and intellectuals that became known as the Camerata de' Bardi. See his entry in *The New Grove Dictionary of Music*, 2:150–2.

24 ASF, Crs 162.22/23, f. 108r–111v at date February 1623/4 between the 11th and 18th; published in Burchi, 'Vita musicale,' 21–6; a much shorter note appears in ASF, Crs 160.8/9 at date 5 February 1623/4.

25 Cicognini, p.n.n. 4.

26 Cicognini, p.n.n. 4.

27 See ch. 12, pp. 155–7 for a discussion of the ritual for this feast.

28 ASF, Crs 162.21/22 at date 28 July 1585.

29 Both composed in 1580–87. Manuscript copies are at the BCI, MS H.XI.56, pp. 1–16, and BCI, MS I.VII.29, pp. 195–203, for the *Disprezzo*; BCI, MS H.XI.56, pp. 16–24 and BCI, MS I.VII.29, pp. 205–17 for the *Duello*. The title pages of the manu-

scripts point out that they works were composed for the feast of St Mary Magdalene at the confraternity of the Arcangelo Raffaello. Both plays were edited by Michele dello Russo in Cecchi, *Commedie*, 121–40 and 97–120 respectively. See also Ferraro, 61–2. For passing references to these plays, see Eisenbichler, 'The Religious Drama of Giovan Maria Cecchi,' *passim*.

30 ASF, Crs 162.22/23, ff. 115r–116v, where there is a long description of the play. The 1690 inventory lists a number of books and manuscripts stored in the *armadio* in the *stanzone* and, among a listing of plays, specifically mentions 'Various works on St Mary Magdalene the penitent'; see ASF, Crs 164.37, p. 17. I should note that Jacopo Cicognini had already taken this play and adapted it for performance after vespers at court on 22 July 1622; see Tinghi, 'Diario' 2:523 transcribed in Solerti, 163.

31 The *sagrestani maggiori* at the time were Lorenzo Stefani, Ruberto Manieri, Giulio Buonaccorsi, Forese Falconieri, while the *sagrestani minori* were Andrea Cavalcanti, Alessandro Galli, Stefano Nemi, and Lorenzo Gabbrielli (ASF, Crs 162.22/23, ff. 106v and 113v). The description that follows is a translation and paraphrase of ASF, Crs 162.22/23, ff. 115r–116v at date 28 July 1624.

32 ASF, Crs 163.25/26, f. 35v at date 24 July 1644. and ASF, Crs 160.8/9 at date.

## Chapter 17

1 *Rappresentazione della natività di Cristo* in D'Ancona, *Sacre rappresentazioni*, 1:191–210.

2 First published in Venice by Gabriel Giolito de' Ferrari in 1550; translated as *The Horned Owl* (1981).

3 Cecchi, *The Horned Owl*, III.iv, p. 38. For St Benedict and the archer see above, ch. 15, p. 192.

4 For a modern description of the event see Nagler, 14–21, where he also lists contemporary published descriptions. See also Herrick, 63–5.

5 ASF, Crs 254.2, f. 13r at date 1570.

6 See my introduction to Cecchi, *Ragionamenti spirituali*, 6–8, for a discussion of Cecchi's change of attitude.

7 ASF, Crs 160.7/8, f. 27r at date 11 January 1572/3.

8 The archbishop's visit is recorded in the confraternity's *ricordi*; ASF, Crs 160.7/8 at date 11 January 1572/3. The decision to undertake work to repair the leaky roof was taken shortly thereafter, on 22 February; the entry into the confraternity of Ser Girolamo da San Miniato 'prete di Mons. Arcivechovo Antonio Altoviti d'età d'anni 28' took place on 1 March; and the St John's procession on 23 June (same document, at dates).

9 D'Addario, 277–8.

10 ASF, Crs 160.8/9 at date 27 January 1584/5.

11 It may be of interest to note that Raffaello Carraresi's two sons, Giuliano and Bernardo, joined the Arcangelo Raffaello and not the confraternity of San Bernardino, paying their entrance fees on 1 January 1580/1; ASF, Crs 165.40/48 at date.

12 ASF, Crs 254.2, f. 13v at date 1580.

13 AAF, Compagnie, vii.ii.1, 'Memoria' of the Compagnia del Vangelista, ff.n.n. 1v–2r.

14 ASF, Crs 162.21/22, at date 31 December 1589.

15 ASF, Crs 162.21/22, at date.

16 ASF, Crs 162.21/22 at date 31 December 1591; see also the entry fee payment for Cosimo II recorded in ASF, Crs 165.40/48 at date 6 January 591/2.

17 For the records of enrolment fees for the Medici, see ASF, Crs 165.40/48, and ASF, Crs 165.41/49 *passim*.

18 ASF, Crs 162.21/22 at date 6 January 1586/7.

19 'Lettere di Alessandro Strozzi,' in Carnesecchi, 117–18. I wish to thank dott.ssa Ludovica Sebregondi for bringing this item to my attention. For references to this confraternity see Sebregondi, *Tre confraternite*, *passim*.

20 ASF, Crs 134.2 f. 18r.

21 ASF, Crs 162.22/23, ff. 93v–95v. The description that follows is drawn from these pages. Cecchi's play survives in two manuscripts, BCS MS I.VII.27 pp. 165–90 and Rosselli del Turco, MS 44, 2. Published in Cecchi, *Drammi spirituali inediti*, 1:93–159.

22 Federigo d'Urbino married Claudia de' Medici, sister of the recently deceased Cosimo II, on 29 April 1621.

After Alessandro d'Ottaviano de' Medici was elected pope in 1605 as Leo XI, Alessandro Marzi Medici, who had been bishop of Fiesole (1596–1605), was transferred to the Florentine see. He took possession on 2 July 1605 and remained there until his death on 13 August 1630. See Ceracchini, 208. Alessandro Marzi Medici had been a member of the Arcangelo Raffaello; he is listed as one of the novices accepted into the confraternity on 23 May 1566, and a later marginal note identifies him as 'Arcivescovo di Firenze' (ASF, Crs 160.7/8 f. xxiii$^{v}$).

23 Jacopo Cignoni had joined the Arcangelo Raffaello just that year; see his payment of the entrance fee of 12 *lire* in ASF, Crs 165.40/48, f. 129v.

24 For the grand-ducal attendance, see ASF, MS Tinghi, 2:557, transcribed in Solerti, 164. The published version appeared in Florence, Appresso i Giunti, 1626.

25 The play was first staged shortly after its composition sometime between 1580 and 1587. It was then restaged on 28 July 1624; see ASF, Crs 160.8/9 at date; ASF, Crs 162.22/23, ff. 115r–116v (where the scribe describes the play and the stage

set, and then provides a list of the individuals that acted in it). See above, ch. 16, pp. 215–17, for a discussion of Cecchi's play. The 1624 play was probably a remake by Jacopo Cicognini, who had already remade it for a performance after Vespers at court on 22 July 1622; Tinghi, 2:523 transcribed by Solerti, 163.

26 Cicognini, sig. [A2r–v].

27 Cicognini, p. 24. Dell'Antella was a member of the Council of Regency that governed Tuscany in the minority of Grand Duke Ferdinando II and as such authorized the publication on behalf of the government. The archbishop and the inquisitor authorized it, of course, on behalf of the diocese and of the Inquisition.

28 *Rappresentazione dei Pastori.* See ASF, Crs 160.8/9 at date; ASF, Crs 162.23/24, f. 157v (the following description is drawn from this second document).

29 ASF, Crs 155.1/3, fasc. B, doc. 13, 'Inventario di robbe spettanti alla Compagnia dell'Agnolo Raffaello fattosi al tempo del Guardiano Messer Antonio Pasci questo dì 25 d'Aprile 1583.'

30 ASF, Crs 164.37, pp. 23–4.

31 ASF, Crs 162.23/24, f. 109.

32 ASF, Crs 162.23/24, f. 102.

33 ASF, Crs 163.25/26, f. 68r at date 7 October 1646.

34 Lorenzo del Turco may be the younger brother of Giovanni del Turco (1577–1647); he is mentioned as such in *The New Grove Dictionary of Music*, 5:354, but no further information is available on him. Agnolo is not mentioned at all.

35 The jurist Sforza Oddi (Perugia 1540–Parma 1611) composed three comedies (*Erofilomachia*, 1572; *Commedia dei morti vivi*, 1576; *La prigione d'amore*, 1576) that add pathetic and romantic elements to the comic motifs of traditional Renaissance comedy. See Herrick, 188–90. For earlier revivals of the play, see Solerti, 28–9, for revivals in 1577 and 1602.

36 The Casino, on today's Via Cavour, was directly west of the convent of San Marco. It was built by Buontalenti in 1576 for the marquis of Capestrano, the illegitimate son of Grand Duke Francesco I de' Medici. It later became the residence of Cardinal Leopoldo de' Medici and of his nephew Lorenzo de' Medici, who used it to house his extensive collection of ancient statues and sculptures. Today it houses the Corte d'Assise e d'Appello (Court of Appeals). For a quasi-contemporary description of the Casino, see Del Migliore, *Firenze città nobilissima illustrata*, 229–30.

37 Lorenzo Guardini served as *cerimoniere maggiore* in January–April 1645.

38 Giovanni Casini was active in the confraternity, holding several positions over the course of many years; he served as *sottoprovveditore* from May 1642 to April 1643; as *governatore* May–August 1644, September–December 1657; as *cerimoniere maggiore* May–August 1645, May–August 1646, May–August 1647,

January–April 1648, January–April 1650; as *infermiere* September–December 1645, September–December 1648, January–April 1651; as *sagrestano maggiore* September–December 1651; and as *consigliere* September–December 1655.

39 ASF, Crs 162.23/24, ff. 67v–68r at date 24 February 1633/4.

40 ASF, Crs 160.8/9 at date 18 February 1645/6; ASF, Crs 163.25/26, f. 61v. See also the transcription in Burchi, 'Musica e musicisti,' 2:178–9, and the passing references to it in Burchi, 'Vita musicale,' 45, 50.

41 See ASF, Crs 162.23/24, ff. 122v–123r, at date 14 December 1637 for his election, and ff. 123v–124r for his assumption of duties. He resigned on 1 August 1645 for reasons of advanced age; ASF, Crs 163.25/26, f. 51r–v.

42 ASF, Crs 160.8/9 at date 3 June 1638; ASF, Crs 162.23/24, f. 133r.

43 The play was staged three times over the course of three separate weeks. The first was a dress rehearsal in front of a mixed public of 'men and women' on 9 February; then it was presented to Don Lorenzo, Don Mattias de' Medici, the court, and invited guests on Wednesday, 15 February; and finally to Don Lorenzo, Don Giovanni Carlo de' Medici, Don Mattias de' Medici, and other prelates, ladies, and gentlemen on Thursday, 23 February. See ASF, Crs 160.8/9 at date; ASF, Crs 162.22/23, ff. 161r–162v; ASF, Crs 163.24/25, f.n.n. 1. ASF, Crs 163.24/25, f.n.n. 4v at date 11 April 1640 has a record of payment of 10 *scudi* to M.o Felice Gamberai for his 'fatiche e spese' for the play, and 10 *scudi* to Agnolo Conti, *maestro di cappella*, for his contribution to the music. See appendix 4 for a list of plays performed that year.

44 ASF, Crs 160.8/9 and ASF, Crs 163.24/25 at date 24 August 1642; ASF, Crs 163.25/26, f. 9v.

45 ASF, Crs 160.8/9 and ASF, Crs 163.25/26, f. 15v.

46 ASF, Crs 163.25/26, f. 15v.

47 ASF, Crs 163.25/26, f. 30v. The four *fanciulli* are identified by surname only: Carnesecchi, Bonsi, Neretti, and Strozzi. See also ASF, Crs 163.24/25 at date 20 March 1643/4.

48 ASF, Crs 160.8/9 and ASF, Crs 163.25/26, f. 35v at date 24 July 1644.

49 ASF, Crs 160.8/9 and ASF, Crs 163.25/26, f. 36r at date 7 August 1644.

50 ASF, Crs 160.8/9 at date 24 February 1644/5; ASF, Crs 163.25/26, ff. 43v–44r. Giacinto Andrea Cicognini (1606–51) was the son of Jacopo Cicognini and joined the confraternity at the same time his father did (1622; ASF, Crs 165.40/48, f. 129v). They both wrote plays that were performed at the Arcangelo Raffaello, and they both had illustrious careers as dramatists.

51 César de Bourbon (1594–1665) was the illegitimate son of King Henry IV of France.

52 ASF, Crs 160.8/9 at date 18 February 1645/6 and ASF, Crs 163.25/26, f. 61v. I have been unable to identify Camillo Lenzoni or his 'opera morale.'

53 Crinò, 273, says she has not been able to locate this play, and neither have I.
54 Transcribed in Crinò, 273.
55 ASF, Crs 160.8/9 at date; ASF, Crs 163.25/26, f. 181r–v.
56 ASF, Crs 163.25/26, f. 181r–v.
57 ASF, Cap. Crs 627, pt. 2, ch. 9, p. 41.
58 The process began on 25 March 1635, when the confraternity elected four brothers to rewrite the statutes. The final document was presented to the confraternity by Archbishop Niccolini on 25 December 1636. ASF, Crs 160.8/9 at dates; ASF, Crs 162.23/24, ff. 83r and 107r.

## Chapter 18

1 Rinuccini/Peri's *Dafne* was first staged for Carnival 1598 and then revived for three successive years; see Carter, 'Non occorre,' 93. For Hill's claim on behalf of the Arcangelo Raffaello performance, see his 'Oratory Music in Florence, I,' 116 and 134 doc. 12. Hill also points out that the madrigal that was sung can be found in BNCF, Magliab. XIX, 66, and in Brussels at the Conservatoire Royale de Musique, MS 704; he then adds that the 'music shows traits more characteristic of Caccini's early solo madrigals than those that survive of Peri's' (117).
2 Mode, 67, 71.
3 ASF, Cap. Crs 882 as copied in ASF, Cap. Crs 752.
4 See, for example, the *lauda* 'Levate su pastori' sung on 24 December 1581; a 'lauda della Natività' sung by Pompeo Caccini for Christmas 1609; a *lauda* sung by a choir of angels hovering over a manger scene (*capanna*) on 31 December 1610; another for Christmas 1613; and so forth.
5 Note, for example, Hill's comment in his 'Oratory Music in Florence, I,' 108, that 'For their indoctrination and inspiration [the youth confraternities] relied principally on sermon ..., *laude* sung by all, and *sacre rappresentazioni*,' with no mention of the Latin hymns at all.
6 ASF, Cap. Crs 627, ch. 8, p. 17.
7 ASF, Crs 160.7/8, f. 4v at date 1 July 1563; transcribed in Burchi, 'Musica e musicisti,' vol. 2, doc. 5.
8 ASF, Crs 162.21, f. 44v at date; Burchi, 'Musica e musicisti,' vol. 2, doc. 22. As Burchi notes, we have no other information on Mollazzi as a musician except for what is to be found in the records of the Arcangelo Raffaello; Burchi, 'Musica e musicisti,' 1:50n5bis. He does not appear in Kirkendale.
9 Burchi, 'Musica e musicisti,' 1:15
10 Burchi, 'Musica e musicisti,' 1:15. For the archival references to performances by these individuals, see ASF, Crs 160.21/22, *passim*.
11 ASF, Crs 160.7/8, f. 28r; see my comments above, ch. 7, p. 91.

12 Gucci died on 13 January 1609/10; the confraternity celebrated the Office for the Dead in his honour on 17 January; ASF, Crs 162.21/22, f. 286r.

13 ASF, Crs 162.21/22, f. 23r at date 20 February 1582/3.

14 ASF, Crs 162.21/22, ff. 53v–54r, transcribed in Burchi, 'Musica e musicisti,' vol. 2, doc. 24; Burchi, 'Vita musicale,' 12–13; Hill, 'Oratory Music in Florence, I,' 133, doc. 3; see also ASF, Crs 160.8/9, f.n.n. at date 1 November 1584, transcribed in Burchi, 'Vita musicale,' 13.

The literature on Giulio Caccini (1551–1618) is vast; for a start, see *The New Grove Dictionary of Music*, 3:576–81, and Kirkendale, 119–80. With respect to the young castrato, Hill, 'Oratory Music in Florence, I,' 114n29, suggests that he may be the Niccolò castrato mentioned in other documents and that he could be identified with Niccolò Bartolini da Pistoia, *eunuco*, who was employed by Grand Duke Ferdinando in 1588 and sang at his wedding festivities in 1589. On castrati in general, see Rosselli. Caccini's son, Giulio, was also active in the Arcangelo Raffaello.

15 Hill, 'Oratory Music in Florence, I,' 115n32, referring back to Aby Warburg, *I costumi teatrali per gli intermedi del 1589: i disegni di Bernardo Buontalenti e il 'libro dei conti' di Emilio de' Cavalieri: saggio storico-critico* (1895), 77, rpt. in *La rinascita del paganesimo antico*, ed. Gertrud Bing (Florence, 1966).

16 ASF, Crs 162.21/22, ff. 114v–115r at date 31 December 1589, transcribed in Burchi, 'Musica e musicisti,' vol. 2, doc. 57; Burchi, 'Vita musicale,' 13. Burchi points out that Jacomelli, born about 1550, played a 'lira grande' at the première of Jacopo Peri's *Euridice* performed in Florence for the wedding of Ferdinando de' Medici with Christine of Lorraine (1589) and later for that of Maria de' Medici with Henri IV of France (6 October 1600).

17 ASF, Crs 162.21/22, f. 143v at date 31 December 1591, transcribed by Burchi, 'Musica e musicisti,' vol. 2, doc. 71; Burchi, 'Vita musicale,' 14–15; Hill, 'Oratory Music in Florence, I,' 133, doc. 10.

18 ASF, Crs 162.21/22, f. 54r at date 1 November 1584, All Souls'. Giulio Caccini is described in the records as 'musico di Sua Altezza Serenissima e nostro fratello,' and the castrato he brought along as 'un suo putto castrato che a requisitione di Sua Altezza Serenissima tiene in casa, et l'insegnia.' The records for all these occasions have been transcribed by Burchi, 'Musica e musicisti,' vol. 2, docs. 25, 26, 40, and by Hill, 'Oratory Music in Florence, I,' 133, docs. 4, 5, 7.

19 ASF, Crs 162.21/22 at dates; transcribed in Burchi, 'Musica e musicisti,' docs. 43, 51, and Hill, 'Oratory Music in Florence, I,' 134, docs. 8, 9. For Gucci's 'retirement' I draw my date from Burchi, 'musica e musicisti,' 1:50 who says he performed 'fino ai primi del 1600.'

I have a suspicion that Raffaello Gucci may have been a castrato, but I have no evidence for it. The suspicion is based on his late entry into the confraternity (at age thirty) and his long and valued service as a singer. I also suspect he was never married, for though he asks the confraternity to pray for his recently deceased mother and father, he never asks the youths to pray for a wife or a child. But all this is, admittedly, speculation.

20 See ASF, Crs 162.21/22, f. 130v for Malespini's first appearance in the records on 3 March 1590/1; ibid., f. 133r at date 21 April 1591 for the hiring agreement; and ibid. f.n.n. at date summer 1609 for the resignation. Burchi, 'Musica e musicisti,' transcribes the entries as docs. 64, 65, and 99.

21 ASF, Crs 165.40/48, f. 22v; Hill, 'Oratory Music in Florence, I,' 119, who corrects Strainchamps's slip with the Florentine *ab incarnatione* calendar. Marco's older brother Lionardo had joined the Arcangelo Raffaello four years earlier, on 17 November 1585; their youngest brother, Giovan Battista, joined on 27 July 1599 and eventually replaced Marco as *maestro di musica*. For all their entrance fee payments, see ASF, Crs 165.40/48.

22 ASF, Crs 155.1/3 fasc. H, f.n.n., at date 1 May 1599.

23 Cardinal Ferdinando Gonzaga had joined the Arcangelo Raffaello on 1 November 1605 during a visit to Florence; ASF, Crs 165.40/48, f. 87v at date; Hill 'Oratory Music in Florence, I,' 119n41.

24 For the entire episode, see Strainchamps, 'Marco da Gagliano,' 473–87. The confraternity records that deal with this episode are found in ASF, Crs 162.21/22, f. 269r–v at date 2 and 31 December 1607; they have been transcribed in Burchi, 'Musica e musicisti,' vol. 2, docs. 97–8. For Malespini's salary see ASF, Crs 160.8/9, f. 7r at date 21 April 1591.

25 See his entry in *The New Grove Dictionary of Music*, 7:81–7; Kirkendale, *passim.*

26 ASF, Crs 162.22/23, f. 83r. For Marco's work at the Arcangelo Raffaello, see Burchi, 'Vita musicale,' 48, and Hill 'Oratory Music in Florence, I,' 119–21 (with the date for the obsequies reported incorrectly as 14 March 1622; p. 121). Marco's own obsequies were held at the Arcangelo Raffaello on 22 March 1642/3; ASF, Crs 163.25/26, f. 16v at date.

27 ASF, Crs 165.40/48, f. 65v; Hill, 'Oratory Music in Florence, I,' 121n54. The confraternity celebrated the Office for the Dead for him on 22 January 1650/1; ASF, Crs 163.25/26, f. 111r. Burchi, 'Vita musicale,' 48, reports that Giovan Battista's first involvement with music at the Arcangelo Raffaello dates from December 1619.

28 For these and all the other *maestri di cappella* at the Arcangelo Raffaello, see appendix 3.

29 'si celebrò il S.mo vespro con gli organi molto solennemente; si cantò ancora molte lalde su gli organi.' ASF, Crs 160.6/7, f. 32v; Burchi, 'Musica e musicisti,' vol. 2, doc. 3.

30 'S. Silvestro ... et mentre si cantava Lauda Hyerusalem d.num pervenit musichalmente in versetto, et Salmo poi e Cori rispondevano ... si cantò musichalmente da nostri Giovanetti ... Si cantava Te Deum Laudamus musichalmente da nostri giovanetti, e Cori rispondevano ... si disse musichalmente el nostro Vespro et sonoronsi gli organi como la mattina.' ASF, Crs 160.7/8, ff. 8v–9r at date 31 December 1563; transcribed in Burchi, 'Musica e musicisti,' vol. 2, doc. 6.
31 ASF, Crs 162.21/22, f. 28r at date 12 April 1583; Burchi, 'Musica e musicisti,' vol. 2, doc. 21.
32 Domenico Torsi, 'Descrizione dell'esequie fatte nella morte del Signor Jacopo Corsi nella Compagnia dell'Arcangelo Raffaello, 1603.' MS in the library of the villa Corsi-Salviati, ff. [41v–42r], cited in Carter 'Music and Patronage' (1985), 93n34.
33 A plaque in honour of Baccio Comi (d. 18 March 1604/5) was placed in the oratory on 30 December 1643 to commemorate his and his brother Domenico's largesse. Baccio supported other groups as well, in particular the Compagnia dei Vanchetoni, contributing generously to the construction of its oratory; see BNCF, MS Magliab. XXV, cod. 418, f. 126.
34 Galileo's affidavit is in ASF, Crs 156.2/4, fasc. C; published in Burchi, 'Vita musicale,' 43n23. On Vincenzo Galilei (late 1520s–1591), theorist, composer, lutenist, singer and music teacher, see the entry by Claude V. Palisca in *The New Grove Dictionary of Music*, 7:96–8. For our interests, it should be noted that Vincenzo enjoyed the patronage of Giovanni de' Bardi and Jacopo Corsi, among others. Although neither Vincenzo nor his son Galileo appears to have joined the Arcangelo Raffaello, his grandson and namesake Vincenzo di Galileo Galilei did become a member sometime before 1615; ASF, Crs 162.21/22, f. 33r, also noted by Hill, 'Oratory Music in Florence, I,' 111n12. For Jacopo Corsi (1561–1602) and his connections with the Florentine musical world, see Carter 'Music and Patronage,' 57–104, and specifically 64–5 for Corsi's membership in Florentine confraternities, 70–1 for his musical training and performance skills, 72–3 for his support of Florentine musicians, etc.
35 ASF, Crs 156.2/4, fasc. C at date; transcribed in Burchi, 'Vita musicale,' 42n23.
36 ASF, Crs 156.2/4, fasc. A, f.n.n. 58r at date 3 October 1620; transcribed in Burchi, 'Musica e musicisti,' 2:379–80. 'Vincentio the organist' may well be the 'Vincenzio organista' mentioned in Jacopo Corsi's account book for 16 April 1599, cited in Kirkendale, 196–7.
37 ASF, Crs 156.2/4, fasc. A, f.n.n. 27r at date 16 November 1615; transcribed in Burchi, 'Musica e musicisti,' 2:378–9.
38 ASF, Crs 156.2/4, fasc. A, f.n.n. at date 4 November 1615, affidavit of Cosimo del Bianco.

39 The documents for the legal battle are found in ASF, Crs 156.2/4, fasc. A.

40 Filippo del Riccio Comi served the confraternity as its *provveditore* in 1604–6 and again in 1609–14. When he disappears from the listing, Lionardo di Zanobi da Gagliano (Marco and Giovan Battista's older brother) continues as *sottoprovveditore*. Because the hand does not change, it appears that the records were kept by Lionardo da Gagliano, and not Filippo Comi.

41 See ASF, Crs 156.2/4, fasc. A, f.n.n. at date 17 November 1615 for Cosimo del Bianco's affidavit and f.n.n. at date 20 November 1615 for that of Pasquino di Francesco. Domenico Comi (d. 13 December 1605) was also a generous donor to the Arcangelo Raffaello, leaving it a house in Borgo Ognissanti and an annuity from his farm La Casellina in Ponte a Greve.

42 ASF, Crs 156.2/4, fasc. A, f.n.n. 15r (no date given) for the affidavit of Pietro Mannucci regarding the organ; f.n.n. 17r–v at date 31 August 1615 for that of Bernardo di Jacopo Chiti and Jacopo di Antonio Diconesi; f.n.n. at date 8 November 1615 for that of fra Santi Contini, sacristan of Santa Maria Novella, regarding the back-boards and the paintings; f.n.n. at date 9 November 1615 for that of Giulio di Bastiano Berni, a painter located at Ponte a Santa Trinita, for the tapestry back-rests; f.n.n. at date 16 November 1615 for those of Marco da Gagliano for the back-rests and the organ; and so forth.

43 ASF, Crs 156.2/4, fasc. A, f.n.n. at date 12 August 1616 for Alessandro Benci and f.n.n. at date 24 October 1620 for Cesare Pollini.

44 Bolcioni remains unknown. Stefano di Giovanni Soldini, however, is listed in Kirkendale, 377, as a *strumentaio* hired at court on 1 October 1629 'to keep in order the instruments of all their Serene Highnesses.' He served until at least 1648 and died on 8 October 1650.

45 ASF, Crs 155.2/4, fasc. A, f.n.n. at date 25 October 1620; transcribed in Burchi, 'Musica e musicisti,' 2:381–2 and 'Vita musicale,' 43n23.

46 See ASF, Crs 155.2/4, fasc. A, f.n.n. (no date given) for the description and f.n.n. at date 16 October 1620 for Cinganelli's affidavit about the commission.

47 Not only Filippo but his son Domenico Comi the Younger and subsequent generations of the family were to experience economic difficulties that led to their chronic inability to provide the Arcangelo Raffaello with the annuities stipulated in the wills of Baccio and Domenico Comi the Elder. Legal wrangling on these matters is documented as late as March 1735/6; see ASF, Crs 156.2/4 fasc. A, *passim*.

48 ASF, Crs 163.25/26, f. 59r–v at date 21 January 1645/6.

49 ASF, Crs 162.23/24, f. 6r at date 14 April 1630; Burchi, 'Musica e musicisti,' vol. 2, doc. 145.

50 ASF, Crs 163.25/26, f. 59r–v at date 21 January 1645/6.

51 Referring back to Biscioni, Hill, 'Oratory Music in Florence, I,' 126n70, says

that del Vivaio 'was a mathematician as well as a composer. Being the last of his family, he left the Compagnia dell'Arcangelo Raffaello, on his death in 1659, a large endowment for musical performances. ... Vivaio published a book of madrigals in Florence, but all that is known of his music are the madrigals included in the collections of Santi Orlandi (1602 and 1605) and Filippo Vitali (1616 and 1629).' For the endowment to the confraternity, see ASF, Crs 156.2/4, fasc. C, 'Comp.a dell'Arcangiolo Raffaello d.a la Scala e Cepperelli e PP. di S. Giuseppe 1659–1663.'

52 ASF, Crs 162.23/24, f. 188r at date 6 October 1641; Burchi, 'Musica e musicisti,' vol. 2, doc. 161.

53 ASF, Crs 162.23/24, f. 188v at date 1 November 1641; Burchi, 'Musica e musicisti,' vol. 2, doc. 162.

54 ASF, Crs 162.23/24, ff. 188v–189r at date November 1641; Burchi, 'Musica e musicisti,' vol. 2, doc. 163.

55 ASF, Crs 156.2/4, fasc. C; transcribed in Burchi, 'Musica e musicisti,' 1:51n19 and 'Vita musicale,' 41n23, where, however, he gives the date in *stile fiorentino* as 1647 rather than 1647/8 or 1648.

56 I am indebted to fellow members of the 'med-and-ren-music' electronic discussion group for their assistance in translating the passage above and for explaining to me the intricate technical aspects of the organ described; in particular Ross W. Duffin, Julia Harlow, John Harper, Robert F. Judd, John Ogasapian, Chantal Phan, Richard Rastall, Timothy Tikker, and Mary Wolinski. To cite Professor Ogasapian's e-mail, 'The description is fragmentary, but what's there is typical of good organ building practice of the period (and, in fact, of any period).'

57 ASF, Crs 161.13/14, ff. 46v–47r at date 23 April 1650; Burchi, 'Musica e musicisti,' vol. 2, doc. 192. In 1651 Palmieri worked on the organ at SS. Annunziata; see Kirkendale, 391.

58 The literature on *intermedi* is vast. Suffice it to point out, for our purposes, Hill's 'Florentine *Intermedi sacri e morali*, 1549–1622,' 265–301, for its pertinence to music in confraternal plays and moralities.

59 ASF, Crs 160.8/9, f. 6r at date 2 February 1584/5.

60 On the date of Jacopo Peri's *Dafne*, see Kirkendale, 194–5.

61 ASF, Crs 162.22/23, f. 95v at date 1 November 1622; transcribed in Burchi, 'Musica e musicisti,' vol. 2, doc. 126. Hill, 'Oratory Music in Florence, I,' 135, docs. 21 and 122–4, transcribes and translates into English the text of this dialogue, which he identifies as the 'Coro d'anime del Purgatorio' attributed to Jacopo Cicognini and contained in BNCF, Magliab. VII.358, ff. 110r–112v.

62 ASF, Crs 160.8/9 at date 24 July 1644; see also the description at ASF, Crs 163.25/26, f. 35v, transcribed in Burchi, 'Musica e musicisti,' vol. 2, doc. 170, and Burchi, 'Vita musicale,' 44.

63 ASF, Crs 162.21/22 at dates.

64 ASF, Crs 162.22/23, ff. 94r–95v; transcribed in Burchi, 'Musica e musicisti,' vol. 2, doc. 125; Burchi, 'Vita musicale,' 15–17. On this performance see also above, ch. 17, pp. 224–5.

65 ASF, Crs 163.25/26, f. 155r at date 31 December 1655.

66 Hill, 'Oratory Music in Florence, III,' 135. Hill also points out that among all the confraternities in Florence, only the Arcangelo Raffaello retained a paid chapel master; the others simply hired one on an ad hoc basis; ibid., 147.

67 Hill, 'Oratory Music in Florence, II,' 250.

68 Hill, 'Oratory Music in Florence, II,' 247. Oratorios were at first an occasional event and did not become a 'regular feature of the Florentine Congregation's evening service for one or more seasons' until 'by at least 1663' (ibid., 252); see also Smither, 1:284. The Oratorians had, of course, been regularly performing oratorios in Rome since the late sixteenth century – the Florentine congregations simply lagged behind in the practice; Hill, 'Oratory Music in Florence, II,' 251. The standard work on St Philip Neri and oratorios is still Smither, where, however, the section on Florence is very brief (283–9).

69 For all these references, see Hill, 'Oratory Music in Florence, III,' 137–8 (with footnote reference to ASF, Crs 254.3 f. 85r for San Bernardino e Santa Caterina) and the detailed list of performances in his appendix on pp. 153–78.

70 Hill argues for a continuity of oratorio performance from the first into the second half of the seventeenth century; see Hill, 'Oratory Music in Florence, II,' 251–2 and 'Oratory Music in Florence, III,' 136.

71 Since oratories were not considered to be churches, they were free from the restriction against instrumental or organ music during Lent or Passiontide, and this allowed the youths to use not only organs but also other instruments such as harpsichords, viols, trumpets, lutes, and so forth. For a similar observation, see O'Regan, 896.

72 Burchi, 'Musica e musicisti,' 2:392–3; Hill, 'Oratory Music in Florence, III,' 154. In his earlier article, 'Oratory Music in Florence, II,' 247, Hill had pointed out that composers of oratorios in Florence 'were, with rare exceptions, native by birth and training.' In the case of Rome, O'Regan comments that 'indeed virtually all Roman composers of note provided music for these oratories at one time or another' (895).

73 Hill, 'Oratory Music in Florence, III,' 133. Hill's description is drawn mostly from the records of the youth confraternity of the Purificazione, or of San Marco, which became the foremost confraternity for the performance of oratorios in Florence. For the slightly different manner used by the Oratorians at their church of San Firenze, see Hill, 'Oratory Music in Florence, II,' 251–4, and, for the musical aspects, 256–9. For a fascinating and detailed description of

the performance of an oratorio at the confraternity of San Jacopo detta del Nicchio, see ASF, Crs 1246.10, ff. 299v–300r, translated in Smither, 1:286–8.

74 Smither, 1:286.

75 ASF, Crs 1246.10, ff. 299v–300r at date 27 March 1712; translated, with comment at the end, in Smither, 1:286–7. Hill, 'Oratory Music in Florence, II,' 267, concludes the contrary, saying that oratorios 'continued to serve more as a vehicle for religious inspiration and education than as a thinly disguised form of musical entertainment, a Lenten substitute for opera, at least more so than in Rome.' Because his focus is on the Oratorians at San Firenze, he may well be correct. My impression from confraternity records, however, is that in lay confraternities the devotional was subservient to the recreational aspect.

76 ASF, Crs 1246.10, ff. 299v–300r, translated in Smither, 1:287–8.

77 ASF, Crs 164.37bis/40, f. 5v at date 10 April 1691.

78 As reported by Hill, 'Oratory Music in Florence, III,' 133 n17, referring back to ASF, Ospizio dei Melani 9, filza E, no. 321. In the same article see n. 19 for references to expenses incurred by other confraternities performing oratorios.

79 Hill, 'Oratory Music in Florence, III,' 132.

80 For the increases in performances, see Hill, 'Oratory Music in Florence, III,' 140 and appendix on 153–65. For a brief comment on competition for attendance at Lenten oratorios in Roman confraternities as early as 1572, see O'Regan, 894.

81 ASF, Crs 163.26/27, f. 57r. See also the entry under Sanmartini's name in *The New Grove Dictionary of Music*, 16:472 (by Argia Bertini), from which I draw my biographical information on him. For the general interest of confraternity members in oratorios, see Hill, 'Oratory Music in Florence, III,' 132.

82 On oratorios at San Firenze see Hill, 'Oratory Music in Florence, II.'

83 ASF, Crs 163.23/24, f. 60v; Burchi, 'Musica e musicisti,' vol. 2, doc. 346.

84 Hill, 'Oratory Music in Florence, III,' 142, 148–51.

85 Bartolomeo Felici (Florence, 1695–1776) served the confraternity from 1744 to 1762. For biographical information see his entry by James L. Jackman in *The New Grove Dictionary of Music*, 6:457.

86 ASF, Crs 164.32/33, pp. 40–1; Burchi, 'Musica e musicisti,' vol. 2, docs. 676–7.

87 ASF, Crs 164.33/34, p. 190 at date 30 March 1763; Burchi, 'Musica e musicisti,' vol. 2, doc. 699.

## Chapter 19

1 See, for example, the descriptions in Bocchi and Cinelli, 265–6; Cambiagi, *L'antiquari fiorentino*, 146; and in *Firenze antica e moderna illustrata*, 7:24.

2 'Inventario ... 1690,' ASF, Crs 164.37, p. 25. Current location unknown.

3 'Inventario ... 1690,' ASF, Crs 164.37, p. 21. For their use, see ASF, 156.2/4, f.n.n. 68r. Until Baccio Comi's death, the sixteen canvases were kept at his house, but were then moved to a storage room built within the confraternity complex by his brother, Domenico; ASF, Crs 156.2/4, f.n.n. at date 17 November 1615 'fede' by Cosimo di Raffaello del Bianco and f.n.n. at date 20 November 1615 'fede' by Pasquino di Francesco, the confraternity's servant. Their current locations are unknown.

4 See below, ch. 20. See also ASF, Crs 162.22/23, ff. 79v–83v, and Giglioli, 178–84.

5 For Cosimo di Lorenzo Rosselli and his appointment as temporary guardian in the spring of 1489/90, see ASF, Crs 155.1/3, fasc. B, doc. 1, dated 8 March 1489/90. For Antonio di Tommaso *miniatore* and his appointment in 1525, see ASF, Crs 155.1/3, fasc. F, doc. 1, dated 19 February 1524/5; at the time of his appointment, Antonio was a member of the Compagnia della Vergine Maria, and therefore required permission from Fra Zanobi Pieri, prior of San Marco and father corrector of the confraternity of the Vergine Maria, to become guardian at the Arcangelo Raffaello.

6 In later documents, the list of guardian fathers refers to Rosselli's predecessor, Lorenzo Vitelli, as the fourth guardian and his successor, Domenico di Giovanni Tasselli, as the fifth, thus ignoring Rosselli's service in the interim between the two; see, for example, ASF, Crs 164.38/41, f. 7v, and ASF, Crs 160.8/9, f. 6v, at dates 18 February 1585/6 and 9 March 1585/6.

7 See the several articles by Anna Padoa Rizzo, including 'La cappella della Compagnia di Santa Barbara della "Nazione tedesca" alla Santissima Annunziata di Firenze nel secolo XV. Cosimo Rosselli e la sua "impresa" artistica,' *Antichità viva* 3 (sett.–ott. 1987), 3–18; 'La cappella della Compagnia di Santa Barbara dei Tedeschi e Fiamminghi alla Santissima Annunziata di Firenze. Opere d'arte e di arredo sec. XVI–XVIII,' *Antichità viva* 3 (nov.–dic. 1987), 10–20; 'L'altare della compagnia dei Tessitori in San Marco a Firenze: Dalla cerchia di Cosimo Rosselli al Cigoli,' *Antichità viva* 4 (maggio–giugno 1989), 17–24; 'Cosimo Rosselli, 15–16.

8 See ASF, Crs 155.1/3, fasc. B, f.n.n. at date 3–15 January 1491/2.

9 For the *Crucifixion*, see ASF, Crs 160.8/9, f.n.n. at date 28 July 1647, ASF Crs 163.25/26, f. 76r, and 'Inventario ... 1690,' ASF, Crs 164.37, p. 1. The work is an oil on canvas measuring 370 × 190 cm. and is now at the Museo di San Marco, Florence, inv. 1890, no. 2115.

10 For the *Crucifix*, the *paliotto*, and the 'quadri grandi dipinti a fresco su la tela' that were part of a ten-picture series illustrating episodes from the stories of the Archangel Raphael, see 'Inventario ... 1690,' ASF, Crs 164.37, pp. 9, 7, and 25 respectively. For all, the current location is unknown.

11 The volume is now at the ASF, Cap. Crs 627. For Valerio Spada (Siena 1613–

Florence 1688), see the biographical entry by Maria Pia Mannini in *Il Seicento Fiorentino. Biografie*, 165, and Massar.

12 ASF, Crs 160.6/7, f. 34r at date 10 August 1561. Current location unknown.

13 ASF, Crs 160.6/7, f. 33r at date May 1561. Current location unknown. Because funds for the necessary niche or pedestal were not yet available, the two busts were temporarily placed on the storage shelf inside the guardian father's desk, and from there they disappear, for they are not listed in subsequent inventories or descriptions of the oratory.

14 ASF, Crs 160.6/7, f. 19r–v at date 25 March 1560.

15 See Venturini, and also Padoa, 'Cosimo Rosselli,' 15–16.

16 ASF, Crs 160.7/8, at dates 20 May 1563 and 12 March 1563/4 respectively.

17 For the restructuring of the confraternity complex, see Del Migliore, 'Registro,' BNCF, MS Magliab. XXV, cod. 418, f. 412. Del Migliore does not give the exact dates, but says it was done 'at the time of the guardian father Girolamo di M.o Luca,' which would place the work in the years 1573–77. For the stalls, see ASF, Crs 162.21/22 at dates 1 June 1586 and 29 September 1586. For the six oil paintings see ASF, Crs 156.2/4, f.n.n., no date given. For the façade, see ASF, Crs 160.8/9 at date 8 September 1595. For the vault, see ASF, Crs 160.8/9 at date 25 December 1596. For Cinganelli and the organ, see ASF, Crs 156.2/4, f.n.n. at date 16 October 1620.

18 For Fidani's painting, see ASF, Crs 164.37, p. 1. For Neri's fresco, see ASF, Crs 160.8/9 at date 8 September 1647 and ASF, Crs 163.25/26, f. 77r at dates 8 September 1647 and 15 December 1647; and also Laur. MS Antinori 155, 'Alcune notizie delle chiese fiorentine' f. 8v. For Cinganelli's work, see Del Migliore, 'Registro,' BNCF, MS Magliab. XXV, cod. 418, f. 412.

19 For the organ loft, see ASF, Crs 160.8/9 at dates 6 October and 1 November 1641; ASF, Crs 162.23/24, ff. 188r–189r; and also above, ch. 18, pp. 247–9. For the bequest, see ASF, Crs 160.8/9 at date February–July 1644; and also ASF, Crs 163.25/26, f. 35.

20 ASF, Crs 160.8/9, ff.n.n. at date 26 July 1592.

21 ASF, Crs 160.8/9, f.n.n. at date 18 August 1561.

22 I should mention that some of these confraternity objects do appear in the extensive work edited by Dora Liscia Bemporad, *Argenti fiorentini dal XV al XIX secolo. Tipologie e marchi* (Firenze: SPES, 1992–3), 3 vols.

23 For the background and iconology of the Archangel Raphael, see Eisenbichler, 'Devotion to the Archangel Raphael.'

24 ASF Crs 160.8/9, f. 1 and ASF, Crs 164.36/38, title page. A cut-out of a black and white illustration from a published book has been pasted in ASF, Crs 155.1/3, fasc. B (on the first sheet of the fascicule containing a copy of the 1690 inventory), and it, too, depicts the archangel, Tobias, and the dog walking along; see ill. 6.

25 In 1690, when the inventory was drawn up, the father corrector was Fra Giovanni Domenico Turriti. He served the confraternity in 1679–82 and again in 1685–93. I have been unable to determine the order to which he belonged.

26 ASF, Crs 155.1/3, fasc. , f.n.n., loose leaf, 'Inventario di maseritie della compagnia di S.to Vincentio.'

27 ASF, Crs 160.6/7, f. 19v. See also Eisenbichler, 'The Acquisition of Art by a Youth Confraternity,' forthcoming.

28 Letter to me from Kristin Lister, chief conservator, Yale University Art Gallery, dated 23 March 1993. I am very grateful to Ms Lister for her kindness in offering me this valuable information.

29 ASF, Crs 155.1/3, fasc. B, f.n.n., loose leaf, 'Inventario di maseritie della compagnia di S.to Vincentio.'

30 For Lapicini's doors, see ASF, Crs 160.6/7, f. 19r–v at date March 1560. For Comi's organ, see ASF, Crs 156.2/4. f.n.n.; for the marble plaque see ASF, Crs 163.25/26, f. 25r at date 28 October 1643. For Vanni's *pianeta* see the 'Inventario ... 1690,' ASF, Crs 164.37, p. 3. For Del Chiaro's *piviale* see ASF, Crs 163.25/26, f. 37r at date 8 September 1644.

31 For Weissman and *nobilizzazione*, see his *Ritual Brotherhood*, esp. ch. 5, 'The Courtiers of God.' See also above, ch. 9, pp. 123–5.

32 The bibliography on this topic is truly vast, but it has been limited, so far, by an interest in tracing individual works or artists, rather than in examining the entirety of a confraternity's collection or the unity of a confraternity's pictorial program. Some research in this direction has, however, been carried out recently by Florentine scholars such as Sebregondi in her *La compagnia e l'oratorio* and *Tre confraternite fiorentine*, and Pagliarulo. For the variety of objects with artistic merit held by confraternities, see Sebregondi, 'Religious Furnishings.' For religious furnishings, see the section on confraternities in *La Chiesa e la Città*.

33 ASF, Crs 162.22/23, ff. 162r–164v at date 27 February 1628/9. The description is published in Burchi, 'Vita musicale,' 26–30. The play was published in 1633 by Cicognini with a title page that read: 'Trionfo | di David | Rappresentazione | sacra | del | Dott. Jacopo Cicognini | Accademico instancabile | Recitata nella Venerabile Compagnia | dell'Arcangelo Raffaello | detta la Scala | alla presenza dell'Altezze Serenissime | di Toscana l'anno 1628 | in Fiorenza | Dedicata agli onorandi Padri e Fratelli | di essa Compagnia | In Firenze | appresso Zanobi Pignoni 1633 | Con licenza de' Superiori.'

34 ASF, Crs 160.8/9 at date 20 February 1633/4 and ASF Crs 162.23/24, ff. 67v–68r at date 24 February 1633/4. See above, ch. 17. This is probably the Casino Medici next to San Marco, and not the current Palazzo Medici-Riccardi.

35 ASF, Crs 160.8/9 and ASF, Crs 162.22/23, ff. 93v–95v at date 25 September 1622. Cosimo Del Bianco had been active in the confraternity since his youth. He

paid his entrance fee into the confraternity on 4 June 1581; ASF, Crs 165.40/48 at date. In the years that followed, he continued to be very involved in the confraternity, holding a variety of posts in the roster of officers.

36 Both youngsters were by then members of the Arcangelo Raffaello. Lorenzo Lippi had joined the confraternity five years earlier, paying his entrance fee on 27 September 1616; ASF, Crs 165.40/48 at date. I have not been able to find Baccio del Bianco's date of entrance.

37 Burchi, 'Musica e musicisti,' 1:43–4. For the membership and contributions of Baccio and Cosimo del Bianco in the *buca* of San Girolamo, see Sebregondi, *Tre confraternite, passim.*

## Chapter 20

1 Very little work has been done on Cosimo II. Because he falls on the cusp between the early grand dukes (Cosimo I, Francesco I, Ferdinando I) and the later ones (Ferdinando II, Cosimo III, and Gian Gastone), he fails to enter significantly into either area of interest. Readers might be directed to Napier's few pages on him in his *Florentine History*, 5:407–23; Young's brief ch. in his *The Medici*, 649–60, where one ought to be careful, however, not to follow his incorrect dating of Cosimo's death (28 February 1620 instead of 1621), caused by ignorance of the Florentine *ab incarnatione* calendar (his perplexity at how scholars 'like Napier' could have been 'wrong on such a point' is both amusing and sad; see 659–60). See also Municchi, 122–30, for Cosimo II's attempt to marry one of his sisters to the widowed king of Spain, Philip III.

2 Maria Maddalena of Austria was eighteen, as was Cosimo's sister Eleonora. His sister Caterina was sixteen, his brother Francesco fifteen, his brother Carlo fourteen, the twins Lorenzo and Maddalena were nine, and his youngest sister, Claudia, a mere five years old.

3 Fakhr ad-Din II (c.1572–1635) is sometimes regarded as the father of modern Lebanon because of his success in uniting the Druze and Maronite areas. His alliance with Tuscany was struck in 1608.

4 See Buonarroti.

5 Napier, 5:421.

6 For Niccolò Dell'Antella (1560–1630), see *DBI*, 37:121–4.

7 Archbishop of Pisa from 15 June 1620 to 6 January 1635.

8 Napier, 5:424. 'un consiglio di reggenza presieduto da due donne bigotte ... non poteva non facilitare l'inserimento del granducato toscano nello spirito di cortigianeria aulica, immobilistica e feudaleggiante che diviene caratteristico dell'assolutismo monarchico in Europa negli anni centrali del '600,' and '[il Concilio] era un'accolta di ecclesiastici e di aristocratici.' Diaz, 365–6

9 De' Ricci, 108–9. The editor points out that the oration appears to be unpublished. The Arcangelo Raffaello records for 1574 do not mention the event, and that is probably because the scribe at the time was not doing his job – the *ricordi* jump from April 1573 to July 1575, then briefly to March 1577 and finally to November 1581, when the new scribe picks up his pen and laments that the *ricordi* had been 'carelessly neglected' (ASF, Crs 160.8/9, f. 1r).

There is scarcely any biographical information available on Andrea di Vincenzo Alamanni (1557–1616). His father was Vincenzo di Andrea di Tommaso Alamanni (1536–90), Florentine ambassador to France (1568, 1572–6), Venice (1578), Savoy (1580), and Spain (1586–90). At the end of his father's entry in the *DBI* 1:573 there is a brief note on the son that says Andrea was made baron of Loriano and marquis of Trentola, in the Kingdom of Naples; he was made a senator in 1615 and served also as ambassador to Spain. The confraternity records mention his name in 1564 in conjunction with the entry of the twenty-two-year-old Matteo di Giuliano Gherardi, from Volterra, who was apprenticed to him ('sta in casa Andrea Alamanni per maestro, nel fondaccio,' ASF, Crs 160.7/8, f. n.n. at date 11 May 1564, Ascension Thursday). Giuliano de' Ricci mentions him a second time in his *Cronaca* in June 1582 as a business partner of Filippo Antinori, and adds that they were swindled by their cashier Galeotto Arrigucci, who ran away with a Slavic servant and an estimated six thousand *scudi* of their money.

10 De' Ricci, 246. The confraternity of the Arcangelo Raffaello in via Maffia is the one for adults, not to be confused with the youth confraternity we are describing in this volume. De' Ricci's editor notes that the Palla di Bernardo Rucellai in question is the one who died in 1596, not the senator with the same name who preceded him (1473–1543), and that neither of these orations has been published.

11 ASF, Crs 160.8/9 and Crs 162.22/23, ff. 80–3, both at date 14 March 1620/1. The actual oration is transcribed in ASF, Crs 155.1/3, fasc. G, doc. 1, 3 ff.n.n. under the title 'Orazione di Gio: Francesco Ghiberti da lui recitata nell'esequie ... del S.mo D. Cosimo 2.do.' See below for a discussion of the oration.

12 ASF, Crs 134.2, f. 20v at date 14 March 1620/1. There were, of course, orations delivered in other associations and locales, not only in Florence but also abroad. Some of these were even published. See, for example, Gualterotti, Buonarroti, or Giulio Strozzi.

13 ASF, Crs 155.1/3, fasc. G, docs. 2 and following. By way of comparison, it could be noted that the event at the confraternity of Sant'Antonio da Padova, held that same evening, cost only *lire* 42.10.0, that is, one seventy-fifth of the Arcangelo Raffaello total; ASF, Crs 134.2, f. 20v at date 14 March 1620/1.

14 The following description is, in many places, a liberal paraphrase of the Italian original found in ASF, Crs 162.22/23, ff. 79v–83v. The description was published in Giglioli, 178–84, and then in Burchi 'Musica e musicisti,' 2:48–68.

15 Giovanni Pieroni is not listed in either Bolaffi, Colnaghi, or Thieme-Becker. He is identified as the son of Alessandro di Benedetto di Girolamo Pieroni (c.1550–1607) in Thieme-Becker's entry for Alessandro.

16 On the architect and engineer Giovanni di Regolo Coccapani (1582–1649) see Thieme-Becker, 7:131; Baldinucci, 4:400–13; *Il Seicento fiorentino. Biografie*, 59–60; *DBI*, 26:435–6; Chappel. He is not listed in either Bolaffi or Colnaghi.
Giovanni had been a member of the youth confraternity of the Purificazione detta di San Marco, which he joined at age seventeen on the same day as his sixteen-year-old brother Sigismondo, 2 January 1599/1600; see ASF, Crs 1647.10, f. 37r. Their younger brothers Vincenzo and Giovan Battista also enrolled in this group – Vincenzo at age sixteen on 4 January 1603/4 and Giovan Battista at age seventeen on 6 March 1615/16 (sponsored by Parigi Parigi); see ASF, Crs 1647.10, ff. 43r and 56r respectively.

17 Giovan Battista Strozzi the Younger (1551–1634) was a founder of the academy of the Alterati (1569), a member of the Accademia Fiorentina (joined in 1570), a poet, and a generous patron of the arts, especially literature. His two major published works are a history of the Medici family (*Della famiglia de' Medici*) and a treatise on the Tuscan language (*Osservazioni intorno al parlare e scriver toscano*). His poetry has been published posthumously (*Madrigali di G.B. Strozzi il Giovane*, Firenze: Carnesecchi, 1899). He is mentioned in many works, but no monographic study has been devoted to him since the brief and now very dated work by Barbi. Barbi mentions that Strozzi 'godeva stare tra i giovani e tra gli artisti: le sue sale apriva ad ognuno o nobile o popolano o forestiero o cittadino, purché amasse le lettere o le arti, e l'onorava splendidamente alla sua tavola. La Firenze colta nei primi anni del '600 si raccoglieva intorno a due vecchi, ambedue ciechi: il Galilei e lo Strozzi' (63).

18 Filippo del Nero (d. 1648) is the dedicatee of a music manuscript now at the Biblioteca Comunale di Bologna (Q.49); see Kirkendale, 346n73.

19 Possibly the Filippo Magalotti who was rector of the University of Pisa in 1659.

20 Giovanni Battista Quaratesi attended the University of Pisa from 1617 to 1622; *Libri matricularum studii pisani*, 55, and Volpi, *Acta gradvvm*, 128. He subsequently became *provveditore* at the University of Pisa (1658–62) and tried, unsuccessfully, to establish a chair of Galilean philosophy with Carlo Rinaldini, who was already on site teaching 'filosofia ordinaria,' as its first holder; see Diaz, 456n1.

21 Jacopo Soldani (1579–1641) became a 'Jesuit, mathematician and astronomer'; see Diaz, 444.

22 Cosimo del Bianco is not listed in Bolaffi, Colnaghi, or Thieme-Becker.

23 The painter Pandolfo Sacchi is also not listed in Bolaffi, Colnaghi, or Thieme-Becker.

24 For the painter Anastagio di Piero di Stagio Fontebuoni (1580–1626), see the entries in Bolaffi 5:55–6; Colnaghi, 101, and Thieme-Becker, 12:191–2.

25 Ripa, 271–5.

26 For the painter Giovanni Mannozzi, also known as Giovanni da San Giovanni (1592–1636), see the entries in Bolaffi, 7:148–50 and Thieme-Becker, 24:26–7. He is not listed in Colnaghi.

27 For the sculptor and architect Felice Palma (1583–1625), see the entry in Thieme-Becker, 26:172. He is not listed in either Bolaffi or Colnaghi.

28 For the sculptor Orazio di Francesco Mochi (d. 1625), see the entries in Thieme-Becker, 24:602, and Colnaghi, 184. He is not listed in Bolaffi.

29 For Agostino Ubaldini (b. 1590), see Thieme-Becker, 5:207, under the name Agostino Bugiardini.

30 For the sculptor Francesco Susini (d. 1646), see the entry in Thieme-Becker, 32:305–6. He is not listed in Bolaffi or Colnaghi.

31 Ripa, 441–3, 179.

32 For the painter Ottavio Vannini (1585–1643), see the entries in Thieme-Becker, 34:100, and Bolaffi, 11:242–53. He is not listed in Colnaghi.

33 For the architect and painter Sigismondo di Regolo Coccapani (1583–1642), younger brother of Giovanni, see the entry in Thieme-Becker, 7:131–2; *DBI*, 26:436–8; Baldinucci, 4:414–20; *Il Seicento fiorentino. Biografie*, 59–60; and Chappel, 32–7. The seventeen-year-old Sigismondo enrolled in the youth confraternity of San Marco on the same day as his younger brother Giovanni, 2 January 1599/1600 (see above, note 16); ASF, Crs 1647.10, f. 37r.

34 Location unknown for these sketches. See Acanfora, 74–5, for a denial of Chappel's claim that sketches no. 2651A, 2652A, 1948S at the Gabinetto Disegni e Stampe, Uffizi, Firenze, are drawings for the obsequies of Cosimo II. She does, however, agree with Chappel that the drawings are by Sigismondo, and not by his brother Giovanni or by Ludovico Cardi detto il Cigoli. See also her biographical entry for Sigismondo in *Il Seicento fiorentino. Biografie*, 59–60.

35 Antonio di Jacopo Peri (d. 23 March 1627), son of the composer; see Kirkendale, 234.

36 The *mappamondo* that hung in the *stanzone* went not to a donor, but to the principal architect of the set, Giovanni Pieroni.

37 The painter Francesco Corniccieri is not listed in either Bolaffi, Colnaghi, or Thieme-Becker.

38 For the painter Giovan Battista Lupicini (d. 1648), see Thieme-Becker, 23:171 and Colnaghi, 165. He is not listed in Bolaffi.

39 The painter Paulantonio Guerrini is not listed in either Bolaffi, Colnaghi, or Thieme-Becker.

40 The painter Giuseppe Buonaiuti is not listed in either Bolaffi, Colnaghi, or Thieme-Becker.

41 For all the payments mentioned in this section, see ASF, Crs 155.1/3, fasc. G, unnumbered folios, at dates ranging from 30 March to 26 April 1621.

42 ASF, Crs 165.40/48, f. 22v at date 24 February 1589.

43 *The New Grove Dictionary of Music*, 7:81–7.

44 ASF, Crs 155.1/3, fasc. G, f.n.n. at date 21 March 1620/1; see also ASF, Crs 162.22/23, f. 83r.

45 See appendix 3, pp. 324–5. See also Hill, 'Oratory Music in Florence, I,' 121, who points out that this is Marco da Gagliano's last appearance in the confraternity records.

46 Giovan Battista da Gagliano joined the Arcangelo Raffaello on 24 July 1599; see ASF, Crs 165.40/48, f. 65v. See also Hill, 'Oratory Music in Florence, I,' 121n54; Burchi, 'Vita musicale,' 48.

47 ASF, Crs 155.1/3, fasc. G, f.n.n. at date 27 March 1621. I have not been able to identify Signor Loreto.

48 For all these, see ASF, Crs 155.1/3, fasc. G.

49 'A un garzone d'un legnaiolo per arbitrio, che si mandò via per fuggire scandoli, havendo usato sopruto ad un'altro garzone di legnaiolo mentre lavoravano insieme 1 lire.' ASF, Crs 155.1/3, fasc. G, ff.n.n. at date 11 March 1620/1.

50 'per fichi secchi, noce, caviale, e pesciolini marinati per dar magnare alli huomini *lire* 7.7.8, per pane per li suddetti *lire* 6.16, per vino per detti *lire* 12.6.' ASF, Crs 155.1/3, fasc. G, f.n.n. at date 12 March 1620/1. Or 'per pesce marinato, fichi secchi, noce, tinche, insalata, limoni, et caviale per desinare per li lavoranti, pittori, e scultori *lire* 15.19, per un boccale di greco per detti scultori, e pittori *lire* 1.' ASF, Crs 155.1/3, fasc. G, f.n.n at date 13 March 1620/1.

51 I am indebted to Professors Giovanna Casagrande, Elizabeth Pilliod, and Benjamin Arbel for many valuable references to caviar (in Andrea Calmo, Bartolomeo Scappi, Baldassare Pisanelle, Pontormo, Michelangelo, Maestro Martino da Como, Bartolomeo Platina, Cristoforo Messisburgo, Bartolomeo Stefani) during a lively discussion on this topic on the electronic list FICINO.

52 ASF, Crs 155.1/3 fasc. G, f.n.n. at dates 16 and 20 March 1621 respectively.

53 Cesare Tinghi, 'Diario cerimoniale,' BNCF, MS Capponi 261, f. 327r.

54 The register of entrance fees for 1620 includes the payments for Cosimo II's other four sons, Giovanni Carlo (1611–62), Mattias (1613–67), Francesco (1614–34), and Leopoldo (1617–75); see ASF, Crs 165.40/48 at date.

55 ASF Crs 162.22/23, f. 83r; Giglioli, 184.

56 The description of the obsequies is in the *ricordi* ASF, Crs 162.22/23, ff. 79v–83r, while the oration is in 'Memorie di curiosità,' ASF, Crs 155.1/3, fasc. G, f.n.n. 5r–8v.

57 For published versions of orations delivered on the death of Cosimo II, see those by Michelangelo Buonarroti the Younger, recited on 21 December 1621 at the Accademia fiorentina, and by Giulio Strozzi, recited as part of the memorial service held in Venice by the local Florentine community on 25 May 1621. The published version of Francesco Maria Gualterotti's oration, which was apparently delivered in public, does not indicate the context for which it was composed. See the bibliography for fuller entries on these three works. For orations delivered in confraternities on the death of previous grand dukes, see De' Ricci, 108–9 and 246 and *passim*.

58 ASF, Crs 155.1/3, fasc. G, f.n.n. 5r.

59 ASF, Crs 155.1/3, fasc. G, f.n.n. 5r–v.

60 Gualterotti, 8; Buonarroti, 7.

61 ASF, Crs 155.1/3, fasc. G, f.n.n. 6v.

62 ASF, Crs 155.1/3, fasc. G, f.n.n. 7r.

63 ASF, Crs 162.21/22 at date 31 December 1591; see also his entry fee payment recorded in Crs 165.40/48 at date 6 January 1591/2.

64 ASF, Crs 155.1/3, fasc. G, f.n.n. 8r.

65 Diaz, 365 and 367.

66 ASF, Crs 163.25/26, f. 9r–v at date 24 August 1642. The following description is drawn from these *ricordi*.

67 Diaz refers to him as a 'galilciano,' that is, a supporter of Galileo's new scientific theories and methodology; see 451.

## Chapter 21

1 ASF, Crs 163.30/31. The decision to begin work was reached on 15 July 1736 (p. 365), a *muratore* was hired on 22 July (p. 366), and a committee of five confraternity members to oversee the work was struck on 26 July (p. 367). The committee consisted of the guardian father, Sigismondo Landini, the *governatore*, Abbot Rocco Niccolini, the Balì senator Tommaso Gaetano de' Medici, the *provveditore* Gaetano Pasquali, and Giuseppe Landini. For the Forty Hours of 1737 see p. 389 at date 20 April 1737.

2 ASF, Crs 163.30/31, p. 25 at date 7 April 1739. The confraternity held 4.75 *luoghi* in the Monte Redimibile, 6 at the Monte del Sale, 2.25 at the Monte della Pietà.

3 For the payments to Cerroti, Ciurini, and the Duomo Chapter, see ASF, Crs 161.16/17, ff. 128v–136v. For the 1751 windows and walls see ASF, Crs 161.17/18, ff. 55–6. For the lawsuit see ASF, Crs 155.1/3, fasc. A, ff.n.n. 262r–266r, dated 26 April 1754, and ASF, Crs 164.31/32, ff. 77–81, 89–91, 100. For the Landini debt, see ASF, Crs 155.1/3, fasc. B, docs. 9, 10, and 11. For the annual rental

income of 280 *lire* from Anna Nardi Valenti, see ASF, Crs 161.17/18, f. 284v and ASF, Crs 155.1/3, fasc. B, f.n.n. 213r.
4 ASF, Crs 163.30/31, *passim.*
5 ASF, Crs 163.31/32, p. 27.
6 ASF, Crs 164.32/33, pp. 59–68.
7 ASF, Crs 164.32/33, pp. 63–4.
8 ASF, Crs 164.32/33, pp. 64–82.
9 ASF, Crs 1648.12, ff. 2v–34 at date 29 June 1743. The Purificazione at first awarded three *candelotti*, but then, when the revenue from the Del Chiaro bequest was not enough to pay for all of them, the candles were reduced to two per *tornata*; ASF, Crs 1648.12, f. 37r at date 23 January 1744/5.
10 ASF, Crs 907.3, ff.n.n.
11 ASF, Crs 165.42/50.
12 The presentation copy of this book from the author to the grand duke is now at ASF, Gabinetto di Segreteria, 51. On Mehus, see Rosa. For Mehus's friendship with Filippo Stosch, see Borroni Salvadori, 599–606 and *passim.*
13 Mehus, 5–6.
14 Mehus, 11, 'Delle profane Confraternite del secolo duo-decimo,' 70–3.
15 Mehus, 105.
16 Mehus, 105.
17 Pullan, 'Support and Redeem,' 184.
18 Mehus, 167–8, citing Durant's 'Tractatus de modo Generali Concilii celebrandi, etc.' (Paris, 1545), part. II, tit. 35, 'Quod Confratriae, in quibus tam Clerici, quam Laici se ingurgitant, tollerentus, sed daretur pauperibus, quod expenderetur in eiusdem.' The first edition of this treatise was 1531. This Guglielmus Durante should not be confused with his immediate predecessor and namesake, Guglielmus Durante 'Speculator,' bishop of Mende from 1290 to 1295, whom he succeeded to the bishopric in 1296.
19 Mehus, 170–3. For Ludovico Antonio Muratori's historical summary of the confraternal movement in Italy, see his Dissertation 75, 'Delle pie Confraternità de' Laici, e dell'origine d'esse, de' Flagellanti, e delle sacre Missioni,' in *Dissertazioni sopra le antichità italiane* (1751), 3:592–607; originally published in Latin in volume 6 of his *Antiquitates italicae medii aevi, sive dissertationes ...* (1742) under the title 'De piis laicorum confraternitatibus ...'
20 Mehus, 173–85.
21 Mehus, 185–94.
22 ASF, Crs 164.34/35, pp. 258–9. Similar inquiries were made by other parish priests to the confraternities meeting in their churches. See, for example, the inquiry of Fr Gaspero Bertelli, prior of Santa Felicita, to the youth confraternity of Sant'Antonio da Padova detta di San Giorgio dei Fanciulli, dated 7 July 1784,

and the response by the guardian father, Leonardo Checcaci, on the following 1 August; ASF, Crs 135.9/10, ff. 52–3.

23 ASF, Crs 164.34/35, p. 264. Arnaldi's membership figure of 166 does not even come close to the actual paid membership of 60 recorded in the 'Registro di tasse, 1746–1785' for 1783. ASF, Crs 165.42/50. This is the register that lists the payment of the annual membership dues of 1 *lira*. Arnaldi was inflating his figures probably by counting both paid and lapsed members.

24 ASF, Segreteria di Gabinetto 51, fasc. 7, 'Nota di tutte le Compagnie della città e regola loro.' Within this fascicule there is another fascicule entitled 'Relazione sopra tutte le Compagnie, Congregazioni, Centurie, Buche esistenti in Firenze attualmente. Li 22 Ottobre 1783.' The information on the Arcangelo Raffaello appears on ff. 48v–49r.

25 In some Florentine confraternities at the time, officers were given a gift of pepper on leaving their post.

26 ASF, Segreteria di Gabinetto 51, fasc. 7, f. 87r.

27 ASF, Patr. Eccl. 43, fasc. 32, 'Stato della Comp.a dell'Arcangelo Raffaello d.a la Scala' and 'Inventario degl'arredi sacri e mobili ... 22 luglio 1784.'

28 ASF, Crs 164.34/35, pp. 276–7.

29 ASF, Segreteria di Gabinetto 51, fasc. 8bis 'Nota data dall'Arcivescovo di Firenze delle Compagnie che crederebbe utili da conservarsi in Città,' and ASF, Segreteria di Gabinetto 51, fasc. 9, 'Seconda nota data posteriormente dall'Arcivescovo di Firenze di altre Compagnie che crederebbe utili di Conservarsi.'

30 *Bandi e ordini del Granducato di Toscana*, vol. 12, no. 99. There is a manuscript copy from the grand-ducal cabinet in ASF, Segreteria di Gabinetto 51, fasc. 12, 'Editto approvato e pubblicato per la Soppressione di tutte le Compagnie'; fasc. 13, 'Motuproprio per le Compagnie che dovranno restare in Firenze, e loro Regolamento'; fasc. 14, 'Capitoli e Sistema dato alle nuove Compagnie in tutte le Cure.' See also the *Gazzetta toscana* no. 14 (2 Aprile 1785), 53–6. See also Mehus, ch. 25, pp. 185–94, for a ten-point résumé of the decree.

31 The other confraternities exempted from the suppression were the *buca* of S. Girolamo in via della Sapienza, the *buca* of S. Iacopo nel Popolo di Santa Felicita, the confraternities of the Misericordia, the Bacchetoni (or Vanchetoni), the Stimate, San Benedetto Bianco, San Salvadore, and San Filippo Neri. *Bandi e ordini del Granducato di Toscana*, vol. 12, no. 102. For the confraternity of San Niccolò del Ceppo, see the monograph by Ludovica Sebregondi Fiorentini.

32 The paragraphs that follow are a paraphrase and somewhat free translation of the edict. The original is to be found in *Bandi e ordini del Granducato di Toscana*, vol. 12, no. 99.

33 See Annalisa Innocenti; Lapucci; and Sebregondi, 'Tracce per la ricostruzione del patrimonio artistico' and 'La soppressione delle confraternite fiorentine.'

34 *Bandi e ordini del Granducato di Toscana*, vol. 12, no. 99, 'Capitoli Generali per le Compagnie di Carità.'
35 Leopold II, *Relazioni sul governo della Toscana*, 1:176–7.
36 Ibid., 1:231, 1:7.
37 ASF, Crs 164.34/35, p. 286.
38 ASF, Crs 165.43/51 and Crs 164.44/52 at date 28 March 1785.
39 AAF, Filza di cancelleria 1785 (3), doc. 62, letter 1. In his *Relazioni sul governo della Toscana*, Grand Duke Peter Leopold describes Huart as a 'Segretario ... ottimo, fidatissimo, onestissimo, esatto e vero galantuomo' (vol. 1, p. 85).
40 AAF, Filza di Cancelleria 1785, doc. 62, letter 2.
41 ASF, Patr. Eccles. 220, 'Vendite dal 1785 al 1788, Firenze.' The sale contract was drawn up by Luigi Rossi and is found in ASF, Notarile Moderno 29463. 'Luigi Rossi. Contratti 1786–1790,' contract no. 5, ff. 3r–4v.

## Epilogue

1 Bottoni, 'Le confraternite milanesi.'

# Bibliography of Manuscript Sources Cited


**Florence, Archivio Arcivescovile di Firenze (AAF)**

Compagnie VI[1], insert 'Compagnie'
Compagnie VII.II.1–2
Compagnie Religiose 02–05
Compagnie Religiose. Capitoli 02, 04
Filze di cancelleria 1782, 1785

**Florence, Archivio della Compagnia di San Girolamo (ACSG)**

Capitoli 1413/14
Deliberationi e Partiti 1500–62
Deliberazioni e Partiti 1723–51
Memorie

**Florence, Archivio di Stato di Firenze (ASF)**

Archivio delle Tratte
  11 'Deliberazioni. 1482–1491'
  44 'Notizie Antiche'
  401 'Registro dello squittinio del 1484'
  823 'Tratte. 1482 al 1485'
Carte Strozziane
  Ser. 3, vol. 233. Strozzi, Carlo. 'Breve notizia delle fondazioni, juspatronato, e altro, delle Chiese, Monasteri, Oratori, Cappelle, Spedali, &c. Opera del Sig.r Senatore Carlo Strozzi'
Catasto
  76 Campioni 1427, Santa Maria Novella, Lion rosso

79 Campioni 1427, San Giovanni, Gonfalone Drago
828 Catasto del 1457. Portate dei cittadini. San Giovanni, Gonfalone Chiavi
Capitoli, Compagnie Religiose Soppresse
314 Compagnia dell'Annunziata e della Vergine Maria
613 Compagnia del SS. Nome di Gesù
627 Compagnia dell'Arcangelo Raffaello
752 Compagnia dell'Arcangelo Raffaello
882 Compagnia dell'Arcangelo Raffaello
Compagnie Religiose Soppresse da Pietro Leopoldo
134–7 Sant'Antonio da Padova detta di San Giorgio
143–55 Arcangelo Raffaello detta il Raffa
155–65 Arcangelo Raffaello detta della Scala
254–5 San Bernardino e Santa Caterina
903, 907 Gesù Pellegrino in Santa Maria Novella
1237–43 San Giovanni Evangelista
1579 Buca di San Paolo
1640–86 Purificazione, detta di S. Marco
Compagnie Sopprese incamerate nel Bigallo, Compagnia della Dottrina dell'Assunta e S. Alberto dei Fanciulli detta del SS. Crocifisso e S. Alberto Bianco, fasc. 13, 'Filza di documenti'
Conventi Soppressi, 102
Decima Granducale, 3782 'Descrizione del Q.re di S.ta M.a Novella, 1561'
Diplomatico, Patrimonio Ecclesiastico di Firenze, 1442 giugno 24
Mannelli-Galilei-Riccardi 439, 'Fogli attenenti alla Compagnia del Vangelista e alla Buca di S. Paolo'
Manoscritti
129 Francesco Settimani, 'Memorie fiorentine'
183 G.B. Dei 'Notizie'
199 Tommaso Forti 'Il foro fiorentino, ovvero notizie e ricordi bellissimi della Repubblica Fiorentina. Usi antichi e magistrati di essa ridotti in capitoli.'
253 Lorenzo Maria Mariani, 'Priorista fiorentino'
Miscellanea Medicea
755 Cesare Tinghi, 'Diario e Cerimoniale della Corte Medicea, tenuta da Cesare di Bastiano Tinghi, ajutante di Camera del Gran Duca Ferdinado I (dal 22 luglio 1600 al 9 novembre 1623).' [vol. 3 of Tinghi's *Diario di Ferdinando I e Cosimo II …* ; vols. 1–2 are at the BNCF, MS Capponi, 261 as per below]
Notarile Antecosimiano
2532 Michele Benincasa, 1433–62
Notarile Moderno
5499 Andreini Andrea. Testamenti, 1601–5

22,456 Dal Poggio Silvestro Antonio. Protocolli, 1730–4
29,463 Luigi Rossi. Contratti, 1786–90

Patrimonio Ecclesiastico
43 'Filza I degli Stati delle Soppresse Compagnie Riunite al Patrimonio Ecclesiastico di Firenze, Loro Giustificazioni annesse'
220 'Vendite dal 1785 al 1788, Firenze'

Provvisioni, Registri 109

Raccolta Ceramelli Papiani, fasc. 3326

Raccolta Sebregondi, 3721

Segreteria di Gabinetto, filza 51

Signoria e Balia, Carte di Corredo 45

**Florence, Biblioteca Nazionale Centrale di Firenze** (BNCF)

Baldovinetti 124. 'Memorie del convento, chiesa e confraternite di Santa Maria Novella'

Capponi 261 Tinghi, Cesare. *Diario di Ferdinando I e Cosimo II gran Duca di Toscana scritto da Cesare Tinghi, suo aiutante di Camera da' 22 luglio 1600 sino a' 12 settembre 1615*. 3 vols. [vols. 1–2 are at the BNCF, MS Capponi 261, available only on microfilm; vol. 3 is at the ASF, Misc. Med. 755; partially published in Solerti.

Cirri. 13 volumes plus 2 volumes of indices and 1 volume of illustrations. Cirri, Alfredo. 'Sepoltuario'

Conventi Soppressi
B.9.432 Ducci, Domenico, OP. 'Istorie del convento di Santa Maria Novella e delle Compagnie poste nei chiostri del S° Convento' [dated 1691]
D.3.270 'Capitoli della Compagnia di San Niccolò'

Conventi Soppressi da ordinare
Badia Fiorentina 33 'Capitoli di Compagnia di San Bernadino da Siena e di Santa Caterina d'Alessandria'

Magliabecchiana
VIII, cod. 1500, fasc. 11 Del Migliore, Ferdinando Leopoldo. '1444, Istorie della Scuola o Compagnia della Purificazione di fra G.B: Bartoli'
XXV, cod. 409 Del Migliore, Ferdinando Leopoldo. 'Zibaldone Istorico, 4'
XXV, cod. 417 Del Migliore, Ferdinando Leopoldo. 'Zibaldone Istorico, 27. Compagnie'
XXV, cod. 418 Del Migliore, Ferdinando Leopoldo. 'Zibaldone Istorico, 28. Compagnie' and 'Registro delle compagnie di Firenze'
XXV, cod. 423 Del Migliore, Ferdinando Leopoldo. 'Compagnie o confraternite di Firenze. Fondazioni, dotazioni, cc. delle medesime'

xxvi, cod. 137 Del Migliore, Ferdinando Leopoldo. 'Zibaldone Genealogico settimo, G'
xxxi, cod. 11 Anonymous. 'Capitoli della Scuola delli Ingesuati, 1427'
Magliab. Strozz. xxxv, cod. 211
Nuovi Acquisti (NA)
987 'Descrizione dei Quattro Quartieri [di Firenze]'
Poligrafo Gargani
II.IV.373 'Repertorio generale de' libri di spoglio di memorie di diverse famiglie fiorentine e luoghi sacri e profani'
II.IV.374 'Raccolta cavata dal sen. Carlo Strozzi da diverse scritture'
II.IV.375 'Memorie fiorentine, luoghi sacri e profani cavate dalle scritture ... del sen. Carlo Strozzi'
II.IV.376 'Spoglie e copie di scritture fatte dal sen. Carlo Strozzi'

**Florence, Biblioteca Riccardiana** (Ricc.)

MS 2204 'Oratione del corpo di Cristo'
Moreni, 287 'Registro di compagnie, pievi e priorie della diocesi fiorentina' [cart., sec. XVII; 18 cc.]

**Florence, Biblioteca Marucelliana** (Maruc.)

Cod. A.147 'Contratto della Compagnia della Scala per conto del trattare con i Mazzinghi confinanti a detta Compagnia di 26 luglio 1573 rogato da Angiolo di Ser Lorenzo Favilla'

**Florence, Biblioteca Laurenziana** (Laur.)

Biblioteca S. Marco, 370 'Chronica convenctus [*sic*] Sancti Marci de Florentia or. pr.' 220 ff.
Antinori, 155 'Alcune notizie delle chiese fiorentine'

**Florence, Private Archive of the Marchese Rosselli del Turco**

MS 43, 2 Giovan Maria Cecchi, 'Il Tobia'

**Florence, Santa Maria Novella, Convent Library** (SMN)

Bilioctus. Biliotti, Modesto and L. Maraffi, R. Badii, 'Chronica pulcherrimae aedis magnique coenobii S. Mariae cognomento Novellae Florentinae civitatis, A.D. 1586' (seen thanks to Fr I.P. Grossi, OP)

**Siena, Biblioteca Comunale degli Intronati di Siena (BCI)**

A.X.18 Compagnia dei fanciulli sotto il titolo di s. Bernardino di Siena. Capitoli
H.XI.55 Giovan Maria Cecchi, Miscellanea
H.XI.56 Giovan Maria Cecchi, Miscellanea
I.VII.27 Giovan Maria Cecchi, Commedie
I.VII.29 Giovan Maria Cecchi, Commedie

**UK. British Library (BL)**

Addit. 28, 178 (Note: this BL manuscript is a copy of ASF, Signoria e Balia, Carte di Corredo 45, f. 18v)

**USA. University of Pennsylvania, Library**
MS 226 Ital. Fontana, Bartolomeo. 'Itinerari'

# Bibliography of Published Works Cited


Acanfora, Elisa. 'Sigismondo Coccapani disegnatore e trattatista.' *Paragone. Arte* 40:477 (1989): 71–99.

*Acta Sanctorum*. Paris, 1680.

Acton, Harold. *The Last Medici*. New York: Thames and Hudson, 1980.

Ademollo, Agostino. *Marietta de' Ricci ovvero Firenze al tempo dell'Assedio. Racconto storico*. Con correzioni e aggiunte per cura di Luigi Passerini. 2nd ed. Firenze: Stabilimento Chiari, 1845. 6 vols.

Aiazzi, Giuseppe. *Narrazioni istoriche delle più considerevoli inondazioni dell'Arno e notizie scientifiche sul medesimo*. Verona: L'Arco dei Gavi, [1967].

Alberigo, G. 'Contributi alla storia delle confraternite dei disciplinati e della spiritualità laicale nei secoli XV e XVI.' In *Il movimento dei disciplinati* ... (1962): 156–252.

Amati, Antonietta. 'Cosimo I e i frati di S. Marco.' *Archivio storico italiano* 81 (1923; published 1925): 227–77.

Ammirato, Scipione (the Younger). *Delle famiglie nobili fiorentine*. Firenze: Appresso G. Donato e B. Giunti & Compagni, 1615; rpt. Bologna: Forni, 1969.

– *Vescovi di Fiesole, di Volterra, e d'Arezzo*. Firenze: A. Mazzi, 1637.

Ansaldi, Jacopo. *Discorsi spirituali et civili, secondo il catechismo per instruttione di giovani desiderosi far profitto nella vita spirituale et civile, fatti da messer Jacopo Ansaldi, dottor di legge*. In Firenze: Appresso Giorgio Marescotti, 1583.

– *Dottrina cristiana. Nuovamente ristampata, & publicata per ordine dell'Illustriss. & Reverendiss. Cardinal di Firenze. Da insegnarsi, & esercitarsi dalli Curati, & Guardiani di Compagnie de' Fanciulli della suo [*sic*] Diocesi per publica utilità*. In Firenze: Appresso Francesco Tosi, e Comp., 1585.

Ansidei, Vincenzo. *Regestum reformationum communis Perusinis ab anno 1256 ad annum 1300*. Perugia: Deputazione di Storia Patria, 1935.

Aranci, Gilberto. *Formazione religiosa e santità laicale a Firenze tra Cinque e Seicento. Ippolito Galantini fondatore della Congregazione di San Francesco della

*Dottrina Cristiana di Firenze (1565–1620)*. Pubblicazioni dell'Archivio Arcivescovile di Firenze, Studi e Testi 2. Firenze: Giampiero Pagnini Editore, 1997.

*Archivio delle Tratte*. Introduzione e inventario a cura di Paolo Viti e Raffaella Maria Zaccaria. Pubblicazioni degli Archivi di Stato. Strumenti CV. Roma: Ufficio Centrale per i Beni Archivistici, 1989.

Arditi, Bastiano. *Diario di Firenze e di altre parti della cristianità (1574–1579)*. Firenze: Istituto Nazionale di Studi sul Rinascimento, 1970.

Ariès, Philippe. *Centuries of Childhood. A Social History of Family Life*, trans. Robert Baldick. New York: Alfred A. Knopf, 1962.

Artusi, Luciano, and Antonio Patruno. *Deo gratias. Storia, tradizioni, culti e personaggi delle antiche confraternitie fiorentine*. Roma: Newton Compton Editori, 1994.

Baccini, Giuseppe. *Notizie di alcune commedie sacre rappresentate in Firenze nel secolo XVII*. Firenze: Libreria Dante, 1889.

Baldinucci, Filippo. *Notizie dei professori del disegno da Cimabue in qua*. Firenze: Batelli, 1846. 6 vols.

Baldocci Nigetti, Dionisio. *Vita del venerabile servo di Dio Ippolito Galantini, fondatore della Congregazione di S. Francesco della dottrina cristiana*. Roma, 1657.

*Bandi e ordini del Granducato di Toscana*. Firenze: Per Gaetano Cambiagi, 1786.

Bandini, Angelo Maria. *Specimen literaturae florentinae saeculi XV*. Florentiae: Sumptibus Iosephi Rigacci, 1751.

– *Vita di Amerigo Vespucci*. Firenze: Auspice il Comune, 1898.

Barbi, Adrasto Silvio. *Un accademico mecenate e poeta*. Firenze: Sansoni, 1900.

Barnes, Andrew E. 'Religious Anxiety and Devotional Change in Sixteenth Century French Penitential Confraternities.' *Sixteenth Century Journal* 19:3 (1988): 389–405.

– 'Poor Relief and Brotherhood,' *Journal of Social History* 24:3 (1991): 603–11.

– *The Social Dimension of Piety. Associative Life and Devotional Change in the Penitent Confraternities of Marseilles (1499–1792)*. New York: Paulist Press, 1994.

Barr, Cyrilla. *The Monophonic Lauda and the Lay Religious Confraternities of Tuscany and Umbria in the Late Middle Ages*. Kalamazoo, Mich.: Western Michigan University/Medieval Institute, 1988.

Benvenuti Papi, Anna. 'Fonti e problemi per la storia dei penitenti a Firenze nel secolo XIII.' In *L'ordine della penitenza di San Francesco d'Assisi nel secolo XIII*. Atti del convegno di studi francescani, Assisi 3–5 luglio 1972 [special issue of] *Collectanea franciscana* 43:1–3 (1974): 279–301.

– 'L'impianto mendicante in Firenze, un problema aperto.' *Mélanges de l'Ecole Française de Rome-Moyen Age, Temps Modernes* 89:2 (1977): 597–608.

– 'I frati della penitenza nella società fiorentina del Due-Trecento.' In *I frati penitenti di San Francesco nella società del Due e Trecento.* Atti del 2° convegno di Studi Francescani, Roma 12–14 ottobre 1976, ed. Mariano D'Alatri. Roma: Istituto Storico dei Cappuccini, 1977, pp. 191–220.

– 'Penitenza e penitenti in Toscana. Stato della questione e prospettive della ricerca.' *Ricerche di storia sociale e religiosa* n.s. 17/18 (1980): 107–20.

Bertoldi Lenoci, Liana. 'Confraternite e comitati antoniani nella realtà pugliese.' In *Sant'Antonio oggi. Presenza viva nella pietà, nella pastorale, nell'impegno caritativo, sociale e culturale.* Atti del convegno di studio, Padova, 12–20 maggio 1989. Padova: Edizioni Messaggero, 1990, pp. 80–9.

*Bibliotheca sanctorum.* Vatican City: Istituto Giovanni XXIII, 1961–8.

Bisticci, Vespasiano da. *Vite di uomini illustri del secolo XV*, ed. Paolo D'Ancona and Erhard Aeschlimann. Milano: Ulrico Hoepli, 1951.

Black, Christopher F. *Italian Confraternities in the Sixteenth Century.* Cambridge: Cambridge University Press, 1989.

Black, Robert. *Benedetto Accolti and the Florentine Renaissance.* Cambridge: Cambridge University Press, 1985.

Bocchi, Francesco, and Giovanni Cinelli. *Le bellezze della città di Firenze ... ora da M. Giovanni Cinelli ampliate, ed accresciute.* Firenze: G. Gugliantini, 1677; rpt. Bologna: Forni, 1974.

Bolzoni, Roberto. 'Dalla fine del XII agli inizi del XV secolo. Tra movimenti religiosi e confraternite in Italia.' In *Storia vissuta del popolo cristiano*, ed. Jean Delumeau, Italian edition ed. Franco Bolgiani. Torino: Società editrice internazionale, 1985, pp. 331–47.

Bornstein, Daniel E. *The Bianchi of 1399. Popular Devotion in Late Medieval Italy.* Ithaca: Cornell University Press, 1993.

Borroni Salvadori, Fabia. 'Tra la fine del Granducato e la Reggenza. Filippo Stosch a Firenze.' *Annali della Scuola normale superiore, Classe di Lettere e Filosofia*, ser. 3, 8:2 (1978): 565–614.

Bossy, John. *Christianity and the West 1400–1700.* Oxford and New York: Oxford University Press, 1985.

Bottoni, Riccardo. 'Le confraternite milanesi nell'età di Maria Teresa: aspetti e problemi.' In *Economia, istituzioni, cultura in Lombardia nell'età di Maria Teresa.* Bologna: Il Mulino, 1982, 3:595–607.

Brackett, John. *Criminal Justice and Crime in Late Renaissance Florence, 1537–1609.* Cambridge: Cambridge University Press, 1992.

Brocchi, Giuseppe Maria. *Vite de' Santi e Beati fiorentini.* Firenze: Gaetano Albizzini, 1742, 1762, 1761 [*sic*]. 3 vols.

Brown, Alison. *Bartolomeo Scala, 1430–1497, Chancellor of Florence.* Princeton: Princeton University Press, 1979.

Bucci, Mario, and Raffaello Bencini. *I Palazzi di Firenze. Quartiere di Santa Maria Novella*. Firenze: Vallecchi, 1973.

Buonarroti the Younger, Michel Angelo. *Delle lodi del Granduca di Toscana, Cosimo II. Orazione di Michelagnol Buonarroti, recitata da lui nell'Accademia fiorentina il dì 21 di dicembre 1621*. In Firenze: Appresso Pietro Cecconcelli, 1622.

Buoninsegni, Tommaso. *Descrizzione della traslazione del corpo di santo Antonino arcivescovo di Firenze fatta nella Chiesa di San Marco l'anno MDLXXXIX*. Firenze: Bartolommeo Sermartelli, 1589.

Burchi, Guido. 'Musica e musicisti nella Compagnia della "Scala" di Firenze (1556–1785).' Tesi di Laurea, Facoltà di Lettere e Filosofia, Università degli Studi di Firenze, Anno Accademico 1971/2. 2 vols.

– 'Vita musicale e spettacoli alla Compagnia della Scala di Firenze fra il 1560 e il 1675.' *Note d'Archivio per la Storia Musicale* n.s. 1 (1983): 9–50.

Burlamacchi, Pacifico (pseud.) *La vita del beato Ieronimo Savonarola*, ed. Pietro Ginori Conti, intro. R. Ridolfi. Firenze: Olschki, 1937.

Calzolai, Carlo Celso. 'L'Archivio arcivescovile fiorentino, inventario sommario' *Rassegna storica toscana* 3 (1957): 127–81.

– 'L'archivio arcivescovile fiorentino,' *Rassegna storica toscana* 3 (1957): 127–81.

– 'S. Antonino e "le buche."' *Sant'Antonino* 1:5 (1958): 9–11.

– 'Opere minori di S. Antonino. La *Dottrina Cristiana* e *De ornatu mulierum*.' *Sant'Antonino nel V centenario della morte* 11 (April 1959): 9–11.

– *Frate Antonino Pierozzi*. Roma: 1960.

– *Fra Antonio, Arcivescovo di Firenze*. N.p., 1961.

– 'Archivio arcivescovile.' *Archivio storico italiano* 114 (1965): 400–3.

Cambi, Giovanni. *Istorie*, in *Delizie degli eruditi toscani* vols. 20–3. Firenze: Gateano Cambiagi, 1785–6.

Cambiagi, Gaetano. *Memorie istoriche riguardanti le feste solite farsi in Firenze per la Natività di San Gio. Batista Protettore della Città, e Dominio Fiorentino*. In Firenze: nella Stamperia Granducale, 1766; rpt. Firenze: Mediocredito Toscano, 1985.

– *L'antiquario fiorentino o sia guida per osservar con metodo le cose notabili della città di Firenze*. 3rd ed. Firenze: Nella Stamperia Granducale, 1778.

*Canons and Decrees of the Council of Trent*, trans. H.J. Schroeder. Rockford, Ill.: Tan Books and Publishers, 1978.

Cantelli, Giuseppe. *Repertorio della pittura fiorentina del Seicento*. Firenze: Opus-Libri, 1983.

Cappelli, Eugenio. *La Compagnia dei Neri. L'arciconfraternita dei battuti di Santa Maria della Croce al Tempio*. Firenze: Felice Le Monnier, [1927].

Carnesecchi, C. 'Notizie di Firenze del 1605–1608.' In *L'Illustratore fiorentino*. Firenze: Tipografia Domenicana, 1908, pp. 109–20.

Carocci, Guido. *San Martino in via della Scala. Ricordo storico.* Firenze: [n.p.], 1898.

– *I dintorni di Firenze.* Firenze: Galletti e Cocci, 1907.

Carter, Tim. 'Music and Patronage in Late Sixteenth-Century Florence. The Case of Jacopo Corsi (1561–1602).' *I Tatti Studies* 1 (1985): 57–104.

– '"Non occorre nominare tanti musici." Private Patronage and Public Ceremony in Late Sixteenth-Century Florence.' *I Tatti Studies* 4 (1991): 89–104.

Casagrande, Giovanna. 'Gli iscritti della Confraternita dei Disciplinati di San Francesco in Perugia.' *Annali della Facoltà di Lettere e Filosofia. Università degli Studi di Perugia* 16/17, n.s. 2/3 (1978–80): 101–63.

Cecchi, Giovan Maria. *Commedie*, ed. Michele dello Russo. Napoli: F. Ferrante, 1869.

– *Drammi spirituali inediti di Giovan Maria Cecchi*, ed. Raffaello Rocchi. Firenze: Le Monnier, 1895. 2 vols.

– *The Horned Owl*, trans. Konrad Eisenbichler. Carleton Renaissance Plays in Translation, 3. Waterloo, Ont.: Wilfrid Laurier University/Ottawa: Dovehouse Editions Canada, 1981.

– *Ragionamenti spirituali*, ed. and intro. Konrad Eisenbichler. Ottawa: Dovehouse Editions Canada, 1986.

Centi, Tito S. 'S. Antonino Pierozzi (fondatore di S. Marco).' In *La Chiesa e il Convento di San Marco a Firenze.* Firenze: Giunti, 1989.

Ceracchini, A. *Cronologia sacra dei vescovi e arcivescovi di Firenze.* Firenze, Jacopo Guiducci e Santi Franchi, 1761.

Chappel, Miles L. 'The Shaping of Giovanni and Sigismondo Coccapani.' *Antichità viva* (1994): 32–8.

Châtellier, Louis. *The Europe of the Devout. The Catholic Reformation and the Formation of a New Society*, trans. Jean Birrell. Cambridge and New York: Cambridge University Press, 1989.

*La Chiesa e la Città a Firenze nel XV secolo. Catalogo della mostra, Firenze, Sotterranei di San Lorenzo, 6 giugno–6 settembre 1992.* A cura di Gianfranco Rolfi, Ludovica Sebregondi, Paolo Viti. Milano: Silvana Editoriale, 1992.

Chiffoleau, Jacques. *La comptabilité de l'au-delà: Les hommes, la mort et la religion dans la région d'Avignon à la fin du Moyen-Age.* Rome: Ecole française de Rome, 1980.

– 'Entre le religieux et le politique: les confréries du Saint-Esprit en Provence et en Comtat Venaissin à la fin du Moyen Age.' In *Le mouvement confraternel au Moyen Age. France, Italie, Suisse.* Rome. Ecole Française de Rome: 1987, pp. 9–40.

Chojnacki, Stanley. 'Political Adulthood in Fifteenth-Century Venice.' *American Historical Review* 91:4 (1986): 791–810.

– 'Measuring Adulthood: Adolescence and Gender in Renaissance Venice.' *Journal of Family History* 17:4 (1992): 371–95.

*Christianity and the Renaissance. Image and Religious Imagination in the Renaissance*, ed. Timothy Verdon and John Henderson. Syracuse: Syracuse University Press, 1990.

Cicero. *De officiis*, trans. Walter Miller, Loeb Classical Library. Cambridge, Mass.: Harvard University Library, 1975.

Cicognini, Jacopo. *La celeste guida o vere, l'Arcangelo Raffaello*. Venice: Bernardo Giunti, 1625.

Cistellini, A. 'Una pagina di storia religiosa di Firenze nel secolo XVII.' *Archivio storico italiano* 125 (1967): 186–245.

– 'San Filippo Neri e la sua patria.' *Rivista di storia della Chiesa in Italia* 23 (1969): 54–111.

*La città degli Uffizi. I musei del futuro*. Exhibition catalogue. Firenze: Sansoni, 1982.

Colnaghi, Dominic Ellis. *A Dictionary of Florentine Painters from the 13th to the 17th Centuries*, intro. Harold Acton, Mina Gregory, Piero Marchi, Carlo Malvani. Firenze: Archivi Colnaghi, 1986.

*La comunità cristiana fiorentina e toscana nella dialettica religiosa del Cinquecento*. Exhibition catalogue. Firenze: Becocci, 1980.

*Conciliorum Oecumenicorum Decreta*, ed. Giuseppe Josepho Alberigo, Giuseppe A. Dossetti, Perikle-P. Joannou, Claudio Leonardi, Paolo Prodi. 3rd ed. Bologna: Istituto per le Scienze Religiose, 1973.

Corradi, Alfonso. *Annali delle epidemie occorse in Italia dalle prime memorie fino al 1850*. Bologna, 1865–94; rpt. Bologna: Forni, 1972. 5 vols.

Cosenza, Mario Emilio. *Biographical and Bibliographical Dictionary of the Italian Humanists and of the World of Classical Scholarship in Italy, 1300–1800*. 2nd ed. rev. and enlarged. Boston: G.K. Hall, 1962. 5+1 vols.

Crinò, Anna Maria. *Documenti inediti sulla vita e l'opera di Jacopo e di Giacinto Andrea Cicognini*. Firenze: Leo S. Olschki, 1962.

*Crossing the Boundaries: Christian Piety and the Arts in Italian Medieval and Renaissance Confraternities*, ed. Konrad Eisenbichler. Kalamazoo: Western Michigan University, 1991.

D'Addario, Arnaldo. *Aspetti della Controriforma a Firenze*. Pubblicazioni degli Archivi di Stato, 77. Roma: Ministero dell'Interno; Firenze: Tip. Giuntina, 1972.

da Empoli, Giovanni. 'Lettera di Giovanni da Empoli a Leonardo suo padre intorno al viagio da lui fatto a Malacca e frammenti di altre lettere del medesimo aggiuntavi la vita di esso Giovanni scritta da Girolamo da Empoli suo zio.' *Archivio storico italiano. Appendice* 3 (1846): 7–92.

D'Afflitto, Chiara. 'Precisazioni sulla fase giovanile di Lorenzo Lippi.' *Paragone* 30:353 (1979): 61–76.

– 'La "conversione" di Lorenzo Lippi.' *Paradigma* (1992): 111–34.

D'Ancona, Alessandro. *Sacre rappresentazioni dei secoli XIV, XV e XVI*. Firenze: Le Monnier, 1872. 3 vols.

– *Origini del teatro italiano*. Torino: Ermanno Loescher, 1891. 3 vols.

Davidson, Nicholas. 'Theology, Nature and the Law: Sexual Sin and Sexual Crime in Italy from the Fourteenth to the Seventeenth Century.' In *Crime, Society and the Law in Renaissance Italy*, ed. Trevor Dean and K.J.P. Lowe. Cambridge: Cambridge University Press, 1994, pp. 74–98.

Dei, Benedetto. *La cronica dall'anno 1400 all'anno 1500*, ed. Roberto Barducci, pref. Anthony Molho. Firenze: Francesco Papafava, 1984.

De la Roncière, Charles M. 'La place des confréries dans l'encadrement religieux du contado florentin au xiv$^{e}$ siècle. I. L'example de la Val d'Elsa. ii. Appendices.' *Mélanges de l'Ecole Française de Rome. Moyen Age-Temps Modernes* 85:1–2 (1973): 31–77, 633–71.

– 'Les confréries à Florence et dans son contado aux xiv$^{e}$–xv$^{e}$ siècles.' In *Le mouvement confraternel au Moyen Age. France, Italie, Suisse*. Rome: Ecole Française de Rome, 1987, pp. 297–342.

Del Campana, D. 'La biblioteca ascetica del b. Ippolito Galantini (m. 1619), terziario francescano.' In *Studi francescani* ser. 3, vol. 18 (1946): 66–78.

Della Torre, Arnaldo. *Storia dell'Accademia Platonica di Firenze*. Firenze: G. Carnesecchi e Figli, 1902.

Del Lungo, Isidoro. *Florentia. Uomini e cose del Quattrocento*. Florence: Barbera, 1897.

Del Migliore, Ferdinando Leopoldo. *Firenze città nobilissima illustrata*. Firenze: Nella Stamperia della Stella, 1684; rpt. Bologna: Forni, 1968.

De' Ricci, Giuliano. *Cronaca (1532–1606)*, ed. Giuliana Sapori. Documenti di filologia, 17. Milano-Napoli: Riccardo Ricciardi, 1972.

De Sandre Gasparini, Giuseppina. 'Benedettini, francescani e confraternite nel Quattrocento padovano.' In *Riforma della chiesa, cultura e spiritualità nel Quattrocento veneto*. Cesena: N.p., 1984, pp. 257–83.

– 'Movimento dei disciplinati. Confraternite e ordini mendicanti.' In *I Frati Minori e il Terzo Ordine. Problemi e discussioni storiografiche*. Todi: Accademia Tudertina, 1985, pp. 79–114.

Dezzi Bardeschi, Marco. 'Il complesso monumentale di San Pancrazio a Firenze e il suo restauro.' *Quaderni dell'Istituto di storia dell'architettura* 13 (Roma, 1966), 73–8.

Diaz, Furio. *Il Granducato di Toscana – I Medici*. Torino: UTET, 1987.

*Dictionnaire des cardinaux*. Paris: J.P. Migne, 1857.

*Dictionnaire d'histoire et de géographie ecclésiastiques*. Paris: Letouzey et Ané, 1912–current. 25+ vols.

*Dizionario biografico degli italiani.* Roma: Istituto dell'Enciclopedia Italiana, 1960–current.

*Dizionario Bolaffi dei pittori e degli incisori italiani.* Torino, 1976.

*Dizionario degli istituti di perfezione.* Roma: Edizioni Paoline, 1974–88.

*Dizionario Enciclopedico dei pittori e degli incisori italiani dall'XI al XX secolo.* Milano: G. Mondadori, 1983–90. 11 vols.

Dondaine, Antoine. 'St. Pierre Martyr.' *Archivium Fratres Praedicatorum* 23 (1953): 66–162.

Edgerton, Samuel Y., Jr. 'A Little Known "Purpose of Art" in the Italian Renaissance.' *Art History* 2 (1979): 5–61.

– *Pictures and Punishment: Art and Criminal Prosecution during the Florentine Renaissance.* Ithaca: Cornell University Press, 1985.

Eisenbichler, Konrad. 'The Religious Drama of Giovan Maria Cecchi.' PhD dissertation. University of Toronto, 1981.

– 'Spazi e luoghi nel teatro fiorentino del Cinquecento.' *Yearbook of Italian Studies* 6 (Montreal, 1987): 51–62.

– 'Plays at the Archangel Raphael's.' *Fifteenth-Century Studies* 13 (1988): 519–34.

– 'Political Posturing in Some "Triumphs of Love" in Quattrocento Florence.' In *Petrarch's 'Triumphs.' Allegory and Spectacle*, ed. Konrad Eisenbichler and Amilcare Iannucci. University of Toronto Italian Studies, 4. Ottawa: Dovehouse Editions Canada, 1990, pp. 369–81.

– 'Lorenzo de' Medici e la Congregazione dei Neri nella Compagnia della Croce al Tempio.' *Archivio Storico Italiano* 150:2 (1992): 343–70.

– 'Confraternities and Carnival: The Context of Lorenzo de' Medici's *Rappresentazione di SS. Giovanni e Paolo.*' In *Medieval Drama on the Continent of Europe*, ed. Clifford Davidson and John H. Stroupe. Kalamazoo: Medieval Institute Publications, Western Michigan University, 1993, pp. 128–39; published contemporaneously in *Comparative Drama* 27:1 (1993): 128–39.

– 'Le confraternite laicali al tempo del concilio.' In *Firenze e il Concilio del 1439.* Convegno di Studi, Firenze, 29 novembre–2 dicembre 1989. Firenze: Olschki, 1994, pp. 221–41.

– 'Lorenzo de' Medici and the Confraternity of the Blacks in Florence.' *Fides et Historia* 26:1 (1994): 85–98.

– 'Ricerche nord-americane sulle confraternite italiane.' In *Confraternite, Chiese e Società.* Fasano: Schena, 1994, pp. 293–303.

– 'Devotion to the Archangel Raphael in Renaissance Florence.' *Saints. Studies in Hagiography*, ed. Sandro Sticca. Binghamton, NY: Medieval and Renaissance Texts and Studies, 1995, pp. 251–67.

– 'Angelo Poliziano e le confraternite di giovani a Firenze.' In *Poliziano nel suo mondo*. Atti del VI Convegno Internazionale, Chianciano-Montepulciano, 18–21 luglio 1994. Firenze: Ffranco Cesati Editore, 1996, pp. 297–308.

– 'Italian Scholarship on Pre-Modern Confraternities in Italy.' *Renaissance Quarterly* 50 (1997): 567–80.

– 'The Acquisition of Art by a Youth Confraternity.' In *Ritual, Spectacle, Image: Confraternities and the Visual Arts in the Italian Renaissance*, ed. Diane Cole Ahl and Barbara Wisch. Toronto: Centre for Reformation and Renaissance Studies, forthcoming.

*Elogj degli uomini illustri di Toscana*. Lucca: [s.n.], 1771–2. 4 vols.

*Enciclopedia cattolica*. Città del Vaticano and Firenze: Sansoni, 1948–53. 12 vols.

Esposito, Anna. 'Le "confraternite" del Gonfalone (secoli XIV–XV).' In *Le confraternite romane: esperienza religiosa, società, committenza artistica*, special issue of *Ricerche per la storia religiosa di Roma* 5 (1984): 91–136.

*Etruria sacra. Triplici monumentorum codice canonico, liturgico, diplomatico*. Florentiae: Apud Caietanum Camblasium, 1782. folio.

Falvey, Kathleen. 'Early Italian Dramatic Traditions and Comforting Rituals: Some Initial Considerations.' In *Crossing the Boundaries* ... (1991), pp. 33–55.

– 'Confraternities and the History of Mystical Traditions. An Invitation.' *Confraternitas* 4:1 (1993): 3–7.

Fanti, Mario. 'Gli inizi del movimento dei Disciplinati a Bologna e la confraternita di Santa Maria della Vita.' *Quaderni del Centro di Documentazione sul Movimento dei Disciplinati* 8 (1969): 3–54.

– *La Chiesa e la Compagnia dei Poveri in Bologna. Una istituzione di mutuo soccorso nella società bolognese fra il Cinquecento e il Seicento*. Bologna: Edizioni Dehoniane, 1977.

– 'Santa Maria della Carità. Il convento e la parrocchia dal XV al XVIII secolo.' In *S. Maria della Carità in Bologna*. Bologna: N.p., 1991, pp. 13–55.

Fantozzi Micali, Osanna, and Piero Roselli. *Le soppressioni dei conventi a Firenze. Riuso e trasformazioni dal sec. XVIII in poi*. Florence: Libreria Editrice Fiorentina, 1980.

Ferraro, Bruno. 'Catalogo delle opere di G.M. Cecchi.' *Studi e problemi di critica testuale* 23 (October 1981): 39–75.

Fineschi, Vincenzo. *S. Maria Novella. Memorie sull'antico cimitero della chiesa. Il forestiero istruito*. Roma: Multigrafica Editrice, 1977. This is a facsimile reprint of two books originally printed separately in Florence, the first, *Memorie* ..., in 1787, the second, *Il forestiero* ..., in 1836.

Finnegan, Charles V. *Priest's Manual for the Forty Hours' Devotion. History, Law and Indulgences, Ceremonies, Prayers*. Paterson, NJ: St Anthony Guild Press, 1958.

*Firenze antica e moderna illustrata*. Attributed to Vincenzo Follini and Modesto Rastrelli. Firenze, 1797; rpt. Sala Bolognese: Forni, 1975.

*Firenze e il Concilio del 1439*. Convegno di Studi. Firenze, 29 novembre–2 dicembre 1989, ed. Paolo Viti. Firenze: Leo S. Olschki, 1994.

*Firenze e la sua immagine. Cinque secoli di vedutismo*, ed. Marco Chiarini and Alessandro Marabottini. Venezia: Marsilio Editori, 1994.

Fontana, Bartolomeo. *Itinerari*, ed. Robert C. Melzi. Geneva: Slatkine, 1995.

Franza, Gerardo. *Il Catechismo a Roma dal Concilio di Trento a Pio VI*. Roma: Edizioni Paoline, 1958.

Frugoni, A. 'Sui flagellanti del 1260.' *Bullettino dell'Istituto storico italiano per il Medio Evo e Archivio Muratoriano* 75 (1963): 211–37.

Fubini, Riccardo. 'Il "Teatro del Mondo" nelle prospettive morali e storico-politiche di Poggio Bracciolini.' In *Poggio Bracciolini 1380–1980 nel VI centenario della nascita*. Firenze: Sansoni, 1982, pp. 1–135.

Gams, Pius Bonifacius. *Series episcoporum ecclesiae catholicae*. Leipzig: Karl W. Hiersemann, 1931.

Garin, Eugenio, ed. *Il pensiero pedagogico dell'umanesimo*. Firenze: Sansoni, 1958.

Gavitt, Philip. *Charity and Children in Renaissance Florence. The Ospedale degli Innocenti, 1410–1536*. Ann Arbor: University of Michigan Press, 1990.

Giamboni, Lodovico Antonio. *Diario sacro e guida perpetua per visitare le chiese della città di Firenze*. Firenze: Iacopo Guiducci, 1700.

Giglioli, Odoardo Hillyer. *Giovanni da San Giovanni (Giovanni Mannozzi 1592–1636)*. Firenze: Edizioni STET, 1949.

Godin, André. 'Les confréries dans le monde mediterranéen (xv$^{e}$–xx$^{e}$ siècle).' *Confraternitas* 3:2 (1992): 15–21.

Goldthwaite, R.A., and W.R. Rearick. 'Michelozzo and the Ospedale di San Paolo in Florence.' *Mitteilungen des Kunsthistorischen Institutes in Florenz* 21 (1977): 221–306.

Goodich, Michael. *The Unmentionable Vice. Homosexuality in the Later Medieval Period*. Santa Barbara: ABC-Clio, 1979.

Gori, Pietro. *Le feste fiorentine attraverso i secoli. v. 1 Le feste per San Giovanni*. v. 2 *Firenze magnifica*. Prato: Bemporad, 1926; rpt. Firenze: Bemporad, 1987.

Grazzini, Anton Francesco. *Rime*. Firenze: Stamperia di F. Möcke, 1741–2. 2 vols.

Grendi, Edoardo. 'Morfologia e dinamica della vita associativa urbana. Le confraternite a Genova fra i secoli XVI e XVIII.' Atti della Società Ligure di Storia Patria, n.s. 5 (1965): 238–311.

– 'Le società dei giovani a Genova fra il 1460 e la riforma del 1528.' *Quaderni storici* 80 n.s. 27:2 (1992): 509–28.

Grendler, Paul F. 'The Schools of Christian Doctrine in Sixteenth-Century Italy.' *Church History* 53:3 (1984): 319–31.

– *Schooling in Renaissance Italy. Literacy and Learning, 1300–1600*. Baltimore and London: Johns Hopkins University Press, 1989.

Grossi, I.P., OP. '"Breve e util modo del viver christiano" di fra Benedetto Onesti OP. Un trattatello di vita spirituale scritto in S. Maria Novella nel 1568.' In *Santa Maria Novella. Un convento nella città. Studi e Fonti* [special issue of] *Memorie domenicane* n.s. 11 (1980): 505–73.

Gualterotti, Francesco Maria. *Orazione in morte del Serenissimo Granduca di Toscana Cosimo Secondo*. In Firenze: Appresso Zanobi Pignoni, 1622. 8vo.

Guasti, Cesare. *Le feste di San Giovanni Battista in Firenze*. Firenze: R. Società di S. Giovanni Batista, 1908.

Hall, Marcia B. *Renovation and Counter-Reformation. Vasari and Duke Cosimo in S.ta Maria Novella and S.ta Croce 1565–1577*. Oxford and New York: Oxford University Press, 1979.

Harding, Robert. 'The Mobilization of Confraternities against the Reformation in France.' *Sixteenth Century Journal* 16 (1980): 85–107.

Härth-Ragaller, Isolde. 'Kirche und Kloster "Madonna della Pace" in Florenz.' In *Kunst des Barock in der Toskan. Studien zur Kunst unter den letzten Medici*. Munich: Bruckmann, 1976, pp. 289–95.

Hatfield, Rab. 'The Compagnia de' Magi.' *Journal of the Warburg and Courtauld Institutes* 33 (1970): 107–61.

Hay, D. *The Church in Italy in the Fifteenth Century*. Cambridge: Cambridge University Press, 1977.

Henderson, John. 'The Flagellant Movement and Flagellant Confraternities in Central Italy, 1260–400.' In *Religious Motivation. Biographical and Sociological Problems for the Church Historian*, ed. Derek Barber. Studies in Church History, 15. Oxford: Basil Blackwell, 1978, pp. 147–60.

– 'Piety and Charity in Late Medieval Florence. Religious Confraternities from the Middle of the Thirteenth Century to the Late Fifteenth Century.' PhD dissertation, Westfield College, University of London, 1983.

– 'Confraternities and the Church in Late Medieval Florence.' In *Voluntary Religion ...* (1986), pp. 69–83.

– 'The Hospitals of Late-Medieval Florence: A Preliminary Survey.' In *The Hospital in History*, ed. L. Granshaw and R. Porter. London: Routledge, 1989, pp. 63–92.

– 'Penitence and the Laity in Fifteenth-Century Florence.' In *Christianity and the Renaissance ...* (1990), pp. 229–49.

– *Piety and Charity in Late Medieval Florence*. Oxford: Clarendon Press, 1994.

Herrick, Marvin T. *Italian Comedy in the Renaissance*. Urbana and London: University of Illinois Press, 1966.

Hill, John Walter. 'Oratory Music in Florence, I: "Recitar Cantando" 1583–1655.' *Acta Musicologica* 51:1 (January–June 1979): 108–36.

– 'Oratory Music in Florence, II: At San Firenze in the Seventeenth and Eighteenth Centuries.' *Acta Musicologica* 51:2 (1979): 247–67.

– 'Florentine *Intermedi sacri e morali*, 1549–1622.' In *La musique et le rite sacré et profane*. Actes du XIII^e Congrès de la Société Internationale de Musicologie. Strasbourg: Université de Strasbourg, 1986, 2:265–301.

– 'Oratory Music in Florence, III: The Confraternities from 1655 to 1785.' *Acta Musicologica* 58:1 (1986): 129–79.

*History of the Church*, ed. Hubert Jedin and John Dolan. Vol. 5: Erwin Iserloh, Joseph Glazik, and Hubert Jedin, *Reformation and Counter Reformation*, trans. Anselm Biggs and Peter W. Becker. New York: Crossroad, 1980.

Hoberg, H. 'Das Bruderschaftswesen ams Obernhein im Spätmittelalter.' *Historisches Jahrbuch* 72 (1953): 238–52.

Horowitz, Elliott. 'A Jewish Youth Confraternity in Seventeenth-Century Italy.' *Italia. Studi e ricerche sulla storia, la cultura e la letteratura degli Ebrei d'Italia* 5:1–2 (Jerusalem, 1985): 36–74.

Housley, N.J. 'Politics and Heresy in Italy: Anti-heretical Crusades, Orders and Fraternities, 1200–1500.' *Journal of Ecclesiastical History* 33 (1982): 193–208.

Hvelsen, Christian. *Le chiese di Roma nel Medio Evo. Cataloghi ed appunti.* Firenze: L.S. Olschki, 1927.

*Infanzie. Funzioni di un gruppo liminale dal mondo classico all'Età moderna*, ed. Ottavia Niccoli. Firenze: Ponte alle Grazie, 1993.

Innocenti, Annalisa. 'Dispersione degli oggetti d'arte durante la soppressione leopoldina.' *Rivista d'arte* 44 (1992): 351–85.

Innocenti, Clarice. 'Orazio Fidani: caratteri ed evoluzione della tematica profana.' *Paradigma* 6 (1985): 85–105.

Kirkendale, Warren. *The Court Musicians in Florence during the Principate of the Medici. With a Reconstruction of the Artistic Establishment*. Firenze: Leo S. Olschki, 1993.

Kirshner, Julius. *Pursuing Honor while Avoiding Sin. The Monte delle Doti of Florence*. Quaderni di Studi Senesi, 41. Milano: A. Giuffre, 1978; originally published in *Studi Senesi* 89 (1977): 177–25.

Klapisch-Zuber, Christiane. *Women, Family, and Ritual in Renaissance Italy*, trans. Lydia Cochrane. Chicago and London: University of Chicago Press, 1985.

Kristeller, Paul Oskar. *Studies in Renaissance Thought and Letters*. Roma: Edizioni di storia e letteratura, 1956; rpt. 1984.

– *Iter Italicum*. London: Warburg Institute, 1963–93. 6 vols.

Lami, Giovanni. *Sanctae Ecclesiae florentinae monumenta*. Florentiae: Ex typographio Deiparae ab Angelo Salutatae, 1758. 3 vols.

Landucci, Luca. *Diario fiorentino dal 1450 al 1516*, ed. Iodoco Del Badia. Firenze: Sansoni, 1883.

– *A Florentine Diary from 1450 to 1516*, trans. Alice de Rosen Jervis. London: J.M. Dent and Sons, 1927.

Lapucci, Roberta. 'Storia di alcuni dipinti estratti dalle compagnie soppresse da Pietro Leopoldo nel 1785.' *Rivista d'arte* 41 (1989): 209–47.

Lastri, Marco. *Ricerche sull'antica e moderna popolazione della città di Firenze per mezzo dei registri del battistero di San Giovanni dal 1451 al 1774*. Firenze: 1775.

Le Bras, G. 'Les confréries chrétiennes.' In his *Etudes de sociologie religieuse*. Paris: Presses universitaires de France, 1956, 2:423–62.

Lee, Arthur Gould. *The Son of Leicester. The Story of Sir Robert Dudley Titular Earl of Warwick, Early of Leicester, and Duke of Northumberland* ... London: Victor Gollancz, 1964.

Leoncini, Giovanni. 'Una "Vita di Jacopo Chiavistelli pittore di figure et eccellente nell'architettura a fresco."' *Rivista d'arte* 37 (1984): 269–346.

Leopold II, Holy Roman Emperor. *Relazioni sul governo della Toscana*, ed. Arnaldo Salvestrini. Firenze: Olschki, 1969. 3 vols.

Lercaro, Giacomo. 'La riforma catechista post-tridentina a Bologna.' *Ravennatensia* 2 (1971): 11–23.

Lesnick, Daniel R. *Preaching in Medieval Florence. The Social World of Franciscan and Dominican Spirituality*. Athens and London: University of Georgia Press, 1989.

*Libri matricularum studii pisani (1543–1737)*, ed. Rodolfo Del Gratta. Pisa: Università di Pisa, 1983.

Limburger, Walther. *Die Gebäude von Florenz*. Leipzig: F.A. Brockhaus, 1910. 2 vols.

Liscia Bemporad, Dora. 'La Scuola Italiana e la Scuola Levantina nel ghetto di Firenze: prima ricostruzione.' *Rivista d'arte* 38:2 (1986): 3–48.

Little, Lester K. 'Una confraternita di giovani in un paese bergamasco, 1474.' In *Società, istituzioni, spiritualità. Studi in onore di Cinzio Violante*. Spoleto: Centro Italiano di studi sull'Alto Medioevo, 1994, pp. 489–502.

Luschino, Benedetto. 'Cedrus Libani ossia vita di fra Girolamo Savonarola,' ed. Vincenzo Marchese. In *Archivio storico italiano*, appendix 7 (1849): 39–95.

Luther, Martin. 'The Brotherhoods.' In *Luther's Works*, ed. E. Theodore Bachmann. Philadelphia: Muhlenberg Press, 1960, 35:67–73.

Maccarani, Domenico. *Vita di Sant'Antonino, arcivescovo di Firenze*. Firenze, 1708; rpt. Florence: Giuliani, 1876.

Mackenney, R. 'Devotional Confraternities in Renaissance Venice.' In *Voluntary Religion* ... (1986), pp. 85–96.

– *Tradesmen and Traders. The World of the Guilds in Venice and Europe, c. 1250–c. 1650*. London and Sydney: Croom Helm, 1987.

Magli, Ida. *Gli uomini della penitenza. Lineamenti antropologici del Medioevo italiano*. Rocca San Casciano: Licinio Cappelli, 1967; Milano: Garzanti, 1977

Maïer, Ida. *Ange Politien. La formation d'un poète humaniste (1469–1480)*. Geneva: Libraire Droz, 1966.

Manni, Domenico Maria. *Osservazioni istoriche sopra i sigilli antichi de' secoli bassi*. Firenze, 1739–82. 28 vols.

Marangoni, Giovanni. 'Breve notizia di alcuni compagni del P. Buonsignore Cacciaguerra.' Appendix to his *Vita del servo di Dio il P. Buonsignore Cacciaguerra*. Roma: Per Gio. Francesco Buagni, 1712, pp. 52–62.

Marchetti, Valerio. *Gruppi ereticali senesi del Cinquecento*. Firenze: La Nuova Italia, 1975.

Marcus, Jacob Rader. *Communal Sick-Care in the German Ghetto*. Cincinnatti: Hebrew Union College Press, 1947.

Martin, abbé. *Répertoire des anciennes confréries et charités du diocèse de Rouen approuvées de 1434 à 1610*. Paris: Fécamp, 1936.

Marzi, Demetrio. *La cancelleria della repubblica fiorentina*. Rocca S. Casciano: L. Cappelli, 1910.

Masi, Bartolomeo. *Ricordanze di Bartolomeo Masi, calderaio fiorentino, dal 1478 al 1526*, ed. G.O. Corazzini. Firenze: G.C. Sansoni, 1906.

Massar, Phyllis Dearborn. 'Valerio Spada, Seventeeth-Century Florentine Calligrapher and Draughtsman.' *Master Drawing* 19 (1981): 251–75.

Masseron, Alexandre. *Saint Antonin (1389–1459)*. Paris: J. Gablada, 1926.

Mazzuchelli, Giovan Maria. *Gli scrittori d'Italia*. Brescia: Giambattista Bossini, 1763.

Medici, Lorenzo de.' *Rime sacre del Magnifico Lorenzo de' Medici il Vecchio, di Madonna Lucrezia sua madre e d'altri della stessa famiglia*, ed. Francesco Cionacci. Florence: Torre dei Donati, 1680.

– *Opere*, ed. Attilio Simioni. Bari: Laterza, 1913–14. 2 vols.

– *Scritti scelti*, ed. Emilio Givi. Torino: UTET, 1955, pp. 549–601.

– *Selected Writings*, trans. Corinna Salvadori. Dublin: Belfield Italian Library, 1992.

Meersseman, Gilles Gerard. 'Etudes sur les anciennes confréries dominicaines. Les Confréries de St. Pierre Martyr.' *Archivium Fratres Praedicatorum* 21 (1951): 51–196.

– 'La riforma delle confraternite laicali in Italia prima del concilio di Trento.' In *Problemi di vita religiosa in Italia nel Cinquecento*. Atti del convegno di storia della Chiesa in Italia. Bologna, 2–6 settembre 1958. Padova: Antenore, 1960, pp. 17–30.

– 'Disciplinati e penitenti nel Duecento.' In *Il movimento dei disciplinati nel settimo centenario del suo inizio, 1260*. Perugia: Deputazione di storia patria per l'Umbria, 1962, pp. 43–72.

– *Ordo fraternitatis. Confraternite e pietà dei laici nel Medioevo*. Rome: Herder, 1977. 3 vols.

Mehus, Lorenzo. *Dell'origine, progresso, abusi, e riforma delle confraternite laicali*. Firenze: Per Gaetano Cambiagi, 1785.

Meneghin, Vittorino. 'Due compagnie sul modello di quelle del "Divino Amore" fondate da francescani a Feltre e a Verona (1499, 1503).' *Archivum Franciscanum Historicum* 62 (1969): 518–64.

Meschini Pontani, Anna. 'Firenze nelle fonti greche del Concilio.' In *Firenze e il Concilio del 1439*, ed. Paolo Viti. Firenze: Leo S. Olschki, 1994, pp. 776–97.

Mode, Robert L. 'Adolescent *Confratelli* and the *Cantoria* of Luca della Robbia.' *Art Bulletin* 68:1 (1987): 67–71.

Moisè, F. *Santa Croce di Firenze. Illustrazione storico-artistica*. Firenze: Presso Molini, Piatti, Vieusseux e Ricordi e Jauhau, 1845.

Monti, Gennaro Maria. *Le confraternite medievali nell'alta e media Italia*. Venezia: La Nuova Italia, 1927. 2 vols.

Monticone, Alberto. 'L'applicazione del Concilio di Trento a Roma. I 'Riformatori' e l'Oratorio (1566–1572).' *Rivista di storia della chiesa in Italia* 8 (1954): 23–48.

Morçay, Raoul. *Saint Antonin fondateur du couvent de Saint-Marc Archevêque de Florence (1389–1459)*. Paris: Librairie Gabalda, 1914.

Moreni, Domenico. *Bibliografia storico-ragonata della Toscana o sia catalogo degli scrittori che hanno illustrata la storia delle città, luoghi, e persone della medesima*. Firenze: Domenico Ciardetti, 1805; rpt. Bologna: Arnaldo Forni, 1974. 2 vols.

Morghen, Raffaello. *Medioevo cristiano*. Bari: Laterza, 1951.

Mori, Attilio, and Giuseppe Boffito. *Firenze nelle vedute e piante. Studio storico topografico cartografico*. Firenze: Tip. Giuntina, 1926; rpt. Roma: Multigrafica editrice, 1973.

Moroni, Gaetano. *Dizionario di erudizione storico-ecclesiastica*. Venezia: Tipografia Emiliana, 1840–79. 103+6 vols.

*Le mouvement confraternel au Moyen Age. France, Italie, Suisse*. Actes de la table ronde ... Lausanne, 9–11 mai 1985. Rome: Ecole Française de Rome, 1987.

*Il movimento dei disciplinati nel settimo centenario dal suo inizio (Perugia – 1260)*. Convegno internazionale, Perugia 25–8 settembre 1960. [Spoleto]: Deputazione di storia patria per l'Umbria, 1962.

Muir, Ed. *Civic Ritual in Renaissance Venice*. Princeton: Princeton University Press, 1981.

Municchi, A. 'Un episodio della politica internazionale di Cosimo II de' Medici.' *Rivista delle biblioteche e degli archivi* 23 (1912): 122–30.

Muraro, Maria Teresa. 'la festa a Venezia e le sue manifestazioni rappresentative: Le

Compagnie della Calza e le momarie.' In *Storia della cultura veneta* 3:3 *Dal primo Quattrocento al Concilio di Trento*, ed. G. Arnaldi and M. Pastore. Stocchi. Vicenza: Neri Pozza, 1981, 315–41.

Muratori, Ludovico Antonio. *Antiquitates italicae medii aevi, sive dissertationes ...* Mediolani: Ex typographia societatis palatinae, 1742. Rpt. Bologna: Arnaldo Forni, 1965.

– *Dissertazioni sopra le antichità italiane*. Milano: Giambatista Pasquali, 1751.

Nagler, A.M. *Theatre Festivals of the Medici. 1539–1637*. New Haven and London: Yale University Press, 1964.

Napier, Henry Edward. *Florentine History from the Earliest Authentic Records to the Accession of Ferdinand the Third*. London Edward Moxon, 1846–7. 6 vols.

Nelson, Jonathan. 'Aggiunte alla cronologia di Filippino Lippi.' *Rivista d'Arte* Anno 43, Ser. Quarta vol. 7 (1991): 33–57.

Nencini, Franco. *Florence: The Days of the Flood*, pref. Enrico Mattei. London: George Allen and Unwin 1967.

Neri, Benedetto. *Un sermone inedito di Angelo Ambrogini Poliziano*. Montepulciano: Lippi e Brencioni, 1902.

*New Catholic Encyclopedia*. New York: McGraw-Hill, 1967.

*The New Grove Dictionary of Music*, ed. Stanley Sadie. London: Macmillan, 1980. 20 vols.

*The New Grove Dictionary of Opera*, ed. Stanley Sadie. London: Macmillan, 1992. 4 vols.

Newbigin, Nerida. 'The Word Made Flesh. The Rappresentation of Mysteries and Miracles in Fifteenth-Century Florence.' In *Christianity and the Renaissance ...* (1990), pp. 361–75.

– '*Cene* and *Cenacoli* in the Ascension and Pentecost Companies of Fifteenth-Century Florence.' In *Crossing the Boundaries ...* (1991), pp. 90–107.

– 'Piety and Politics in the *feste* of Lorenzo's Florence.' In *Lorenzo il Magnifico e il suo mondo*. Convegno internazionale di studi, Firenze 9–13 giugno 1992, ed. Gian Carlo Garfagnini. Firenze: L.S. Olschki, 1994, pp. 17–41.

Niccoli, Ottavia. 'Compagnie di bambini nell'Italia del Rinascimento.' *Rivista storica italiana* 101 (1989): 346–74.

*Il notaio nella civiltà fiorentina. Secoli XIII–XIV*. Mostra nella Biblioteca Medicea Laurenziana. Firenze, 1 ottobre–10 novembre 1984. Firenze: Vallecchi Editore, 1984.

*Nuovo Corpus di Sacre Rappresentazioni fiorentine del Quattrocento*, ed. Nerida Newbigin. Collezione di opere inedite o rare pubblicate dalla Commissione per i Testi di Lingua, vol. 139. Bologna: Commissione per i Testi di Lingua, 1983.

O'Regan, Noel. 'Roman Confraternities and Their Oratories, 1550–1600.' In *Tra-*

*smissione e recezione delle forme di cultura musicale*. Atti del XIV congresso della Società internazionale di musicologia, ed. Angelo Pompilio, Lorenzo Bianconi, Donatella Restani, F. Alberto Gallo. Torino: EDT, 1990, 3:891–8.

Orlandi, Stefano. *Il VII centenario della predicazione e ricordi di S. Pietro Martire a Firenze (1245–1945)*. Firenze: Il Rosario, 1946.

– *'Necrologio' di S. Maria Novella*. Firenze: Leo S. Olschki, 1955. 2 vols.

– *S. Antonino. Studi bibliografici*. Firenze: Edizioni Il Rosario, 1960. 2 vols.

Owen, D.M. *Church and Society in Medieval Lincolnshire*. Lincoln: Lincolnshire Historical Committee, 1971.

*The Oxford English Dictionary*, 2nd ed. Oxford: Clarendon Press, 1989.

Paatz, Walter and Elizabeth. *Die Kirchen von Florenz. Ein kunstgeschichtliche Handbuch*. Frankfurt am Main: Vittorio Klosterman, 1940–55. 6 vols.

Padoa, Anna. 'Cosimo Rosselli e la tavola per la Compagnia dei SS. Innocenti.' *Antichità viva* 6 (1991): 15–16.

Paglia, Vincenzo. *'La Pietà dei Carcerati.' Confraternite e società a Roma nei secoli XVI-XVIII*. Roma: Edizioni di storia e letteratura, 1980.

Pagliarulo, Giovanni. 'Dipinti fiorentini del Seicento per la Compagnia di San Paolo di Notte.' *Paragone. Arte* 40:471 (1989): 53–71.

*Palazzo Ruspoli*, ed. Carlo Pietrangeli. Rome: Editalia, 1992.

Palmieri, Matteo. *Liber de Temporibus* [alternative titles *Annales* or *Historia fiorentina (1429–1474)*], ed. Gino Scaramella. In *Rerum Italicarum Scriptores*, vol. 26; 2nd ed. Città di Castello: Lapi, 1906.

Papi, Massimo D. 'Per un censimento delle fonti relative alle confraternite laiche fiorentine: primi risultati.' In *Da Dante a Cosimo I. Ricerche di storia religiosa e culturale toscana nei secoli XIV–XVI*, ed. Domenico Maselli. Pistoia: Libreria Editrice Tellini, 1976, pp. 92–121.

– 'Le associazioni laiche di ispirazione francescana nella Firenze del Due-Trecento.' In *I Frati Penitenti di San Francesco nella società del Due e Trecento*, ed. Mariano D'Alatri. Roma: Istituto Storico dei Cappuccini, 1977, pp. 221–43.

– 'Confraternite ed ordini mendicanti a Firenze. Aspetti di una ricerca quantitativa.' *Mélanges de l'Ecole Française de Rome. Temps Modernes* 89 (1977): 723–32.

– 'Santa Maria Novella di Firenze e l'*outremer* domenicano.' In *Toscana e Terrasanta nel Medioevo*. Vol. 1: *Italia, Oriente, Mediterraneo*, ed. F. Cardini. Firenze: Alinea Editrice, 1982, pp. 87–101.

Passerini, Luigi. *Storia degli stabilimenti di beneficenza e d'istruzione elementare gratuita della città di Firenze*. Firenze: Le Monnier, 1853.

– *Genealogia e storia della famiglia Altoviti*. Firenze: Cellini, 1871.

– *Genealogia della famiglia Ginori*. Firenze: Cellini, 1876.

Pastor, Ludwig von. *The History of the Popes from the Close of the Middle Ages*, ed. Frederick Ignatius Antrobius. London: Kegan Paul, Trench, Trubner, 1913–32. 22 vols.

Pelliccia, Guerrino. 'Scuole di catechismo e scuole rionali per fanciulle nella Roma del Seicento.' *Ricerche per la storia religiosa di Roma. Studi, documenti, inventari* 4 (1980): 237–68.

Penco, Gregorio. *Storia della Chiesa in Italia.* Vol. 1: *Dalle origini al Concilio di Trento.* Milano: Jaca Book, 1977. 2 vols.

Peretto, Elio. *Movimenti spirituali laicali del Medioevo. Tra ortodossia e eresia.* Roma: Edizioni Studium 1985.

Peterson, David Spencer. 'Archbishop Antoninus: Florence and the Church in the Early Fifteenth Century.' PhD Thesis, Cornell University, 1985. Ann Arbor: University Microfilms International, 1985.

Poccianti, Michele. *Vite de' sette beati fiorentini fondatori del Sacro Ordine de' Servi.* Firenze: Giorgio Marescotti, 1589.

Poggi, Giovanni. *Il Duomo di Firenze. Documenti sulla decorazione della chiesa e del campanile tratti dall'archivio dell'Opera*, ed. Margaret Haynes. Firenze: Edizioni Medicea, 1988. 2 vols.

Poliziano, Angelo. *Prose Volgari inedite e Poesie latine e greche edite e inedite*, ed. Isidoro Del Lungo. Firenze: G. Barbera, 1867; rpt. Hildesheim and New York: G. Olms, 1976.

– *Opera omnia*, ed. Ida Maïer. Torino: Bottega d'Erasmo, 1971. 3 vols.

Polizzotto, Lorenzo. 'Confraternities, Conventicles and Political Dissent: The Case of the Savonarolan "Capi rossi."' In *Politica e vita religiosa a Firenze tra '300 e '500, Memorie domenicane* n.s. 16 (1985): 235–83.

– 'Confraternities, Conventicles and Political Dissent: The Case of the Savonarolan "Capi rossi". Documents.' *Memorie domenicane* n.s. 17 (1986): 285–300.

– 'When Saints Fall Out: Women and the Savonarolan Reform in Early Sixteenth-Century Florence.' *Renaissance Quarterly* 46 (1993): 486–525.

– *The Elect Nation. The Savonarolan Movement in Florence 1494–1545.* Oxford: Clarendon Press, 1994.

Ponnelle, Louis, and Bordet Louis. *St. Philip Neri and the Roman Society of His Times*, trans. and intro. R.F. Kerr. London: Sheed, 1932; rpt. 1979.

Pontani, Anna. 'Firenze nelle fonti greche del Concilio.' In *Firenze e il Concilio del 1439.* Convegno di studi. Firenze, 29 novembre–2 dicembre 1989, ed. Paolo Viti. Firenze: Leo S. Olschki, 1994, pp. 753–812. 2 vols.

Puccinelli, Placido. *Istoria delle eroiche attioni di Ugo il Grande con la Cronica dell'insigne ed Imperial Abbadia di Fiorenza.* Milano: Giulio Cesare Malatesta, 1664.

Pugliese, Olga Zorzi. 'Two Sermons by Giovanni Nesi and the Language of Spirituality in Late Fifteenth-Century Florence.' *Bibliothèque d'Humanisme et Renaissance* 42 (1980) 641–56.

Pullan, Brian S. *Rich and Poor in Renaissance Venice. The Social Institutions of a Catholic State, to 1620*. Cambridge, Mass.: Harvard University Press, 1971.

– 'Le Scuole Grandi e la loro opera nel quadro della Controriforma.' *Studi Veneziani* 14 (1976): 83–109.

– *The Jews of Europe and the Inquisition of Venice 1550–1670*. Totowa, NJ: Barnes and Noble, 1983.

– 'Support and Redeem: Charity and Poor Relief in Italian Cities from the Fourteenth to the Seventeenth Century.' *Continuity and Change* 3:2 (1988): 177–208.

*The Pursuit of Holiness in Late Medieval and Renaissance Religion*, ed. Charles Trinkaus and Heiko A. Oberman. Leiden: E.J. Brill, 1974.

Quintillian. *Istitutio oratoria*, trans. H.E. Butler. Loeb Classical Library. Cambridge, Mass.: Harvard University Press, 1980.

Razzi, Serafino. *Historia degli huomini illustri ... del sacro ordine degli Predicatori*. In Lucca: Per il Busdrago, 1596.

*Revised English Bible with the Apocrypha*. Oxford and Cambridge: Oxford University Press and Cambridge University Press, 1989.

Richa, Giuseppe. *Notizie istoriche delle chiese fiorentine divise ne' suoi quartieri*. Firenze: Pietro Gaetano Viviani, 1754–1762; rpt. Roma: Multigrafica, 1972, 10 vols.

Ricozzi, Paolo, OP. 'Necrologio di S. Maria Novella (1505–1666).' In *Santa Maria Novella. Un convento nella città. Studi e Fonti*, special issue of *Memorie Domenicane* n.s. 11 (1980): 219–324.

Ridolfi, Roberto. *Vita di Girolamo Savonarola*. Roma: Angelo Belardetti, 1952. 2 vols.

– *The Life of Girolamo Savonarola*, trans. Cecil Grayson. New York: Alfred A. Knopf, 1959.

Ripa, Cesare. *Iconologia*. Padova: Per Pietro Paolo Tozzi, 1611; rpt. New York and London: Garland Publishing, 1976.

*Risultati e prospettive di ricerca sul movimento dei disciplinati*. Atti del Convegno Internazionale di Studio, Perugia 5–7 dicembre 1969. Perugia: Deputazione di storia patria per l'Umbria/Centro di documentazione sul movimento dei disciplinati, 1972.

Rocke, Michael J. 'Il controllo dell'omosessualità a Firenze nel XV secolo: Gli Ufficiali di Notte.' *Quaderni storici* 66 (1987) 701–23.

– 'Male Homosexuality and Its Regulation in Late Medieval Florence.' PhD dissertation, State University of New York at Binghamton, 1990. 2 vols.

Rosa, Mario. 'Per la storia dell'erudizione toscana del '700: profilo di Lorenzo Mehus.' *Annali della Scuola speciale per archivisti e bibliotecari dell'Università di Roma* 2:2 (1962): 41–96.

Rosselli, John. 'The Castrati as a Professional Group and a Social Phenomenon, 1550–1850.' *Acta Musicologica* 60:2 (1988): 143–79.

Rostirolla, Giancarlo. 'La musica nelle istituzioni religiose romane al tempo di Stradella dal Diario N. 93 (1675) della Cappella Pontificia e dalle *Memorie dell'anno santo* di R. Caetano, con alcune precisazioni storiche sulla "Stagione" di oratori a S. Giovanni dei Fiorentini.' *Chigiana* 39, n.s. 19 (1982) 2:575–831.

Ruderman, David B. 'The Founding of a *Gemilut Hasadim* Society in Ferrara in 1515.' *AJS Review* 1 (1976): 233–67.

Rusconi, Roberto. 'Tra movimenti religiosi e confraternite in Italia. Dalla fine del XII agli inizi del XV secolo.' In *Storia vissuta del popolo cristiano*, ed. Jean Delumeau. Torino: Società Editrice Internazionale, 1985.

– 'Confraternite, compagnie e devozioni.' In *Storia d'Italia. Annali* 9 (1987): 469–506.

– 'Pratica cultuale ed istruzione religiosa nelle confraternite italiane del tardo medio evo: "libri di compagnia" e libri di pietà.' In *Le mouvement confraternel au Moyen Age. France, Italie, Suisse*. Rome: École Française de Rome, 1987, pp. 133–53.

Saalman, H. *The Bigallo. The Oratory and Residence of the Compagnia del Bigallo e della Misericordia in Florence*. New York: New York University Press, 1969.

*Sacrorum conciliorum nova et amplissima collectio*, ed. Giovanni Domenico Mansi. Paris: Welter, 1903–27. 53 vols. in 58.

Sanesi, Emilio. 'L'insegnamento religioso della Dottrina Cristiana in Firenze da S. Antonino al B. Ippolito Galantini.' In *Atti del Congresso catechistico diocesano (1940)*. Firenze: 1940.

– 'Sant'Antonino e l'umanesimo.' *La Rinascita* 3 (1940): 105–16.

– *La vita di S. Antonino Arcivescovo di Firenze*. Fkirenze: Libhreria Editrice Fiorentina, 1940.

*San Lorenzo. I documenti e i tesori nascosti*. Venezia: Marsilio, 1993.

Schnitzer, Joseph. *Savonarola*. Milano: Treves, 1931.

Schultz, James A. 'Medieval Adolescence: The Claims of History and the Silence of German Narrative.' *Speculum* 66 (1991): 519–39.

Sebregondi, G. *Repertorio delle famiglie patrizie e nobili fiorentine*. Firenze, 1951.

Sebregondi Fiorentini, Ludovica. *La compagnia e l'oratorio di San Niccolò del Ceppo*. Firenze: Salimbeni, 1985.

– 'Francesco Buonarroti, Cavaliere Gerosolimitani e architetto dilettante.' *Rivista d'arte* 38:2 (1986): 49–86.

Sebregondi, Ludovica. *Tre confraternite fiorentine. Santa Maria della Pietà, detta 'Buca' di San Girolamo. San Filippo Benizi. San Francesco Poverino*. Firenze: Salimbeni, 1991.

– 'Religious Furnishings and Devotional Objects in Renaissance Florentine Confraternities.' In *Crossing the Boundaries ...* (1991), pp. 141–60.
– 'Lorenzo de' Medici confratello illustre.' *Archivio Storico Italiano*, 150:2 (1992): 319–41.
– 'Tracce per la ricostruzione del patrimonio artistico delle confraternite fiorentine soppresse da Pietro Leopoldo.' *Rivista d'arte* 43 (1991): 229–44.
– 'La soppressione delle confraternite fiorentine: la dispersione di un patrimonio, le possibilità residue della sua salvaguardia.' *Confraternite, chiesa e società. Aspetti e problemi dell'associazionismo laicale europeo in età moderna e contemporanea*. Fasano (BR): Schena Editore, 1994, pp. 457–501.
Sebregondi, Ludovica, and Gorizio Viti, *Ordo equestris Sancti Sepulchri Hierosolymitani. Sezione Toscana. Sede Attività Componenti*. Firenze: n.p., 1994.
*Il Seicento fiorentino. Arte a Firenze da Ferdinando I a Cosimo III*. Palazzo Strozzi, 21 dicembre 1986–4 maggio 1987. Vol. 1: *Pittura*. Vol. 2: *Disegno, incisione, scultura, arti minori*. Vol. 3: *Biografie*. Firenze: Cantini, 1987.
Sensi, Mario. 'Fraternite disciplinate e sacre rappresentazioni a Foligno nel secolo xv.' *Bollettino della Deputazione di Storia Patria per l'Umbria* 71 (1974): 139–217.
Smither, Howard E. *A History of the Oratorio*. Vol. 1: *The Oratorio in the Baroque Era. Italy. Vienna. Paris*. Chapel Hill: University of North Carolina Press, 1977.
Solerti, Angelo. *Musica, ballo e drammatica alla Corte dal 1600 al 1637*. Firenze: 1905; rpt. New York and London: Benjamin Blom, 1968.
Sorgenti, Fabio. *The Lives of St. Joseph Calasanctius, founder of the Pious schools, and of the Blessed Ippolito Galantini, founder of the Congregation of Christian Doctrine*. [trans. anon.] London: Thomas Richardson, 1850.
Spallanzani, Marco. *Giovanni da Empoli, mercante navigatore fiorentino*. Firenze: SPES, 1984.
Spinillo, Angelico, OP. 'La dottrina cristiana di S. Antonino.' *Sant'Antonino nel V centenario della morte* 17 (1959): 5–6.
Sricchia, Fiorella. 'Lorenzo Lippi nello svolgimento della pittura fiorentina della prima metà del '600.' *Proporzioni* (1963): 242–70.
Stefani, Marchionne di Coppo. *Cronaca fiorentina*, ed. Niccolò Rodolico. In *Rerum Italicarum Scriptores*, n.s. 30:1. Città di Castello: S. Lapi, 1903.
Strainchamps, Edmond. 'Marco da Gagliano and the *Compagnia dell'Arcangelo Raffaello* in Florence: An Unknown Episode in the Composer's Life.' In *Essays Presented to Myron P. Gilmore*, ed. Sergio Bertelli and Gloria Ramakus. Firenze: La Nuova Italia, 1978 [1977], 2.473–487.
– 'Music in a Florentine Confraternity: The Memorial Madrigals for Jacopo Corsi in the Company of the Archangel Raphael.' In *Crossing the Boundaries ...* (1991), pp. 161–78.

Strozzi, Alessandro. 'Lettere di Alessandro Strozzi.' In C. Carnesecchi, 'Notizie di Firenze del 1605–1608.' *L'Illustratore fiorentino*. Firenze: Tipografia Domenicana, 1908, pp. 109–20.

Strozzi, Giulio. *Esequie fatte in Venetia dalla natione fiorentina al Serenissimo D. Cosimo II quarto gran duca di Toscana il dì 25 di maggio 1621*. Venetia: Appreso il Ciotti, 1621. Folio.

Tarugi, Giovannangiola. 'Scritti religiosi di Angelo Poliziano.' In *Il pensiero italiano del Rinascimento e il tempo nostro*, Atti del v Convegno Internazionale del Centro di Studi Umanistici, Montepulciano, 8–13 agosto 1968. Firenze: Olschki, 1970, pp. 43–108.

Terpstra, Nicholas. *Lay Confraternities and Civic Religion in Renaissance Bologna*. Cambridge: Cambridge University Press, 1995.

Thiem, Christel. *Florentiner Zeichner des Frühbarock*. München: Bruchmann, 1977.

Thieme, Ulrich, and Felix Becker, *Allgemeines Lexikon der bildenden Künstler von der Antike bis zur Gegenwart*. Leipzig, E.A. Seemann, 1909–50; rpt. 1965–6. 37 vols.

Tinalli, Giuseppe. *S. Antonino arcivescovo di Firenze*. Firenze: Sordomuti, 1923.

Tordi, Domenico. *Compagnia di S. Jacopo d'Oltrarno detta del Nicchio o della Notte*. Firenze, 1927.

*La Toscana nell'età di Cosimo III*. Atti del Convegno. Pisa–San Domenico di Fiesole, 4–5 giugno 1990, ed. Franco Angiolini, Vieri Becagli, Marcello Verga. Ospedaletto (PI): EDIFIR, 1993.

Traversari, Ambrogio. *Latinae epistolae*, ed. L. Mehus. Firenze: Ex Typ. Caesareo, 1759; rpt. Bologna: A. Forni, 1968. 2 vols.

Trevor, Meriol. *Apostle of Rome. A Life of Philip Neri 1515–1595*. London: Macmillan, 1966.

Trexler, Richard C. 'Florentine Religious Experience: The Sacred Image.' *Studies in the Renaissance* 19 (1972): 7–41.

– 'Hospital Patients in Florence: San Paolo 1567–68.' *Bulletin of the History of Medicine* 48 (1974): 41–59.

– 'Ritual in Florence: Adolescence and Salvation in the Renaissance.' *The Pursuit of Holiness ...* (1974): 200–64.

– *The Spiritual Power. Republican Florence under Interdict*. Leiden: Brill, 1974.

– 'Lorenzo de' Medici and Savonarola, Martyrs for Florence.' *Renaissance Quarterly* 31:3 (1978): 293–308.

– 'The Episcopal Constitutions of Antoninus of Florence.' *Quellen und Forschungen aus italienischen Archiven und Bibliotheken* 59 (1979): 244–72.

– *Public Life in Renaissance Florence*. New York–London: Academic Press, 1980.

Turrini, Miriam. '"Riformare il mondo a vera vita christiana": le scuole di catechismo nell'Italia del Cinquecento.' *Annali dell'Istituto storico italo-germanico in Trento* 8 (1982): 407–98.

Uccelli, Giovanni Battista. *Della compagnia di S. Maria della Croce al Tempio*. Firenze: Dalla Tipografia Calasanziana, 1864.

– *Il convento di S. Giusto alle Mura e i Gesuati. Aggiungonsi i Capitoli della loro Regola*. Firenze: Tipografia delle Murate, 1865.

Ughelli, Ferdinando. *Italia sacra, sive de episcopis Italiae et insularum adiacentiu, rebusque ab iis praeclare gestis, deducta serie ad nostram usque aetatem*. Romae: Apud B. Tanum, 1644–1722. 2nd ed. Venetiis: S. Coleti, 1722; rpt. Bologna: A. Forni, 1972–74. 10 vols.

Unger, Dominic J. *Handbook for Forty Hours' Adoration. Legislation, Ceremonies, and Litany with Chant*. Westminster, Maryland: Newman Press, 1949.

Vaglienti, Piero. *Storia dei suoi tempi, 1492–1514*, ed. Giuliana Berti, Michele Luzzati, Ezio Tongiorgi. Pisa: Nistri-Lischi e Pacini, 1982.

Varchi, Benedetto. *Storia fiorentina*. Firenze: Salani, 1963. 2 vols.

Vasari, Giorgio. *Le vite de' più eccellenti pittori, scultori ed architettori*, ed. Gaetano Milanesi. Firenze: G.C. Sansoni, 1878–85. 9 vols.

Vasoli, Cesare. 'Giovanni Nesi tra Donato Acciaiuoli e Girolamo Savonarola.' *Umanesimo e teologia tra '400 e '500*. Special issue of *Memorie Domenicane* n.s. 4 (1973): 103–79.

– *I miti e gli astri*. Napoli: Guida, 1977.

Vauchez, André. *Les Laïcs au Moyen Age. Pratiques et expériences Religieuses*. Paris: Cerf, 1987.

Venturi, Lionello. 'Le Compagnie della Calza (sec. xv–xvi).' *Nuovo archivio veneto* n.s. 16 (1908), 161–221 and n.s. 17 (1909), 140–233.

Venturini, Lisa. 'Piero di Cosimo e la pala della Compagnia di San Vincenzo.' *Paragone. Arte* 45:529–31–33 (1994): 60–7.

Vigo, Pietro. *Una confraternita di giovanetti pistoiesi al principio del secolo XVI: Compagnia della Purità*. Scelta di curiosità letterarie inedite o rare, 220. Bologna: Romagnoli, 1887.

Villani, Giovanni. *Cronica*. Turin: Einaudi, 1979.

Volpi, Giuliana. *Acta gradvvm academiae pisanae. II. (1600–1699)*. Pisa: n.p. 1979.

*Voluntary Religion. Papers read at the 1985 Summer Meeting and the 1986 Winter Meeting of the Ecclesiastical History Society*, ed. W.J. Sheils and D. Wood. Studies in Church History, vol. 23. Oxford: B. Blackwell, 1986.

von Greyerz, K. *The Late City Reformation in Germany: The case of Colmar, 1522–1628*. Weisbaden. Steiner, 1980.

Wackernagel, Martin. *The World of the Florentine Renaissance Artist. Projects and Patrons, Workshop and Art Market*, trans. A. Luchs. Princeton: Princeton University Press, 1981.

Weil, M.S. 'The Devotion of the Forty Hours and Roman Baroque Illusions.' *Journal of the Warburg and Courtauld Institutes* 37 (1974): 218–48.

Weinstein, Donald. *Savonarola and Florence*. Princeton: Princeton University Press, 1970.

Weissman, Ronald F.E. *Ritual Brotherhood in Renaissance Florence*. New York–London: Academic Press, 1981.

– 'Sacred Eloquence. Humanist Preaching and Lay Piety in Renaissance Florence.' In *Christianity and the Renaissance* ... (1990), pp. 250–71.

– 'Lorenzo de' Medici and the Confraternity of San Paolo.' In *Lorenzo de' Medici. New Perspectives*, ed. Bernard Toscani. New York: Peter Land, 1993, pp. 315–29.

Weisz, Jean S. '*Caritas/Controriforma*: The Changing Role of a Confraternity's Ritual.' In *Crossing the Boundaries* ... (1991), pp. 221–36.

Young, G.F. *The Medici*. New York: Modern Library, [1930?].

Zardin, Danilo. 'Le confraternite in Italia settentrionale fra XV e XVIII secolo.' *Società e storia* 35 (1987): 81–137.

# Index

www.ingramcontent.com/pod-product-compliance
Lightning Source LLC
LaVergne TN
LVHW020435080826
844660LV00033B/1290

* 9 7 8 1 4 4 2 6 1 3 0 3 4 *